Department of Economic
and Social Affairs
Statistics Division

No. 42

D1482707

World
Statistics
Pocketbook
2018 edition

Containing data available
as of 31 May 2018

United Nations, New York, 2018

The **Department of Economic and Social Affairs** of the United Nations Secretariat is a vital interface between global policies in the economic, social and environmental spheres and national action. The Department works in three main interlinked areas: (i) it compiles, generates and analyses a wide range of economic, social and environmental data and information on which Member States of the United Nations draw to review common problems and to take stock of policy options; (ii) it facilitates the negotiations of Member States in many intergovernmental bodies on joint courses of action to address ongoing or emerging global challenges; and (iii) it advises interested Governments on the ways and means of translating policy frameworks developed in United Nations conferences and summits into programmes at the country level and, through technical assistance, helps build national capacities.

Note

The designations employed and the presentation of material in this publication do not imply the expression of any opinion whatsoever on the part of the Secretariat of the United Nations concerning the legal status of any country, territory, city or area; or of its authorities, or concerning the delimitation of its frontiers or boundaries.

The term "country" as used in the text of this publication also refers, as appropriate, to territories or areas.

Visit the United Nations World Wide Web site on the Internet:
For the Department of Economic and Social Affairs,
    http://www.un.org/esa/desa/
For statistics and statistical publications,
    http://unstats.un.org/unsd/
For UN publications, https://shop.un.org/

ST/ESA/STAT/SER.V/42
United Nations Publication
Sales No. E.18.XVII.16
ISBN: 978-92-1-161642-2
eISBN: 978-92-1-045169-7
Print ISSN: 2411 – 8915
Online ISSN: 2411 – 894X

Contents

World, Regional and Country /Area profiles

Contents (*continued*)

Contents (*continued*)

Explanatory notes

The following symbols and abbreviations have been used in the *World Statistics Pocketbook*:

.	A point is used to indicate decimals.
...	Data are not available or not applicable.
~0.0	Not zero, but less than half of the unit employed.
—0.0	Not zero, but negative and less than half of the unit employed.
%	Percentage
000	Thousands
Assist.	Assistance
Bol. Rep.	Bolivarian Republic
CIF	Cost, Insurance and Freight
CO_2	Carbon dioxide
const.	Constant
CPI	Consumer price index
Dem. Rep.	Democratic Republic
est.	Estimate
F	Females
FOB	Free on board
GDP	Gross domestic product
GNI	Gross national income
GVA	Gross value added
ISIC	International Standard Industrial Classification
ISO	International Organization for Standardization
Km^2	Square kilometres
M	Males
nes	Not elsewhere specified
pop.	Population
Rep.	Republic
SAR	Special Administrative Region
UN	United Nations
UNHCR	Office of the UN High Commissioner for Refugees
United Kingdom	United Kingdom of Great Britain and Northern Ireland
United States	United States of America
UNSD	United Nations Statistics Division
US$/USD	United States dollars

The metric system of weights and measures has been employed in the *World Statistics Pocketbook*.

Introduction

The *World Statistics Pocketbook* is an annual compilation of key economic, social and environmental indicators, presented in one-page profiles. This edition includes profiles for the 30 world geographical regions and 232 countries or areas. Prepared by the United Nations Statistics Division of the Department of Economic and Social Affairs, it responds to General Assembly resolution 2626 (XXV), in which the Secretary-General is requested to supply basic national data that will increase international public awareness of countries' development efforts.

The indicators shown are selected from the wealth of international statistical information compiled regularly by the Statistics Division and the Population Division of the United Nations, the statistical services of the United Nations specialized agencies and other international organizations and institutions. Special recognition is gratefully given for their assistance in continually providing data.

Organization of the Pocketbook

The profiles are presented first with the world and its geographical regions and sub-regions, based on the M49 regional classification[1], and then countries and areas alphabetically according to their names in English. Each profile is organised into 5 sections, where relevant and/or available:

- *General information:* includes data on surface area, population and population density, sex ratio of the population, capital city and its population, national currency and its exchange rate to the US dollar, location by geographical region and the date of admission to the United Nations.

- *Economic indicators:* includes data on national accounts Gross domestic product (GDP), GDP per capita, GDP growth rate, Gross Value Added (GVA) share by industry, employment share by industry, unemployment rate, labour force participation rate, consumer price index, production indices (industry and agriculture), the value of total exports, imports and the trade balance and balance of payments.

- *Major trading partners:* shows a country's main trading partners

- *Social indicators:* includes data on population (growth rates, including for the urban population), total fertility rate, life expectancy at birth, population age distribution, international migrant stock, refugees, infant mortality rate, health (expenditure and physicians), education (expenditure and gross enrolment ratios), intentional homicide rate and seats held by women in the National Parliament.

- *Environmental and infrastructure indicators:* includes data on internet users, Research & Development expenditure, threatened species, forested area, CO_2 emission estimates, energy production and energy supply per capita, tourist/visitor arrivals, important sites for terrestrial biodiversity protected,

---

[1] See UNSD website: https://unstats.un.org/unsd/methodology/m49/

population using improved drinking water sources and improved sanitation facilities and Official Development Assistance received or disbursed.

The complete set of indicators, listed by category and in the order in which they appear in the profiles, is shown before the country profile section (see page ix). Not all indicators are shown for each country or area due to different degrees of data availability.

The technical notes section, which follows the country profile pages, contains brief descriptions of the concepts and methodologies used in the compilation of the indicators as well as information on the statistical sources for the indicators. Readers interested in longer time-series data or more detailed descriptions of the concepts or methodologies should consult the primary sources of the data and the references listed in the section following the technical notes.

For brevity the Pocketbook omits specific information on the source or methodology for individual data points, and when a data point is estimated no distinction is made between whether the estimation was done by the international or national organization. See the technical notes section for the primary source which may provide this information.

Time period

This issue of the *World Statistics Pocketbook* presents data for the economic, social, environmental and infrastructure sections for three reference years - 2005, 2010 and 2018 - when available or the most recent data previous to these years, back to 2000. These instances are footnoted in each profile. For the general information and major trading partners sections the reference year is 2018 and 2017 respectively, unless otherwise footnoted.

Acknowledgement

The *World Statistics Pocketbook* is prepared annually by the Statistical Services Branch of the Statistics Division, Department of Economic and Social Affairs of the United Nations Secretariat. The programme managers are Matthias Reister and Ian Rutherford. Anuradha Chimata is the editor; David Carter, Mohamed Nabassoua Jaspreet Doung and Zin Lin provided production assistance; and Eduardo Belinchon provided IT support. Comments on this publication are welcome and may be sent by e-mail to statistics@un.org.

Profile information and indicator list*

General information

Region	UN membership date
Population (000)	Surface area (km^2)
Population density (per km^2)	Sex ratio (males per 100 females)
Capital city	National currency
Capital city population (000)	Exchange rate (per US$)

Economic indicators

GDP: Gross domestic product (million current US$)
GDP growth rate (annual %, constant 2010 prices)
GDP per capita (current US$)
Economy: Agriculture, industry and services and other activity (% of GVA)
Employment in agriculture, industry and services & other sectors (% of employed)
Unemployment rate (% of labour force)
Labour force participation rate (% of female/male population)
CPI: Consumer Price Index (2010=100)
Agricultural production index (2004-2006=100)
Index of industrial production (2005=100)
International trade: Exports, imports and balance (million current US$)
Balance of payments, current account (million current US$)

Major trading partners (% of exports and imports)

Social indicators

Population growth rate (average annual %)
Urban population (% of total population)
Urban population growth rate (average annual %)
Fertility rate, total (live births per woman)
Life expectancy at birth (females/males, years)
Population age distribution (0-14/60+ years old, %)
International migrant stock (000/% of total population)
Refugees and others of concern to the UNHCR (000)
Infant mortality rate (per 1 000 live births)
Health: Current expenditure (% of GDP)
Health: Physicians (per 1 000 population)
Education: Government expenditure (% of GDP)
Education: Primary, Secondary and Tertiary gross enrolment ratio (females/males per 100 population)
Intentional homicide rate (per 100 000 population)
Seats held by women in the National Parliament (% of total seats)

Environmental and infrastructure indicators

Individuals using the Internet (per 100 inhabitants)
Research & Development expenditure (% of GDP)
Threatened species (number)
Forested area (% of land area)
CO_2 emission estimates (million tons/tons per capita)
Energy production, primary (Petajoules)
Energy supply per capita (Gigajoules)
Tourist/visitor arrivals at national borders (000)
Important sites for terrestrial biodiversity protected (%)
Population using improved drinking water sources (urban/rural, %)
Population using improved sanitation facilities (urban/rural, %)
Net Official Development Assistance disbursed (% of GNI of donor)
Net Official Development Assistance received (% of GNI of recipient)

* The complete set of information and indicators listed here may not be shown for each country or area depending upon data availability. The technical notes provide a brief description of each information item and indicator.

World

Population (000, 2018)	7 632 819[a]	Surface area (km2)	136 162 000[b]
Pop. density (per km2, 2018)	58.7[a]	Sex ratio (m per 100 f)	101.8[a]

Economic indicators

	2005	2010	2018
GDP: Gross domestic product (million current US$)	47 601 561	66 010 167	75 648 868[c]
GDP growth rate (annual %, const. 2010 prices)	3.8	4.3	2.4[c]
GDP per capita (current US$)	7 278.0	9 489.0	10 134.0[c]
Employment in agriculture (% of employed)[d]	35.2	30.8	26.0
Employment in industry (% of employed)[d]	22.6	23.0	22.4
Employment in services & other sectors (% employed)[d]	42.1	46.2	51.7
Unemployment rate (% of labour force)[d]	6.0	5.8	5.5
Labour force participation rate (female/male pop. %)[d]	51.1 / 77.4	49.4 / 76.2	48.5 / 75.0
Agricultural production index (2004-2006=100)	100	113	127[c]
International trade: exports (million current US$)	10 373 445	15 100 194	17 177 323[e]
International trade: imports (million current US$)	10 577 013	15 261 844	17 507 492[e]
International trade: balance (million current US$)	- 203 568	- 161 649	- 330 169[e]

Social indicators

	2005	2010	2018
Population growth rate (average annual %)[f]	1.3	1.2	1.2[b]
Urban population (% of total population)	49.2	51.7	55.3
Urban population growth rate (average annual %)[f]	2.3	2.2	2.0[b]
Fertility rate, total (live births per woman)[f]	2.6	2.6	2.5[b]
Life expectancy at birth (females/males, years)[f]	69.5 / 65.0	71.3 / 66.9	73.1 / 68.6[b]
Population age distribution (0-14/60+ years old, %)	28.0 / 10.3	26.8 / 11.1	25.8 / 13.0[a]
International migrant stock (000/% of total pop.)	190 531.6 / 2.9	220 019.3 / 3.2	257 715.4 / 3.4[a]
Refugees and others of concern to the UNHCR (000)	...	...	67 408.4[e]
Infant mortality rate (per 1 000 live births)[f]	49.1	41.3	35.0[b]
Education: Primary gross enrol. ratio (f/m per 100 pop.)	99.8 / 104.8	103.0 / 105.9	104.6 / 104.1[c]
Education: Secondary gross enrol. ratio (f/m per 100 pop.)	62.1 / 65.7	69.8 / 72.4	75.9 / 76.9[c]
Education: Tertiary gross enrol. ratio (f/m per 100 pop.)	24.8 / 23.7	30.4 / 28.3	39.0 / 34.7[c]
Intentional homicide rate (per 100 000 pop.)	...	...	5.3[g,b]
Seats held by women in the National Parliament (%)	15.9	19.0	23.4

Environment and infrastructure indicators

	2005	2010	2018
Individuals using the Internet (per 100 inhabitants)	15.6	28.7	45.7[c]
Research & Development expenditure (% of GDP)	1.5	1.6	1.7[h]
Forested area (% of land area)	31.0	30.9	30.7[b]
CO2 emission estimates (million tons/tons per capita)	29 490.0 / 4.5	33 472.4 / 4.8	36 138.3 / 5.0[h]
Energy production, primary (Petajoules)	476 469	530 321	572 353[b]
Energy supply per capita (Gigajoules)	71	75	75[b]
Important sites for terrestrial biodiversity protected (%)	40.1	44.4	46.6
Pop. using improved drinking water (urban/rural, %)	95.8 / 75.7	96.1 / 80.2	96.4 / 84.5[b]
Pop. using improved sanitation facilities (urban/rural, %)	80.4 / 44.2	81.4 / 47.6	82.2 / 50.5[b]

a Projected estimate (medium fertility variant). b 2015. c 2016. d Estimate. e 2017. f Data refers to a 5-year period preceding the reference year. g Data is for 2015, or latest available data from 2010 onwards. h 2014. i Including regional aid disbursements in addition to the disbursements made to individual countries and areas.

Africa

Region	World	Population (000, 2018)	1 287 920[a]
Surface area (km2)	30 311 000[b]	Pop. density (per km2, 2018)	43.4[a]
Sex ratio (m per 100 f)	99.8[a]		

Economic indicators	2005	2010	2018
GDP: Gross domestic product (million current US$)	1 120 031	1 948 202	2 143 440[c]
GDP growth rate (annual %, const. 2010 prices)	6.0	5.3	1.8[c]
GDP per capita (current US$)	1 213.0	1 859.0	1 752.0[c]
Employment in agriculture (% of employed)[d]	58.7	54.1	52.9
Employment in industry (% of employed)[d]	12.0	13.3	13.5
Employment in services & other sectors (% employed)[d]	29.3	32.6	33.6
Unemployment rate (% of labour force)[d]	8.4	7.8	7.9
Labour force participation rate (female/male pop. %)[d]	53.4 / 74.5	54.4 / 74.4	55.7 / 73.6
Agricultural production index (2004-2006=100)	100	117	130[c]
International trade: exports (million current US$)	306 656	496 498	355 742[e]
International trade: imports (million current US$)	246 228	468 146	480 744[e]
International trade: balance (million current US$)	60 428	28 352	- 125 002[e]

Social indicators	2005	2010	2018
Population growth rate (average annual %)[f]	2.5	2.5	2.6[b]
Urban population (% of total population)	36.9	38.9	42.5
Urban population growth rate (average annual %)[f]	3.5	3.6	3.7[b]
Fertility rate, total (live births per woman)[f]	5.1	4.9	4.7[b]
Life expectancy at birth (females/males, years)[f]	55.2 / 52.2	58.4 / 55.5	61.9 / 58.6[b]
Population age distribution (0-14/60+ years old, %)	41.8 / 5.2	41.4 / 5.2	40.6 / 5.5[a]
International migrant stock (000/% of total pop.)	15 462.3 / 1.7	17 007.2 / 1.6	24 650.2 / 2.0[e]
Refugees and others of concern to the UNHCR (000)	...	...	21 927.2[e]
Infant mortality rate (per 1 000 live births)[f]	80.7	68.1	57.2[b]
Seats held by women in the National Parliament (%)	13.9	17.4	23.4

Environment and infrastructure indicators	2005	2010	2018
Forested area (% of land area)	22.1	21.5	21.0[b]
Energy production, primary (Petajoules)	44 963	47 676	45 242[b]
Energy supply per capita (Gigajoules)	27	27	27[b]

a Projected estimate (medium fertility variant). **b** 2015. **c** 2016. **d** Estimate. **e** 2017. **f** Data refers to a 5-year period preceding the reference year. **g** Including regional aid disbursements in addition to the disbursements made to individual countries and areas.

Northern Africa

Region	Africa	Population (000, 2018)	237 785[a]
Surface area (km2)	7 880 000[b]	Pop. density (per km2, 2018)	30.6[a]
Sex ratio (m per 100 f)	101.0[a]		

Economic indicators	2005	2010	2018
GDP: Gross domestic product (million current US$)	373 106	648 507	700 350[c]
GDP growth rate (annual %, const. 2010 prices)	5.7	4.6	3.4[c]
GDP per capita (current US$)	1 908.0	3 182.0	3 060.0[c]
Employment in agriculture (% of employed)[d]	34.0	30.4	28.1
Employment in industry (% of employed)[d]	24.0	27.5	28.0
Employment in services & other sectors (% employed)[d]	42.1	42.1	44.0
Unemployment rate (% of labour force)[d]	12.5	11.5	11.5
Labour force participation rate (female/male pop. %)[d]	21.0 / 73.3	22.0 / 73.9	21.9 / 72.0
Agricultural production index (2004-2006=100)	99	112	118[c]
International trade: exports (million current US$)	114 104	165 544	103 249[e]
International trade: imports (million current US$)	87 571	181 147	182 306[e]
International trade: balance (million current US$)	26 533	- 15 603	- 79 057[e]

Social indicators	2005	2010	2018
Population growth rate (average annual %)[f]	1.7	1.7	1.9[b]
Urban population (% of total population)	49.3	50.5	52.0
Urban population growth rate (average annual %)[f]	2.1	2.1	2.3[b]
Fertility rate, total (live births per woman)[f]	3.2	3.1	3.3[b]
Life expectancy at birth (females/males, years)[f]	69.9 / 66.0	71.6 / 67.7	72.8 / 69.4[b]
Population age distribution (0-14/60+ years old, %)	33.3 / 7.0	31.9 / 7.4	32.3 / 8.5[a]
International migrant stock (000/% of total pop.)[g]	1 731.9 / 0.9	1 893.6 / 0.9	2 410.1 / 1.0[e]
Infant mortality rate (per 1 000 live births)[f]	39.3	33.3	28.1[b]
Education: Primary gross enrol. ratio (f/m per 100 pop.)	90.3 / 97.5	98.0 / 101.4	97.7 / 101.1[c]
Education: Secondary gross enrol. ratio (f/m per 100 pop.)	67.8 / 68.7[d]	70.4 / 72.2	78.4 / 79.3[d,c]
Education: Tertiary gross enrol. ratio (f/m per 100 pop.)	23.0 / 23.8	27.7 / 25.8	35.2 / 30.5[c]
Seats held by women in the National Parliament (%)	8.7	10.9	22.6

Environment and infrastructure indicators	2005	2010	2018
Individuals using the Internet (per 100 inhabitants)	9.6	24.6	41.7[c]
Research & Development expenditure (% of GDP)	0.3	0.4	0.5[h]
Forested area (% of land area)	4.4	4.4	3.4[b]
Important sites for terrestrial biodiversity protected (%)	21.1	24.8	38.0
Pop. using improved drinking water (urban/rural, %)	92.6 / 76.8	91.5 / 76.8	94.9 / 90.2[b]
Pop. using improved sanitation facilities (urban/rural, %)	86.0 / 59.3	85.8 / 62.9	92.2 / 86.1[b]

a Projected estimate (medium fertility variant). b 2015. c 2016. d Estimate. e 2017. f Data refers to a 5-year period preceding the reference year. g Excluding Sudan. h 2014. i Including regional aid disbursements in addition to the disbursements made to individual countries and areas.

Sub-Saharan Africa

Region	Africa	Population (000, 2018)	1 050 136[a]
Surface area (km2)	22 431 000[b,c]	Pop. density (per km2, 2018)	48.0[a]
Sex ratio (m per 100 f)	99.5[a]		

Economic indicators	2005	2010	2018
GDP: Gross domestic product (million current US$)	746 926	1 299 694	1 443 090[d]
GDP growth rate (annual %, const. 2010 prices)	6.1	5.6	1.1[d]
GDP per capita (current US$)	1 026.0	1 540.0	1 451.0[d]
Employment in agriculture (% of employed)[e]	63.6	58.7	57.1
Employment in industry (% of employed)[e]	9.7	10.6	11.0
Employment in services & other sectors (% employed)[e]	26.8	30.8	31.8
Unemployment rate (% of labour force)[e]	7.5	7.1	7.2
Labour force participation rate (female/male pop. %)[e]	63.1 / 74.9	63.8 / 74.5	64.6 / 74.0
International trade: exports (million current US$)	192 552	330 954	252 493[f]
International trade: imports (million current US$)	158 657	287 000	298 438[f]
International trade: balance (million current US$)	33 895	43 955	- 45 945[f]

Social indicators	2005	2010	2018
Population growth rate (average annual %)[g]	2.7	2.7	2.7[c]
Urban population (% of total population)	33.7	36.1	40.4
Urban population growth rate (average annual %)[g]	4.1	4.1	4.1[c]
Fertility rate, total (live births per woman)[g]	5.6	5.4	5.1[c]
Life expectancy at birth (females/males, years)[g]	52.1 / 49.3	55.7 / 52.9	59.5 / 56.2[c]
Population age distribution (0-14/60+ years old, %)	44.0 / 4.7	43.7 / 4.7	42.5 / 4.8[a]
International migrant stock (000/% of total pop.)[h]	14 272.4 / 1.9	15 692.0 / 1.8	22 976.0 / 2.2[f]
Infant mortality rate (per 1 000 live births)[g]	87.3	73.7	62.1[c]
Education: Primary gross enrol. ratio (f/m per 100 pop.)	88.1 / 99.9	93.3 / 100.8	95.5 / 100.8[e,d]
Education: Secondary gross enrol. ratio (f/m per 100 pop.)	27.8 / 35.6	35.5 / 43.3	39.4 / 45.6[e,d]
Education: Tertiary gross enrol. ratio (f/m per 100 pop.)	4.7 / 7.0	5.9 / 8.9	7.0 / 9.9[e,d]
Intentional homicide rate (per 100 000 pop.)	...	...	9.6[i,c]
Seats held by women in the National Parliament (%)	14.4	18.4	23.6

Environment and infrastructure indicators	2005	2010	2018
Individuals using the Internet (per 100 inhabitants)	2.1	6.6	19.6[d]
Research & Development expenditure (% of GDP)	0.4	0.4	0.4[i]
Forested area (% of land area)[b]	29.0	28.3	28.0[c]
Important sites for terrestrial biodiversity protected (%)	34.9	40.2	42.0
Pop. using improved drinking water (urban/rural, %)	85.1 / 46.0	86.1 / 51.0	86.8 / 56.1[c]
Pop. using improved sanitation facilities (urban/rural, %)	40.0 / 20.6	40.4 / 22.1	40.3 / 23.3[c]

a Projected estimate (medium fertility variant). b Calculated by the United Nations Statistics Division. c 2015. d 2016. e Estimate. f 2017. g Data refers to a 5-year period preceding the reference year. h Including Sudan. i Data is for 2015, or latest available data from 2010 onwards. j 2014. k Including regional aid disbursements in addition to the disbursements made to individual countries and areas.

Eastern Africa

Region	Sub-Saharan Africa	Population (000, 2018)	433 643[a]
Surface area (km2)	7 005 000[b]	Pop. density (per km2, 2018)	65.0[a]
Sex ratio (m per 100 f)	98.5[a]		

Economic indicators	2005	2010	2018
GDP: Gross domestic product (million current US$)	111 507	215 107	320 971[c]
GDP growth rate (annual %, const. 2010 prices)	6.4	7.3	4.8[c]
GDP per capita (current US$)	382.0	622.0	784.0[c]
Employment in agriculture (% of employed)[d]	74.5	71.2	66.2
Employment in industry (% of employed)[d]	7.2	7.6	9.0
Employment in services & other sectors (% employed)[d]	18.3	21.2	24.8
Unemployment rate (% of labour force)[d]	6.8	7.1	6.5
Labour force participation rate (female/male pop. %)[d]	73.6 / 83.1	73.6 / 82.6	73.0 / 81.5
Agricultural production index (2004-2006=100)	100	124	140[c]
International trade: exports (million current US$)	16 297	31 652	39 658[e]
International trade: imports (million current US$)	31 243	62 688	83 747[e]
International trade: balance (million current US$)	- 14 945	- 31 036	- 44 090[e]

Social indicators	2005	2010	2018
Population growth rate (average annual %)[f]	2.8	2.9	2.8[b]
Urban population (% of total population)	22.5	24.4	28.0
Urban population growth rate (average annual %)[f]	4.2	4.4	4.8[b]
Fertility rate, total (live births per woman)[f]	5.8	5.3	4.9[b]
Life expectancy at birth (females/males, years)[f]	53.5 / 50.4	58.5 / 55.5	63.4 / 59.5[b]
Population age distribution (0-14/60+ years old, %)	45.5 / 4.5	44.8 / 4.5	42.4 / 4.7[a]
International migrant stock (000/% of total pop.)	4 745.8 / 1.6	4 657.1 / 1.3	7 591.8 / 1.8[e]
Infant mortality rate (per 1 000 live births)[f]	77.4	62.8	52.2[b]
Seats held by women in the National Parliament (%)	16.6	21.6	30.0

Environment and infrastructure indicators	2005	2010	2018
Individuals using the Internet (per 100 inhabitants)	1.3	5.4	15.3[b]
Forested area (% of land area)	33.6	32.4	32.6[b]
Pop. using improved drinking water (urban/rural, %)	84.7 / 43.6	85.3 / 49.3	85.7 / 55.9[b]
Pop. using improved sanitation facilities (urban/rural, %)	34.8 / 18.5	35.6 / 21.5	35.3 / 24.0[b]

a Projected estimate (medium fertility variant). b 2015. c 2016. d Estimate. e 2017. f Data refers to a 5-year period preceding the reference year.

Middle Africa

Region	Sub-Saharan Africa	Population (000, 2018)	168 538[a]
Surface area (km2)	6 613 000[b]	Pop. density (per km2, 2018)	25.9[a]
Sex ratio (m per 100 f)	99.3[a]		

Economic indicators	2005	2010	2018
GDP: Gross domestic product (million current US$)	99 285	184 993	225 212[c]
GDP growth rate (annual %, const. 2010 prices)	8.8	4.2	0.0[c]
GDP per capita (current US$)	887.0	1 408.0	1 420.0[c]
Employment in agriculture (% of employed)[d]	70.8	70.5	71.6
Employment in industry (% of employed)[d]	11.1	10.5	10.1
Employment in services & other sectors (% employed)[d]	18.1	19.0	18.3
Unemployment rate (% of labour force)[d]	7.9	5.7	5.4
Labour force participation rate (female/male pop. %)[d]	70.1 / 76.2	70.3 / 76.2	70.6 / 76.0
Agricultural production index (2004-2006=100)	102	132	150[c]
International trade: exports (million current US$)	48 958	90 717	30 798[e]
International trade: imports (million current US$)	18 680	43 623	35 120[e]
International trade: balance (million current US$)	30 278	47 094	- 4 322[e]

Social indicators	2005	2010	2018
Population growth rate (average annual %)[f]	3.1	3.2	3.1[b]
Urban population (% of total population)	42.6	45.2	49.5
Urban population growth rate (average annual %)[f]	4.4	4.4	4.3[b]
Fertility rate, total (live births per woman)[f]	6.4	6.2	5.9[b]
Life expectancy at birth (females/males, years)[f]	52.2 / 49.3	55.9 / 52.9	59.1 / 55.8[b]
Population age distribution (0-14/60+ years old, %)	45.6 / 4.6	45.7 / 4.5	45.3 / 4.6[a]
International migrant stock (000/% of total pop.)	1 928.8 / 1.7	2 140.0 / 1.6	3 539.7 / 2.2[e]
Infant mortality rate (per 1 000 live births)[f]	100.1	84.6	72.2[b]
Seats held by women in the National Parliament (%)	11.2	13.5	16.4

Environment and infrastructure indicators	2005	2010	2018
Individuals using the Internet (per 100 inhabitants)	0.7	2.0	8.3[b]
Forested area (% of land area)	47.8	47.2	46.7[b]
Pop. using improved drinking water (urban/rural, %)	82.2 / 34.6	83.4 / 35.7	83.8 / 36.5[b]
Pop. using improved sanitation facilities (urban/rural, %)	43.1 / 19.4	44.7 / 21.6	45.7 / 23.6[b]

a Projected estimate (medium fertility variant). **b** 2015. **c** 2016. **d** Estimate. **e** 2017. **f** Data refers to a 5-year period preceding the reference year.

Southern Africa

Region	Sub-Saharan Africa	Population (000, 2018)	65 974[a]
Surface area (km2)	2 675 000[b]	Pop. density (per km2, 2018)	24.9[a]
Sex ratio (m per 100 f)	96.2[a]		

Economic indicators

	2005	2010	2018
GDP: Gross domestic product (million current US$)	279 559	406 247	328 201[c]
GDP growth rate (annual %, const. 2010 prices)	5.1	3.3	0.5[c]
GDP per capita (current US$)	5 013.0	6 884.0	5 105.0[c]
Employment in agriculture (% of employed)[d]	10.6	8.1	8.5
Employment in industry (% of employed)[d]	24.9	23.9	23.2
Employment in services & other sectors (% employed)[d]	64.5	67.9	68.4
Unemployment rate (% of labour force)[d]	24.2	24.4	27.8
Labour force participation rate (female/male pop. %)[d]	46.9 / 62.7	45.8 / 61.4	49.2 / 63.2
Agricultural production index (2004-2006=100)	103	116	115[c]
International trade: exports (million current US$)	56 076	95 227	101 898[e]
International trade: imports (million current US$)	63 786	97 572	98 505[e]
International trade: balance (million current US$)	- 7 711	- 2 345	3 393[e]

Social indicators

	2005	2010	2018
Population growth rate (average annual %)[f]	1.3	1.1	1.4[b]
Urban population (% of total population)	56.5	59.4	63.6
Urban population growth rate (average annual %)[f]	2.3	2.1	2.3[b]
Fertility rate, total (live births per woman)[f]	2.9	2.7	2.6[b]
Life expectancy at birth (females/males, years)[f]	55.8 / 50.7	55.4 / 50.6	62.7 / 56.0[b]
Population age distribution (0-14/60+ years old, %)	32.6 / 6.6	31.2 / 7.0	29.6 / 8.2[a]
International migrant stock (000/% of total pop.)	1 439.4 / 2.6	2 357.1 / 4.0	4 338.2 / 6.7[e]
Infant mortality rate (per 1 000 live births)[f]	62.4	53.7	38.0[b]
Seats held by women in the National Parliament (%)	24.6	33.4	33.7

Environment and infrastructure indicators

	2005	2010	2018
Individuals using the Internet (per 100 inhabitants)	7.0	22.0	48.3[b]
Forested area (% of land area)	11.1	10.7	10.4[b]
Pop. using improved drinking water (urban/rural, %)	98.7 / 74.1	99.1 / 77.8	99.4 / 81.1[b]
Pop. using improved sanitation facilities (urban/rural, %)	66.6 / 46.4	67.8 / 51.0	68.9 / 55.1[b]

a Projected estimate (medium fertility variant). b 2015. c 2016. d Estimate. e 2017. f Data refers to a 5-year period preceding the reference year.

Western Africa

Region	Sub-Saharan Africa	Population (000, 2018)	381 981 [a,b]
Surface area (km2)	6 138 000 [c]	Pop. density (per km2, 2018)	63.0 [a,b]
Sex ratio (m per 100 f)	101.4 [a,b]		

Economic indicators	2005	2010	2018
GDP: Gross domestic product (million current US$)	256 575	493 347	568 706 [d]
GDP growth rate (annual %, const. 2010 prices)	6.0	7.3	0.3 [d]
GDP per capita (current US$)	955.0	1 603.0	1 570.0 [d]
Employment in agriculture (% of employed) [e]	54.8	43.8	44.1
Employment in industry (% of employed) [e]	9.6	12.5	12.7
Employment in services & other sectors (% employed) [e]	35.6	43.6	43.3
Unemployment rate (% of labour force) [e]	4.5	4.3	5.3
Labour force participation rate (female/male pop. %) [e]	52.7 / 68.7	54.3 / 67.9	55.6 / 66.8
Agricultural production index (2004-2006=100)	100	113	131 [d]
International trade: exports (million current US$)	71 221	113 358	80 140 [f]
International trade: imports (million current US$)	44 948	83 116	81 066 [f]
International trade: balance (million current US$)	26 273	30 241	- 926 [f]

Social indicators	2005	2010	2018
Population growth rate (average annual %) [g]	2.6	2.7	2.7 [c]
Urban population (% of total population)	37.8	41.1	46.4
Urban population growth rate (average annual %) [g]	4.4	4.4	4.3 [c]
Fertility rate, total (live births per woman) [b,g]	6.0	5.8	5.5 [c]
Life expectancy at birth (females/males, years) [b,g]	50.2 / 48.4	53.2 / 51.5	55.6 / 53.9 [c]
Population age distribution (0-14/60+ years old, %) [b]	44.0 / 4.6	44.1 / 4.6	43.6 / 4.6 [a]
International migrant stock (000/% of total pop.)	5 616.3 / 2.1	5 959.5 / 1.9	6 770.5 / 1.8 [f]
Infant mortality rate (per 1 000 live births) [b,g]	95.7	82.7	70.5 [c]
Seats held by women in the National Parliament (%)	10.2	11.6	14.8

Environment and infrastructure indicators	2005	2010	2018
Individuals using the Internet (per 100 inhabitants)	2.5	14.3	31.1 [c]
Forested area (% of land area)	12.2	11.6	11.1 [c]
Pop. using improved drinking water (urban/rural, %)	82.3 / 49.8	84.1 / 56.0	85.7 / 61.5 [c]
Pop. using improved sanitation facilities (urban/rural, %)	33.8 / 20.3	34.2 / 19.3	34.3 / 18.3 [c]

a Projected estimate (medium fertility variant). **b** Including Saint Helena. **c** 2015. **d** 2016. **e** Estimate. **f** 2017. **g** Data refers to a 5-year period preceding the reference year.

Americas

Region	World	Population (000, 2018)	1 015 856[a,b]
Surface area (km2)	42 322 000[a,c]	Pop. density (per km2, 2018)	26.2[a,b]
Sex ratio (m per 100 f)	97.8[a,b]		

Economic indicators	2005	2010	2018
GDP: Gross domestic product (million current US$)	17 129 485	21 925 902	25 404 270[d]
GDP growth rate (annual %, const. 2010 prices)	3.5	3.4	0.7[d]
GDP per capita (current US$)	19 289.0	23 343.0	25 496.0[d]
Employment in agriculture (% of employed)[e]	12.2	11.1	9.4
Employment in industry (% of employed)[e]	21.3	20.4	20.4
Employment in services & other sectors (% employed)[e]	66.4	68.5	70.2
Unemployment rate (% of labour force)[e]	6.9	8.1	6.6
Labour force participation rate (female/male pop. %)[e]	53.6 / 76.7	53.9 / 75.4	53.2 / 73.8
Agricultural production index (2004-2006=100)	100	111	124[d]
International trade: exports (million current US$)	1 835 325	2 550 360	2 956 598[f]
International trade: imports (million current US$)	2 557 150	3 228 657	3 815 365[f]
International trade: balance (million current US$)	- 721 825	- 678 297	- 858 767[f]

Social indicators	2005	2010	2018
Population age distribution (0-14/60+ years old, %)[a]	26.5 / 11.8	24.8 / 13.0	22.4 / 15.7[b]
Seats held by women in the National Parliament (%)	18.8	22.1	28.5

Environment and infrastructure indicators	2005	2010	2018
Forested area (% of land area)	41.7	41.3	41.1[c]

a Calculated by the United Nations Statistics Division. b Projected estimate (medium fertility variant). c 2015. d 2016. e Estimate. f 2017. g Including regional aid disbursements in addition to the disbursements made to individual countries and areas.

Northern America

Region	Americas	Population (000, 2018)	363 844[a,b]
Surface area (km2)	21 776 000[c]	Pop. density (per km2, 2018)	19.5[a,b]
Sex ratio (m per 100 f)	98.1[a,b]		

Economic indicators	2005	2010	2018
GDP: Gross domestic product (million current US$)	14 269 644	16 585 997	20 162 646[d]
GDP growth rate (annual %, const. 2010 prices)	3.3	2.6	1.5[d]
GDP per capita (current US$)	43 566.0	48 365.0	56 228.0[d]
Employment in agriculture (% of employed)[e]	1.7	1.7	1.7
Employment in industry (% of employed)[e]	21.2	18.6	18.9
Employment in services & other sectors (% employed)[e]	77.2	79.7	79.4
Unemployment rate (% of labour force)[e]	5.3	9.5	4.5
Labour force participation rate (female/male pop. %)[e]	58.5 / 72.2	58.0 / 70.1	56.0 / 68.1
Agricultural production index (2004-2006=100)	100	106	116[d]
International trade: exports (million current US$)	1 265 374	1 665 222	1 967 911[f]
International trade: imports (million current US$)	2 048 668	2 362 939	2 845 929[f]
International trade: balance (million current US$)	- 783 295	- 697 718	- 878 017[f]

Social indicators	2005	2010	2018
Population growth rate (average annual %)[g]	0.9	0.9	0.7[c]
Urban population (% of total population)	80.0	80.8	82.2
Urban population growth rate (average annual %)[g]	1.1	1.1	1.0[c]
Fertility rate, total (live births per woman)[b,g]	2.0	2.0	1.9[c]
Life expectancy at birth (females/males, years)[b,g]	80.0 / 74.8	80.9 / 75.9	81.5 / 76.8[c]
Population age distribution (0-14/60+ years old, %)[b]	20.6 / 16.8	19.8 / 18.5	18.6 / 22.2[a]
International migrant stock (000/% of total pop.)	45 363.4 / 13.8	50 971.0 / 14.9	57 664.2 / 16.0[f]
Refugees and others of concern to the UNHCR (000)	...	...	1 106.0[f]
Infant mortality rate (per 1 000 live births)[b,g]	6.9	6.7	5.9[c]
Education: Primary gross enrol. ratio (f/m per 100 pop.)	98.0 / 99.0	99.1 / 99.9	99.6 / 99.3[e,d]
Education: Secondary gross enrol. ratio (f/m per 100 pop.)	95.9 / 94.3	94.3 / 93.5	99.1 / 98.0[e,d]
Education: Tertiary gross enrol. ratio (f/m per 100 pop.)	95.0 / 67.8	105.4 / 75.7	96.5 / 71.7[e,d]
Seats held by women in the National Parliament (%)	17.5	19.0	22.8

Environment and infrastructure indicators	2005	2010	2018
Individuals using the Internet (per 100 inhabitants)	68.3	72.5	77.6[d]
Research & Development expenditure (% of GDP)	2.5	2.7	2.6[h]
Forested area (% of land area)	34.9	35.2	35.2[c]
Important sites for terrestrial biodiversity protected (%)	21.8	25.5	26.2
Pop. using improved drinking water (urban/rural, %)	99.6 / 96.9	99.5 / 97.8	99.5 / 98.2[c]
Pop. using improved sanitation facilities (urban/rural, %)	99.9 / 99.5	100.0 / 99.8	100.0 / 99.9[c]

a Projected estimate (medium fertility variant). b Including Bermuda, Greenland, and Saint Pierre and Miquelon. c 2015. d 2016. e Estimate. f 2017. g Data refers to a 5-year period preceding the reference year. h 2014.

Latin America and the Caribbean

Region	Americas	Population (000, 2018)	652 012[a]
Surface area (km2)	20 546 000[b]	Pop. density (per km2, 2018)	32.4[a]
Sex ratio (m per 100 f)	97.7[a]		

Economic indicators	2005	2010	2018
GDP: Gross domestic product (million current US$)	2 859 841	5 339 905	5 241 624[c]
GDP growth rate (annual %, const. 2010 prices)	4.3	5.8	- 1.6[c]
GDP per capita (current US$)	5 102.0	8 954.0	8 218.0[c]
Employment in agriculture (% of employed)[d]	19.5	16.9	14.1
Employment in industry (% of employed)[d]	21.5	21.5	21.3
Employment in services & other sectors (% employed)[d]	59.1	61.6	64.5
Unemployment rate (% of labour force)[d]	8.0	7.3	7.9
Labour force participation rate (female/male pop. %)[d]	50.3 / 79.6	51.3 / 78.8	51.5 / 77.2
International trade: exports (million current US$)	569 951	885 138	988 687[e]
International trade: imports (million current US$)	508 481	865 718	969 436[e]
International trade: balance (million current US$)	61 470	19 420	19 250[e]

Social indicators	2005	2010	2018
Population growth rate (average annual %)[f]	1.3	1.2	1.1[b]
Urban population (% of total population)	77.1	78.6	80.7
Urban population growth rate (average annual %)[f]	1.7	1.6	1.5[b]
Fertility rate, total (live births per woman)[f]	2.5	2.3	2.1[b]
Life expectancy at birth (females/males, years)[f]	75.5 / 68.8	76.8 / 70.1	78.0 / 71.4[b]
Population age distribution (0-14/60+ years old, %)	29.9 / 8.8	27.6 / 9.8	24.5 / 12.1[a]
International migrant stock (000/% of total pop.)	7 237.5 / 1.3	8 246.7 / 1.4	9 508.2 / 1.5[e]
Refugees and others of concern to the UNHCR (000)	...	...	8 215.7[e]
Infant mortality rate (per 1 000 live births)[f]	25.4	21.4	18.7[b]
Education: Primary gross enrol. ratio (f/m per 100 pop.)	114.0 / 117.5	111.9 / 115.4	107.7 / 109.6[d,c]
Education: Secondary gross enrol. ratio (f/m per 100 pop.)	90.3 / 83.5	92.8 / 85.7	97.2 / 92.1[d,c]
Education: Tertiary gross enrol. ratio (f/m per 100 pop.)	33.8 / 27.6	45.3 / 34.7	55.1 / 41.9[d,c]
Intentional homicide rate (per 100 000 pop.)	...	...	22.3[g,b]
Seats held by women in the National Parliament (%)	19.0	22.7	29.5

Environment and infrastructure indicators	2005	2010	2018
Individuals using the Internet (per 100 inhabitants)	16.6	34.7	56.8[c]
Research & Development expenditure (% of GDP)	0.6	0.6	0.7[h]
Forested area (% of land area)[i]	47.9	47.0	46.7[i]
Important sites for terrestrial biodiversity protected (%)	33.6	36.9	39.1
Pop. using improved drinking water (urban/rural, %)	96.3 / 75.7	96.9 / 80.2	97.4 / 83.9[b]
Pop. using improved sanitation facilities (urban/rural, %)	85.1 / 53.6	86.7 / 59.4	87.9 / 64.1[b]

a Projected estimate (medium fertility variant). b 2015. c 2016. d Estimate. e 2017. f Data refers to a 5-year period preceding the reference year. g Data is for 2015, or latest available data from 2010 onwards. h 2014. i Calculated by the United Nations Statistics Division. j 2013.

Caribbean

Region	Latin America & Caribbean	Population (000, 2018)	44 155[a]
Surface area (km2)	234 000[b]	Pop. density (per km2, 2018)	195.4[a]
Sex ratio (m per 100 f)	97.9[a,c]		

Economic indicators	2005	2010	2018
GDP: Gross domestic product (million current US$)	221 428	288 787	347 035[d]
GDP growth rate (annual %, const. 2010 prices)	3.4	1.8	0.5[d]
GDP per capita (current US$)	5 655.0	7 086.0	8 139.0[d]
Employment in agriculture (% of employed)[e]	22.4	21.8	20.2
Employment in industry (% of employed)[e]	18.7	16.1	16.1
Employment in services & other sectors (% employed)[e]	58.9	62.1	63.7
Unemployment rate (% of labour force)[e]	8.1	8.6	8.1
Labour force participation rate (female/male pop. %)[e]	47.3 / 71.5	49.2 / 71.4	51.1 / 71.2
Agricultural production index (2004-2006=100)	98	105	121[d]
International trade: exports (million current US$)	21 331	24 192	43 533[f]
International trade: imports (million current US$)	36 923	51 238	49 571[f]
International trade: balance (million current US$)	- 15 592	- 27 045	- 6 037[f]

Social indicators	2005	2010	2018
Population growth rate (average annual %)[g]	0.9	0.8	0.7[b]
Urban population (% of total population)	65.4	67.8	71.3
Urban population growth rate (average annual %)[g]	1.7	1.5	1.4[b]
Fertility rate, total (live births per woman)[c,g]	2.5	2.4	2.3[b]
Life expectancy at birth (females/males, years)[c,g]	72.6 / 67.4	74.0 / 68.7	75.2 / 69.8[b]
Population age distribution (0-14/60+ years old, %)[c]	28.2 / 11.1	26.5 / 12.0	24.3 / 14.1[a]
International migrant stock (000/% of total pop.)	1 333.1 / 3.3	1 353.6 / 3.2	1 399.7 / 3.2[f]
Infant mortality rate (per 1 000 live births)[c,g]	33.0	30.4	27.0[b]
Seats held by women in the National Parliament (%)	26.0	29.4	33.7

Environment and infrastructure indicators	2005	2010	2018
Individuals using the Internet (per 100 inhabitants)	12.6	23.8	41.5[b]
Forested area (% of land area)	28.1	29.8	32.2[b]
Pop. using improved drinking water (urban/rural, %)	90.5 / 71.5	88.2 / 73.0	85.8 / 74.5[b]
Pop. using improved sanitation facilities (urban/rural, %)	81.1 / 57.0	80.2 / 60.0	79.1 / 62.3[b]

a Projected estimate (medium fertility variant). b 2015. c Including Anguilla, Bonaire, Sint Eustatius and Saba, British Virgin Islands, Cayman Islands, Dominica, Montserrat, Saint Kitts and Nevis, Sint Maarten (Dutch part) and Turks and Caicos Islands. d 2016. e Estimate. f 2017. g Data refers to a 5-year period preceding the reference year.

Central America

Region	Latin America & Caribbean	Population (000, 2018)	179 616[a]
Surface area (km2)	2 480 000[b]	Pop. density (per km2, 2018)	73.2[a]
Sex ratio (m per 100 f)	98.6[a]		

Economic indicators	2005	2010	2018
GDP: Gross domestic product (million current US$)	974 370	1 212 738	1 321 586[c]
GDP growth rate (annual %, const. 2010 prices)	2.5	5.0	3.0[c]
GDP per capita (current US$)	6 574.0	7 553.0	7 552.0[c]
Employment in agriculture (% of employed)[d]	18.4	18.0	16.0
Employment in industry (% of employed)[d]	24.4	22.8	24.3
Employment in services & other sectors (% employed)[d]	57.2	59.2	59.7
Unemployment rate (% of labour force)[d]	4.0	5.4	3.8
Labour force participation rate (female/male pop. %)[d]	41.9 / 81.9	43.6 / 80.8	44.9 / 79.8
Agricultural production index (2004-2006=100)	99	110	128[c]
International trade: exports (million current US$)	233 506	336 529	458 759[e]
International trade: imports (million current US$)	259 847	366 171	492 280[e]
International trade: balance (million current US$)	- 26 340	- 29 642	- 33 522[e]

Social indicators	2005	2010	2018
Population growth rate (average annual %)[f]	1.4	1.6	1.5[b]
Urban population (% of total population)	70.3	72.1	74.7
Urban population growth rate (average annual %)[f]	1.9	2.1	1.9[b]
Fertility rate, total (live births per woman)[f]	2.8	2.5	2.4[b]
Life expectancy at birth (females/males, years)[f]	76.5 / 71.3	77.4 / 72.3	78.4 / 73.2[b]
Population age distribution (0-14/60+ years old, %)	33.6 / 7.5	31.0 / 8.2	27.3 / 10.0[a]
International migrant stock (000/% of total pop.)	1 385.7 / 0.9	1 749.9 / 1.1	2 092.8 / 1.2[e]
Infant mortality rate (per 1 000 live births)[f]	23.3	21.8	20.0[b]
Seats held by women in the National Parliament (%)	17.4	21.6	32.5

Environment and infrastructure indicators	2005	2010	2018
Forested area (% of land area)	36.4	35.7	35.2[b]
Pop. using improved drinking water (urban/rural, %)	95.3 / 78.5	96.5 / 84.3	97.4 / 88.9[b]
Pop. using improved sanitation facilities (urban/rural, %)	83.5 / 56.6	85.4 / 63.4	86.8 / 68.6[b]

a Projected estimate (medium fertility variant). b 2015. c 2016. d Estimate. e 2017. f Data refers to a 5-year period preceding the reference year.

South America

Region	Latin America & Caribbean	Population (000, 2018)	428 240[a]
Surface area (km2)	17 832 000[b]	Pop. density (per km2, 2018)	24.5[a]
Sex ratio (m per 100 f)	97.3[a,c]		

Economic indicators	2005	2010	2018
GDP: Gross domestic product (million current US$)	1 664 043	3 838 379	3 573 003[d]
GDP growth rate (annual %, const. 2010 prices)	5.0	6.4	- 3.3[d]
GDP per capita (current US$)	4 460.0	9 716.0	8 504.0[d]
Employment in agriculture (% of employed)[e]	19.6	16.1	12.8
Employment in industry (% of employed)[e]	20.7	21.5	20.6
Employment in services & other sectors (% employed)[e]	59.8	62.4	66.6
Unemployment rate (% of labour force)[e]	9.4	7.8	9.4
Labour force participation rate (female/male pop. %)[e]	53.7 / 79.6	54.5 / 78.7	54.2 / 76.8
Agricultural production index (2004-2006=100)	100	118	132[d]
International trade: exports (million current US$)	315 113	524 416	486 394[f]
International trade: imports (million current US$)	211 711	448 308	427 585[f]
International trade: balance (million current US$)	103 402	76 108	58 809[f]

Social indicators	2005	2010	2018
Population growth rate (average annual %)[g]	1.3	1.1	1.0[b]
Urban population (% of total population)	81.1	82.4	84.1
Urban population growth rate (average annual %)[g]	1.7	1.5	1.3[b]
Fertility rate, total (live births per woman)[c,g]	2.4	2.1	2.0[b]
Life expectancy at birth (females/males, years)[c,g]	75.5 / 68.1	76.9 / 69.6	78.1 / 71.0[b]
Population age distribution (0-14/60+ years old, %)[c]	28.6 / 9.1	26.4 / 10.2	23.4 / 12.8[a]
International migrant stock (000/% of total pop.)	4 518.6 / 1.2	5 143.1 / 1.3	6 015.6 / 1.4[f]
Infant mortality rate (per 1 000 live births)[c,g]	25.5	20.3	17.1[b]
Seats held by women in the National Parliament (%)	15.8	19.2	24.8

Environment and infrastructure indicators	2005	2010	2018
Forested area (% of land area)	49.7	48.8	48.2[b]
Energy production, primary (Petajoules)	26 630	29 391	31 660[b]
Energy supply per capita (Gigajoules)	51	56	57[b]
Pop. using improved drinking water (urban/rural, %)	97.0 / 74.7	97.7 / 78.9	98.2 / 82.3[b]
Pop. using improved sanitation facilities (urban/rural, %)	86.0 / 51.0	87.7 / 56.7	89.1 / 61.5[b]

a Projected estimate (medium fertility variant). **b** 2015. **c** Including Falkland Islands (Malvinas). **d** 2016. **e** Estimate. **f** 2017. **g** Data refers to a 5-year period preceding the reference year. **h** Including regional aid disbursements in addition to the disbursements made to individual countries and areas.

Asia

Region	World	Population (000, 2018)	4 545 133[a]
Surface area (km2)	31 915 000[b]	Pop. density (per km2, 2018)	146.5[a]
Sex ratio (m per 100 f)	104.8[a]		

Economic indicators	2005	2010	2018
GDP: Gross domestic product (million current US$)	12 349 162	20 837 705	27 538 651[c]
GDP growth rate (annual %, const. 2010 prices)	5.7	7.4	4.7[c]
GDP per capita (current US$)	3 115.0	4 968.0	6 172.0[c]
Agricultural production index (2004-2006=100)	100	118	135[c]
International trade: exports (million current US$)	3 569 857	5 893 417	6 963 850[d]
International trade: imports (million current US$)	3 172 210	5 444 317	6 577 637[d]
International trade: balance (million current US$)	397 647	449 100	386 213[d]

Social indicators	2005	2010	2018
Population growth rate (average annual %)[e]	1.2	1.1	1.0[b]
Urban population (% of total population)	41.2	44.8	49.9
Urban population growth rate (average annual %)[e]	3.1	2.8	2.4[b]
Fertility rate, total (live births per woman)[e]	2.4	2.3	2.2[b]
Life expectancy at birth (females/males, years)[e]	70.3 / 67.0	72.2 / 68.6	73.8 / 69.9[b]
Population age distribution (0-14/60+ years old, %)	27.4 / 9.3	25.6 / 10.1	24.0 / 12.5[a]
International migrant stock (000/% of total pop.)	53 243.7 / 1.3	65 921.8 / 1.6	79 586.7 / 1.8[d]
Refugees and others of concern to the UNHCR (000)	...	...	29 820.9[d]
Infant mortality rate (per 1 000 live births)[e]	45.6	37.2	30.5[b]
Seats held by women in the National Parliament (%)	13.4	16.8	17.9

Environment and infrastructure indicators	2005	2010	2018
Individuals using the Internet (per 100 inhabitants)	9.1	22.7	42.0[c]
Forested area (% of land area)	18.7	19.0	19.1[b]
Energy production, primary (Petajoules)	192 204	236 026	263 383[b]
Energy supply per capita (Gigajoules)	46	56	62[b]

a Projected estimate (medium fertility variant). b 2015. c 2016. d 2017. e Data refers to a 5-year period preceding the reference year. f Including regional aid disbursements in addition to the disbursements made to individual countries and areas.

Central Asia

Region	Asia	Population (000, 2018)	71 860[a]
Surface area (km2)	4 103 000[b,c]	Pop. density (per km2, 2018)	18.3[a]
Sex ratio (m per 100 f)	97.9[a]		

Economic indicators	2005	2010	2018
GDP: Gross domestic product (million current US$)	90 474	220 593	252 467[d]
GDP growth rate (annual %, const. 2010 prices)	9.2	7.5	2.8[d]
GDP per capita (current US$)	1 540.0	3 493.0	3 618.0[d]
Employment in agriculture (% of employed)[e]	35.0	29.0	22.6
Employment in industry (% of employed)[e]	25.4	29.0	30.2
Employment in services & other sectors (% employed)[e]	39.5	42.0	47.2
Unemployment rate (% of labour force)[e]	8.1	7.5	6.5
Labour force participation rate (female/male pop. %)[e]	55.5 / 74.4	55.7 / 75.4	55.4 / 77.1
Agricultural production index (2004-2006=100)	100	115	145[d]
International trade: exports (million current US$)	36 890	74 861	69 031[f]
International trade: imports (million current US$)	25 644	40 686	52 271[f]
International trade: balance (million current US$)	11 246	34 175	16 760[f]

Social indicators	2005	2010	2018
Population growth rate (average annual %)[g]	1.1	1.5	1.7[c]
Urban population (% of total population)	46.8	48.0	48.2
Urban population growth rate (average annual %)[g]	1.6	1.9	1.7[c]
Fertility rate, total (live births per woman)[g]	2.5	2.7	2.7[c]
Life expectancy at birth (females/males, years)[g]	70.1 / 61.7	71.6 / 63.5	73.3 / 66.3[c]
Population age distribution (0-14/60+ years old, %)	31.0 / 7.3	28.7 / 7.0	29.6 / 8.5[a]
International migrant stock (000/% of total pop.)	5 238.7 / 8.9	5 262.4 / 8.3	5 463.0 / 7.7[f]
Infant mortality rate (per 1 000 live births)[g]	48.0	38.0	28.5[c]
Seats held by women in the National Parliament (%)	13.4	20.0	21.3

Environment and infrastructure indicators	2005	2010	2018
Individuals using the Internet (per 100 inhabitants)	3.3	18.4	43.5[c]
Research & Development expenditure (% of GDP)	0.2	0.2	0.2[h]
Forested area (% of land area)	3.1	3.0	3.0[c]
Important sites for terrestrial biodiversity protected (%)	12.3	15.7	16.5
Pop. using improved drinking water (urban/rural, %)	96.9 / 74.8	98.0 / 78.8	98.1 / 79.0[c]
Pop. using improved sanitation facilities (urban/rural, %)	95.1 / 92.1	97.4 / 98.0	97.4 / 98.4[c]

a Projected estimate (medium fertility variant). b Calculated by the United Nations Statistics Division. c 2015. d 2016. e Estimate. f 2017. g Data refers to a 5-year period preceding the reference year. h 2014.

Eastern Asia

Region	Asia	Population (000, 2018)	1 653 884 [a]
Surface area (km2)	11 799 000 [b]	Pop. density (per km2, 2018)	143.1 [a]
Sex ratio (m per 100 f)	104.8 [a]		

Economic indicators	2005	2010	2018
GDP: Gross domestic product (million current US$)	8 547 753	13 584 987	16 489 486 [c]
GDP growth rate (annual %, const. 2010 prices)	5.1	7.4	4.4 [c]
GDP per capita (current US$)	5 497.0	8 513.0	11 262.0 [c]
Employment in agriculture (% of employed) [d]	32.8	24.4	15.8
Employment in industry (% of employed) [d]	29.2	29.4	26.1
Employment in services & other sectors (% employed) [d]	38.0	46.1	58.1
Unemployment rate (% of labour force) [d]	4.2	4.3	4.5
Labour force participation rate (female/male pop. %) [d]	64.3 / 78.9	61.9 / 77.1	59.7 / 75.1
Agricultural production index (2004-2006=100)	100	118	136 [c]
International trade: exports (million current US$)	1 937 757	3 219 245	4 069 183 [e]
International trade: imports (million current US$)	1 744 378	2 967 396	3 600 614 [e]
International trade: balance (million current US$)	193 379	251 849	468 569 [e]

Social indicators	2005	2010	2018
Population growth rate (average annual %) [f]	0.6	0.5	0.5 [b]
Urban population (% of total population)	48.3	54.4	62.9
Urban population growth rate (average annual %) [f]	3.3	2.9	2.4 [b]
Fertility rate, total (live births per woman) [f]	1.5	1.6	1.6 [b]
Life expectancy at birth (females/males, years) [f]	76.2 / 72.3	77.8 / 73.8	78.7 / 74.9 [b]
Population age distribution (0-14/60+ years old, %)	19.4 / 12.4	17.5 / 14.1	17.1 / 18.1 [a]
International migrant stock (000/% of total pop.)	6 229.5 / 0.4	7 061.8 / 0.4	7 776.7 / 0.5 [e]
Infant mortality rate (per 1 000 live births) [f]	23.2	15.7	11.0 [b]
Education: Primary gross enrol. ratio (f/m per 100 pop.)	104.6 / 104.7 [d]	105.9 / 107.4	100.5 / 100.0 [c]
Education: Secondary gross enrol. ratio (f/m per 100 pop.)	68.7 / 69.9 [d]	89.2 / 89.3	91.5 / 89.8 [c]
Education: Tertiary gross enrol. ratio (f/m per 100 pop.)	21.6 / 25.1	27.7 / 27.6	54.2 / 47.4 [c]
Seats held by women in the National Parliament (%)	18.1	18.7	20.9

Environment and infrastructure indicators	2005	2010	2018
Individuals using the Internet (per 100 inhabitants)	16.1	39.5	54.4 [b]
Research & Development expenditure (% of GDP)	2.1	2.2	2.5 [g]
Forested area (% of land area)	20.9	21.7	22.2 [b]
Important sites for terrestrial biodiversity protected (%)	48.7	49.5	51.1
Pop. using improved drinking water (urban/rural, %)	97.8 / 79.0	97.9 / 86.0	97.9 / 93.1 [b]
Pop. using improved sanitation facilities (urban/rural, %)	83.3 / 55.9	86.0 / 60.3	88.8 / 64.8 [b]

a Projected estimate (medium fertility variant). b 2015. c 2016. d Estimate. e 2017. f Data refers to a 5-year period preceding the reference year. g 2014.

South-eastern Asia

Region	Asia	Population (000, 2018)	655 637 [a]
Surface area (km2)	4 495 000 [b]	Pop. density (per km2, 2018)	151.0 [a]
Sex ratio (m per 100 f)	99.7 [a]		

Economic indicators	2005	2010	2018
GDP: Gross domestic product (million current US$)	958 929	1 980 866	2 558 569 [c]
GDP growth rate (annual %, const. 2010 prices)	5.7	7.8	4.7 [c]
GDP per capita (current US$)	1 707.0	3 316.0	3 987.0 [c]
Employment in agriculture (% of employed) [d]	46.4	41.1	31.8
Employment in industry (% of employed) [d]	18.1	18.9	21.7
Employment in services & other sectors (% employed) [d]	35.5	40.0	46.5
Unemployment rate (% of labour force) [d]	4.9	3.5	3.3
Labour force participation rate (female/male pop. %) [d]	56.4 / 82.4	57.0 / 81.5	56.3 / 80.0
Agricultural production index (2004-2006=100)	99	120	133 [c]
International trade: exports (million current US$)	655 071	1 051 556	1 299 270 [e]
International trade: imports (million current US$)	584 010	950 481	1 265 884 [e]
International trade: balance (million current US$)	71 061	101 076	33 386 [e]

Social indicators	2005	2010	2018
Population growth rate (average annual %) [f]	1.4	1.2	1.2 [b]
Urban population (% of total population)	41.1	44.3	48.9
Urban population growth rate (average annual %) [f]	3.0	2.7	2.5 [b]
Fertility rate, total (live births per woman) [f]	2.5	2.4	2.3 [b]
Life expectancy at birth (females/males, years) [f]	70.9 / 65.4	72.3 / 66.5	73.4 / 67.7 [b]
Population age distribution (0-14/60+ years old, %)	30.0 / 7.6	28.0 / 8.1	26.0 / 10.2 [a]
International migrant stock (000/% of total pop.)	6 522.3 / 1.2	8 673.7 / 1.5	9 873.6 / 1.5 [e]
Infant mortality rate (per 1 000 live births) [f]	34.1	28.6	24.0 [b]
Education: Primary gross enrol. ratio (f/m per 100 pop.)	103.9 / 106.9	107.8 / 107.2	104.8 / 108.2 [c]
Education: Secondary gross enrol. ratio (f/m per 100 pop.)	62.1 / 62.4	71.0 / 70.0	81.7 / 80.3 [d,c]
Education: Tertiary gross enrol. ratio (f/m per 100 pop.)	20.4 / 20.7 [d]	26.9 / 25.3	33.0 / 27.1 [c]
Seats held by women in the National Parliament (%)	15.5	19.3	19.1

Environment and infrastructure indicators	2005	2010	2018
Individuals using the Internet (per 100 inhabitants)	8.7	18.8	34.2 [b]
Research & Development expenditure (% of GDP)	0.6	0.8	0.8 [g]
Forested area (% of land area)	50.0	49.4	48.6 [b]
Important sites for terrestrial biodiversity protected (%)	31.4	33.7	35.2
Pop. using improved drinking water (urban/rural, %)	93.1 / 76.7	94.4 / 81.4	95.5 / 85.6 [b]
Pop. using improved sanitation facilities (urban/rural, %)	76.2 / 54.9	78.8 / 60.0	80.8 / 64.3 [b]

a Projected estimate (medium fertility variant). **b** 2015. **c** 2016. **d** Estimate. **e** 2017. **f** Data refers to a 5-year period preceding the reference year. **g** 2014.

Southern Asia

Region	Asia	Population (000, 2018)	1 891 454[a]
Surface area (km2)	6 688 000[b,c]	Pop. density (per km2, 2018)	295.5[a]
Sex ratio (m per 100 f)	106.1[a]		

Economic indicators	2005	2010	2018
GDP: Gross domestic product (million current US$)	1 258 642	2 524 007	3 317 296[d]
GDP growth rate (annual %, const. 2010 prices)	7.4	8.4	7.8[d]
GDP per capita (current US$)	795.0	1 480.0	1 797.0[d]
Employment in agriculture (% of employed)[e]	53.5	49.7	41.2
Employment in industry (% of employed)[e]	18.6	21.3	23.4
Employment in services & other sectors (% employed)[e]	27.9	29.0	35.5
Unemployment rate (% of labour force)[e]	5.0	3.7	4.1
Labour force participation rate (female/male pop. %)[e]	34.0 / 83.1	28.2 / 80.4	27.8 / 79.1
Agricultural production index (2004-2006=100)	100	120	139[d]
International trade: exports (million current US$)	193 182	354 892	317 138[f]
International trade: imports (million current US$)	229 179	497 340	514 174[f]
International trade: balance (million current US$)	- 35 997	- 142 448	- 197 036[f]

Social indicators	2005	2010	2018
Population growth rate (average annual %)[g]	1.7	1.5	1.3[c]
Urban population (% of total population)	30.7	32.5	35.8
Urban population growth rate (average annual %)[g]	2.8	2.6	2.5[c]
Fertility rate, total (live births per woman)[g]	3.2	2.9	2.5[c]
Life expectancy at birth (females/males, years)[g]	65.0 / 63.1	67.0 / 64.9	69.4 / 66.5[c]
Population age distribution (0-14/60+ years old, %)	33.4 / 7.1	31.5 / 7.5	28.3 / 9.1[a]
International migrant stock (000/% of total pop.)	13 722.0 / 0.9	14 307.6 / 0.8	13 582.4 / 0.7[f]
Infant mortality rate (per 1 000 live births)[g]	61.4	51.9	44.1[c]
Education: Primary gross enrol. ratio (f/m per 100 pop.)	100.6 / 106.1[e]	107.0 / 107.5	117.8 / 107.8[d]
Education: Secondary gross enrol. ratio (f/m per 100 pop.)	46.8 / 55.3	57.4 / 61.9	71.4 / 71.5[d]
Education: Tertiary gross enrol. ratio (f/m per 100 pop.)	8.7 / 11.7	14.9 / 19.5	24.4 / 25.5[d]
Seats held by women in the National Parliament (%)	8.8	18.2	13.9

Environment and infrastructure indicators	2005	2010	2018
Individuals using the Internet (per 100 inhabitants)	2.8	7.6	24.6[c]
Research & Development expenditure (% of GDP)	0.7	0.7	0.7[h]
Forested area (% of land area)	14.3	14.6	14.7[c]
Important sites for terrestrial biodiversity protected (%)	29.2	30.3	32.8
Pop. using improved drinking water (urban/rural, %)	93.4 / 81.3	94.6 / 86.6	95.5 / 91.0[c]
Pop. using improved sanitation facilities (urban/rural, %)	62.0 / 25.8	65.0 / 31.3	67.2 / 36.0[c]

a Projected estimate (medium fertility variant). b Calculated by the United Nations Statistics Division. c 2015. d 2016. e Estimate. f 2017. g Data refers to a 5-year period preceding the reference year. h 2014.

Western Asia

Region	Asia	Population (000, 2018)	272 298[a]
Surface area (km2)	4 831 000[b]	Pop. density (per km2, 2018)	56.7[a]
Sex ratio (m per 100 f)	109.7[a]		

Economic indicators	2005	2010	2018
GDP: Gross domestic product (million current US$)	1 493 364	2 527 253	2 920 834[c]
GDP growth rate (annual %, const. 2010 prices)	6.9	5.8	3.0[c]
GDP per capita (current US$)	7 269.0	10 872.0	11 122.0[c]
Employment in agriculture (% of employed)[d,e]	13.7	10.7	13.3
Employment in industry (% of employed)[d,e]	22.8	25.6	26.2
Employment in services & other sectors (% employed)[d,e]	63.4	63.7	60.5
Unemployment rate (% of labour force)[d,e]	11.1	9.0	8.3
Labour force participation rate (female/male pop. %)[d,e]	17.4 / 74.5	18.2 / 76.2	18.9 / 77.2
Agricultural production index (2004-2006=100)	101	106	117[c]
International trade: exports (million current US$)	557 564	919 156	891 649[f]
International trade: imports (million current US$)	407 407	737 099	884 788[f]
International trade: balance (million current US$)	150 158	182 058	6 861[f]

Social indicators	2005	2010	2018
Population growth rate (average annual %)[g]	2.1	2.5	2.1[b]
Urban population (% of total population)	65.8	68.2	71.6
Urban population growth rate (average annual %)[g]	2.7	3.2	2.7[b]
Fertility rate, total (live births per woman)[g]	3.2	3.0	2.9[b]
Life expectancy at birth (females/males, years)[g]	73.5 / 68.4	74.8 / 69.5	75.7 / 70.1[b]
Population age distribution (0-14/60+ years old, %)	33.4 / 7.2	31.0 / 7.3	29.1 / 8.4[a]
International migrant stock (000/% of total pop.)	21 531.2 / 10.5	30 616.2 / 13.2	42 891.0 / 16.0[f]
Infant mortality rate (per 1 000 live births)[g]	30.9	25.0	22.8[b]
Education: Primary gross enrol. ratio (f/m per 100 pop.)	95.7 / 105.1	98.3 / 105.7	96.4 / 103.0[a,c]
Education: Secondary gross enrol. ratio (f/m per 100 pop.)	68.2 / 79.0	71.7 / 79.3	78.2 / 85.2[a,c]
Education: Tertiary gross enrol. ratio (f/m per 100 pop.)	25.1 / 27.9	33.7 / 36.1	50.5 / 52.2[a,c]
Seats held by women in the National Parliament (%)	5.7	9.3	14.3

Environment and infrastructure indicators	2005	2010	2018
Individuals using the Internet (per 100 inhabitants)	11.1	32.5	50.3[b]
Research & Development expenditure (% of GDP)	0.5	0.5	0.6[h]
Forested area (% of land area)	3.8	4.0	4.1[b]
Important sites for terrestrial biodiversity protected (%)	11.1	13.9	15.4
Pop. using improved drinking water (urban/rural, %)	95.5 / 75.7	95.7 / 78.7	96.7 / 89.9[b]
Pop. using improved sanitation facilities (urban/rural, %)	94.6 / 69.6	95.4 / 74.3	95.9 / 88.6[b]

a Projected estimate (medium fertility variant). b 2015. c 2016. d Data excludes Armenia, Azerbaijan, Cyprus, Georgia, Israel and Turkey. e Estimate. f 2017. g Data refers to a 5-year period preceding the reference year. h 2014. i Excluding Armenia, Azerbaijan, Cyprus, Georgia and Turkey. Includes Iran (Islamic Rep. of). j Including regional aid disbursements in addition to the disbursements made to individual countries and areas.

Europe

Region	World	Population (000, 2018)	742 648[a]
Surface area (km2)	23 049 000[b]	Pop. density (per km2, 2018)	33.6[a]
Sex ratio (m per 100 f)	93.5[a]		

Economic indicators	2005	2010	2018
GDP: Gross domestic product (million current US$)	16 100 999	19 821 579	19 026 676[c]
GDP growth rate (annual %, const. 2010 prices)	2.5	2.3	1.7[c]
GDP per capita (current US$)	21 996.0	26 824.0	25 596.0[c]
Agricultural production index (2004-2006=100)	99	100	110[c]
International trade: exports (million current US$)	4 527 059	5 907 021	6 619 661[d]
International trade: imports (million current US$)	4 439 990	5 873 573	6 348 032[d]
International trade: balance (million current US$)	87 068	33 447	271 629[d]

Social indicators	2005	2010	2018
Population growth rate (average annual %)[e]	0.1	0.2	0.1[b]
Urban population (% of total population)	71.9	72.9	74.5
Urban population growth rate (average annual %)[e]	0.3	0.5	0.3[b]
Fertility rate, total (live births per woman)[e]	1.4	1.5	1.6[b]
Life expectancy at birth (females/males, years)[e]	78.1 / 69.6	79.3 / 71.3	80.7 / 73.7[b]
Population age distribution (0-14/60+ years old, %)	15.9 / 20.6	15.5 / 22.0	15.9 / 25.0[a]
International migrant stock (000/% of total pop.)	63 201.3 / 8.7	70 747.9 / 9.6	77 895.2 / 10.5[d]
Refugees and others of concern to the UNHCR (000)	...	...	6 244.0[d]
Infant mortality rate (per 1 000 live births)[e]	8.4	6.5	5.3[b]
Education: Primary gross enrol. ratio (f/m per 100 pop.)	101.5 / 102.3	102.1 / 102.7	102.4 / 102.3[f,c]
Education: Secondary gross enrol. ratio (f/m per 100 pop.)	98.0 / 98.1	101.0 / 101.8	108.4 / 108.7[f,c]
Education: Tertiary gross enrol. ratio (f/m per 100 pop.)	70.9 / 55.3	77.3 / 60.1	77.6 / 63.4[f,c]
Seats held by women in the National Parliament (%)	20.5	23.2	28.9

Environment and infrastructure indicators	2005	2010	2018
Individuals using the Internet (per 100 inhabitants)	40.2	61.4	77.5[c]
Research & Development expenditure (% of GDP)	1.6	1.7	1.8[g]
Forested area (% of land area)	45.4	45.8	45.9[b]
Energy production, primary (Petajoules)	102 546	102 514	101 099[b]
Energy supply per capita (Gigajoules)	154	152	141[b]
Important sites for terrestrial biodiversity protected (%)	57.6	63.6	65.6
Pop. using improved drinking water (urban/rural, %)	99.4 / 95.4	99.5 / 96.7	99.5 / 97.6[b]
Pop. using improved sanitation facilities (urban/rural, %)	93.9 / 86.5	94.1 / 87.4	94.2 / 88.1[b]

a Projected estimate (medium fertility variant). **b** 2015. **c** 2016. **d** 2017. **e** Data refers to a 5-year period preceding the reference year. **f** Estimate. **g** 2014. **h** Including Turkey and Cyprus. **i** Including regional aid disbursements in addition to the disbursements made to individual countries and areas.

Eastern Europe

Region	Europe	Population (000, 2018)	291 953[a]
Surface area (km2)	18 814 000[b]	Pop. density (per km2, 2018)	16.2[a]
Sex ratio (m per 100 f)	88.9[a]		

Economic indicators	2005	2010	2018
GDP: Gross domestic product (million current US$)	1 621 006	2 849 342	2 515 689[c]
GDP growth rate (annual %, const. 2010 prices)	5.6	3.5	1.2[c]
GDP per capita (current US$)	5 449.0	9 674.0	8 589.0[c]
Employment in agriculture (% of employed)[d]	13.8	11.7	9.2
Employment in industry (% of employed)[d]	29.9	28.7	28.1
Employment in services & other sectors (% employed)[d]	56.2	59.7	62.8
Unemployment rate (% of labour force)[d]	8.5	7.8	5.3
Labour force participation rate (female/male pop. %)[d]	51.9 / 65.3	52.3 / 66.9	52.1 / 67.4
Agricultural production index (2004-2006=100)	99	99	127[c]
International trade: exports (million current US$)	594 285	993 297	1 178 501[e]
International trade: imports (million current US$)	490 657	867 387	1 003 499[e]
International trade: balance (million current US$)	103 628	125 910	175 002[e]

Social indicators	2005	2010	2018
Population growth rate (average annual %)[f]	- 0.4	- 0.2	- 0.1[b]
Urban population (% of total population)	68.5	68.9	69.6
Urban population growth rate (average annual %)[f]	- 0.4	- 0.1	-0.0[b]
Fertility rate, total (live births per woman)[f]	1.3	1.4	1.6[b]
Life expectancy at birth (females/males, years)[f]	73.8 / 62.4	75.1 / 64.1	77.1 / 67.3[b]
Population age distribution (0-14/60+ years old, %)	15.4 / 18.2	14.8 / 19.3	16.6 / 22.9[a]
International migrant stock (000/% of total pop.)	19 747.4 / 6.6	19 127.8 / 6.5	20 121.7 / 6.9[e]
Infant mortality rate (per 1 000 live births)[f]	13.8	9.8	7.6[b]
Seats held by women in the National Parliament (%)	14.1	15.2	20.0

Environment and infrastructure indicators	2005	2010	2018
Forested area (% of land area)	47.2	47.6	47.7[b]
Pop. using improved drinking water (urban/rural, %)	98.7 / 90.5	98.7 / 93.2	98.6 / 95.1[b]
Pop. using improved sanitation facilities (urban/rural, %)	86.0 / 73.0	86.1 / 74.7	86.2 / 76.0[b]

a Projected estimate (medium fertility variant). b 2015. c 2016. d Estimate. e 2017. f Data refers to a 5-year period preceding the reference year.

Northern Europe

Region	Europe	Population (000, 2018)	104 762[a]
Surface area (km2)	1 810 000[b]	Pop. density (per km2, 2018)	61.5[a]
Sex ratio (m per 100 f)	97.4[a,c]		

Economic indicators	2005	2010	2018
GDP: Gross domestic product (million current US$)	3 972 776	4 244 137	4 497 618[d]
GDP growth rate (annual %, const. 2010 prices)	3.2	2.1	2.2[d]
GDP per capita (current US$)	41 341.0	42 431.0	43 520.0[d]
Employment in agriculture (% of employed)[e]	2.8	2.2	2.0
Employment in industry (% of employed)[e]	23.1	19.9	18.9
Employment in services & other sectors (% employed)[e]	74.1	77.9	79.1
Unemployment rate (% of labour force)[e]	5.5	8.6	5.1
Labour force participation rate (female/male pop. %)[e]	55.5 / 68.9	56.1 / 68.1	57.2 / 67.5
Agricultural production index (2004-2006=100)	101	101	106[d]
International trade: exports (million current US$)	913 599	1 045 978	1 070 228[f]
International trade: imports (million current US$)	937 990	1 122 240	1 204 673[f]
International trade: balance (million current US$)	- 24 391	- 76 262	- 134 445[f]

Social indicators	2005	2010	2018
Population growth rate (average annual %)[g]	0.4	0.8	0.5[b]
Urban population (% of total population)	78.9	80.1	82.2
Urban population growth rate (average annual %)[g]	0.6	1.1	0.9[b]
Fertility rate, total (live births per woman)[c,g]	1.7	1.9	1.8[b]
Life expectancy at birth (females/males, years)[c,g]	80.5 / 75.2	81.6 / 76.6	82.7 / 78.3[b]
Population age distribution (0-14/60+ years old, %)[c]	18.0 / 21.1	17.4 / 22.6	17.7 / 24.4[a]
International migrant stock (000/% of total pop.)	9 588.8 / 9.9	11 810.7 / 11.8	13 946.4 / 13.4[f]
Infant mortality rate (per 1 000 live births)[c,g]	5.0	4.4	3.7[b]
Seats held by women in the National Parliament (%)	28.0	29.6	33.8

Environment and infrastructure indicators	2005	2010	2018
Forested area (% of land area)	43.7	43.8	44.0[b]
Pop. using improved drinking water (urban/rural, %)	99.8 / 98.7	99.9 / 99.0	99.9 / 99.2[b]
Pop. using improved sanitation facilities (urban/rural, %)	98.4 / 96.2	98.5 / 96.5	90.6 / 96.8[h]

a Projected estimate (medium fertility variant). b 2015. c Including the Faroe Islands and the Isle of Man. d 2016. e Estimate. f 2017. g Data refers to a 5-year period preceding the reference year.

Southern Europe

Region	Europe	Population (000, 2018)	151 860[a]
Surface area (km2)	1 317 000[b]	Pop. density (per km2, 2018)	117.3[a]
Sex ratio (m per 100 f)	95.5[a,c]		

Economic indicators	2005	2010	2018
GDP: Gross domestic product (million current US$)	3 606 121	4 304 357	3 693 991[d]
GDP growth rate (annual %, const. 2010 prices)	1.9	0.6	1.8[d]
GDP per capita (current US$)	23 983.0	27 967.0	24 281.0[d]
Employment in agriculture (% of employed)[e]	8.7	7.7	6.7
Employment in industry (% of employed)[e]	29.3	25.6	23.0
Employment in services & other sectors (% employed)[e]	62.0	66.8	70.2
Unemployment rate (% of labour force)[e]	10.4	14.3	13.4
Labour force participation rate (female/male pop. %)[e]	43.0 / 64.4	44.6 / 62.9	45.4 / 60.6
Agricultural production index (2004-2006=100)	98	100	99[d]
International trade: exports (million current US$)	660 817	830 354	996 859[f]
International trade: imports (million current US$)	861 881	1 039 442	1 045 973[f]
International trade: balance (million current US$)	- 201 064	- 209 088	- 49 114[f]

Social indicators	2005	2010	2018
Population growth rate (average annual %)[g]	0.6	0.5	- 0.2[b]
Urban population (% of total population)	67.8	69.2	71.5
Urban population growth rate (average annual %)[g]	1.0	0.9	0.2[b]
Fertility rate, total (live births per woman)[c,g]	1.4	1.4	1.4[b]
Life expectancy at birth (females/males, years)[c,g]	81.8 / 75.6	82.9 / 77.1	83.7 / 78.4[b]
Population age distribution (0-14/60+ years old, %)[c]	15.1 / 22.5	14.8 / 24.1	14.2 / 27.3[a]
International migrant stock (000/% of total pop.)	11 974.3 / 8.0	16 205.4 / 10.5	15 957.6 / 10.5[f]
Infant mortality rate (per 1 000 live births)[c,g]	5.8	4.7	4.0[b]
Seats held by women in the National Parliament (%)	17.1	23.0	29.9

Environment and infrastructure indicators	2005	2010	2018
Forested area (% of land area)	33.4	34.8	35.2[b]
Pop. using improved drinking water (urban/rural, %)	99.9 / 99.2	99.9 / 99.5	99.9 / 99.7[b]
Pop. using improved sanitation facilities (urban/rural, %)	99.2 / 97.2	99.3 / 97.8	99.4 / 98.0[b]

a Projected estimate (medium fertility variant). b 2015. c Including Andorra, Gibraltar, Holy See, and San Marino. d 2016. e Estimate. f 2017. g Data refers to a 5-year period preceding the reference year.

Western Europe

Region	Europe	Population (000, 2018)	194 073[a]
Surface area (km2)	1 108 000[b]	Pop. density (per km2, 2018)	178.9[a]
Sex ratio (m per 100 f)	97.2[a,c]		

Economic indicators	2005	2010	2018
GDP: Gross domestic product (million current US$)	6 901 095	8 423 742	8 319 377[d]
GDP growth rate (annual %, const. 2010 prices)	1.5	2.9	1.7[d]
GDP per capita (current US$)	36 704.0	44 223.0	42 669.0[d]
Employment in agriculture (% of employed)[e]	3.1	2.4	2.1
Employment in industry (% of employed)[e]	26.2	24.6	23.2
Employment in services & other sectors (% employed)[e]	70.7	72.9	74.7
Unemployment rate (% of labour force)[e]	9.0	7.2	5.9
Labour force participation rate (female/male pop. %)[e]	51.1 / 65.8	52.7 / 65.4	53.7 / 64.1
Agricultural production index (2004-2006=100)	100	102	103[d]
International trade: exports (million current US$)	2 358 357	3 037 392	3 374 073[f]
International trade: imports (million current US$)	2 149 462	2 844 504	3 093 887[f]
International trade: balance (million current US$)	208 895	192 888	280 185[f]

Social indicators	2005	2010	2018
Population growth rate (average annual %)[g]	0.3	0.3	0.4[b]
Urban population (% of total population)	77.3	78.5	79.9
Urban population growth rate (average annual %)[g]	0.7	0.6	0.8[b]
Fertility rate, total (live births per woman)[c,g]	1.6	1.6	1.7[b]
Life expectancy at birth (females/males, years)[c,g]	82.0 / 75.8	83.0 / 77.3	83.7 / 78.4[b]
Population age distribution (0-14/60+ years old, %)[c]	16.4 / 22.6	15.9 / 24.3	15.4 / 26.8[a]
International migrant stock (000/% of total pop.)	21 890.7 / 11.8	23 604.0 / 12.5	27 869.5 / 14.4[f]
Infant mortality rate (per 1 000 live births)[c,g]	4.3	3.7	3.4[b]
Seats held by women in the National Parliament (%)	25.8	28.4	34.0

Environment and infrastructure indicators	2005	2010	2018
Forested area (% of land area)	30.8	31.4	32.0[b]
Pop. using improved drinking water (urban/rural, %)	100.0 / 100.0	100.0 / 100.0	100.0 / 100.0[b]
Pop. using improved sanitation facilities (urban/rural, %)	99.0 / 99.1	98.9 / 99.1	98.9 / 99.1[b]

a Projected estimate (medium fertility variant). b 2015. c Including Liechtenstein and Monaco. d 2016. e Estimate. f 2017. g Data refers to a 5-year period preceding the reference year.

Oceania

Region	World	Population (000, 2018)	41 261[a]
Surface area (km2)	8 564 000[b]	Pop. density (per km2, 2018)	4.9[a]
Sex ratio (m per 100 f)	100.1[a]		

Economic indicators	2005	2010	2018
GDP: Gross domestic product (million current US$)	901 884	1 476 780	1 535 831[c]
GDP growth rate (annual %, const. 2010 prices)	3.0	2.3	2.1[c]
GDP per capita (current US$)	27 109.0	40 627.0	38 561.0[c]
Employment in agriculture (% of employed)[d]	14.6	9.7	8.5
Employment in industry (% of employed)[d]	18.2	18.3	16.7
Employment in services & other sectors (% employed)[d]	67.1	72.0	74.8
Unemployment rate (% of labour force)[d]	4.5	5.0	5.1
Labour force participation rate (female/male pop. %)[d]	59.0 / 72.8	60.2 / 72.7	60.8 / 71.1
Agricultural production index (2004-2006=100)	99	98	109[c]
International trade: exports (million current US$)	134 548	252 899	281 470[e]
International trade: imports (million current US$)	161 435	247 151	285 713[e]
International trade: balance (million current US$)	- 26 888	5 748	- 4 243[e]

Social indicators	2005	2010	2018
Population growth rate (average annual %)[f]	1.4	1.7	1.5[b]
Urban population (% of total population)	68.0	68.1	68.2
Urban population growth rate (average annual %)[f]	1.3	1.8	1.5[b]
Fertility rate, total (live births per woman)[f]	2.4	2.5	2.4[b]
Life expectancy at birth (females/males, years)[f]	78.2 / 73.1	79.4 / 74.6	80.2 / 75.7[b]
Population age distribution (0-14/60+ years old, %)	24.9 / 14.1	24.0 / 15.3	23.5 / 17.2[a]
International migrant stock (000/% of total pop.)	6 023.4 / 17.9	7 124.6 / 19.4	8 410.9 / 20.7[a]
Refugees and others of concern to the UNHCR (000)	...	...	94.6[e]
Infant mortality rate (per 1 000 live births)[f]	25.2	22.4	20.8[b]
Education: Primary gross enrol. ratio (f/m per 100 pop.)	89.7 / 91.7	98.5 / 101.5	103.4 / 107.0[c]
Education: Secondary gross enrol. ratio (f/m per 100 pop.)[d]	109.5 / 112.8	108.2 / 115.9	100.9 / 113.7[c]
Education: Tertiary gross enrol. ratio (f/m per 100 pop.)	73.4 / 58.7[d]	84.5 / 62.5[d]	92.6 / 65.4[c]
Seats held by women in the National Parliament (%)	11.2	13.2	15.5

Environment and infrastructure indicators	2005	2010	2018
Individuals using the Internet (per 100 inhabitants)	47.2	57.6	68.6[c]
Research & Development expenditure (% of GDP)	1.9	2.2	2.0[g]
Forested area (% of land area)	20.8	20.3	20.4[b]
Energy production, primary (Petajoules)	12 214	14 500	16 897[b]
Energy supply per capita (Gigajoules)	171	179	185[b]
Important sites for terrestrial biodiversity protected (%)	26.1	32.8	36.6
Pop. using improved drinking water (urban/rural, %)	99.4 / 60.0	99.5 / 60.1	99.5 / 59.4[b]
Pop. using improved sanitation facilities (urban/rural, %)	97.5 / 43.7	97.5 / 42.8	97.4 / 41.1[b]

a Projected estimate (medium fertility variant). b 2015. c 2016. d Estimate. e 2017. f Data refers to a 5-year period preceding the reference year. g 2014. h Including regional aid disbursements in addition to the disbursements made to individual countries and areas.

Region	Oceania	Population (000, 2018)	29 522[a]
Surface area (km2)	8 012 000[b]	Pop. density (per km2, 2018)	3.7[a]
Sex ratio (m per 100 f)	98.9[a]		

Economic indicators	2005	2010	2018
GDP: Gross domestic product (million current US$)	877 210	1 440 378	1 491 980[c]
GDP growth rate (annual %, const. 2010 prices)	3.0	2.2	2.1[c]
GDP per capita (current US$)	35 989.0	54 374.0	51 829.0[c]
Agricultural production index (2004-2006=100)	99	97	108[c]
International trade: exports (million current US$)	127 740	243 041	268 213[d]
International trade: imports (million current US$)	151 453	231 861	268 570[d]
International trade: balance (million current US$)	- 23 714	11 179	- 357[d]

Social indicators	2005	2010	2018
Population growth rate (average annual %)[e]	1.2	1.7	1.4[b]
Urban population (% of total population)	84.9	85.3	86.1
Urban population growth rate (average annual %)[e]	1.3	1.8	1.5[b]
Fertility rate, total (live births per woman)[e]	1.8	2.0	1.9[b]
Life expectancy at birth (females/males, years)[e]	82.6 / 77.6	83.5 / 79.0	84.2 / 80.1[b]
Population age distribution (0-14/60+ years old, %)	20.1 / 17.3	19.3 / 18.8	19.2 / 21.2[a]
International migrant stock (000/% of total pop.)	5 718.0 / 23.5	6 830.4 / 25.8	8 103.0 / 27.8[d]
Infant mortality rate (per 1 000 live births)[e]	5.0	4.5	4.0[b]
Intentional homicide rate (per 100 000 pop.)	...	...	1.0[f,b]
Seats held by women in the National Parliament (%)	26.3	30.1	33.0

Environment and infrastructure indicators	2005	2010	2018
Individuals using the Internet (per 100 inhabitants)	63.0	76.7	88.3[c]
Research & Development expenditure (% of GDP)	1.9	2.2	2.1[g]
Forested area (% of land area)	17.3	16.8	17.0[b]
Important sites for terrestrial biodiversity protected (%)	40.0	45.7	51.4
Pop. using improved drinking water (urban/rural, %)	100.0 / 100.0	100.0 / 100.0	100.0 / 100.0[b]
Pop. using improved sanitation facilities (urban/rural, %)	100.0 / 100.0	100.0 / 100.0	100.0 / 100.0[b]

a Projected estimate (medium fertility variant). **b** 2015. **c** 2016. **d** 2017. **e** Data refers to a 5-year period preceding the reference year. **f** Data is for 2015, or latest available data from 2010 onwards. **g** 2014.

Melanesia

Region	Oceania	Population (000, 2018)	10 516[a]
Surface area (km2)	541 000[b]	Pop. density (per km2, 2018)	19.9[a]
Sex ratio (m per 100 f)	103.4[a]		

Economic indicators	2005	2010	2018
GDP: Gross domestic product (million current US$)	17 353	28 121	35 782[c]
GDP growth rate (annual %, const. 2010 prices)	3.6	8.5	2.5[c]
GDP per capita (current US$)	2 156.0	3 130.0	3 534.0[c]
Agricultural production index (2004-2006=100)	99	110	119[c]
International trade: exports (million current US$)	5 199	8 112	11 193[d]
International trade: imports (million current US$)	5 397	9 665	9 398[d]
International trade: balance (million current US$)	- 197	- 1 553	1 795[d]

Social indicators	2005	2010	2018
Population growth rate (average annual %)[e]	2.2	2.2	2.0[b]
Urban population (% of total population)	18.9	19.0	19.4
Urban population growth rate (average annual %)[e]	2.2	2.3	2.2[b]
Fertility rate, total (live births per woman)[e]	4.2	3.9	3.7[b]
Life expectancy at birth (females/males, years)[e]	66.1 / 61.4	67.7 / 62.9	68.7 / 63.8[b]
Population age distribution (0-14/60+ years old, %)	38.1 / 5.4	37.1 / 5.8	34.8 / 6.8[a]
International migrant stock (000/% of total pop.)	103.9 / 1.3	105.7 / 1.2	118.1 / 1.1[d]
Infant mortality rate (per 1 000 live births)[e]	51.0	47.3	44.3[b]
Seats held by women in the National Parliament (%)	3.2	1.4	3.5

Environment and infrastructure indicators	2005	2010	2018
Forested area (% of land area)	71.9	71.9	71.8[b]
Pop. using improved drinking water (urban/rural, %)	91.9 / 38.3	92.6 / 40.1	92.8 / 40.6[b]
Pop. using improved sanitation facilities (urban/rural, %)	72.8 / 19.2	72.7 / 19.7	72.4 / 19.3[b]

a Projected estimate (medium fertility variant). b 2015. c 2016. d 2017. e Data refers to a 5-year period preceding the reference year.

Micronesia

Region	Oceania	Population (000, 2018)	532[a]	
Surface area (km2)	3 000[b]	Pop. density (per km2, 2018)	167.8[a]	
Sex ratio (m per 100 f)	101.5[a,c]			

Economic indicators	2005	2010	2018
GDP: Gross domestic product (million current US$)	718	860	1 100[d]
GDP growth rate (annual %, const. 2010 prices)	1.5	3.5	3.2[d]
GDP per capita (current US$)	2 560.0	2 975.0	3 605.0[d]
Agricultural production index (2004-2006=100)	97	79	76[d]
International trade: exports (million current US$)	1 295	1 508	1 833[e]
International trade: imports (million current US$)	2 379	3 292	5 340[e]
International trade: balance (million current US$)	- 1 084	- 1 783	- 3 507[e]

Social indicators	2005	2010	2018
Population growth rate (average annual %)[f]	0.2	−0.0	0.6[b]
Urban population (% of total population)	65.9	66.6	68.7
Urban population growth rate (average annual %)[f]	0.3	0.2	1.0[b]
Fertility rate, total (live births per woman)[c,f]	3.2	3.0	3.0[b]
Life expectancy at birth (females/males, years)[c,f]	73.1 / 68.9	74.3 / 69.7	75.3 / 70.5[b]
Population age distribution (0-14/60+ years old, %)[c]	33.3 / 6.5	32.1 / 7.8	28.8 / 10.8[a]
International migrant stock (000/% of total pop.)	120.4 / 25.5	115.9 / 23.0	117.6 / 22.3[e]
Infant mortality rate (per 1 000 live births)[c,f]	31.0	29.1	27.9[b]
Seats held by women in the National Parliament (%)	2.4	2.4	7.8

Environment and infrastructure indicators	2005	2010	2018
Forested area (% of land area)	58.4	58.2	58.0[b]
Pop. using improved drinking water (urban/rural, %)	95.7 / 77.2	96.1 / 77.0	96.4 / 76.6[h]

a Projected estimate (medium fertility variant). **b** 2015. **c** Including Marshall Islands, Nauru, Northern Mariana Islands and Palau. **d** 2016. **e** 2017. **f** Data refers to a 5-year period preceding the reference year.

Polynesia

Region	Oceania	Population (000, 2018)	692[a,b]
Surface area (km2)	8 000[c]	Pop. density (per km2, 2018)	85.5[a,b]
Sex ratio (m per 100 f)	103.4[b,d]		

Economic indicators	2005	2010	2018
GDP: Gross domestic product (million current US$)	6 603	7 421	6 969[e]
GDP growth rate (annual %, const. 2010 prices)	1.6	- 1.6	2.3[a]
GDP per capita (current US$)	11 674.0	12 636.0	11 406.0[e]
Agricultural production index (2004-2006=100)	101	111	117[e]
International trade: exports (million current US$)	314	238	231[f]
International trade: imports (million current US$)	2 206	2 333	2 405[f]
International trade: balance (million current US$)	- 1 893	- 2 095	- 2 174[f]

Social indicators	2005	2010	2018
Population growth rate (average annual %)[a,g]	0.9	0.5	0.5[c]
Urban population (% of total population)	43.5	44.3	44.4
Urban population growth rate (average annual %)[g]	1.3	0.9	0.6[c]
Fertility rate, total (live births per woman)[d,g]	3.3	3.2	3.0[c]
Life expectancy at birth (females/males, years)[d,g]	74.6 / 68.9	76.1 / 70.6	77.4 / 72.0[c]
Population age distribution (0-14/60+ years old, %)[d]	33.9 / 7.7	31.9 / 8.4	29.5 / 10.6[b]
International migrant stock (000/% of total pop.)	73.2 / 11.4	72.6 / 11.0	72.3 / 10.5[f]
Infant mortality rate (per 1 000 live births)[d,g]	19.9	17.6	15.2[c]
Seats held by women in the National Parliament (%)	3.2	5.2	8.7

Environment and infrastructure indicators	2005	2010	2018
Forested area (% of land area)	45.8	48.8	48.7[c]
Pop. using improved drinking water (urban/rural, %)	99.3 / 97.7	99.5 / 98.9	99.6 / 99.6[c]
Pop. using improved sanitation facilities (urban/rural, %)	89.7 / 92.8	89.7 / 92.7	89.5 / 92.9[c]

a Including Pitcairn. b Projected estimate (medium fertility variant). c 2015. d Including American Samoa, Cook Islands, Niue, Pitcairn, Tokelau, Tuvalu, and Wallis and Futuna Islands. e 2016. f 2017. g Data refers to a 5-year period preceding the reference year.

Afghanistan

Region	Southern Asia	UN membership date	19 November 1946
Population (000, 2018)	36 373 [a]	Surface area (km2)	652 864 [b]
Pop. density (per km2, 2018)	55.7 [a]	Sex ratio (m per 100 f)	106.2 [a]
Capital city	Kabul	National currency	Afghani (AFN)
Capital city pop. (000, 2018)	4 011.8	Exchange rate (per US$)	69.5 [c]

Economic indicators	2005	2010	2018
GDP: Gross domestic product (million current US$)	6 622	16 078	20 235 [d]
GDP growth rate (annual %, const. 2010 prices)	9.9	3.2	3.6 [d]
GDP per capita (current US$)	264.0	558.0	584.0 [d]
Economy: Agriculture (% of Gross Value Added)	35.2	28.8	24.1 [d]
Economy: Industry (% of Gross Value Added)	26.0	21.3	22.0 [d]
Economy: Services and other activity (% of GVA)	38.8	49.8	53.9 [d]
Employment in agriculture (% of employed) [e]	71.8	64.5	62.0
Employment in industry (% of employed) [e]	6.6	6.1	6.8
Employment in services & other sectors (% employed) [e]	21.7	29.4	31.3
Unemployment rate (% of labour force)	8.5	7.8 [e]	8.8 [e]
Labour force participation rate (female/male pop. %) [e]	16.1 / 87.1	14.7 / 86.5	19.5 / 86.7
CPI: Consumer Price Index (2010=100)	71	100	145 [c]
Agricultural production index (2004-2006=100)	107	116	125 [d]
International trade: exports (million current US$)	...	388	700 [e,c]
International trade: imports (million current US$)	...	5 154	7 384 [e,c]
International trade: balance (million current US$)	...	- 4 766	- 6 684 [e,c]
Balance of payments, current account (million US$)	...	- 1 505	- 4 683 [c]

Major trading partners						2017
Export partners (% of exports)	Pakistan	47.5 [e]	India	38.6	Iran (Islamic Rep.)	3.2 [e]
Import partners (% of imports) [e]	Iran (Islamic Rep.)	19.4	Pakistan	18.3	China	16.7

Social indicators	2005	2010	2018
Population growth rate (average annual %) [f]	4.4	2.8	3.2 [b]
Urban population (% of total population)	22.7	23.7	25.5
Urban population growth rate (average annual %) [f]	5.0	3.7	4.0 [b]
Fertility rate, total (live births per woman) [f]	7.2	6.4	5.3 [b]
Life expectancy at birth (females/males, years) [f]	58.1 / 55.8	61.3 / 58.9	63.5 / 61.0 [b]
Population age distribution (0-14/60+ years old, %)	47.6 / 3.6	47.8 / 3.9	42.6 / 4.2 [a]
International migrant stock (000/% of total pop.)	87.3 / 0.3	102.2 / 0.4	133.6 / 0.4 [c]
Refugees and others of concern to the UNHCR (000)	159.6 [g]	1 200.0 [g]	2 189.2 [c]
Infant mortality rate (per 1 000 live births) [f]	89.4	76.7	68.6 [b]
Health: Current expenditure (% of GDP)	9.9	8.6	10.3 [b]
Health: Physicians (per 1 000 pop.)	0.2 [h]	0.2	0.3 [d]
Education: Government expenditure (% of GDP)	...	3.5	3.2 [b]
Education: Primary gross enrol. ratio (f/m per 100 pop.)	74.5 / 126.9	82.7 / 120.6	84.3 / 124.0 [c]
Education: Secondary gross enrol. ratio (f/m per 100 pop.)	9.3 / 28.6	34.3 / 68.6	39.7 / 69.6 [c]
Education: Tertiary gross enrol. ratio (f/m per 100 pop.)	0.5 / 1.9 [j]	1.4 / 6.1 [j]	3.6 / 13.0 [k]
Intentional homicide rate (per 100 000 pop.)	...	3.4	6.3 [l]
Seats held by women in the National Parliament (%)	...	27.3	27.7

Environment and infrastructure indicators	2005	2010	2018
Individuals using the Internet (per 100 inhabitants)	1.2	4.0 [e]	10.6 [e,d]
Threatened species (number)	33 [i]	34	42 [c]
Forested area (% of land area) [e]	2.1	2.1	2.1 [b]
CO2 emission estimates (million tons/tons per capita)	1.3 / ~0.0	8.5 / 0.3	9.8 / 0.3 [k]
Energy production, primary (Petajoules)	23	41	60 [b]
Energy supply per capita (Gigajoules)	1	5	4 [b]
Important sites for terrestrial biodiversity protected (%)	~0.0	6.1	6.1
Pop. using improved drinking water (urban/rural, %)	61.5 / 32.4	70.7 / 40.5	78.2 / 47.0 [b]
Pop. using improved sanitation facilities (urban/rural, %)	36.1 / 23.3	41.1 / 25.4	45.1 / 27.0 [b]
Net Official Development Assist. received (% of GNI)	45.15	40.44	20.64 [d]

a Projected estimate (medium fertility variant). b 2015. c 2017. d 2016. e Estimate. f Data refers to a 5-year period preceding the reference year. g Data as at the end of December. h 2001. i 2004. j 2009. k 2014. l 2012.

Albania

Region	Southern Europe	UN membership date	14 December 1955
Population (000, 2018)	2 934[a]	Surface area (km2)	28 748[b]
Pop. density (per km2, 2018)	107.1[a]	Sex ratio (m per 100 f)	101.8[a]
Capital city	Tirana	National currency	Lek (ALL)
Capital city pop. (000, 2018)	475.6	Exchange rate (per US$)	111.1[c]

Economic indicators

	2005	2010	2018
GDP: Gross domestic product (million current US$)	8 052	11 927	11 864[d]
GDP growth rate (annual %, const. 2010 prices)	5.5	3.7	3.4[d]
GDP per capita (current US$)	2 615.0	4 056.0	4 054.0[d]
Economy: Agriculture (% of Gross Value Added)[e]	21.5	20.7	22.7[d]
Economy: Industry (% of Gross Value Added)[e]	28.7	28.7	23.7[d]
Economy: Services and other activity (% of GVA)[e]	49.8	50.7	53.6[d]
Employment in agriculture (% of employed)[f]	54.0	43.9	38.9
Employment in industry (% of employed)[f]	19.9	19.4	18.7
Employment in services & other sectors (% employed)[f]	26.2	36.7	42.4
Unemployment rate (% of labour force)	17.5[f]	14.2	15.1[f]
Labour force participation rate (female/male pop. %)[f]	48.1 / 67.9	45.7 / 63.0	47.0 / 64.7
CPI: Consumer Price Index (2010=100)[g]	87	100	115[c]
Agricultural production index (2004-2006=100)	98	119	143[d]
Index of industrial production (2005=100)	100	200	355[h]
International trade: exports (million current US$)	658	1 550	2 262[c]
International trade: imports (million current US$)	2 614	4 603	5 826[c]
International trade: balance (million current US$)	- 1 956	- 3 053	- 3 565[c]
Balance of payments, current account (million US$)	- 571	- 1 356	- 909[c]

Major trading partners

						2017
Export partners (% of exports)	Italy	54.5	Serbia	7.8	Spain	5.6
Import partners (% of imports)	Italy	26.0	Areas nes[i]	13.0	Turkey	7.4

Social indicators

	2005	2010	2018
Population growth rate (average annual %)[j]	- 0.3	- 0.9	- 0.1[b]
Urban population (% of total population)	46.7	52.2	60.3
Urban population growth rate (average annual %)[j]	2.0	1.3	1.8[b]
Fertility rate, total (live births per woman)[j]	1.9	1.6	1.7[b]
Life expectancy at birth (females/males, years)[j]	77.8 / 72.2	78.5 / 73.2	79.9 / 75.6[b]
Population age distribution (0-14/60+ years old, %)	26.5 / 12.3	22.5 / 15.0	17.1 / 19.7[a]
International migrant stock (000/% of total pop.)	64.7 / 2.1	52.8 / 1.8	52.5 / 1.8[c]
Refugees and others of concern to the UNHCR (000)	0.1[k]	0.1[k]	7.7[c]
Infant mortality rate (per 1 000 live births)[j]	21.1	16.8	14.6[b]
Health: Current expenditure (% of GDP)	6.3	5.0	6.8[b]
Health: Physicians (per 1 000 pop.)	...	1.3	1.3[l]
Education: Government expenditure (% of GDP)	3.2	3.3[m]	3.5[b]
Education: Primary gross enrol. ratio (f/m per 100 pop.)	100.6 / 101.6	93.0 / 94.6	108.3 / 111.1[d]
Education: Secondary gross enrol. ratio (f/m per 100 pop.)	76.4 / 80.2	88.1 / 89.1	91.5 / 98.3[d]
Education: Tertiary gross enrol. ratio (f/m per 100 pop.)	27.2 / 19.1	51.6 / 38.6	76.1 / 48.2[d]
Intentional homicide rate (per 100 000 pop.)	5.0	4.3	2.7[d]
Seats held by women in the National Parliament (%)	6.4	16.4	27.9

Environment and infrastructure indicators

	2005	2010	2018
Individuals using the Internet (per 100 inhabitants)	6.0	45.0	66.4[f,d]
Research & Development expenditure (% of GDP)	...	0.2[n,o]	...
Threatened species (number)	37[p]	100	130[c]
Forested area (% of land area)[f]	28.6	28.3	28.2[b]
CO2 emission estimates (million tons/tons per capita)	4.3 / 1.4	4.6 / 1.6	5.7 / 2.0[h]
Energy production, primary (Petajoules)	48	69	87[b]
Energy supply per capita (Gigajoules)	29	31	32[b]
Tourist/visitor arrivals at national borders (000)[q]	...	2 191	4 070[d]
Important sites for terrestrial biodiversity protected (%)	44.0	58.8	67.0
Pop. using improved drinking water (urban/rural, %)	98.4 / 94.0	96.5 / 94.7	94.9 / 95.2[b]
Pop. using improved sanitation facilities (urban/rural, %)	95.0 / 80.7	95.3 / 86.1	95.5 / 90.2[b]
Net Official Development Assist. received (% of GNI)	3.79	3.09	1.42[d]

a Projected estimate (medium fertility variant). **b** 2015. **c** 2017. **d** 2016. **e** Data classified according to ISIC Rev. 4. **f** Estimate. **g** Calculated by the Statistics Division of the United Nations from national indices. **h** 2014. **i** Areas not elsewhere specified. **j** Data refers to a 5-year period preceding the reference year. **k** Data as at the end of December. **l** 2013. **m** 2007. **n** Partial data. **o** 2008. **p** 2004. **q** Excluding nationals residing abroad.

Algeria

Region	Northern Africa	UN membership date	08 October 1962
Population (000, 2018)	42 008[a]	Surface area (km2)	2 381 741[b]
Pop. density (per km2, 2018)	17.6[a]	Sex ratio (m per 100 f)	102.0[a]
Capital city	Algiers	National currency	Algerian Dinar (DZD)
Capital city pop. (000, 2018)	2 693.5[c]	Exchange rate (per US$)	114.9[d]

Economic indicators

	2005	2010	2018
GDP: Gross domestic product (million current US$)	103 198	161 207	159 049[e]
GDP growth rate (annual %, const. 2010 prices)	5.9	3.6	3.8[e]
GDP per capita (current US$)	3 100.0	4 463.0	3 917.0[e]
Economy: Agriculture (% of Gross Value Added)	8.0	8.6	12.7[e]
Economy: Industry (% of Gross Value Added)	59.7	51.4	36.1[e]
Economy: Services and other activity (% of GVA)	32.3	40.0	51.1[e]
Employment in agriculture (% of employed)[f]	20.0	16.5	12.8
Employment in industry (% of employed)[f]	29.8	39.4	46.5
Employment in services & other sectors (% employed)[f]	50.2	44.0	40.7
Unemployment rate (% of labour force)	15.3	10.0	9.9[f]
Labour force participation rate (female/male pop. %)[f]	12.8 / 71.8	14.4 / 70.0	15.3 / 67.2
CPI: Consumer Price Index (2010=100)[g]	82	100	142[d]
Agricultural production index (2004-2006=100)	99	130	151[e]
Index of industrial production (2005=100)[h]	100	97	104[i]
International trade: exports (million current US$)	46 002	57 051	35 191[d]
International trade: imports (million current US$)	20 357	41 000	46 053[d]
International trade: balance (million current US$)	25 645	16 051	- 10 862[d]
Balance of payments, current account (million US$)	21 180	12 220[j]	- 26 179[e]

Major trading partners

							2017
Export partners (% of exports)	Italy	16.0	France	12.6	Spain	11.7
Import partners (% of imports)	China	18.1	France	9.3	Italy	8.2

Social indicators

	2005	2010	2018
Population growth rate (average annual %)[k]	1.3	1.6	2.0[b]
Urban population (% of total population)	63.8	67.5	72.6
Urban population growth rate (average annual %)[k]	2.8	2.8	2.9[b]
Fertility rate, total (live births per woman)[k]	2.4	2.7	3.0[b]
Life expectancy at birth (females/males, years)[k]	72.9 / 70.1	75.2 / 72.6	76.5 / 74.1[b]
Population age distribution (0-14/60+ years old, %)	29.1 / 7.0	27.2 / 7.8	29.5 / 9.6[a]
International migrant stock (000/% of total pop.)[l]	197.4 / 0.6	217.0 / 0.6	248.6 / 0.6[d]
Refugees and others of concern to the UNHCR (000)	94.4[m]	94.4[m]	100.2[d]
Infant mortality rate (per 1 000 live births)[k]	37.3	32.6	27.7[b]
Health: Current expenditure (% of GDP)	3.2	5.1	7.1[b]
Health: Physicians (per 1 000 pop.)	1.0	1.2[n]	...
Education: Government expenditure (% of GDP)	...	4.3[o]	...
Education: Primary gross enrol. ratio (f/m per 100 pop.)	103.4 / 111.8	111.4 / 118.9	110.6 / 116.6[e]
Education: Secondary gross enrol. ratio (f/m per 100 pop.)	82.4 / 75.2	98.7 / 95.3	101.5 / 97.8[p]
Education: Tertiary gross enrol. ratio (f/m per 100 pop.)	23.3 / 18.2	35.3 / 24.4	53.6 / 32.1[e]
Intentional homicide rate (per 100 000 pop.)	0.6	0.7	1.4[b]
Seats held by women in the National Parliament (%)	6.2	7.7	25.6

Environment and infrastructure indicators

	2005	2010	2018
Individuals using the Internet (per 100 inhabitants)	5.8	12.5	42.9[f,e]
Research & Development expenditure (% of GDP)	0.1[q]	...	...
Threatened species (number)	50[r]	105	135[d]
Forested area (% of land area)	0.6	0.8	0.8[b]
CO2 emission estimates (million tons/tons per capita)	107.3 / 3.3	119.2 / 3.3	145.4 / 3.7[i]
Energy production, primary (Petajoules)	7 534	6 200	5 883[b]
Energy supply per capita (Gigajoules)	48	46	56[b]
Tourist/visitor arrivals at national borders (000)[s]	1 443	2 070	2 039[e]
Important sites for terrestrial biodiversity protected (%)	38.4	38.4	38.8
Pop. using improved drinking water (urban/rural, %)	90.3 / 83.3	87.3 / 82.5	84.3 / 81.8[b]
Pop. using improved sanitation facilities (urban/rural, %)	90.7 / 75.6	90.3 / 78.9	89.8 / 82.2[b]
Net Official Development Assist. received (% of GNI)	0.35	0.13	0.10[e]

a Projected estimate (medium fertility variant). b 2015. c Refers to the Governorate of Grand Algiers. d 2017. e 2016. f Estimate. g Algiers h Data classified according to ISIC Rev. 3. i 2014. j Break in the time series. k Data refers to a 5-year period preceding the reference year. l Including refugees. m Data as at the end of December. n 2007. o 2008. p 2011. q Partial data. r 2004. s Including nationals residing abroad.

American Samoa

Region	Polynesia	Population (000, 2018)	56[a]
Surface area (km2)	199[b]	Pop. density (per km2, 2018)	278.4[a]
Sex ratio (m per 100 f)	103.6[c,d]	Capital city	Pago Pago
National currency	US Dollar (USD)	Capital city pop. (000, 2018)	48.5

Economic indicators	2005	2010	2018
Employment in agriculture (% of employed)[e,f]	3.1[g]	3.0[c]	...
Employment in industry (% of employed)[e,f]	41.7[g]	23.2[c]	...
Employment in services & other sectors (% employed)[e,f]	51.9[g]	73.8[c]	...
Unemployment rate (% of labour force)[e]	5.1[g]	9.2[c]	...
Labour force participation rate (female/male pop. %)	41.2 / 58.8[e,g]	... / ...	... / ...
Agricultural production index (2004-2006=100)	100	110	116[d]

Social indicators	2005	2010	2018
Population growth rate (average annual %)[h]	0.5	- 1.2	-- 0.0[b]
Urban population (% of total population)	88.1	87.6	87.2
Urban population growth rate (average annual %)[h]	0.4	- 1.3	- 0.1[b]
Fertility rate, total (live births per woman)	...	...	2.6[i]
Life expectancy at birth (females/males, years)	... / ...	76.2 / 68.5[j]	77.8 / 71.1[k]
Population age distribution (0-14/60+ years old, %)	38.8 / 5.4[l,m,g]	35.0 / 6.7[l,m]	33.3 / 9.0[c,d]
International migrant stock (000/% of total pop.)	24.2 / 41.0	23.6 / 42.3	23.6 / 42.3[n]
Infant mortality rate (per 1 000 live births)	...	...	9.6[o,p]
Intentional homicide rate (per 100 000 pop.)	10.1	9.0	5.4[d]

Environment and infrastructure indicators	2005	2010	2018
Threatened species (number)	24[q]	79	92[n]
Forested area (% of land area)[r]	89.4	88.6	87.7[b]
Tourist/visitor arrivals at national borders (000)	24	23	20[d]
Important sites for terrestrial biodiversity protected (%)	61.5	61.5	61.5
Pop. using improved drinking water (urban/rural, %)	99.9 / 99.9	100.0 / 100.0	100.0 / 100.0[b]
Pop. using improved sanitation facilities (urban/rural, %)	61.9 / 61.9	62.3 / 62.3	62.5 / 62.5[b]

a Projected estimate (medium fertility variant). b 2015. c Break in the time series. d 2016. e Population aged 16 years and over. f Data classified according to ISIC Rev. 3. g 2000. h Data refers to a 5-year period preceding the reference year. i 2013. j 2006. k 2011. l De jure population. m Including armed forces stationed in the area. n 2017. o Data refers to a 2-year period up to and including the reference year. p 2012. q 2004. r Estimate.

Andorra

Region	Southern Europe	UN membership date	28 July 1993
Population (000, 2018)	77 [a]	Surface area (km2)	468 [b]
Pop. density (per km2, 2018)	163.7 [a]	Sex ratio (m per 100 f)	102.3 [c,d,e]
Capital city	Andorra la Vella	National currency	Euro (EUR)
Capital city pop. (000, 2018)	22.6	Exchange rate (per US$)	0.8 [f]

Economic indicators

	2005	2010	2018
GDP: Gross domestic product (million current US$)	3 256	3 355	2 858 [e]
GDP growth rate (annual %, const. 2010 prices)	7.4	- 5.4	1.2 [e]
GDP per capita (current US$)	41 281.0	39 734.0	36 987.0 [e]
Economy: Agriculture (% of Gross Value Added) [g]	0.4	0.5	0.6 [e]
Economy: Industry (% of Gross Value Added) [g]	17.3	14.6	11.1 [e]
Economy: Services and other activity (% of GVA) [g]	82.3	84.8	88.4 [e]
CPI: Consumer Price Index (2010=100) [h]	90	100	105 [f]
International trade: exports (million current US$)	143	92	120 [i,f]
International trade: imports (million current US$)	1 796 [i]	1 541	1 480 [i,f]
International trade: balance (million current US$)	- 1 653 [i]	- 1 448	- 1 360 [i,f]

Major trading partners
						2017
Export partners (% of exports)	Spain	29.6 [i]	Sri Lanka	15.3	United States	13.0 [i]
Import partners (% of imports) [i]	Spain	67.3	France	18.8	Germany	3.0

Social indicators

	2005	2010	2018
Population growth rate (average annual %) [j]	3.7	1.4	- 1.6 [b]
Urban population (% of total population)	90.3	88.8	88.1
Urban population growth rate (average annual %) [j]	3.3	1.0	- 1.7 [b]
Fertility rate, total (live births per woman)	1.2	1.2	1.2 [k]
Population age distribution (0-14/60+ years old, %) [d,c]	15.1 / 16.1	14.0 / 18.6	14.4 / 19.0 [e]
International migrant stock (000/% of total pop.) [l]	50.3 / 63.8	52.1 / 61.6	41.0 / 53.3 [f]
Health: Current expenditure (% of GDP)	9.8	11.6	12.0 [b]
Health: Physicians (per 1 000 pop.)	3.3 [m]	...	3.7 [b]
Education: Government expenditure (% of GDP)	1.6	3.1	3.3 [e]
Intentional homicide rate (per 100 000 pop.)	1.3 [n]	1.2 [o]	1.2 [p]
Seats held by women in the National Parliament (%)	14.3	35.7	32.1

Environment and infrastructure indicators

	2005	2010	2018
Individuals using the Internet (per 100 inhabitants)	37.6	81.0	97.9 [i,e]
Threatened species (number)	5 [n]	8	13 [f]
Forested area (% of land area)	34.0	34.0	34.0 [b]
CO2 emission estimates (million tons/tons per capita)	0.6 / 7.4	0.5 / 6.2	0.5 / 6.4 [q]
Energy production, primary (Petajoules)	0	1	1 [b]
Energy supply per capita (Gigajoules)	130	114	124 [b]
Tourist/visitor arrivals at national borders (000)	2 418	1 808 [f]	2 831 [r,e]
Important sites for terrestrial biodiversity protected (%)	17.9	17.9	26.1
Pop. using improved drinking water (urban/rural, %)	100.0 / 100.0	100.0 / 100.0	100.0 / 100.0 [b]
Pop. using improved sanitation facilities (urban/rural, %)	100.0 / 100.0	100.0 / 100.0	100.0 / 100.0 [b]

a Projected estimate (medium fertility variant). b 2015. c De jure population. d Population statistics are compiled from registers. e 2016. f 2017. g Data classified according to ISIC Rev. 4. h Calculated by the Statistics Division of the United Nations from national indices. i Estimate. j Data refers to a 5-year period preceding the reference year. k 2012. l Refers to foreign citizens. m 2003. n 2004. o 2008. p 2011. q 2014. r Break in the time series.

Angola

Region	Middle Africa	UN membership date	01 December 1976
Population (000, 2018)	30 774 [a]	Surface area (km2)	1 246 700 [b]
Pop. density (per km2, 2018)	24.7 [a]	Sex ratio (m per 100 f)	96.3 [a]
Capital city	Luanda	National currency	Kwanza (AOA)
Capital city pop. (000, 2018)	7 774.2 [c]	Exchange rate (per US$)	165.9 [d]

Economic indicators

	2005	2010	2018
GDP: Gross domestic product (million current US$)	36 971	83 799	106 918 [e]
GDP growth rate (annual %, const. 2010 prices)	15.0	4.7	- 0.7 [e]
GDP per capita (current US$)	1 891.0	3 586.0	3 711.0 [e]
Economy: Agriculture (% of Gross Value Added)	5.0	6.1	8.0 [e]
Economy: Industry (% of Gross Value Added)	59.7	51.2	46.0 [e]
Economy: Services and other activity (% of GVA)	35.3	42.7	46.0 [e]
Employment in agriculture (% of employed) [f]	37.5	47.2	50.4
Employment in industry (% of employed) [f]	8.8	8.8	8.7
Employment in services & other sectors (% employed) [f]	53.7	44.0	40.9
Unemployment rate (% of labour force) [f]	21.4	9.9	8.5
Labour force participation rate (female/male pop. %) [f]	74.9 / 80.6	75.3 / 80.5	75.3 / 80.0
CPI: Consumer Price Index (2010=100) [f,g]	54	100	281 [d]
Agricultural production index (2004-2006=100)	102	167	192 [e]
International trade: exports (million current US$) [f,h]	23 835	52 612	13 311 [d]
International trade: imports (million current US$) [f,h]	8 321	18 143	3 845 [d]
International trade: balance (million current US$) [h]	15 514 [f]	34 469	9 466 [f,d]
Balance of payments, current account (million US$)	5 138	7 506	- 3 071 [e]

Major trading partners

						2017
Export partners (% of exports) [f]	China	43.2 [f]	India	8.1	Spain	6.8 [f]
Import partners (% of imports) [f]	China	16.9	Portugal	14.6	Republic of Korea	8.6

Social indicators

	2005	2010	2018
Population growth rate (average annual %) [i]	3.5	3.6	3.5 [b]
Urban population (% of total population)	56.0	59.8	65.5
Urban population growth rate (average annual %) [i]	5.7	4.9	4.7 [b]
Fertility rate, total (live births per woman) [i]	6.6	6.4	6.0 [b]
Life expectancy at birth (females/males, years) [i]	52.5 / 47.5	58.2 / 53.0	63.0 / 57.4 [b]
Population age distribution (0-14/60+ years old, %)	47.2 / 3.7	47.3 / 3.6	46.6 / 4.1 [a]
International migrant stock (000/% of total pop.) [i]	61.3 / 0.3	76.5 / 0.3	638.5 / 2.1 [d]
Refugees and others of concern to the UNHCR (000)	14.9 [k]	19.4 [k]	78.4 [d]
Infant mortality rate (per 1 000 live births) [i]	108.3	83.8	65.4 [b]
Health: Current expenditure (% of GDP)	4.0	2.7	2.9 [b]
Health: Physicians (per 1 000 pop.)	0.1 [l]	0.1 [m]	...
Education: Government expenditure (% of GDP)	2.8	3.5	...
Education: Primary gross enrol. ratio (f/m per 100 pop.)	... / ...	92.8 / 117.6	91.2 / 146.7 [n]
Education: Secondary gross enrol. ratio (f/m per 100 pop.)	13.6 / 16.7 [f,o]	21.2 / 31.9	20.7 / 32.9 [n]
Education: Tertiary gross enrol. ratio (f/m per 100 pop.)	0.6 / 0.9 [f,o]	... / ...	7.4 / 9.6 [b]
Intentional homicide rate (per 100 000 pop.)	...	...	4.8 [p]
Seats held by women in the National Parliament (%)	15.0	38.6	30.5

Environment and infrastructure indicators

	2005	2010	2018
Individuals using the Internet (per 100 inhabitants)	1.1	2.8 [f]	13.0 [f,e]
Threatened species (number)	76 [l]	117	146 [d]
Forested area (% of land area)	47.4	46.9	46.4 [b]
CO2 emission estimates (million tons/tons per capita)	19.2 / 1.2	29.1 / 1.4	34.8 / 1.4 [q]
Energy production, primary (Petajoules)	2 934	4 057	4 137 [b]
Energy supply per capita (Gigajoules)	22	24	24 [b]
Tourist/visitor arrivals at national borders (000)	210	425	397 [d]
Important sites for terrestrial biodiversity protected (%)	28.4	28.4	28.4
Pop. using improved drinking water (urban/rural, %)	66.1 / 34.6	71.9 / 30.6	75.4 / 28.2 [b]
Pop. using improved sanitation facilities (urban/rural, %)	79.0 / 16.3	85.0 / 20.2	88.6 / 22.5 [b]
Net Official Development Assist. received (% of GNI)	1.71	0.32	0.24 [e]

a Projected estimate (medium fertility variant). b 2015. c Refers to the urban population of the province of Luanda. d 2017. e 2016. f Estimate. g Luanda h Imports FOB. i Data refers to a 5-year period preceding the reference year. j Including refugees. k Data as at the end of December. l 2004. m 2009. n 2011. o 2002. p 2012. q 2014.

Anguilla

Region	Caribbean	Population (000, 2018)	15[a]
Surface area (km2)	91[b]	Pop. density (per km2, 2018)	167.2[a]
Sex ratio (m per 100 f)	97.6[c,d]	Capital city	The Valley
National currency	E. Caribbean Dollar (XCD)[e]	Capital city pop. (000, 2018)	1.4
Exchange rate (per US$)	2.7[f]		

Economic indicators	2005	2010	2018
GDP: Gross domestic product (million current US$)	229	268	338[g]
GDP growth rate (annual %, const. 2010 prices)	13.1	- 4.5	1.1[g]
GDP per capita (current US$)	18 129.0	19 459.0	22 861.0[g]
Economy: Agriculture (% of Gross Value Added)	2.7	2.0	2.8[g]
Economy: Industry (% of Gross Value Added)	19.3	15.8	14.3[g]
Economy: Services and other activity (% of GVA)	78.0	82.2	82.9[g]
Employment in agriculture (% of employed)	2.9[h,i,j]	...	...
Employment in industry (% of employed)	18.9[h,i,j]	...	...
Employment in services & other sectors (% employed)	76.7[h,i,j]	...	...
Unemployment rate (% of labour force)	7.8[k]	...	...
Labour force participation rate (female/male pop. %)	67.2 / 77.2[k]	... / ...	... / ...
CPI: Consumer Price Index (2010=100)	82	100	105[g]
International trade: exports (million current US$)[l]	7	12	3[f]
International trade: imports (million current US$)[l]	133	150	194[f]
International trade: balance (million current US$)[l]	- 126	- 137	- 191[f]
Balance of payments, current account (million US$)	- 52	- 51	- 99[g]

Major trading partners						2017
Export partners (% of exports)	United States	26.5[l]	Thailand	26.4	Saint Lucia	8.3[l]
Import partners (% of imports)[l]	United States	69.2	Trinidad and Tobago	5.1	Poland	4.2

Social indicators	2005	2010	2018
Population growth rate (average annual %)[m]	2.6	1.7	1.2[b]
Urban population (% of total population)	100.0	100.0	100.0
Urban population growth rate (average annual %)[m]	2.6	1.7	1.2[b]
Fertility rate, total (live births per woman)	1.8	2.0[n]	...
Life expectancy at birth (females/males, years)	81.1 / 76.5[o,p]	... / ...	... / ...
Population age distribution (0-14/60+ years old, %)	27.7 / 10.2[j]	... / ...	23.3 / 7.6[c,d,q]
International migrant stock (000/% of total pop.)	4.7 / 37.1	5.1 / 37.1	5.6 / 37.4[f]
Refugees and others of concern to the UNHCR (000)	...	...	~0.0[g]
Education: Government expenditure (% of GDP)	...	2.8[r]	...
Intentional homicide rate (per 100 000 pop.)	8.1[p]	7.4[s]	27.7[t]

Environment and infrastructure indicators	2005	2010	2018
Individuals using the Internet (per 100 inhabitants)[l]	29.0	49.6	81.6[g]
Threatened species (number)	18[p]	33	52[f]
Forested area (% of land area)[l]	61.1	61.1	61.1[b]
CO2 emission estimates (million tons/tons per capita)	0.1 / 9.5	0.2 / 10.9	0.1 / 9.8[t]
Energy production, primary (Petajoules)[l]	0	0	0[b]
Energy supply per capita (Gigajoules)[l]	132	155	151[b]
Tourist/visitor arrivals at national borders (000)[u]	62	62	79[g]
Important sites for terrestrial biodiversity protected (%)	0.2	0.2	0.2
Pop. using improved drinking water (urban/rural, %)	94.0 / ...	94.5 / ...	94.6 / ...[b]
Pop. using improved sanitation facilities (urban/rural, %)	94.7 / ...	97.3 / ...	97.9 / ...[b]

a Projected estimate (medium fertility variant). b 2015. c Provisional data. d 2011. e East Caribbean Dollar. f 2017. g 2016. h Break in the time series. i Data classified according to ISIC Rev. 3. j 2001. k 2002. l Estimate. m Data refers to a 5-year period preceding the reference year. n 2006. o Data refers to a 3-year period up to and including the reference year. p 2004. q Population aged 65 years and over. r 2008. s 2009. t 2014. u Excluding nationals residing abroad.

Antigua and Barbuda

Region	Caribbean	UN membership date	11 November 1981
Population (000, 2018)	103 [a]	Surface area (km2)	442 [b]
Pop. density (per km2, 2018)	234.2 [a]	Sex ratio (m per 100 f)	92.3 [a]
Capital city	Saint John's	National currency	E. Caribbean Dollar (XCD) [c]
Capital city pop. (000, 2018)	20.8	Exchange rate (per US$)	2.7 [d]

Economic indicators

	2005	2010	2018
GDP: Gross domestic product (million current US$)	1 015	1 148	1 460 [e]
GDP growth rate (annual %, const. 2010 prices)	6.4	- 7.2	5.3 [e]
GDP per capita (current US$)	11 372.0	12 127.0	14 462.0 [e]
Economy: Agriculture (% of Gross Value Added)	2.0	1.8	1.9 [e]
Economy: Industry (% of Gross Value Added)	16.3	18.2	19.8 [e]
Economy: Services and other activity (% of GVA)	81.7	80.0	78.3 [e]
Employment in agriculture (% of employed) [f]	2.8	2.8 [g]	...
Employment in industry (% of employed) [f]	15.6	15.6 [g]	...
Employment in services & other sectors (% employed) [f]	81.6	81.6 [g]	...
Unemployment rate (% of labour force)	8.4 [h]	...	...
Labour force participation rate (female/male pop. %)	65.9 / 78.4 [h]	... / ...	... / ...
CPI: Consumer Price Index (2010=100)	89	100	112 [d]
Agricultural production index (2004-2006=100)	95	73	70 [e]
International trade: exports (million current US$)	121	35	62 [d]
International trade: imports (million current US$)	525	501	630 [d]
International trade: balance (million current US$)	- 405	- 466	- 567 [d]
Balance of payments, current account (million US$)	- 171	- 167	2 [e]

Major trading partners

						2017
Export partners (% of exports)	United Kingdom	52.5	United States	16.2	Spain	12.8
Import partners (% of imports)	United States	44.3	Undisclosed	14.5	Japan	4.7

Social indicators

	2005	2010	2018
Population growth rate (average annual %) [i]	1.3	1.2	1.1 [b]
Urban population (% of total population)	29.2	26.2	24.6
Urban population growth rate (average annual %) [i]	- 0.6	- 1.0	0.1 [b]
Fertility rate, total (live births per woman) [i]	2.3	2.2	2.1 [b]
Life expectancy at birth (females/males, years) [i]	76.4 / 71.5	77.4 / 72.6	78.2 / 73.3 [b]
Population age distribution (0-14/60+ years old, %)	28.4 / 9.3	26.6 / 8.9	23.6 / 11.3 [a]
International migrant stock (000/% of total pop.)	24.7 / 27.7	26.4 / 27.9	28.6 / 28.1 [a]
Refugees and others of concern to the UNHCR (000)	...	...	~0.0 [d]
Infant mortality rate (per 1 000 live births) [i]	12.2	10.0	9.1 [b]
Health: Current expenditure (% of GDP)	4.4	5.5	4.8 [b]
Education: Government expenditure (% of GDP)	3.4 [j]	2.5 [k]	...
Education: Primary gross enrol. ratio (f/m per 100 pop.)	... / ...	89.9 / 98.1	85.1 / 90.2 [b]
Education: Secondary gross enrol. ratio (f/m per 100 pop.)	65.7 / 72.6 [l,m]	100.0 / 98.6	94.6 / 92.7 [b]
Education: Tertiary gross enrol. ratio (f/m per 100 pop.)	... / ...	20.9 / 8.3	29.2 / 14.1 [n]
Intentional homicide rate (per 100 000 pop.)	3.4	6.3	10.3 [n]
Seats held by women in the National Parliament (%)	10.5	10.5	11.1

Environment and infrastructure indicators

	2005	2010	2018
Individuals using the Internet (per 100 inhabitants) [i]	27.0	47.0	73.0 [e]
Threatened species (number)	22 [o]	38	55 [d]
Forested area (% of land area) [i]	22.3	22.3	22.3 [b]
CO2 emission estimates (million tons/tons per capita)	0.4 / 5.1	0.5 / 6.0	0.5 / 5.8 [p]
Energy production, primary (Petajoules)	...	0	0 [q]
Energy supply per capita (Gigajoules) [i]	75	86	85 [b]
Tourist/visitor arrivals at national borders (000) [r]	245	230	265 [s,e]
Important sites for terrestrial biodiversity protected (%)	18.4	18.4	18.4
Pop. using improved drinking water (urban/rural, %)	97.8 / 97.8	97.9 / 97.9	97.9 / 97.9 [b]
Pop. using improved sanitation facilities (urban/rural, %)	89.5 / 89.5	91.4 / 91.4	91.4 / 91.4 [q]
Net Official Development Assist. received (% of GNI)	0.83	1.76	0.00 [e]

a Projected estimate (medium fertility variant). **b** 2015. **c** East Caribbean Dollar. **d** 2017. **e** 2016. **f** Data classified according to ISIC Rev. 3. **g** 2008. **h** 2001. **i** Data refers to a 5-year period preceding the reference year. **j** 2002. **k** 2009. **l** Estimate. **m** 2000. **n** 2012. **o** 2004. **p** 2014. **q** 2011. **r** Excluding nationals residing abroad. **s** Arrivals by air.

Argentina

Region	South America	UN membership date	24 October 1945	
Population (000, 2018)	44 689[a]	Surface area (km2)	2 780 400[b]	
Pop. density (per km2, 2018)	16.3[a]	Sex ratio (m per 100 f)	95.9[a]	
Capital city	Buenos Aires	National currency	Argentine Peso (ARS)	
Capital city pop. (000, 2018)	14 966.5[c]	Exchange rate (per US$)	18.6[d]	

Economic indicators

	2005	2010	2018
GDP: Gross domestic product (million current US$)	200 622	426 487	545 866[e]
GDP growth rate (annual %, const. 2010 prices)	8.9	10.1	- 2.3[e]
GDP per capita (current US$)	5 125.0	10 346.0	12 449.0[e]
Economy: Agriculture (% of Gross Value Added)	9.3	8.5	7.6[e]
Economy: Industry (% of Gross Value Added)	33.7	30.1	26.7[e]
Economy: Services and other activity (% of GVA)	57.0	61.4	65.8[e]
Employment in agriculture (% of employed)[f]	1.3	1.3	0.5
Employment in industry (% of employed)[f]	23.3	23.3	23.2
Employment in services & other sectors (% employed)[f]	75.5	75.4	76.3
Unemployment rate (% of labour force)	11.5	7.4	8.4[f]
Labour force participation rate (female/male pop. %)[f]	49.4 / 75.6	46.4 / 74.0	47.2 / 73.1
CPI: Consumer Price Index (2010=100)	...	...	113[g,d]
Agricultural production index (2004-2006=100)	105	112	131[e]
International trade: exports (million current US$)	40 106	68 174	58 384[d]
International trade: imports (million current US$)	28 689	56 792	66 899[d]
International trade: balance (million current US$)	11 418	11 382	- 8 515[d]
Balance of payments, current account (million US$)	5 274	- 1 623	- 30 792[d]

Major trading partners

							2017
Export partners (% of exports)	Brazil	15.9	United States	7.7	China	7.4	
Import partners (% of imports)	Brazil	26.7	China	18.4	United States	11.4	

Social indicators

	2005	2010	2018
Population growth rate (average annual %)[h]	1.1	1.0	1.0[b]
Urban population (% of total population)	90.0	90.8	91.9
Urban population growth rate (average annual %)[h]	1.3	1.2	1.2[b]
Fertility rate, total (live births per woman)[h]	2.5	2.4	2.3[b]
Life expectancy at birth (females/males, years)[h]	78.1 / 70.6	79.0 / 71.3	79.8 / 72.2[b]
Population age distribution (0-14/60+ years old, %)	26.9 / 13.8	25.9 / 14.4	24.7 / 15.6[a]
International migrant stock (000/% of total pop.)	1 673.1 / 4.3	1 806.0 / 4.4	2 164.5 / 4.9[d]
Refugees and others of concern to the UNHCR (000)	3.9[i]	4.2[i]	7.7[d]
Infant mortality rate (per 1 000 live births)[h]	15.0	14.6	13.7[b]
Health: Current expenditure (% of GDP)	6.4	6.8	6.8[b]
Health: Physicians (per 1 000 pop.)	3.2[j]	...	3.9[k]
Education: Government expenditure (% of GDP)	3.9	5.0	5.9[b]
Education: Primary gross enrol. ratio (f/m per 100 pop.)	116.6 / 117.7	115.9 / 117.5	109.7 / 110.1[b]
Education: Secondary gross enrol. ratio (f/m per 100 pop.)	98.4 / 89.8	106.6 / 97.1	110.2 / 104.0[b]
Education: Tertiary gross enrol. ratio (f/m per 100 pop.)	75.8 / 52.1	89.2 / 59.1	106.8 / 65.3[b]
Intentional homicide rate (per 100 000 pop.)	...	...	5.9[e]
Seats held by women in the National Parliament (%)	33.7	38.5	38.9

Environment and infrastructure indicators

	2005	2010	2018
Individuals using the Internet (per 100 inhabitants)	17.7	45.0[f]	70.2[f,a]
Research & Development expenditure (% of GDP)	0.4	0.6	0.6[l]
Threatened species (number)	186[i]	213	256[d]
Forested area (% of land area)[f]	11.0	10.4	9.9[b]
CO2 emission estimates (million tons/tons per capita)	162.1 / 4.2	187.9 / 4.5	204.0 / 4.7[l]
Energy production, primary (Petajoules)	3 609	3 343	3 100[b]
Energy supply per capita (Gigajoules)	75	80	83[b]
Tourist/visitor arrivals at national borders (000)	3 823	5 325	5 559[m,e]
Important sites for terrestrial biodiversity protected (%)	29.7	32.0	33.2
Pop. using improved drinking water (urban/rural, %)	98.4 / 87.5	98.7 / 93.7	99.0 / 100.0[b]
Pop. using improved sanitation facilities (urban/rural, %)	93.7 / 87.9	95.0 / 93.9	96.2 / 98.3[b]
Net Official Development Assist. received (% of GNI)	0.05	0.03	0.00[e]

a Projected estimate (medium fertility variant). b 2015. c Refers to Gran Buenos Aires. d 2017. e 2016. f Estimate. g Index base: December 2016=100. h Data refers to a 5-year period preceding the reference year. i Data as at the end of December. j 2004. k 2013. l 2014. m Break in the time series.

Armenia

Region	Western Asia
Population (000, 2018)	2 934 [a]
Pop. density (per km2, 2018)	103.1 [a]
Capital city	Yerevan
Capital city pop. (000, 2018)	1 080.3

UN membership date	02 March 1992
Surface area (km2)	29 743 [b]
Sex ratio (m per 100 f)	88.8 [a]
National currency	Armenian Dram (AMD)
Exchange rate (per US$)	484.1 [c]

Economic indicators

	2005	2010	2018
GDP: Gross domestic product (million current US$)	5 226	9 875	10 572 [d]
GDP growth rate (annual %, const. 2010 prices)	13.9	2.2	0.2 [d]
GDP per capita (current US$)	1 753.0	3 432.0	3 615.0 [d]
Economy: Agriculture (% of Gross Value Added) [e]	19.9	17.8	17.4 [d]
Economy: Industry (% of Gross Value Added) [e]	43.8	34.7	26.9 [d]
Economy: Services and other activity (% of GVA) [e]	36.3	47.4	55.7 [d]
Employment in agriculture (% of employed) [f]	40.6	38.6	33.2
Employment in industry (% of employed) [f]	17.7	17.4	16.3
Employment in services & other sectors (% employed) [f]	41.7	44.0	50.4
Unemployment rate (% of labour force)	8.2	19.0	18.0 [f]
Labour force participation rate (female/male pop. %) [f]	47.5 / 65.9	49.6 / 71.6	51.6 / 70.8
CPI: Consumer Price Index (2010=100) [f]	76	100 [g]	124 [c]
Agricultural production index (2004-2006=100)	108	96	127 [d]
Index of industrial production (2005=100) [h]	100	105	...
International trade: exports (million current US$)	937	1 011	2 041 [c]
International trade: imports (million current US$)	1 692	3 782	4 077 [c]
International trade: balance (million current US$)	- 755	- 2 770	- 2 035 [c]
Balance of payments, current account (million US$)	- 124	- 1 261	- 400 [c]

Major trading partners

						2017
Export partners (% of exports)	Russian Federation	26.5	Bulgaria	14.0	Switzerland	11.8
Import partners (% of imports)	Russian Federation	28.7	China	11.7	Turkey	5.6

Social indicators

	2005	2010	2018
Population growth rate (average annual %) [i]	- 0.6	- 0.7	0.3 [b]
Urban population (% of total population)	63.9	63.4	63.1
Urban population growth rate (average annual %) [i]	- 0.8	- 0.9	0.2 [b]
Fertility rate, total (live births per woman) [i]	1.6	1.7	1.6 [b]
Life expectancy at birth (females/males, years) [i]	75.3 / 69.1	75.8 / 69.4	77.0 / 70.6 [b]
Population age distribution (0-14/60+ years old, %)	21.5 / 14.4	19.5 / 14.8	20.1 / 17.5 [a]
International migrant stock (000/% of total pop.) [j]	469.1 / 15.7	221.6 / 7.7	190.7 / 6.5 [c]
Refugees and others of concern to the UNHCR (000)	219.6 [k]	85.8 [k]	18.6 [c]
Infant mortality rate (per 1 000 live births) [i]	27.0	21.0	13.2 [b]
Health: Current expenditure (% of GDP)	7.0	5.3	10.1 [b]
Health: Physicians (per 1 000 pop.)	...	2.8	2.8 [l]
Education: Government expenditure (% of GDP)	2.7	3.2	2.8 [d]
Education: Primary gross enrol. ratio (f/m per 100 pop.)	96.3 / 94.6	112.8 / 109.2 [m]	94.8 / 94.0 [d]
Education: Secondary gross enrol. ratio (f/m per 100 pop.)	96.5 / 87.8 [n]	99.0 / 101.2 [m]	88.4 / 84.0 [b]
Education: Tertiary gross enrol. ratio (f/m per 100 pop.)	46.0 / 32.8	58.0 / 47.6	57.1 / 45.0 [d]
Intentional homicide rate (per 100 000 pop.)	1.9	1.9	3.0 [d]
Seats held by women in the National Parliament (%)	5.3	9.2	18.1

Environment and infrastructure indicators

	2005	2010	2018
Individuals using the Internet (per 100 inhabitants)	5.3	25.0 [f]	62.0 [f,d]
Research & Development expenditure (% of GDP)	0.3 [o]	0.2 [o]	0.3 [p,q,b]
Threatened species (number)	35 [f]	36	114 [c]
Forested area (% of land area)	11.7	11.6	11.7 [f,b]
CO2 emission estimates (million tons/tons per capita)	4.4 / 1.4	4.2 / 1.4	5.5 / 1.8 [l]
Energy production, primary (Petajoules)	36	52	46 [b]
Energy supply per capita (Gigajoules)	34	40 [f]	43 [b]
Tourist/visitor arrivals at national borders (000)	319	684	1 260 [d]
Important sites for terrestrial biodiversity protected (%)	24.8	30.5	30.5
Pop. using improved drinking water (urban/rural, %)	99.1 / 89.1	99.6 / 96.5	100.0 / 100.0 [b]
Pop. using improved sanitation facilities (urban/rural, %)	95.7 / 78.3	95.9 / 78.2	96.2 / 78.2 [b]
Net Official Development Assist. received (% of GNI)	3.38	3.52	3.03 [d]

a Projected estimate (medium fertility variant). **b** 2015. **c** 2017. **d** 2016. **e** Data classified according to ISIC Rev. 4. **f** Estimate. **g** Break in the time series. **h** Data classified according to ISIC Rev. 3. **i** Data refers to a 5-year period preceding the reference year. **j** Including refugees. **k** Data as at the end of December. **l** 2014. **m** 2009. **n** 2000. **o** Partial data. **p** Excluding private non-profit. **q** Excluding business enterprise. **r** 2004.

Aruba

Region	Caribbean	Population (000, 2018)	106[a]	
Surface area (km2)	180[b]	Pop. density (per km2, 2018)	587.1[a]	
Sex ratio (m per 100 f)	90.3[a]	Capital city	Oranjestad	
National currency	Aruban Florin (AWG)	Capital city pop. (000, 2018)	29.9	
Exchange rate (per US$)	1.8[c]			

Economic indicators

	2005	2010	2018
GDP: Gross domestic product (million current US$)	2 331	2 391	2 667[d]
GDP growth rate (annual %, const. 2010 prices)	1.2	- 3.4	- 0.2[d]
GDP per capita (current US$)	23 303.0	23 513.0	25 444.0[d]
Economy: Agriculture (% of Gross Value Added)[e]	0.4	0.5	0.5[d]
Economy: Industry (% of Gross Value Added)[f]	19.6	15.4	15.4[d]
Economy: Services and other activity (% of GVA)	80.0	84.2	84.2[d]
Employment in agriculture (% of employed)[g,h]	0.5[i]	0.6[j]	0.6[k]
Employment in industry (% of employed)[g,h]	16.4[i]	14.5[j]	14.0[k]
Employment in services & other sectors (% employed)[g,h]	82.3[i]	84.4[j]	85.1[k]
Unemployment rate (% of labour force)	6.9[l]	10.6[g,j]	...
Labour force participation rate (female/male pop. %)[g]	... / ...	59.5 / 68.9[j,m]	58.8 / 69.6[k]
CPI: Consumer Price Index (2010=100)[n]	84	100	102[c]
International trade: exports (million current US$)	106	125	95[o,c]
International trade: imports (million current US$)	1 030	1 071	1 152[o,c]
International trade: balance (million current US$)	- 924	- 947	- 1 057[o,c]
Balance of payments, current account (million US$)	105	- 460	141[d]

Major trading partners

							2017
Export partners (% of exports)[o]	Colombia	24.2	United States	19.5	Netherlands	16.6	
Import partners (% of imports)[o]	United States	55.1	Netherlands	12.8	Areas nes[p]	12.1	

Social indicators

	2005	2010	2018
Population growth rate (average annual %)[q]	1.9	0.3	0.5[b]
Urban population (% of total population)	44.9	43.1	43.4
Urban population growth rate (average annual %)[q]	1.1	- 0.5	0.5[b]
Fertility rate, total (live births per woman)[q]	1.8	1.8	1.8[b]
Life expectancy at birth (females/males, years)[q]	76.4 / 71.5	77.1 / 72.2	77.8 / 72.9[b]
Population age distribution (0-14/60+ years old, %)	21.5 / 12.6	20.9 / 15.5	17.7 / 20.4[a]
International migrant stock (000/% of total pop.)	32.5 / 32.5	34.3 / 33.8	36.4 / 34.5[c]
Refugees and others of concern to the UNHCR (000)	...	~0.0[r]	~0.0[c]
Infant mortality rate (per 1 000 live births)	17.8	16.2	14.8[b]
Education: Government expenditure (% of GDP)	4.7	6.7	6.5[b]
Education: Primary gross enrol. ratio (f/m per 100 pop.)	107.8 / 114.9	113.0 / 114.5	115.2 / 118.9[e]
Education: Secondary gross enrol. ratio (f/m per 100 pop.)	96.1 / 95.8	98.3 / 93.5	112.1 / 110.2[t]
Education: Tertiary gross enrol. ratio (f/m per 100 pop.)	37.3 / 25.9	43.9 / 31.1	21.4 / 9.4[b]
Intentional homicide rate (per 100 000 pop.)	6.0	3.9	1.9[s]

Environment and infrastructure indicators

	2005	2010	2018
Individuals using the Internet (per 100 inhabitants)[o]	25.4	62.0	93.5[d]
Threatened species (number)	18[u]	22	32[c]
Forested area (% of land area)[q]	2.3	2.3	2.3[b]
CO2 emission estimates (million tons/tons per capita)	2.7 / 26.9	2.5 / 24.7	0.9 / 8.4[s]
Energy production, primary (Petajoules)[o]	5	5	1[b]
Energy supply per capita (Gigajoules)	299	273[o]	123[o,b]
Tourist/visitor arrivals at national borders (000)[v]	733	824	1 102[d]
Important sites for terrestrial biodiversity protected (%)	47.8	47.8	47.8
Pop. using improved drinking water (urban/rural, %)	95.8 / 95.8	97.4 / 97.4	98.1 / 98.1[b]
Pop. using improved sanitation facilities (urban/rural, %)	98.0 / 98.0	97.7 / 97.7	97.7 / 97.7[b]

a Projected estimate (medium fertility variant). b 2015. c 2017. d 2016. e Including mining and quarrying. f Excluding mining and quarrying. g Break in the time series. h Data classified according to ISIC Rev.3. i 2000. j Population aged 14 years and over. k 2011. l 2001. m Resident population (de jure). n Calculated by the Statistics Division of the United Nations from national indices. o Estimate. p Areas not elsewhere specified. q Data refers to a 5-year period preceding the reference year. r Data as at the end of December. s 2014. t 2012. u 2004. v Arrivals by air.

Australia

Region	Oceania	UN membership date	01 November 1945
Population (000, 2018)	24 772[a,b]	Surface area (km2)	7 692 060[c,d]
Pop. density (per km2, 2018)	3.2[a,b]	Sex ratio (m per 100 f)	99.3[a,b]
Capital city	Canberra	National currency	Australian Dollar (AUD)
Capital city pop. (000, 2018)	447.7[e]	Exchange rate (per US$)	1.3[f]

Economic indicators	2005	2010	2018
GDP: Gross domestic product (million current US$)	762 488	1 293 794	1 304 463[g]
GDP growth rate (annual %, const. 2010 prices)	3.0	2.4	2.0[g]
GDP per capita (current US$)	37 674.0	58 490.0	54 069.0[g]
Economy: Agriculture (% of Gross Value Added)[h]	3.0	2.5	2.5[g]
Economy: Industry (% of Gross Value Added)[h]	27.9	28.5	25.7[g]
Economy: Services and other activity (% of GVA)[h]	69.1	69.0	71.8[g]
Employment in agriculture (% of employed)[i]	3.6	3.2	2.6
Employment in industry (% of employed)[i]	21.1	21.0	19.0
Employment in services & other sectors (% employed)[i]	75.3	75.8	78.5
Unemployment rate (% of labour force)	5.0	5.2	5.6[i]
Labour force participation rate (female/male pop. %)[i]	57.0 / 72.2	58.7 / 72.4	59.2 / 70.4
CPI: Consumer Price Index (2010=100)[j,k]	86	100[l]	116[f]
Agricultural production index (2004-2006=100)	99	95	104[g]
Index of industrial production (2005=100)[m]	100	111	123[n]
International trade: exports (million current US$)[o]	106 011	212 109	230 163[f]
International trade: imports (million current US$)[o]	125 221	201 703	228 442[f]
International trade: balance (million current US$)[o]	- 19 210	10 405	1 721[f]
Balance of payments, current account (million US$)	- 43 343	- 44 714	- 32 653[f]

Major trading partners						2017
Export partners (% of exports)	China	29.6	Areas nes[p]	15.0[i]	Japan	10.4
Import partners (% of imports)	China	21.9	United States	10.3	Japan	7.2

Social indicators	2005	2010	2018
Population growth rate (average annual %)[a,q]	1.2	1.8	1.5[d]
Urban population (% of total population)[a]	84.6	85.2	86.0
Urban population growth rate (average annual %)[a,q]	1.3	1.9	1.6[d]
Fertility rate, total (live births per woman)[a,q]	1.8	2.0	1.9[d]
Life expectancy at birth (females/males, years)[a,q]	82.8 / 77.8	83.8 / 79.2	84.4 / 80.2[d]
Population age distribution (0-14/60+ years old, %)[a]	19.8 / 17.4	19.0 / 18.9	19.1 / 21.2[b]
International migrant stock (000/% of total pop.)[e]	4 878.0 / 24.1	5 883.0 / 26.6	7 035.6 / 28.8[f]
Refugees and others of concern to the UNHCR (000)	66.8[r]	25.6[r]	82.4[f]
Infant mortality rate (per 1 000 live births)[e,q]	4.9	4.4	3.9[d]
Health: Current expenditure (% of GDP)	8.0	8.5	9.4[d]
Health: Physicians (per 1 000 pop.)	2.5[s]	2.9[t]	3.5[d]
Education: Government expenditure (% of GDP)	4.9	5.6	5.2[n]
Education: Primary gross enrol. ratio (f/m per 100 pop.)	103.3 / 101.8	105.8 / 106.0	101.3 / 101.4[g]
Education: Secondary gross enrol. ratio (f/m per 100 pop.)	... / ...	... / ...	142.7 / 164.5[g]
Education: Tertiary gross enrol. ratio (f/m per 100 pop.)	... / ...	... / ...	144.1 / 100.8[g]
Intentional homicide rate (per 100 000 pop.)	1.3	1.0	0.9[g]
Seats held by women in the National Parliament (%)	24.7	27.3	28.7

Environment and infrastructure indicators	2005	2010	2018
Individuals using the Internet (per 100 inhabitants)	63.0[u]	76.0[i]	88.2[i,g]
Research & Development expenditure (% of GDP)	1.9[v]	2.4[i]	2.2[i,w]
Threatened species (number)[x]	621[v]	853	948[f]
Forested area (% of land area)	16.6	16.0	16.2[i,d]
CO2 emission estimates (million tons/tons per capita)	350.2 / 17.2	390.9 / 17.6	361.3 / 15.3[n]
Energy production, primary (Petajoules)[x]	11 451	13 620	15 938[d]
Energy supply per capita (Gigajoules)[x]	233	245	220[d]
Tourist/visitor arrivals at national borders (000)[y]	5 499	5 790	8 263[g]
Important sites for terrestrial biodiversity protected (%)	38.7	46.2	54.3
Pop. using improved drinking water (urban/rural, %)	100.0 / 100.0	100.0 / 100.0	100.0 / 100.0[d]
Pop. using improved sanitation facilities (urban/rural, %)	100.0 / 100.0	100.0 / 100.0	100.0 / 100.0[d]
Net Official Development Assist. disbursed (% of GNI)[z]	0.25	0.32	0.23[f,f]

a Including Christmas Island, Cocos (Keeling) Islands and Norfolk Island. b Projected estimate (medium fertility variant). c Including Norfolk Island. d 2015. e Refers to Significant Urban Areas as of 2001. f 2017. g 2016. h Data classified according to ISIC Rev. 4. i Estimate. j Weighted average of index values computed for the eight capital cities. k Calculated by the Statistics Division of the United Nations from national indices. l Break in the time series. m Twelve months ending 30 June of the year stated. n 2014. o Imports FOB. p Areas not elsewhere specified. q Data refers to a 5-year period preceding the reference year. r Data as at the end of December. s 2001. t 2009. u Population aged 15 years and over. v 2004. w 2013. x Excluding overseas territories. y Excluding nationals residing abroad and crew members. z Development Assistance Committee member (OECD). { Provisional data.

Austria

Region	Western Europe	UN membership date		14 December 1955
Population (000, 2018)	8 752[a]	Surface area (km2)		83 871[b]
Pop. density (per km2, 2018)	106.2[a]	Sex ratio (m per 100 f)		96.3[a]
Capital city	Vienna	National currency		Euro (EUR)
Capital city pop. (000, 2018)	1 900.5	Exchange rate (per US$)		0.8[c]

Economic indicators	2005	2010	2018
GDP: Gross domestic product (million current US$)	315 967	391 893	390 800[d]
GDP growth rate (annual %, const. 2010 prices)	2.1	1.9	1.5[d]
GDP per capita (current US$)	38 282.0	46 599.0	44 857.0[d]
Economy: Agriculture (% of Gross Value Added)[e]	1.4	1.4	1.2[d]
Economy: Industry (% of Gross Value Added)[e]	30.5	28.7	27.7[d]
Economy: Services and other activity (% of GVA)[e]	68.1	69.9	71.0[d]
Employment in agriculture (% of employed)[f]	5.3	5.2[f]	4.2[f]
Employment in industry (% of employed)[f]	27.6	24.9	25.5
Employment in services & other sectors (% employed)[f]	67.2	69.9	70.3
Unemployment rate (% of labour force)	5.6	4.8	5.3[f]
Labour force participation rate (female/male pop. %)[f]	50.7 / 66.1	53.5 / 66.9	54.9 / 65.8
CPI: Consumer Price Index (2010=100)	91	100	114[c]
Agricultural production index (2004-2006=100)	100	98	100[d]
Index of industrial production (2005=100)	100	110	119[g]
International trade: exports (million current US$)	117 722	144 882	159 785[f,c]
International trade: imports (million current US$)	119 950	150 593	166 551[f,c]
International trade: balance (million current US$)	- 2 228	- 5 711	- 6 766[f,c]
Balance of payments, current account (million US$)	6 245	11 478	7 709[c]

Major trading partners						2017
Export partners (% of exports)[f]	Germany	30.0	United States	6.5	Italy	6.2
Import partners (% of imports)[f]	Germany	36.8	Italy	6.1	China	5.9

Social indicators	2005	2010	2018
Population growth rate (average annual %)[h]	0.5	0.4	0.6[b]
Urban population (% of total population)	58.8	57.4	58.3
Urban population growth rate (average annual %)[h]	—0.0	- 0.1	0.7[b]
Fertility rate, total (live births per woman)[h]	1.4	1.4	1.4[b]
Life expectancy at birth (females/males, years)[h]	81.7 / 75.9	82.8 / 77.3	83.5 / 78.4[b]
Population age distribution (0-14/60+ years old, %)	16.0 / 22.1	14.7 / 23.3	14.1 / 25.5[a]
International migrant stock (000/% of total pop.)	1 136.3 / 13.8	1 276.0 / 15.2	1 660.3 / 19.0[c]
Refugees and others of concern to the UNHCR (000)	62.8[i]	68.7[i]	170.9[c]
Infant mortality rate (per 1 000 live births)[h]	4.5	3.8	3.3[b]
Health: Current expenditure (% of GDP)	9.6	10.1	10.3[b]
Health: Physicians (per 1 000 pop.)	...	4.8	5.2[d]
Education: Government expenditure (% of GDP)	5.2	5.7	5.4[g]
Education: Primary gross enrol. ratio (f/m per 100 pop.)	100.8 / 100.9	99.1 / 100.5	102.0 / 102.5[d]
Education: Secondary gross enrol. ratio (f/m per 100 pop.)	97.8 / 102.8	96.8 / 100.8	98.9 / 102.9[d]
Education: Tertiary gross enrol. ratio (f/m per 100 pop.)	... / ...	... / ...	90.8 / 76.4[d]
Intentional homicide rate (per 100 000 pop.)	0.7	0.7	0.7[d]
Seats held by women in the National Parliament (%)	33.9	27.9	34.4

Environment and infrastructure indicators	2005	2010	2018
Individuals using the Internet (per 100 inhabitants)	58.0[i]	75.2[i]	84.3[d]
Research & Development expenditure (% of GDP)[f]	2.4	2.7	3.1[b]
Threatened species (number)	67[k]	82	118[c]
Forested area (% of land area)	46.6[f]	46.7	46.9[f,b]
CO2 emission estimates (million tons/tons per capita)	74.2 / 9.0	67.5 / 8.0	58.7 / 6.9[g]
Energy production, primary (Petajoules)	414	503	500[b]
Energy supply per capita (Gigajoules)	172	170	161[b]
Tourist/visitor arrivals at national borders (000)[l]	19 952	22 004	28 121[d]
Important sites for terrestrial biodiversity protected (%)	63.5	66.1	66.3
Pop. using improved drinking water (urban/rural, %)	100.0 / 100.0	100.0 / 100.0	100.0 / 100.0[b]
Pop. using improved sanitation facilities (urban/rural, %)	100.0 / 100.0	100.0 / 100.0	100.0 / 100.0[b]
Net Official Development Assist. disbursed (% of GNI)[m]	0.52	0.32	0.30[n,c]

a Projected estimate (medium fertility variant). b 2015. c 2017. d 2016. e Data classified according to ISIC Rev. 4. f Estimate. g 2014. h Data refers to a 5-year period preceding the reference year. i Data as at the end of December. j Population aged 16 to 74 years. k 2004. l Only paid accommodation; excluding stays at friends and relatives and second homes. m Development Assistance Committee member (OECD). n Provisional data.

Azerbaijan

Region	Western Asia	UN membership date	02 March 1992
Population (000, 2018)	9 924 [a,b]	Surface area (km2)	86 600 [c]
Pop. density (per km2, 2018)	120.1 [a,b]	Sex ratio (m per 100 f)	99.3 [a,b]
Capital city	Baku	National currency	Azerbaijan manat (AZN)
Capital city pop. (000, 2018)	2 285.7 [d]	Exchange rate (per US$)	1.7 [e]

Economic indicators	2005	2010	2018
GDP: Gross domestic product (million current US$)	13 245	52 906	37 847 [f]
GDP growth rate (annual %, const. 2010 prices)	28.0	4.6	- 2.5 [f]
GDP per capita (current US$)	1 551.0	5 857.0	3 892.0 [f]
Economy: Agriculture (% of Gross Value Added) [g]	9.8	5.9	6.0 [f]
Economy: Industry (% of Gross Value Added) [g]	63.2	64.0	51.3 [f]
Economy: Services and other activity (% of GVA) [g]	27.0	30.1	42.7 [f]
Employment in agriculture (% of employed) [h]	40.5	38.2	37.5
Employment in industry (% of employed) [h]	12.6	13.7	13.8
Employment in services & other sectors (% employed) [h]	46.9	48.0	48.7
Unemployment rate (% of labour force)	7.3	5.6	5.1 [h]
Labour force participation rate (female/male pop. %) [h]	61.1 / 66.0	61.4 / 66.8	62.8 / 69.2
CPI: Consumer Price Index (2010=100)	61	100	149 [e]
Agricultural production index (2004-2006=100)	104	117	141 [f]
Index of industrial production (2005=100)	100	200	188 [i]
International trade: exports (million current US$)	4 347	21 278	13 798 [e]
International trade: imports (million current US$)	4 211	6 597	8 767 [e]
International trade: balance (million current US$)	136	14 682	5 031 [e]
Balance of payments, current account (million US$)	167	15 040	1 685 [e]

Major trading partners						2017
Export partners (% of exports)	Italy	31.9	Turkey	9.9 [h]	Israel	4.6
Import partners (% of imports)	Russian Federation	16.8	Turkey	14.7	China	11.2

Social indicators	2005	2010	2018
Population growth rate (average annual %) [b,j]	1.0	1.1	1.3 [c]
Urban population (% of total population) [b]	52.4	53.4	55.7
Urban population growth rate (average annual %) [b,j]	1.4	1.5	1.7 [c]
Fertility rate, total (live births per woman) [b,j]	1.9	1.8	2.1 [c]
Life expectancy at birth (females/males, years) [b,j]	70.3 / 64.6	73.4 / 66.9	74.6 / 68.6 [c]
Population age distribution (0-14/60+ years old, %) [b]	26.2 / 8.5	22.8 / 8.1	23.3 / 10.6 [a]
International migrant stock (000/% of total pop.) [b,k]	302.2 / 3.5	276.9 / 3.1	259.2 / 2.6 [a]
Refugees and others of concern to the UNHCR (000)	584.3 [l]	596.9 [l]	618.3 [e]
Infant mortality rate (per 1 000 live births) [b,j]	54.2	40.7	31.4 [c]
Health: Current expenditure (% of GDP)	7.4	4.9	6.7 [c]
Health: Physicians (per 1 000 pop.)	...	3.6	3.4 [l]
Education: Government expenditure (% of GDP)	3.0	2.8	3.0 [c]
Education: Primary gross enrol. ratio (f/m per 100 pop.) [h]	92.8 / 98.2	93.2 / 94.2	105.9 / 106.9 [f]
Education: Tertiary gross enrol. ratio (f/m per 100 pop.) [h]	... / ...	19.2 / 19.4	29.7 / 25.0 [f]
Intentional homicide rate (per 100 000 pop.)	2.2	2.3	2.1 [f]
Seats held by women in the National Parliament (%)	10.5	11.4	16.8

Environment and infrastructure indicators	2005	2010	2018
Individuals using the Internet (per 100 inhabitants)	8.0	46.0 [m]	78.2 [f]
Research & Development expenditure (% of GDP)	0.2 [n]	0.2	0.2 [c]
Threatened species (number)	38 [o]	45	97 [e]
Forested area (% of land area) [h]	10.6	12.2	13.8 [c]
CO2 emission estimates (million tons/tons per capita)	34.3 / 4.0	30.7 / 3.4	37.5 / 3.9 [i]
Energy production, primary (Petajoules)	1 155	2 759	2 472 [c]
Energy supply per capita (Gigajoules)	67	53	62 [c]
Tourist/visitor arrivals at national borders (000)	693	1 280	2 044 [f]
Important sites for terrestrial biodiversity protected (%)	33.3	39.4	39.4
Pop. using improved drinking water (urban/rural, %)	90.5 / 65.3	92.6 / 71.5	94.7 / 77.8 [c]
Pop. using improved sanitation facilities (urban/rural, %)	81.9 / 64.6	86.8 / 75.6	91.6 / 86.6 [c]
Net Official Development Assist. disbursed (% of GNI)	...	...	0.04 [f]
Net Official Development Assist. received (% of GNI)	1.82	0.33	0.22 [f]

a Projected estimate (medium fertility variant). b Including Nagorno-Karabakh. c 2015. d Including communities under the authority of the Town Council. e 2017. f 2016. g Data classified according to ISIC Rev. 4. h Estimate. i 2014. j Data refers to a 5-year period preceding the reference year. k Including refugees. l Data as at the end of December. m Population aged 7 years and over. n Data have been converted from the former national currency using the appropriate conversion rate. o 2004.

Bahamas

Region	Caribbean	
Population (000, 2018)	399[a]	
Pop. density (per km2, 2018)	39.9[a]	
Capital city	Nassau	
Capital city pop. (000, 2018)	279.7	

UN membership date	18 September 1973
Surface area (km2)	13 940[b]
Sex ratio (m per 100 f)	96.0[a]
National currency	Bahamian Dollar (BSD)
Exchange rate (per US$)	1.0[c]

Economic indicators	2005	2010	2018
GDP: Gross domestic product (million current US$)	9 836	10 096	11 262[d]
GDP growth rate (annual %, const. 2010 prices)	3.4	1.5	0.2[d]
GDP per capita (current US$)	29 875.0	27 979.0	28 785.0[d]
Economy: Agriculture (% of Gross Value Added)[e,f]	1.1	1.2	1.0[d]
Economy: Industry (% of Gross Value Added)[e,f]	11.7	12.4	12.8[d]
Economy: Services and other activity (% of GVA)[e,f]	87.1	86.4	86.2[d]
Employment in agriculture (% of employed)[g]	3.5	3.3	4.0
Employment in industry (% of employed)[g]	17.8	14.7	11.7
Employment in services & other sectors (% employed)[g]	78.7	82.0	84.3
Unemployment rate (% of labour force)	10.2	14.3[g]	12.3[g]
Labour force participation rate (female/male pop. %)[g]	69.9 / 81.6	70.1 / 82.0	70.1 / 82.0
CPI: Consumer Price Index (2010=100)[g,h]	88	100	111[c]
Agricultural production index (2004-2006=100)	99	123	131[d]
International trade: exports (million current US$)[i]	271	620	200[g,o]
International trade: imports (million current US$)[i]	2 567	2 862	2 660[g,c]
International trade: balance (million current US$)[i]	- 2 296	- 2 242	- 2 380[g,c]
Balance of payments, current account (million US$)	- 701	- 814	- 1 106[d]

Major trading partners						2017
Export partners (% of exports)	United States	83.1[g]	France	4.4	Finland	3.2[g]
Import partners (% of imports)[g]	United States	81.9	Areas nes[j]	3.0	Dominica	1.5

Social indicators	2005	2010	2018
Population growth rate (average annual %)[k]	2.0	1.8	1.4[b]
Urban population (% of total population)	82.2	82.4	83.0
Urban population growth rate (average annual %)[k]	2.1	1.9	1.5[b]
Fertility rate, total (live births per woman)[k]	1.9	1.9	1.8[b]
Life expectancy at birth (females/males, years)[k]	76.2 / 70.0	77.3 / 71.2	78.1 / 72.0[b]
Population age distribution (0-14/60+ years old, %)	25.6 / 9.4	22.5 / 10.5	20.5 / 14.0[a]
International migrant stock (000/% of total pop.)	45.6 / 13.8	54.7 / 15.2	61.8 / 15.6[c]
Refugees and others of concern to the UNHCR (000)	...	~0.0[l]	~0.0[c]
Infant mortality rate (per 1 000 live births)[k]	11.6	10.0	9.1[b]
Health: Current expenditure (% of GDP)	5.9	7.4	7.4[b]
Health: Physicians (per 1 000 pop.)	...	2.7[m]	2.3[n]
Education: Government expenditure (% of GDP)	2.8[g,o]	...	...
Education: Primary gross enrol. ratio (f/m per 100 pop.)	108.4 / 109.9	109.0 / 106.9	97.9 / 92.9[d]
Education: Secondary gross enrol. ratio (f/m per 100 pop.)	89.1 / 89.4	95.1 / 90.2	93.1 / 87.9[d]
Intentional homicide rate (per 100 000 pop.)	15.8	26.1	28.4[d]
Seats held by women in the National Parliament (%)	20.0	12.2	12.8

Environment and infrastructure indicators	2005	2010	2018
Individuals using the Internet (per 100 inhabitants)[g]	25.0	43.0	80.0[d]
Threatened species (number)	42[p]	62	86[c]
Forested area (% of land area)[g]	51.4	51.4	51.4[b]
CO2 emission estimates (million tons/tons per capita)	1.7 / 5.5	1.7 / 4.6	2.4 / 6.3[q]
Energy production, primary (Petajoules)	0	0	0[b]
Energy supply per capita (Gigajoules)	83[g]	96	87[g,b]
Tourist/visitor arrivals at national borders (000)	1 608	1 370	1 482[d]
Important sites for terrestrial biodiversity protected (%)	7.0	7.0	24.7
Pop. using improved drinking water (urban/rural, %)	97.3 / 97.3	98.1 / 98.1	98.4 / 98.4[b]
Pop. using improved sanitation facilities (urban/rural, %)	90.0 / 90.0	91.4 / 91.4	92.0 / 92.0[b]

a Projected estimate (medium fertility variant). b 2015. c 2017. d 2016. e Data classified according to ISIC Rev. 4. f At producers' prices. g Estimate. h New Providence. i Trade statistics exclude certain oil and chemical products. j Areas not elsewhere specified. k Data refers to a 5-year period preceding the reference year. l Data as at the end of December. m 2008. n 2011. o 2000. p 2004. q 2014.

Bahrain

Region	Western Asia	UN membership date	21 September 1971
Population (000, 2018)	1 567 [a]	Surface area (km2)	771 [b]
Pop. density (per km2, 2018)	2 061.8 [a]	Sex ratio (m per 100 f)	173.0 [a]
Capital city	Manama	National currency	Bahraini Dinar (BHD)
Capital city pop. (000, 2018)	564.6 [c]	Exchange rate (per US$)	0.4 [d]

Economic indicators

	2005	2010	2018
GDP: Gross domestic product (million current US$)	15 969	25 713	32 179 [e]
GDP growth rate (annual %, const. 2010 prices)	6.8	4.3	3.3 [e]
GDP per capita (current US$)	17 959.0	20 722.0	22 579.0 [e]
Economy: Agriculture (% of Gross Value Added) [f]	0.3	0.3	0.3 [e]
Economy: Industry (% of Gross Value Added) [f]	42.8	45.5	39.8 [e]
Economy: Services and other activity (% of GVA) [f]	56.9	54.2	59.8 [e]
Employment in agriculture (% of employed) [g]	1.3	1.1	1.0
Employment in industry (% of employed) [g]	30.7	35.7	35.6
Employment in services & other sectors (% employed) [g]	68.0	63.2	63.4
Unemployment rate (% of labour force)	7.8 [g]	1.1	1.4 [g]
Labour force participation rate (female/male pop. %) [g]	38.9 / 86.2	43.8 / 87.4	44.2 / 87.0
CPI: Consumer Price Index (2010=100) [h]	87	100	115 [d]
Agricultural production index (2004-2006=100)	91	118	198 [e]
Index of industrial production (2005=100) [i]	100	117	134 [j]
International trade: exports (million current US$)	10 239	16 059	9 666 [g,d]
International trade: imports (million current US$)	9 339	16 002	12 613 [g,d]
International trade: balance (million current US$)	899	58	- 2 947 [g,d]
Balance of payments, current account (million US$)	1 474	770	- 1 600 [d]

Major trading partners

								2017
Export partners (% of exports) [g]	Saudi Arabia	18.1	United Arab Emirates	17.3		United States	11.0
Import partners (% of imports) [g]	Areas nes [k]	21.4	China		9.7	United States	8.6

Social indicators

	2005	2010	2018
Population growth rate (average annual %) [l]	5.8	6.7	2.0 [b]
Urban population (% of total population)	88.4	88.6	89.3
Urban population growth rate (average annual %) [l]	5.8	6.7	2.1 [b]
Fertility rate, total (live births per woman) [l]	2.6	2.2	2.1 [b]
Life expectancy at birth (females/males, years) [l]	75.8 / 74.2	76.7 / 74.9	77.5 / 75.6 [b]
Population age distribution (0-14/60+ years old, %)	25.7 / 3.4	20.3 / 3.5	19.2 / 4.9 [a]
International migrant stock (000/% of total pop.) [m]	404.0 / 45.4	657.9 / 53.0	722.6 / 48.4 [d]
Refugees and others of concern to the UNHCR (000)	~0.0 [n]	0.2 [n]	0.4 [d]
Infant mortality rate (per 1 000 live births) [l]	9.8	8.0	6.9 [b]
Health: Current expenditure (% of GDP)	3.0	3.3	5.2 [b]
Health: Physicians (per 1 000 pop.)	1.1	0.9	0.9 [b]
Education: Government expenditure (% of GDP)	...	2.5 [o]	2.7 [e]
Education: Primary gross enrol. ratio (f/m per 100 pop.)	97.5 / 94.1	101.0 / 96.1 [p]	102.2 / 100.1 [a]
Education: Secondary gross enrol. ratio (f/m per 100 pop.)	101.5 / 91.5	93.5 / 92.2	104.3 / 103.4 [e]
Education: Tertiary gross enrol. ratio (f/m per 100 pop.)	39.9 / 13.0	38.3 / 12.2 [p]	63.0 / 33.7 [a]
Intentional homicide rate (per 100 000 pop.)	0.4	0.9	0.5 [j]
Seats held by women in the National Parliament (%)	0.0	2.5	7.5

Environment and infrastructure indicators

	2005	2010	2018
Individuals using the Internet (per 100 inhabitants)	21.3	55.0	98.0 [e]
Research & Development expenditure (% of GDP)	...	...	0.1 [j]
Threatened species (number)	18 [q]	32	38 [d]
Forested area (% of land area) [g]	0.6	0.7	0.8 [b]
CO2 emission estimates (million tons/tons per capita)	19.2 / 26.5	29.3 / 23.2	31.3 / 23.0 [j]
Energy production, primary (Petajoules)	672	849	957 [b]
Energy supply per capita (Gigajoules)	480	407	420 [b]
Tourist/visitor arrivals at national borders (000) [r]	6 313	11 952	10 158 [s,e]
Important sites for terrestrial biodiversity protected (%)	19.6	27.5	27.5
Pop. using improved drinking water (urban/rural, %)	100.0 / 100.0	100.0 / 100.0	100.0 / 100.0 [b]
Pop. using improved sanitation facilities (urban/rural, %)	99.2 / 99.2	99.2 / 99.2	99.2 / 99.2 [b]

a Projected estimate (medium fertility variant). b 2015. c Refers to the urban area of the municipality of Al-Manamah. d 2017. e 2016. f At producers' prices. g Estimate. h Calculated by the Statistics Division of the United Nations from national indices. i Data classified according to ISIC Rev. 3. j 2014. k Areas not elsewhere specified. l Data refers to a 5-year period preceding the reference year. m Refers to foreign citizens. n Data as at the end of December. o 2008. p 2006. q 2004. r Excluding nationals residing abroad. s Break in the time series.

Bangladesh

Region	Southern Asia	UN membership date	17 September 1974
Population (000, 2018)	166 368[a]	Surface area (km2)	147 570[b]
Pop. density (per km2, 2018)	1 278.1[a]	Sex ratio (m per 100 f)	101.6[a]
Capital city	Dhaka	National currency	Taka (BDT)
Capital city pop. (000, 2018)	19 578.4[c]	Exchange rate (per US$)	82.7[d]

Economic indicators	2005	2010	2018
GDP: Gross domestic product (million current US$)	57 628	114 508	220 837[e]
GDP growth rate (annual %, const. 2010 prices)	6.0	5.6	7.1[e]
GDP per capita (current US$)	402.0	753.0	1 355.0[e]
Economy: Agriculture (% of Gross Value Added)	20.1	17.8	14.8[e]
Economy: Industry (% of Gross Value Added)	27.2	26.1	28.8[e]
Economy: Services and other activity (% of GVA)	52.6	56.0	56.5[e]
Employment in agriculture (% of employed)	48.1[f]	47.3	37.6[f]
Employment in industry (% of employed)[f]	14.5	17.6	21.4
Employment in services & other sectors (% employed)[f]	37.4	35.1	41.0
Unemployment rate (% of labour force)	4.2	3.4	4.4[f]
Labour force participation rate (female/male pop. %)[f]	28.0 / 86.2	30.0 / 83.6	33.2 / 79.8
CPI: Consumer Price Index (2010=100)	69	100	161[d]
Agricultural production index (2004-2006=100)	103	128	144[e]
Index of industrial production (2005=100)[g,h]	100	148	206[i]
International trade: exports (million current US$)	9 332	19 231	31 367[f,d]
International trade: imports (million current US$)	12 631	30 504	47 743[f,d]
International trade: balance (million current US$)	- 3 299	- 11 273	- 16 376[f,d]
Balance of payments, current account (million US$)	508[j]	2 109	- 6 365[d]

Major trading partners						2017
Export partners (% of exports)[f]	United States	19.3	Germany	14.7	United Kingdom	11.0
Import partners (% of imports)[f]	China	21.5	India	12.2	Singapore	9.2

Social indicators	2005	2010	2018
Population growth rate (average annual %)[k]	1.7	1.2	1.2[b]
Urban population (% of total population)	26.8	30.5	36.6
Urban population growth rate (average annual %)[k]	4.3	3.7	3.5[b]
Fertility rate, total (live births per woman)[k]	2.9	2.5	2.2[b]
Life expectancy at birth (females/males, years)[k]	67.3 / 66.2	70.0 / 68.2	72.9 / 69.8[b]
Population age distribution (0-14/60+ years old, %)	34.4 / 6.6	32.1 / 6.9	27.8 / 7.5[a]
International migrant stock (000/% of total pop.)[l]	1 166.7 / 0.8	1 345.5 / 0.9	1 500.9 / 0.9[d]
Refugees and others of concern to the UNHCR (000)	271.2[m]	229.3[m]	307.5[d]
Infant mortality rate (per 1 000 live births)[k]	56.0	43.3	33.3[b]
Health: Current expenditure (% of GDP)[n,o]	2.8	2.7	2.6[b]
Health: Physicians (per 1 000 pop.)	0.3	0.4	0.5[b]
Education: Government expenditure (% of GDP)	1.9[p]	1.9[q]	2.5[f,e]
Education: Primary gross enrol. ratio (f/m per 100 pop.)	100.8 / 96.3	105.5 / 99.2[f]	122.1 / 115.2[e]
Education: Secondary gross enrol. ratio (f/m per 100 pop.)	46.9 / 44.0	53.0 / 47.2	72.5 / 65.6[e]
Education: Tertiary gross enrol. ratio (f/m per 100 pop.)	4.2 / 8.1	7.8 / 13.1[q]	14.2 / 20.3[e]
Intentional homicide rate (per 100 000 pop.)	2.5	2.6	2.5[b]
Seats held by women in the National Parliament (%)	2.0	18.6	20.3

Environment and infrastructure indicators	2005	2010	2018
Individuals using the Internet (per 100 inhabitants)[f]	0.2	3.7	18.2[e]
Threatened species (number)	85[p]	122	151[d]
Forested area (% of land area)	11.2	11.1[f]	11.0[f,b]
CO2 emission estimates (million tons/tons per capita)	39.5 / 0.3	59.9 / 0.4	73.2 / 0.5[r]
Energy production, primary (Petajoules)	1 027	1 304	1 509[b]
Energy supply per capita (Gigajoules)	8	10	11[b]
Tourist/visitor arrivals at national borders (000)	208	303	125[r]
Important sites for terrestrial biodiversity protected (%)	37.9	48.0	48.0
Pop. using improved drinking water (urban/rural, %)	84.3 / 78.2	85.4 / 82.6	86.5 / 87.0[b]
Pop. using improved sanitation facilities (urban/rural, %)	53.3 / 49.8	55.5 / 55.9	57.7 / 62.1[b]
Net Official Development Assist. received (% of GNI)	1.82	1.13	1.07[e]

a Projected estimate (medium fertility variant). b 2015. c Mega city. d 2017. e 2016. f Estimate. g Data classified according to ISIC Rev. 3. h Twelve months ending 30 June of the year stated. i 2013. j Break in the time series. k Data refers to a 5-year period preceding the reference year. l Including refugees. m Data as at the end of December. n Data revision. o Data refer to fiscal years beginning 1 July. p 2004. q 2009. r 2014.

Barbados

Region	Caribbean	UN membership date	09 December 1966
Population (000, 2018)	286[a]	Surface area (km2)	431[b]
Pop. density (per km2, 2018)	666.0[a]	Sex ratio (m per 100 f)	91.8[a]
Capital city	Bridgetown	National currency	Barbados Dollar (BBD)
Capital city pop. (000, 2018)	89.2	Exchange rate (per US$)	2.0[c]

Economic indicators

	2005	2010	2018
GDP: Gross domestic product (million current US$)	3 897	4 365	4 553[d]
GDP growth rate (annual %, const. 2010 prices)	4.0	0.3	1.7[d]
GDP per capita (current US$)	14 223.0	15 613.0	15 975.0[d]
Economy: Agriculture (% of Gross Value Added)	1.8	1.5	1.6[d]
Economy: Industry (% of Gross Value Added)	16.9	15.5	15.5[d]
Economy: Services and other activity (% of GVA)	81.3	83.0	83.0[d]
Employment in agriculture (% of employed)[e]	2.4	2.8	2.9
Employment in industry (% of employed)[e]	20.6	28.0	19.2
Employment in services & other sectors (% employed)[e]	77.0	69.2	78.0
Unemployment rate (% of labour force)	9.1	10.7	9.5[e]
Labour force participation rate (female/male pop. %)[e]	64.2 / 75.4	63.5 / 73.1	61.9 / 69.5
CPI: Consumer Price Index (2010=100)[f,g]	...	100	124[c]
Agricultural production index (2004-2006=100)	106	91	85[d]
Index of industrial production (2005=100)[h]	100	88	80[i]
International trade: exports (million current US$)	361	314	485[c]
International trade: imports (million current US$)	1 672	1 196	1 600[c]
International trade: balance (million current US$)	- 1 311	- 883	- 1 114[c]
Balance of payments, current account (million US$)	- 466	- 218	...

Major trading partners   2017

Export partners (% of exports)	United States	25.8	Areas nes[j]	19.5	Trinidad and Tobago 7.5
Import partners (% of imports)	United States	39.5	Trinidad and Tobago 16.8		China 5.8

Social indicators

	2005	2010	2018
Population growth rate (average annual %)[k]	0.3	0.4	0.3[b]
Urban population (% of total population)	32.8	31.9	31.1
Urban population growth rate (average annual %)[k]	- 0.3	- 0.2	- 0.1[b]
Fertility rate, total (live births per woman)[k]	1.8	1.8	1.8[b]
Life expectancy at birth (females/males, years)[k]	76.0 / 71.4	76.9 / 72.1	77.7 / 72.9[b]
Population age distribution (0-14/60+ years old, %)	20.7 / 15.5	19.9 / 17.3	18.9 / 21.6[a]
International migrant stock (000/% of total pop.)	30.6 / 11.2	32.8 / 11.7	34.7 / 12.1[c]
Refugees and others of concern to the UNHCR (000)	...	...	~0.0[c]
Infant mortality rate (per 1 000 live births)[k]	12.4	11.0	9.6[b]
Health: Current expenditure (% of GDP)	6.3	6.9	7.5[b]
Health: Physicians (per 1 000 pop.)	1.8	...	...
Education: Government expenditure (% of GDP)	5.6	6.1	5.1[d]
Education: Primary gross enrol. ratio (f/m per 100 pop.)	96.0 / 96.3	100.6 / 98.9[e]	93.2 / 92.0[d]
Education: Secondary gross enrol. ratio (f/m per 100 pop.)	108.0 / 109.1	102.2 / 101.6[e]	109.6 / 104.7[d]
Education: Tertiary gross enrol. ratio (f/m per 100 pop.)	57.0 / 23.0[i]	95.9 / 43.9	90.6 / 40.3[m]
Intentional homicide rate (per 100 000 pop.)	10.6	11.1	10.9[b]
Seats held by women in the National Parliament (%)	13.3	10.0	16.7

Environment and infrastructure indicators

	2005	2010	2018
Individuals using the Internet (per 100 inhabitants)[e]	52.5	65.1	79.5[d]
Threatened species (number)	20[n]	36	56[c]
Forested area (% of land area)	14.7	14.7	14.7[b]
CO2 emission estimates (million tons/tons per capita)	1.4 / 5.0	1.5 / 5.3	1.3 / 4.5[i]
Energy production, primary (Petajoules)	5	4	3[b]
Energy supply per capita (Gigajoules)	65	72	58[b]
Tourist/visitor arrivals at national borders (000)	548	532	632[d]
Important sites for terrestrial biodiversity protected (%)	2.1	2.1	2.1
Pop. using improved drinking water (urban/rural, %)	98.4 / 98.4	99.1 / 99.1	99.7 / 99.7[b]
Pop. using improved sanitation facilities (urban/rural, %)	90.1 / 90.1	93.5 / 93.5	96.2 / 96.2[b]
Net Official Development Assist. received (% of GNI)	- 0.06	0.37	...

a Projected estimate (medium fertility variant). **b** 2015. **c** 2017. **d** 2016. **e** Estimate. **f** Calculated by the Statistics Division of the United Nations from national indices. **g** Data refer to the Retail Price Index. **h** Data classified according to ISIC Rev. 3. **i** 2014. **j** Areas not elsewhere specified. **k** Data refers to a 5-year period preceding the reference year. **l** 2001. **m** 2011. **n** 2004.

Belarus

Region	Eastern Europe	UN membership date	24 October 1945
Population (000, 2018)	9 452 [a]	Surface area (km2)	207 600 [b]
Pop. density (per km2, 2018)	46.6 [a]	Sex ratio (m per 100 f)	87.0 [a]
Capital city	Minsk	National currency	Belarusian Ruble (BYN)
Capital city pop. (000, 2018)	2 004.7 [c]	Exchange rate (per US$)	2.0 [d]

Economic indicators

	2005	2010	2018
GDP: Gross domestic product (million current US$)	31 310	57 232	47 408 [e]
GDP growth rate (annual %, const. 2010 prices)	9.4	7.7	- 2.6 [e]
GDP per capita (current US$)	3 254.0	6 042.0	5 001.0 [e]
Economy: Agriculture (% of Gross Value Added) [f]	9.7	10.1	7.9 [e]
Economy: Industry (% of Gross Value Added) [f]	43.1	40.3	36.1 [e]
Economy: Services and other activity (% of GVA) [f]	47.2	49.5	56.0 [e]
Employment in agriculture (% of employed) [g]	13.9	10.8	9.7
Employment in industry (% of employed) [g]	35.6	34.6	31.0
Employment in services & other sectors (% employed) [g]	50.5	54.6	59.3
Unemployment rate (% of labour force)	0.9 [g]	1.2	0.5 [g]
Labour force participation rate (female/male pop. %) [g]	55.4 / 67.3	57.5 / 69.5	58.2 / 70.3
CPI: Consumer Price Index (2010=100)	62 [g]	100 [g]	459 [d]
Agricultural production index (2004-2006=100)	98	117	120 [e]
Index of industrial production (2005=100) [h]	100	146	163 [i]
International trade: exports (million current US$)	15 977	25 283	29 207 [g,d]
International trade: imports (million current US$)	16 699	34 884	34 235 [g,d]
International trade: balance (million current US$)	- 722	- 9 601	- 5 027 [g,d]
Balance of payments, current account (million US$)	459	- 8 280	- 931 [d]

Major trading partners

							2017
Export partners (% of exports)	Russian Federation	46.3 [g]	Ukraine	12.0	United Kingdom	4.6 [g]
Import partners (% of imports) [g]	Russian Federation	54.2	China	7.7	Germany	4.8

Social indicators

	2005	2010	2018
Population growth rate (average annual %) [j]	- 0.6	- 0.3	-0.0 [b]
Urban population (% of total population)	72.4	74.7	78.6
Urban population growth rate (average annual %) [j]	-0.0	0.3	0.7 [b]
Fertility rate, total (live births per woman) [j]	1.3	1.4	1.6 [b]
Life expectancy at birth (females/males, years) [j]	73.6 / 62.3	75.2 / 63.6	77.7 / 66.5 [b]
Population age distribution (0-14/60+ years old, %)	15.6 / 18.6	14.8 / 19.1	17.0 / 21.8 [a]
International migrant stock (000/% of total pop.)	1 107.0 / 11.5	1 090.4 / 11.5	1 078.7 / 11.4 [d]
Refugees and others of concern to the UNHCR (000)	13.2 [k]	8.4 [k]	8.0 [d]
Infant mortality rate (per 1 000 live births) [j]	9.6	6.3	3.8 [b]
Health: Current expenditure (% of GDP)	6.3	5.3	6.1 [b]
Health: Physicians (per 1 000 pop.)	...	3.5	4.1 [i]
Education: Government expenditure (% of GDP)	5.9	5.2	5.0 [e]
Education: Primary gross enrol. ratio (f/m per 100 pop.)	96.1 / 99.4	103.6 / 103.8	102.1 / 101.7 [e]
Education: Secondary gross enrol. ratio (f/m per 100 pop.)	... / ...	105.8 / 109.3	103.5 / 105.2 [e]
Education: Tertiary gross enrol. ratio (f/m per 100 pop.)	77.8 / 56.8	94.0 / 65.0 [g]	98.4 / 76.3 [e]
Intentional homicide rate (per 100 000 pop.)	8.6	4.2	3.6 [i]
Seats held by women in the National Parliament (%)	29.4	31.8	34.5

Environment and infrastructure indicators

	2005	2010	2018
Individuals using the Internet (per 100 inhabitants)	1.9 [i]	31.8 [m]	71.1 [e]
Research & Development expenditure (% of GDP)	0.7	0.7	0.5 [b]
Threatened species (number)	18 [n]	16	25 [d]
Forested area (% of land area)	41.6	42.1	42.5 [g,b]
CO2 emission estimates (million tons/tons per capita)	59.2 / 6.0	63.0 / 6.6	63.5 / 6.7 [i]
Energy production, primary (Petajoules)	159	166	146 [b]
Energy supply per capita (Gigajoules)	115	122	111 [b]
Tourist/visitor arrivals at national borders (000)	91 [o,p]	119 [o,p]	9 424 [q,e]
Important sites for terrestrial biodiversity protected (%)	35.0	35.4	49.1
Pop. using improved drinking water (urban/rural, %)	99.7 / 99.1	99.8 / 99.1	99.9 / 99.1 [b]
Pop. using improved sanitation facilities (urban/rural, %)	94.0 / 96.4	94.0 / 95.8	94.1 / 95.2 [b]
Net Official Development Assist. received (% of GNI)	0.19	0.24	- 0.05 [e]

a Projected estimate (medium fertility variant). b 2015. c Including communities under the authority of the Town Council. d 2017. e 2016. f Data classified according to ISIC Rev. 4. g Estimate. h Data classified according to ISIC Rev. 3. i 2014. j Data refers to a 5-year period preceding the reference year. k Data as at the end of December. l 2000. m Population aged 16 years and over. n 2004. o Package tour only. p Excludes the Belarusian-Russian border segment. q Includes estimation of the Belarusian-Russian border segment.

Belgium

Region	Western Europe		UN membership date	27 December 1945	
Population (000, 2018)	11 498[a]		Surface area (km2)	30 528[b]	
Pop. density (per km2, 2018)	379.7[a]		Sex ratio (m per 100 f)	97.7[a]	
Capital city	Brussels		National currency	Euro (EUR)	
Capital city pop. (000, 2018)	2 049.5[c]		Exchange rate (per US$)	0.8[d]	

Economic indicators	2005	2010	2018
GDP: Gross domestic product (million current US$)	387 356	483 549	467 955[e]
GDP growth rate (annual %, const. 2010 prices)	2.1	2.7	1.5[e]
GDP per capita (current US$)	36 727.0	44 205.0	41 199.0[e]
Economy: Agriculture (% of Gross Value Added)[f]	0.9	0.9	0.7[e]
Economy: Industry (% of Gross Value Added)[f]	25.1	23.2	22.2[e]
Economy: Services and other activity (% of GVA)[f]	74.0	76.0	77.2[e]
Employment in agriculture (% of employed)	2.0	1.49	1.2[g]
Employment in industry (% of employed)[g]	24.7	23.4	21.3
Employment in services & other sectors (% employed)[g]	73.3	75.3	77.5
Unemployment rate (% of labour force)	8.4	8.3	7.2[g]
Labour force participation rate (female/male pop. %)[g]	45.5 / 61.3	47.5 / 60.8	47.8 / 58.5
CPI: Consumer Price Index (2010=100)[h]	90	100	113[d]
Agricultural production index (2004-2006=100)	100	100	101[e]
Index of industrial production (2005=100)	100	117	121[i]
International trade: exports (million current US$)	335 692	407 596	429 980[d]
International trade: imports (million current US$)	319 085	391 256	406 412[d]
International trade: balance (million current US$)	16 606	16 340	23 568[d]
Balance of payments, current account (million US$)	7 703	7 977	- 790[d]

Major trading partners					2017
Export partners (% of exports)	Germany	16.6	France	14.9	Netherlands 12.0
Import partners (% of imports)	Netherlands	17.2	Germany	13.8	France 9.5

Social indicators	2005	2010	2018
Population growth rate (average annual %)[j]	0.5	0.7	0.6[b]
Urban population (% of total population)	97.4	97.7	98.0
Urban population growth rate (average annual %)[j]	0.6	0.8	0.7[b]
Fertility rate, total (live births per woman)[j]	1.7	1.8	1.8[b]
Life expectancy at birth (females/males, years)[j]	81.4 / 75.3	82.3 / 76.8	83.0 / 78.0[b]
Population age distribution (0-14/60+ years old, %)	17.2 / 22.1	16.9 / 23.2	17.2 / 24.9[a]
International migrant stock (000/% of total pop.)[k]	882.0 / 8.4	1 119.1 / 10.2	1 268.4 / 11.1[d]
Refugees and others of concern to the UNHCR (000)[l]	34.6	36.9	68.9[e]
Infant mortality rate (per 1 000 live births)[j]	4.2	3.8	3.5[b]
Health: Current expenditure (% of GDP)	9.0	9.9	10.5[b]
Health: Physicians (per 1 000 pop.)	2.0	2.9	3.0[b]
Education: Government expenditure (% of GDP)	5.8	6.4	6.6[i]
Education: Primary gross enrol. ratio (f/m per 100 pop.)	100.2 / 100.7	101.8 / 102.0	103.1 / 103.2[b]
Education: Secondary gross enrol. ratio (f/m per 100 pop.)	169.1 / 151.1	167.3 / 146.9	174.7 / 153.6[b]
Education: Tertiary gross enrol. ratio (f/m per 100 pop.)	67.9 / 54.5	75.9 / 60.0	84.7 / 64.8[b]
Intentional homicide rate (per 100 000 pop.)[m]	2.1	1.7	1.9[b]
Seats held by women in the National Parliament (%)	34.7	38.0	38.0

Environment and infrastructure indicators	2005	2010	2018
Individuals using the Internet (per 100 inhabitants)	55.8[g]	75.0	86.5[n,o,e]
Research & Development expenditure (% of GDP)	1.8	2.1	2.5[p,e]
Threatened species (number)	36[q]	27	37[d]
Forested area (% of land area)	22.3	22.5	22.6[g,b]
CO2 emission estimates (million tons/tons per capita)	108.5 / 10.4	110.8 / 10.2	93.4 / 8.3[i]
Energy production, primary (Petajoules)	577	646	444[b]
Energy supply per capita (Gigajoules)	234	230	197[b]
Tourist/visitor arrivals at national borders (000)	6 747	7 186	7 481[r,e]
Important sites for terrestrial biodiversity protected (%)	80.5	80.6	80.8
Pop. using improved drinking water (urban/rural, %)	100.0 / 100.0	100.0 / 100.0	100.0 / 100.0[b]
Pop. using improved sanitation facilities (urban/rural, %)	99.5 / 99.5	99.5 / 99.4	99.5 / 99.4[b]
Net Official Development Assist. disbursed (% of GNI)[s]	0.53	0.64	0.45[p,d]

a Projected estimate (medium fertility variant). b 2015. c Refers to the population of Brussels-Capital Region and "communes" of the agglomeration and suburbs. d 2017. e 2016. f Data classified according to ISIC Rev. 4. g Estimate. h Calculated by the Statistics Division of the United Nations from national indices. i 2014. j Data refers to a 5-year period preceding the reference year. k Refers to foreign citizens. l Data as at the end of December. m Data refer to offences, not victims, of intentional homicide. n Population aged 16 to 74 years. o Users in the last 3 months. p Provisional data. q 2004. r Break in the time series. s Development Assistance Committee member (OECD).

Belize

Region	Central America	UN membership date	25 September 1981
Population (000, 2018)	382[a]	Surface area (km2)	22 966[b]
Pop. density (per km2, 2018)	16.8[a]	Sex ratio (m per 100 f)	99.0[a]
Capital city	Belmopan	National currency	Belize Dollar (BZD)
Capital city pop. (000, 2018)	23.0	Exchange rate (per US$)	2.0[c]

Economic indicators

	2005	2010	2018
GDP: Gross domestic product (million current US$)	1 114	1 397	1 741[d]
GDP growth rate (annual %, const. 2010 prices)	3.0	3.3	- 0.6[d]
GDP per capita (current US$)	3 933.0	4 344.0	4 745.0[d]
Economy: Agriculture (% of Gross Value Added)	14.7	12.6	10.9[d]
Economy: Industry (% of Gross Value Added)	16.5	20.7	18.0[d]
Economy: Services and other activity (% of GVA)	68.8	66.7	71.1[d]
Employment in agriculture (% of employed)[e]	19.6	17.2	15.5
Employment in industry (% of employed)[e]	17.9	18.0	15.4
Employment in services & other sectors (% of employed)[e]	62.6	64.8	69.1
Unemployment rate (% of labour force)	11.0	11.3[e]	7.6[e]
Labour force participation rate (female/male pop. %)[e]	45.9 / 81.9	52.4 / 82.1	53.7 / 81.4
CPI: Consumer Price Index (2010=100)[f]	88	100	106[c]
Agricultural production index (2004-2006=100)	101	97	97[d]
Index of industrial production (2005=100)	100[g]	...	...
International trade: exports (million current US$)	208	282	278[c]
International trade: imports (million current US$)	439	700	913[c]
International trade: balance (million current US$)	- 231	- 418	- 636[c]
Balance of payments, current account (million US$)	- 151	- 46	- 131[c]

Major trading partners

							2017
Export partners (% of exports)	United Kingdom	27.7	United States	26.3	Jamaica	5.4	
Import partners (% of imports)	United States	35.6	China	11.2	Mexico	11.2	

Social indicators

	2005	2010	2018
Population growth rate (average annual %)[h]	2.7	2.5	2.2[b]
Urban population (% of total population)	45.3	45.2	45.7
Urban population growth rate (average annual %)[h]	2.7	2.5	2.3[b]
Fertility rate, total (live births per woman)[h]	3.4	2.8	2.6[b]
Life expectancy at birth (females/males, years)[h]	71.6 / 65.7	72.4 / 67.0	72.7 / 67.2[b]
Population age distribution (0-14/60+ years old, %)	39.0 / 4.7	35.7 / 5.7	30.9 / 6.3[a]
International migrant stock (000/% of total pop.)[i]	41.4 / 14.6	46.4 / 14.4	60.0 / 16.0[c]
Refugees and others of concern to the UNHCR (000)	0.6[j]	0.2[j]	5.1[c]
Infant mortality rate (per 1 000 live births)[h]	19.7	17.0	14.3[b]
Health: Current expenditure (% of GDP)	4.4	5.8	6.2[b]
Health: Physicians (per 1 000 pop.)	1.0[k]	0.8[l]	...
Education: Government expenditure (% of GDP)	5.3[m]	6.6	7.4[c]
Education: Primary gross enrol. ratio (f/m per 100 pop.)	110.8 / 115.8	110.3 / 114.8	111.7 / 117.5[d]
Education: Secondary gross enrol. ratio (f/m per 100 pop.)	77.7 / 75.3	78.2 / 72.5	87.8 / 86.6[d]
Education: Tertiary gross enrol. ratio (f/m per 100 pop.)	19.7 / 12.5	26.9 / 16.8	30.0 / 18.5[d]
Intentional homicide rate (per 100 000 pop.)	28.6	40.1	37.6[d]
Seats held by women in the National Parliament (%)	6.7	0.0	9.4

Environment and infrastructure indicators

	2005	2010	2018
Individuals using the Internet (per 100 inhabitants)	17.0[e]	28.2[n]	44.6[e,d]
Threatened species (number)	67[m]	92	117[c]
Forested area (% of land area)[e]	62.1	61.0	59.9[b]
CO2 emission estimates (million tons/tons per capita)	0.4 / 1.5	0.5 / 1.7	0.5 / 1.4[o]
Energy production, primary (Petajoules)	4	14	9[b]
Energy supply per capita (Gigajoules)	39	40	41[b]
Tourist/visitor arrivals at national borders (000)	237	242	386[d]
Important sites for terrestrial biodiversity protected (%)	45.8	45.8	46.0
Pop. using improved drinking water (urban/rural, %)	94.9 / 87.8	97.4 / 97.1	98.9 / 100.0[b]
Pop. using improved sanitation facilities (urban/rural, %)	88.8 / 83.5	92.6 / 86.5	93.5 / 88.2[b]
Net Official Development Assist. received (% of GNI)	1.20	2.02	2.09[d]

a Projected estimate (medium fertility variant). b 2015. c 2017. d 2016. e Estimate. f Calculated by the Statistics Division of the United Nations from national indices. g Data classified according to ISIC Rev. 3. h Data refers to a 5-year period preceding the reference year. i Including refugees. j Data as at the end of December. k 2000. l 2009. m 2004. n Population aged 5 years and over. o 2014.

Benin

Region	Western Africa	UN membership date	20 September 1960
Population (000, 2018)	11 486[a]	Surface area (km2)	114 763[b]
Pop. density (per km2, 2018)	101.9[a]	Sex ratio (m per 100 f)	99.6[a]
Capital city	Porto-Novo[c]	National currency	CFA Franc, BCEAO (XOF)[d]
Capital city pop. (000, 2018)	285.3	Exchange rate (per US$)	546.9[e]

Economic indicators

	2005	2010	2018
GDP: Gross domestic product (million current US$)	4 804	6 970	8 894[f]
GDP growth rate (annual %, const. 2010 prices)	1.7	2.1	5.0[f]
GDP per capita (current US$)	602.0	758.0	818.0[f]
Economy: Agriculture (% of Gross Value Added)	27.1	25.4	23.0[f]
Economy: Industry (% of Gross Value Added)	30.3	24.7	24.1[f]
Economy: Services and other activity (% of GVA)	42.5	49.9	52.9[f]
Employment in agriculture (% of employed)[g]	47.5	45.3	42.4
Employment in industry (% of employed)[g]	11.9	10.5	18.6
Employment in services & other sectors (% employed)[g]	40.6	44.2	39.0
Unemployment rate (% of labour force)	0.9[g]	1.0	2.4[g]
Labour force participation rate (female/male pop. %)[g]	67.3 / 76.6	69.2 / 73.0	68.9 / 73.1
CPI: Consumer Price Index (2010=100)[g,h]	84	100	109[e]
Agricultural production index (2004-2006=100)	104	118	153[f]
Index of industrial production (2005=100)[i,j]	100	129	148[k]
International trade: exports (million current US$)	288	534	160[g,e]
International trade: imports (million current US$)	899	2 134	2 690[g,e]
International trade: balance (million current US$)	- 611	- 1 600	- 2 530[g,e]
Balance of payments, current account (million US$)	- 226	- 530	- 809[f]

Major trading partners

							2017
Export partners (% of exports)	India	15.4[g]	Malaysia	13.2	Bangladesh	10.2[g]
Import partners (% of imports)[g]	India	14.9	Thailand	12.4	France	10.1

Social indicators

	2005	2010	2018
Population growth rate (average annual %)[l]	3.0	2.8	2.8[b]
Urban population (% of total population)	40.5	43.1	47.3
Urban population growth rate (average annual %)[l]	4.1	4.1	4.0[b]
Fertility rate, total (live births per woman)[l]	5.8	5.5	5.2[b]
Life expectancy at birth (females/males, years)[l]	57.7 / 54.6	60.0 / 57.1	61.4 / 58.5[b]
Population age distribution (0-14/60+ years old, %)	44.4 / 5.0	43.8 / 4.9	42.4 / 5.0[a]
International migrant stock (000/% of total pop.)[m,n]	171.5 / 2.1	209.3 / 2.3	253.3 / 2.3[e]
Refugees and others of concern to the UNHCR (000)	32.1[o]	7.3[o]	1.2[e]
Infant mortality rate (per 1 000 live births)[l]	84.1	74.5	67.7[b]
Health: Current expenditure (% of GDP)	4.0	4.1	4.0[b]
Health: Physicians (per 1 000 pop.)	-0.0[p]	0.1[q]	0.2[f]
Education: Government expenditure (% of GDP)	3.6	5.0	4.4[b]
Education: Primary gross enrol. ratio (f/m per 100 pop.)	89.0 / 112.4	113.2 / 126.9	127.6 / 137.2[b]
Education: Secondary gross enrol. ratio (f/m per 100 pop.)	18.4 / 39.2[p]	... / ...	48.9 / 68.5[b]
Education: Tertiary gross enrol. ratio (f/m per 100 pop.)	1.8 / 7.2[g,r]	7.2 / 20.3	7.9 / 18.4[f]
Intentional homicide rate (per 100 000 pop.)	7.2	6.6	6.2[b]
Seats held by women in the National Parliament (%)	7.2	10.8	7.2

Environment and infrastructure indicators

	2005	2010	2018
Individuals using the Internet (per 100 inhabitants)	1.3	3.1	12.0[g,f]
Threatened species (number)	31[p]	62	88[e]
Forested area (% of land area)[g]	42.7	40.4	38.2[b]
CO2 emission estimates (million tons/tons per capita)	2.4 / 0.3	5.1 / 0.6	6.3 / 0.6[s]
Energy production, primary (Petajoules)	70	86	114[b]
Energy supply per capita (Gigajoules)	14	16	17[b]
Tourist/visitor arrivals at national borders (000)	176	199	267[f]
Important sites for terrestrial biodiversity protected (%)	77.4	77.4	77.4
Pop. using improved drinking water (urban/rural, %)	80.6 / 63.4	83.2 / 68.3	85.2 / 72.1[b]
Pop. using improved sanitation facilities (urban/rural, %)	29.0 / 4.9	32.7 / 6.2	35.6 / 7.3[b]
Net Official Development Assist. received (% of GNI)	7.29	9.96	5.74[f]

a Projected estimate (medium fertility variant). **b** 2015. **c** Porto-Novo is the constitutional capital and Cotonou is the economic capital. **d** African Financial Community (CFA) Franc, Central Bank of West African States (BCEAO). **e** 2017. **f** 2016. **g** Estimate. **h** Cotonou **i** Data classified according to ISIC Rev. 3. **j** Country data supplemented with data from the Observatoire Economique et Statistique d'Afrique Subsaharienne (Afristat). **k** 2013. **l** Data refers to a 5-year period preceding the reference year. **m** Refers to foreign citizens. **n** Including refugees. **o** Data as at the end of December. **p** 2004. **q** 2008. **r** 2001. **s** 2014.

Bermuda

Region	Northern America	Population (000, 2018)	61 [a]
Surface area (km2)	53 [b]	Pop. density (per km2, 2018)	1 221.4 [a]
Sex ratio (m per 100 f)	91.4 [c,d,e]	Capital city	Hamilton
National currency	Bermudian Dollar (BMD)	Capital city pop. (000, 2018)	10.1
Exchange rate (per US$)	1.0 [e]		

Economic indicators	2005	2010	2018
GDP: Gross domestic product (million current US$)	4 868	5 855	6 127 [f]
GDP growth rate (annual %, const. 2010 prices)	1.7	- 2.5	- 0.1 [f]
GDP per capita (current US$)	74 745.0	91 552.0	99 363.0 [f]
Economy: Agriculture (% of Gross Value Added)	0.8	0.7	0.8 [f]
Economy: Industry (% of Gross Value Added)	9.7	7.1	5.6 [f]
Economy: Services and other activity (% of GVA)	89.5	92.2	93.6 [f]
Employment in agriculture (% of employed)	1.7 [g,h]	1.4 [i,j,k]	1.6 [i,j,k,l,m]
Employment in industry (% of employed)	12.1 [g,h]	12.9 [i,j,k]	10.3 [i,j,k,l,m]
Employment in services & other sectors (% employed)	86.2 [g,h]	85.7 [i,j,k]	87.6 [i,j,k,l,m]
Unemployment rate (% of labour force) [i]	2.7 [n]	4.5 [j,o]	6.7 [l,m]
Labour force participation rate (female/male pop. %)	67.4 / 79.2 [n]	81.0 / 87.0 [i]	72.6 / 80.0 [i,j,p]
CPI: Consumer Price Index (2010=100)	...	...	148 [q,r]
Agricultural production index (2004-2006=100)	98	109	112 [f]
International trade: exports (million current US$)	49 [s]	15 [s]	12 [e]
International trade: imports (million current US$)	988	970	1 078 [e]
International trade: balance (million current US$)	- 939 [s]	- 955 [s]	- 1 066 [e]
Balance of payments, current account (million US$)	...	696	766 [f]

Major trading partners						2017
Export partners (% of exports)	United States	81.2	Canada	4.9 [s]	United Kingdom	4.4
Import partners (% of imports)	United States	66.5	Canada	9.5	United Kingdom	4.0

Social indicators	2005	2010	2018
Population growth rate (average annual %) [t]	0.3	- 0.4	- 0.6 [b]
Urban population (% of total population)	100.0	100.0	100.0
Urban population growth rate (average annual %) [t]	0.3	- 0.4	- 0.6 [b]
Fertility rate, total (live births per woman)	1.8	1.7	1.5 [f]
Life expectancy at birth (females/males, years)	... / ...	82.3 / 76.9	85.1 / 77.5 [f]
Population age distribution (0-14/60+ years old, %) [c]	18.4 / 16.4	17.4 / 18.7	14.8 / 24.9 [d,e]
International migrant stock (000/% of total pop.)	18.3 / 28.1	18.9 / 29.5	19.0 / 30.9 [e]
Education: Government expenditure (% of GDP)	2.0	2.6	1.5 [e]
Education: Primary gross enrol. ratio (f/m per 100 pop.)	101.5 / 96.8	100.7 / 93.7 [u]	89.4 / 91.3 [b]
Education: Secondary gross enrol. ratio (f/m per 100 pop.)	85.9 / 76.0	85.4 / 72.3	75.5 / 67.7 [b]
Education: Tertiary gross enrol. ratio (f/m per 100 pop.)	... / ...	40.6 / 19.3	21.3 / 12.7 [e]
Intentional homicide rate (per 100 000 pop.)	3.1	10.9	13.0 [f]

Environment and infrastructure indicators	2005	2010	2018
Individuals using the Internet (per 100 inhabitants)	65.4	84.2 [s]	98.0 [s,f]
Research & Development expenditure (% of GDP) [w]	...	0.2 [v]	0.2 [b]
Threatened species (number)	47 [h]	50	72 [e]
Forested area (% of land area) [s]	20.0	20.0	20.0 [b]
CO2 emission estimates (million tons/tons per capita)	0.6 / 9.1	0.6 / 9.5	0.6 / 9.2 [r]
Energy production, primary (Petajoules) [s]	...	1	1 [b]
Energy supply per capita (Gigajoules)	124 [s]	138 [s]	133 [b]
Tourist/visitor arrivals at national borders (000) [x,y]	270	232	244 [f]
Important sites for terrestrial biodiversity protected (%)	16.2	16.2	16.2

a Projected estimate (medium fertility variant). b 2015. c De jure population. d Data refer to projections based on the 2010 Population Census. e 2017. f 2016. g Data classified according to ISIC Rev. 2. h 2004. i Population aged 16 years and over. j Break in the time series. k Data classified according to ISIC Rev. 3. l Excluding the institutional population. m 2013. n 2000. o 2009. p 2012. q Index base: 2000=100. r 2014. s Estimate. t Data refers to a 5-year period preceding the reference year. u 2006. v Excluding most or all capital expenditures. w Overestimated or based on overestimated data. x Arrivals by air. y Excluding nationals residing abroad.

Bhutan

Region	Southern Asia	UN membership date	21 September 1971
Population (000, 2018)	817[a]	Surface area (km2)	38 394[b]
Pop. density (per km2, 2018)	21.4[a]	Sex ratio (m per 100 f)	112.9[a]
Capital city	Thimphu	National currency	Ngultrum (BTN)
Capital city pop. (000, 2018)	203.3	Exchange rate (per US$)	63.9[c]

Economic indicators	2005	2010	2018
GDP: Gross domestic product (million current US$)	819	1 585	2 213[d]
GDP growth rate (annual %, const. 2010 prices)	7.1	11.7	8.0[d]
GDP per capita (current US$)	1 247.0	2 179.0	2 774.0[d]
Economy: Agriculture (% of Gross Value Added)	23.2	17.5	17.3[d]
Economy: Industry (% of Gross Value Added)	37.3	44.6	43.5[d]
Economy: Services and other activity (% of GVA)	39.5	37.9	39.2[d]
Employment in agriculture (% of employed)[e]	70.3	59.6	55.6
Employment in industry (% of employed)[e]	4.8	6.6	9.7
Employment in services & other sectors (% employed)[e]	24.9	33.8	34.7
Unemployment rate (% of labour force)	3.1	3.3	2.4[e]
Labour force participation rate (female/male pop. %)[e]	65.4 / 75.4	64.6 / 74.3	58.5 / 74.3
CPI: Consumer Price Index (2010=100)	75	100	158[c]
Agricultural production index (2004-2006=100)	106	95	102[d]
International trade: exports (million current US$)	258	413	520[e,c]
International trade: imports (million current US$)	387	854	983[e,c]
International trade: balance (million current US$)	- 129	- 440	- 463[e,c]
Balance of payments, current account (million US$)	...	- 323	- 546[c]

Major trading partners						2017
Export partners (% of exports)	India	77.2[e]	Bangladesh	12.7	Nepal	2.6[e]
Import partners (% of imports)[e]	India	80.2	Thailand	5.7	Republic of Korea	2.5

Social indicators	2005	2010	2018
Population growth rate (average annual %)[f]	2.7	2.1	1.6[b]
Urban population (% of total population)	31.0	34.8	40.9
Urban population growth rate (average annual %)[f]	6.7	4.4	3.7[b]
Fertility rate, total (live births per woman)[f]	3.1	2.6	2.2[b]
Life expectancy at birth (females/males, years)[f]	63.1 / 62.7	66.7 / 66.3	68.9 / 68.6[b]
Population age distribution (0-14/60+ years old, %)	34.9 / 5.7	30.6 / 6.2	26.2 / 7.5[a]
International migrant stock (000/% of total pop.)	40.3 / 6.1	48.4 / 6.7	52.3 / 6.5[c]
Infant mortality rate (per 1 000 live births)[f]	51.9	39.5	30.5[b]
Health: Current expenditure (% of GDP)[g,h]	3.5	3.2	3.5[b]
Health: Physicians (per 1 000 pop.)	0.2[i]	0.2[j]	0.4[d]
Education: Government expenditure (% of GDP)	7.1	4.0	7.4[b]
Education: Primary gross enrol. ratio (f/m per 100 pop.)	90.0 / 92.2	107.9 / 105.2	95.3 / 94.7[d]
Education: Secondary gross enrol. ratio (f/m per 100 pop.)	41.7 / 46.7	64.2 / 63.0	87.8 / 80.2[d]
Education: Tertiary gross enrol. ratio (f/m per 100 pop.)	3.7 / 5.7	5.1 / 8.4	8.9 / 12.1[k]
Intentional homicide rate (per 100 000 pop.)	1.7	2.2	1.1[d]
Seats held by women in the National Parliament (%)	9.3	8.5	8.5

Environment and infrastructure indicators	2005	2010	2018
Individuals using the Internet (per 100 inhabitants)	3.8	13.6[e]	41.8[e,d]
Threatened species (number)	48[i]	59	71[c]
Forested area (% of land area)	69.7	71.0	72.3[b]
CO2 emission estimates (million tons/tons per capita)	0.4 / 0.6	0.5 / 0.7	1.0 / 1.3[l]
Energy production, primary (Petajoules)	53	73	77[b]
Energy supply per capita (Gigajoules)	73	81	82[b]
Tourist/visitor arrivals at national borders (000)	14	41[m,n]	210[d]
Important sites for terrestrial biodiversity protected (%)	38.6	41.2	42.9
Pop. using improved drinking water (urban/rural, %)	98.9 / 86.6	99.5 / 94.1	100.0 / 100.0[b]
Pop. using improved sanitation facilities (urban/rural, %)	67.2 / 26.4	76.0 / 31.2	77.9 / 33.1[b]
Net Official Development Assist. received (% of GNI)	11.16	8.78	2.50[d]

a Projected estimate (medium fertility variant). **b** 2015. **c** 2017. **d** 2016. **e** Estimate. **f** Data refers to a 5-year period preceding the reference year. **g** Data refer to fiscal years beginning 1 July. **h** Data revision. **i** 2004. **j** 2008. **k** 2013. **l** 2014. **m** Break in the time series. **n** Including regional high end tourists.

Bolivia (Plurinational State of)

Region	South America	UN membership date	14 November 1945
Population (000, 2018)	11 216[a]	Surface area (km2)	1 098 581[b,c]
Pop. density (per km2, 2018)	10.4[a]	Sex ratio (m per 100 f)	100.2[a]
Capital city	Sucre[d]	National currency	Boliviano (BOB)
Capital city pop. (000, 2018)	277.9	Exchange rate (per US$)	6.9[e]

Economic indicators	2005	2010	2018
GDP: Gross domestic product (million current US$)	9 549	19 650	33 806[f]
GDP growth rate (annual %, const. 2010 prices)	4.4	4.1	4.3[f]
GDP per capita (current US$)	1 046.0	1 981.0	3 105.0[f]
Economy: Agriculture (% of Gross Value Added)	13.9	12.4	12.9[f]
Economy: Industry (% of Gross Value Added)	30.9	35.8	29.3[f]
Economy: Services and other activity (% of GVA)	55.2	51.8	57.7[f]
Employment in agriculture (% of employed)	35.2	30.0[g]	26.4[g]
Employment in industry (% of employed)[g]	20.4	20.6	22.5
Employment in services & other sectors (% employed)[g]	44.4	49.3	51.1
Unemployment rate (% of labour force)	5.1	2.5[g]	3.1[g]
Labour force participation rate (female/male pop. %)[g]	62.5 / 82.6	62.0 / 82.0	55.3 / 79.9
CPI: Consumer Price Index (2010=100)[h]	73	100	142[e]
Agricultural production index (2004-2006=100)	100	120	147[f]
International trade: exports (million current US$)	2 797	8 985	7 852[o]
International trade: imports (million current US$)	2 343	5 604	9 302[e]
International trade: balance (million current US$)	454	1 361	- 1 450[e]
Balance of payments, current account (million US$)	622	874	- 2 377[e]

Major trading partners						2017
Export partners (% of exports)	Brazil	18.5	Argentina	15.7[g]	Republic of Korea	7.8
Import partners (% of imports)	China	21.8	Brazil	16.8	Argentina	12.5

Social indicators	2005	2010	2018
Population growth rate (average annual %)[i]	1.8	1.7	1.6[c]
Urban population (% of total population)	64.2	66.4	69.4
Urban population growth rate (average annual %)[i]	2.6	2.4	2.1[c]
Fertility rate, total (live births per woman)[i]	3.8	3.4	3.0[c]
Life expectancy at birth (females/males, years)[i]	64.3 / 60.0	67.3 / 62.7	70.2 / 65.3[c]
Population age distribution (0-14/60+ years old, %)	36.6 / 7.8	34.7 / 8.3	31.3 / 9.6[a]
International migrant stock (000/% of total pop.)	107.7 / 1.2	122.8 / 1.2	148.8 / 1.3[a]
Refugees and others of concern to the UNHCR (000)	0.5[j]	0.7[j]	0.8[e]
Infant mortality rate (per 1 000 live births)[i]	61.2	51.0	42.9[c]
Health: Current expenditure (% of GDP)	5.0	5.1	6.4[c]
Health: Physicians (per 1 000 pop.)	1.2[k]	0.4	0.5[f]
Education: Government expenditure (% of GDP)	6.4[m]	7.6	7.3[n]
Education: Primary gross enrol. ratio (f/m per 100 pop.)	114.4 / 115.5	103.6 / 105.7	96.5 / 98.8[f]
Education: Secondary gross enrol. ratio (f/m per 100 pop.)	84.3 / 89.6	82.6 / 83.6	85.6 / 87.3[f]
Intentional homicide rate (per 100 000 pop.)	5.2	12.8	6.3[f]
Seats held by women in the National Parliament (%)	19.2	22.3	53.1

Environment and infrastructure indicators	2005	2010	2018
Individuals using the Internet (per 100 inhabitants)	5.2	22.4[g]	39.7[g,f]
Research & Development expenditure (% of GDP)	0.3[o]	0.2[p,q]	...
Threatened species (number)	150[r]	163	231[e]
Forested area (% of land area)	54.2	51.9[g]	50.6[g,c]
CO2 emission estimates (million tons/tons per capita)	12.2 / 1.3	15.2 / 1.5	20.4 / 1.9[h]
Energy production, primary (Petajoules)	586	656	871[c]
Energy supply per capita (Gigajoules)	24	26	31[c]
Tourist/visitor arrivals at national borders (000)	524	679	959[f]
Important sites for terrestrial biodiversity protected (%)	52.8	54.6	56.2
Pop. using improved drinking water (urban/rural, %)	94.4 / 62.4	95.6 / 69.7	96.7 / 75.6[c]
Pop. using improved sanitation facilities (urban/rural, %)	53.8 / 21.4	57.7 / 24.8	60.8 / 27.5[c]
Net Official Development Assist. received (% of GNI)	7.01	3.82	2.10[f]

a Projected estimate (medium fertility variant). **b** Data updated according to "Superintendencia Agraria". Interior waters correspond to natural or artificial bodies of water or snow. **c** 2015. **d** La Paz is the seat of government and Sucre is the constitutional capital. **e** 2017. **f** 2016. **g** Estimate. **h** Calculated by the Statistics Division of the United Nations from national indices. **i** Data refers to a 5-year period preceding the reference year. **j** Data as at the end of December. **k** 2001. **l** 2011. **m** 2003. **n** 2014. **o** 2002. **p** Break in the time series. **q** 2009. **r** 2004.

Bonaire, Sint Eustatius and Saba

Region	Caribbean	Population (000, 2018)	26 [a]
Pop. density (per km2, 2018)	78.4 [a]	Capital city	Kralendijk
National currency	US Dollar (USD)	Capital city pop. (000, 2018)	11.3 [b]

Social indicators	2005	2010	2018
Population growth rate (average annual %) [c]	-0.0	7.5	3.2 [d]
Urban population (% of total population)	74.8	74.7	74.9
Urban population growth rate (average annual %) [c]	-0.0	7.5	3.2 [d]
International migrant stock (000/% of total pop.)	... / ...	11.4 / 54.7	13.5 / 53.2 [e]
Refugees and others of concern to the UNHCR (000)	...	~0.0 [f,g]	...

Environment and infrastructure indicators	2005	2010	2018
Threatened species (number)	...	...	56 [e]
CO2 emission estimates (million tons/tons per capita)	... / ...	... / ...	0.3 / 13.3 [h]
Energy production, primary (Petajoules)	...	...	0 [d]
Energy supply per capita (Gigajoules)	...	...	212 [i,d]
Important sites for terrestrial biodiversity protected (%)	39.3	39.3	39.3

a Projected estimate (medium fertility variant). **b** Refers to the island of Bonaire. **c** Data refers to a 5-year period preceding the reference year. **d** 2015. **e** 2017. **f** Bonaire only. **g** Data as at the end of December. **h** 2014. **i** Estimate.

Bosnia and Herzegovina

Region	Southern Europe	UN membership date	22 May 1992
Population (000, 2018)	3 504[a]	Surface area (km2)	51 209[b]
Pop. density (per km2, 2018)	68.7[a]	Sex ratio (m per 100 f)	96.5[a]
Capital city	Sarajevo	National currency	Convertible Mark (BAM)
Capital city pop. (000, 2018)	342.6[c]	Exchange rate (per US$)	1.6[d]

Economic indicators	2005	2010	2018
GDP: Gross domestic product (million current US$)	11 223	17 176	16 910[e]
GDP growth rate (annual %, const. 2010 prices)	3.9	0.9	3.2[e]
GDP per capita (current US$)	2 968.0	4 615.0	4 808.0[e]
Economy: Agriculture (% of Gross Value Added)[f]	9.8	8.0	7.5[e]
Economy: Industry (% of Gross Value Added)[f]	25.3	26.4	27.2[e]
Economy: Services and other activity (% of GVA)[f]	64.9	65.6	65.3[e]
Employment in agriculture (% of employed)[g]	24.6	19.6	18.6
Employment in industry (% of employed)[g]	28.4	29.1	32.1
Employment in services & other sectors (% employed)[g]	47.1	51.2	49.3
Unemployment rate (% of labour force)	29.8[g]	27.2	26.0[g]
Labour force participation rate (female/male pop. %)[g]	37.9 / 60.5	37.1 / 59.9	35.1 / 58.5
CPI: Consumer Price Index (2010=100)	85	100	104[d]
Agricultural production index (2004-2006=100)	98	107	118[e]
Index of industrial production (2005=100)[h]	100	135	143[i]
International trade: exports (million current US$)	2 388	4 803	6 367[d]
International trade: imports (million current US$)	7 054	9 223	10 444[d]
International trade: balance (million current US$)	- 4 665	- 4 420	- 4 078[d]
Balance of payments, current account (million US$)	- 1 844	- 1 031	- 875[d]

Major trading partners						2017
Export partners (% of exports)	Germany	14.4	Croatia	11.6[g]	Italy	10.9
Import partners (% of imports)	Germany	11.6	Italy	11.4	Serbia	11.2

Social indicators	2005	2010	2018
Population growth rate (average annual %)[j]	0.1	- 0.3	- 1.0[b]
Urban population (% of total population)	44.0	45.6	48.2
Urban population growth rate (average annual %)[j]	0.8	0.4	- 0.3[b]
Fertility rate, total (live births per woman)[j]	1.3	1.3	1.3[b]
Life expectancy at birth (females/males, years)[j]	77.5 / 72.0	78.1 / 72.9	78.8 / 73.7[b]
Population age distribution (0-14/60+ years old, %)	17.7 / 17.4	15.7 / 19.2	14.2 / 23.9[a]
International migrant stock (000/% of total pop.)[a,k]	47.3 / 1.3	38.8 / 1.0	37.1 / 1.1[d]
Refugees and others of concern to the UNHCR (000)	199.5[l]	179.0[l]	156.4[d]
Infant mortality rate (per 1 000 live births)[j]	9.9	9.0	7.6[b]
Health: Current expenditure (% of GDP)	9.1	9.0	9.4[b]
Health: Physicians (per 1 000 pop.)	...	1.7	1.9[m]
Intentional homicide rate (per 100 000 pop.)	1.9	1.5	1.3[b]
Seats held by women in the National Parliament (%)	16.7	19.0	21.4

Environment and infrastructure indicators	2005	2010	2018
Individuals using the Internet (per 100 inhabitants)	21.3	42.8[g]	69.3[g,e]
Research & Development expenditure (% of GDP)	~0.0[n]	~0.0[n,o]	0.2[b]
Threatened species (number)	40[p]	67	91[d]
Forested area (% of land area)[g]	42.7	42.7	42.7[b]
CO2 emission estimates (million tons/tons per capita)	16.2 / 4.3	21.3 / 5.5	22.2 / 5.8[q]
Energy production, primary (Petajoules)	152	182	257[b]
Energy supply per capita (Gigajoules)	54	70	87[b]
Tourist/visitor arrivals at national borders (000)	217	365	777[e]
Important sites for terrestrial biodiversity protected (%)	0.0	12.0	12.0
Pop. using improved drinking water (urban/rural, %)	99.5 / 97.6	99.6 / 98.9	99.7 / 100.0[b]
Pop. using improved sanitation facilities (urban/rural, %)	98.6 / 92.5	98.8 / 92.2	98.9 / 92.0[b]
Net Official Development Assist. received (% of GNI)	4.62	2.93	2.67[e]

a Projected estimate (medium fertility variant). b 2015. c Refers to the municipalities of Stari Grad Sarajevo, Centar Sarajevo, Novo Sarajevo, Novi Grad Sarajevo and Ilidza. d 2017. e 2016. f Data classified according to ISIC Rev. 4. g Estimate. h Data classified according to ISIC Rev. 3. i 2011. j Data refers to a 5-year period preceding the reference year. k Including refugees. l Data as at the end of December. m 2013. n Partial data. o 2009. p 2004. q 2014.

Botswana

Region	Southern Africa	UN membership date	17 October 1966
Population (000, 2018)	2 333[a]	Surface area (km2)	582 000[b]
Pop. density (per km2, 2018)	4.1[a]	Sex ratio (m per 100 f)	97.8[a]
Capital city	Gaborone	National currency	Pula (BWP)
Capital city pop. (000, 2018)	269.3	Exchange rate (per US$)	9.9[c]

Economic indicators	2005	2010	2018
GDP: Gross domestic product (million current US$)	9 931	12 787	15 566[d]
GDP growth rate (annual %, const. 2010 prices)	4.6	8.6	4.3[d]
GDP per capita (current US$)	5 351.0	6 346.0	6 917.0[d]
Economy: Agriculture (% of Gross Value Added)	2.0	2.8	2.2[d]
Economy: Industry (% of Gross Value Added)	47.6	35.7	34.7[d]
Economy: Services and other activity (% of GVA)	50.3	61.6	63.1[d]
Employment in agriculture (% of employed)[e]	27.0	26.4	25.8
Employment in industry (% of employed)[e]	17.2	13.8	13.6
Employment in services & other sectors (% employed)[e]	55.9	59.8	60.6
Unemployment rate (% of labour force)	20.7[e]	17.9	18.3[e]
Labour force participation rate (female/male pop. %)[e]	54.4 / 71.5	53.5 / 67.3	66.0 / 78.5
CPI: Consumer Price Index (2010=100)[f]	64	100	141[c]
Agricultural production index (2004-2006=100)	101	125	120[d]
International trade: exports (million current US$)	4 431	4 693	5 898[c]
International trade: imports (million current US$)	3 162	5 657	5 283[c]
International trade: balance (million current US$)	1 268	- 964	615[c]
Balance of payments, current account (million US$)	1 598	- 533[g]	2 149[c]

Major trading partners						2017
Export partners (% of exports)	Belgium	22.8	India	19.7	United Arab Emirates	16.6
Import partners (% of imports)	South Africa	64.3	Canada	8.8	Namibia	6.7

Social indicators	2005	2010	2018
Population growth rate (average annual %)[h]	1.4	1.6	1.8[b]
Urban population (% of total population)	55.9	62.4	69.4
Urban population growth rate (average annual %)[h]	2.4	3.8	3.3[b]
Fertility rate, total (live births per woman)[h]	3.2	2.9	2.9[b]
Life expectancy at birth (females/males, years)[h]	51.0 / 47.3	58.5 / 54.4	66.1 / 59.8[b]
Population age distribution (0-14/60+ years old, %)	35.1 / 5.0	33.0 / 5.3	31.2 / 6.5[a]
International migrant stock (000/% of total pop.)	88.8 / 4.8	120.9 / 6.0	166.4 / 7.3[c]
Refugees and others of concern to the UNHCR (000)	3.7[i]	3.3[i]	2.9[c]
Infant mortality rate (per 1 000 live births)[h]	65.4	46.5	35.2[b]
Health: Current expenditure (% of GDP)	5.3	5.6	6.0[b]
Health: Physicians (per 1 000 pop.)	0.2	0.3[k]	0.4[i]
Education: Government expenditure (% of GDP)	10.7	9.6[k]	...
Education: Primary gross enrol. ratio (f/m per 100 pop.)	107.8 / 109.5	107.4 / 111.4[k]	103.5 / 107.2[m]
Education: Secondary gross enrol. ratio (f/m per 100 pop.)	82.4 / 80.0	81.9 / 75.0[n]	... / ...
Education: Tertiary gross enrol. ratio (f/m per 100 pop.)	8.6 / 9.7	9.1 / 11.1[o]	27.3 / 19.5[c]
Intentional homicide rate (per 100 000 pop.)	15.7	15.0	...
Seats held by women in the National Parliament (%)	11.1	7.9	9.5

Environment and infrastructure indicators	2005	2010	2018
Individuals using the Internet (per 100 inhabitants)	3.3[a]	6.0	39.4[e,d]
Research & Development expenditure (% of GDP)	0.5	...	0.5[p]
Threatened species (number)	15[q]	18	28[c]
Forested area (% of land area)[e]	21.1	20.0	19.1[b]
CO2 emission estimates (million tons/tons per capita)	4.1 / 2.2	4.7 / 2.3	7.0 / 3.2[m]
Energy production, primary (Petajoules)	29	30	56[b]
Energy supply per capita (Gigajoules)	35	36	35[b]
Tourist/visitor arrivals at national borders (000)	1 474	1 973	1 528[b]
Important sites for terrestrial biodiversity protected (%)	47.1	47.1	47.1
Pop. using improved drinking water (urban/rural, %)	99.4 / 90.4	99.2 / 91.6	99.2 / 92.3[b]
Pop. using improved sanitation facilities (urban/rural, %)	72.9 / 36.1	76.4 / 40.4	78.5 / 43.1[b]
Net Official Development Assist. received (% of GNI)	0.53	1.26	0.61[d]

a Projected estimate (medium fertility variant). b 2015. c 2017. d 2016. e Estimate. f Calculated by the Statistics Division of the United Nations from national indices. g Break in the time series. h Data refers to a 5-year period preceding the reference year. i Refers to foreign citizens. j Data as at the end of December. k 2009. l 2012. m 2014. n 2008. o 2006. p 2013. q 2004.

Brazil

Region	South America	UN membership date	24 October 1945
Population (000, 2018)	210 868[a]	Surface area (km2)	8 515 767[b]
Pop. density (per km2, 2018)	25.2[a]	Sex ratio (m per 100 f)	96.6[a]
Capital city	Brasilia	National currency	Brazilian Real (BRL)
Capital city pop. (000, 2018)	4 469.6[c]	Exchange rate (per US$)	3.3[d]

Economic indicators

	2005	2010	2018
GDP: Gross domestic product (million current US$)	891 634	2 208 838	1 795 926[e]
GDP growth rate (annual %, const. 2010 prices)	3.2	7.5	- 3.6[e]
GDP per capita (current US$)	4 770.0	11 224.0	8 649.0[e]
Economy: Agriculture (% of Gross Value Added)[f]	5.5	4.8	5.1[e]
Economy: Industry (% of Gross Value Added)[f]	28.5	27.4	24.8[e]
Economy: Services and other activity (% of GVA)[f]	66.0	67.8	70.1[e]
Employment in agriculture (% of employed)[g]	20.5	16.0	10.2
Employment in industry (% of employed)[g]	21.4	22.3	20.9
Employment in services & other sectors (% employed)[g]	58.1	61.7	69.0
Unemployment rate (% of labour force)[g]	9.3	8.4	11.9
Labour force participation rate (female/male pop. %)[g]	55.4 / 79.2	54.6 / 77.7	53.1 / 74.5
CPI: Consumer Price Index (2010=100)[h]	80	100	156[d]
Agricultural production index (2004-2006=100)	99	122	136[d]
Index of industrial production (2005=100)	100	115	111[i]
International trade: exports (million current US$)	118 529	201 915	217 739[d]
International trade: imports (million current US$)	73 600	181 768	150 749[d]
International trade: balance (million current US$)	44 928	20 147	66 990[d]
Balance of payments, current account (million US$)	13 985	- 75 760[j]	- 9 762[d]

Major trading partners

							2017
Export partners (% of exports)	China	21.8	United States	12.5	Argentina	8.1
Import partners (% of imports)	China	18.1	United States	16.7	Argentina	6.3

Social indicators

	2005	2010	2018
Population growth rate (average annual %)[k]	1.3	1.0	0.9[b]
Urban population (% of total population)	82.8	84.3	86.6
Urban population growth rate (average annual %)[k]	1.7	1.4	1.2[b]
Fertility rate, total (live births per woman)[k]	2.1	1.9	1.8[b]
Life expectancy at birth (females/males, years)[k]	75.0 / 67.3	76.7 / 69.2	78.4 / 71.0[b]
Population age distribution (0-14/60+ years old, %)	27.4 / 8.7	24.9 / 10.0	21.4 / 13.1[a]
International migrant stock (000/% of total pop.)	030.6 / 0.3	592.6 / 0.3	736.8 / 0.4[d]
Refugees and others of concern to the UNHCR (000)	7.7[l]	5.2[l]	108.0[d]
Infant mortality rate (per 1 000 live births)[k]	28.2	20.4	15.8[b]
Health: Current expenditure (% of GDP)	8.0	8.0	8.9[b]
Health: Physicians (per 1 000 pop.)	1.6	1.8	1.9[m]
Education: Government expenditure (% of GDP)	4.5	5.6[n]	5.9[i]
Education: Primary gross enrol. ratio (f/m per 100 pop.)[g]	129.2 / 137.2	128.2 / 133.9[n]	113.8 / 116.8[b]
Education: Secondary gross enrol. ratio (f/m per 100 pop.)[g]	106.2 / 96.5	102.1 / 91.5[n]	102.2 / 97.2[b]
Education: Tertiary gross enrol. ratio (f/m per 100 pop.)[g]	29.3 / 22.8	42.2 / 31.9[n]	59.3 / 42.4[b]
Intentional homicide rate (per 100 000 pop.)	23.3	22.0	29.5[e]
Seats held by women in the National Parliament (%)	8.6	8.8	10.7

Environment and infrastructure indicators

	2005	2010	2018
Individuals using the Internet (per 100 inhabitants)	21.0[o,p]	40.6[o,p]	59.7[p,e]
Research & Development expenditure (% of GDP)	1.0	1.2	1.2[i]
Threatened species (number)	697[q]	773	990[d]
Forested area (% of land area)[g]	60.6	59.6	59.0[b]
CO2 emission estimates (million tons/tons per capita)	347.3 / 1.9	419.8 / 2.1	529.8 / 2.6[i]
Energy production, primary (Petajoules)	8 344	10 050	11 456[b]
Energy supply per capita (Gigajoules)	50	55	59[b]
Tourist/visitor arrivals at national borders (000)[r]	5 358	5 161	6 578[e]
Important sites for terrestrial biodiversity protected (%)	42.3	47.5	47.6
Pop. using improved drinking water (urban/rural, %)	98.4 / 79.7	99.3 / 83.8	100.0 / 87.0[b]
Pop. using improved sanitation facilities (urban/rural, %)	84.7 / 43.8	86.5 / 48.1	88.0 / 51.5[b]
Net Official Development Assist. received (% of GNI)	0.02	0.02	0.04[e]

a Projected estimate (medium fertility variant). b 2015. c Refers to the "Região Integrada de Desenvolvimento do Distrito Federal e Entorno". d 2017. e 2016. f Data classified according to ISIC Rev. 4. g Estimate. h Calculated by the Statistics Division of the United Nations from national indices. i 2014. j Break in the time series. k Data refers to a 5-year period preceding the reference year. l Data as at the end of December. m 2013. n 2009. o Population aged 10 years and over. p Users in the last 3 months. q 2004. r Including nationals residing abroad.

British Virgin Islands

Region	Caribbean
Surface area (km2)	151[b]
Sex ratio (m per 100 f)	97.1[c]
National currency	US Dollar (USD)

Population (000, 2018)	32[a]
Pop. density (per km2, 2018)	211.5[a]
Capital city	Road Town
Capital city pop. (000, 2018)	15.1

Economic indicators	2005	2010	2018
GDP: Gross domestic product (million current US$)	853	876	971[d]
GDP growth rate (annual %, const. 2010 prices)	15.5	- 0.1	0.3[d]
GDP per capita (current US$)	36 802.0	32 183.0	31 677.0[d]
Economy: Agriculture (% of Gross Value Added)[e]	0.2	0.2	0.2[d]
Economy: Industry (% of Gross Value Added)[e]	6.1	5.3	6.5[d]
Economy: Services and other activity (% of GVA)[e]	93.7	94.5	93.3[d]
Employment in agriculture (% of employed)	...	0.5[f]	...
Employment in industry (% of employed)	...	11.1[f]	...
Employment in services & other sectors (% employed)	...	87.4[f]	...
Agricultural production index (2004-2006=100)	100	102	103[d]
International trade: exports (million current US$)[g]	~0	~0	~0[h]
International trade: imports (million current US$)[g]	227	313	403[h]
International trade: balance (million current US$)[g]	- 226	- 313	- 403[h]

Major trading partners						2017
Export partners (% of exports)[g]	Ghana	60.0	Mexico	8.4	United States	3.1
Import partners (% of imports)[g]	United States	39.5	Areas nes[i]	38.5	Switzerland	5.1

Social indicators	2005	2010	2018
Population growth rate (average annual %)[j]	2.3	3.2	2.0[b]
Urban population (% of total population)	43.2	44.8	47.7
Urban population growth rate (average annual %)[j]	3.0	4.0	2.8[b]
Fertility rate, total (live births per woman)	2.0[k]	...	...
Life expectancy at birth (females/males, years)	78.5 / 69.9[k]	... / ...	... / ...
Population age distribution (0-14/60+ years old, %)	26.3 / 7.4[l]	22.3 / 9.7	... / ...
International migrant stock (000/% of total pop.)	15.0 / 64.8	17.1 / 62.7	20.0 / 64.0[h]
Refugees and others of concern to the UNHCR (000)	...	~0.0[m]	~0.0[h]
Education: Government expenditure (% of GDP)	...	4.4	6.3[b]
Intentional homicide rate (per 100 000 pop.)	17.7[k]	8.4[n]	...

Environment and infrastructure indicators	2005	2010	2018
Individuals using the Internet (per 100 inhabitants)	...	37.0	37.6[o]
Threatened species (number)	30[k]	43	67[h]
Forested area (% of land area)[g]	24.4	24.3	24.1[b]
CO2 emission estimates (million tons/tons per capita)	0.1 / 6.0	0.2 / 6.3	0.2 / 6.0[p]
Energy production, primary (Petajoules)	0	0	0[b]
Energy supply per capita (Gigajoules)[g]	85	89	84[b]
Tourist/visitor arrivals at national borders (000)	337	330	408[d]
Important sites for terrestrial biodiversity protected (%)	9.4	9.4	9.4
Pop. using improved drinking water (urban/rural, %)	94.9 / 94.9	... / ...	... / ...
Pop. using improved sanitation facilities (urban/rural, %)	97.5 / 97.5	97.5 / 97.5	97.5 / 97.5[b]

a Projected estimate (medium fertility variant). b 2015. c 2010. d 2016. e Data classified according to ISIC Rev. 4. f Data classified according to ISIC Rev. 3. g Estimate. h 2017. i Areas not elsewhere specified. j Data refers to a 5-year period preceding the reference year. k 2004. l 2001. m Data as at the end of December. n 2006. o 2012. p 2014.

Brunei Darussalam

Region	South-eastern Asia	UN membership date	21 September 1984
Population (000, 2018)	434ᵃ	Surface area (km2)	5 765ᵇ
Pop. density (per km2, 2018)	82.4ᵃ	Sex ratio (m per 100 f)	106.0ᵃ
Capital city	Bandar Seri Begawan	National currency	Brunei Dollar (BND)
Capital city pop. (000, 2018)	40.8	Exchange rate (per US$)	1.3ᶜ

Economic indicators

	2005	2010	2018
GDP: Gross domestic product (million current US$)	10 561	13 707	11 400ᵈ
GDP growth rate (annual %, const. 2010 prices)	0.4	2.6	- 2.5ᵈ
GDP per capita (current US$)	28 923.0	35 267.0	26 939.0ᵈ
Economy: Agriculture (% of Gross Value Added)ᵉ	0.9	0.7	1.2ᵈ
Economy: Industry (% of Gross Value Added)ᵉ	72.0	67.4	56.5ᵈ
Economy: Services and other activity (% of GVA)ᵉ	27.1	31.9	42.4ᵈ
Employment in agriculture (% of employed)ᶠ	1.0	0.7	0.5
Employment in industry (% of employed)ᶠ	19.2	19.2	17.6
Employment in services & other sectors (% employed)ᶠ	79.8	80.0	81.9
Unemployment rate (% of labour force)ᶠ	5.9	6.2	7.1
Labour force participation rate (female/male pop. %)ᶠ	56.6 / 78.0	58.0 / 76.4	59.0 / 74.5
CPI: Consumer Price Index (2010=100)	96ᵍ	100	99ᶜ
Agricultural production index (2004-2006=100)	75	139	169ᵈ
Index of industrial production (2005=100)ʰ	100	88	79ⁱ
International trade: exports (million current US$)	6 242ᶠ	8 908	5 571ᶜ
International trade: imports (million current US$)	1 447ᶠ	2 539	3 085ᶜ
International trade: balance (million current US$)	4 794ᶠ	6 369	2 486ᶜ
Balance of payments, current account (million US$)	4 033	5 016ᵍ	1 766ᵈ

Major trading partners

							2017
Export partners (% of exports)	Japan	29.3	Republic of Korea	14.2	Malaysia	11.2
Import partners (% of imports)	China	20.8	Singapore	18.5	Malaysia	18.2

Social indicators

	2005	2010	2018
Population growth rate (average annual %)ʲ	1.8	1.2	1.4ᵇ
Urban population (% of total population)	73.2	75.0	77.6
Urban population growth rate (average annual %)ʲ	2.4	1.7	1.9ᵇ
Fertility rate, total (live births per woman)ʲ	2.0	1.8	1.9ᵇ
Life expectancy at birth (females/males, years)ʲ	77.4 / 74.2	78.4 / 75.1	78.4 / 75.1ᵇ
Population age distribution (0-14/60+ years old, %)	27.8 / 4.8	26.0 / 5.4	22.6 / 8.5ᵃ
International migrant stock (000/% of total pop.)	98.4 / 27.0	100.6 / 25.9	108.6 / 25.3ᶜ
Refugees and others of concern to the UNHCR (000)	...	21.0ᵏ	20.5ᶜ
Infant mortality rate (per 1 000 live births)ʲ	8.2	6.5	6.5ᵇ
Health: Current expenditure (% of GDP)ˡ	2.2	2.3	2.6ᵇ
Health: Physicians (per 1 000 pop.)	1.1	1.4	1.7ᵇ
Education: Government expenditure (% of GDP)	3.7ᵐ	2.0	4.4ᵈ
Education: Primary gross enrol. ratio (f/m per 100 pop.)	108.4 / 112.8	106.3 / 106.8	106.2 / 107.1ᵈ
Education: Secondary gross enrol. ratio (f/m per 100 pop.)	95.8 / 97.3	99.5 / 98.9	94.0 / 92.8ᵈ
Education: Tertiary gross enrol. ratio (f/m per 100 pop.)	19.4 / 9.7	20.4 / 10.9	38.3 / 23.8ᵈ
Intentional homicide rate (per 100 000 pop.)	0.5	0.3	0.5ⁿ
Seats held by women in the National Parliament (%)	...	...	9.1

Environment and infrastructure indicators

	2005	2010	2018
Individuals using the Internet (per 100 inhabitants)	36.5	53.0ᶠ	75.0ᵈ
Research & Development expenditure (% of GDP)	–0.0ᵍ,ᵒ,ᵖ	...	...
Threatened species (number)	148ᵖ	170	193ᶜ
Forested area (% of land area)ᶠ	73.8	72.1	72.1ᵇ
CO2 emission estimates (million tons/tons per capita)	5.0 / 13.8	8.2 / 20.9	9.1 / 21.8ⁱ
Energy production, primary (Petajoules)	848	775	673ᵇ
Energy supply per capita (Gigajoules)	210	345	269ᵇ
Tourist/visitor arrivals at national borders (000)ᑫ	126	214	219ᵈ
Important sites for terrestrial biodiversity protected (%)	62.9	62.9	62.9

a Projected estimate (medium fertility variant). b 2015. c 2017. d 2016. e Data classified according to ISIC Rev. 4. f Estimate. g Break in the time series. h Data classified according to ISIC Rev. 3. i 2014. j Data refers to a 5-year period preceding the reference year. k Data as at the end of December. l Data refer to fiscal years beginning 1 April. m 2000. n 2013. o Partial data. p 2004. q Arrivals by air.

Bulgaria

Region	Eastern Europe
Population (000, 2018)	7 037[a]
Pop. density (per km2, 2018)	64.8[a]
Capital city	Sofia
Capital city pop. (000, 2018)	1 272.4

UN membership date	14 December 1955
Surface area (km2)	111 002[b]
Sex ratio (m per 100 f)	94.6[a]
National currency	Bulgarian Lev (BGN)
Exchange rate (per US$)	1.6[c]

Economic indicators

	2005	2010	2018
GDP: Gross domestic product (million current US$)	29 636	50 610	53 240[d]
GDP growth rate (annual %, const. 2010 prices)	7.1	1.3	3.9[d]
GDP per capita (current US$)	3 857.0	6 835.0	7 465.0[d]
Economy: Agriculture (% of Gross Value Added)[e]	8.6	4.8	4.7[d]
Economy: Industry (% of Gross Value Added)[e]	28.4	27.4	28.3[d]
Economy: Services and other activity (% of GVA)[e]	63.0	67.8	67.0[d]
Employment in agriculture (% of employed)[f]	8.9	6.8	6.1[f]
Employment in industry (% of employed)[f]	34.2	33.0	29.0
Employment in services & other sectors (% employed)[f]	56.8	60.2	64.9
Unemployment rate (% of labour force)	10.1	10.3	5.9[f]
Labour force participation rate (female/male pop. %)[f]	44.7 / 56.4	47.7 / 59.5	47.8 / 59.5
CPI: Consumer Price Index (2010=100)[g]	73	100	108[c]
Agricultural production index (2004-2006=100)	90	106	114[d]
Index of industrial production (2005=100)	100	98[h]	105[h,i]
International trade: exports (million current US$)	11 739	20 608	30 182[c]
International trade: imports (million current US$)	18 162	25 360	34 149[c]
International trade: balance (million current US$)	- 6 423	- 4 752	- 3 967[c]
Balance of payments, current account (million US$)	- 3 347	- 965[j]	2 628[c]

Major trading partners

					2017
Export partners (% of exports)	Germany	13.4	Italy	8.3[f]	Romania	8.2
Import partners (% of imports)	Germany	12.2	Russian Federation	10.2	Italy	7.3

Social indicators

	2005	2010	2018
Population growth rate (average annual %)[k]	- 0.8	- 0.7	- 0.6[b]
Urban population (% of total population)	70.6	72.3	75.0
Urban population growth rate (average annual %)[k]	- 0.3	- 0.3	- 0.2[b]
Fertility rate, total (live births per woman)[k]	1.2	1.4	1.5[b]
Life expectancy at birth (females/males, years)[k]	75.8 / 68.8	76.7 / 69.7	77.8 / 70.8[b]
Population age distribution (0-14/60+ years old, %)	13.6 / 23.1	13.3 / 25.3	14.4 / 27.9[a]
International migrant stock (000/% of total pop.)	61.1 / 0.8	76.3 / 1.0	153.8 / 2.2[c]
Refugees and others of concern to the UNHCR (000)	5.2[l]	6.9[l]	27.7[c]
Infant mortality rate (per 1 000 live births)[k]	12.7	9.5	8.3[b]
Health: Current expenditure (% of GDP)[m]	6.9	7.1	8.2[b]
Health: Physicians (per 1 000 pop.)	...	3.8	4.0[i]
Education: Government expenditure (% of GDP)	4.1	3.9	4.1[n]
Education: Primary gross enrol. ratio (f/m per 100 pop.)	102.8 / 103.8	108.3 / 108.7	94.3 / 95.3[d]
Education: Secondary gross enrol. ratio (f/m per 100 pop.)	87.3 / 91.0	88.2 / 92.1	98.3 / 101.4[d]
Education: Tertiary gross enrol. ratio (f/m per 100 pop.)	48.9 / 42.1	66.1 / 50.0	79.3 / 63.7[d]
Intentional homicide rate (per 100 000 pop.)	2.6	2.0	1.1[d]
Seats held by women in the National Parliament (%)	26.3	20.8	23.8

Environment and infrastructure indicators

	2005	2010	2018
Individuals using the Internet (per 100 inhabitants)	20.0[o]	46.2[o]	59.8[d]
Research & Development expenditure (% of GDP)	0.4	0.6	1.0[p,b]
Threatened species (number)	44[q]	66	104[c]
Forested area (% of land area)	33.6	34.4[f]	35.2[f,b]
CO2 emission estimates (million tons/tons per capita)	47.9 / 6.2	44.1 / 5.9	42.4 / 5.9[i]
Energy production, primary (Petajoules)	444	442	505[b]
Energy supply per capita (Gigajoules)	107	100	108[b]
Tourist/visitor arrivals at national borders (000)	4 837	6 047	8 252[d]
Important sites for terrestrial biodiversity protected (%)	41.2	95.5	95.6
Pop. using improved drinking water (urban/rural, %)	99.8 / 99.3	99.7 / 99.1	99.6 / 99.0[b]
Pop. using improved sanitation facilities (urban/rural, %)	86.8 / 83.6	86.8 / 83.7	86.8 / 83.7[b]
Net Official Development Assist. disbursed (% of GNI)	...	0.09	0.11[p,c]

a Projected estimate (medium fertility variant). b 2015. c 2017. d 2016. e Data classified according to ISIC Rev. 4. f Estimate. g Calculated by the Statistics Division of the United Nations from national indices. h Excluding water and waste management. i 2014. j Break in the time series. k Data refers to a 5-year period preceding the reference year. l Data as at the end of December. m Health expenditure data do not include funds from foreign origin flowing in the health financing system. n 2013. o Population aged 16 to 74 years. p Provisional data. q 2004.

Burkina Faso

Region	Western Africa	UN membership date	20 September 1960
Population (000, 2018)	19 752[a]	Surface area (km2)	272 967[b]
Pop. density (per km2, 2018)	72.2[a]	Sex ratio (m per 100 f)	99.6[a]
Capital city	Ouagadougou	National currency	CFA Franc, BCEAO (XOF)[c]
Capital city pop. (000, 2018)	2 531.4	Exchange rate (per US$)	546.9[d]

Economic indicators

	2005	2010	2018
GDP: Gross domestic product (million current US$)	5 463	8 980	11 695[e]
GDP growth rate (annual %, const. 2010 prices)	8.7	8.4	5.9[e]
GDP per capita (current US$)	407.0	575.0	627.0[e]
Economy: Agriculture (% of Gross Value Added)	38.5	35.1	30.3[e]
Economy: Industry (% of Gross Value Added)	17.7	20.2	25.7[e]
Economy: Services and other activity (% of GVA)	43.8	44.7	44.0[e]
Employment in agriculture (% of employed)[f]	82.0	60.9	27.6
Employment in industry (% of employed)[f]	5.1	11.4	32.0
Employment in services & other sectors (% employed)[f]	12.9	27.7	40.4
Unemployment rate (% of labour force)	4.0	4.7[f]	6.2[f]
Labour force participation rate (female/male pop. %)[f]	62.4 / 86.8	59.7 / 81.7	57.9 / 75.0
CPI: Consumer Price Index (2010=100)[g]	87	100	108[d]
Agricultural production index (2004-2006=100)	104	118	125[e]
International trade: exports (million current US$)	332	1 288	2 262[f,d]
International trade: imports (million current US$)	1 161	2 048	4 083[f,d]
International trade: balance (million current US$)	- 828	- 760	- 1 821[f,d]
Balance of payments, current account (million US$)	- 634	- 181	- 780[e]

Major trading partners

					2017
Export partners (% of exports)	Switzerland	59.4[f]	Singapore	9.1	India	5.2[f]
Import partners (% of imports)[f]	China	14.5	Côte d'Ivoire	8.6	France	8.1

Social indicators

	2005	2010	2018
Population growth rate (average annual %)[h]	2.9	3.0	3.0[b]
Urban population (% of total population)	21.5	24.6	29.4
Urban population growth rate (average annual %)[h]	6.7	5.7	5.2[h]
Fertility rate, total (live births per woman)[h]	6.4	6.1	5.6[b]
Life expectancy at birth (females/males, years)[h]	52.6 / 50.5	55.8 / 54.6	59.3 / 58.0[b]
Population age distribution (0-14/60+ years old, %)	46.5 / 4.1	46.2 / 3.9	44.9 / 3.9[a]
International migrant stock (000/% of total pop.)[i]	597.0 / 4.4	673.9 / 4.3	708.9 / 3.7[d]
Refugees and others of concern to the UNHCR (000)	1.3[j]	1.1[j]	34.2[d]
Infant mortality rate (per 1 000 live births)[h]	90.0	77.6	64.8[b]
Health: Current expenditure (% of GDP)	4.4	5.9	5.4[b]
Health: Physicians (per 1 000 pop.)	0.1[k]	~0.0	~0.0[l]
Education: Government expenditure (% of GDP)	4.4	3.9	4.2[b]
Education: Primary gross enrol. ratio (f/m per 100 pop.)	51.8 / 64.6	74.3 / 81.6	90.1 / 92.1[e]
Education: Secondary gross enrol. ratio (f/m per 100 pop.)	11.8 / 16.7	18.9 / 24.8	34.9 / 36.7[e]
Education: Tertiary gross enrol. ratio (f/m per 100 pop.)	1.4 / 3.2	2.3 / 4.8	3.8 / 7.3[e]
Intentional homicide rate (per 100 000 pop.)	0.5	0.6	0.4[b]
Seats held by women in the National Parliament (%)	11.7	15.3	11.0

Environment and infrastructure indicators

	2005	2010	2018
Individuals using the Internet (per 100 inhabitants)	0.5	2.4[f]	14.0[f,a]
Research & Development expenditure (% of GDP)	0.2[m]	0.2[n]	...
Threatened species (number)	11[k]	24	31[d]
Forested area (% of land area)[f]	21.7	20.6	19.6[b]
CO2 emission estimates (million tons/tons per capita)	1.1 / 0.1	2.0 / 0.1	2.8 / 0.1[e]
Energy production, primary (Petajoules)	98	118	126[b]
Energy supply per capita (Gigajoules)	8	9	9[b]
Tourist/visitor arrivals at national borders (000)	245	274	152[e]
Important sites for terrestrial biodiversity protected (%)	66.7	71.8	71.8
Pop. using improved drinking water (urban/rural, %)	90.0 / 63.4	95.3 / 72.3	97.5 / 75.8[b]
Pop. using improved sanitation facilities (urban/rural, %)	48.3 / 5.1	49.8 / 6.2	50.4 / 6.7[b]
Net Official Development Assist. received (% of GNI)	12.83	11.35	8.66[e]

a Projected estimate (medium fertility variant). **b** 2015. **c** African Financial Community (CFA) Franc, Central Bank of West African States (BCEAO). **d** 2017. **e** 2016. **f** Estimate. **g** Ouagadougou **h** Data refers to a 5-year period preceding the reference year. **i** Including refugees. **j** Data as at the end of December. **k** 2004. **l** 2012. **m** Partial data. **n** 2009. **o** 2014.

Burundi

Region	Eastern Africa	UN membership date	18 September 1962
Population (000, 2018)	11 216[a]	Surface area (km2)	27 830[b]
Pop. density (per km2, 2018)	436.8[a]	Sex ratio (m per 100 f)	97.0[a]
Capital city	Bujumbura	National currency	Burundi Franc (BIF)
Capital city pop. (000, 2018)	899.0	Exchange rate (per US$)	1 766.7[c]

Economic indicators	2005	2010	2018
GDP: Gross domestic product (million current US$)	1 117	2 032	2 874[d]
GDP growth rate (annual %, const. 2010 prices)	0.9	5.1	1.7[d]
GDP per capita (current US$)	150.0	232.0	273.0[d]
Economy: Agriculture (% of Gross Value Added)	43.0	40.7	37.7[d]
Economy: Industry (% of Gross Value Added)	17.8	16.3	15.2[d]
Economy: Services and other activity (% of GVA)	39.1	43.0	47.1[d]
Employment in agriculture (% of employed)[e]	91.8	91.4	91.5
Employment in industry (% of employed)[e]	2.6	2.6	2.5
Employment in services & other sectors (% employed)[e]	5.6	6.1	6.0
Unemployment rate (% of labour force)[e]	1.7	1.6	1.5
Labour force participation rate (female/male pop. %)[e]	82.1 / 80.2	80.4 / 78.2	80.3 / 77.5
CPI: Consumer Price Index (2010=100)[f]	61	100	189[c]
Agricultural production index (2004-2006=100)	92	108	108[d]
International trade: exports (million current US$)	114	118	142[c]
International trade: imports (million current US$)	258	404	725[c]
International trade: balance (million current US$)	- 144	- 286	- 583[c]
Balance of payments, current account (million US$)	- 6[g]	- 301	- 355[d]

Major trading partners					2017
Export partners (% of exports)	United Arab Emirates	27.1	Dem. Rep. of Congo 17.0	Pakistan	9.2
Import partners (% of imports)	India	14.2	China 13.8	Saudi Arabia	9.1

Social indicators	2005	2010	2018
Population growth rate (average annual %)[h]	3.0	3.3	3.0[b]
Urban population (% of total population)	9.4	10.6	13.0
Urban population growth rate (average annual %)[h]	5.5	5.9	5.6[b]
Fertility rate, total (live births per woman)[h]	6.8	6.5	6.0[b]
Life expectancy at birth (females/males, years)[h]	53.7 / 50.3	55.4 / 52.0	58.0 / 54.2[b]
Population age distribution (0-14/60+ years old, %)	45.7 / 4.2	44.1 / 4.0	45.1 / 4.4[a]
International migrant stock (000/% of total pop.)[i]	172.9 / 2.3	235.3 / 2.7	299.6 / 2.8[c]
Refugees and others of concern to the UNHCR (000)	53.6[j]	200.8[j]	186.9[c]
Infant mortality rate (per 1 000 live births)[h]	94.6	86.2	77.8[b]
Health: Current expenditure (% of GDP)[k]	9.4	11.3	8.2[b]
Health: Physicians (per 1 000 pop.)	~0.0[l]	...	...
Education: Government expenditure (% of GDP)	3.6	6.8	5.4[m]
Education: Primary gross enrol. ratio (f/m per 100 pop.)	75.4 / 89.7	137.0 / 141.8	131.3 / 130.5[d]
Education: Secondary gross enrol. ratio (f/m per 100 pop.)	11.2 / 15.8[e]	19.5 / 28.7	47.6 / 49.2[d]
Education: Tertiary gross enrol. ratio (f/m per 100 pop.)	1.4 / 3.7[e]	2.3 / 4.6	2.5 / 8.3[n]
Intentional homicide rate (per 100 000 pop.)	...	4.0	6.0[d]
Seats held by women in the National Parliament (%)	18.4	31.4	36.4

Environment and infrastructure indicators	2005	2010	2018
Individuals using the Internet (per 100 inhabitants)	0.5	1.0[e]	5.2[e,d]
Research & Development expenditure (% of GDP)[o]	...	0.1	0.1[p]
Threatened species (number)	28[l]	52	61[c]
Forested area (% of land area)[e]	7.0	9.9	10.7[b]
CO2 emission estimates (million tons/tons per capita)	0.2 / ~0.0	0.2 / ~0.0	0.4 / ~0.0[n]
Energy production, primary (Petajoules)	79	86	56[b]
Energy supply per capita (Gigajoules)	11	9	5[b]
Tourist/visitor arrivals at national borders (000)[q]	148	142[g]	187[g,d]
Important sites for terrestrial biodiversity protected (%)	51.0	51.0	51.2
Pop. using improved drinking water (urban/rural, %)	92.9 / 71.2	91.9 / 72.6	91.1 / 73.8[b]
Pop. using improved sanitation facilities (urban/rural, %)	39.1 / 46.3	41.7 / 47.6	43.8 / 48.6[b]
Net Official Development Assist. received (% of GNI)	33.23	31.15	24.84[d]

a Projected estimate (medium fertility variant). b 2015. c 2017. d 2016. e Estimate. f Bujumbura g Break in the time series. h Data refers to a 5-year period preceding the reference year. i Including refugees. j Data as at the end of December. k Data revision. l 2004. m 2013. n 2014. o Partial data. p 2011. q Including nationals residing abroad.

Cabo Verde

Region	Western Africa	UN membership date	16 September 1975
Population (000, 2018)	553[a]	Surface area (km2)	4 033[b]
Pop. density (per km2, 2018)	137.3[a]	Sex ratio (m per 100 f)	99.4[a]
Capital city	Praia	National currency	Cabo Verde Escudo (CVE)
Capital city pop. (000, 2018)	167.5	Exchange rate (per US$)	92.4[c]

Economic indicators	2005	2010	2018
GDP: Gross domestic product (million current US$)	1 105	1 664	1 639[d]
GDP growth rate (annual %, const. 2010 prices)	6.5	1.5	3.8[d]
GDP per capita (current US$)	2 329.0	3 313.0	3 038.0[d]
Economy: Agriculture (% of Gross Value Added)	11.7	9.2	9.4[d]
Economy: Industry (% of Gross Value Added)	22.8	20.8	19.9[d]
Economy: Services and other activity (% of GVA)	65.5	70.1	70.6[d]
Employment in agriculture (% of employed)[e]	73.2	69.7	67.2
Employment in industry (% of employed)[e]	6.8	7.3	6.9
Employment in services & other sectors (% employed)[e]	20.0	23.0	25.9
Unemployment rate (% of labour force)	11.2[e]	10.7	10.4[e]
Labour force participation rate (female/male pop. %)[e]	44.2 / 75.7	46.0 / 72.8	50.0 / 71.6
CPI: Consumer Price Index (2010=100)[f]	83	100	108[c]
Agricultural production index (2004-2006=100)	99	106	97[d]
International trade: exports (million current US$)	89	220	50[c]
International trade: imports (million current US$)	438	731	794[c]
International trade: balance (million current US$)	- 349	- 511	- 744[c]
Balance of payments, current account (million US$)	- 41	- 223	- 125[c]

Major trading partners						2017
Export partners (% of exports)	Spain	70.8	Portugal	24.8[e]	United States	2.3
Import partners (% of imports)	Portugal	42.9	Spain	12.6	Italy	6.1

Social indicators	2005	2010	2018
Population growth rate (average annual %)[g]	1.7	1.1	1.2[b]
Urban population (% of total population)	57.7	61.8	65.7
Urban population growth rate (average annual %)[g]	3.3	2.5	2.0[b]
Fertility rate, total (live births per woman)[g]	3.4	2.9	2.5[b]
Life expectancy at birth (females/males, years)[g]	72.8 / 69.5	73.4 / 69.9	74.0 / 70.1[b]
Population age distribution (0-14/60+ years old, %)	38.1 / 7.2	34.0 / 6.7	29.8 / 7.0[a]
International migrant stock (000/% of total pop.)	12.7 / 2.7	14.4 / 2.9	15.3 / 2.8[c]
Refugees and others of concern to the UNHCR (000)	~0.0[h]	...	0.1[c]
Infant mortality rate (per 1 000 live births)[g]	25.0	23.5	22.5[b]
Health: Current expenditure (% of GDP)	4.8	4.5	4.8[b]
Health: Physicians (per 1 000 pop.)	...	0.6	0.8[b]
Education: Government expenditure (% of GDP)	7.5[i]	5.6	5.4[d]
Education: Primary gross enrol. ratio (f/m per 100 pop.)	110.1 / 114.7	99.0 / 106.1	93.4 / 99.9[d]
Education: Secondary gross enrol. ratio (f/m per 100 pop.)	75.3 / 66.7	94.0 / 79.1	88.4 / 80.7[d]
Education: Tertiary gross enrol. ratio (f/m per 100 pop.)	7.8 / 7.3	20.2 / 15.7	26.0 / 17.9[d]
Intentional homicide rate (per 100 000 pop.)	9.3	7.8	11.5[d]
Seats held by women in the National Parliament (%)	11.1	18.1	23.6

Environment and infrastructure indicators	2005	2010	2018
Individuals using the Internet (per 100 inhabitants)	6.1	30.0[e]	48.2[e,d]
Research & Development expenditure (% of GDP)	...	...	0.1[j,k,l]
Threatened species (number)	23[i]	31	65[c]
Forested area (% of land area)	20.7	21.1	22.3[b]
CO2 emission estimates (million tons/tons per capita)	0.4 / 0.9	0.6 / 1.1	0.5 / 1.0[m]
Energy production, primary (Petajoules)	2	1	2[e,b]
Energy supply per capita (Gigajoules)	16	19	17[e,b]
Tourist/visitor arrivals at national borders (000)	198	336	598[d]
Important sites for terrestrial biodiversity protected (%)	15.0	15.0	15.1
Pop. using improved drinking water (urban/rural, %)	87.5 / 83.1	91.1 / 85.4	94.0 / 87.3[b]
Pop. using improved sanitation facilities (urban/rural, %)	67.8 / 35.2	75.5 / 45.8	81.6 / 54.3[b]
Net Official Development Assist. received (% of GNI)	17.36	20.55	7.38[d]

a Projected estimate (medium fertility variant). b 2015. c 2017. d 2016. e Estimate. f Calculated by the Statistics Division of the United Nations from national indices. g Data refers to a 5-year period preceding the reference year. h Data as at the end of December. i 2004. j Higher Education only. k Partial data. l 2011. m 2014.

Cambodia

Region	South-eastern Asia
Population (000, 2018)	16 246[a]
Pop. density (per km2, 2018)	92.0[a]
Capital city	Phnom Penh
Capital city pop. (000, 2018)	1 952.3[c]

UN membership date	14 December 1955
Surface area (km2)	181 035[b]
Sex ratio (m per 100 f)	95.3[a]
National currency	Riel (KHR)
Exchange rate (per US$)	4 041.5[d]

Economic indicators	2005	2010	2018
GDP: Gross domestic product (million current US$)	6 293	11 242	20 017[a]
GDP growth rate (annual %, const. 2010 prices)	13.2	6.0	6.9[e]
GDP per capita (current US$)	474.0	786.0	1 270.0[e]
Economy: Agriculture (% of Gross Value Added)	32.4	36.0	26.3[e]
Economy: Industry (% of Gross Value Added)	26.4	23.3	31.3[e]
Economy: Services and other activity (% of GVA)	41.2	40.7	42.4[e]
Employment in agriculture (% of employed)[f]	70.8	54.2	25.7
Employment in industry (% of employed)[f]	9.8	16.2	26.9
Employment in services & other sectors (% employed)[f]	19.4	29.6	47.4
Unemployment rate (% of labour force)	2.0[f]	0.4	0.2[f]
Labour force participation rate (female/male pop. %)[f]	76.9 / 86.7	81.8 / 89.3	81.2 / 88.9
CPI: Consumer Price Index (2010=100)[g]	68	100	125[d]
Agricultural production index (2004-2006=100)	105	148	186[e]
International trade: exports (million current US$)	3 019	5 590	12 440[f,d]
International trade: imports (million current US$)	2 552	4 903	13 155[f,d]
International trade: balance (million current US$)	467	688	- 716[f,d]
Balance of payments, current account (million US$)	- 307	- 538[h]	- 1 775[e]

Major trading partners						2017
Export partners (% of exports)	United States	21.3[f]	United Kingdom	9.5	Germany	9.0[f]
Import partners (% of imports)	China	36.8[f]	Thailand	15.4	Viet Nam	11.4

Social indicators	2005	2010	2018
Population growth rate (average annual %)[i]	1.8	1.5	1.6[b]
Urban population (% of total population)	19.2	20.3	23.4
Urban population growth rate (average annual %)[i]	2.4	2.6	3.4[b]
Fertility rate, total (live births per woman)[i]	3.4	3.1	2.7[b]
Life expectancy at birth (females/males, years)[i]	63.0 / 58.5	67.4 / 62.7	69.6 / 65.5[b]
Population age distribution (0-14/60+ years old, %)	37.1 / 5.3	33.3 / 5.9	31.2 / 7.2[a]
International migrant stock (000/% of total pop.)	114.0 / 0.9	82.0 / 0.6	76.3 / 0.5[d]
Refugees and others of concern to the UNHCR (000)	0.4[j]	0.2[j]	0.1[d]
Infant mortality rate (per 1 000 live births)[i]	65.9	45.0	29.9[b]
Health: Current expenditure (% of GDP)[k,l]	7.1	6.9	6.0[b]
Health: Physicians (per 1 000 pop.)	0.2[m]	0.2	0.1[n]
Education: Government expenditure (% of GDP)	1.7[o]	1.5	1.9[n]
Education: Primary gross enrol. ratio (f/m per 100 pop.)	126.0 / 135.6	120.2 / 127.4	108.8 / 111.6[e]
Education: Secondary gross enrol. ratio (f/m per 100 pop.)	25.7 / 36.7[f,o]	41.6 / 48.7[f,p]	... / ...
Education: Tertiary gross enrol. ratio (f/m per 100 pop.)	2.1 / 4.7	10.5 / 17.7	11.8 / 14.4[b]
Intentional homicide rate (per 100 000 pop.)	3.4	2.3	1.8[q]
Seats held by women in the National Parliament (%)	9.8	21.1	20.3

Environment and infrastructure indicators	2005	2010	2018
Individuals using the Internet (per 100 inhabitants)	0.3	1.3	25.6[e]
Research & Development expenditure (% of GDP)	~0.0[r,s]	...	0.1[h,b]
Threatened species (number)	103[o]	204	255[d]
Forested area (% of land area)	60.8	57.2[f]	53.6[f,b]
CO2 emission estimates (million tons/tons per capita)	2.8 / 0.2	5.0 / 0.4	6.7 / 0.4[h]
Energy production, primary (Petajoules)	105	152	184[b]
Energy supply per capita (Gigajoules)	11	16	19[b]
Tourist/visitor arrivals at national borders (000)	1 422	2 508	5 012[e]
Important sites for terrestrial biodiversity protected (%)	38.1	39.5	39.5
Pop. using improved drinking water (urban/rural, %)	71.6 / 48.4	86.1 / 58.8	100.0 / 69.1[b]
Pop. using improved sanitation facilities (urban/rural, %)	58.6 / 16.9	73.8 / 23.7	88.1 / 30.5[b]
Net Official Development Assist. received (% of GNI)	8.97	6.84	3.88[e]

a Projected estimate (medium fertility variant). **b** 2015. **c** Refers to the municipality of Phnom Penh including suburban areas. **d** 2017. **e** 2016. **f** Estimate. **g** Phnom Penh **h** Break in the time series. **i** Data refers to a 5-year period preceding the reference year. **j** Data as at the end of December. **k** 2012 data are based on a health accounts study based on SHA2011. Numbers were converted to SHA 1.0 format for comparability. **l** Data refer to fiscal years beginning 1 July. **m** 2000. **n** 2014. **o** 2004. **p** 2008. **q** 2011. **r** Partial data. **s** 2002.

Cameroon

Region	Middle Africa	UN membership date	20 September 1960
Population (000, 2018)	24 678[a]	Surface area (km2)	475 650[b]
Pop. density (per km2, 2018)	52.2[a]	Sex ratio (m per 100 f)	100.2[a]
Capital city	Yaoundé	National currency	CFA Franc, BEAC (XAF)[c]
Capital city pop. (000, 2018)	3 655.7	Exchange rate (per US$)	546.9[d]

Economic indicators

	2005	2010	2018
GDP: Gross domestic product (million current US$)	17 944	26 144	32 217[e]
GDP growth rate (annual %, const. 2010 prices)	2.0	3.4	4.5[e]
GDP per capita (current US$)	1 030.0	1 309.0	1 374.0[e]
Economy: Agriculture (% of Gross Value Added)[f]	15.2	15.1	16.7[e]
Economy: Industry (% of Gross Value Added)[f]	30.3	29.1	26.6[e]
Economy: Services and other activity (% of GVA)[f]	54.6	55.8	56.7[e]
Employment in agriculture (% of employed)[g]	64.9	64.9	61.6
Employment in industry (% of employed)[g]	9.6	9.3	9.3
Employment in services & other sectors (% employed)[g]	25.5	25.8	29.1
Unemployment rate (% of labour force)	4.4	4.1	4.2[g]
Labour force participation rate (female/male pop. %)[g]	70.4 / 81.4	70.6 / 81.4	71.3 / 81.2
CPI: Consumer Price Index (2010=100)[g]	86	100	115[d]
Agricultural production index (2004-2006=100)	103	140	175[e]
Index of industrial production (2005=100)[h]	100[i]	102[j]	112[j,k]
International trade: exports (million current US$)	2 849	3 878	2 433[g,d]
International trade: imports (million current US$)	2 800	5 133	4 224[g,d]
International trade: balance (million current US$)	49	- 1 255	- 1 791[g,d]
Balance of payments, current account (million US$)	- 495	- 856	- 1 037[l,e]

Major trading partners

						2017
Export partners (% of exports)	Netherlands	15.7[g]	India	11.5	China	10.9[g]
Import partners (% of imports)	China	21.4	France	12.0	Nigeria	4.6

Social indicators

	2005	2010	2018
Population growth rate (average annual %)[m]	2.6	2.7	2.7[b]
Urban population (% of total population)	48.5	51.6	56.4
Urban population growth rate (average annual %)[m]	3.9	3.9	3.8[b]
Fertility rate, total (live births per woman)[m]	5.4	5.2	5.0[b]
Life expectancy at birth (females/males, years)[m]	52.3 / 50.6	55.4 / 53.4	57.7 / 55.1[b]
Population age distribution (0-14/60+ years old, %)	44.0 / 5.0	43.5 / 4.9	42.5 / 4.8[a]
International migrant stock (000/% of total pop.)	258.7 / 1.5	289.1 / 1.4	540.3 / 2.2[d]
Refugees and others of concern to the UNHCR (000)	66.3[n]	106.7[n]	553.4[d]
Infant mortality rate (per 1 000 live births)[m]	88.5	77.2	67.5[b]
Health: Current expenditure (% of GDP)[g]	4.5	5.0	5.1[b]
Health: Physicians (per 1 000 pop.)	0.1	0.1	...
Education: Government expenditure (% of GDP)	2.9	3.0	2.8[o]
Education: Primary gross enrol. ratio (f/m per 100 pop.)	96.6 / 115.1[g]	102.8 / 118.9	112.9 / 125.3[e]
Education: Secondary gross enrol. ratio (f/m per 100 pop.)	24.5 / 31.0	37.9 / 45.2[p]	57.1 / 66.4[e]
Education: Tertiary gross enrol. ratio (f/m per 100 pop.)	4.7 / 7.2[q]	10.3 / 12.6	15.5 / 19.3[b]
Intentional homicide rate (per 100 000 pop.)	6.1[q]	5.0	4.2[k]
Seats held by women in the National Parliament (%)	8.9	13.9	31.1

Environment and infrastructure indicators

	2005	2010	2018
Individuals using the Internet (per 100 inhabitants)	1.4	4.3[g]	25.0[g,e]
Threatened species (number)	484[r]	624	775[d]
Forested area (% of land area)	44.5	42.1[g]	39.8[g,b]
CO2 emission estimates (million tons/tons per capita)	3.7 / 0.2	6.8 / 0.3	7.0 / 0.3[s]
Energy production, primary (Petajoules)	442	351	446[b]
Energy supply per capita (Gigajoules)	17	14	14[b]
Tourist/visitor arrivals at national borders (000)	...	573	822[s]
Important sites for terrestrial biodiversity protected (%)	25.4	28.4	36.3
Pop. using improved drinking water (urban/rural, %)	89.1 / 46.0	92.6 / 50.2	94.8 / 52.7[b]
Pop. using improved sanitation facilities (urban/rural, %)	61.1 / 26.7	61.5 / 26.7	61.8 / 26.8[b]
Net Official Development Assist. received (% of GNI)	2.59	2.31	3.16[e]

a Projected estimate (medium fertility variant). b 2015. c African Financial Community (CFA) Franc, Bank of Central African States (BEAC). d 2017. e 2016. f Data classified according to ISIC Rev. 4. g Estimate. h Data classified according to ISIC Rev. 3. i Country data supplemented with data from the Observatoire Economique et Statistique d'Afrique Subsaharienne (Afristat). j Data refers to manufacturing and utilities only. k 2012. l Break in the time series. m Data refers to a 5-year period preceding the reference year. n Data as at the end of December. o 2013. p 2009. q 2003. r 2004. s 2014.

Canada

Region	Northern America	UN membership date	09 November 1945
Population (000, 2018)	36 954[a]	Surface area (km2)	9 984 670[b]
Pop. density (per km2, 2018)	4.1[a]	Sex ratio (m per 100 f)	98.5[a]
Capital city	Ottawa	National currency	Canadian Dollar (CAD)
Capital city pop. (000, 2018)	1 363.2[c]	Exchange rate (per US$)	1.3[d]

Economic indicators

	2005	2010	2018
GDP: Gross domestic product (million current US$)	1 169 393	1 613 463	1 529 760[a]
GDP growth rate (annual %, const. 2010 prices)	3.2	3.1	1.5[e]
GDP per capita (current US$)	36 218.0	47 221.0	42 154.0[a]
Economy: Agriculture (% of Gross Value Added)	1.8	1.4[f]	1.7[f,e]
Economy: Industry (% of Gross Value Added)	32.4	28.6[f]	28.5[f,e]
Economy: Services and other activity (% of GVA)	65.8	70.0[f]	69.8[f,e]
Employment in agriculture (% of employed)[g]	2.7	2.3	1.9
Employment in industry (% of employed)[g]	22.0	19.8	19.5
Employment in services & other sectors (% employed)[g]	75.2	77.9	78.6
Unemployment rate (% of labour force)	6.8	8.1	6.3[g]
Labour force participation rate (female/male pop. %)[g]	60.9 / 72.6	61.9 / 71.4	60.6 / 69.6
CPI: Consumer Price Index (2010=100)[h]	92	100	112[d]
Agricultural production index (2004-2006=100)	102	103	113[a]
Index of industrial production (2005=100)[i]	100	88	92[j]
International trade: exports (million current US$)[k]	360 552	386 580	420 502[d]
International trade: imports (million current US$)[k]	314 444	392 109	432 721[d]
International trade: balance (million current US$)[k]	46 108	- 5 529	- 12 219[d]
Balance of payments, current account (million US$)	21 931	- 58 160	- 48 800[d]

Major trading partners

						2017
Export partners (% of exports)	United States	76.0	China	4.3	United Kingdom	3.2
Import partners (% of imports)	United States	51.4	China	12.6	Mexico	6.3

Social indicators

	2005	2010	2018
Population growth rate (average annual %)[l]	1.0	1.1	1.0[b]
Urban population (% of total population)	80.1	80.9	81.4
Urban population growth rate (average annual %)[l]	1.1	1.3	1.1[b]
Fertility rate, total (live births per woman)[l]	1.5	1.6	1.6[b]
Life expectancy at birth (females/males, years)[l]	82.1 / 77.2	83.0 / 78.4	83.8 / 79.7[b]
Population age distribution (0-14/60+ years old, %)	17.7 / 17.9	16.5 / 20.0	16.1 / 24.0[a]
International migrant stock (000/% of total pop.)	6 079.0 / 18.8	6 761.2 / 19.8	7 861.2 / 21.5[d]
Refugees and others of concern to the UNHCR (000)	167.7[m]	216.6[m]	134.5[d]
Infant mortality rate (per 1 000 live births)[l]	5.3	5.1	4.7[b]
Health: Current expenditure (% of GDP)	9.1	10.6	10.4[b]
Health: Physicians (per 1 000 pop.)	1.9[n]	2.0	2.5[b]
Education: Government expenditure (% of GDP)	4.8	5.4	5.3[j]
Education: Primary gross enrol. ratio (f/m per 100 pop.)	96.6 / 97.4	98.9 / 98.4	101.5 / 101.4[e]
Education: Secondary gross enrol. ratio (f/m per 100 pop.)	99.8 / 102.1	101.1 / 103.5	113.9 / 112.2[e]
Intentional homicide rate (per 100 000 pop.)	2.1	1.6	1.7[e]
Seats held by women in the National Parliament (%)	21.1	22.1	27.0

Environment and infrastructure indicators

	2005	2010	2018
Individuals using the Internet (per 100 inhabitants)	71.7[o]	80.3[o,p]	89.8[q,e]
Research & Development expenditure (% of GDP)	2.0	1.8	1.6[q,q]
Threatened species (number)	74[n]	77	122[q]
Forested area (% of land area)	38.2	38.2	38.2[b]
CO2 emission estimates (million tons/tons per capita)	557.4 / 17.3	534.7 / 15.7	537.2 / 15.1[q]
Energy production, primary (Petajoules)	16 597	16 450	19 321[b]
Energy supply per capita (Gigajoules)	348	319	310[b]
Tourist/visitor arrivals at national borders (000)	18 771	16 219	19 824[e]
Important sites for terrestrial biodiversity protected (%)	21.2	25.4	25.7
Pop. using improved drinking water (urban/rural, %)	100.0 / 99.0	100.0 / 99.0	100.0 / 99.0[b]
Pop. using improved sanitation facilities (urban/rural, %)	100.0 / 99.0	100.0 / 99.0	100.0 / 99.0[b]
Net Official Development Assist. disbursed (% of GNI)[r]	0.34	0.34	0.26[s,d]

a Projected estimate (medium fertility variant). **b** 2015. **c** Refers to Ottawa-Gatineau, the Census Metropolitan Area. **d** 2017. **e** 2016. **f** Data classified according to ISIC Rev. 4. **g** Estimate. **h** Calculated by the Statistics Division of the United Nations from national indices. **i** Data classified according to ISIC Rev. 3. **j** 2011. **k** Imports FOB. **l** Data refers to a 5-year period preceding the reference year. **m** Data as at the end of December. **n** 2004. **o** Population aged 16 years and over. **p** Break in the time series. **q** 2014. **r** Development Assistance Committee member (OECD). **s** Provisional data.

Cayman Islands

Region	Caribbean	Population (000, 2018)	62 [a]
Surface area (km2)	264 [b]	Pop. density (per km2, 2018)	259.8 [a]
Sex ratio (m per 100 f)	100.4 [c,b]	Capital city	George Town
National currency	Cayman Islands Dollar (KYD)	Capital city pop. (000, 2018)	34.9
Exchange rate (per US$)	0.8 [d,e]		

Economic indicators	2005	2010	2018
GDP: Gross domestic product (million current US$)	3 042	3 267	3 844 [f]
GDP growth rate (annual %, const. 2010 prices)	6.5	- 2.7	1.8 [f]
GDP per capita (current US$)	62 559.0	58 859.0	63 261.0 [f]
Economy: Agriculture (% of Gross Value Added) [g]	0.2	0.3	0.3 [f]
Economy: Industry (% of Gross Value Added) [g]	9.1	7.7	7.5 [f]
Economy: Services and other activity (% of GVA) [g]	90.6	92.0	92.2 [f]
Employment in agriculture (% of employed)	1.7 [h]	0.6 [i]	0.8 [i,j]
Employment in industry (% of employed)	22.2 [h]	14.9 [i]	15.5 [i,j]
Employment in services & other sectors (% employed)	75.5 [h]	84.2 [i]	83.6 [i,j]
Unemployment rate (% of labour force)	3.5	6.7	6.3 [i]
Labour force participation rate (female/male pop. %)	... / ...	80.6 / 88.0 [i,k,l]	80.6 / 85.6 [i]
CPI: Consumer Price Index (2010=100) [m]	...	100	103 [f]
Agricultural production index (2004-2006=100)	101	100	103 [f]
International trade: exports (million current US$) [n]	52	13	79 [e]
International trade: imports (million current US$) [n]	1 191	828	988 [e]
International trade: balance (million current US$) [n]	- 1 138	- 815	- 909 [e]

Major trading partners						2017
Export partners (% of exports) [n]	Netherlands	33.3	Malta	30.0	Seychelles	28.5
Import partners (% of imports)	United States	85.4	Bahamas	2.9	Denmark	2.0

Social indicators	2005	2010	2018
Population growth rate (average annual %) [o]	3.1	2.6	1.5 [b]
Urban population (% of total population)	100.0	100.0	100.0
Urban population growth rate (average annual %) [o]	3.1	2.6	1.5 [b]
Fertility rate, total (live births per woman)	...	1.6 [p]	...
Life expectancy at birth (females/males, years)	... / ...	83.8 / 76.3 [q,r]	... / ...
Population age distribution (0-14/60+ years old, %) [c]	... / ...	18.1 / 8.6 [s]	18.3 / 6.7 [b,t]
International migrant stock (000/% of total pop.) [u]	21.7 / 44.5	24.1 / 43.3	24.4 / 39.6 [a]
Refugees and others of concern to the UNHCR (000)	...	~0.0 [v]	0.1 [e]
Intentional homicide rate (per 100 000 pop.)	6.2	16.2	8.4 [w]

Environment and infrastructure indicators	2005	2010	2018
Individuals using the Internet (per 100 inhabitants)	38.0	66.0 [n]	79.0 [n,f]
Threatened species (number)	19 [x]	34	74 [e]
Forested area (% of land area) [n]	52.9	52.9	52.9 [b]
CO2 emission estimates (million tons/tons per capita)	0.5 / 9.1	0.6 / 10.1	0.5 / 9.2 [w]
Energy supply per capita (Gigajoules)	130	144	132 [b]
Tourist/visitor arrivals at national borders (000) [y]	168	288	385 [f]
Important sites for terrestrial biodiversity protected (%)	31.6	31.7	32.5
Pop. using improved drinking water (urban/rural, %)	95.0 / ...	96.7 / ...	97.4 / ... [b]
Pop. using improved sanitation facilities (urban/rural, %)	95.5 / ...	95.6 / ...	95.6 / ... [b]

a Projected estimate (medium fertility variant). b 2015. c De jure population. d UN operational exchange rate. e 2017. f 2016. g Data classified according to ISIC Rev. 4. h Data classified according to ISIC Rev. 3. i Break in the time series. j 2013. k Resident population (de jure). l 2009. m Calculated by the Statistics Division of the United Nations from national indices. n Estimate. o Data refers to a 5-year period preceding the reference year. p 2007. q Data are based on a small number of deaths. r 2006. s Excluding the institutional population. t Population aged 65 years and over. u Refers to foreign citizens. v Data as at the end of December. w 2014. x 2004. y Arrivals by air.

Central African Republic

Region	Middle Africa	UN membership date	20 September 1960
Population (000, 2018)	4 737[a]	Surface area (km2)	622 984[b]
Pop. density (per km2, 2018)	7.6[a]	Sex ratio (m per 100 f)	97.3[a]
Capital city	Bangui	National currency	CFA Franc, BEAC (XAF)[c]
Capital city pop. (000, 2018)	850.9	Exchange rate (per US$)	546.9[d]

Economic indicators	2005	2010	2018
GDP: Gross domestic product (million current US$)	1 413	2 034	1 810[e]
GDP growth rate (annual %, const. 2010 prices)	2.4	3.6	4.5[e]
GDP per capita (current US$)	342.0	457.0	394.0[e]
Economy: Agriculture (% of Gross Value Added)	45.0	41.2	31.9[e]
Economy: Industry (% of Gross Value Added)	18.6	24.0	25.5[e]
Economy: Services and other activity (% of GVA)	36.5	34.8	42.6[e]
Employment in agriculture (% of employed)[f]	86.4	86.2	85.6
Employment in industry (% of employed)[f]	7.0	7.1	7.9
Employment in services & other sectors (% employed)[f]	6.6	6.8	6.5
Unemployment rate (% of labour force)[f]	6.2	6.3	5.8
Labour force participation rate (female/male pop. %)[f]	64.1 / 78.8	64.1 / 79.0	63.3 / 80.0
CPI: Consumer Price Index (2010=100)[f,g]	81	100	187[b]
Agricultural production index (2004-2006=100)	101	115	122[e]
Index of industrial production (2005=100)[h,i]	100	126	86[j]
International trade: exports (million current US$)	111	90	41[f,d]
International trade: imports (million current US$)	185	210	333[f,d]
International trade: balance (million current US$)	- 75	- 120	- 292[f,d]

Major trading partners							2017
Export partners (% of exports)	France	48.6[f]	Burundi	14.2	China	10.2[f]
Import partners (% of imports)	France	21.1	Japan	11.3	United States	9.9

Social indicators	2005	2010	2018
Population growth rate (average annual %)[k]	1.9	1.5	0.4[b]
Urban population (% of total population)	38.1	38.9	41.4
Urban population growth rate (average annual %)[k]	2.1	1.9	1.1[b]
Fertility rate, total (live births per woman)[k]	5.4	5.3	5.1[b]
Life expectancy at birth (females/males, years)[k]	44.9 / 42.5	47.4 / 44.6	51.0 / 47.8[b]
Population age distribution (0-14/60+ years old, %)	42.2 / 5.7	42.5 / 5.5	42.8 / 5.5[a]
International migrant stock (000/% of total pop.)[l]	94.4 / 2.3	93.5 / 2.1	88.8 / 1.9[d]
Refugees and others of concern to the UNHCR (000)	28.7[m]	215.3[m]	649.6[d]
Infant mortality rate (per 1 000 live births)[k]	113.4	105.9	93.5[b]
Health: Current expenditure (% of GDP)[f]	4.5	3.8	4.8[b]
Health: Physicians (per 1 000 pop.)	0.1[n]	-0.0[o]	...
Education: Government expenditure (% of GDP)	1.6	1.2	1.2[p]
Education: Primary gross enrol. ratio (f/m per 100 pop.)	52.3 / 76.0	74.2 / 104.3	91.5 / 120.0[e]
Education: Secondary gross enrol. ratio (f/m per 100 pop.)	8.1 / 15.5[f,q]	9.7 / 17.5[o]	12.0 / 18.8[e]
Education: Tertiary gross enrol. ratio (f/m per 100 pop.)	0.6 / 3.1[r]	1.3 / 4.0	1.6 / 4.3[e]
Intentional homicide rate (per 100 000 pop.)	...	...	19.8[e]
Seats held by women in the National Parliament (%)	7.3[f]	9.6	8.6

Environment and infrastructure indicators	2005	2010	2018
Individuals using the Internet (per 100 inhabitants)[f]	0.3	2.0	4.0[e]
Threatened species (number)	30[n]	36	60[d]
Forested area (% of land area)	35.8	35.7	35.6[b]
CO2 emission estimates (million tons/tons per capita)	0.2 / 0.1	0.3 / 0.1	0.3 / 0.1[t]
Energy production, primary (Petajoules)	19	19	19[b]
Energy supply per capita (Gigajoules)	5	5	5[b]
Tourist/visitor arrivals at national borders (000)[u]	12	54	120[b]
Important sites for terrestrial biodiversity protected (%)	74.2	74.4	74.4
Pop. using improved drinking water (urban/rural, %)	86.2 / 51.6	88.6 / 53.6	89.6 / 54.4[b]
Pop. using improved sanitation facilities (urban/rural, %)	35.3 / 8.8	41.2 / 7.7	43.6 / 7.2[b]
Net Official Development Assist. received (% of GNI)	6.64	13.08	28.42[e]

a Projected estimate (medium fertility variant). b 2015. c African Financial Community (CFA) Franc, Bank of Central African States (BEAC). d 2017. e 2016. f Estimate. g Bangui h Data classified according to ISIC Rev. 3. i Country data supplemented with data from the Observatoire Economique et Statistique d'Afrique Subsaharienne (Afristat). j 2013. k Data refers to a 5-year period preceding the reference year. l Refers to foreign citizens. m Data as at the end of December. n 2004. o 2009. p 2011. q 2001. r 2000. s 2012. t 2014. u Arrivals by air at Bangui only.

Chad

Region	Middle Africa	UN membership date	20 September 1960
Population (000, 2018)	15 353[a]	Surface area (km2)	1 284 000[b]
Pop. density (per km2, 2018)	12.2[a]	Sex ratio (m per 100 f)	100.2[a]
Capital city	N'Djamena	National currency	CFA Franc, BEAC (XAF)[c]
Capital city pop. (000, 2018)	1 322.7	Exchange rate (per US$)	546.9[d]

Economic indicators	2005	2010	2018
GDP: Gross domestic product (million current US$)	6 681	9 791	11 267[e]
GDP growth rate (annual %, const. 2010 prices)	7.9	13.4	- 3.4[e]
GDP per capita (current US$)	664.0	824.0	780.0[e]
Economy: Agriculture (% of Gross Value Added)	26.0	35.9	27.5[e]
Economy: Industry (% of Gross Value Added)	35.1	36.7	32.6[e]
Economy: Services and other activity (% of GVA)	38.9	27.4	39.9[e]
Employment in agriculture (% of employed)[f]	87.2	86.8	87.0
Employment in industry (% of employed)[f]	5.3	6.1	4.9
Employment in services & other sectors (% employed)[f]	7.5	7.1	8.0
Unemployment rate (% of labour force)[f]	5.7	5.7	5.9
Labour force participation rate (female/male pop. %)[f]	64.9 / 79.9	64.8 / 79.1	64.8 / 77.5
CPI: Consumer Price Index (2010=100)[f,g]	86	100	116[b]
Agricultural production index (2004-2006=100)	106	147	150[e]
Index of industrial production (2005=100)[h,i]	100	79	65[j]
International trade: exports (million current US$)[f]	3 095	3 410	1 344[d]
International trade: imports (million current US$)[f]	953	2 507	844[d]
International trade: balance (million current US$)[f]	2 142	904	499[d]

Major trading partners						2017
Export partners (% of exports)[f]	United States	47.4	United Arab Emirates	12.9	China	11.7
Import partners (% of imports)	France	21.6	China	16.5	Cameroon	12.4

Social indicators	2005	2010	2018
Population growth rate (average annual %)[k]	3.8	3.3	3.3[b]
Urban population (% of total population)	21.8	22.0	23.1
Urban population growth rate (average annual %)[k]	3.9	3.5	3.8[b]
Fertility rate, total (live births per woman)[k]	7.2	6.9	6.3[b]
Life expectancy at birth (females/males, years)[k]	48.5 / 46.8	49.7 / 48.0	52.8 / 50.5[b]
Population age distribution (0-14/60+ years old, %)	49.1 / 4.2	48.6 / 4.0	46.9 / 4.0[a]
International migrant stock (000/% of total pop.)[l]	352.1 / 3.5	416.9 / 3.5	489.7 / 3.3[d]
Refugees and others of concern to the UNHCR (000)	275.5[m]	533.0[m]	563.7[d]
Infant mortality rate (per 1 000 live births)[k]	110.8	105.2	91.2[b]
Health: Current expenditure (% of GDP)[f]	4.9	4.1	4.6[b]
Health: Physicians (per 1 000 pop.)	~0.0[n]	~0.0[o]	~0.0
Education: Government expenditure (% of GDP)	1.7	2.0	2.9[j]
Education: Primary gross enrol. ratio (f/m per 100 pop.)	58.0 / 85.5	69.8 / 94.9	77.0 / 99.0[e]
Education: Secondary gross enrol. ratio (f/m per 100 pop.)	8.1 / 23.2[f]	13.4 / 31.7	14.3 / 31.0[e]
Education: Tertiary gross enrol. ratio (f/m per 100 pop.)	0.2 / 2.7	0.6 / 3.6[f]	1.1 / 5.7[f,p]
Intentional homicide rate (per 100 000 pop.)	10.7	9.7	9.0[b]
Seats held by women in the National Parliament (%)	6.5	5.2	12.8

Environment and infrastructure indicators	2005	2010	2018
Individuals using the Internet (per 100 inhabitants)	0.4	1.7[f]	5.0[f,a]
Threatened species (number)	21[n]	30	43[d]
Forested area (% of land area)	4.9	4.4	3.9[f,b]
CO2 emission estimates (million tons/tons per capita)	0.4 / ~0.0	0.5 / ~0.0	0.7 / ~0.0[p]
Energy production, primary (Petajoules)	433	324	225[f,b]
Energy supply per capita (Gigajoules)	7	6	6[f,b]
Tourist/visitor arrivals at national borders (000)	...	71	120[b]
Important sites for terrestrial biodiversity protected (%)	70.6	70.6	70.6
Pop. using improved drinking water (urban/rural, %)	64.7 / 42.4	69.8 / 44.1	71.8 / 44.8[b]
Pop. using improved sanitation facilities (urban/rural, %)	28.1 / 5.8	30.5 / 6.3	31.4 / 6.5[b]
Net Official Development Assist. received (% of GNI)	6.87	4.76	6.63[b]

a Projected estimate (medium fertility variant). b 2015. c African Financial Community (CFA) Franc, Bank of Central African States (BEAC). d 2017. e 2016. f Estimate. g N'Djamena h Data classified according to ISIC Rev. 3. i Country data supplemented with data from the Observatoire Economique et Statistique d'Afrique Subsaharienne (Afristat). j 2013. k Data refers to a 5-year period preceding the reference year. l Including refugees. m Data as at the end of December. n 2004. o 2006. p 2014.

Channel Islands

Region	Northern Europe	Population (000, 2018)	166[a,b]
Surface area (km2)	180[a,c]	Pop. density (per km2, 2018)	874.1[a,b]
Sex ratio (m per 100 f)	98.5[a,b]	Capital city	Saint Helier[d]
National currency	Pound Sterling (GBP)	Capital city pop. (000, 2018)	34.4
Exchange rate (per US$)	0.7[e]		

Economic indicators	2005	2010	2018
Employment in agriculture (% of employed)[f]	20.9	21.0	19.9
Employment in industry (% of employed)[f]	30.2	30.0	29.7
Employment in services & other sectors (% employed)[f]	48.9	49.0	50.4
Unemployment rate (% of labour force)[f]	9.3	9.7	9.3
Labour force participation rate (female/male pop. %)[f]	50.0 / 68.9	50.2 / 67.4	49.2 / 65.2

Social indicators	2005	2010	2018
Population growth rate (average annual %)[a,g]	0.7	0.7	0.5[c]
Urban population (% of total population)[a]	30.7	31.1	30.9
Urban population growth rate (average annual %)[a,g]	0.9	0.9	0.5[c]
Fertility rate, total (live births per woman)[a,g]	1.4	1.4	1.5[c]
Life expectancy at birth (females/males, years)[a,g]	80.5 / 76.0	81.7 / 77.5	82.4 / 78.7[c]
Population age distribution (0-14/60+ years old, %)[a]	16.3 / 20.4	15.3 / 21.7	14.5 / 25.0[b]
International migrant stock (000/% of total pop.)[a]	70.9 / 46.0	77.6 / 48.6	83.1 / 50.3[g]
Infant mortality rate (per 1 000 live births)[a,g]	10.3	8.7	7.9[c]
Intentional homicide rate (per 100 000 pop.)	0.6	0.0	...

Environment and infrastructure indicators	2005	2010	2018
Forested area (% of land area)[f]	4.2	4.2	4.2[c]

a Refers to Guernsey and Jersey. **b** Projected estimate (medium fertility variant). **c** 2015. **d** The capital of the Bailiwick of Jersey. **e** 2017. **f** Estimate. **g** Data refers to a 5-year period preceding the reference year.

Region	South America	UN membership date	24 October 1945
Population (000, 2018)	18 197 [a]	Surface area (km2)	756 102 [b]
Pop. density (per km2, 2018)	24.5 [a]	Sex ratio (m per 100 f)	98.2 [a]
Capital city	Santiago	National currency	Chilean Peso (CLP)
Capital city pop. (000, 2018)	6 680.4 [c]	Exchange rate (per US$)	615.2 [d]

Economic indicators

	2005	2010	2018
GDP: Gross domestic product (million current US$)	122 965	218 538	247 046 [e]
GDP growth rate (annual %, const. 2010 prices)	6.2	5.8	1.6 [e]
GDP per capita (current US$)	7 615.0	12 860.0	13 794.0 [e]
Economy: Agriculture (% of Gross Value Added) [f]	4.6	3.9	4.3 [e]
Economy: Industry (% of Gross Value Added) [f]	39.1	38.8	31.3 [e]
Economy: Services and other activity (% of GVA) [f]	56.3	57.3	64.4 [e]
Employment in agriculture (% of employed) [g]	13.2	10.6	9.4
Employment in industry (% of employed) [g]	23.0	23.0	22.7
Employment in services & other sectors (% employed) [g]	63.9	66.4	67.9
Unemployment rate (% of labour force)	8.0	8.4	7.1 [g]
Labour force participation rate (female/male pop. %) [g]	38.3 / 73.0	47.1 / 75.0	50.8 / 74.5
CPI: Consumer Price Index (2010=100)	...	101 [h]	116 [i,d]
Agricultural production index (2004-2006=100)	100	108	114 [e]
International trade: exports (million current US$)	41 973	71 106	69 229 [d]
International trade: imports (million current US$)	32 927	59 007	65 062 [d]
International trade: balance (million current US$)	9 046	12 099	4 168 [d]
Balance of payments, current account (million US$)	1 825	3 069	- 4 146 [d]

Major trading partners

					2017
Export partners (% of exports)	China	27.6	United States	14.4 [g]	Japan 9.3
Import partners (% of imports)	China	23.8	United States	18.0	Brazil 8.6

Social indicators

	2005	2010	2018
Population growth rate (average annual %) [j]	1.1	1.0	0.9 [b]
Urban population (% of total population)	86.8	87.1	87.6
Urban population growth rate (average annual %) [j]	1.3	1.1	1.0 [b]
Fertility rate, total (live births per woman) [j]	2.0	1.9	1.8 [b]
Life expectancy at birth (females/males, years) [j]	80.3 / 74.3	80.8 / 75.3	81.3 / 76.2 [b]
Population age distribution (0-14/60+ years old, %)	24.6 / 11.8	22.5 / 13.2	20.1 / 16.5 [a]
International migrant stock (000/% of total pop.)	273.4 / 1.7	369.4 / 2.2	488.6 / 2.7 [d]
Refugees and others of concern to the UNHCR (000)	0.9 [k]	1.9 [k]	6.9 [d]
Infant mortality rate (per 1 000 live births) [j]	8.4	7.8	7.4 [b]
Health: Current expenditure (% of GDP)	6.6	6.8	8.1 [b]
Health: Physicians (per 1 000 pop.)	1.0	1.0 [i]	...
Education: Government expenditure (% of GDP)	3.3	4.2	4.9 [b]
Education: Primary gross enrol. ratio (f/m per 100 pop.)	104.3 / 109.2	99.9 / 102.8	96.4 / 101.2 [e]
Education: Secondary gross enrol. ratio (f/m per 100 pop.)	96.0 / 94.8	94.3 / 91.4	100.2 / 99.1 [e]
Education: Tertiary gross enrol. ratio (f/m per 100 pop.)	47.7 / 49.7	71.5 / 66.2	96.4 / 84.5 [e]
Intentional homicide rate (per 100 000 pop.)	3.6	3.2	3.5 [e]
Seats held by women in the National Parliament (%)	12.5	14.2	15.8 [d]

Environment and infrastructure indicators

	2005	2010	2018
Individuals using the Internet (per 100 inhabitants) [g]	31.2 [m]	45.0 [m]	66.0 [e]
Research & Development expenditure (% of GDP)	...	0.3	0.4 [n,b]
Threatened species (number)	123 [o]	145	197 [d]
Forested area (% of land area)	21.6	21.8	23.9 [g,b]
CO2 emission estimates (million tons/tons per capita)	61.8 / 3.8	72.3 / 4.3	82.6 / 4.7 [p]
Energy production, primary (Petajoules)	390	384	540 [b]
Energy supply per capita (Gigajoules)	72	75	84 [b]
Tourist/visitor arrivals at national borders (000)	2 027	2 801 [q]	5 641 [q,e]
Important sites for terrestrial biodiversity protected (%)	33.4	35.2	35.7
Pop. using improved drinking water (urban/rural, %)	99.4 / 77.6	99.6 / 87.4	99.7 / 93.3 [b]
Pop. using improved sanitation facilities (urban/rural, %)	97.3 / 77.6	99.2 / 85.9	100.0 / 90.9 [b]
Net Official Development Assist. received (% of GNI)	0.15	0.09	0.07 [e]

a Projected estimate (medium fertility variant). b 2015. c Refers to the urban population of Santiago Metropolitan Area Region. d 2017. e 2016. f Data classified according to ISIC Rev. 4. g Estimate. h Index base: 2009=100. i Index base: 2013=100. j Data refers to a 5-year period preceding the reference year. k Data as at the end of December. l 2009. m Population aged 5 years and over. n Provisional data. o 2004. p 2014. q Including nationals residing abroad.

China

Region	Eastern Asia	UN membership date	24 October 1945
Population (000, 2018)	1 415 046[a,b]	Surface area (km2)	9 600 000[c]
Pop. density (per km2, 2018)	150.7[a,b]	Sex ratio (m per 100 f)	106.3[a,b]
Capital city	Beijing	National currency	Yuan Renminbi (CNY)
Capital city pop. (000, 2018)	19 618.0[d]	Exchange rate (per US$)	6.5[e]

Economic indicators

	2005	2010	2018
GDP: Gross domestic product (million current US$)[a]	2 308 800	6 066 351	11 218 281[f]
GDP growth rate (annual %, const. 2010 prices)[a]	11.4	10.6	7.3[f]
GDP per capita (current US$)[a]	1 747.0	4 461.0	7 993.0[f]
Economy: Agriculture (% of Gross Value Added)[a,g]	12.0	9.8	8.9[f]
Economy: Industry (% of Gross Value Added)[a,g]	47.2	46.6	40.0[f]
Economy: Services and other activity (% of GVA)[a,g]	40.9	43.6	51.2[f]
Employment in agriculture (% of employed)[a,h]	35.8	26.2	16.4
Employment in industry (% of employed)[a,h]	29.6	30.2	26.3
Employment in services & other sectors (% employed)[a,h]	34.6	43.6	57.2
Unemployment rate (% of labour force)[a,h]	4.1	4.2	4.7
Labour force participation rate (female/male pop. %)[a,h]	66.8 / 79.7	63.8 / 77.9	60.9 / 75.7
CPI: Consumer Price Index (2010=100)[a]	...	100	104[i,e]
Agricultural production index (2004-2006=100)[a]	100	120	139[f]
International trade: exports (million current US$)[a]	761 953	1 577 764	2 238 669[h,e]
International trade: imports (million current US$)[a]	659 953	1 396 002	1 844 183[h,e]
International trade: balance (million current US$)[a]	102 001	181 762	394 485[h,e]
Balance of payments, current account (million US$)[a]	132 378[j]	237 810	164 887[e]

Major trading partners

						2017
Export partners (% of exports)	United States	18.4[h]	China, Hong Kong SAR	13.7	Japan	6.2[h]
Import partners (% of imports)	Republic of Korea	10.0	Japan	9.2	Asia nes[k]	8.7

Social indicators

	2005	2010	2018
Population growth rate (average annual %)[a,l]	0.6	0.6	0.5[c]
Urban population (% of total population)[a]	42.5	49.2	59.2
Urban population growth rate (average annual %)[a,l]	4.0	3.5	2.9[c]
Fertility rate, total (live births per woman)[a,l]	1.6	1.6	1.6[c]
Life expectancy at birth (females/males, years)[a,l]	74.7 / 71.7	76.3 / 73.2	77.2 / 74.2[c]
Population age distribution (0-14/60+ years old, %)[a]	19.9 / 11.0	17.8 / 12.6	17.6 / 16.6[b]
International migrant stock (000/% of total pop.)[a,m]	678.9 / 0.1	849.9 / 0.1	999.5 / 0.1[e]
Refugees and others of concern to the UNHCR (000)[a]	301.1[n]	301.1[n]	318.0[e]
Infant mortality rate (per 1 000 live births)[a,l]	25.3	16.7	11.6[c]
Health: Current expenditure (% of GDP)[o]	4.3	4.5	5.3[c]
Health: Physicians (per 1 000 pop.)	1.1[p]	1.5	3.6[c]
Education: Primary gross enrol. ratio (f/m per 100 pop.)[a]	118.6 / 119.2[q]	106.6 / 108.2	101.2 / 100.6[f]
Education: Secondary gross enrol. ratio (f/m per 100 pop.)[a]	60.0 / 63.6[q]	88.0 / 88.1	95.9 / 94.2[r]
Education: Tertiary gross enrol. ratio (f/m per 100 pop.)[a]	17.9 / 19.8	24.8 / 23.3	53.3 / 44.2[f]
Intentional homicide rate (per 100 000 pop.)[a]	1.6	1.0	0.6[f]
Seats held by women in the National Parliament (%)	20.2	21.3	24.2

Environment and infrastructure indicators

	2005	2010	2018
Individuals using the Internet (per 100 inhabitants)[e]	8.5	34.3	53.2[f]
Research & Development expenditure (% of GDP)[a]	1.3	1.7	2.1[c]
Threatened species (number)[a]	773[s]	859	1 080[a]
Forested area (% of land area)[h,a]	20.6	21.4	22.2[c]
CO2 emission estimates (million tons/tons per capita)[e]	5 897.0 / 4.5	8 776.0 / 6.5	10 291.9 / 7.5[t]
Energy production, primary (Petajoules)[a]	63 831	88 642	100 864[c]
Energy supply per capita (Gigajoules)[a]	53	76	87[c]
Tourist/visitor arrivals at national borders (000)[a]	46 809	55 664	59 270[f]
Important sites for terrestrial biodiversity protected (%)[e]	46.6	47.1	47.6
Pop. using improved drinking water (urban/rural, %)[a]	97.3 / 78.2	97.4 / 85.6	97.5 / 93.0[c]
Pop. using improved sanitation facilities (urban/rural, %)[a]	79.1 / 54.3	82.9 / 59.0	86.6 / 63.7[c]
Net Official Development Assist. received (% of GNI)[a]	0.08	0.01	- 0.01[f]

a For statistical purposes, the data for China do not include those for the Hong Kong Special Administrative Region (Hong Kong SAR), Macao Special Administrative Region (Macao SAR) and Taiwan Province of China. b Projected estimate (medium fertility variant). c 2015. d Refers to all city districts (excluding Yanqing District) meeting the criteria such as contiguous built-up areas, being the location of the local government, being a Street or Having a Resident Committee. e 2017. f 2016. g At producers' prices. h Index base: 2015=100. i Index base: 2010=100. j Break in the time series. k Asia not elsewhere specified. l Data refers to a 5-year period preceding the reference year. m Refers to foreign citizens. n Data as at the end of December. o Data revision. p 2002. q 2003. r 2013. s 2004. t 2014.

China, Hong Kong SAR

Region	Eastern Asia	Population (000, 2018)	7 429[a]
Surface area (km2)	1 106[b]	Pop. density (per km2, 2018)	7 075.1[a]
Sex ratio (m per 100 f)	84.8[a]	Capital city	Hong Kong
National currency	Hong Kong Dollar (HKD)	Capital city pop. (000, 2018)	7 428.9[c]
Exchange rate (per US$)	7.8[d]		

Economic indicators	2005	2010	2018
GDP: Gross domestic product (million current US$)	181 569	228 639	320 912[e]
GDP growth rate (annual %, const. 2010 prices)	7.4	6.8	2.0[e]
GDP per capita (current US$)	26 593.0	32 545.0	43 943.0[e]
Economy: Agriculture (% of Gross Value Added)[f,g]	0.1	0.1	0.1[e]
Economy: Industry (% of Gross Value Added)[h,i]	8.7	7.0	7.2[e]
Economy: Services and other activity (% of GVA)[j]	91.3	93.0	92.7[e]
Employment in agriculture (% of employed)[k]	0.3	0.2	0.2
Employment in industry (% of employed)[k]	15.1	13.3	13.0
Employment in services & other sectors (% employed)[k]	84.7	86.4	86.8
Unemployment rate (% of labour force)	5.6	4.3	3.2[k]
Labour force participation rate (female/male pop. %)[k]	51.7 / 71.1	51.4 / 68.1	53.8 / 67.8
CPI: Consumer Price Index (2010=100)	90	100	128[d]
Agricultural production index (2004-2006=100)	99	55	59[e]
International trade: exports (million current US$)	292 119	400 692	550 240[d]
International trade: imports (million current US$)	300 160	441 369	589 824[d]
International trade: balance (million current US$)	- 8 042	- 40 677	- 39 584[d]
Balance of payments, current account (million US$)	21 575	16 012	14 736[d]

Major trading partners							2017
Export partners (% of exports)	China	54.2	United States	7.7	India	3.8
Import partners (% of imports)	China	44.6	Asia nes	7.2	Singapore	6.4

Social indicators	2005	2010	2018
Population growth rate (average annual %)[l]	0.5	0.6	0.6[b]
Urban population (% of total population)	100.0	100.0	100.0
Urban population growth rate (average annual %)[l]	0.5	0.6	0.6[b]
Fertility rate, total (live births per woman)[l]	1.0	1.0	1.2[b]
Life expectancy at birth (females/males, years)[l]	84.4 / 78.5	85.5 / 79.5	86.4 / 80.5[b]
Population age distribution (0-14/60+ years old, %)	14.4 / 15.6	11.9 / 18.4	11.9 / 24.3[a]
International migrant stock (000/% of total pop.)	2 721.2 / 39.9	2 780.0 / 39.6	2 883.1 / 39.1[d]
Refugees and others of concern to the UNHCR (000)	3.0[m]	0.6[m]	0.1[d]
Infant mortality rate (per 1 000 live births)[l]	2.5	1.9	1.6[b]
Education: Government expenditure (% of GDP)	4.1	3.5	3.3[d]
Education: Primary gross enrol. ratio (f/m per 100 pop.)	... / ...	... / ...	106.0 / 108.3[e]
Education: Secondary gross enrol. ratio (f/m per 100 pop.)	81.9 / 81.3	87.1 / 87.5	100.9 / 104.4[e]
Education: Tertiary gross enrol. ratio (f/m per 100 pop.)	33.3 / 33.0	58.9 / 59.2[k]	76.6 / 67.2[a]
Intentional homicide rate (per 100 000 pop.)	0.5	0.5	0.4[e]

Environment and infrastructure indicators	2005	2010	2018
Individuals using the Internet (per 100 inhabitants)	56.9[n]	72.0[n]	87.3[k,e]
Research & Development expenditure (% of GDP)	0.8	0.7	0.8[b]
Threatened species (number)	39[o]	49	64[d]
CO2 emission estimates (million tons/tons per capita)	43.9 / 6.5	40.7 / 5.8	46.2 / 6.4[p]
Energy supply per capita (Gigajoules)	85	79	80[b]
Tourist/visitor arrivals at national borders (000)	14 773	20 085	26 553[e]
Important sites for terrestrial biodiversity protected (%)	56.7	56.7	56.7

a Projected estimate (medium fertility variant). **b** 2015. **c** Consists of the population of Hong Kong Island, New Kowloon the new towns in New Territories and the marine areas. **d** 2017. **e** 2016. **f** Excluding hunting and forestry. **g** Including mining and quarrying. **h** Excluding mining and quarrying. **i** Includes waste management. **j** Excluding waste management. **k** Estimate. **l** Data refers to a 5-year period preceding the reference year. **m** Data as at the end of December. **n** Population aged 10 years and over. **o** 2004. **p** 2014.

China, Macao SAR

Region	Eastern Asia
Surface area (km2)	30[b,c]
Sex ratio (m per 100 f)	92.4[a]
National currency	Pataca (MOP)
Exchange rate (per US$)	8.1[d]

Population (000, 2018)	632[a]
Pop. density (per km2, 2018)	21 151.1[a]
Capital city	Macao
Capital city pop. (000, 2018)	632.4

Economic indicators	2005	2010	2018
GDP: Gross domestic product (million current US$)	12 092	28 124	45 311[a]
GDP growth rate (annual %, const. 2010 prices)	8.1	25.3	- 0.9[a]
GDP per capita (current US$)	25 059.0	52 375.0	74 018.0[a]
Economy: Industry (% of Gross Value Added)	14.9	7.4	8.0[a]
Economy: Services and other activity (% of GVA)	85.1	92.6	92.0[a]
Employment in agriculture (% of employed)[f]	0.1	0.2	0.5
Employment in industry (% of employed)[f]	25.0	13.7	20.0
Employment in services & other sectors (% employed)[f]	74.8	86.0	79.5
Unemployment rate (% of labour force)	4.2	2.8	1.9[f]
Labour force participation rate (female/male pop. %)[f]	57.3 / 72.5	65.3 / 76.9	66.0 / 76.1
CPI: Consumer Price Index (2010=100)	80	100	136[g,d]
Agricultural production index (2004-2006=100)	100	95	90[e]
Index of industrial production (2005=100)[h]	100	45[i]	42[i,j]
International trade: exports (million current US$)	2 474	870	1 406[f,d]
International trade: imports (million current US$)	4 514	5 629	9 449[f,d]
International trade: balance (million current US$)	- 2 040	- 4 760	- 8 043[f,d]
Balance of payments, current account (million US$)	2 902	11 089	12 215[e]

Major trading partners						2017
Export partners (% of exports)	Areas nes[k]	61.9[f]	China, Hong Kong SAR	29.8	China	5.9[f]
Import partners (% of imports)[f]	China	31.4	Areas nes[k]	11.6	China, Hong Kong SAR	8.5

Social indicators	2005	2010	2018
Population growth rate (average annual %)[l]	2.4	2.1	2.3[c]
Urban population (% of total population)	100.0	100.0	100.0
Urban population growth rate (average annual %)[l]	2.4	2.1	2.3[c]
Fertility rate, total (live births per woman)[l]	0.8	0.9	1.2[c]
Life expectancy at birth (females/males, years)[l]	83.6 / 78.2	84.9 / 79.1	86.2 / 80.3[c]
Population age distribution (0-14/60+ years old, %)	16.9 / 9.6	12.7 / 11.0	13.8 / 17.0[a]
International migrant stock (000/% of total pop.)	279.3 / 57.9	318.5 / 59.3	353.7 / 56.8[d]
Refugees and others of concern to the UNHCR (000)	...	~0.0[m]	~0.0[d]
Infant mortality rate (per 1 000 live births)[l]	4.9	3.8	3.0[c]
Education: Government expenditure (% of GDP)	2.3	2.6	3.0[c]
Education: Primary gross enrol. ratio (f/m per 100 pop.)	96.6 / 102.8	94.8 / 96.6	105.1 / 106.5[e]
Education: Secondary gross enrol. ratio (f/m per 100 pop.)	83.2 / 89.3	86.2 / 89.0	99.1 / 99.5[e]
Education: Tertiary gross enrol. ratio (f/m per 100 pop.)	44.2 / 65.7	54.0 / 56.0	89.4 / 67.3[e]
Intentional homicide rate (per 100 000 pop.)	0.8	0.4	0.2[e]

Environment and infrastructure indicators	2005	2010	2018
Individuals using the Internet (per 100 inhabitants)	34.9[f]	55.2[n]	81.6[a]
Research & Development expenditure (% of GDP)[o]	0.1	0.1	0.1[c]
Threatened species (number)	5[p]	9	11[d]
CO2 emission estimates (million tons/tons per capita)	1.8 / 3.8	1.4 / 2.6	1.3 / 2.2[q]
Energy production, primary (Petajoules)[f]	2	2	2[c]
Energy supply per capita (Gigajoules)	58	57	68[c]
Tourist/visitor arrivals at national borders (000)[f]	9 014	11 926	15 704[a]
Important sites for terrestrial biodiversity protected (%)	0.0	0.0	0.0

a Projected estimate (medium fertility variant). b Inland waters include the reservoirs. c 2015. d 2017. e 2016. f Estimate. g Calculated by the Statistics Division of the United Nations from national indices. h Data classified according to ISIC Rev. 3. i Data refers to manufacturing and utilities only. j 2012. k Areas not elsewhere specified. l Data refers to a 5-year period preceding the reference year. m Data as at the end of December. n Population aged 3 years and over. o Partial data. p 2004. q 2014.

Colombia

Region	South America	UN membership date	05 November 1945	
Population (000, 2018)	49 465[a]	Surface area (km2)	1 141 748[b]	
Pop. density (per km2, 2018)	44.6[a]	Sex ratio (m per 100 f)	96.8[a]	
Capital city	Bogota	National currency	Colombian Peso (COP)	
Capital city pop. (000, 2018)	10 574.4[c]	Exchange rate (per US$)	2 971.6[d]	

Economic indicators	2005	2010	2018
GDP: Gross domestic product (million current US$)	146 566	287 018	282 463[e]
GDP growth rate (annual %, const. 2010 prices)	4.7	4.0	2.0[e]
GDP per capita (current US$)	3 366.0	6 251.0	5 806.0[e]
Economy: Agriculture (% of Gross Value Added)	8.4	7.1	7.1[e]
Economy: Industry (% of Gross Value Added)	32.8	35.0	32.6[e]
Economy: Services and other activity (% of GVA)	58.8	57.9	60.3[e]
Employment in agriculture (% of employed)	20.7[f]	18.3	16.0[f]
Employment in industry (% of employed)[f]	20.0	19.6	19.2
Employment in services & other sectors (% of employed)[f]	59.2	62.1	64.8
Unemployment rate (% of labour force)	11.9	10.9	9.1[f]
Labour force participation rate (female/male pop. %)[j]	49.3 / 81.7	56.2 / 82.5	59.0 / 82.6
CPI: Consumer Price Index (2010=100)[g]	80	100	132[d]
Agricultural production index (2004-2006=100)	99	100	115[e]
International trade: exports (million current US$)	21 190	39 820	38 463[f,d]
International trade: imports (million current US$)	21 204	40 683	45 878[f,d]
International trade: balance (million current US$)	- 14	- 863	- 7 414[f,d]
Balance of payments, current account (million US$)	- 1 891	- 8 732	- 10 359[d]

Major trading partners						2017
Export partners (% of exports)[f]	United States	32.9	Panama	6.2	Netherlands	3.9
Import partners (% of imports)	United States	26.7	China	19.3	Mexico	7.6

Social indicators	2005	2010	2018
Population growth rate (average annual %)[h]	1.4	1.2	1.0[b]
Urban population (% of total population)	76.0	78.0	80.8
Urban population growth rate (average annual %)[h]	1.9	1.7	1.4[h]
Fertility rate, total (live births per woman)[h]	2.3	2.1	1.9[b]
Life expectancy at birth (females/males, years)[h]	75.4 / 68.0	76.6 / 69.2	77.4 / 70.2[b]
Population age distribution (0-14/60+ years old, %)	28.9 / 7.6	26.4 / 9.0	23.1 / 12.1[a]
International migrant stock (000/% of total pop.)	107.6 / 0.2	124.3 / 0.3	142.3 / 0.3[d]
Refugees and others of concern to the UNHCR (000)	2 000.2[i]	3 672.4[i]	7 524.8[d]
Infant mortality rate (per 1 000 live births)[h]	20.5	19.0	17.9[b]
Health: Current expenditure (% of GDP)	5.5	6.1	6.2[b]
Health: Physicians (per 1 000 pop.)	1.5	1.6	1.8[i]
Education: Government expenditure (% of GDP)	4.0	4.8	4.5[e]
Education: Primary gross enrol. ratio (f/m per 100 pop.)	126.2 / 128.7	123.1 / 125.4	112.2 / 115.7[a]
Education: Secondary gross enrol. ratio (f/m per 100 pop.)	87.7 / 79.3	106.9 / 97.3	101.2 / 95.2[e]
Education: Tertiary gross enrol. ratio (f/m per 100 pop.)	30.4 / 28.0	41.3 / 37.6	63.1 / 54.4[a]
Intentional homicide rate (per 100 000 pop.)	41.8	33.7	25.5[e]
Seats held by women in the National Parliament (%)	12.0	8.4	18.7

Environment and infrastructure indicators	2005	2010	2018
Individuals using the Internet (per 100 inhabitants)	11.0	36.5[k]	58.1[e]
Research & Development expenditure (% of GDP)	0.2	0.2	0.2[b]
Threatened species (number)	593[l]	681	835[d]
Forested area (% of land area)	54.3	52.8	52.7[b]
CO2 emission estimates (million tons/tons per capita)	60.9 / 1.4	76.2 / 1.7	84.1 / 1.8[i]
Energy production, primary (Petajoules)	3 335	4 486	5 593[b]
Energy supply per capita (Gigajoules)	27	31	31[b]
Tourist/visitor arrivals at national borders (000)	933[m]	1 405	3 317[e]
Important sites for terrestrial biodiversity protected (%)	25.0	30.3	38.0
Pop. using improved drinking water (urban/rural, %)	97.1 / 72.1	96.9 / 73.2	96.8 / 73.8[b]
Pop. using improved sanitation facilities (urban/rural, %)	84.0 / 57.8	84.6 / 63.4	85.2 / 67.9[b]
Net Official Development Assist. received (% of GNI)	0.44	0.24	0.40[e]

a Projected estimate (medium fertility variant). b 2015. c Refers to the nuclei of Santa Fe de Bogotá, Soacha, Chia and Funza. d 2017. e 2016. f Estimate. g Calculated by the Statistics Division of the United Nations from national indices. h Data refers to a 5-year period preceding the reference year. i Data as at the end of December. j 2014. k Population aged 5 years and over. l 2004. m Break in the time series.

Comoros

Region	Eastern Africa	UN membership date	12 November 1975
Population (000, 2018)	832 [a]	Surface area (km2)	2 235 [b]
Pop. density (per km2, 2018)	447.3 [a]	Sex ratio (m per 100 f)	101.8 [a]
Capital city	Moroni	National currency	Comorian Franc (KMF)
Capital city pop. (000, 2018)	62.4	Exchange rate (per US$)	410.2 [c]

Economic indicators

	2005	2010	2018
GDP: Gross domestic product (million current US$)	787	1 068	1 150 [d]
GDP growth rate (annual %, const. 2010 prices)	2.8	3.8	2.2 [d]
GDP per capita (current US$)	1 287.0	1 549.0	1 445.0 [d]
Economy: Agriculture (% of Gross Value Added)	37.3	41.4	42.0 [d]
Economy: Industry (% of Gross Value Added)	10.9	8.3	11.8 [d]
Economy: Services and other activity (% of GVA)	51.8	50.3	46.2 [d]
Employment in agriculture (% of employed) [e]	55.8	55.9	54.7
Employment in industry (% of employed) [e]	14.3	14.7	15.4
Employment in services & other sectors (% employed) [e]	29.8	29.5	29.9
Unemployment rate (% of labour force) [e]	4.5	4.4	4.3
Labour force participation rate (female/male pop. %) [e]	33.3 / 50.2	34.4 / 49.8	36.1 / 50.3
CPI: Consumer Price Index (2010=100)	84	100	104 [f]
Agricultural production index (2004-2006=100)	96	106	109 [d]
International trade: exports (million current US$)	4	14	18 [e,c]
International trade: imports (million current US$)	85	181	167 [e,c]
International trade: balance (million current US$)	- 81	- 167	- 149 [e,c]
Balance of payments, current account (million US$)	- 27	- 39	...

Major trading partners

							2017
Export partners (% of exports)	India	25.2 [e]	France	12.2	United Arab Emirates	11.8 [e]
Import partners (% of imports)	United Rep. Tanzania	38.4	China	12.1	France	11.4

Social indicators

	2005	2010	2018
Population growth rate (average annual %) [g]	2.4	2.4	2.4 [b]
Urban population (% of total population)	27.9	28.0	29.0
Urban population growth rate (average annual %) [g]	2.3	2.5	2.7 [b]
Fertility rate, total (live births per woman) [g]	5.2	4.9	4.6 [b]
Life expectancy at birth (females/males, years) [e]	61.2 / 58.0	62.5 / 59.3	64.5 / 61.2 [b]
Population age distribution (0-14/60+ years old, %)	42.3 / 4.6	41.0 / 4.5	39.5 / 5.0 [a]
International migrant stock (000/% of total pop.)	13.2 / 2.2	12.6 / 1.8	12.6 / 1.5 [c]
Refugees and others of concern to the UNHCR (000)	~0.0 [h]	...	...
Infant mortality rate (per 1 000 live births) [g]	72.6	66.7	58.1 [b]
Health: Current expenditure (% of GDP) [i]	10.1	8.7	8.0 [b]
Health: Physicians (per 1 000 pop.)	0.2 [j]	...	...
Education: Government expenditure (% of GDP)	3.9 [k]	7.7 [l]	4.3 [b]
Education: Primary gross enrol. ratio (f/m per 100 pop.)	101.6 / 114.5 [j]	104.1 / 113.0 [l]	101.2 / 108.6 [m]
Education: Secondary gross enrol. ratio (f/m per 100 pop.)	38.0 / 49.8 [j]	... / ...	63.1 / 59.1 [m]
Education: Tertiary gross enrol. ratio (f/m per 100 pop.)	2.7 / 3.5 [n]	4.9 / 6.6	8.0 / 9.9 [m]
Intentional homicide rate (per 100 000 pop.)	9.5	8.5	7.7 [b]
Seats held by women in the National Parliament (%)	3.0	3.0	6.1

Environment and infrastructure indicators

	2005	2010	2018
Individuals using the Internet (per 100 inhabitants) [e]	2.0	5.1	7.9 [d]
Threatened species (number)	27 [j]	89	114 [c]
Forested area (% of land area) [e]	22.6	21.0	19.9 [b]
CO2 emission estimates (million tons/tons per capita)	0.1 / 0.2	0.2 / 0.2	0.2 / 0.2 [m]
Energy production, primary (Petajoules)	2	2	3 [b]
Energy supply per capita (Gigajoules)	6 [e]	7 [e]	7 [b]
Tourist/visitor arrivals at national borders (000) [o]	26	15	27 [d]
Important sites for terrestrial biodiversity protected (%)	5.0	10.4	10.4
Pop. using improved drinking water (urban/rural, %)	93.8 / 88.6	93.1 / 86.9	92.6 / 89.1 [b]
Pop. using improved sanitation facilities (urban/rural, %)	41.7 / 23.9	45.4 / 27.8	48.3 / 30.9 [b]
Net Official Development Assist. received (% of GNI)	6.11	13.19	8.68 [d]

a Projected estimate (medium fertility variant). b 2015. c 2017. d 2016. e Estimate. f 2013. g Data refers to a 5-year period preceding the reference year. h Data as at the end of December. i Data revision. j 2004. k 2002. l 2008. m 2014. n 2003. o Arrivals by air.

Congo

Region	Middle Africa	UN membership date	20 September 1960
Population (000, 2018)	5 400[a]	Surface area (km2)	342 000[b]
Pop. density (per km2, 2018)	15.8[a]	Sex ratio (m per 100 f)	100.1[a]
Capital city	Brazzaville	National currency	CFA Franc, BEAC (XAF)[c]
Capital city pop. (000, 2018)	2 229.7	Exchange rate (per US$)	546.9[d]

Economic indicators

	2005	2010	2018
GDP: Gross domestic product (million current US$)	6 087	12 281	7 778[e]
GDP growth rate (annual %, const. 2010 prices)	7.6	8.7	- 1.9[e]
GDP per capita (current US$)	1 637.0	2 800.0	1 517.0[e]
Economy: Agriculture (% of Gross Value Added)	4.6	3.7	9.3[e]
Economy: Industry (% of Gross Value Added)	73.4	78.1	51.9[e]
Economy: Services and other activity (% of GVA)	22.0	18.2	38.8[e]
Employment in agriculture (% of employed)[f]	40.0	39.1	37.9
Employment in industry (% of employed)[f]	23.4	23.3	25.4
Employment in services & other sectors (% employed)[f]	36.6	37.6	36.7
Unemployment rate (% of labour force)	19.8	14.6[f]	11.3[f]
Labour force participation rate (female/male pop. %)[f]	66.7 / 70.6	67.5 / 71.5	67.3 / 71.9
CPI: Consumer Price Index (2010=100)[f,g]	79	100	119[b]
Agricultural production index (2004-2006=100)	100	122	138[e]
Index of industrial production (2005=100)[h,i]	100	159[j,k]	...
International trade: exports (million current US$)	4 744[f]	6 918	1 397[f,d]
International trade: imports (million current US$)	1 342[f]	4 369	12 380[f,d]
International trade: balance (million current US$)	3 402[f]	2 548	- 10 993[f,d]
Balance of payments, current account (million US$)	696	900	- 4 627[b]

Major trading partners

						2017
Export partners (% of exports)	China	47.8[f]	United Arab Emirates	10.9	Italy	9.4[f]
Import partners (% of imports)	China	25.9	France	20.3	Norway	4.4

Social indicators

	2005	2010	2018
Population growth rate (average annual %)[l]	2.8	3.3	2.6[b]
Urban population (% of total population)	61.0	63.3	66.9
Urban population growth rate (average annual %)[l]	3.6	4.0	3.3[b]
Fertility rate, total (live births per woman)[l]	5.1	5.0	4.9[b]
Life expectancy at birth (females/males, years)[l]	53.1 / 51.1	59.2 / 56.7	64.1 / 61.0[b]
Population age distribution (0-14/60+ years old, %)	41.6 / 5.2	41.7 / 5.0	42.1 / 5.2[a]
International migrant stock (000/% of total pop.)	315.2 / 8.5	419.6 / 9.6	398.9 / 7.6[d]
Refugees and others of concern to the UNHCR (000)	77.6[m]	138.7[m]	138.7[d]
Infant mortality rate (per 1 000 live births)[l]	81.1	61.0	46.5[b]
Health: Current expenditure (% of GDP)	1.9	2.0	3.4[b]
Health: Physicians (per 1 000 pop.)	0.2[n]	0.1[o]	...
Education: Government expenditure (% of GDP)	1.8	6.2	...
Education: Primary gross enrol. ratio (f/m per 100 pop.)	103.5 / 111.4	103.8 / 110.0	107.8 / 100.6[p]
Education: Secondary gross enrol. ratio (f/m per 100 pop.)	40.7 / 48.2[f,n]	... / ...	48.4 / 55.8[p]
Education: Tertiary gross enrol. ratio (f/m per 100 pop.)	2.1 / 5.3[f,q]	2.2 / 10.3[k]	8.0 / 10.6[f]
Intentional homicide rate (per 100 000 pop.)	10.6	9.9	9.3[b]
Seats held by women in the National Parliament (%)	8.5	7.3	11.3

Environment and infrastructure indicators

	2005	2010	2018
Individuals using the Internet (per 100 inhabitants)[f]	1.5	5.0	8.1[e]
Threatened species (number)	65[n]	103	134[d]
Forested area (% of land area)[f]	65.8	65.6	65.4[b]
CO2 emission estimates (million tons/tons per capita)	1.0 / 0.3	2.0 / 0.5	3.1 / 0.7[s]
Energy production, primary (Petajoules)	563	724	623[b]
Energy supply per capita (Gigajoules)	13	17	24[b]
Tourist/visitor arrivals at national borders (000)[t]	35	194	211[e]
Important sites for terrestrial biodiversity protected (%)	51.5	61.2	72.1
Pop. using improved drinking water (urban/rural, %)	95.5 / 34.6	95.6 / 37.6	95.8 / 40.0[b]
Pop. using improved sanitation facilities (urban/rural, %)	18.4 / 5.6	19.3 / 5.6	20.0 / 5.6[b]
Net Official Development Assist. received (% of GNI)	35.36	14.57	1.19[b]

a Projected estimate (medium fertility variant). b 2015. c African Financial Community (CFA) Franc, Bank of Central African States (BEAC). d 2017. e 2016. f Estimate. g Brazzaville h Data classified according to ISIC Rev. 3. i Country data supplemented with data from the Observatoire Economique et Statistique d'Afrique Subsaharienne (Afristat). j Data refers to manufacturing and utilities only. k 2009. l Data refers to a 5-year period preceding the reference year. m Data as at the end of December. n 2004. o 2007. p 2012. q 2003. r 2013. s 2014. t Including nationals residing abroad.

Cook Islands

Region	Polynesia	Population (000, 2018)	17 [a]
Surface area (km2)	236 [b]	Pop. density (per km2, 2018)	72.5 [a]
Sex ratio (m per 100 f)	97.4 [c,d]	Capital city	Avarua
National currency	New Zealand Dollar (NZD)	Capital city pop. (000, 2018)	13.1 [e]
Exchange rate (per US$)	1.4 [f]		

Economic indicators	2005	2010	2018
GDP: Gross domestic product (million current US$)	183	255	290 [d]
GDP growth rate (annual %, const. 2010 prices)	- 1.1	- 3.0	3.7 [d]
GDP per capita (current US$)	9 262.0	13 758.0	16 698.0 [d]
Economy: Agriculture (% of Gross Value Added) [g]	6.9	4.9	7.9 [d]
Economy: Industry (% of Gross Value Added) [g]	9.6	8.5	8.1 [d]
Economy: Services and other activity (% of GVA) [g]	83.5	86.6	84.0 [d]
Employment in agriculture (% of employed)	...	...	4.3 [h,i]
Employment in industry (% of employed)	...	...	11.7 [h,i]
Employment in services & other sectors (% employed)	...	...	84.0 [h,i]
Unemployment rate (% of labour force)	13.1 [i]	6.9 [c,h,k]	8.2 [h,i]
Labour force participation rate (female/male pop. %)	63.0 / 75.5 [i,j]	64.2 / 76.1 [c,h,k]	65.4 / 76.6 [h,i]
CPI: Consumer Price Index (2010=100) [m,n,o]	...	100	111 [f]
Agricultural production index (2004-2006=100)	100	94	91 [d]
International trade: exports (million current US$)	5	5	21 [p,f]
International trade: imports (million current US$)	81	91	130 [p,f]
International trade: balance (million current US$)	- 76	- 85	- 109 [p,f]

Major trading partners						2017
Export partners (% of exports)	Japan	40.2 [p]	Thailand	11.0	Greece	8.4 [p]
Import partners (% of imports)	New Zealand	54.2	Fiji	8.7	Italy	5.8

Social indicators	2005	2010	2018
Population growth rate (average annual %) [q]	1.7	- 1.2	- 1.2 [b]
Urban population (% of total population)	71.0	73.3	75.1
Urban population growth rate (average annual %) [q]	3.4	- 0.6	- 0.9 [b]
Fertility rate, total (live births per woman)	...	...	2.6 [i]
Life expectancy at birth (females/males, years)	74.0 / 68.0 [i]	76.2 / 69.5 [k]	79.6 / 71.7 [c,r,e]
Population age distribution (0-14/60+ years old, %)	30.0 / 10.6 [i]	26.1 / 11.9 [t,k]	26.9 / 14.2 [c,d]
International migrant stock (000/% of total pop.)	3.3 / 18.6	3.8 / 20.3	4.2 / 24.2 [f]
Infant mortality rate (per 1 000 live births)	...	...	3.6 [r,s]
Health: Current expenditure (% of GDP) [u]	4.2	3.5	2.7 [b]
Health: Physicians (per 1 000 pop.)	1.0 [v]	1.2 [w]	...
Education: Government expenditure (% of GDP)	...	...	4.7 [d]
Education: Primary gross enrol. ratio (f/m per 100 pop.) [p]	113.0 / 110.2	103.6 / 104.6	105.2 / 111.7 [d]
Education: Secondary gross enrol. ratio (f/m per 100 pop.) [p]	84.9 / 75.1	88.1 / 80.7	90.1 / 84.9 [d]
Education: Tertiary gross enrol. ratio (f/m per 100 pop.)	... / ...	... / ...	50.1 / 41.2 [p,x]
Intentional homicide rate (per 100 000 pop.)	...	...	3.5 [x]

Environment and infrastructure indicators	2005	2010	2018
Individuals using the Internet (per 100 inhabitants)	26.2 [p]	35.7	54.0 [p,d]
Threatened species (number)	23 [v]	53	75 [f]
Forested area (% of land area)	62.9	62.9	62.9 [b]
CO2 emission estimates (million tons/tons per capita)	0.1 / 3.2	0.1 / 3.5	0.1 / 3.4 [y]
Energy production, primary (Petajoules)	...	...	0 [p,b]
Energy supply per capita (Gigajoules)	39	36 [p]	41 [p,b]
Tourist/visitor arrivals at national borders (000)	88	104	146 [d]
Important sites for terrestrial biodiversity protected (%)	7.6	7.6	22.4
Pop. using improved drinking water (urban/rural, %)	99.9 / 99.9	99.9 / 99.9	99.9 / 99.9 [b]
Pop. using improved sanitation facilities (urban/rural, %)	94.2 / 94.2	96.4 / 96.4	97.6 / 97.6 [b]

a Projected estimate (medium fertility variant). **b** 2015. **c** Break in the time series. **d** 2016. **e** Refers to the island of Rarotonga. **f** 2017. **g** At producers' prices. **h** Resident population (de jure). **i** 2011. **j** 2001. **k** 2006. **l** Population aged 15 to 69 years. **m** Rarotonga **n** Calculated by the Statistics Division of the United Nations from national indices. **o** Index base: 2006=100. **p** Estimate. **q** Data refers to a 5-year period preceding the reference year. **r** Data refers to a 5-year period up to and including the reference year. **s** 2013. **t** Provisional data. **u** Data refer to fiscal years beginning 1 July. **v** 2004. **w** 2009. **x** 2012. **y** 2014.

Costa Rica

Region	Central America	UN membership date	02 November 1945
Population (000, 2018)	4 953[a]	Surface area (km2)	51 100[b]
Pop. density (per km2, 2018)	97.0[a]	Sex ratio (m per 100 f)	100.0[a]
Capital city	San José	National currency	Costa Rican Colon (CRC)
Capital city pop. (000, 2018)	1 357.7[c]	Exchange rate (per US$)	569.5[d]

Economic indicators

	2005	2010	2018
GDP: Gross domestic product (million current US$)	19 952	37 269	57 436[e]
GDP growth rate (annual %, const. 2010 prices)	3.9	5.0	4.3[e]
GDP per capita (current US$)	4 697.0	8 199.0	11 825.0[e]
Economy: Agriculture (% of Gross Value Added)[f]	9.6	7.2	5.5[e]
Economy: Industry (% of Gross Value Added)[f]	26.9	25.4	21.5[e]
Economy: Services and other activity (% of GVA)[f]	63.6	67.4	73.0[e]
Employment in agriculture (% of employed)[g]	15.2	15.1	11.6
Employment in industry (% of employed)[g]	21.6	19.6	18.6
Employment in services & other sectors (% employed)[g]	63.1	65.3	69.8
Unemployment rate (% of labour force)	6.6	8.9	8.4[g]
Labour force participation rate (female/male pop. %)[g]	44.7 / 80.5	44.1 / 77.1	45.6 / 73.9
CPI: Consumer Price Index (2010=100)[h,j]	63[i]	100	123[d]
Agricultural production index (2004-2006=100)	98	113	129[e]
International trade: exports (million current US$)	7 151	9 045	10 642[g,d]
International trade: imports (million current US$)	9 173	13 920	15 907[g,d]
International trade: balance (million current US$)	- 2 023	- 4 875	- 5 265[g,d]
Balance of payments, current account (million US$)	- 860	- 1 214	- 1 717[d]

Major trading partners

					2017
Export partners (% of exports)	United States	41.0[g]	Netherlands	5.8	Panama	5.7[g]
Import partners (% of imports)	United States	37.3	China	13.6	Mexico	7.0

Social indicators

	2005	2010	2018
Population growth rate (average annual %)[k]	1.6	1.4	1.1[b]
Urban population (% of total population)	65.7	71.7	79.3
Urban population growth rate (average annual %)[k]	3.7	3.1	2.5[b]
Fertility rate, total (live births per woman)[k]	2.2	2.0	1.9[b]
Life expectancy at birth (females/males, years)[k]	80.2 / 75.5	80.8 / 76.1	81.7 / 76.7[b]
Population age distribution (0-14/60+ years old, %)	27.4 / 9.4	24.6 / 11.1	21.4 / 14.1[a]
International migrant stock (000/% of total pop.)[l]	358.2 / 8.4	405.4 / 8.9	414.2 / 8.4[d]
Refugees and others of concern to the UNHCR (000)	11.5[m]	19.9[m]	10.2[d]
Infant mortality rate (per 1 000 live births)[k]	10.9	10.0	9.3[b]
Health: Current expenditure (% of GDP)	6.7	8.1	8.1[b]
Health: Physicians (per 1 000 pop.)	1.3[n]	...	1.2[o]
Education: Government expenditure (% of GDP)	4.9[p]	6.6	7.1[e]
Education: Primary gross enrol. ratio (f/m per 100 pop.)	111.5 / 114.4	115.8 / 118.1	110.3 / 109.7[e]
Education: Secondary gross enrol. ratio (f/m per 100 pop.)	86.2 / 82.6	104.3 / 100.1	129.5 / 122.8[e]
Education: Tertiary gross enrol. ratio (f/m per 100 pop.)	30.2 / 24.5[p]	... / ...	59.8 / 48.4[e]
Intentional homicide rate (per 100 000 pop.)	7.9	11.6	11.9[e]
Seats held by women in the National Parliament (%)	35.1	36.8	35.1

Environment and infrastructure indicators

	2005	2010	2018
Individuals using the Internet (per 100 inhabitants)	22.1[q]	36.5[q,r]	66.0[e]
Research & Development expenditure (% of GDP)	0.4[p]	0.5	0.6[s]
Threatened species (number)	231[p]	285	340[d]
Forested area (% of land area)[g]	48.8	51.0	54.0[b]
CO2 emission estimates (million tons/tons per capita)	6.9 / 1.6	7.6 / 1.7	7.8 / 1.6[s]
Energy production, primary (Petajoules)	93	104	110[b]
Energy supply per capita (Gigajoules)	41	45	43[b]
Tourist/visitor arrivals at national borders (000)	1 679	2 100	2 925[e]
Important sites for terrestrial biodiversity protected (%)	44.8	45.3	45.3
Pop. using improved drinking water (urban/rural, %)	99.4 / 90.0	99.5 / 91.2	99.6 / 91.9[b]
Pop. using improved sanitation facilities (urban/rural, %)	94.8 / 88.9	95.1 / 91.0	95.2 / 92.3[b]
Net Official Development Assist. received (% of GNI)	0.14	0.14	0.19[e]

a Projected estimate (medium fertility variant). b 2015. c Refers to the urban population of cantons. d 2017. e 2016.
f Data classified according to ISIC Rev. 4. g Estimate. h Central area. i Break in the time series. j Calculated by the Statistics Division of the United Nations from national indices. k Data refers to a 5-year period preceding the reference year. l Including refugees. m Data as at the end of December. n 2000. o 2013. p 2004. q Population aged 5 years and over. r Users in the last 3 months. s 2014.

Côte d'Ivoire

Region	Western Africa	UN membership date	20 September 1960
Population (000, 2018)	24 906 [a]	Surface area (km2)	322 463 [b]
Pop. density (per km2, 2018)	78.3 [a]	Sex ratio (m per 100 f)	102.5 [a]
Capital city	Yamoussoukro [c]	National currency	CFA Franc, BCEAO (XOF) [d]
Capital city pop. (000, 2018)	231.1	Exchange rate (per US$)	546.9 [e]

Economic indicators

	2005	2010	2018
GDP: Gross domestic product (million current US$)	17 085	24 885	36 768 [f]
GDP growth rate (annual %, const. 2010 prices)	1.7	2.0	8.8 [f]
GDP per capita (current US$)	932.0	1 220.0	1 552.0 [f]
Economy: Agriculture (% of Gross Value Added)	24.3	26.0	20.8 [f]
Economy: Industry (% of Gross Value Added)	24.5	23.8	32.8 [f]
Economy: Services and other activity (% of GVA)	51.3	50.2	46.3 [f]
Employment in agriculture (% of employed) [g]	50.6	49.5	47.4
Employment in industry (% of employed) [g]	6.1	5.9	6.3
Employment in services & other sectors (% employed) [g]	43.3	44.6	46.2
Unemployment rate (% of labour force) [g]	3.5	3.1	2.6
Labour force participation rate (female/male pop. %) [g]	48.3 / 76.9	48.2 / 72.3	48.2 / 66.1
CPI: Consumer Price Index (2010=100) [g,h]	88	100	112 [e]
Agricultural production index (2004-2006=100)	100	107	127 [f]
Index of industrial production (2005=100) [i,j]	100	103	140 [k]
International trade: exports (million current US$)	7 248	10 284	12 437 [g,e]
International trade: imports (million current US$)	5 865	7 849	9 555 [g,e]
International trade: balance (million current US$)	1 383	2 434	2 881 [g,e]
Balance of payments, current account (million US$)	40	465	- 414 [f]

Major trading partners

						2017
Export partners (% of exports) [g]	Netherlands	12.1	United States	8.1	Belgium	6.5
Import partners (% of imports) [g]	Nigeria	15.2	France	13.8	China	11.7

Social indicators

	2005	2010	2018
Population growth rate (average annual %) [l]	1.9	2.1	2.5 [b]
Urban population (% of total population)	45.2	47.3	50.8
Urban population growth rate (average annual %) [l]	2.8	3.0	3.4 [b]
Fertility rate, total (live births per woman) [l]	5.7	5.4	5.1 [b]
Life expectancy at birth (females/males, years) [l]	47.6 / 45.9	50.0 / 48.5	53.2 / 50.4 [b]
Population age distribution (0-14/60+ years old, %)	44.1 / 4.6	43.7 / 4.7	42.3 / 4.8 [a]
International migrant stock (000/% of total pop.) [m]	2 010.8 / 11.0	2 095.2 / 10.3	2 197.2 / 9.0 [e]
Refugees and others of concern to the UNHCR (000)	115.1 [n]	564.5 [n]	700.2 [e]
Infant mortality rate (per 1 000 live births) [l]	91.6	84.6	71.6 [b]
Health: Current expenditure (% of GDP)	5.4	6.1	5.4 [b]
Health: Physicians (per 1 000 pop.)	0.1	0.1 [o]	...
Education: Government expenditure (% of GDP)	4.1	4.6	4.8 [g,b]
Education: Primary gross enrol. ratio (f/m per 100 pop.)	63.5 / 79.3 [g,p]	64.8 / 79.4 [g]	91.3 / 102.1 [f]
Education: Secondary gross enrol. ratio (f/m per 100 pop.)	... / ...	... / ...	38.8 / 53.3 [f]
Education: Tertiary gross enrol. ratio (f/m per 100 pop.)	... / ...	5.4 / 10.4	7.2 / 10.8 [b]
Intentional homicide rate (per 100 000 pop.)	14.7	12.6	11.6 [b]
Seats held by women in the National Parliament (%)	8.5	8.9	10.6

Environment and infrastructure indicators

	2005	2010	2018
Individuals using the Internet (per 100 inhabitants)	1.0	2.7 [q]	26.5 [g,f]
Threatened species (number)	167 [r]	210	249 [e]
Forested area (% of land area) [g]	32.7	32.7	32.7 [b]
CO2 emission estimates (million tons/tons per capita)	7.8 / 0.4	7.0 / 0.3	11.0 / 0.5 [k]
Energy production, primary (Petajoules)	451	467	526 [b]
Energy supply per capita (Gigajoules)	23	21	24 [b]
Tourist/visitor arrivals at national borders (000) [s]	...	252	1 583 [f]
Important sites for terrestrial biodiversity protected (%)	79.1	79.1	79.1
Pop. using improved drinking water (urban/rural, %)	92.0 / 68.0	92.6 / 68.4	93.1 / 68.8 [b]
Pop. using improved sanitation facilities (urban/rural, %)	30.9 / 8.9	32.0 / 9.7	32.8 / 10.3 [b]
Net Official Development Assist. received (% of GNI)	0.56	3.53	1.88 [f]

a Projected estimate (medium fertility variant). b 2015. c Yamoussoukro is the capital and Abidjan is the administrative capital. d African Financial Community (CFA) Franc, Central Bank of West African States (BCEAO). e 2017. f 2016. g Estimate. h Abidjan i Data classified according to ISIC Rev. 3. j Country data supplemented with data from the Observatoire Économique et Statistique d'Afrique Subsaharienne (Afristat). k 2014. l Data refers to a 5-year period preceding the reference year. m Refers to foreign citizens. n Data as at the end of December. o 2008. p 2003. q 2009. r 2004. s Arrivals to Félix Houphouët Boigny Airport only.

Croatia

Region	Southern Europe	UN membership date	22 May 1992
Population (000, 2018)	4 165[a]	Surface area (km2)	56 594[b]
Pop. density (per km2, 2018)	74.4[a]	Sex ratio (m per 100 f)	93.1[a]
Capital city	Zagreb	National currency	Kuna (HRK)
Capital city pop. (000, 2018)	685.6[c]	Exchange rate (per US$)	6.3[d]

Economic indicators

	2005	2010	2018
GDP: Gross domestic product (million current US$)	45 416	59 829	51 231[e]
GDP growth rate (annual %, const. 2010 prices)	4.2	- 1.4	3.0[e]
GDP per capita (current US$)	10 374.0	13 823.0	12 159.0[e]
Economy: Agriculture (% of Gross Value Added)[f]	5.0	4.8	4.1[e]
Economy: Industry (% of Gross Value Added)[f]	29.0	26.9	26.4[e]
Economy: Services and other activity (% of GVA)[f]	66.0	68.2	69.6[e]
Employment in agriculture (% of employed)	17.3	14.2[g]	7.3[g]
Employment in industry (% of employed)[g]	28.6	27.4	26.8
Employment in services & other sectors (% employed)[g]	54.1	58.3	65.8
Unemployment rate (% of labour force)	12.6	11.6	9.2[g]
Labour force participation rate (female/male pop. %)[g]	46.2 / 61.1	46.2 / 59.8	45.4 / 57.4
CPI: Consumer Price Index (2010=100)	86	100	107[d]
Agricultural production index (2004-2006=100)	100	111	121[e]
Index of industrial production (2005=100)	100	99[h]	92[h,i]
International trade: exports (million current US$)	8 773	11 811	15 732[d]
International trade: imports (million current US$)	18 560	20 067	24 513[d]
International trade: balance (million current US$)	- 9 788	- 8 256	- 8 780[d]
Balance of payments, current account (million US$)	- 2 479	- 894	2 363[d]

Major trading partners

						2017
Export partners (% of exports)	Italy	13.6	Germany	12.3	Slovenia	10.7
Import partners (% of imports)	Germany	15.8	Italy	12.9	Slovenia	10.7

Social indicators

	2005	2010	2018
Population growth rate (average annual %)[j]	- 0.2	- 0.2	- 0.4[b]
Urban population (% of total population)	54.3	55.2	56.9
Urban population growth rate (average annual %)[j]	0.1	0.1	- 0.1[b]
Fertility rate, total (live births per woman)[j]	1.4	1.5	1.5[b]
Life expectancy at birth (females/males, years)[j]	78.4 / 71.4	79.5 / 72.6	80.4 / 73.6[b]
Population age distribution (0-14/60+ years old, %)	15.7 / 21.9	15.4 / 23.8	14.7 / 27.2[a]
International migrant stock (000/% of total pop.)[k]	579.3 / 13.2	573.2 / 13.2	560.5 / 13.4[d]
Refugees and others of concern to the UNHCR (000)	10.9[l]	25.5[l]	13.4[d]
Infant mortality rate (per 1 000 live births)[j]	6.5	5.7	3.9[b]
Health: Current expenditure (% of GDP)	6.9	8.1	7.4[b]
Health: Physicians (per 1 000 pop.)	...	2.9	3.1[l]
Education: Government expenditure (% of GDP)	3.8[m]	4.3	4.6[n]
Education: Primary gross enrol. ratio (f/m per 100 pop.)	103.4 / 103.3	92.0 / 91.9	95.8 / 95.0[e]
Education: Secondary gross enrol. ratio (f/m per 100 pop.)	94.8 / 91.7	103.4 / 96.5	100.0 / 95.6[e]
Education: Tertiary gross enrol. ratio (f/m per 100 pop.)	49.2 / 40.5	62.1 / 46.3	78.5 / 57.0[e]
Intentional homicide rate (per 100 000 pop.)	1.6	1.4	1.0[e]
Seats held by women in the National Parliament (%)	21.7	23.5	18.5

Environment and infrastructure indicators

	2005	2010	2018
Individuals using the Internet (per 100 inhabitants)	33.1[o]	56.6[o]	72.7[e]
Research & Development expenditure (% of GDP)	0.9	0.7	0.9[b]
Threatened species (number)	57[m]	101	176[d]
Forested area (% of land area)	34.0	34.3	34.3[g,b]
CO2 emission estimates (million tons/tons per capita)	22.6 / 5.1	20.2 / 4.7	16.8 / 4.0[i]
Energy production, primary (Petajoules)	199	215	184[b]
Energy supply per capita (Gigajoules)	92	90	83[b]
Tourist/visitor arrivals at national borders (000)	7 743[p]	9 111[q]	13 809[q,e]
Important sites for terrestrial biodiversity protected (%)	22.8	24.4	72.0
Pop. using improved drinking water (urban/rural, %)	99.8 / 97.4	99.7 / 98.6	99.6 / 99.7[b]
Pop. using improved sanitation facilities (urban/rural, %)	98.1 / 96.1	98.0 / 95.9	97.8 / 95.8[b]
Net Official Development Assist. disbursed (% of GNI)	...	...	0.09[r,d]
Net Official Development Assist. received (% of GNI)	0.28	0.23	

a Projected estimate (medium fertility variant). b 2015. c Refers to the settlement of Zagreb. d 2017. e 2016. f Data classified according to ISIC Rev. 4. g Estimate. h Excluding water and waste management. i 2014. j Data refers to a 5-year period preceding the reference year. k Including refugees. l Data as at the end of December. m 2004. n 2013. o Population aged 16 to 74 years. p Data revision. q Excluding arrivals in ports of nautical tourism. r Provisional data.

Cuba

Region	Caribbean	UN membership date	24 October 1945
Population (000, 2018)	11 489[a]	Surface area (km2)	109 884[b]
Pop. density (per km2, 2018)	107.9[a]	Sex ratio (m per 100 f)	100.1[a]
Capital city	Havana	National currency	Cuban Peso (CUP)[c]
Capital city pop. (000, 2018)	2 136.5	Exchange rate (per US$)	1.0[d,e]

Economic indicators

	2005	2010	2018
GDP: Gross domestic product (million current US$)	42 644	64 328	89 689[f]
GDP growth rate (annual %, const. 2010 prices)	11.2	2.4	- 0.9[f]
GDP per capita (current US$)	3 779.0	5 676.0	7 815.0[f]
Economy: Agriculture (% of Gross Value Added)	4.4	3.7	3.9[f]
Economy: Industry (% of Gross Value Added)	21.8	23.1	22.9[f]
Economy: Services and other activity (% of GVA)	73.8	73.2	73.2[f]
Employment in agriculture (% of employed)[g]	20.2	18.6	18.4
Employment in industry (% of employed)[g]	19.1	17.1	16.5
Employment in services & other sectors (% employed)[g]	60.6	64.3	65.0
Unemployment rate (% of labour force)	1.9	2.5	2.7[g]
Labour force participation rate (female/male pop. %)[g]	38.3 / 67.4	42.3 / 68.7	41.3 / 67.3
Agricultural production index (2004-2006=100)	97	88	103[f]
International trade: exports (million current US$)	2 319	4 945[g]	22 329[g,a]
International trade: imports (million current US$)	8 084	10 913[g]	4 304[g,e]
International trade: balance (million current US$)	- 5 766	- 5 968[g]	18 025[g,e]

Major trading partners

						2017
Export partners (% of exports)[g]	Canada	21.6	China	16.9	Spain	10.1
Import partners (% of imports)	China	26.2[g]	Spain	14.0[g]	Mexico	5.0

Social indicators

	2005	2010	2018
Population growth rate (average annual %)[h]	0.2	0.1	0.2[b]
Urban population (% of total population)	76.1	76.6	77.0
Urban population growth rate (average annual %)[h]	0.5	0.2	0.3[b]
Fertility rate, total (live births per woman)[h]	1.6	1.6	1.7[b]
Life expectancy at birth (females/males, years)[h]	79.1 / 75.3	80.7 / 76.6	81.3 / 77.1[b]
Population age distribution (0-14/60+ years old, %)	19.4 / 15.2	17.4 / 17.0	15.9 / 20.5[a]
International migrant stock (000/% of total pop.)	17.0 / 0.2	14.8 / 0.1	13.1 / 0.1[e]
Refugees and others of concern to the UNHCR (000)	0.7[i]	0.4[i]	0.3[e]
Infant mortality rate (per 1 000 live births)[h]	6.1	5.7	5.5[b]
Health: Physicians (per 1 000 pop.)	6.3	6.8	7.5[j]
Education: Government expenditure (% of GDP)	10.6	12.8	...
Education: Primary gross enrol. ratio (f/m per 100 pop.)	96.8 / 99.7	102.2 / 104.0	97.9 / 103.8[b]
Education: Secondary gross enrol. ratio (f/m per 100 pop.)	93.1 / 91.6	91.4 / 90.8	102.2 / 98.6[b]
Education: Tertiary gross enrol. ratio (f/m per 100 pop.)	78.8 / 46.6[g]	119.2 / 72.4	40.1 / 28.4[f]
Intentional homicide rate (per 100 000 pop.)	6.1	4.5	5.0[f]
Seats held by women in the National Parliament (%)	36.0	43.2	48.9

Environment and infrastructure indicators

	2005	2010	2018
Individuals using the Internet (per 100 inhabitants)	9.7[k]	15.9[k]	38.8[g,f]
Research & Development expenditure (% of GDP)	0.5	0.6	0.4[b]
Threatened species (number)	272[l]	304	339[e]
Forested area (% of land area)	25.3	27.5[g]	30.8[g,b]
CO2 emission estimates (million tons/tons per capita)	26.0 / 2.3	38.4 / 3.4	34.8 / 3.0[j]
Energy production, primary (Petajoules)	205	200	212[b]
Energy supply per capita (Gigajoules)	37	44	42[b]
Tourist/visitor arrivals at national borders (000)[m]	2 261	2 507	3 968[f]
Important sites for terrestrial biodiversity protected (%)	42.1	68.3	73.4
Pop. using improved drinking water (urban/rural, %)	95.4 / 81.5	95.9 / 85.6	96.4 / 89.8[b]
Pop. using improved sanitation facilities (urban/rural, %)	91.5 / 81.9	93.3 / 86.4	94.4 / 89.1[b]
Net Official Development Assist. received (% of GNI)	0.22	0.21	0.13[n]

a Projected estimate (medium fertility variant). **b** 2015. **c** The national currency of Cuba is the Cuban Peso (CUP). The convertible peso (CUC) is used by foreigners and tourists in Cuba. **d** UN operational exchange rate. **e** 2017. **f** 2016. **g** Estimate. **h** Data refers to a 5-year period preceding the reference year. **i** Data as at the end of December. **j** 2014. **k** Including users of the international network and also those having access only to the Cuban network. **l** 2004. **m** Arrivals by air. **n** 2013.

Curaçao

Region	Caribbean	Population (000, 2018)	162[a]
Surface area (km2)	444[b]	Pop. density (per km2, 2018)	363.9[a]
Sex ratio (m per 100 f)	84.7[a]	Capital city	Willemstad
National currency	Neth. Ant. Guilder (ANG)[c]	Capital city pop. (000, 2018)	144.0[d]
Exchange rate (per US$)	1.8[e]		

Economic indicators	2005	2010	2018
GDP: Gross domestic product (million current US$)	2 345	2 951	3 121[f]
GDP growth rate (annual %, const. 2010 prices)	...	0.1	- 1.0[f]
GDP per capita (current US$)	18 120.0	19 994.0	19 586.0[f]
Economy: Agriculture (% of Gross Value Added)[g]	0.6	0.5	0.4[f]
Economy: Industry (% of Gross Value Added)	16.4	16.0	19.8[f]
Economy: Services and other activity (% of GVA)	83.0	83.5	79.8[f]
Employment in agriculture (% of employed)[h]	0.9	1.1[i]	...
Employment in industry (% of employed)[h]	15.3	17.6[i]	...
Employment in services & other sectors (% employed)[h]	83.8	81.3[i]	...
Unemployment rate (% of labour force)	18.2	9.6[j,k,l]	13.0[j,m]
Labour force participation rate (female/male pop. %)	54.8 / 65.4	53.2 / 66.5[i]	... / ...
CPI: Consumer Price Index (2010=100)[n]	84	100	110[e]
Balance of payments, current account (million US$)	...	...	- 690[e]

Social indicators	2005	2010	2018
Population growth rate (average annual %)[o]	- 0.4	2.6	1.4[b]
Urban population (% of total population)	90.5	89.9	89.1
Urban population growth rate (average annual %)[o]	- 0.5	2.5	1.2[b]
Fertility rate, total (live births per woman)[o]	2.1	2.0	2.1[b]
Life expectancy at birth (females/males, years)[o]	78.6 / 71.2	79.4 / 72.6	80.7 / 74.5[b]
Population age distribution (0-14/60+ years old, %)	21.1 / 17.2	19.9 / 18.8	18.5 / 23.4[a]
International migrant stock (000/% of total pop.)	... / ...	34.6 / 23.5	38.4 / 23.9[e]
Refugees and others of concern to the UNHCR (000)	...	~0.0[p]	0.2[e]
Infant mortality rate (per 1 000 live births)[o]	14.7	13.0	10.3[b]
Education: Government expenditure (% of GDP)	...	...	4.9[m]
Education: Primary gross enrol. ratio (f/m per 100 pop.)	... / ...	... / ...	169.2 / 176.3[m]
Education: Secondary gross enrol. ratio (f/m per 100 pop.)	... / ...	... / ...	91.1 / 84.1[m]
Education: Tertiary gross enrol. ratio (f/m per 100 pop.)	... / ...	... / ...	29.6 / 13.0[m]
Intentional homicide rate (per 100 000 pop.)	20.1	19.2[q]	...

Environment and infrastructure indicators	2005	2010	2018
Threatened species (number)	...	...	51[e]
CO2 emission estimates (million tons/tons per capita)	... / ...	... / ...	5.9 / 37.8[r]
Energy production, primary (Petajoules)	...	...	0[b]
Energy supply per capita (Gigajoules)	...	...	592[b]
Tourist/visitor arrivals at national borders (000)[s]	222	342	441[f]
Important sites for terrestrial biodiversity protected (%)	6.1	6.1	40.4

a Projected estimate (medium fertility variant). b 2015. c Netherlands Antillean Guilder. d Total population of Curaçao excluding some neighborhoods (see source). e 2017. f 2016. g Including mining and quarrying. h Data classified according to ISIC Rev. 3. i 2008. j Excluding the institutional population. k Break in the time series. l 2009. m 2013. n Calculated by the Statistics Division of the United Nations from national indices. o Data refers to a 5-year period preceding the reference year. p Data as at the end of December. q 2007. r 2014. s Arrivals by air.

Cyprus

Region	Western Asia	UN membership date	20 September 1960
Population (000, 2018)	1 189 [a,b]	Surface area (km2)	9 251 [c]
Pop. density (per km2, 2018)	128.7 [a,b]	Sex ratio (m per 100 f)	100.1 [a,b]
Capital city	Nicosia	National currency	Euro (EUR)
Capital city pop. (000, 2018)	269.5	Exchange rate (per US$)	0.8 [d]

Economic indicators

	2005	2010	2018
GDP: Gross domestic product (million current US$) [e]	18 694	25 561	20 046 [f]
GDP growth rate (annual %, const. 2010 prices) [e]	3.7	1.3	3.0 [f]
GDP per capita (current US$) [e]	25 311.0	30 817.0	23 631.0 [f]
Economy: Agriculture (% of Gross Value Added) [e,g]	3.1	2.4	2.1 [f]
Economy: Industry (% of Gross Value Added) [e,g]	20.5	16.7	11.4 [f]
Economy: Services and other activity (% of GVA) [e,g]	76.4	80.9	86.5 [f]
Employment in agriculture (% of employed)	4.7	3.8 [h]	3.5 [h]
Employment in industry (% of employed) [h]	24.0	20.4	16.9
Employment in services & other sectors (% employed) [h]	71.2	75.8	79.6
Unemployment rate (% of labour force)	5.3	6.3	10.5 [h]
Labour force participation rate (female/male pop. %) [h]	53.2 / 72.7	57.6 / 70.6	58.1 / 67.3
CPI: Consumer Price Index (2010=100) [e,i]	89	100	101 [d]
Agricultural production index (2004-2006=100)	98	84	79 [f]
Index of industrial production (2005=100) [j]	100	100	72 [k]
International trade: exports (million current US$)	1 546	1 506	3 368 [d]
International trade: imports (million current US$)	6 382	8 645	9 292 [d]
International trade: balance (million current US$)	- 4 836	- 7 138	- 5 924 [d]
Balance of payments, current account (million US$)	- 971	- 2 906	- 1 452 [d]

Major trading partners

						2017
Export partners (% of exports)	Libya	9.0	Bunkers	8.2	Greece	7.7
Import partners (% of imports)	Greece	18.6	Italy	7.3	China	7.1

Social indicators

	2005	2010	2018
Population growth rate (average annual %) [b,l]	1.7	1.6	0.9 [c]
Urban population (% of total population) [b]	68.3	67.6	66.8
Urban population growth rate (average annual %) [b,i]	1.6	1.4	0.7 [c]
Fertility rate, total (live births per woman) [b,l]	1.6	1.5	1.4 [c]
Life expectancy at birth (females/males, years) [b,l]	80.4 / 76.2	81.1 / 76.8	82.2 / 77.7 [c]
Population age distribution (0-14/60+ years old, %) [b]	20.0 / 14.9	17.8 / 16.1	16.8 / 18.9 [a]
International migrant stock (000/% of total pop.) [m]	117.2 / 11.4	188.5 / 16.9	189.0 / 16.0 [d]
Refugees and others of concern to the UNHCR (000)	13.8 [n]	8.8 [n]	19.0 [d]
Infant mortality rate (per 1 000 live births) [b,l]	5.6	4.4	4.2 [c]
Health: Current expenditure (% of GDP)	5.3	6.3	6.8 [c]
Health: Physicians (per 1 000 pop.)	...	2.2	2.5 [k]
Education: Government expenditure (% of GDP)	6.2	6.6	6.1 [k]
Education: Primary gross enrol. ratio (f/m per 100 pop.) [h]	100.8 / 100.9	101.6 / 101.6	99.3 / 99.3 [c]
Education: Secondary gross enrol. ratio (f/m per 100 pop.) [h]	97.5 / 95.7	92.0 / 90.9	99.4 / 100.1 [c]
Education: Tertiary gross enrol. ratio (f/m per 100 pop.) [h]	35.3 / 31.2	45.6 / 50.9	69.4 / 51.1 [c]
Intentional homicide rate (per 100 000 pop.)	1.9	0.7	1.1 [f]
Seats held by women in the National Parliament (%)	16.1	12.5	17.9

Environment and infrastructure indicators

	2005	2010	2018
Individuals using the Internet (per 100 inhabitants)	32.8 [o]	53.0 [o]	75.9 [f]
Research & Development expenditure (% of GDP)	0.4	0.4	0.5 [p,c]
Threatened species (number)	25 [q]	43	72 [d]
Forested area (% of land area)	18.7	18.7	18.7 [c]
CO2 emission estimates (million tons/tons per capita)	7.5 / 7.3	7.7 / 7.0	6.1 / 5.2 [k]
Energy production, primary (Petajoules)	0	4	5 [c]
Energy supply per capita (Gigajoules)	89	94	73 [c]
Tourist/visitor arrivals at national borders (000)	2 470	2 173	3 187 [f]
Important sites for terrestrial biodiversity protected (%)	35.1	54.5	57.8
Pop. using improved drinking water (urban/rural, %)	100.0 / 100.0	100.0 / 100.0	100.0 / 100.0 [c]
Pop. using improved sanitation facilities (urban/rural, %)	100.0 / 100.0	100.0 / 100.0	100.0 / 100.0 [c]
Net Official Development Assist. disbursed (% of GNI) [j]	0.09	0.23	0.09 [c]

a Projected estimate (medium fertility variant). b Refers to the whole country. c 2015. d 2017. e Excluding northern Cyprus. f 2016. g Data classified according to ISIC Rev. 4. h Estimate. i Calculated by the Statistics Division of the United Nations from national indices. j Data refer to government controlled areas. k 2014. l Data refers to a 5-year period preceding the reference year. m Including northern Cyprus. n Data as at the end of December. o Population aged 16 to 74 years. p Provisional data. q 2004.

Czechia

Region	Eastern Europe	
Population (000, 2018)	10 625[a]	
Pop. density (per km2, 2018)	137.6[a]	
Capital city	Prague	
Capital city pop. (000, 2018)	1 291.6	

UN membership date	19 January 1993	
Surface area (km2)	78 868[b]	
Sex ratio (m per 100 f)	96.7[a]	
National currency	Czech Koruna (CZK)	
Exchange rate (per US$)	21.3[c]	

Economic indicators

	2005	2010	2018
GDP: Gross domestic product (million current US$)	135 990	207 016	195 305[d]
GDP growth rate (annual %, const. 2010 prices)	6.4	2.3	2.6[d]
GDP per capita (current US$)	13 257.0	19 648.0	18 406.0[d]
Economy: Agriculture (% of Gross Value Added)[e]	2.4	1.7	2.5[d]
Economy: Industry (% of Gross Value Added)[e]	37.7	36.8	37.6[d]
Economy: Services and other activity (% of GVA)[e]	59.8	61.5	59.9[d]
Employment in agriculture (% of employed)[f]	4.0	3.1[f]	2.8[f]
Employment in industry (% of employed)[f]	39.5	38.0	37.4
Employment in services & other sectors (% employed)[f]	56.5	58.9	59.8
Unemployment rate (% of labour force)	7.9	7.3	3.5[f]
Labour force participation rate (female/male pop. %)[i]	50.8 / 68.9	49.2 / 68.0	51.8 / 68.0
CPI: Consumer Price Index (2010=100)	87	100	111[c]
Agricultural production index (2004-2006=100)	100	91	100[d]
Index of industrial production (2005=100)	100	110[g]	122[g,h]
International trade: exports (million current US$)	78 209	132 141	180 010[c]
International trade: imports (million current US$)	76 527	125 691	162 058[c]
International trade: balance (million current US$)	1 681	6 450	17 952[c]
Balance of payments, current account (million US$)	- 2 810	- 7 351	1 918[c]

Major trading partners

						2017
Export partners (% of exports)	Germany	32.8	Slovakia	7.8	Poland	6.1
Import partners (% of imports)	Germany	25.8	China	12.6	Poland	7.7

Social indicators

	2005	2010	2018
Population growth rate (average annual %)[j]	- 0.1	0.5	0.1[b]
Urban population (% of total population)	73.6	73.3	73.8
Urban population growth rate (average annual %)[j]	- 0.2	0.4	0.2[b]
Fertility rate, total (live births per woman)[j]	1.2	1.4	1.5[b]
Life expectancy at birth (females/males, years)[j]	78.8 / 72.2	80.1 / 73.8	81.2 / 75.1[b]
Population age distribution (0-14/60+ years old, %)	14.7 / 19.8	14.2 / 22.4	15.5 / 25.8[a]
International migrant stock (000/% of total pop.)[j]	322.5 / 3.1	398.5 / 3.8	433.3 / 4.1[c]
Refugees and others of concern to the UNHCR (000)	2.7[k]	3.5[k]	6.0[c]
Infant mortality rate (per 1 000 live births)[j]	3.9	3.1	2.5[b]
Health: Current expenditure (% of GDP)	6.4	6.9	7.3[b]
Health: Physicians (per 1 000 pop.)	...	3.6	3.7[l]
Education: Government expenditure (% of GDP)	3.9	4.1	4.0[h]
Education: Primary gross enrol. ratio (f/m per 100 pop.)	98.5 / 99.9	103.6 / 104.0	99.7 / 99.3[b]
Education: Secondary gross enrol. ratio (f/m per 100 pop.)	96.6 / 94.8	94.9 / 94.4	105.6 / 104.6[b]
Education: Tertiary gross enrol. ratio (f/m per 100 pop.)	52.0 / 44.8	74.9 / 53.6	75.7 / 53.8[b]
Intentional homicide rate (per 100 000 pop.)	1.1	1.0	0.6[d]
Seats held by women in the National Parliament (%)	17.0	15.5	22.0

Environment and infrastructure indicators

	2005	2010	2018
Individuals using the Internet (per 100 inhabitants)	35.3[m]	68.8[m]	76.5[n,d]
Research & Development expenditure (% of GDP)	1.2	1.3	1.9[o,b]
Threatened species (number)	45[p]	33	53[c]
Forested area (% of land area)	34.3	34.4	34.5[b]
CO2 emission estimates (million tons/tons per capita)	120.1 / 11.7	111.6 / 10.6	96.5 / 9.2[h]
Energy production, primary (Petajoules)	1 387	1 339	1 213[b]
Energy supply per capita (Gigajoules)	186	180	167[b]
Tourist/visitor arrivals at national borders (000)	9 404	8 629	12 090[d]
Important sites for terrestrial biodiversity protected (%)	87.8	92.3	92.3
Pop. using improved drinking water (urban/rural, %)	99.9 / 99.7	100.0 / 99.9	100.0 / 100.0[b]
Pop. using improved sanitation facilities (urban/rural, %)	99.1 / 99.2	99.1 / 99.2	99.1 / 99.2[b]
Net Official Development Assist. disbursed (% of GNI)[q]	0.11	0.13	0.13[o,c]

a Projected estimate (medium fertility variant). b 2015. c 2017. d 2016. e Data classified according to ISIC Rev. 4. f Estimate. g Excluding water and waste management. h 2014. i Data refers to a 5-year period preceding the reference year. j Refers to foreign citizens. k Data as at the end of December. l 2013. m Population aged 16 to 74 years. n Population aged 16 years and over. o Provisional data. p 2004. q Development Assistance Committee member (OECD).

Democratic People's Republic of Korea

Region	Eastern Asia	UN membership date	17 September 1991
Population (000, 2018)	25 611[a]	Surface area (km2)	120 538[b]
Pop. density (per km2, 2018)	212.7[a]	Sex ratio (m per 100 f)	95.7[a]
Capital city	Pyongyang	National currency	North Korean Won (KPW)
Capital city pop. (000, 2018)	3 037.9	Exchange rate (per US$)	105.0[c,d]

Economic indicators

	2005	2010	2018
GDP: Gross domestic product (million current US$)	13 031	13 945	16 789[e]
GDP growth rate (annual %, const. 2010 prices)	3.8	- 0.5	3.9[e]
GDP per capita (current US$)	548.0	570.0	665.0[e]
Economy: Agriculture (% of Gross Value Added)	25.0	20.8	21.7[e]
Economy: Industry (% of Gross Value Added)	42.8	48.2	47.2[e]
Economy: Services and other activity (% of GVA)	32.2	31.0	31.1[e]
Employment in agriculture (% of employed)[f]	67.6	66.8	67.0
Employment in industry (% of employed)[f]	16.3	17.4	17.5
Employment in services & other sectors (% employed)[f]	16.1	15.8	15.5
Unemployment rate (% of labour force)[f]	4.5	4.6	4.7
Labour force participation rate (female/male pop. %)[f]	75.5 / 87.9	74.9 / 87.2	74.4 / 86.9
Agricultural production index (2004-2006=100)	101	98	102[e]
International trade: exports (million current US$)[f]	787	882	1 033[d]
International trade: imports (million current US$)[f]	1 466	1 957	2 920[d]
International trade: balance (million current US$)[f]	- 679	- 1 075	- 1 887[d]

Major trading partners

						2017
Export partners (% of exports)[f]	China	92.2	Pakistan	0.9	India	0.8
Import partners (% of imports)[f]	China	91.4	Russian Federation	2.2	Thailand	1.5

Social indicators

	2005	2010	2018
Population growth rate (average annual %)[g]	0.8	0.6	0.5[b]
Urban population (% of total population)	59.8	60.4	61.9
Urban population growth rate (average annual %)[g]	1.0	0.8	0.8[b]
Fertility rate, total (live births per woman)[g]	2.0	2.0	2.0[b]
Life expectancy at birth (females/males, years)[g]	71.5 / 64.2	71.8 / 64.8	74.1 / 67.2[b]
Population age distribution (0-14/60+ years old, %)	24.7 / 11.9	22.8 / 12.9	20.4 / 14.1[a]
International migrant stock (000/% of total pop.)[f]	40.1 / 0.2	44.0 / 0.2	48.9 / 0.2[d]
Infant mortality rate (per 1 000 live births)[g]	28.5	27.3	18.5[b]
Health: Physicians (per 1 000 pop.)	3.2[h]	3.3[i]	3.5[i]
Education: Primary gross enrol. ratio (f/m per 100 pop.)	... / ...	99.4 / 99.4[k]	... / ...
Education: Secondary gross enrol. ratio (f/m per 100 pop.)	... / ...	102.1 / 102.1[k]	93.5 / 92.5[b]
Education: Tertiary gross enrol. ratio (f/m per 100 pop.)	... / ...	20.6 / 40.8[k]	19.9 / 36.0[b]
Intentional homicide rate (per 100 000 pop.)[f]	5.0	4.8	4.4[b]
Seats held by women in the National Parliament (%)	20.1	15.6	16.3

Environment and infrastructure indicators

	2005	2010	2018
Individuals using the Internet (per 100 inhabitants)	0.0[l]	0.0[f]	0.0[f,m]
Threatened species (number)	44[n]	52	78[d]
Forested area (% of land area)[f]	52.3	47.1	41.8[b]
CO2 emission estimates (million tons/tons per capita)	75.6 / 3.2	66.5 / 2.7	40.5 / 1.6[j]
Energy production, primary (Petajoules)	923	872	788[b]
Energy supply per capita (Gigajoules)	38	32	13[b]
Important sites for terrestrial biodiversity protected (%)	10.2	10.2	10.2
Pop. using improved drinking water (urban/rural, %)	99.9 / 99.6	99.9 / 99.4	99.9 / 99.4[b]
Pop. using improved sanitation facilities (urban/rural, %)	75.5 / 62.8	85.9 / 70.9	87.9 / 72.5[b]

a Projected estimate (medium fertility variant). **b** 2015. **c** UN operational exchange rate. **d** 2017. **e** 2016. **f** Estimate.
g Data refers to a 5-year period preceding the reference year. **h** 2003. **i** 2008. **j** 2014. **k** 2009. **l** Commercially not available. Local Intranet available in country. **m** 2012. **n** 2004.

Democratic Republic of the Congo

Region	Middle Africa	UN membership date	20 September 1960
Population (000, 2018)	84 005[a]	Surface area (km2)	2 344 858[b]
Pop. density (per km2, 2018)	37.1[a]	Sex ratio (m per 100 f)	99.6[a]
Capital city	Kinshasa	National currency	Congolese Franc (CDF)
Capital city pop. (000, 2018)	13 171.3	Exchange rate (per US$)	1 592.2[c]

Economic indicators

	2005	2010	2018
GDP: Gross domestic product (million current US$)	11 965	21 566	40 337[d]
GDP growth rate (annual %, const. 2010 prices)	6.1	7.1	2.4[d]
GDP per capita (current US$)	219.0	334.0	512.0[d]
Economy: Agriculture (% of Gross Value Added)	22.3	22.4	20.6[d]
Economy: Industry (% of Gross Value Added)	32.9	40.5	43.1[d]
Economy: Services and other activity (% of GVA)	44.9	37.0	36.2[d]
Employment in agriculture (% of employed)[e]	81.4	79.6	82.0
Employment in industry (% of employed)[e]	13.0	11.7	11.0
Employment in services & other sectors (% employed)[e]	5.7	8.7	7.0
Unemployment rate (% of labour force)	3.7	3.7[e]	3.7[e]
Labour force participation rate (female/male pop. %)[e]	71.2 / 73.4	71.2 / 73.6	71.4 / 73.5
CPI: Consumer Price Index (2010=100)	59	100	134[d]
Agricultural production index (2004-2006=100)	100	104	109[d]
International trade: exports (million current US$)[e]	2 190	5 300	4 491[c]
International trade: imports (million current US$)[e]	2 268	4 500	5 655[c]
International trade: balance (million current US$)[e]	- 78	800	- 1 165[c]
Balance of payments, current account (million US$)	- 389	- 2 174	- 1 334[d]

Major trading partners

						2017
Export partners (% of exports)[e]	China	37.4	Zambia	15.9	Republic of Korea	9.2
Import partners (% of imports)	China	19.7	South Africa	16.4	Zambia	11.6

Social indicators

	2005	2010	2018
Population growth rate (average annual %)[f]	3.0	3.3	3.3[b]
Urban population (% of total population)	37.5	40.0	44.5
Urban population growth rate (average annual %)[f]	4.3	4.6	4.6[b]
Fertility rate, total (live births per woman)[f]	6.7	6.6	6.4[b]
Life expectancy at birth (females/males, years)[f]	53.3 / 50.4	56.9 / 54.0	59.5 / 56.7[b]
Population age distribution (0-14/60+ years old, %)	45.8 / 4.7	46.1 / 4.7	46.2 / 4.7[a]
International migrant stock (000/% of total pop.)[g]	622.9 / 1.1	589.0 / 0.9	879.2 / 1.1[c]
Refugees and others of concern to the UNHCR (000)	251.9[h]	2 363.9[h]	4 533.4[c]
Infant mortality rate (per 1 000 live births)[f]	99.5	83.9	73.2[b]
Health: Current expenditure (% of GDP)	3.0	4.0	4.3[b]
Health: Physicians (per 1 000 pop.)	...	0.1[i]	...
Education: Government expenditure (% of GDP)	...	1.6	2.3[b]
Education: Primary gross enrol. ratio (f/m per 100 pop.)	59.1 / 74.9	93.1 / 107.0	107.6 / 108.4[b]
Education: Secondary gross enrol. ratio (f/m per 100 pop.)	... / ...	30.1 / 52.2	36.0 / 56.3[b]
Education: Tertiary gross enrol. ratio (f/m per 100 pop.)	... / ...	3.2 / 10.3[i]	4.3 / 9.5[k]
Intentional homicide rate (per 100 000 pop.)	14.6	14.3	13.5[b]
Seats held by women in the National Parliament (%)	12.0	8.4	8.9

Environment and infrastructure indicators

	2005	2010	2018
Individuals using the Internet (per 100 inhabitants)[e]	0.2	0.7	6.2[d]
Research & Development expenditure (% of GDP)[l,m]	0.1[n]	0.1[i]	...
Threatened species (number)	171[o]	296	349[c]
Forested area (% of land area)[e]	68.7	68.0	67.3[b]
CO2 emission estimates (million tons/tons per capita)	1.5 / ~0.0	2.0 / ~0.0	4.7 / 0.1[p]
Energy production, primary (Petajoules)	866	855	1 218[b]
Energy supply per capita (Gigajoules)	14	13	16[b]
Tourist/visitor arrivals at national borders (000)	61	81[q]	191[r,k]
Important sites for terrestrial biodiversity protected (%)	36.6	38.5	40.1
Pop. using improved drinking water (urban/rural, %)	83.5 / 28.2	82.3 / 29.7	81.1 / 31.2[b]
Pop. using improved sanitation facilities (urban/rural, %)	29.2 / 22.2	28.9 / 25.5	28.5 / 28.7[b]
Net Official Development Assist. received (% of GNI)	16.43	17.76	6.57[d]

a Projected estimate (medium fertility variant). b 2015. c 2017. d 2016. e Estimate. f Data refers to a 5-year period preceding the reference year. g Including refugees. h Data as at the end of December. i 2009. j 2002. k 2013. l S&T budget instead of R&D expenditure. m Government only. n Break in the time series. o 2004. p 2014. q Arrivals by air. r The arrivals data relate only to three border posts (N'Djili airport in Kinshasa, the Luano airport in Lubumbashi, and the land border-crossing of Kasumbalesa in Katanga province).

Denmark

Region	Northern Europe
Population (000, 2018)	5 754[a]
Pop. density (per km2, 2018)	135.6[a]
Capital city	Copenhagen
Capital city pop. (000, 2018)	1 320.8[c]

UN membership date	24 October 1945
Surface area (km2)	42 921[b]
Sex ratio (m per 100 f)	99.0[a]
National currency	Danish Krone (DKK)
Exchange rate (per US$)	6.2[d]

Economic indicators	2005	2010	2018
GDP: Gross domestic product (million current US$)	264 467	321 995	306 900[e]
GDP growth rate (annual %, const. 2010 prices)	2.3	1.9	2.0[e]
GDP per capita (current US$)	48 779.0	57 967.0	53 730.0[e]
Economy: Agriculture (% of Gross Value Added)[f]	1.3	1.4	0.9[e]
Economy: Industry (% of Gross Value Added)[f]	26.2	22.8	23.5[e]
Economy: Services and other activity (% of GVA)[f]	72.5	75.8	75.6[e]
Employment in agriculture (% of employed)	3.2	2.4[g]	2.5[g]
Employment in industry (% of employed)[g]	23.9	19.6	18.6
Employment in services & other sectors (% employed)[g]	72.9	78.0	78.8
Unemployment rate (% of labour force)	4.8	7.5	5.9[g]
Labour force participation rate (female/male pop. %)[g]	60.5 / 71.4	59.8 / 69.1	59.1 / 67.0
CPI: Consumer Price Index (2010=100)[h]	90	100	109[d]
Agricultural production index (2004-2006=100)	101	101	101[e]
Index of industrial production (2005=100)	100	86[i]	89[i,j]
International trade: exports (million current US$)	82 278	96 217	101 646[d]
International trade: imports (million current US$)	72 716	82 724	92 248[d]
International trade: balance (million current US$)	9 562	13 492	9 398[d]
Balance of payments, current account (million US$)	11 007[k]	21 051	25 798[d]

Major trading partners						2017
Export partners (% of exports)	Undisclosed[l]	15.0	Germany	14.2[g]	Sweden	10.6
Import partners (% of imports)	Germany	21.4	Sweden	11.9	Netherlands	7.7

Social indicators	2005	2010	2018
Population growth rate (average annual %)[m]	0.3	0.5	0.5[b]
Urban population (% of total population)	85.9	86.8	87.9
Urban population growth rate (average annual %)[m]	0.5	0.7	0.6[b]
Fertility rate, total (live births per woman)[m]	1.8	1.9	1.7[b]
Life expectancy at birth (females/males, years)[m]	79.6 / 75.0	80.8 / 76.4	82.2 / 78.1[b]
Population age distribution (0-14/60+ years old, %)	18.7 / 21.2	17.9 / 23.3	16.4 / 25.6[a]
International migrant stock (000/% of total pop.)	440.4 / 8.1	509.7 / 9.2	656.8 / 11.5[d]
Refugees and others of concern to the UNHCR (000)	45.5[n]	24.5[n]	47.1[d]
Infant mortality rate (per 1 000 live births)[m]	4.5	3.7	3.5[b]
Health: Current expenditure (% of GDP)	9.1	10.4	10.3[b]
Health: Physicians (per 1 000 pop.)	3.2	3.6	3.7[j]
Education: Government expenditure (% of GDP)	8.1	8.6	7.6[j]
Education: Primary gross enrol. ratio (f/m per 100 pop.)	98.7 / 98.8	99.7 / 99.5	101.2 / 102.4[e]
Education: Secondary gross enrol. ratio (f/m per 100 pop.)	126.5 / 121.9	120.0 / 119.0	131.0 / 127.3[e]
Education: Tertiary gross enrol. ratio (f/m per 100 pop.)	93.4 / 67.7	87.4 / 60.4	94.0 / 68.8[e]
Intentional homicide rate (per 100 000 pop.)	1.0	0.8	1.0[e]
Seats held by women in the National Parliament (%)	38.0	38.0	37.4

Environment and infrastructure indicators	2005	2010	2018
Individuals using the Internet (per 100 inhabitants)	82.7[o]	88.7[o]	97.0[e]
Research & Development expenditure (% of GDP)	2.4	2.9	3.0[p,b]
Threatened species (number)	35[q]	33	47[d]
Forested area (% of land area)	13.1	13.8	14.6[g,b]
CO2 emission estimates (million tons/tons per capita)	47.1 / 8.7	46.6 / 8.4	33.5 / 5.9[j]
Energy production, primary (Petajoules)[r]	1 298	968	662[b]
Energy supply per capita (Gigajoules)[r]	145	146	118[b]
Tourist/visitor arrivals at national borders (000)	9 587[k]	9 425	10 781[e]
Important sites for terrestrial biodiversity protected (%)	89.2	89.6	89.7
Pop. using improved drinking water (urban/rural, %)	100.0 / 100.0	100.0 / 100.0	100.0 / 100.0[b]
Pop. using improved sanitation facilities (urban/rural, %)	99.6 / 99.6	99.6 / 99.6	99.6 / 99.6[b]
Net Official Development Assist. disbursed (% of GNI)[s]	0.81	0.91	0.72[p,d]

a Projected estimate (medium fertility variant). b 2015. c Refers to the Greater Copenhagen Region, consisting of (parts of) 16 municipalities. d 2017. e 2016. f Data classified according to ISIC Rev. 4. g Estimate. h Calculated by the Statistics Division of the United Nations from national indices. i Excluding water and waste management. j 2014. k Break in the time series. l Undisclosed (Special categories). m Data refers to a 5-year period preceding the reference year. n Data as at the end of December. o Population aged 16 to 74 years. p Provisional data. q 2004. r Excluding the Faroe Islands and Greenland. s Development Assistance Committee member (OECD).

Djibouti

Region	Eastern Africa
Population (000, 2018)	971 [a]
Pop. density (per km2, 2018)	41.9 [a]
Capital city	Djibouti
Capital city pop. (000, 2018)	561.6 [c]

UN membership date	20 September 1977
Surface area (km2)	23 200 [b]
Sex ratio (m per 100 f)	100.7 [a]
National currency	Djibouti Franc (DJF)
Exchange rate (per US$)	177.7 [d]

Economic indicators	2005	2010	2018
GDP: Gross domestic product (million current US$)	709	1 067	1 892 [e]
GDP growth rate (annual %, const. 2010 prices)	3.2	3.5	6.3 [e]
GDP per capita (current US$)	905.0	1 254.0	2 007.0 [e]
Economy: Agriculture (% of Gross Value Added)	3.6	3.6	3.3 [e]
Economy: Industry (% of Gross Value Added)	16.2	19.0	21.8 [e]
Economy: Services and other activity (% of GVA)	80.2	77.4	74.9 [e]
Employment in agriculture (% of employed) [f]	36.1	33.2	29.0
Employment in industry (% of employed) [f]	24.4	27.4	29.8
Employment in services & other sectors (% employed) [f]	39.6	39.4	41.1
Unemployment rate (% of labour force) [f]	6.4	6.2	5.8
Labour force participation rate (female/male pop. %) [f]	46.7 / 73.8	47.6 / 71.1	49.5 / 68.6
CPI: Consumer Price Index (2010=100)	78	100	116 [d]
Agricultural production index (2004-2006=100)	95	116	133 [e]
International trade: exports (million current US$) [f]	39	470	137 [d]
International trade: imports (million current US$) [f]	277	603	1 094 [d]
International trade: balance (million current US$) [f]	- 238	- 133	- 956 [d]
Balance of payments, current account (million US$)	20	50	- 170 [e]

Major trading partners						2017
Export partners (% of exports) [f]	United States	25.3	Saudi Arabia	19.9	United Arab Emirates	7.3
Import partners (% of imports) [f]	China	50.6	Indonesia	4.5	United Arab Emirates	4.3

Social indicators	2005	2010	2018
Population growth rate (average annual %) [g]	1.8	1.7	1.7 [b]
Urban population (% of total population)	76.8	77.0	77.8
Urban population growth rate (average annual %) [g]	1.8	1.7	1.8 [b]
Fertility rate, total (live births per woman) [g]	4.2	3.6	3.1 [b]
Life expectancy at birth (females/males, years) [g]	58.8 / 55.8	60.5 / 57.6	63.2 / 60.0 [b]
Population age distribution (0-14/60+ years old, %)	37.9 / 5.2	34.8 / 5.8	30.6 / 6.6 [a]
International migrant stock (000/% of total pop.) [h]	92.1 / 11.8	101.6 / 11.9	116.1 / 12.1 [d]
Refugees and others of concern to the UNHCR (000)	18.1 [i]	15.8 [i]	27.2 [d]
Infant mortality rate (per 1 000 live births) [g]	68.1	63.4	55.3 [b]
Health: Current expenditure (% of GDP)	4.5	4.3	4.4 [b]
Health: Physicians (per 1 000 pop.)	0.2	0.2 [j]	0.2 [k]
Education: Government expenditure (% of GDP)	8.4	4.5	...
Education: Primary gross enrol. ratio (f/m per 100 pop.)	39.4 / 47.8	53.0 / 58.9 [i]	60.2 / 67.5 [d]
Education: Secondary gross enrol. ratio (f/m per 100 pop.)	18.3 / 27.4	28.4 / 38.5 [i]	40.1 / 48.1 [d]
Education: Tertiary gross enrol. ratio (f/m per 100 pop.)	1.9 / 2.7	2.8 / 4.1	4.0 / 6.0 [m]
Intentional homicide rate (per 100 000 pop.)	8.1	7.4	6.5 [b]
Seats held by women in the National Parliament (%)	10.8	13.8	10.8

Environment and infrastructure indicators	2005	2010	2018
Individuals using the Internet (per 100 inhabitants)	1.0	6.5 [f]	13.1 [f,a]
Threatened species (number)	21 [n]	81	98 [d]
Forested area (% of land area) [f]	0.2	0.2	0.2 [b]
CO2 emission estimates (million tons/tons per capita)	0.4 / 0.5	0.5 / 0.6	0.7 / 0.8 [k]
Energy production, primary (Petajoules)	3	3	4 [b]
Energy supply per capita (Gigajoules)	11 [f]	13	11 [f,b]
Tourist/visitor arrivals at national borders (000)	30	51	63 [o]
Important sites for terrestrial biodiversity protected (%)	0.0	0.0	0.9
Pop. using improved drinking water (urban/rural, %)	92.5 / 63.3	96.6 / 64.5	97.4 / 64.7 [b]
Pop. using improved sanitation facilities (urban/rural, %)	64.5 / 18.9	60.6 / 7.4	59.8 / 5.1 [b]
Net Official Development Assist. received (% of GNI)	9.56	...	...

a Projected estimate (medium fertility variant). **b** 2015. **c** Refers to the population of the "cercle". **d** 2017. **e** 2016. **f** Estimate. **g** Data refers to a 5-year period preceding the reference year. **h** Including refugees. **i** Data as at the end of December. **j** 2006. **k** 2014. **l** 2009. **m** 2011. **n** 2004. **o** 2013.

Dominica

Region	Caribbean	UN membership date	18 December 1978
Population (000, 2018)	74[a]	Surface area (km2)	750[b]
Pop. density (per km2, 2018)	99.1[a]	Sex ratio (m per 100 f)	103.0[c]
Capital city	Roseau	National currency	E. Caribbean Dollar (XCD)[d]
Capital city pop. (000, 2018)	14.9	Exchange rate (per US$)	2.7[e]

Economic indicators	2005	2010	2018
GDP: Gross domestic product (million current US$)	370	494	581[f]
GDP growth rate (annual %, const. 2010 prices)	- 0.3	1.2	2.6[f]
GDP per capita (current US$)	5 245.0	6 912.0	7 907.0[f]
Economy: Agriculture (% of Gross Value Added)	13.2	13.8	18.0[f]
Economy: Industry (% of Gross Value Added)	15.0	14.4	13.6[f]
Economy: Services and other activity (% of GVA)	71.9	71.8	68.4[f]
Employment in agriculture (% of employed)	21.0[g,h,i]	...	...
Employment in industry (% of employed)	20.0[g,h,i]	...	...
Employment in services & other sectors (% employed)	58.8[g,h,i]	...	...
Unemployment rate (% of labour force)	11.0[i]	...	...
Labour force participation rate (female/male pop. %)	45.0 / 70.2[i]	... / ...	... / ...
CPI: Consumer Price Index (2010=100)	86	100	103[e]
Agricultural production index (2004-2006=100)	99	108	113[f]
International trade: exports (million current US$)	42	34	21[i,e]
International trade: imports (million current US$)	165	225	231[i,e]
International trade: balance (million current US$)	- 124	- 190	- 210[i,e]
Balance of payments, current account (million US$)	- 76	- 80	5[f]

Major trading partners					2017
Export partners (% of exports)	Bahamas	40.3[j]	Indonesia	14.1	Saudi Arabia	6.7[j]
Import partners (% of imports)[j]	United States	57.0	China	8.3	Mexico	7.1

Social indicators	2005	2010	2018
Population growth rate (average annual %)[k]	0.3	0.2	0.5[b]
Urban population (% of total population)	66.6	68.1	70.5
Urban population growth rate (average annual %)[k]	0.7	0.7	0.9[b]
Fertility rate, total (live births per woman)	3.0[i]	...	...
Life expectancy at birth (females/males, years)	... / ...	78.2 / 73.8[f]	... / ...
Population age distribution (0-14/60+ years old, %)	29.0 / 13.2[m,i]	29.5 / 13.3[n]	... / ...
International migrant stock (000/% of total pop.)	4.7 / 6.7	5.8 / 8.1	6.8 / 9.2[e]
Health: Current expenditure (% of GDP)	4.6	5.1	5.4[b]
Health: Physicians (per 1 000 pop.)	1.8[i]	...	...
Education: Government expenditure (% of GDP)	...	...	3.4[b]
Education: Primary gross enrol. ratio (f/m per 100 pop.)	99.4 / 99.4	107.6 / 110.0	110.5 / 114.1[f]
Education: Secondary gross enrol. ratio (f/m per 100 pop.)	111.7 / 103.3	101.4 / 92.8	99.8 / 101.2[b]
Intentional homicide rate (per 100 000 pop.)	11.3	21.0	8.4[o]
Seats held by women in the National Parliament (%)	19.4	14.3	25.0

Environment and infrastructure indicators	2005	2010	2018
Individuals using the Internet (per 100 inhabitants)	38.5[i]	47.4	67.0[i,f]
Threatened species (number)	33[p]	48	66[e]
Forested area (% of land area)[i]	61.3	59.5	57.8[b]
CO2 emission estimates (million tons/tons per capita)	0.1 / 1.7	0.1 / 1.9	0.1 / 1.9[c]
Energy production, primary (Petajoules)	0	0	0[b]
Energy supply per capita (Gigajoules)	31[j]	34	37[j,b]
Tourist/visitor arrivals at national borders (000)	79	77	78[f]
Important sites for terrestrial biodiversity protected (%)	44.3	44.3	44.3
Pop. using improved drinking water (urban/rural, %)	95.7 / 91.8	95.7 / ...	95.7 / ...[b]
Pop. using improved sanitation facilities (urban/rural, %)	79.6 / 84.3	... / ...	... / ...
Net Official Development Assist. received (% of GNI)	6.19	6.71	1.69[f]

a Projected estimate (medium fertility variant). b 2015. c 2014. d East Caribbean Dollar. e 2017. f 2016. g Break in the time series. h Data classified according to ISIC Rev. 2. i 2001. j Estimate. k Data refers to a 5-year period preceding the reference year. l 2008. m Data have not been adjusted for underenumeration, estimated at 1.4 per cent. n 2006. o 2011. p 2004.

Dominican Republic

Region	Caribbean	UN membership date	24 October 1945
Population (000, 2018)	10 883[a]	Surface area (km2)	48 671[b]
Pop. density (per km2, 2018)	225.2[a]	Sex ratio (m per 100 f)	99.1[a]
Capital city	Santo Domingo	National currency	Dominican Peso (DOP)
Capital city pop. (000, 2018)	3 172.2[c]	Exchange rate (per US$)	48.5[d]

Economic indicators

	2005	2010	2018
GDP: Gross domestic product (million current US$)	35 510	53 132	71 584[e]
GDP growth rate (annual %, const. 2010 prices)	9.3	8.3	6.6[e]
GDP per capita (current US$)	3 844.0	5 368.0	6 722.0[e]
Economy: Agriculture (% of Gross Value Added)[f]	7.7	6.4	6.1[e]
Economy: Industry (% of Gross Value Added)[f]	32.5	30.0	28.5[e]
Economy: Services and other activity (% of GVA)[f]	59.8	63.6	65.5[e]
Employment in agriculture (% of employed)	15.3[g]	14.4	11.9[g]
Employment in industry (% of employed)[g]	23.4	18.2	17.6
Employment in services & other sectors (% employed)[g]	61.3	67.4	70.6
Unemployment rate (% of labour force)	6.5	5.0	5.5[g]
Labour force participation rate (female/male pop. %)[g]	48.8 / 81.3	49.3 / 78.7	54.4 / 79.3
CPI: Consumer Price Index (2010=100)[h]	73	100	129[d]
Agricultural production index (2004-2006=100)	98	123	145[e]
Index of industrial production (2005=100)[i]	100	114	129[j]
International trade: exports (million current US$)[k,l]	6 183	4 767	8 856[d]
International trade: imports (million current US$)[k,l]	6 804	15 138	19 524[d]
International trade: balance (million current US$)[k,l]	- 621	- 10 371	- 10 669[d]
Balance of payments, current account (million US$)	- 473	- 4 024[m]	- 165[d]

Major trading partners

						2017
Export partners (% of exports)	United States	53.3	Haiti	9.6	Canada	8.9
Import partners (% of imports)	United States	44.4	China	13.2	Mexico	4.6

Social indicators

	2005	2010	2018
Population growth rate (average annual %)[n]	1.5	1.4	1.2[b]
Urban population (% of total population)	67.4	73.8	81.1
Urban population growth rate (average annual %)[n]	3.3	3.2	2.5[b]
Fertility rate, total (live births per woman)[n]	2.8	2.7	2.5[b]
Life expectancy at birth (females/males, years)[n]	74.4 / 68.1	75.4 / 69.2	76.4 / 70.2[b]
Population age distribution (0-14/60+ years old, %)	33.2 / 8.0	31.4 / 8.7	29.0 / 10.5[a]
International migrant stock (000/% of total pop.)	376.0 / 4.1	393.7 / 4.0	425.0 / 3.9[d]
Refugees and others of concern to the UNHCR (000)	...	2.4[o]	1.4[d]
Infant mortality rate (per 1 000 live births)[n]	34.9	29.6	25.1[b]
Health: Current expenditure (% of GDP)	4.6	5.6	6.2[b]
Health: Physicians (per 1 000 pop.)	1.8[p]	1.1[q]	1.5[r]
Education: Government expenditure (% of GDP)	1.9[g,s]	2.0[t]	...
Education: Primary gross enrol. ratio (f/m per 100 pop.)	103.3 / 108.6	100.5 / 114.1	97.7 / 105.7[e]
Education: Secondary gross enrol. ratio (f/m per 100 pop.)	76.0 / 63.6	80.6 / 71.5	80.7 / 73.7[e]
Education: Tertiary gross enrol. ratio (f/m per 100 pop.)	40.7 / 25.9[e]	... / ...	68.2 / 38.0[e]
Intentional homicide rate (per 100 000 pop.)	25.9	25.0	15.2[e]
Seats held by women in the National Parliament (%)	17.3	19.7	26.8

Environment and infrastructure indicators

	2005	2010	2018
Individuals using the Internet (per 100 inhabitants)	11.5	31.4[g]	61.3[g,e]
Threatened species (number)	104[u]	126	184[d]
Forested area (% of land area)	34.2	37.6	41.0[g,b]
CO2 emission estimates (million tons/tons per capita)	18.6 / 2.0	21.0 / 2.1	21.5 / 2.1[v]
Energy production, primary (Petajoules)	28	27	25[b]
Energy supply per capita (Gigajoules)	29	30	31[b]
Tourist/visitor arrivals at national borders (000)[w]	3 691	4 125	5 959[e]
Important sites for terrestrial biodiversity protected (%)	72.9	72.9	76.2
Pop. using improved drinking water (urban/rural, %)	89.9 / 79.4	87.7 / 80.7	85.4 / 81.9[b]
Pop. using improved sanitation facilities (urban/rural, %)	84.6 / 70.0	85.4 / 72.9	86.2 / 75.7[b]
Net Official Development Assist. received (% of GNI)	0.24	0.34	0.26[e]

a Projected estimate (medium fertility variant). b 2015. c Refers to the urban population of the Municipalities of Santo Domingo de Guzmán, Santo Domingo Este, Santo Domingo Oeste, and Santo Domingo Norte. d 2017. e 2016. f Data classified according to ISIC Rev. 4. g Estimate. h Calculated by the Statistics Division of the United Nations from national indices. i Data classified according to ISIC Rev. 3. j 2013. k Imports FOB. l Export and import values exclude trade in the processing zone. m Break in the time series. n Data refers to a 5-year period preceding the reference year. o Data as at the end of December. p 2000. q 2008. r 2011. s 2003. t 2007. u 2004. v 2014. w Arrivals by air.

Ecuador

Region	South America	UN membership date	21 December 1945
Population (000, 2018)	16 863[a]	Surface area (km2)	257 217[b]
Pop. density (per km2, 2018)	67.9[a]	Sex ratio (m per 100 f)	99.9[a]
Capital city	Quito	National currency	US Dollar (USD)
Capital city pop. (000, 2018)	1 822.4		

Economic indicators

	2005	2010	2018
GDP: Gross domestic product (million current US$)	41 507	69 555	98 010[d]
GDP growth rate (annual %, const. 2010 prices)	5.3	3.5	- 2.2[d]
GDP per capita (current US$)	3 022.0	4 657.0	5 982.0[d]
Economy: Agriculture (% of Gross Value Added)[e]	10.0	10.2	9.6[d]
Economy: Industry (% of Gross Value Added)[e]	33.4	36.3	37.3[d]
Economy: Services and other activity (% of GVA)[e]	56.6	53.5	53.1[d]
Employment in agriculture (% of employed)[f]	29.1[f]	27.9	26.8[f]
Employment in industry (% of employed)[f]	18.5	18.5	18.6
Employment in services & other sectors (% employed)[f]	52.4	53.6	54.6
Unemployment rate (% of labour force)	7.7	4.1	5.1[f]
Labour force participation rate (female/male pop. %)[f]	55.3 / 83.2	49.9 / 80.5	55.0 / 81.2
CPI: Consumer Price Index (2010=100)	80	100	124[c]
Agricultural production index (2004-2006=100)	98	123	115[d]
International trade: exports (million current US$)	9 869	17 490	19 122[c]
International trade: imports (million current US$)	9 609	20 591	19 845[c]
International trade: balance (million current US$)	261	- 3 101	- 722[c]
Balance of payments, current account (million US$)	474	- 1 583	- 255[c]

Major trading partners

							2017
Export partners (% of exports)	United States	31.7	Viet Nam	7.6	Peru	6.7
Import partners (% of imports)	United States	20.0	China	18.6	Colombia	8.1

Social indicators

	2005	2010	2018
Population growth rate (average annual %)[g]	1.7	1.7	1.6[b]
Urban population (% of total population)	61.7	62.7	63.8
Urban population growth rate (average annual %)[g]	2.1	2.0	1.8[b]
Fertility rate, total (live births per woman)[g]	2.9	2.7	2.6[b]
Life expectancy at birth (females/males, years)[g]	76.8 / 70.6	77.5 / 71.7	78.4 / 72.8[b]
Population age distribution (0-14/60+ years old, %)	32.7 / 8.0	30.7 / 8.7	28.2 / 10.7[a]
International migrant stock (000/% of total pop.)[h]	187.4 / 1.4	325.4 / 2.2	399.1 / 2.4[c]
Refugees and others of concern to the UNHCR (000)	262.6[i]	171.1[i]	121.6[c]
Infant mortality rate (per 1 000 live births)[g]	27.1	23.4	21.1[b]
Health: Current expenditure (% of GDP)	5.6	7.5	8.5[b]
Health: Physicians (per 1 000 pop.)	1.5[i]	1.6[k]	1.7[l]
Education: Government expenditure (% of GDP)	1.2[m]	4.5	5.0[b]
Education: Primary gross enrol. ratio (f/m per 100 pop.)	111.5 / 112.0	116.0 / 115.7	104.7 / 103.7[c]
Education: Secondary gross enrol. ratio (f/m per 100 pop.)	62.2 / 61.5	91.0 / 86.6	108.6 / 105.6[c]
Education: Tertiary gross enrol. ratio (f/m per 100 pop.)	... / ...	41.5 / 36.0[n]	49.0 / 42.2[b]
Intentional homicide rate (per 100 000 pop.)	15.4	17.6	5.9[d]
Seats held by women in the National Parliament (%)	16.0	32.3	38.0

Environment and infrastructure indicators

	2005	2010	2018
Individuals using the Internet (per 100 inhabitants)	6.0[f]	29.0[o]	54.1[d]
Research & Development expenditure (% of GDP)	0.1[j]	0.4	0.4[p]
Threatened species (number)	2 151[q]	2 255	2 358[c]
Forested area (% of land area)	53.7	52.1	50.5[f,b]
CO2 emission estimates (million tons/tons per capita)	30.3 / 2.2	36.5 / 2.5	43.9 / 2.8[p]
Energy production, primary (Petajoules)	1 251	1 077	1 297[b]
Energy supply per capita (Gigajoules)	35	38	40[b]
Tourist/visitor arrivals at national borders (000)[r]	860	1 047	1 418[d]
Important sites for terrestrial biodiversity protected (%)	25.5	27.9	29.0
Pop. using improved drinking water (urban/rural, %)	89.8 / 70.2	91.8 / 73.2	93.4 / 75.5[b]
Pop. using improved sanitation facilities (urban/rural, %)	82.2 / 64.1	85.0 / 73.3	87.0 / 80.7[b]
Net Official Development Assist. received (% of GNI)	0.59	0.22	0.25[d]

a Projected estimate (medium fertility variant). b 2015. c 2017. d 2016. e Data classified according to ISIC Rev. 4. f Estimate. g Data refers to a 5-year period preceding the reference year. h Including refugees. i Data as at the end of December. j 2003. k 2009. l 2011. m 2000. n 2008. o Population aged 5 years and over. p 2014. q 2004. r Excluding nationals residing abroad.

Egypt

Region	Northern Africa	UN membership date	24 October 1945
Population (000, 2018)	99 376[a]	Surface area (km2)	1 002 000[b]
Pop. density (per km2, 2018)	99.8[a]	Sex ratio (m per 100 f)	102.3[a]
Capital city	Cairo	National currency	Egyptian Pound (EGP)
Capital city pop. (000, 2018)	20 076.0[c]	Exchange rate (per US$)	17.7[d]

Economic indicators	2005	2010	2018
GDP: Gross domestic product (million current US$)	94 456	214 630	270 144[e]
GDP growth rate (annual %, const. 2010 prices)	4.5	5.1	4.3[e]
GDP per capita (current US$)	1 230.0	2 552.0	2 823.0[e]
Economy: Agriculture (% of Gross Value Added)[f]	14.4	14.0	11.9[e]
Economy: Industry (% of Gross Value Added)[f]	36.9	37.5	32.9[e]
Economy: Services and other activity (% of GVA)[f]	48.8	48.5	55.2[e]
Employment in agriculture (% of employed)[g]	30.9	29.1	24.5
Employment in industry (% of employed)[g]	21.5	24.0	25.6
Employment in services & other sectors (% employed)[g]	47.6	46.9	49.9
Unemployment rate (% of labour force)	11.2	11.8	11.8[g]
Labour force participation rate (female/male pop. %)[g]	20.2 / 73.0	22.8 / 75.8	22.3 / 73.8
CPI: Consumer Price Index (2010=100)[h]	58	100	231[d]
Agricultural production index (2004-2006=100)	99	109	124[e]
International trade: exports (million current US$)[i]	10 646	26 332	25 943[d]
International trade: imports (million current US$)[i]	19 812	53 003	66 339[d]
International trade: balance (million current US$)[i]	- 9 166	- 26 672	- 40 396[d]
Balance of payments, current account (million US$)	2 103	- 4 504	- 9 336[d]

Major trading partners						2017
Export partners (% of exports)	United Arab Emirates	10.6	Italy	8.5	Turkey	7.2
Import partners (% of imports)	China	12.2	Germany	6.8	Italy	6.3

Social indicators	2005	2010	2018
Population growth rate (average annual %)[j]	1.9	1.8	2.2[b]
Urban population (% of total population)	43.0	43.0	42.7
Urban population growth rate (average annual %)[j]	2.0	1.8	2.1[b]
Fertility rate, total (live births per woman)[j]	3.2	3.0	3.4[b]
Life expectancy at birth (females/males, years)[j]	71.4 / 66.6	72.2 / 67.6	73.0 / 68.7[b]
Population age distribution (0-14/60+ years old, %)	33.3 / 7.1	32.1 / 7.5	33.3 / 8.0[a]
International migrant stock (000/% of total pop.)[k]	274.0 / 0.4	295.7 / 0.4	478.3 / 0.5[d]
Refugees and others of concern to the UNHCR (000)	100.2[l]	109.9[l]	278.4[d]
Infant mortality rate (per 1 000 live births)[j]	29.4	23.5	18.9[b]
Health: Current expenditure (% of GDP)	5.2	4.4	4.2[b]
Health: Physicians (per 1 000 pop.)	2.4	2.8[m]	0.8[n]
Education: Government expenditure (% of GDP)	4.8	3.8[o]	...
Education: Primary gross enrol. ratio (f/m per 100 pop.)	94.2 / 99.4	102.0 / 105.1	103.7 / 103.6[e]
Education: Secondary gross enrol. ratio (f/m per 100 pop.)	76.8 / 81.0[g,p]	68.2 / 70.1	85.2 / 86.7[e]
Education: Tertiary gross enrol. ratio (f/m per 100 pop.)	26.8 / 31.8	28.9 / 31.5	34.8 / 34.0[e]
Intentional homicide rate (per 100 000 pop.)	0.7	2.2	2.5[q]
Seats held by women in the National Parliament (%)	2.9	1.8	14.9

Environment and infrastructure indicators	2005	2010	2018
Individuals using the Internet (per 100 inhabitants)	12.8	21.6[r]	39.2[g,e]
Research & Development expenditure (% of GDP)	0.2[s,t]	0.4[u,v]	0.7[b]
Threatened species (number)	46[p]	121	156[d]
Forested area (% of land area)	0.1	0.1[g]	0.1[g,b]
CO2 emission estimates (million tons/tons per capita)	167.2 / 2.2	202.7 / 2.5	201.9 / 2.2[n]
Energy production, primary (Petajoules)	3 383	3 692	3 051[b]
Energy supply per capita (Gigajoules)	37	40	38[b]
Tourist/visitor arrivals at national borders (000)	8 244	14 051	5 258[e]
Important sites for terrestrial biodiversity protected (%)	37.9	39.6	39.6
Pop. using improved drinking water (urban/rural, %)	98.9 / 95.8	99.6 / 97.4	100.0 / 99.0[b]
Pop. using improved sanitation facilities (urban/rural, %)	95.8 / 85.5	96.8 / 93.1	96.8 / 93.1[b]
Net Official Development Assist. received (% of GNI)	1.17	0.28	0.64[e]

a Projected estimate (medium fertility variant). b 2015. c Refers to Greater Cairo as the sum of the Governorate of Al-Qahirah (Cairo) and the surrounding districts of the Governorates of Al-Jizah (Giza) and Al-Qalyūbyah (Qalyubia). d 2017. e 2016. f At factor cost. g Estimate. h Urban areas. i Imports exclude petroleum imported without stated value. Exports cover domestic exports. j Data refers to a 5-year period preceding the reference year. k Including refugees. l Data as at the end of December. m 2009. n 2014. o 2008. p 2004. q 2012. r Population aged 6 years and over. s Government only. t Partial data. u Excluding private non-profit. v Excluding business enterprise.

El Salvador

Region	Central America	UN membership date	24 October 1945
Population (000, 2018)	6 412[a]	Surface area (km2)	21 041 [b,c]
Pop. density (per km2, 2018)	309.4[a]	Sex ratio (m per 100 f)	88.4[a]
Capital city	San Salvador	National currency	US Dollar (USD)
Capital city pop. (000, 2018)	1 106.7[d]		

Economic indicators

	2005	2010	2018
GDP: Gross domestic product (million current US$)	17 094	21 418	26 797[f]
GDP growth rate (annual %, const. 2010 prices)	3.6	1.4	2.4[f]
GDP per capita (current US$)	2 835.0	3 474.0	4 224.0[f]
Economy: Agriculture (% of Gross Value Added)[g]	10.2	12.1	10.6[f]
Economy: Industry (% of Gross Value Added)[g]	28.7	25.9	25.5[f]
Economy: Services and other activity (% of GVA)[g]	61.1	62.1	63.9[f]
Employment in agriculture (% of employed)[h]	20.0	20.8	18.6
Employment in industry (% of employed)[h]	22.2	21.4	21.1
Employment in services & other sectors (% employed)[h]	57.8	57.9	60.3
Unemployment rate (% of labour force)	7.2	4.9	4.6[h]
Labour force participation rate (female/male pop. %)[h]	45.5 / 79.0	46.4 / 79.1	47.3 / 79.1
CPI: Consumer Price Index (2010=100)[i]	84	100	110[e]
Agricultural production index (2004-2006=100)	99	107	111[f]
Index of industrial production (2005=100)[j]	100	106	116[k]
International trade: exports (million current US$)	3 436	4 499	5 760[e]
International trade: imports (million current US$)	6 809	8 416	10 593[e]
International trade: balance (million current US$)	- 3 373	- 3 917	- 4 833[e]
Balance of payments, current account (million US$)	- 622	- 533	- 501[e]

Major trading partners

							2017
Export partners (% of exports)	United States	44.9	Honduras	13.8	Guatemala	13.8
Import partners (% of imports)	United States	31.8	China	13.7	Guatemala	9.9

Social indicators

	2005	2010	2018
Population growth rate (average annual %)[l]	0.5	0.4	0.5[c]
Urban population (% of total population)	61.6	65.5	72.0
Urban population growth rate (average annual %)[l]	1.5	1.6	1.7[c]
Fertility rate, total (live births per woman)[l]	2.7	2.4	2.2[c]
Life expectancy at birth (females/males, years)[l]	74.1 / 65.0	75.6 / 66.4	77.1 / 67.9[c]
Population age distribution (0-14/60+ years old, %)	34.8 / 9.1	31.6 / 10.0	27.1 / 11.8[a]
International migrant stock (000/% of total pop.)[m]	36.0 / 0.6	40.3 / 0.7	42.3 / 0.7[e]
Refugees and others of concern to the UNHCR (000)	0.1[n]	0.1[n]	3.4[e]
Infant mortality rate (per 1 000 live births)[l]	23.6	20.7	17.0[c]
Health: Current expenditure (% of GDP)	7.2	6.9	6.9[c]
Health: Physicians (per 1 000 pop.)	1.7	1.9[c]	
Education: Government expenditure (% of GDP)	2.7[h]	3.5	3.5[f]
Education: Primary gross enrol. ratio (f/m per 100 pop.)	116.6 / 120.7	112.8 / 118.1	98.2 / 102.2[f]
Education: Secondary gross enrol. ratio (f/m per 100 pop.)	68.0 / 68.0	69.2 / 69.6	74.2 / 74.3[f]
Education: Tertiary gross enrol. ratio (f/m per 100 pop.)	24.3 / 21.8	27.5 / 24.9	29.6 / 26.4[f]
Intentional homicide rate (per 100 000 pop.)	64.4	64.7	82.8[f]
Seats held by women in the National Parliament (%)	10.7	19.0	32.1

Environment and infrastructure indicators

	2005	2010	2018
Individuals using the Internet (per 100 inhabitants)	4.2[h,p]	15.9[p]	29.0[h,f]
Research & Development expenditure (% of GDP)	...	0.1	0.1[c]
Threatened species (number)	49[q]	72	86[e]
Forested area (% of land area)[h]	14.9	13.9	12.8[c]
CO2 emission estimates (million tons/tons per capita)	6.5 / 1.1	6.5 / 1.1	6.3 / 1.0[k]
Energy production, primary (Petajoules)	104	95	87[c]
Energy supply per capita (Gigajoules)	31	29	29[c]
Tourist/visitor arrivals at national borders (000)	1 127	1 150	1 434[f]
Important sites for terrestrial biodiversity protected (%)	9.9	22.4	26.6
Pop. using improved drinking water (urban/rural, %)	94.7 / 72.2	96.1 / 79.4	97.5 / 86.5[c]
Pop. using improved sanitation facilities (urban/rural, %)	78.4 / 48.3	80.4 / 54.2	82.4 / 60.0[c]
Net Official Development Assist. received (% of GNI)	1.20	1.35	0.51[f]

a Projected estimate (medium fertility variant). b The total surface is 21 040.79 square kilometres, without taking into account the last ruling of The Hague. c 2015. d Refers to the urban parts of the municipalities San Salvador, Mejicanos, Soyapango, Delgado, Ilopango, Cuscatancingo, Ayutuxtepeque and San Marcos. e 2017. f 2016. g At producers' prices. h Estimate. i Urban areas. j Data classified according to ISIC Rev. 3. k 2014. l Data refers to a 5-year period preceding the reference year. m Including refugees. n Data as at the end of December. o 2008. p Population aged 10 years and over. q 2004.

Equatorial Guinea

Region	Middle Africa	UN membership date	12 November 1968
Population (000, 2018)	1 314[a]	Surface area (km2)	28 052[b]
Pop. density (per km2, 2018)	46.8[a]	Sex ratio (m per 100 f)	124.3[a]
Capital city	Malabo	National currency	CFA Franc, BEAC (XAF)[c]
Capital city pop. (000, 2018)	296.8	Exchange rate (per US$)	546.9[d]

Economic indicators	2005	2010	2018
GDP: Gross domestic product (million current US$)	8 520	16 299	10 678[e]
GDP growth rate (annual %, const. 2010 prices)	8.9	- 8.9	- 8.9[e]
GDP per capita (current US$)	11 250.0	17 136.0	8 742.0[e]
Economy: Agriculture (% of Gross Value Added)	1.5	1.1	2.5[e]
Economy: Industry (% of Gross Value Added)	81.3	74.3	50.0[e]
Economy: Services and other activity (% of GVA)	17.2	24.6	47.5[e]
Employment in agriculture (% of employed)[f]	57.2	54.9	60.4
Employment in industry (% of employed)[f]	6.8	8.0	6.4
Employment in services & other sectors (% employed)[f]	36.1	37.1	33.2
Unemployment rate (% of labour force)[f]	5.7	5.6	7.6
Labour force participation rate (female/male pop. %)[f]	53.8 / 61.5	55.4 / 61.5	55.7 / 61.7
CPI: Consumer Price Index (2010=100)	77	100[g]	121[d]
Agricultural production index (2004-2006=100)	101	109	115[e]
International trade: exports (million current US$)[f]	7 062	9 964	6 196[d]
International trade: imports (million current US$)[f]	1 309	5 679	4 887[d]
International trade: balance (million current US$)[f]	5 753	4 285	1 309[d]

Major trading partners						2017
Export partners (% of exports)[f]	China	16.5	India	12.7	Republic of Korea	11.4
Import partners (% of imports)[f]	Spain	19.6	China	17.6	United States	12.4

Social indicators	2005	2010	2018
Population growth rate (average annual %)[h]	4.2	4.6	4.2[b]
Urban population (% of total population)	57.7	65.9	72.1
Urban population growth rate (average annual %)[h]	7.4	7.2	5.6[b]
Fertility rate, total (live births per woman)[h]	5.7	5.4	5.0[b]
Life expectancy at birth (females/males, years)[h]	54.9 / 52.3	56.2 / 53.8	58.4 / 55.5[b]
Population age distribution (0-14/60+ years old, %)	39.5 / 5.3	38.4 / 4.8	37.0 / 4.4[a]
International migrant stock (000/% of total pop.)[i]	6.6 / 0.9	8.7 / 0.9	221.9 / 17.5[d]
Infant mortality rate (per 1 000 live births)[h]	89.7	80.4	70.0[b]
Health: Current expenditure (% of GDP)[f]	0.8	1.5	2.7[b]
Health: Physicians (per 1 000 pop.)	0.3[j]	...	...
Education: Primary gross enrol. ratio (f/m per 100 pop.)	87.7 / 90.8	68.4 / 69.4	61.3 / 61.8[b]
Education: Secondary gross enrol. ratio (f/m per 100 pop.)	22.0 / 29.8	... / ...	... / ...
Education: Tertiary gross enrol. ratio (f/m per 100 pop.)	1.2 / 2.4[k]	... / ...	... / ...
Intentional homicide rate (per 100 000 pop.)	2.9	2.6	2.3[b]
Seats held by women in the National Parliament (%)	18.0	10.0	20.0

Environment and infrastructure indicators	2005	2010	2018
Individuals using the Internet (per 100 inhabitants)	1.1	6.0	23.8[f,e]
Threatened species (number)	101[j]	130	177[d]
Forested area (% of land area)	60.1	58.0	55.9[b]
CO2 emission estimates (million tons/tons per capita)	4.7 / 7.7	4.7 / 6.4	5.3 / 6.5[l]
Energy production, primary (Petajoules)	823	813	879[b]
Energy supply per capita (Gigajoules)	86	94	84[f,b]
Important sites for terrestrial biodiversity protected (%)	100.0	100.0	100.0
Pop. using improved drinking water (urban/rural, %)	64.1 / 36.7	69.3 / 33.5	72.5 / 31.5[b]
Pop. using improved sanitation facilities (urban/rural, %)	80.4 / 76.4	80.1 / 73.0	79.9 / 71.0[b]
Net Official Development Assist. received (% of GNI)	0.91	0.89	0.10[e]

a Projected estimate (medium fertility variant). b 2015. c African Financial Community (CFA) Franc, Bank of Central African States (BEAC). d 2017. e 2016. f Estimate. g Break in the time series. h Data refers to a 5-year period preceding the reference year. i Refers to foreign citizens. j 2004. k 2000. l 2014.

Eritrea

Region	Eastern Africa	UN membership date	28 May 1993
Population (000, 2018)	5 188[a]	Surface area (km2)	117 600[b]
Pop. density (per km2, 2018)	51.4[a]	Sex ratio (m per 100 f)	100.5[a]
Capital city	Asmara	National currency	Nakfa (ERN)
Capital city pop. (000, 2018)	895.9	Exchange rate (per US$)	15.4[c]

Economic indicators

	2005	2010	2018
GDP: Gross domestic product (million current US$)	1 098	2 117	5 414[d]
GDP growth rate (annual %, const. 2010 prices)	1.5	2.2	3.7[d]
GDP per capita (current US$)	277.0	482.0	1 093.0[d]
Economy: Agriculture (% of Gross Value Added)	24.2	19.1	17.3[d]
Economy: Industry (% of Gross Value Added)	21.9	23.1	23.5[d]
Economy: Services and other activity (% of GVA)	53.9	57.8	59.1[d]
Employment in agriculture (% of employed)[e]	83.7	84.3	83.8
Employment in industry (% of employed)[e]	7.6	7.3	7.0
Employment in services & other sectors (% employed)[e]	8.6	8.4	9.1
Unemployment rate (% of labour force)[e]	7.0	6.8	6.3
Labour force participation rate (female/male pop. %)[e]	73.8 / 84.9	74.7 / 86.6	75.4 / 87.3
Agricultural production index (2004-2006=100)	108	102	104[d]
International trade: exports (million current US$)[e]	11	13	16[c]
International trade: imports (million current US$)[e]	503	1 187	3 949[c]
International trade: balance (million current US$)[e]	- 493	- 1 175	- 3 932[c]

Major trading partners

							2017
Export partners (% of exports)[e]	China	49.2	Republic of Korea	20.2	United Arab Emirates	20.0
Import partners (% of imports)[e]	Egypt	26.7	China	19.1	United Arab Emirates	10.1

Social indicators

	2005	2010	2018
Population growth rate (average annual %)[f]	3.1	2.0	2.0[b]
Urban population (% of total population)	31.1	35.2	40.1
Urban population growth rate (average annual %)[f]	6.3	4.5	3.6[b]
Fertility rate, total (live births per woman)[f]	5.1	4.8	4.4[b]
Life expectancy at birth (females/males, years)[f]	58.8 / 54.7	62.7 / 58.7	65.6 / 61.4[b]
Population age distribution (0-14/60+ years old, %)	41.0 / 5.5	41.6 / 5.5	41.5 / 5.3[a]
International migrant stock (000/% of total pop.)[e]	14.3 / 0.4	15.7 / 0.4	16.0 / 0.3[c]
Refugees and others of concern to the UNHCR (000)	6.0[g]	5.0[g]	2.4[c]
Infant mortality rate (per 1 000 live births)[f]	59.4	51.7	45.0[b]
Health: Current expenditure (% of GDP)[e]	5.3	3.7	3.3[b]
Health: Physicians (per 1 000 pop.)	0.1[h]	...	...
Education: Government expenditure (% of GDP)	3.1[h]	2.1[i]	...
Education: Primary gross enrol. ratio (f/m per 100 pop.)	68.2 / 84.1	48.7 / 57.1	50.0 / 58.0[b]
Education: Secondary gross enrol. ratio (f/m per 100 pop.)	23.0 / 38.4	32.0 / 41.8	30.4 / 35.8[b]
Education: Tertiary gross enrol. ratio (f/m per 100 pop.)	0.3 / 1.9[h]	1.4 / 3.7	1.9 / 2.7[d]
Intentional homicide rate (per 100 000 pop.)	9.6	8.9	8.0[b]
Seats held by women in the National Parliament (%)	22.0	22.0	22.0

Environment and infrastructure indicators

	2005	2010	2018
Individuals using the Internet (per 100 inhabitants)	0.1[i]	0.6[e]	1.2[e,d]
Threatened species (number)	34[h]	97	122[c]
Forested area (% of land area)[e]	15.4	15.2	15.0[b]
CO2 emission estimates (million tons/tons per capita)	0.8 / 0.2	0.5 / 0.1	0.7 / 0.1[k]
Energy production, primary (Petajoules)	21	24	27[b]
Energy supply per capita (Gigajoules)	7	7	7[b]
Tourist/visitor arrivals at national borders (000)[l]	83	84	142[d]
Important sites for terrestrial biodiversity protected (%)	13.3	13.3	13.3
Pop. using improved drinking water (urban/rural, %)	70.2 / 49.8	72.3 / 52.3	73.2 / 53.3[b]
Pop. using improved sanitation facilities (urban/rural, %)	49.8 / 4.4	46.0 / 6.5	44.6 / 7.3[b]
Net Official Development Assist. received (% of GNI)	32.12	7.74	5.16[m]

a Projected estimate (medium fertility variant). **b** 2015. **c** 2017. **d** 2016. **e** Estimate. **f** Data refers to a 5-year period preceding the reference year. **g** Data as at the end of December. **h** 2004. **i** 2006. **j** 2000. **k** 2014. **l** Including nationals residing abroad. **m** 2011.

Estonia

Region	Northern Europe	UN membership date	17 September 1991	
Population (000, 2018)	1 307 [a]	Surface area (km2)	45 227 [b]	
Pop. density (per km2, 2018)	30.8 [a]	Sex ratio (m per 100 f)	88.3 [a]	
Capital city	Tallinn	National currency	Euro (EUR)	
Capital city pop. (000, 2018)	437.0	Exchange rate (per US$)	0.8 [c]	

Economic indicators

	2005	2010	2018
GDP: Gross domestic product (million current US$)	14 003	19 503	23 338 [d]
GDP growth rate (annual %, const. 2010 prices)	9.6	2.3	2.1 [d]
GDP per capita (current US$)	10 330.0	14 640.0	17 782.0 [d]
Economy: Agriculture (% of Gross Value Added) [e]	3.5	3.2	2.6 [d]
Economy: Industry (% of Gross Value Added) [e]	29.8	28.0	26.9 [d]
Economy: Services and other activity (% of GVA) [e]	66.7	68.8	70.5 [d]
Employment in agriculture (% of employed) [f]	5.2	4.2 [f]	3.8 [f]
Employment in industry (% of employed) [f]	34.1	30.3	29.7
Employment in services & other sectors (% employed) [f]	60.7	65.5	66.5
Unemployment rate (% of labour force)	8.0	16.7	6.7 [f]
Labour force participation rate (female/male pop. %) [f]	53.5 / 64.7	55.0 / 67.1	56.2 / 69.9
CPI: Consumer Price Index (2010=100)	79	100	115 [c]
Agricultural production index (2004-2006=100)	103	110	128 [d]
Index of industrial production (2005=100)	100	104 [g]	134 [g,h]
International trade: exports (million current US$)	8 247	12 811	15 353 [c]
International trade: imports (million current US$)	11 018	13 197	17 320 [c]
International trade: balance (million current US$)	- 2 770	- 385	- 1 967 [c]
Balance of payments, current account (million US$)	- 1 386	344	825 [c]

Major trading partners

						2017
Export partners (% of exports)	Finland	15.2	Sweden	12.7	Russian Federation	10.3
Import partners (% of imports)	Finland	10.7	Germany	10.3	China	8.5

Social indicators

	2005	2010	2018
Population growth rate (average annual %) [i]	- 0.6	- 0.4	- 0.3 [b]
Urban population (% of total population)	68.7	68.1	68.9
Urban population growth rate (average annual %) [i]	- 0.8	- 0.5	- 0.2 [b]
Fertility rate, total (live births per woman) [i]	1.4	1.7	1.6 [b]
Life expectancy at birth (females/males, years) [i]	77.1 / 66.0	79.0 / 68.3	81.2 / 71.8 [b]
Population age distribution (0-14/60+ years old, %)	15.2 / 21.9	15.1 / 23.2	16.6 / 26.2 [a]
International migrant stock (000/% of total pop.)	233.7 / 17.2	217.9 / 16.4	193.0 / 14.7 [c]
Refugees and others of concern to the UNHCR (000)	136.0 [j]	101.0 [j]	81.8 [c]
Infant mortality rate (per 1 000 live births) [i]	7.3	4.7	3.2 [b]
Health: Current expenditure (% of GDP)	5.0	6.3	6.5 [b]
Health: Physicians (per 1 000 pop.)	4.4 [k]	3.2	3.4 [b]
Education: Government expenditure (% of GDP)	4.8	5.5	5.5 [h]
Education: Primary gross enrol. ratio (f/m per 100 pop.)	97.6 / 100.2	102.3 / 103.8	97.0 / 96.9 [b]
Education: Secondary gross enrol. ratio (f/m per 100 pop.)	104.7 / 101.0	105.3 / 105.3	110.7 / 111.1 [b]
Education: Tertiary gross enrol. ratio (f/m per 100 pop.)	85.8 / 50.9	85.9 / 51.6	87.4 / 57.6 [b]
Intentional homicide rate (per 100 000 pop.)	8.3	5.3	3.2 [b]
Seats held by women in the National Parliament (%)	18.8	22.8	26.7

Environment and infrastructure indicators

	2005	2010	2018
Individuals using the Internet (per 100 inhabitants)	61.4 [l]	74.1 [i,m]	87.2 [d]
Research & Development expenditure (% of GDP)	0.9	1.6	1.5 [n,b]
Threatened species (number)	12 [o]	11	23 [c]
Forested area (% of land area)	53.1	52.7	52.7 [f,b]
CO2 emission estimates (million tons/tons per capita)	16.8 / 12.4	18.1 / 13.6	19.5 / 14.8 [h]
Energy production, primary (Petajoules)	163	205	233 [b]
Energy supply per capita (Gigajoules)	164	177	176 [b]
Tourist/visitor arrivals at national borders (000) [p]	1 917 [q]	2 372 [r]	3 147 [r,d]
Important sites for terrestrial biodiversity protected (%)	94.7	94.8	94.9
Pop. using improved drinking water (urban/rural, %)	99.8 / 97.9	99.9 / 98.5	100.0 / 99.0 [b]
Pop. using improved sanitation facilities (urban/rural, %)	97.5 / 96.1	97.5 / 96.4	97.5 / 96.6 [b]
Net Official Development Assist. disbursed (% of GNI)	0.08	0.10	0.17 [n,c]

a Projected estimate (medium fertility variant). **b** 2015. **c** 2017. **d** 2016. **e** Data classified according to ISIC Rev. 4. **f** Estimate. **g** Excluding water and waste management. **h** 2014. **i** Data refers to a 5-year period preceding the reference year. **j** Data as at the end of December. **k** 2000. **l** Population aged 16 to 74 years. **m** Users in the last 3 months. **n** Provisional data. **o** 2004. **p** Border statistics are not collected any more, surveys used instead. **q** Calculated on the basis of accommodation statistics and "Foreign Visitor Survey" carried out by the Statistical Office of Estonia. **r** Based on mobile positioning data.

Eswatini

Region	Southern Africa	UN membership date	24 September 1968
Population (000, 2018)	1 391 [a]	Surface area (km2)	17 363 [b]
Pop. density (per km2, 2018)	80.9 [a]	Sex ratio (m per 100 f)	93.9 [a]
Capital city	Mbabane [c]	National currency	Lilangeni (SZL)
Capital city pop. (000, 2018)	68.0 [c]	Exchange rate (per US$)	12.3 [d]

Economic indicators

	2005	2010	2018
GDP: Gross domestic product (million current US$)	3 176	4 436	4 007 [e]
GDP growth rate (annual %, const. 2010 prices)	1.8	3.8	--0.0 [e]
GDP per capita (current US$)	2 872.0	3 688.0	2 983.0 [e]
Economy: Agriculture (% of Gross Value Added) [f]	11.3	10.4	10.0 [e]
Economy: Industry (% of Gross Value Added) [f]	40.8	38.7	36.9 [e]
Economy: Services and other activity (% of GVA) [f]	47.9	50.9	53.1 [e]
Employment in agriculture (% of employed) [g]	69.1	68.3	69.4
Employment in industry (% of employed) [g]	14.5	13.7	12.2
Employment in services & other sectors (% employed) [g]	16.4	18.0	18.4
Unemployment rate (% of labour force) [g]	22.1	27.8	26.4
Labour force participation rate (female/male pop. %) [g]	38.8 / 68.0	40.3 / 66.3	42.9 / 67.4
CPI: Consumer Price Index (2010=100)	69	100	155 [d]
Agricultural production index (2004-2006=100)	103	106	113 [e]
Index of industrial production (2005=100)	...	132	153 [h]
International trade: exports (million current US$)	1 278	1 557 [g]	1 588 [g,d]
International trade: imports (million current US$)	1 656	1 710 [g]	483 [g,d]
International trade: balance (million current US$)	- 378	- 153 [g]	1 106 [g,d]
Balance of payments, current account (million US$)	- 103	- 388	640 [e]

Major trading partners

						2017
Export partners (% of exports) [g]	South Africa	66.2	Nigeria	5.1	Zimbabwe	2.2
Import partners (% of imports) [g]	South Africa	78.7	Guinea	3.8	China	2.8

Social indicators

	2005	2010	2018
Population growth rate (average annual %) [i]	0.8	1.7	1.8 [b]
Urban population (% of total population)	22.0	22.5	23.8
Urban population growth rate (average annual %) [i]	0.2	2.1	2.6 [b]
Fertility rate, total (live births per woman) [i]	4.0	3.8	3.3 [b]
Life expectancy at birth (females/males, years) [i]	47.6 / 44.2	50.2 / 46.5	58.2 / 51.6 [b]
Population age distribution (0-14/60+ years old, %)	42.1 / 4.6	39.5 / 4.7	37.0 / 4.9 [a]
International migrant stock (000/% of total pop.) [j]	27.1 / 2.5	30.5 / 2.5	33.3 / 2.4 [d]
Refugees and others of concern to the UNHCR (000)	1.0 [k]	0.8 [k]	1.2 [d]
Infant mortality rate (per 1 000 live births) [i]	86.6	75.8	56.3 [b]
Health: Current expenditure (% of GDP)	5.9	8.2	7.0 [b]
Health: Physicians (per 1 000 pop.)	0.2 [l]	0.1 [m]	
Education: Government expenditure (% of GDP)	6.5	6.1	7.1 [h]
Education: Primary gross enrol. ratio (f/m per 100 pop.)	99.1 / 106.2	107.9 / 118.2	102.9 / 112.8 [b]
Education: Secondary gross enrol. ratio (f/m per 100 pop.)	47.5 / 46.9	57.7 / 58.2	66.8 / 67.3 [b]
Education: Tertiary gross enrol. ratio (f/m per 100 pop.)	4.9 / 4.6	4.4 / 4.5 [n]	5.5 / 5.3 [o]
Intentional homicide rate (per 100 000 pop.)	13.7	17.3	...
Seats held by women in the National Parliament (%)	10.8	13.6	6.2

Environment and infrastructure indicators

	2005	2010	2018
Individuals using the Internet (per 100 inhabitants)	3.7 [g]	11.0	28.6 [g,e]
Threatened species (number)	23 [l]	29	34 [d]
Forested area (% of land area) [g]	31.5	32.7	34.1 [b]
CO2 emission estimates (million tons/tons per capita)	1.0 / 0.9	1.0 / 0.9	1.2 / 1.0 [h]
Energy production, primary (Petajoules)	36	33	38 [b]
Energy supply per capita (Gigajoules)	36	37	38 [b]
Tourist/visitor arrivals at national borders (000)	837	868	947 [e]
Important sites for terrestrial biodiversity protected (%)	30.0	30.0	30.3
Pop. using improved drinking water (urban/rural, %)	90.8 / 52.7	92.8 / 64.2	93.6 / 68.9 [b]
Pop. using improved sanitation facilities (urban/rural, %)	62.9 / 51.7	63.0 / 54.7	63.1 / 56.0 [b]
Net Official Development Assist. received (% of GNI)	1.39	2.16	4.14 [e]

a Projected estimate (medium fertility variant). b 2015. c Mbabane is the administrative capital and Lobamba is the legislative capital. d 2017. e 2016. f Data classified according to ISIC Rev. 4. g Estimate. h 2014. i Data refers to a 5-year period preceding the reference year. j Including refugees. k Data as at the end of December. l 2004. m 2009. n 2006. o 2013.

Ethiopia

Region	Eastern Africa	UN membership date	13 November 1945
Population (000, 2018)	107 535[a]	Surface area (km2)	1 104 300[b]
Pop. density (per km2, 2018)	107.5[a]	Sex ratio (m per 100 f)	99.7[a]
Capital city	Addis Ababa	National currency	Ethiopian Birr (ETB)
Capital city pop. (000, 2018)	4 399.7	Exchange rate (per US$)	27.6[c]

Economic indicators	2005	2010	2018
GDP: Gross domestic product (million current US$)	12 164	26 311	70 315[d]
GDP growth rate (annual %, const. 2010 prices)	11.8	12.6	7.6[d]
GDP per capita (current US$)	159.0	300.0	687.0[d]
Economy: Agriculture (% of Gross Value Added)	45.2	45.3	36.8[d]
Economy: Industry (% of Gross Value Added)	13.1	10.4	21.0[d]
Economy: Services and other activity (% of GVA)	41.7	44.3	42.2[d]
Employment in agriculture (% of employed)[e]	80.2	77.2	67.3
Employment in industry (% of employed)[e]	6.6	6.3	9.6
Employment in services & other sectors (% employed)[e]	13.1	16.6	23.1
Unemployment rate (% of labour force)[e]	5.4	5.2	5.3
Labour force participation rate (female/male pop. %)[e]	78.4 / 90.8	77.5 / 90.0	77.4 / 87.9
CPI: Consumer Price Index (2010=100)[e]	45[f]	100	249[c]
Agricultural production index (2004-2006=100)	102	138	164[d]
Index of industrial production (2005=100)[g,h]	100	159	242[i]
International trade: exports (million current US$)	926	2 330	1 385[e,c]
International trade: imports (million current US$)	4 095	8 602	16 252[e,c]
International trade: balance (million current US$)	- 3 169	- 6 272	- 14 867[e,c]
Balance of payments, current account (million US$)	- 1 568	- 425	- 8 269[d]

Major trading partners						2017
Export partners (% of exports)[e]	United States	9.8[e]	Saudi Arabia	9.7	Germany	8.6[e]
Import partners (% of imports)[e]	China	31.9	United States	8.8	India	7.5

Social indicators	2005	2010	2018
Population growth rate (average annual %)[j]	2.8	2.7	2.6[b]
Urban population (% of total population)	15.7	17.3	20.8
Urban population growth rate (average annual %)[j]	4.1	4.6	4.9[b]
Fertility rate, total (live births per woman)[j]	6.1	5.3	4.6[b]
Life expectancy at birth (females/males, years)[j]	55.0 / 52.3	60.6 / 57.6	65.5 / 61.9[b]
Population age distribution (0-14/60+ years old, %)	46.2 / 4.9	44.5 / 5.1	40.0 / 5.3[a]
International migrant stock (000/% of total pop.)[k]	514.2 / 0.7	567.7 / 0.6	1 227.1 / 1.2[c]
Refugees and others of concern to the UNHCR (000)	105.1[l]	155.4[l]	843.8[c]
Infant mortality rate (per 1 000 live births)[j]	78.0	59.9	45.8[b]
Health: Current expenditure (% of GDP)	4.1	5.5	4.0[b]
Health: Physicians (per 1 000 pop.)	~0.0	~0.0[m]	
Education: Government expenditure (% of GDP)	3.6[e,n]	4.5	4.5[i]
Education: Primary gross enrol. ratio (f/m per 100 pop.)	71.9 / 86.0	88.1 / 95.4	97.0 / 106.8[b]
Education: Secondary gross enrol. ratio (f/m per 100 pop.)	18.5 / 30.8	31.5 / 38.0	34.4 / 35.8[b]
Education: Tertiary gross enrol. ratio (f/m per 100 pop.)	1.3 / 4.2	4.4 / 10.2	5.3 / 10.9[o]
Intentional homicide rate (per 100 000 pop.)	9.4	8.5	7.6[b]
Seats held by women in the National Parliament (%)	7.7	21.9	38.8

Environment and infrastructure indicators	2005	2010	2018
Individuals using the Internet (per 100 inhabitants)	0.2	0.8[e]	15.4[d]
Research & Development expenditure (% of GDP)	0.2[p]	0.2[f]	0.6[i]
Threatened species (number)	93[q]	120	148[c]
Forested area (% of land area)[e]	13.0	12.3	12.5[b]
CO2 emission estimates (million tons/tons per capita)	5.1 / 0.1	6.6 / 0.1	11.6 / 0.1[o]
Energy production, primary (Petajoules)	1 070	1 212	1 334[b]
Energy supply per capita (Gigajoules)	15	15	15[b]
Tourist/visitor arrivals at national borders (000)	227	468	871[d]
Important sites for terrestrial biodiversity protected (%)	18.6	19.8	19.8
Pop. using improved drinking water (urban/rural, %)	89.1 / 28.8	91.1 / 38.7	93.1 / 48.6[b]
Pop. using improved sanitation facilities (urban/rural, %)	24.3 / 13.5	25.7 / 20.9	27.2 / 28.2[b]
Net Official Development Assist. received (% of GNI)	15.60	11.58	5.65[d]

a Projected estimate (medium fertility variant). b 2015. c 2017. d 2016. e Estimate. f Break in the time series. g Data classified according to ISIC Rev. 3. h Twelve months ending 30 June of the year stated. i 2013. j Data refers to a 5-year period preceding the reference year. k Including refugees. l Data as at the end of December. m 2009. n 2002. o 2014. p Partial data. q 2004.

Falkland Islands (Malvinas)

Region	South America	Population (000, 2018)	3[a,b]
Surface area (km2)	12 173[b,c]	Pop. density (per km2, 2018)	0.2[a,b]
Sex ratio (m per 100 f)	110.5[b,d,e]	Capital city	Stanley
National currency	Falkland Islands Pound (FKP)	Capital city pop. (000, 2018)	2.3[b]
Exchange rate (per US$)	0.7[f]		

Economic indicators	2005	2010	2018
Unemployment rate (% of labour force)	...	...	1.2[g,h]
Labour force participation rate (female/male pop. %)	... / ...	... / ...	77.2 / 86.0[g,i,h]
Agricultural production index (2004-2006=100)	103	96	96[i]
International trade: exports (million current US$)[k]	11	9	3[f]
International trade: imports (million current US$)[k]	8	50	13[f]
International trade: balance (million current US$)[k]	2	- 41	- 10[f]

Major trading partners						2017
Export partners (% of exports)	Spain	72.6[k]	Namibia	12.5	United States	5.0[k]
Import partners (% of imports)[k]	United Kingdom	47.9	Spain	28.7	Greece	10.6

Social indicators	2005	2010	2018
Population growth rate (average annual %)[l]	0.4	- 0.6	0.3[c]
Urban population (% of total population)[b]	70.8	73.7	77.7
Urban population growth rate (average annual %)[b,l]	1.3	0.2	1.0[c]
Population age distribution (0-14/60+ years old, %)[b]	15.0 / 12.0[m]	15.9 / 14.0[n]	16.4 / 15.7[d,e]
International migrant stock (000/% of total pop.)	1.2 / 39.7	1.4 / 50.4	1.6 / 54.3[f]

Environment and infrastructure indicators	2005	2010	2018
Individuals using the Internet (per 100 inhabitants)	84.0[k]	95.8	99.0[k,l]
Threatened species (number)	26[o]	23	23[f]
Forested area (% of land area)[k]	0.0	0.0	0.0[c]
CO2 emission estimates (million tons/tons per capita)	0.1 / 17.5	0.1 / 19.1	0.1 / 18.9[p]
Energy production, primary (Petajoules)[k]	0	0	0[c]
Energy supply per capita (Gigajoules)[k]	235	261	257[c]
Important sites for terrestrial biodiversity protected (%)	10.9	10.9	10.9

a Projected estimate (medium fertility variant). **b** A dispute exists between the Governments of Argentina and the United Kingdom of Great Britain and Northern Ireland concerning sovereignty over the Falkland Islands (Malvinas). **c** 2015. **d** Excluding military personnel and their families, visitors and transients. **e** 2012. **f** 2017. **g** Population aged 16 to 65 years. **h** 2013. **i** Break in the time series. **j** 2016. **k** Estimate. **l** Data refers to a 5-year period preceding the reference year. **m** 2001. **n** 2006. **o** 2004. **p** 2014.

Faroe Islands

Region	Northern Europe	Population (000, 2018)	50[a]
Surface area (km2)	1 393[b]	Pop. density (per km2, 2018)	35.5[a]
Sex ratio (m per 100 f)	107.2[c,b]	Capital city	Tórshavn
National currency	Danish Krone (DKK)	Capital city pop. (000, 2018)	20.8
Exchange rate (per US$)	6.2[d]		

Economic indicators	2005	2010	2018
Employment in agriculture (% of employed)	11.1[e,f]	...	...
Employment in industry (% of employed)	22.2[e,f]	...	...
Employment in services & other sectors (% employed)	66.7[e,f]	...	...
Unemployment rate (% of labour force)	3.2[e]	6.4[g,h,i]	4.0[g,h,j]
Labour force participation rate (female/male pop. %)[g,h]	... / ...	77.5 / 85.3	79.4 / 86.0[j]
Agricultural production index (2004-2006=100)	100	100	101[k]
International trade: exports (million current US$)	602	839[l]	1 405[l,d]
International trade: imports (million current US$)	747	780[l]	1 066[l,d]
International trade: balance (million current US$)	- 145	59[l]	338[l,d]
Balance of payments, current account (million US$)	31	144	...

Major trading partners						2017
Export partners (% of exports)[l]	Russian Federation	24.1	United Kingdom	17.5	Denmark	13.5
Import partners (% of imports)[l]	Denmark	59.9	Norway	11.5	Germany	6.2

Social indicators	2005	2010	2018
Population growth rate (average annual %)[m]	0.4	0.1	0.2[b]
Urban population (% of total population)	39.8	40.9	42.1
Urban population growth rate (average annual %)[m]	2.2	0.7	0.5[b]
Fertility rate, total (live births per woman)	2.6	2.5	2.4[b]
Life expectancy at birth (females/males, years)	... / ...	82.3 / 76.8[n]	84.5 / 78.3[o,k]
Population age distribution (0-14/60+ years old, %)[c]	... / ...	22.0 / 19.3[n]	21.0 / 22.5[b]
International migrant stock (000/% of total pop.)	4.6 / 9.5	5.1 / 10.5	5.7 / 11.6[d]

Environment and infrastructure indicators	2005	2010	2018
Individuals using the Internet (per 100 inhabitants)	67.9[l]	75.2	95.1[l,k]
Research & Development expenditure (% of GDP)	0.9[p]	...	...
Threatened species (number)	11[q]	13	21[d]
Forested area (% of land area)[l]	0.1	0.1	0.1[b]
CO2 emission estimates (million tons/tons per capita)	0.7 / 15.0	0.6 / 12.9	0.6 / 12.4[r]
Energy production, primary (Petajoules)	0	0	1[b]
Energy supply per capita (Gigajoules)[l]	216	184	188[b]
Important sites for terrestrial biodiversity protected (%)	0.0	0.0	6.7

a Projected estimate (medium fertility variant). b 2015. c De jure population. d 2017. e Population aged 16 years and over. f Data classified according to ISIC Rev. 2. g Excluding the institutional population. h Population aged 15 to 74 years. i Break in the time series. j 2013. k 2016. l Estimate. m Data refers to a 5-year period preceding the reference year. n 2008. o Data refers to a 2-year period up to and including the reference year. p 2003. q 2004. r 2014.

Fiji

Region	Melanesia	UN membership date	13 October 1970
Population (000, 2018)	912[a]	Surface area (km2)	18 272[b]
Pop. density (per km2, 2018)	49.9[a]	Sex ratio (m per 100 f)	102.9[a]
Capital city	Suva	National currency	Fiji Dollar (FJD)
Capital city pop. (000, 2018)	178.3	Exchange rate (per US$)	2.1[c]

Economic indicators	2005	2010	2018
GDP: Gross domestic product (million current US$)	2 980	3 140	4 671[d]
GDP growth rate (annual %, const. 2010 prices)	0.7	3.0	0.4[d]
GDP per capita (current US$)	3 627.0	3 652.0	5 197.0[d]
Economy: Agriculture (% of Gross Value Added)[e]	12.8	10.2	13.6[d]
Economy: Industry (% of Gross Value Added)[e]	17.9	19.9	17.5[d]
Economy: Services and other activity (% of GVA)[e]	69.2	69.9	68.9[d]
Employment in agriculture (% of employed)[f]	44.2	42.9	38.6
Employment in industry (% of employed)[f]	13.4	13.7	13.2
Employment in services & other sectors (% employed)[f]	42.4	43.4	48.1
Unemployment rate (% of labour force)	4.6	8.9	6.2[f]
Labour force participation rate (female/male pop. %)[f]	38.1 / 73.8	39.0 / 73.9	40.7 / 75.2
CPI: Consumer Price Index (2010=100)[h]	81[g]	100	125[c]
Agricultural production index (2004-2006=100)	99	81	84[d]
Index of industrial production (2005=100)[i]	100	101	104[j]
International trade: exports (million current US$)	702	841	956[c]
International trade: imports (million current US$)	1 607	1 808	2 420[c]
International trade: balance (million current US$)	- 906	- 967	- 1 464[c]
Balance of payments, current account (million US$)	- 206[g]	- 149	- 315[c]

Major trading partners						2017
Export partners (% of exports)	United States	19.4	Australia	15.4	New Zealand	6.8
Import partners (% of imports)	Singapore	19.1	New Zealand	17.2	Australia	16.6

Social indicators	2005	2010	2018
Population growth rate (average annual %)[k]	0.3	0.9	0.7[b]
Urban population (% of total population)	49.9	52.2	56.2
Urban population growth rate (average annual %)[k]	1.1	1.8	1.7[b]
Fertility rate, total (live births per woman)[k]	3.0	2.8	2.6[b]
Life expectancy at birth (females/males, years)[k]	70.7 / 65.5	71.9 / 66.1	72.9 / 66.9[b]
Population age distribution (0-14/60+ years old, %)	30.5 / 6.9	29.0 / 7.9	28.3 / 10.3[a]
International migrant stock (000/% of total pop.)	12.4 / 1.5	13.4 / 1.6	13.9 / 1.5[c]
Refugees and others of concern to the UNHCR (000)	...	~0.0[l]	~0.0[c]
Infant mortality rate (per 1 000 live births)[k]	19.0	17.9	16.0[b]
Health: Current expenditure (% of GDP)[m]	3.5	3.6	3.6[b]
Health: Physicians (per 1 000 pop.)	0.5[n]	0.4[o]	0.8[b]
Education: Government expenditure (% of GDP)	5.1	4.5[o]	3.9[p]
Education: Primary gross enrol. ratio (f/m per 100 pop.)	111.8 / 113.4[q]	104.3 / 105.9[o]	105.1 / 106.0[b]
Education: Secondary gross enrol. ratio (f/m per 100 pop.)	93.9 / 88.0[q]	90.9 / 83.1[o]	93.4 / 84.3[r]
Education: Tertiary gross enrol. ratio (f/m per 100 pop.)	17.6 / 14.7[f]	... / ...	... / ...
Intentional homicide rate (per 100 000 pop.)	2.8	2.3	2.3[s]
Seats held by women in the National Parliament (%)	8.5	8.5[t]	16.0

Environment and infrastructure indicators	2005	2010	2018
Individuals using the Internet (per 100 inhabitants)	8.5	20.0[f]	46.5[f,d]
Threatened species (number)	101[q]	192	291[c]
Forested area (% of land area)[f]	54.6	54.3	55.7[b]
CO2 emission estimates (million tons/tons per capita)	1.1 / 1.3	1.2 / 1.4	1.2 / 1.3[s]
Energy production, primary (Petajoules)	9	6	8[b]
Energy supply per capita (Gigajoules)	29	25	43[b]
Tourist/visitor arrivals at national borders (000)[u]	545	632	792[d]
Important sites for terrestrial biodiversity protected (%)	3.3	4.9	4.9
Pop. using improved drinking water (urban/rural, %)	98.0 / 87.9	99.3 / 90.7	99.5 / 91.2[b]
Pop. using improved sanitation facilities (urban/rural, %)	91.1 / 73.6	93.0 / 86.0	93.4 / 88.4[b]
Net Official Development Assist. received (% of GNI)	2.17	2.49	2.65[d]

a Projected estimate (medium fertility variant). **b** 2015. **c** 2017. **d** 2016. **e** Data classified according to ISIC Rev. 4. **f** Estimate. **g** Break in the time series. **h** Calculated by the Statistics Division of the United Nations from national indices. **i** Data classified according to ISIC Rev. 3. **j** 2011. **k** Data refers to a 5-year period preceding the reference year. **l** Data as at the end of December. **m** Data revision. **n** 2003. **o** 2009. **p** 2013. **q** 2004. **r** 2012. **s** 2014. **t** 2006. **u** Excluding nationals residing abroad.

Finland

Region	Northern Europe	UN membership date	14 December 1955
Population (000, 2018)	5 542[a,b]	Surface area (km2)	338 440[b,c]
Pop. density (per km2, 2018)	18.2[a,b]	Sex ratio (m per 100 f)	97.3[a,b]
Capital city	Helsinki	National currency	Euro (EUR)
Capital city pop. (000, 2018)	1 279.1	Exchange rate (per US$)	0.8[d]

Economic indicators

	2005	2010	2018
GDP: Gross domestic product (million current US$)	204 431	247 800	238 503[e]
GDP growth rate (annual %, const. 2010 prices)	2.8	3.0	1.9[e]
GDP per capita (current US$)	38 873.0	46 181.0	43 339.0[e]
Economy: Agriculture (% of Gross Value Added)[f]	2.6	2.7	2.7[e]
Economy: Industry (% of Gross Value Added)[f]	33.5	30.0	27.1[e]
Economy: Services and other activity (% of GVA)[f]	63.8	67.3	70.2[e]
Employment in agriculture (% of employed)[g]	4.8	4.4[g]	3.8[g]
Employment in industry (% of employed)[g]	25.8	23.3	22.1
Employment in services & other sectors (% employed)[g]	69.4	72.3	74.1
Unemployment rate (% of labour force)	8.4	8.4	8.6[g]
Labour force participation rate (female/male pop. %)[g]	56.6 / 64.8	56.0 / 63.9	54.7 / 61.7
CPI: Consumer Price Index (2010=100)[h]	91	100	110[d]
Agricultural production index (2004-2006=100)	102	94	97[e]
Index of industrial production (2005=100)	100	100	94[i]
International trade: exports (million current US$)	65 238	70 117	67 281[d]
International trade: imports (million current US$)	58 473	68 767	70 100[d]
International trade: balance (million current US$)	6 766	1 349	- 2 820[d]
Balance of payments, current account (million US$)	7 788[j]	2 792	1 917[d]

Major trading partners

						2017
Export partners (% of exports)	Germany	14.0	Sweden	10.2[g]	Netherlands	6.7
Import partners (% of imports)	Germany	15.2	Russian Federation	13.1	Sweden	10.9

Social indicators

	2005	2010	2018
Population growth rate (average annual %)[b,k]	0.3	0.4	0.4[c]
Urban population (% of total population)[b]	82.9	83.8	85.4
Urban population growth rate (average annual %)[b,k]	0.4	0.6	0.8[c]
Fertility rate, total (live births per woman)[b,k]	1.8	1.8	1.8[c]
Life expectancy at birth (females/males, years)[b,k]	81.7 / 74.9	82.9 / 76.1	83.7 / 77.7[c]
Population age distribution (0-14/60+ years old, %)[b]	17.3 / 21.5	16.5 / 24.8	16.5 / 28.1[a]
International migrant stock (000/% of total pop.)[b]	192.2 / 3.7	248.1 / 4.6	343.6 / 6.2[d]
Refugees and others of concern to the UNHCR (000)	12.7[l]	14.0[l]	26.1[d]
Infant mortality rate (per 1 000 live births)[b,k]	3.2	2.7	2.3[c]
Health: Current expenditure (% of GDP)	8.0	8.9	9.4[c]
Health: Physicians (per 1 000 pop.)	3.2[m]	3.0	3.2[i]
Education: Government expenditure (% of GDP)	6.0	6.5	7.2[i]
Education: Primary gross enrol. ratio (f/m per 100 pop.)	98.0 / 98.8	99.2 / 99.8	100.2 / 100.6[e]
Education: Secondary gross enrol. ratio (f/m per 100 pop.)	114.3 / 109.3	110.1 / 105.2	159.7 / 145.0[e]
Education: Tertiary gross enrol. ratio (f/m per 100 pop.)	100.5 / 83.3	103.1 / 84.3	94.5 / 79.8[e]
Intentional homicide rate (per 100 000 pop.)	2.3	2.2	1.4[e]
Seats held by women in the National Parliament (%)	37.5	40.0	42.0

Environment and infrastructure indicators

	2005	2010	2018
Individuals using the Internet (per 100 inhabitants)	74.5[n]	86.9[n]	87.7[o,e]
Research & Development expenditure (% of GDP)	3.3	3.7	2.9[c]
Threatened species (number)	25[p]	18	36[d]
Forested area (% of land area)	72.7	73.1	73.1[c]
CO2 emission estimates (million tons/tons per capita)	54.6 / 10.4	62.1 / 11.6	47.3 / 8.6[i]
Energy production, primary (Petajoules)	699	727	734[c]
Energy supply per capita (Gigajoules)	273	284	245[c]
Tourist/visitor arrivals at national borders (000)	2 080[j]	2 319	2 789[e]
Important sites for terrestrial biodiversity protected (%)	72.0	72.2	72.6
Pop. using improved drinking water (urban/rural, %)	100.0 / 100.0	100.0 / 100.0	100.0 / 100.0[c]
Pop. using improved sanitation facilities (urban/rural, %)	99.4 / 88.1	99.4 / 88.1	99.4 / 88.0[c]
Net Official Development Assist. disbursed (% of GNI)[q]	0.46	0.55	0.41[r,d]

a Projected estimate (medium fertility variant). b Including Åland Islands. c 2015. d 2017. e 2016. f Data classified according to ISIC Rev. 4. g Estimate. h Calculated by the Statistics Division of the United Nations from national indices. i 2014. j Break in the time series. k Data refers to a 5-year period preceding the reference year. l Data as at the end of December. m 2002. n Population aged 16 to 74 years. o Population aged 16 to 89 years. p 2004. q Development Assistance Committee member (OECD). r Provisional data.

France

Region	Western Europe	UN membership date	24 October 1945
Population (000, 2018)	65 233[a]	Surface area (km2)	551 500[b]
Pop. density (per km2, 2018)	119.1[a]	Sex ratio (m per 100 f)	96.8[a]
Capital city	Paris	National currency	Euro (EUR)
Capital city pop. (000, 2018)	10 901.0	Exchange rate (per US$)	0.8[c]

Economic indicators

	2005	2010	2018
GDP: Gross domestic product (million current US$)[d]	2 203 624	2 646 837	2 465 454[a]
GDP growth rate (annual %, const. 2010 prices)[d]	1.6	2.0	1.2[e]
GDP per capita (current US$)[d]	34 843.0	40 629.0	36 826.0[e]
Economy: Agriculture (% of Gross Value Added)[d,f]	1.9	1.8	1.6[e]
Economy: Industry (% of Gross Value Added)[d,f]	21.5	19.6	19.6[e]
Economy: Services and other activity (% of GVA)[d,f]	76.6	78.6	78.8[e]
Employment in agriculture (% of employed)[g]	3.6	2.9[g]	2.8[g]
Employment in industry (% of employed)[g]	23.8	22.2	20.3
Employment in services & other sectors (% employed)[g]	72.6	74.8	76.9
Unemployment rate (% of labour force)	8.5	8.9	9.7[g]
Labour force participation rate (female/male pop. %)[g]	50.1 / 62.6	50.9 / 62.0	50.5 / 59.8
CPI: Consumer Price Index (2010=100)[d,h,i]	93	100	107[c]
Agricultural production index (2004-2006=100)	100	99	96[e]
Index of industrial production (2005=100)[j]	100	90	87[k]
International trade: exports (million current US$)[d]	434 354	511 651	526 267[g,c]
International trade: imports (million current US$)[d]	475 857	599 172	617 386[g,c]
International trade: balance (million current US$)[d]	- 41 503	- 87 520	- 91 119[g,c]
Balance of payments, current account (million US$)	- 137	- 22 034	- 18 514[c]

Major trading partners

						2017
Export partners (% of exports)[g]	Germany	16.1[g]	Spain	7.5	United States	7.4[g]
Import partners (% of imports)[g]	Germany	16.9	China	9.1	Italy	7.5

Social indicators

	2005	2010	2018
Population growth rate (average annual %)[l]	0.5	0.6	0.4[b]
Urban population (% of total population)	77.1	78.4	80.4
Urban population growth rate (average annual %)[l]	0.9	0.9	0.8[b]
Fertility rate, total (live births per woman)[l]	1.9	2.0	2.0[b]
Life expectancy at birth (females/males, years)[l]	83.1 / 75.8	84.3 / 77.4	85.0 / 78.8[b]
Population age distribution (0-14/60+ years old, %)	18.4 / 20.9	18.4 / 23.1	18.0 / 26.1[a]
International migrant stock (000/% of total pop.)	6 737.6 / 11.0	7 196.5 / 11.4	7 902.8 / 12.2[c]
Refugees and others of concern to the UNHCR (000)	179.5[m]	250.4[m]	378.1[c]
Infant mortality rate (per 1 000 live births)[l]	4.3	3.7	3.4[b]
Health: Current expenditure (% of GDP)	10.2	10.7	11.1[b]
Health: Physicians (per 1 000 pop.)	...	3.7[n]	3.2[e]
Education: Government expenditure (% of GDP)	5.5	5.7	5.5[k]
Education: Primary gross enrol. ratio (f/m per 100 pop.)	108.2 / 109.6	107.8 / 109.0	107.2 / 107.5[b]
Education: Secondary gross enrol. ratio (f/m per 100 pop.)	114.1 / 113.7	112.8 / 112.0	111.6 / 110.6[b]
Education: Tertiary gross enrol. ratio (f/m per 100 pop.)	62.4 / 48.5	65.0 / 51.0	72.8 / 58.1[b]
Intentional homicide rate (per 100 000 pop.)	1.6	1.3	1.4[e]
Seats held by women in the National Parliament (%)	12.2	18.9	39.0

Environment and infrastructure indicators

	2005	2010	2018
Individuals using the Internet (per 100 inhabitants)	42.9[o,p]	77.3[d,q]	85.6[d,e]
Research & Development expenditure (% of GDP)	2.0	2.2[r]	2.2[s,b]
Threatened species (number)	120[t]	168	278[c]
Forested area (% of land area)[g]	29.0	30.0	31.0[b]
CO2 emission estimates (million tons/tons per capita)[u]	385.4 / 6.3	353.0 / 5.6	303.3 / 4.7[k]
Energy production, primary (Petajoules)[u]	5 692	5 623	5 720[b]
Energy supply per capita (Gigajoules)[u]	186	173	155[b]
Tourist/visitor arrivals at national borders (000)[v]	74 988	76 647	82 570[s,e]
Important sites for terrestrial biodiversity protected (%)	68.8	80.1	81.2
Pop. using improved drinking water (urban/rural, %)	100.0 / 100.0	100.0 / 100.0	100.0 / 100.0[b]
Pop. using improved sanitation facilities (urban/rural, %)	98.6 / 98.9	98.6 / 98.9	98.6 / 98.9[b]
Net Official Development Assist. disbursed (% of GNI)[w]	0.47	0.50	0.43[s,c]

a Projected estimate (medium fertility variant). **b** 2015. **c** 2017. **d** Including French Guiana, Guadeloupe, Martinique and Réunion. **e** 2016. **f** Data classified according to ISIC Rev. 4. **g** Estimate. **h** Calculated by the Statistics Division of the United Nations from national indices. **i** All households. **j** Excluding the Overseas Departments (French Guiana, Guadeloupe, Martinique, Mayotte and Réunion). **k** 2014. **l** Data refers to a 5-year period preceding the reference year. **m** Data as at the end of December. **n** 2007. **o** Population aged 11 years and over. **p** Users in the last month. **q** Population aged 16 to 74 years. **r** Break in the time series. **s** Provisional data. **t** 2004. **u** Including Monaco. **v** Arrivals of non-resident visitors. **w** Development Assistance Committee member (OECD).

French Guiana

Region	South America	Population (000, 2018)	290 [a]
Surface area (km2)	83 534 [b]	Pop. density (per km2, 2018)	3.5 [a]
Sex ratio (m per 100 f)	100.0 [a]	Capital city	Cayenne
National currency	Euro (EUR)	Capital city pop. (000, 2018)	57.5
Exchange rate (per US$)	0.8 [c]		

Economic indicators	2005	2010	2018
Employment in industry (% of employed) [d,e]	...	14.1	14.9 [f]
Employment in services & other sectors (% of employed) [d,e]	...	51.5	58.3 [f]
Unemployment rate (% of labour force) [e]	24.8	21.0	21.3 [g,h]
Labour force participation rate (female/male pop. %) [e]	36.3 / 48.2	43.2 / 54.9	48.4 / 58.8 [g,h]
CPI: Consumer Price Index (2010=100)	...	...	126 [i,j]
Agricultural production index (2004-2006=100)	98	103	127 [k]

Social indicators	2005	2010	2018
Population growth rate (average annual %) [l]	4.5	2.8	2.8 [b]
Urban population (% of total population)	81.1	82.9	85.3
Urban population growth rate (average annual %) [l]	5.0	3.2	3.1 [b]
Fertility rate, total (live births per woman) [l]	3.7	3.6	3.5 [b]
Life expectancy at birth (females/males, years) [l]	80.1 / 72.8	81.4 / 75.0	82.6 / 76.1 [b]
Population age distribution (0-14/60+ years old, %)	36.1 / 5.7	35.3 / 6.5	32.8 / 8.7 [a]
International migrant stock (000/% of total pop.)	86.5 / 42.4	96.3 / 41.1	111.7 / 39.5 [c]
Infant mortality rate (per 1 000 live births) [l]	13.6	10.6	9.3 [b]
Intentional homicide rate (per 100 000 pop.)	22.1	13.2 [m]	...

Environment and infrastructure indicators	2005	2010	2018
Threatened species (number)	49 [n]	56	73 [b]
Forested area (% of land area) [o]	99.4	99.0	98.9 [b]
CO2 emission estimates (million tons/tons per capita)	0.6 / 2.8	0.6 / 2.8	0.7 / 2.8 [i]
Energy production, primary (Petajoules)	2	3	3 [b]
Energy supply per capita (Gigajoules)	49	51 [o]	46 [o,b]
Tourist/visitor arrivals at national borders (000) [p]	95	189	199 [b]
Important sites for terrestrial biodiversity protected (%)	58.6	67.0	67.4
Pop. using improved drinking water (urban/rural, %)	91.8 / 73.4	94.5 / 75.1	94.5 / 75.1 [i]
Pop. using improved sanitation facilities (urban/rural, %)	90.8 / 68.0	94.9 / 75.8	94.9 / 75.8 [i]

a Projected estimate (medium fertility variant). **b** 2015. **c** 2017. **d** Population aged 15 to 64 years. **e** Excluding the institutional population. **f** 2012. **g** Break in the time series. **h** 2013. **i** Index base: 2000=100. **j** 2014. **k** 2016. **l** Data refers to a 5-year period preceding the reference year. **m** 2009. **n** 2004. **o** Estimate. **p** Survey at Cayenne-Rochambeau airport on departure.

French Polynesia

Region	Polynesia	Population (000, 2018)	286[a]	
Surface area (km2)	4 000[b]	Pop. density (per km2, 2018)	78.1[a]	
Sex ratio (m per 100 f)	103.6[a]	Capital city	Papeete	
National currency	CFP Franc (XPF)[c]	Capital city pop. (000, 2018)	136.0[d]	
Exchange rate (per US$)	99.5[e]			

Economic indicators	2005	2010	2018
GDP: Gross domestic product (million current US$)	5 703	6 081	5 418[f]
GDP growth rate (annual %, const. 2010 prices)	1.4	- 2.5	1.8[f]
GDP per capita (current US$)	22 374.0	22 704.0	19 335.0[f]
Economy: Agriculture (% of Gross Value Added)	3.4	2.5	3.1[f]
Economy: Industry (% of Gross Value Added)	12.7	12.3	11.8[f]
Economy: Services and other activity (% of GVA)	83.9	85.2	85.1[f]
Employment in agriculture (% of employed)[g]	9.2	9.2	8.6
Employment in industry (% of employed)[g]	17.5	18.2	17.4
Employment in services & other sectors (% employed)[g]	73.3	72.6	74.0
Unemployment rate (% of labour force)[g]	11.8	18.0	20.5
Labour force participation rate (female/male pop. %)[g]	47.2 / 65.7	48.2 / 63.8	47.7 / 61.2
CPI: Consumer Price Index (2010=100)	...	...	122[h,i]
Agricultural production index (2004-2006=100)	104	99	102[f]
International trade: exports (million current US$)	210	153	153[g,e]
International trade: imports (million current US$)	1 702	1 726	1 638[g,e]
International trade: balance (million current US$)	- 1 491	- 1 573	- 1 485[g,e]
Balance of payments, current account (million US$)	9	- 18	412[f]

Major trading partners						2017
Export partners (% of exports)	Japan	26.1[g]	China, Hong Kong SAR	24.5	United States	18.0[g]
Import partners (% of imports)	France	25.6[g]	China	13.2[g]	United States	10.4

Social indicators	2005	2010	2018
Population growth rate (average annual %)[j]	1.4	1.0	0.7[b]
Urban population (% of total population)	57.4	60.3	61.8
Urban population growth rate (average annual %)[j]	1.9	2.0	1.2[b]
Fertility rate, total (live births per woman)[j]	2.4	2.2	2.1[b]
Life expectancy at birth (females/males, years)[j]	76.0 / 70.6	77.4 / 72.8	78.6 / 74.0[b]
Population age distribution (0-14/60+ years old, %)	27.7 / 8.0	25.2 / 9.3	22.9 / 12.4[a]
International migrant stock (000/% of total pop.)	32.3 / 12.7	31.6 / 11.8	30.7 / 10.8[e]
Infant mortality rate (per 1 000 live births)[j]	9.4	8.8	6.9[b]
Intentional homicide rate (per 100 000 pop.)	...	0.4[k]	...

Environment and infrastructure indicators	2005	2010	2018
Individuals using the Internet (per 100 inhabitants)	21.5	49.0	68.4[g,f]
Threatened species (number)	122[l]	160	175[e]
Forested area (% of land area)[g]	35.5	42.3	42.3[b]
CO2 emission estimates (million tons/tons per capita)	0.8 / 3.2	0.9 / 3.2	0.8 / 2.9[i]
Energy production, primary (Petajoules)	1	1	1[g,b]
Energy supply per capita (Gigajoules)	46	46	41[b]
Tourist/visitor arrivals at national borders (000)[m,n]	208	154	192[f]
Important sites for terrestrial biodiversity protected (%)	4.0	5.4	5.4
Pop. using improved drinking water (urban/rural, %)	100.0 / 100.0	100.0 / 100.0	100.0 / 100.0[b]
Pop. using improved sanitation facilities (urban/rural, %)	98.2 / 98.2	98.4 / 98.4	98.5 / 98.5[b]

a Projected estimate (medium fertility variant). **b** 2015. **c** Communauté financière du Pacifique (CFP) Franc. **d** Refers to the total population in the communes of Arue, Faaa, Mahina, Papara, Papeete, Pirae and Punaauia. **e** 2017. **f** 2016. **g** Estimate. **h** Index base: 2000=100. **i** 2014. **j** Data refers to a 5-year period preceding the reference year. **k** 2009. **l** 2004. **m** Excluding nationals residing abroad. **n** Arrivals by air.

Gabon

Region	Middle Africa	UN membership date	20 September 1960
Population (000, 2018)	2 068[a]	Surface area (km2)	267 668[b]
Pop. density (per km2, 2018)	8.0[a]	Sex ratio (m per 100 f)	105.5[a]
Capital city	Libreville	National currency	CFA Franc, BEAC (XAF)[c]
Capital city pop. (000, 2018)	813.5	Exchange rate (per US$)	546.9[d]

Economic indicators

	2005	2010	2018
GDP: Gross domestic product (million current US$)	9 579	12 882	13 863[e]
GDP growth rate (annual %, const. 2010 prices)	1.1	6.8	3.2[e]
GDP per capita (current US$)	6 827.0	7 854.0	7 002.0[e]
Economy: Agriculture (% of Gross Value Added)	5.2	4.6	4.1[e]
Economy: Industry (% of Gross Value Added)	62.6	55.6	50.8[e]
Economy: Services and other activity (% of GVA)	32.2	39.8	45.2[e]
Employment in agriculture (% of employed)[f]	43.3	43.1	41.8
Employment in industry (% of employed)[f]	12.2	12.6	12.6
Employment in services & other sectors (% employed)[f]	44.5	44.3	45.5
Unemployment rate (% of labour force)	16.9	20.4	19.5[f]
Labour force participation rate (female/male pop. %)[f]	37.8 / 57.3	39.9 / 58.1	43.2 / 59.5
CPI: Consumer Price Index (2010=100)[f,g,h]	89	100	111[e]
Agricultural production index (2004-2006=100)	100	112	123[e]
Index of industrial production (2005=100)[i,j]	100	117[k]	126[k,l]
International trade: exports (million current US$)	5 068	8 539[f]	1 584[f,d]
International trade: imports (million current US$)	1 451	2 969[f]	2 805[f,d]
International trade: balance (million current US$)	3 617	5 570[f]	- 1 220[f,d]
Balance of payments, current account (million US$)	1 983	2 453	...

Major trading partners

						2017
Export partners (% of exports)	China	29.9[f]	Trinidad and Tobago	14.4	Australia	8.2[f]
Import partners (% of imports)[f]	France	26.4	China	19.0	Belgium	7.6

Social indicators

	2005	2010	2018
Population growth rate (average annual %)[m]	2.6	3.1	3.3[b]
Urban population (% of total population)	82.5	85.5	89.4
Urban population growth rate (average annual %)[m]	3.5	3.9	3.9[b]
Fertility rate, total (live births per woman)[m]	4.4	4.2	4.0[b]
Life expectancy at birth (females/males, years)[m]	59.8 / 58.3	61.8 / 60.8	65.8 / 63.1[b]
Population age distribution (0-14/60+ years old, %)	39.0 / 7.7	37.0 / 7.0	35.9 / 6.3[a]
International migrant stock (000/% of total pop.)[n]	214.1 / 15.3	244.0 / 14.9	280.2 / 13.8[d]
Refugees and others of concern to the UNHCR (000)	13.7[o]	13.2[o]	1.1[d]
Infant mortality rate (per 1 000 live births)[m]	58.1	49.3	40.8[b]
Health: Current expenditure (% of GDP)	2.8	2.5	2.7[b]
Health: Physicians (per 1 000 pop.)	0.3[p]	...	0.4[e]
Education: Government expenditure (% of GDP)	3.8[f,q]	3.1	2.7[r]
Education: Primary gross enrol. ratio (f/m per 100 pop.)	138.5 / 139.5[s]	... / ...	136.6 / 140.8[l]
Education: Tertiary gross enrol. ratio (f/m per 100 pop.)	6.1 / 10.5[s]	... / ...	... / ...
Intentional homicide rate (per 100 000 pop.)	11.0	8.7	8.0[b]
Seats held by women in the National Parliament (%)	9.2	14.7	17.1

Environment and infrastructure indicators

	2005	2010	2018
Individuals using the Internet (per 100 inhabitants)	4.9	13.0[f]	48.1[f,e]
Research & Development expenditure (% of GDP)	...	0.6[t]	...
Threatened species (number)	139[p]	204	270[d]
Forested area (% of land area)	85.4	85.4	89.3[b]
CO2 emission estimates (million tons/tons per capita)	4.9 / 3.6	4.8 / 3.1	5.2 / 3.1[f]
Energy production, primary (Petajoules)	622	590	556[b]
Energy supply per capita (Gigajoules)	53	60	62[b]
Tourist/visitor arrivals at national borders (000)	269[u]	...	...
Important sites for terrestrial biodiversity protected (%)	61.2	61.2	61.7
Pop. using improved drinking water (urban/rural, %)	95.4 / 50.0	96.4 / 59.3	97.2 / 66.7[b]
Pop. using improved sanitation facilities (urban/rural, %)	41.0 / 33.7	42.3 / 32.5	43.4 / 31.5[b]
Net Official Development Assist. received (% of GNI)	0.59	0.85	0.32

a Projected estimate (medium fertility variant). b 2015. c African Financial Community (CFA) Franc, Bank of Central African States (BEAC). d 2017. e 2016. f Estimate. g Libreville and Owendo. h African population. i Data classified according to ISIC Rev. 3. j Country data supplemented with data from the Observatoire Economique et Statistique d'Afrique Subsaharienne (Afristat). k Data refers to manufacturing and utilities only. l 2011. m Data refers to a 5-year period preceding the reference year. n Refers to foreign citizens. o Data as at the end of December. p 2004. q 2000. r 2014. s 2003. t 2009. u Arrivals of non-resident tourists at Libreville airport.

Gambia

Region	Western Africa	UN membership date	21 September 1965
Population (000, 2018)	2 164[a]	Surface area (km2)	11 295[b]
Pop. density (per km2, 2018)	213.8[a]	Sex ratio (m per 100 f)	98.0[a]
Capital city	Banjul	National currency	Dalasi (GMD)
Capital city pop. (000, 2018)	437.2[c]	Exchange rate (per US$)	43.9[d]

Economic indicators	2005	2010	2018
GDP: Gross domestic product (million current US$)	624	952	986[d]
GDP growth rate (annual %, const. 2010 prices)	- 0.9	6.5	2.2[d]
GDP per capita (current US$)	432.0	563.0	484.0[d]
Economy: Agriculture (% of Gross Value Added)	28.6	30.7	20.6[d]
Economy: Industry (% of Gross Value Added)	14.9	13.1	13.8[d]
Economy: Services and other activity (% of GVA)	56.5	56.2	65.6[d]
Employment in agriculture (% of employed)[e]	34.2	32.8	26.8
Employment in industry (% of employed)[e]	16.2	14.7	15.4
Employment in services & other sectors (% employed)[e]	49.6	52.5	57.8
Unemployment rate (% of labour force)[e]	9.4	9.4	9.5
Labour force participation rate (female/male pop. %)[e]	48.5 / 68.8	50.3 / 68.7	51.4 / 67.7
CPI: Consumer Price Index (2010=100)[f]	81	100	140[d]
Agricultural production index (2004-2006=100)	94	133	106[d]
International trade: exports (million current US$)	7	68	120[e,g]
International trade: imports (million current US$)	260	284	386[e,g]
International trade: balance (million current US$)	- 252	- 215	- 265[e,g]
Balance of payments, current account (million US$)	- 43	17	- 96[d]

Major trading partners						2017
Export partners (% of exports)	Guinea-Bissau	62.9[e]	Viet Nam	12.0	Senegal	11.1[e]
Import partners (% of imports)[e]	Côte d'Ivoire	16.8	Brazil	11.6	Spain	11.0

Social indicators	2005	2010	2018
Population growth rate (average annual %)[h]	3.2	3.2	3.1[b]
Urban population (% of total population)	52.0	55.7	61.3
Urban population growth rate (average annual %)[h]	4.8	4.5	4.4[b]
Fertility rate, total (live births per woman)[h]	5.9	5.8	5.6[b]
Life expectancy at birth (females/males, years)[h]	58.1 / 55.9	60.2 / 57.6	61.6 / 59.1[b]
Population age distribution (0-14/60+ years old, %)	46.3 / 4.0	46.3 / 3.7	45.1 / 3.8[a]
International migrant stock (000/% of total pop.)	181.9 / 12.6	185.8 / 11.0	205.1 / 9.8[a]
Refugees and others of concern to the UNHCR (000)	8.0[i]	8.5[i]	8.0[g]
Infant mortality rate (per 1 000 live births)[h]	59.4	52.4	49.8[b]
Health: Current expenditure (% of GDP)	4.9	5.7	6.7[b]
Health: Physicians (per 1 000 pop.)	0.1	0.1	0.1[b]
Education: Government expenditure (% of GDP)	1.1	4.2	2.8[k]
Education: Primary gross enrol. ratio (f/m per 100 pop.)	91.5 / 88.7	84.9 / 82.6	101.0 / 93.3[g]
Education: Secondary gross enrol. ratio (f/m per 100 pop.)	... / ...	55.7 / 58.5[e]	... / ...
Education: Tertiary gross enrol. ratio (f/m per 100 pop.)	0.4 / 1.9[i]	1.8 / 2.6	2.5 / 3.7[m]
Intentional homicide rate (per 100 000 pop.)	9.8	9.8	9.1[b]
Seats held by women in the National Parliament (%)	13.2	7.5	10.3

Environment and infrastructure indicators	2005	2010	2018
Individuals using the Internet (per 100 inhabitants)	3.8[e]	9.2	18.5[e,d]
Research & Development expenditure (% of GDP)	...	~0.0[n,o]	0.1[p,q]
Threatened species (number)	21[l]	43	67[g]
Forested area (% of land area)	46.5	47.4	48.2[e,b]
CO2 emission estimates (million tons/tons per capita)	0.3 / 0.2	0.4 / 0.3	0.5 / 0.3[r]
Energy production, primary (Petajoules)	6	6	7[b]
Energy supply per capita (Gigajoules)	7	7	7[e,b]
Tourist/visitor arrivals at national borders (000)[s,t]	108	91	161[d]
Important sites for terrestrial biodiversity protected (%)	34.6	34.6	34.6
Pop. using improved drinking water (urban/rural, %)	91.5 / 79.7	93.5 / 83.0	94.2 / 84.4[b]
Pop. using improved sanitation facilities (urban/rural, %)	60.5 / 57.7	61.2 / 55.8	61.5 / 55.0[b]
Net Official Development Assist. received (% of GNI)	10.26	12.83	9.78[d]

a Projected estimate (medium fertility variant). **b** 2015. **c** Refers to the local government areas of Banjul and Kanifing. **d** 2016. **e** Estimate. **f** Banjul, Kombo St. Mary **g** 2017. **h** Data refers to a 5-year period preceding the reference year. **i** Data as at the end of December. **j** 2008. **k** 2013. **l** 2004. **m** 2012. **n** Partial data. **o** 2009. **p** Overestimated or based on overestimated data. **q** 2011. **r** 2014. **s** Including nationals residing abroad. **t** Charter tourists only.

Georgia

Region	Western Asia	UN membership date	31 July 1992
Population (000, 2018)	3 907[a,b]	Surface area (km2)	69 700[c]
Pop. density (per km2, 2018)	56.2[a,b]	Sex ratio (m per 100 f)	91.3[a,b]
Capital city	Tbilisi	National currency	Lari (GEL)
Capital city pop. (000, 2018)	1 077.3	Exchange rate (per US$)	2.6[d]

Economic indicators

	2005	2010	2018
GDP: Gross domestic product (million current US$)	6 411	11 638	14 333[e]
GDP growth rate (annual %, const. 2010 prices)	9.6	6.2	2.7[e]
GDP per capita (current US$)	1 429.0	2 750.0	3 651.0[e]
Economy: Agriculture (% of Gross Value Added)	16.5	8.3	9.1[e]
Economy: Industry (% of Gross Value Added)	26.5	22.0	24.9[e]
Economy: Services and other activity (% of GVA)	57.0	69.8	66.0[e]
Employment in agriculture (% of employed)[f]	54.3	48.2	39.8
Employment in industry (% of employed)[f]	9.3	10.4	12.7
Employment in services & other sectors (% employed)[f]	36.4	41.5	47.5
Unemployment rate (% of labour force)	13.8	16.3	11.5[f]
Labour force participation rate (female/male pop. %)[f]	55.2 / 72.9	56.0 / 75.1	58.0 / 78.9
CPI: Consumer Price Index (2010=100)[g]	70	100	124[d]
Agricultural production index (2004-2006=100)	121	68	74[e]
Index of industrial production (2005=100)[h]	100	137	185[i]
International trade: exports (million current US$)	865	1 677	2 728[d]
International trade: imports (million current US$)	2 490	5 236	7 982[d]
International trade: balance (million current US$)	- 1 624	- 3 558	- 5 254[d]
Balance of payments, current account (million US$)	- 696	- 1 199	- 1 311[d]

Major trading partners

							2017
Export partners (% of exports)	Russian Federation	14.5	Azerbaijan	10.0[f]	Turkey	7.9
Import partners (% of imports)	Turkey	17.2	Russian Federation	9.9	China	9.2

Social indicators

	2005	2010	2018
Population growth rate (average annual %)[b,j]	- 1.0	- 1.2	- 1.4[c]
Urban population (% of total population)[b]	53.6	55.5	58.6
Urban population growth rate (average annual %)[b,j]	- 0.7	- 0.5	- 0.7[c]
Fertility rate, total (live births per woman)[b,j]	1.6	1.8	2.0[c]
Life expectancy at birth (females/males, years)[b,j]	76.1 / 68.9	76.5 / 68.6	77.0 / 68.5[c]
Population age distribution (0-14/60+ years old, %)[b]	19.5 / 18.2	18.0 / 18.8	19.4 / 21.1[a]
International migrant stock (000/% of total pop.)[b]	72.3 / 1.6	73.0 / 1.7	78.2 / 2.0[d]
Refugees and others of concern to the UNHCR (000)	238.6[k]	362.2[k]	278.8[d]
Infant mortality rate (per 1 000 live births)[b,j]	29.0	20.2	11.2[c]
Health: Current expenditure (% of GDP)[l]	8.3	9.5	7.9[c]
Health: Physicians (per 1 000 pop.)	...	4.3	4.8[i]
Education: Government expenditure (% of GDP)	2.5	3.2[f,m]	3.8[e]
Education: Primary gross enrol. ratio (f/m per 100 pop.)	88.6 / 90.8	102.2 / 101.4	102.8 / 102.4[e]
Education: Secondary gross enrol. ratio (f/m per 100 pop.)	79.1 / 80.8	86.4 / 89.9[n]	105.5 / 103.2[e]
Education: Tertiary gross enrol. ratio (f/m per 100 pop.)	47.0 / 44.9	32.8 / 25.7	55.7 / 48.3[e]
Intentional homicide rate (per 100 000 pop.)	9.0	4.4	1.0[e]
Seats held by women in the National Parliament (%)	9.4	5.1	16.0

Environment and infrastructure indicators

	2005	2010	2018
Individuals using the Internet (per 100 inhabitants)	6.1[f]	26.9	50.0[f,e]
Research & Development expenditure (% of GDP)	0.2	...	0.3[o,p,q,c]
Threatened species (number)	43[r]	46	120[d]
Forested area (% of land area)	39.9	40.6[f]	40.6[f,c]
CO2 emission estimates (million tons/tons per capita)	5.1 / 1.1	6.3 / 1.5	9.0 / 2.2[i]
Energy production, primary (Petajoules)	53	58	58[c]
Energy supply per capita (Gigajoules)	30	33	49[c]
Tourist/visitor arrivals at national borders (000)	...	1 067	2 721[e]
Important sites for terrestrial biodiversity protected (%)	19.2	21.3	28.4
Pop. using improved drinking water (urban/rural, %)	98.3 / 87.2	99.5 / 93.8	100.0 / 100.0[c]
Pop. using improved sanitation facilities (urban/rural, %)	96.0 / 88.6	95.6 / 82.2	95.2 / 75.9[c]
Net Official Development Assist. received (% of GNI)	4.53	5.56	3.42[e]

a Projected estimate (medium fertility variant). b Including Abkhazia and South Ossetia. c 2015. d 2017. e 2016. f Estimate. g Five cities. h Data classified according to ISIC Rev. 3. i 2014. j Data refers to a 5-year period preceding the reference year. k Data as at the end of December. l As a result of recent health-care reforms, public compulsory insurance has since 2008 been implemented by private insurance companies. The voucher cost of this insurance is treated as general government health expenditure. m 2009. n 2008. o Partial data. p Excluding private non-profit. q Excluding business enterprise. r 2004.

Germany

Region	Western Europe	UN membership date	18 September 1973
Population (000, 2018)	82 294[a]	Surface area (km2)	357 376[b]
Pop. density (per km2, 2018)	236.1[a]	Sex ratio (m per 100 f)	97.1[a]
Capital city	Berlin	National currency	Euro (EUR)
Capital city pop. (000, 2018)	3 552.1	Exchange rate (per US$)	0.8[c]

Economic indicators	2005	2010	2018
GDP: Gross domestic product (million current US$)	2 861 339	3 417 095	3 477 796[d]
GDP growth rate (annual %, const. 2010 prices)	0.7	4.1	1.9[d]
GDP per capita (current US$)	35 035.0	42 241.0	42 456.0[d]
Economy: Agriculture (% of Gross Value Added)[e]	0.9	0.9	0.7[d]
Economy: Industry (% of Gross Value Added)[e]	34.8	35.8	35.9[d]
Economy: Services and other activity (% of GVA)[e]	64.3	63.4	63.4[d]
Employment in agriculture (% of employed)[f]	2.4	1.6	1.3[f]
Employment in industry (% of employed)[f]	29.8	28.3	27.0
Employment in services & other sectors (% employed)[f]	67.8	70.0	71.7
Unemployment rate (% of labour force)	11.2	7.0	3.6[f]
Labour force participation rate (female/male pop. %)[f]	50.7 / 66.7	52.8 / 66.5	55.1 / 66.1
CPI: Consumer Price Index (2010=100)	92	100	109[c]
Agricultural production index (2004-2006=100)	100	103	107[d]
Index of industrial production (2005=100)	100	104[g]	112[g,h]
International trade: exports (million current US$)	977 132	1 271 096	1 450 215[c]
International trade: imports (million current US$)	779 819	1 066 817	1 173 628[c]
International trade: balance (million current US$)	197 313	204 280	276 587[c]
Balance of payments, current account (million US$)	131 661	193 034	297 118[c]

Major trading partners						2017
Export partners (% of exports)	United States	8.7	France	8.2[f]	China	6.7
Import partners (% of imports)	China	9.8	Netherlands	8.1	France	6.2

Social indicators	2005	2010	2018
Population growth rate (average annual %)[i]	~0.0	-0.2	0.2[b]
Urban population (% of total population)	76.0	77.0	77.3
Urban population growth rate (average annual %)[i]	0.3	0.1	0.3[b]
Fertility rate, total (live births per woman)[i]	1.4	1.4	1.4[b]
Life expectancy at birth (females/males, years)[i]	81.5 / 75.6	82.4 / 77.0	82.9 / 77.9[b]
Population age distribution (0-14/60+ years old, %)	14.4 / 24.9	13.6 / 26.1	13.1 / 28.4[a]
International migrant stock (000/% of total pop.)	9 402.4 / 11.5	9 812.3 / 12.1	12 165.1 / 14.8[c]
Refugees and others of concern to the UNHCR (000)	784.0[j]	670.6[j]	1 337.1[c]
Infant mortality rate (per 1 000 live births)[i]	4.2	3.7	3.4[b]
Health: Current expenditure (% of GDP)	10.3	11.0	11.2[b]
Health: Physicians (per 1 000 pop.)	...	3.8	4.2[b]
Education: Government expenditure (% of GDP)	...	4.9	4.9[h]
Education: Primary gross enrol. ratio (f/m per 100 pop.)	102.9 / 103.1	102.8 / 103.1	102.1 / 102.7[b]
Education: Secondary gross enrol. ratio (f/m per 100 pop.)	100.8 / 103.3	101.2 / 106.4	98.6 / 103.4[b]
Education: Tertiary gross enrol. ratio (f/m per 100 pop.)	... / ...	... / ...	65.6 / 66.9[b]
Intentional homicide rate (per 100 000 pop.)	1.1	1.0	1.2[d]
Seats held by women in the National Parliament (%)	32.8	32.8	30.7

Environment and infrastructure indicators	2005	2010	2018
Individuals using the Internet (per 100 inhabitants)	68.7[k]	82.0[k]	89.6[d]
Research & Development expenditure (% of GDP)	2.4	2.7	2.9[f,b]
Threatened species (number)	78[l]	79	116[c]
Forested area (% of land area)	32.6	32.7	32.7[f,b]
CO2 emission estimates (million tons/tons per capita)	797.2 / 9.6	758.9 / 9.4	719.9 / 8.9[h]
Energy production, primary (Petajoules)	5 706	5 377	5 007[b]
Energy supply per capita (Gigajoules)	170	170	160[b]
Tourist/visitor arrivals at national borders (000)	21 500	26 875	35 555[d]
Important sites for terrestrial biodiversity protected (%)	70.7	78.1	78.6
Pop. using improved drinking water (urban/rural, %)	100.0 / 100.0	100.0 / 100.0	100.0 / 100.0[b]
Pop. using improved sanitation facilities (urban/rural, %)	99.3 / 99.0	99.3 / 99.0	99.3 / 99.0[b]
Net Official Development Assist. disbursed (% of GNI)[m]	0.36	0.39	0.66[n,c]

a Projected estimate (medium fertility variant). b 2015. c 2017. d 2016. e Data classified according to ISIC Rev. 4. f Estimate. g Excluding water and waste management. h 2014. i Data refers to a 5-year period preceding the reference year. j Data as at the end of December. k Population aged 16 to 74 years. l 2004. m Development Assistance Committee member (OECD). n Provisional data.

Ghana

Region	Western Africa	UN membership date	08 March 1957
Population (000, 2018)	29 464[a]	Surface area (km2)	238 537[b]
Pop. density (per km2, 2018)	129.5[a]	Sex ratio (m per 100 f)	99.4[a]
Capital city	Accra	National currency	Ghana Cedi (GHS)
Capital city pop. (000, 2018)	2 439.4	Exchange rate (per US$)	4.4[c]

Economic indicators

	2005	2010	2018
GDP: Gross domestic product (million current US$)	17 199	32 174	42 794[d]
GDP growth rate (annual %, const. 2010 prices)	6.2	7.9	3.5[d]
GDP per capita (current US$)	798.0	1 313.0	1 517.0[d]
Economy: Agriculture (% of Gross Value Added)	31.8	29.8[e]	18.9[e,d]
Economy: Industry (% of Gross Value Added)	20.3	19.1[e]	24.2[e,d]
Economy: Services and other activity (% of GVA)	47.9	51.1[e]	56.9[e,d]
Employment in agriculture (% of employed)[f]	49.0	42.0	39.7
Employment in industry (% of employed)[f]	15.8	15.2	14.4
Employment in services & other sectors (% employed)[f]	35.2	42.8	46.0
Unemployment rate (% of labour force)	4.7[f]	5.3	2.4[f]
Labour force participation rate (female/male pop. %)[f]	73.1 / 77.7	73.8 / 78.7	74.9 / 79.4
CPI: Consumer Price Index (2010=100)	53	100	232[c]
Agricultural production index (2004-2006=100)	100	127	153[d]
International trade: exports (million current US$)	3 060	5 233	7 982[f,c]
International trade: imports (million current US$)	4 878	8 057	10 124[f,c]
International trade: balance (million current US$)	- 1 819	- 2 824	- 2 141[f,c]
Balance of payments, current account (million US$)	- 1 105	- 2 747	- 2 003[c]

Major trading partners

							2017
Export partners (% of exports)	Switzerland	17.5[f]	India	14.6	United Arab Emirates	13.4[f]
Import partners (% of imports)[f]	China	17.3	United Kingdom	9.7	United States	7.8

Social indicators

	2005	2010	2018
Population growth rate (average annual %)[g]	2.6	2.6	2.4[b]
Urban population (% of total population)	47.3	50.7	56.1
Urban population growth rate (average annual %)[g]	4.1	4.0	3.6[b]
Fertility rate, total (live births per woman)[g]	4.6	4.4	4.2[b]
Life expectancy at birth (females/males, years)[g]	58.3 / 56.7	60.9 / 59.2	62.6 / 60.7[b]
Population age distribution (0-14/60+ years old, %)	40.6 / 5.2	39.6 / 5.4	38.3 / 5.4[a]
International migrant stock (000/% of total pop.)	304.4 / 1.4	337.0 / 1.4	417.6 / 1.4[c]
Refugees and others of concern to the UNHCR (000)	60.2[h]	14.8[h]	13.4[c]
Infant mortality rate (per 1 000 live births)[g]	60.9	55.4	46.5[b]
Health: Current expenditure (% of GDP)	6.3	6.5	5.9[b]
Health: Physicians (per 1 000 pop.)	0.2[i]	0.1	
Education: Government expenditure (% of GDP)	7.4	5.5	6.2[j]
Education: Primary gross enrol. ratio (f/m per 100 pop.)	86.9 / 90.4	100.8 / 102.7[k]	105.5 / 104.1[c]
Education: Secondary gross enrol. ratio (f/m per 100 pop.)	37.2 / 44.9[f]	46.3 / 52.8[k]	59.6 / 61.2[c]
Education: Tertiary gross enrol. ratio (f/m per 100 pop.)	4.1 / 7.7	6.7 / 11.4[k]	13.4 / 18.7[d]
Intentional homicide rate (per 100 000 pop.)	1.8	1.7	1.7[l]
Seats held by women in the National Parliament (%)	10.9	8.3	12.7

Environment and infrastructure indicators

	2005	2010	2018
Individuals using the Internet (per 100 inhabitants)	1.8	7.8[m,n]	34.7[f,d]
Research & Development expenditure (% of GDP)	...	0.4[m]	...
Threatened species (number)	160[i]	202	238[c]
Forested area (% of land area)	39.8[f]	40.4	41.0[f,b]
CO2 emission estimates (million tons/tons per capita)	7.0 / 0.3	10.0 / 0.4	14.5 / 0.6[i]
Energy production, primary (Petajoules)	164	148	372[b]
Energy supply per capita (Gigajoules)	12	11	12[b]
Tourist/visitor arrivals at national borders (000)[o]	429	931	897[b]
Important sites for terrestrial biodiversity protected (%)	85.0	85.0	85.0
Pop. using improved drinking water (urban/rural, %)	89.3 / 66.1	90.9 / 75.1	92.6 / 84.0[b]
Pop. using improved sanitation facilities (urban/rural, %)	17.6 / 6.9	19.2 / 8.0	20.2 / 8.6[b]
Net Official Development Assist. received (% of GNI)	10.87	5.36	3.19[d]

a Projected estimate (medium fertility variant). b 2015. c 2017. d 2016. e Data classified according to ISIC Rev. 4. f Estimate. g Data refers to a 5-year period preceding the reference year. h Data as at the end of December. i 2004. j 2014. k 2009. l 2011. m Break in the time series. n Population aged 12 years and over. o Including nationals residing abroad.

Gibraltar

Region	Southern Europe	Population (000, 2018)	35[a]
Surface area (km2)	6[b]	Pop. density (per km2, 2018)	3 473.3[a]
Sex ratio (m per 100 f)	101.8[c,b]	Capital city	Gibraltar
National currency	Gibraltar Pound (GIP)	Capital city pop. (000, 2018)	34.7
Exchange rate (per US$)	0.7[d]		

Economic indicators	2005	2010	2018
Labour force participation rate (female/male pop. %)	57.5 / 78.8[e]	... / ...	... / ...
CPI: Consumer Price Index (2010=100)	...	...	142[f,g]
International trade: exports (million current US$)[h]	195	259	362[d]
International trade: imports (million current US$)[h]	501	627	743[d]
International trade: balance (million current US$)[h]	- 306	- 368	- 382[d]

Major trading partners						2017
Export partners (% of exports)[h]	Mauritania	27.6	Germany	19.4	Netherlands	13.8
Import partners (% of imports)[h]	Areas nes[i]	38.4	United Kingdom	12.3	Spain	10.9

Social indicators	2005	2010	2018
Population growth rate (average annual %)[j]	0.6	0.7	0.6[b]
Urban population (% of total population)	100.0	100.0	100.0
Urban population growth rate (average annual %)[j]	0.6	0.7	0.6[b]
Life expectancy at birth (females/males, years)	83.3 / 78.5[e]	... / ...	... / ...
Population age distribution (0-14/60+ years old, %)	18.4 / 20.5[k,e]	... / ...	18.1 / 22.4[b,l,m]
International migrant stock (000/% of total pop.)	9.2 / 28.7	10.4 / 31.2	11.2 / 32.3[d]
Intentional homicide rate (per 100 000 pop.)	...	3.0	...

Environment and infrastructure indicators	2005	2010	2018
Individuals using the Internet (per 100 inhabitants)	39.1[h]	65.0	94.4[h,n]
Threatened species (number)	18[o]	22	31[d]
Forested area (% of land area)[h]	0.0	0.0	0.0[b]
CO2 emission estimates (million tons/tons per capita)	0.4 / 13.7	0.5 / 15.2	0.5 / 16.5[g]
Energy supply per capita (Gigajoules)	219	238	272[b]
Important sites for terrestrial biodiversity protected (%)	35.0	35.0	35.0

a Projected estimate (medium fertility variant). b 2015. c Excluding military personnel, visitors and transients. d 2017. e 2001. f Index base: 2000=100. g 2014. h Estimate. i Areas not elsewhere specified. j Data refers to a 5-year period preceding the reference year. k Excluding families of military personnel, visitors and transients. l De jure population. m 2012. n 2016. o 2004.

Greece

Region	Southern Europe	UN membership date	25 October 1945	
Population (000, 2018)	11 142[a]	Surface area (km2)	131 957[b]	
Pop. density (per km2, 2018)	86.4[a]	Sex ratio (m per 100 f)	96.9[a]	
Capital city	Athens	National currency	Euro (EUR)	
Capital city pop. (000, 2018)	3 155.6[c]	Exchange rate (per US$)	0.8[d]	

Economic indicators	2005	2010	2018
GDP: Gross domestic product (million current US$)	247 777	299 362	192 691[e]
GDP growth rate (annual %, const. 2010 prices)	0.6	- 5.5	- 0.2[e]
GDP per capita (current US$)	21 925.0	26 154.0	17 230.0[e]
Economy: Agriculture (% of Gross Value Added)[f]	4.8	3.3	4.0[e]
Economy: Industry (% of Gross Value Added)[f]	19.8	15.7	16.3[e]
Economy: Services and other activity (% of GVA)[f]	75.4	81.1	79.7[e]
Employment in agriculture (% of employed)	12.2	12.4	11.9[g]
Employment in industry (% of employed)[g]	22.4	19.6	15.3
Employment in services & other sectors (% employed)[g]	65.4	68.0	72.8
Unemployment rate (% of labour force)	10.0	12.7	19.5[g]
Labour force participation rate (female/male pop. %)[g]	42.7 / 64.9	44.8 / 64.5	45.3 / 60.2
CPI: Consumer Price Index (2010=100)[h]	85	100	101[d]
Agricultural production index (2004-2006=100)	104	94	93[e]
Index of industrial production (2005=100)	100	84	74[i]
International trade: exports (million current US$)	17 434	27 586	32 155[d]
International trade: imports (million current US$)	54 894	66 453	55 301[d]
International trade: balance (million current US$)	- 37 459	- 38 867	- 23 146[d]
Balance of payments, current account (million US$)	- 18 233	- 30 275	- 1 331[d]

Major trading partners						2017
Export partners (% of exports)	Italy	10.6	Germany	7.1[g]	Turkey	6.9
Import partners (% of imports)	Germany	10.2	Italy	7.6	Russian Federation	7.0

Social indicators	2005	2010	2018
Population growth rate (average annual %)[j]	0.3	0.3	- 0.4[b]
Urban population (% of total population)	74.5	76.3	79.1
Urban population growth rate (average annual %)[j]	0.8	0.7	0.1[b]
Fertility rate, total (live births per woman)[j]	1.3	1.5	1.3[b]
Life expectancy at birth (females/males, years)[j]	81.9 / 76.4	82.8 / 77.3	83.3 / 78.0[b]
Population age distribution (0-14/60+ years old, %)	15.1 / 22.5	14.9 / 24.0	14.1 / 26.9[a]
International migrant stock (000/% of total pop.)	1 190.7 / 10.5	1 321.1 / 11.5	1 220.4 / 10.9[d]
Refugees and others of concern to the UNHCR (000)	14.3[k]	57.4[k]	80.3[d]
Infant mortality rate (per 1 000 live births)[j]	4.6	3.5	3.3[b]
Health: Current expenditure (% of GDP)	9.0	9.6	8.4[b]
Health: Physicians (per 1 000 pop.)		6.2	6.3[i]
Education: Government expenditure (% of GDP)	4.0	...	...
Education: Primary gross enrol. ratio (f/m per 100 pop.)	94.3 / 96.4	94.7 / 96.4	94.6 / 95.5[b]
Education: Secondary gross enrol. ratio (f/m per 100 pop.)	95.8 / 100.4	99.0 / 105.4	95.9 / 102.6[b]
Education: Tertiary gross enrol. ratio (f/m per 100 pop.)	90.0 / 80.8	103.7 / 100.0	116.9 / 118.0[i]
Intentional homicide rate (per 100 000 pop.)	1.2	1.5	0.8[e]
Seats held by women in the National Parliament (%)	14.0	17.3	18.3

Environment and infrastructure indicators	2005	2010	2018
Individuals using the Internet (per 100 inhabitants)	24.0[i]	44.4[i]	69.1[e]
Research & Development expenditure (% of GDP)	0.6	0.6[g]	1.0[m,b]
Threatened species (number)	75[h]	156	374[d]
Forested area (% of land area)[g]	29.1	30.3	31.5[b]
CO2 emission estimates (million tons/tons per capita)	98.7 / 8.8	83.9 / 7.5	67.3 / 6.1[i]
Energy production, primary (Petajoules)	432	396	355[b]
Energy supply per capita (Gigajoules)	115	105	90[b]
Tourist/visitor arrivals at national borders (000)	14 765	15 007	24 799[e]
Important sites for terrestrial biodiversity protected (%)	66.1	73.2	73.2
Pop. using improved drinking water (urban/rural, %)	99.9 / 98.1	100.0 / 100.0	100.0 / 100.0[b]
Pop. using improved sanitation facilities (urban/rural, %)	98.3 / 93.6	98.9 / 97.2	99.2 / 98.1[b]
Net Official Development Assist. disbursed (% of GNI)[o]	0.17	0.17	0.16[m,d]

a Projected estimate (medium fertility variant). b 2015. c Refers to the localities of Calithéa, Peristérion and Piraeus, among others. d 2017. e 2016. f Data classified according to ISIC Rev.4. g Estimate. h Calculated by the Statistics Division of the United Nations from national indices. i 2014. j Data refers to a 5-year period preceding the reference year. k Data as at the end of December. l Population aged 16 to 74 years. m Provisional data. n 2004. o Development Assistance Committee member (OECD).

Greenland

Region	Northern America	Population (000, 2018)	57[a]
Surface area (km2)	2 166 086[b]	Pop. density (per km2, 2018)	0.1[a]
Sex ratio (m per 100 f)	112.1[c,d,e]	Capital city	Nuuk
National currency	Danish Krone (DKK)	Capital city pop. (000, 2018)	18.4
Exchange rate (per US$)	6.2[f]		

Economic indicators		2005	2010	2018
GDP: Gross domestic product (million current US$)		1 656	2 307	2 283[e]
GDP growth rate (annual %, const. 2010 prices)		2.7	2.7	0.2[e]
GDP per capita (current US$)		29 081.0	40 724.0	40 469.0[e]
Economy: Agriculture (% of Gross Value Added)		10.6	8.3	12.8[e]
Economy: Industry (% of Gross Value Added)		15.2	17.5	15.2[e]
Economy: Services and other activity (% of GVA)		74.2	74.3	72.0[e]
Employment in agriculture (% of employed)		...	...	4.6[g,h,i]
Employment in industry (% of employed)		...	...	12.6[g,h,i]
Employment in services & other sectors (% employed)		...	...	82.5[g,h,i]
Unemployment rate (% of labour force)		9.3	8.4[j]	9.7[h,k,l,m]
Agricultural production index (2004-2006=100)		99	98	98[e]
International trade: exports (million current US$)		402	391	549[n,f]
International trade: imports (million current US$)		700	854	743[n,f]
International trade: balance (million current US$)		- 297	- 463	- 194[n,f]

Major trading partners						2017
Export partners (% of exports)	Denmark	81.3[n]	Portugal	8.3	Areas nes[o]	6.0[n]
Import partners (% of imports)[n]	Denmark	72.2	Sweden	9.8	China	2.6

Social indicators	2005	2010	2018
Population growth rate (average annual %)[p]	0.3	- 0.1	- 0.1[b]
Urban population (% of total population)	82.9	84.4	86.8
Urban population growth rate (average annual %)[p]	0.6	0.3	0.3[b]
Fertility rate, total (live births per woman)	2.3	2.3	2.0[q]
Life expectancy at birth (females/males, years)[r]	... / ...	71.0 / 65.7	73.6 / 69.1
Population age distribution (0-14/60+ years old, %)[d,c]	25.0 / 9.6	22.6 / 10.9	21.0 / 13.2[e]
International migrant stock (000/% of total pop.)	6.7 / 11.7	6.2 / 11.0	6.0 / 10.6[f]
Intentional homicide rate (per 100 000 pop.)	17.6	19.4	5.3[e]

Environment and infrastructure indicators	2005	2010	2018
Individuals using the Internet (per 100 inhabitants)	57.7	63.0	68.5[n,e]
Research & Development expenditure (% of GDP)	0.7[s]	...	...
Threatened species (number)	12[s]	14	23[f]
Forested area (% of land area)[n]	~0.0	~0.0	~0.0[b]
CO2 emission estimates (million tons/tons per capita)	0.6 / 10.6	0.7 / 11.7	0.5 / 9.0[q]
Energy production, primary (Petajoules)	1	1	2[b]
Energy supply per capita (Gigajoules)	165	186	158[b]
Important sites for terrestrial biodiversity protected (%)	26.1	26.4	30.3
Pop. using improved drinking water (urban/rural, %)	100.0 / 100.0	100.0 / 100.0	100.0 / 100.0[b]
Pop. using improved sanitation facilities (urban/rural, %)	100.0 / 100.0	100.0 / 100.0	100.0 / 100.0[b]

a Projected estimate (medium fertility variant). b 2015. c De jure population. d Population statistics are compiled from registers. e 2016. f 2017. g Population aged 15 to 64 years. h Nationals, residents. i 2011. j 2006. k Population aged 18 to 64 years. l Break in the time series. m 2013. n Estimate. o Areas not elsewhere specified. p Data refers to a 5-year period preceding the reference year. q 2014. r Data refers to a 5-year period up to and including the reference year. s 2004.

Grenada

Region	Caribbean	UN membership date	17 September 1974
Population (000, 2018)	108[a]	Surface area (km2)	345[b]
Pop. density (per km2, 2018)	318.6[a]	Sex ratio (m per 100 f)	101.0[a]
Capital city	Saint George's	National currency	E. Caribbean Dollar (XCD)[c]
Capital city pop. (000, 2018)	39.3[d]	Exchange rate (per US$)	2.7[e]

Economic indicators	2005	2010	2018
GDP: Gross domestic product (million current US$)	695	771	1 016[f]
GDP growth rate (annual %, const. 2010 prices)	13.3	- 0.5	1.9[f]
GDP per capita (current US$)	6 755.0	7 366.0	9 469.0[f]
Economy: Agriculture (% of Gross Value Added)	3.4	5.2	7.3[f]
Economy: Industry (% of Gross Value Added)	26.1	16.8	15.1[f]
Economy: Services and other activity (% of GVA)	70.5	78.1	77.6[f]
Unemployment rate (% of labour force)	10.2[g]	...	...
CPI: Consumer Price Index (2010=100)	83	100	107[e]
Agricultural production index (2004-2006=100)	78	96	128[f]
International trade: exports (million current US$)	28	25[h]	23[h,e]
International trade: imports (million current US$)	334	306[h]	419[h,e]
International trade: balance (million current US$)	- 306	- 281[h]	- 396[h,e]
Balance of payments, current account (million US$)	- 193	- 204	- 34[f]

Major trading partners						2017
Export partners (% of exports)[h]	United States	31.1	Saint Lucia	9.9	Germany	8.1
Import partners (% of imports)[h]	United States	36.1	Trinidad and Tobago	15.7	United Kingdom	4.6

Social indicators	2005	2010	2018
Population growth rate (average annual %)[i]	0.3	0.3	0.4[b]
Urban population (% of total population)	35.9	35.9	36.3
Urban population growth rate (average annual %)[i]	0.4	0.3	0.5[b]
Fertility rate, total (live births per woman)[i]	2.4	2.3	2.2[b]
Life expectancy at birth (females/males, years)[i]	73.2 / 68.5	74.4 / 69.6	75.6 / 70.8[b]
Population age distribution (0-14/60+ years old, %)	30.0 / 9.9	27.5 / 9.6	26.3 / 10.7[a]
International migrant stock (000/% of total pop.)	6.9 / 6.7	7.0 / 6.7	7.1 / 6.6[e]
Refugees and others of concern to the UNHCR (000)	...	~0.0[j]	~0.0[e]
Infant mortality rate (per 1 000 live births)[i]	12.0	10.2	9.6[b]
Health: Current expenditure (% of GDP)	5.3	6.1	5.0[b]
Health: Physicians (per 1 000 pop.)	0.6[k]	0.7[i]	...
Education: Government expenditure (% of GDP)	3.9[k]	...	10.3[f]
Education: Primary gross enrol. ratio (f/m per 100 pop.)	95.5 / 98.4	101.5 / 105.1	99.6 / 103.1[f]
Education: Secondary gross enrol. ratio (f/m per 100 pop.)	98.7 / 96.9[h]	109.4 / 106.2	102.5 / 98.8[f]
Education: Tertiary gross enrol. ratio (f/m per 100 pop.)	... / ...	60.9 / 44.9[m]	102.7 / 80.3[f]
Intentional homicide rate (per 100 000 pop.)	10.7	9.6	10.2[f]
Seats held by women in the National Parliament (%)	26.7	13.3	33.3

Environment and infrastructure indicators	2005	2010	2018
Individuals using the Internet (per 100 inhabitants)[h]	20.5	27.0	55.9[f]
Threatened species (number)	23[n]	37	54[e]
Forested area (% of land area)[h]	50.0	50.0	50.0[b]
CO2 emission estimates (million tons/tons per capita)	0.2 / 2.1	0.3 / 2.5	0.2 / 2.3[o]
Energy production, primary (Petajoules)	0	0	0[b]
Energy supply per capita (Gigajoules)	33	38	38[b]
Tourist/visitor arrivals at national borders (000)	99	110	156[f]
Important sites for terrestrial biodiversity protected (%)	30.2	30.2	42.7
Pop. using improved drinking water (urban/rural, %)	99.0 / 95.3	99.0 / 95.3	99.0 / 95.3[b]
Pop. using improved sanitation facilities (urban/rural, %)	97.5 / 98.3	97.5 / 98.3	97.5 / 98.3[b]
Net Official Development Assist. received (% of GNI)	7.89	4.63	0.88[f]

a Projected estimate (medium fertility variant). b 2015. c East Caribbean Dollar. d Refers to Saint George Parish. e 2017. f 2016. g 2001. h Estimate. i Data refers to a 5-year period preceding the reference year. j Data as at the end of December. k 2003. l 2006. m 2009. n 2004. o 2014.

Guadeloupe

Region	Caribbean	Population (000, 2018)	449[a,b]
Surface area (km2)	1 705[c]	Pop. density (per km2, 2018)	265.8[a,b]
Sex ratio (m per 100 f)	86.2[a,b]	Capital city	Basse-Terre
National currency	Euro (EUR)	Capital city pop. (000, 2018)	58.4
Exchange rate (per US$)	0.8[d]		

Economic indicators	2005	2010	2018
Employment in agriculture (% of employed)	...	...	3.3[e,f,g]
Employment in industry (% of employed)[e,f]	...	13.8	13.5[g]
Employment in services & other sectors (% employed)[e,f]	...	64.4	65.5[g]
Unemployment rate (% of labour force)[f]	25.9	23.8	26.1[h,i]
Labour force participation rate (female/male pop. %)[f]	37.7 / 46.8	39.5 / 44.2	49.6 / 56.5[h,i]
CPI: Consumer Price Index (2010=100)[j]	...	100	106[k]
Agricultural production index (2004-2006=100)	103	89	92[k]

Social indicators	2005	2010	2018
Population growth rate (average annual %)[a,l]	0.7	0.5	—0.0[c]
Urban population (% of total population)[a]	98.4	98.4	98.5
Urban population growth rate (average annual %)[a,l]	0.7	0.5	—0.0[c]
Fertility rate, total (live births per woman)[a,l]	2.1	2.1	2.0[c]
Life expectancy at birth (females/males, years)[a,l]	81.4 / 74.2	82.9 / 75.7	84.0 / 76.8[c]
Population age distribution (0-14/60+ years old, %)[a]	23.8 / 15.6	22.0 / 19.3	18.2 / 24.3[b]
International migrant stock (000/% of total pop.)[a]	89.1 / 20.3	94.9 / 21.1	99.4 / 22.1[d]
Infant mortality rate (per 1 000 live births)[a,l]	8.7	7.0	5.8[c]
Intentional homicide rate (per 100 000 pop.)	5.2	8.0[m]	...

Environment and infrastructure indicators	2005	2010	2018
Threatened species (number)[n]	33[o]	54	73[d]
Forested area (% of land area)[p]	43.8	43.1	43.0[c]
CO2 emission estimates (million tons/tons per capita)	2.2 / 5.0	2.3 / 5.0	2.6 / 5.5[q]
Energy production, primary (Petajoules)	5	2[p]	5[c]
Energy supply per capita (Gigajoules)	75	71[p]	71[c]
Tourist/visitor arrivals at national borders (000)[n,r]	372	392	581[k]
Important sites for terrestrial biodiversity protected (%)	53.4	80.6	80.8
Pop. using improved drinking water (urban/rural, %)	98.6 / 99.7	99.3 / 99.8	99.3 / 99.8[c]
Pop. using improved sanitation facilities (urban/rural, %)	95.5 / 89.5	97.0 / 89.5	97.0 / 89.5[c,q]

a Including Saint Barthélemy and Saint Martin (French part). b Projected estimate (medium fertility variant). c 2015. d 2017. e Population aged 15 to 64 years. f Excluding the institutional population. g 2012. h Break in the time series. i 2013. j Calculated by the Statistics Division of the United Nations from national indices. k 2016. l Data refers to a 5-year period preceding the reference year. m 2009. n Excluding the north islands, Saint Barthélemy and Saint Martin (French part). o 2004. p Estimate. q 2014. r Arrivals by air.

Guam

Region	Micronesia	Population (000, 2018)	166[a]
Surface area (km2)	549[b]	Pop. density (per km2, 2018)	306.9[a]
Sex ratio (m per 100 f)	102.5[a]	Capital city	Hagåtña
National currency	US Dollar (USD)	Capital city pop. (000, 2018)	146.9

Economic indicators	2005	2010	2018
Employment in agriculture (% of employed)[c]	10.1	9.6	8.8
Employment in industry (% of employed)[c]	15.4	16.6	16.1
Employment in services & other sectors (% employed)[c]	74.5	73.9	75.2
Unemployment rate (% of labour force)	7.0	8.2	5.9[c]
Labour force participation rate (female/male pop. %)[c]	56.1 / 79.9	54.8 / 78.6	52.8 / 76.6
CPI: Consumer Price Index (2010=100)[d]	...	100	115[e]
Agricultural production index (2004-2006=100)	99	95	78[f]

Social indicators	2005	2010	2018
Population growth rate (average annual %)[g]	0.4	0.1	0.3[b]
Urban population (% of total population)	93.6	94.1	94.8
Urban population growth rate (average annual %)[g]	0.5	0.2	0.4[b]
Fertility rate, total (live births per woman)[g]	2.7	2.5	2.4[b]
Life expectancy at birth (females/males, years)[g]	78.5 / 73.6	80.3 / 74.7	81.5 / 76.4[b]
Population age distribution (0-14/60+ years old, %)	29.5 / 9.2	27.5 / 11.1	24.4 / 14.4[a]
International migrant stock (000/% of total pop.)	74.7 / 47.2	75.4 / 47.3	78.0 / 47.5[e]
Infant mortality rate (per 1 000 live births)[g]	13.5	11.4	9.6[b]
Intentional homicide rate (per 100 000 pop.)	4.4	1.9	2.5[h]

Environment and infrastructure indicators	2005	2010	2018
Individuals using the Internet (per 100 inhabitants)	38.6	54.0[c]	77.0[c,f]
Threatened species (number)	24[i]	34	99[e]
Forested area (% of land area)[c]	46.3	46.3	46.3[b]
Tourist/visitor arrivals at national borders (000)	1 228	1 197	1 535[f]
Important sites for terrestrial biodiversity protected (%)	40.2	40.2	40.2
Pop. using improved drinking water (urban/rural, %)	99.6 / 99.6	99.5 / 99.5	99.5 / 99.5[b]
Pop. using improved sanitation facilities (urban/rural, %)	89.4 / 89.4	89.7 / 89.7	89.8 / 89.8[b]

a Projected estimate (medium fertility variant). b 2015. c Estimate. d Calculated by the Statistics Division of the United Nations from national indices. e 2017. f 2016. g Data refers to a 5-year period preceding the reference year. h 2011. i 2004.

Guatemala

Region	Central America	UN membership date	21 November 1945
Population (000, 2018)	17 245[a]	Surface area (km2)	108 889[b]
Pop. density (per km2, 2018)	160.9[a]	Sex ratio (m per 100 f)	97.0[a]
Capital city	Guatemala City	National currency	Quetzal (GTQ)
Capital city pop. (000, 2018)	2 851.1	Exchange rate (per US$)	7.3[c]

Economic indicators

	2005	2010	2018
GDP: Gross domestic product (million current US$)	27 211	41 338	68 763[d]
GDP growth rate (annual %, const. 2010 prices)	3.3	2.9	3.1[d]
GDP per capita (current US$)	2 078.0	2 825.0	4 147.0[d]
Economy: Agriculture (% of Gross Value Added)	13.1	11.4	10.7[d]
Economy: Industry (% of Gross Value Added)	28.6	28.0	26.7[d]
Economy: Services and other activity (% of GVA)	58.3	60.6	62.6[d]
Employment in agriculture (% of employed)[e]	36.0	37.0	29.0
Employment in industry (% of employed)[e]	20.9	19.8	21.1
Employment in services & other sectors (% employed)[e]	43.1	43.2	49.9
Unemployment rate (% of labour force)	2.5[e]	3.7	2.7[e]
Labour force participation rate (female/male pop. %)[e]	44.4 / 87.3	41.7 / 85.6	40.6 / 85.0
CPI: Consumer Price Index (2010=100)	75	100[f]	133[c]
Agricultural production index (2004-2006=100)	100	124	158[d]
International trade: exports (million current US$)	5 381	8 460	11 108[e,c]
International trade: imports (million current US$)	10 500	13 830	18 190[e,c]
International trade: balance (million current US$)	- 5 119	- 5 370	- 7 082[e,c]
Balance of payments, current account (million US$)	- 1 241	- 563	1 134[c]

Major trading partners

							2017
Export partners (% of exports)	United States	34.5[e]	El Salvador	11.4	Honduras	8.6[e]
Import partners (% of imports)[e]	United States	38.5	Mexico	11.4	China	10.9

Social indicators

	2005	2010	2018
Population growth rate (average annual %)[g]	2.3	2.2	2.1[b]
Urban population (% of total population)	46.9	48.4	51.1
Urban population growth rate (average annual %)[g]	3.0	2.8	2.7[b]
Fertility rate, total (live births per woman)[g]	4.3	3.6	3.2[b]
Life expectancy at birth (females/males, years)[g]	72.1 / 65.7	73.7 / 67.2	75.6 / 69.2[b]
Population age distribution (0-14/60+ years old, %)	42.3 / 5.9	39.4 / 6.1	34.4 / 7.0[a]
International migrant stock (000/% of total pop.)[h]	57.3 / 0.4	66.4 / 0.5	81.5 / 0.5[c]
Refugees and others of concern to the UNHCR (000)	0.4[i]	0.1[i]	22.0[c]
Infant mortality rate (per 1 000 live births)[g]	37.3	31.3	26.9[b]
Health: Current expenditure (% of GDP)	6.6	6.4	5.7[b]
Health: Physicians (per 1 000 pop.)	...	0.9[i]	...
Education: Government expenditure (% of GDP)	...	2.8	2.8[d]
Education: Primary gross enrol. ratio (f/m per 100 pop.)	106.3 / 113.3	114.3 / 116.6	99.1 / 102.4[d]
Education: Secondary gross enrol. ratio (f/m per 100 pop.)	47.1 / 51.0	60.2 / 63.9	61.8 / 65.2[d]
Education: Tertiary gross enrol. ratio (f/m per 100 pop.)	7.5 / 10.2[k]	17.1 / 16.6[l]	23.1 / 19.5[b]
Intentional homicide rate (per 100 000 pop.)	40.8	40.7	27.3[d]
Seats held by women in the National Parliament (%)	8.2	12.0	12.7

Environment and infrastructure indicators

	2005	2010	2018
Individuals using the Internet (per 100 inhabitants)	5.7	10.5[e]	34.5[e,d]
Research & Development expenditure (% of GDP)[m]	~0.0	~0.0	~0.0[n]
Threatened species (number)	208[o]	230	290[c]
Forested area (% of land area)	36.7	34.7[e]	33.0[e,b]
CO2 emission estimates (million tons/tons per capita)	12.6 / 1.0	11.7 / 0.8	18.3 / 1.1[p]
Energy production, primary (Petajoules)	255	279	316[b]
Energy supply per capita (Gigajoules)	28	26	29[b]
Tourist/visitor arrivals at national borders (000)	...	1 119	1 585[d]
Important sites for terrestrial biodiversity protected (%)	27.6	30.8	30.8
Pop. using improved drinking water (urban/rural, %)	95.4 / 80.1	97.3 / 84.3	98.4 / 86.8[b]
Pop. using improved sanitation facilities (urban/rural, %)	75.0 / 43.0	76.6 / 46.9	77.5 / 49.3[b]
Net Official Development Assist. received (% of GNI)	0.95	0.97	0.40[d]

a Projected estimate (medium fertility variant). b 2015. c 2017. d 2016. e Estimate. f Break in the time series. g Data refers to a 5-year period preceding the reference year. h Including refugees. i Data as at the end of December. j 2009. k 2002. l 2007. m Partial data. n 2012. o 2004. p 2014.

Guinea

Region	Western Africa	UN membership date	12 December 1958
Population (000, 2018)	13 053[a]	Surface area (km2)	245 857[b]
Pop. density (per km2, 2018)	53.1[a]	Sex ratio (m per 100 f)	100.6[a]
Capital city	Conakry	National currency	Guinean Franc (GNF)
Capital city pop. (000, 2018)	1 843.1	Exchange rate (per US$)	9 225.3[c]

Economic indicators	2005	2010	2018
GDP: Gross domestic product (million current US$)	4 063	6 853	8 476[c]
GDP growth rate (annual %, const. 2010 prices)	3.0	4.2	6.6[c]
GDP per capita (current US$)	420.0	835.0	684.0[c]
Economy: Agriculture (% of Gross Value Added)	14.9	18.6	20.2[c]
Economy: Industry (% of Gross Value Added)	34.9	34.3	36.9[c]
Economy: Services and other activity (% of GVA)	50.3	47.1	42.9[c]
Employment in agriculture (% of employed)[d]	70.1	70.2	68.0
Employment in industry (% of employed)[d]	5.8	6.0	6.0
Employment in services & other sectors (% employed)[d]	24.0	23.8	26.1
Unemployment rate (% of labour force)[d]	4.6	4.5	4.5
Labour force participation rate (female/male pop. %)[d]	62.8 / 67.4	62.8 / 66.6	63.0 / 65.4
CPI: Consumer Price Index (2010=100)[e]	42	100	219[f]
Agricultural production index (2004-2006=100)	100	120	135[c]
International trade: exports (million current US$)	796	1 471[d]	1 942[d,f]
International trade: imports (million current US$)	1 648	1 405[d]	2 065[d,f]
International trade: balance (million current US$)	- 852	66[d]	- 123[d,f]
Balance of payments, current account (million US$)	- 160	- 327	- 2 745[c]

Major trading partners						2017
Export partners (% of exports)[d]	China	86.6	Belgium	6.8	Singapore	1.7
Import partners (% of imports)[d]	Côte d'Ivoire	22.3	China	11.6	Spain	8.8

Social indicators	2005	2010	2018
Population growth rate (average annual %)[g]	1.9	2.2	2.3[b]
Urban population (% of total population)	32.3	33.7	36.1
Urban population growth rate (average annual %)[g]	2.8	3.0	3.1[b]
Fertility rate, total (live births per woman)[g]	5.9	5.5	5.1[b]
Life expectancy at birth (females/males, years)[g]	51.3 / 51.3	56.4 / 54.5	58.4 / 57.4[b]
Population age distribution (0-14/60+ years old, %)	44.0 / 5.1	43.5 / 4.9	42.0 / 5.2[a]
International migrant stock (000/% of total pop.)[h,i]	229.6 / 2.4	178.0 / 1.6	122.8 / 1.0[f]
Refugees and others of concern to the UNHCR (000)	97.0[j]	15.0[j]	5.2[f]
Infant mortality rate (per 1 000 live births)[g]	95.2	77.7	65.7[b]
Health: Current expenditure (% of GDP)	4.5	4.4	4.5[b]
Health: Physicians (per 1 000 pop.)	0.1	...	0.1[c]
Education: Government expenditure (% of GDP)	1.8	2.5	2.4[k]
Education: Primary gross enrol. ratio (f/m per 100 pop.)	70.2 / 87.6	77.5 / 94.1	86.1 / 101.7[k]
Education: Secondary gross enrol. ratio (f/m per 100 pop.)	19.3 / 38.8[d]	25.1 / 43.4[l]	31.9 / 48.6[k]
Education: Tertiary gross enrol. ratio (f/m per 100 pop.)	1.1 / 4.7	5.2 / 15.6	6.9 / 15.5[k]
Intentional homicide rate (per 100 000 pop.)	10.1	9.4	8.8[b]
Seats held by women in the National Parliament (%)	19.3	19.3[m,l]	21.9

Environment and infrastructure indicators	2005	2010	2018
Individuals using the Internet (per 100 inhabitants)	0.5	1.0[d]	9.8[d,c]
Threatened species (number)	67[n]	134	185[f]
Forested area (% of land area)[d]	27.4	26.6	25.9[b]
CO2 emission estimates (million tons/tons per capita)	1.8 / 0.2	2.6 / 0.2	2.4 / 0.2[k]
Energy production, primary (Petajoules)	109	112	116[b]
Energy supply per capita (Gigajoules)	15	13	12[b]
Tourist/visitor arrivals at national borders (000)[o]	45	12	35[b]
Important sites for terrestrial biodiversity protected (%)	76.4	76.4	76.4
Pop. using improved drinking water (urban/rural, %)	90.3 / 56.8	91.7 / 62.7	92.7 / 67.4[b]
Pop. using improved sanitation facilities (urban/rural, %)	27.9 / 9.2	31.3 / 10.6	34.1 / 11.8[b]
Net Official Development Assist. received (% of GNI)	7.26	5.14	9.70[c]

a Projected estimate (medium fertility variant). b 2015. c 2016. d Estimate. e Conakry f 2017. g Data refers to a 5-year period preceding the reference year. h Refers to foreign citizens. i Including refugees. j Data as at the end of December. k 2014, l 2008. m The parliament was dissolved following the December 2008 coup. n 2004. o Arrivals by air at Conakry airport.

Guinea-Bissau

Region	Western Africa	UN membership date	17 September 1974
Population (000, 2018)	1 907 [a]	Surface area (km2)	36 125 [b]
Pop. density (per km2, 2018)	67.8 [a]	Sex ratio (m per 100 f)	96.9 [a]
Capital city	Bissau	National currency	CFA Franc, BCEAO (XOF) [c]
Capital city pop. (000, 2018)	558.4	Exchange rate (per US$)	546.9 [d]

Economic indicators	2005	2010	2018
GDP: Gross domestic product (million current US$)	587	849	1 123 [e]
GDP growth rate (annual %, const. 2010 prices)	4.3	4.6	5.1 [e]
GDP per capita (current US$)	425.0	546.0	618.0 [e]
Economy: Agriculture (% of Gross Value Added)	45.4	46.2	44.2 [e]
Economy: Industry (% of Gross Value Added)	14.7	13.5	14.7 [e]
Economy: Services and other activity (% of GVA)	39.9	40.3	41.1 [e]
Employment in agriculture (% of employed) [f]	84.6	84.5	83.3
Employment in industry (% of employed) [f]	6.9	6.6	6.9
Employment in services & other sectors (% employed) [f]	8.4	9.0	9.7
Unemployment rate (% of labour force) [f]	6.5	6.3	6.1
Labour force participation rate (female/male pop. %) [f]	64.4 / 79.2	64.7 / 78.1	65.7 / 78.1
CPI: Consumer Price Index (2010=100) [g]	84	100	112 [d]
Agricultural production index (2004-2006=100)	100	128	143 [e]
International trade: exports (million current US$)	23	120 [f]	1 430 [f,d]
International trade: imports (million current US$)	112	197 [f]	204 [f,d]
International trade: balance (million current US$)	- 88	- 77 [f]	1 226 [f,d]
Balance of payments, current account (million US$)	- 10	- 71	10 [e]

Major trading partners						2017
Export partners (% of exports) [f]	India	61.1	Viet Nam	21.3	Belarus	10.0
Import partners (% of imports) [f]	Portugal	26.6	Gambia	19.6	Senegal	15.4

Social indicators	2005	2010	2018
Population growth rate (average annual %) [h]	2.1	2.4	2.6 [b]
Urban population (% of total population)	38.2	40.1	43.4
Urban population growth rate (average annual %) [h]	3.1	3.4	3.6 [b]
Fertility rate, total (live births per woman) [h]	5.6	5.2	4.9 [b]
Life expectancy at birth (females/males, years) [h]	53.3 / 52.0	55.6 / 52.8	57.7 / 54.3 [b]
Population age distribution (0-14/60+ years old, %)	43.6 / 4.5	42.3 / 4.6	41.3 / 5.0 [a]
International migrant stock (000/% of total pop.) [i]	20.7 / 1.5	21.1 / 1.4	23.4 / 1.3 [d]
Refugees and others of concern to the UNHCR (000)	7.8 [j]	8.0 [j]	9.4 [d]
Infant mortality rate (per 1 000 live births) [h]	101.0	91.1	80.4 [b]
Health: Current expenditure (% of GDP) [f]	6.3	6.2	6.9 [b]
Health: Physicians (per 1 000 pop.)	0.1 [k]	0.1	...
Education: Government expenditure (% of GDP)	...	1.9	2.1 [m]
Education: Primary gross enrol. ratio (f/m per 100 pop.)	58.9 / 87.6 [n]	114.1 / 122.1	... / ...
Education: Secondary gross enrol. ratio (f/m per 100 pop.)	12.4 / 22.8 [n]	... / ...	... / ...
Intentional homicide rate (per 100 000 pop.)	11.7	10.5	9.5 [b]
Seats held by women in the National Parliament (%)	14.0	10.0	13.7

Environment and infrastructure indicators	2005	2010	2018
Individuals using the Internet (per 100 inhabitants)	1.9	2.4 [f]	3.8 [f,e]
Threatened species (number)	22 [k]	52	77 [d]
Forested area (% of land area) [f]	73.7	71.9	70.1 [b]
CO2 emission estimates (million tons/tons per capita)	0.2 / 0.1	0.2 / 0.1	0.3 / 0.1 [o]
Energy production, primary (Petajoules)	22	24	25 [b]
Energy supply per capita (Gigajoules)	19	17	16 [b]
Tourist/visitor arrivals at national borders (000) [p]	5	22	44 [b]
Important sites for terrestrial biodiversity protected (%)	52.2	52.2	52.6
Pop. using improved drinking water (urban/rural, %)	77.9 / 48.9	88.4 / 54.6	98.8 / 60.3 [b]
Pop. using improved sanitation facilities (urban/rural, %)	29.7 / 5.9	32.4 / 7.8	33.5 / 8.5 [b]
Net Official Development Assist. received (% of GNI)	11.61	15.27	17.75 [e]

a Projected estimate (medium fertility variant). **b** 2015. **c** African Financial Community (CFA) Franc, Central Bank of West African States (BCEAO). **d** 2017. **e** 2016. **f** Estimate. **g** Bissau **h** Data refers to a 5-year period preceding the reference year. **i** Including refugees. **j** Data as at the end of December. **k** 2004. **l** 2009. **m** 2013. **n** 2000. **o** 2014. **p** Arrivals by air.

Guyana

Region	South America	UN membership date	20 September 1966
Population (000, 2018)	782[a]	Surface area (km2)	214 969[b]
Pop. density (per km2, 2018)	4.0[a]	Sex ratio (m per 100 f)	102.1[a]
Capital city	Georgetown	National currency	Guyana Dollar (GYD)
Capital city pop. (000, 2018)	109.9	Exchange rate (per US$)	206.5[c]

Economic indicators	2005	2010	2018
GDP: Gross domestic product (million current US$)	1 315	2 259	3 437[d]
GDP growth rate (annual %, const. 2010 prices)	- 2.0	4.1	3.4[d]
GDP per capita (current US$)	1 752.0	3 026.0	4 444.0[d]
Economy: Agriculture (% of Gross Value Added)	25.7	17.6	14.6[d]
Economy: Industry (% of Gross Value Added)	28.7	34.5	40.3[d]
Economy: Services and other activity (% of GVA)	45.6	47.9	45.1[d]
Employment in agriculture (% of employed)[e]	23.5	17.0	13.2
Employment in industry (% of employed)[e]	23.9	25.0	26.4
Employment in services & other sectors (% employed)[e]	52.6	58.0	60.5
Unemployment rate (% of labour force)[e]	11.8	10.9	11.7
Labour force participation rate (female/male pop. %)[e]	34.1 / 78.0	37.0 / 76.0	40.8 / 74.5
CPI: Consumer Price Index (2010=100)[e,f]	74	100	110[d]
Agricultural production index (2004-2006=100)	94	108	130[d]
International trade: exports (million current US$)	539	901	1 790[c]
International trade: imports (million current US$)	778	1 452	1 762[c]
International trade: balance (million current US$)	- 239	- 551	28[c]
Balance of payments, current account (million US$)	- 96	- 246	128[d]

Major trading partners							2017
Export partners (% of exports)	Canada	22.9	United States	15.9	Trinidad and Tobago	11.4
Import partners (% of imports)	Trinidad and Tobago	27.5	United States	26.5	China	8.9

Social indicators	2005	2010	2018
Population growth rate (average annual %)[g]	- 0.1	- 0.1	0.6[b]
Urban population (% of total population)	27.8	26.6	26.6
Urban population growth rate (average annual %)[g]	- 0.7	- 1.0	0.4[b]
Fertility rate, total (live births per woman)[g]	2.9	2.7	2.6[b]
Life expectancy at birth (females/males, years)[g]	68.1 / 62.6	68.4 / 63.4	68.6 / 64.0[b]
Population age distribution (0-14/60+ years old, %)	36.2 / 6.0	32.7 / 7.2	28.6 / 8.9[a]
International migrant stock (000/% of total pop.)	10.9 / 1.4	13.1 / 1.8	15.5 / 2.0[a]
Refugees and others of concern to the UNHCR (000)	...	~0.0[h]	~0.0[c]
Infant mortality rate (per 1 000 live births)[g]	36.5	34.4	33.2[b]
Health: Current expenditure (% of GDP)	5.4	4.6	4.5[b]
Health: Physicians (per 1 000 pop.)	0.5[i]	0.2	...
Education: Government expenditure (% of GDP)	8.1	3.6	3.2[i]
Education: Primary gross enrol. ratio (f/m per 100 pop.)	100.2 / 99.9	96.7 / 96.7	97.1 / 95.1[i]
Education: Secondary gross enrol. ratio (f/m per 100 pop.)	86.6 / 83.9	92.8 / 87.2	100.9 / 96.6[i]
Education: Tertiary gross enrol. ratio (f/m per 100 pop.)	15.9 / 7.4	16.6 / 6.9	15.6 / 7.6[i]
Intentional homicide rate (per 100 000 pop.)	18.9	18.8	18.4[d]
Seats held by women in the National Parliament (%)	30.8	30.0	31.9

Environment and infrastructure indicators	2005	2010	2018
Individuals using the Internet (per 100 inhabitants)	6.6[i]	29.9	35.7[e,d]
Threatened species (number)	65[k]	69	94[c]
Forested area (% of land area)[e]	84.3	84.2	84.0[b]
CO2 emission estimates (million tons/tons per capita)	1.4 / 1.9	1.7 / 2.3	2.0 / 2.6[l]
Energy production, primary (Petajoules)	9	8	7[b]
Energy supply per capita (Gigajoules)	39	43	45[b]
Tourist/visitor arrivals at national borders (000)[m]	117	152	235[d]
Pop. using improved drinking water (urban/rural, %)	95.9 / 88.0	97.0 / 93.1	98.2 / 98.3[b]
Pop. using improved sanitation facilities (urban/rural, %)	87.0 / 79.0	87.7 / 81.5	87.9 / 82.0[b]
Net Official Development Assist. received (% of GNI)	19.28	7.37	2.02[d]

a Projected estimate (medium fertility variant). **b** 2015. **c** 2017. **d** 2016. **e** Estimate. **f** Georgetown **g** Data refers to a 5-year period preceding the reference year. **h** Data as at the end of December. **i** 2000. **j** 2012. **k** 2004. **l** 2014. **m** Arrivals to Timehri airport only.

Haiti

Region	Caribbean	UN membership date	24 October 1945
Population (000, 2018)	11 113[a]	Surface area (km2)	27 750[b]
Pop. density (per km2, 2018)	403.2[a]	Sex ratio (m per 100 f)	97.8[a]
Capital city	Port-au-Prince	National currency	Gourde (HTG)
Capital city pop. (000, 2018)	2 636.8	Exchange rate (per US$)	67.4[c]

Economic indicators

	2005	2010	2018
GDP: Gross domestic product (million current US$)	4 154	6 708	7 647[c]
GDP growth rate (annual %, const. 2010 prices)	1.8	-5.5	1.4[c]
GDP per capita (current US$)	448.0	671.0	705.0[c]
Economy: Agriculture (% of Gross Value Added)	22.4	21.0	16.7[c]
Economy: Industry (% of Gross Value Added)	32.9	33.7	38.0[c]
Economy: Services and other activity (% of GVA)	44.8	45.4	45.3[c]
Employment in agriculture (% of employed)[d]	49.8	47.2	40.6
Employment in industry (% of employed)[d]	10.4	10.2	12.6
Employment in services & other sectors (% employed)[d]	39.9	42.5	46.8
Unemployment rate (% of labour force)[d]	15.0	15.9	13.9
Labour force participation rate (female/male pop. %)[d]	59.2 / 70.1	60.6 / 71.4	64.1 / 72.8
CPI: Consumer Price Index (2010=100)	67	100	181[e]
Agricultural production index (2004-2006=100)	102	132	155[c]
International trade: exports (million current US$)[d]	470	579	941[e]
International trade: imports (million current US$)[d]	1 449	3 147	3 470[e]
International trade: balance (million current US$)[d]	- 979	- 2 568	- 2 530[e]
Balance of payments, current account (million US$)	7	- 102	- 72[c]

Major trading partners

						2017
Export partners (% of exports)[d]	United States	82.7	Dominican Republic	3.7	Canada	2.9
Import partners (% of imports)[d]	United States	34.1	Dominican Republic	21.0	China	11.9

Social indicators

	2005	2010	2018
Population growth rate (average annual %)[f]	1.6	1.5	1.4[b]
Urban population (% of total population)	42.6	47.5	55.3
Urban population growth rate (average annual %)[f]	5.2	3.7	3.3[b]
Fertility rate, total (live births per woman)[f]	4.0	3.5	3.1[b]
Life expectancy at birth (females/males, years)[f]	60.1 / 56.5	62.3 / 58.2	64.4 / 60.2[b]
Population age distribution (0-14/60+ years old, %)	38.0 / 6.4	35.9 / 6.5	32.6 / 7.4[a]
International migrant stock (000/% of total pop.)	30.5 / 0.3	35.1 / 0.4	40.5 / 0.4[e]
Refugees and others of concern to the UNHCR (000)	...	~0.0[g]	2.7[e]
Infant mortality rate (per 1 000 live births)[f]	56.0	52.2	46.9[b]
Health: Current expenditure (% of GDP)	5.5	10.2	6.9[b]
Intentional homicide rate (per 100 000 pop.)	...	6.8	10.0[h]
Seats held by women in the National Parliament (%)	3.6	4.1	2.5

Environment and infrastructure indicators

	2005	2010	2018
Individuals using the Internet (per 100 inhabitants)[d]	6.4	8.4	12.2[c]
Threatened species (number)	116[i]	137	205[e]
Forested area (% of land area)[d]	3.8	3.7	3.5[b]
CO2 emission estimates (million tons/tons per capita)	2.1 / 0.2	2.1 / 0.2	2.9 / 0.3[j]
Energy production, primary (Petajoules)	115	131	139[b]
Energy supply per capita (Gigajoules)	15	16	17[b]
Tourist/visitor arrivals at national borders (000)[k]	112	255[l]	516[l,b]
Important sites for terrestrial biodiversity protected (%)	10.5	10.5	10.5
Pop. using improved drinking water (urban/rural, %)	75.6 / 48.7	69.7 / 48.1	64.9 / 47.6[b]
Pop. using improved sanitation facilities (urban/rural, %)	33.4 / 16.0	33.5 / 17.7	33.6 / 19.2[b]
Net Official Development Assist. received (% of GNI)	9.96	46.25	13.32[c]

a Projected estimate (medium fertility variant). **b** 2015. **c** 2016. **d** Estimate. **e** 2017. **f** Data refers to a 5-year period preceding the reference year. **g** Data as at the end of December. **h** 2012. **i** 2004. **j** 2014. **k** Arrivals by air. **l** Including nationals residing abroad.

Holy See

Region	Southern Europe	Population (000, 2018)	1 [a]
Surface area (km2)	~0 [b,c]	Pop. density (per km2, 2018)	1 820.5 [a]
Sex ratio (m per 100 f)	219.2 [d]	Capital city	Vatican City
National currency	Euro (EUR)	Capital city pop. (000, 2018)	0.8
Exchange rate (per US$)	0.8 [e]		

Social indicators	2005	2010	2018
Population growth rate (average annual %) [f]	0.3	~0.0	~0.0 [c]
Urban population (% of total population)	100.0	100.0	100.0
Urban population growth rate (average annual %) [f]	0.3	-0.1	0.2 [c]
International migrant stock (000/% of total pop.) [g]	0.8 / 100.0	0.8 / 100.0	0.8 / 100.0 [e]
Intentional homicide rate (per 100 000 pop.)	...	0.0	0.0 [c]

Environment and infrastructure indicators	2005	2010	2018
Threatened species (number)	...	1	1 [e]

a Projected estimate (medium fertility variant). b Surface area is 0.44 Km2. c 2015. d 2009. e 2017. f Data refers to a 5-year period preceding the reference year. g Estimate.

Honduras

Region	Central America	UN membership date	17 December 1945
Population (000, 2018)	9 417[a]	Surface area (km2)	112 492[b]
Pop. density (per km2, 2018)	84.2[a]	Sex ratio (m per 100 f)	99.5[a]
Capital city	Tegucigalpa	National currency	Lempira (HNL)
Capital city pop. (000, 2018)	1 363.0	Exchange rate (per US$)	23.6[c]

Economic indicators

	2005	2010	2018
GDP: Gross domestic product (million current US$)	9 757	15 839	21 517[d]
GDP growth rate (annual %, const. 2010 prices)	6.1	3.7	3.6[d]
GDP per capita (current US$)	1 323.0	1 933.0	2 361.0[d]
Economy: Agriculture (% of Gross Value Added)	13.1	11.9	12.7[d]
Economy: Industry (% of Gross Value Added)	27.6	26.2	26.6[d]
Economy: Services and other activity (% of GVA)	59.3	62.0	60.7[d]
Employment in agriculture (% of employed)[e]	39.3	37.8	28.3
Employment in industry (% of employed)[e]	20.9	18.6	21.4
Employment in services & other sectors (% employed)[e]	39.8	43.6	50.4
Unemployment rate (% of labour force)	4.0	4.1	4.3[e]
Labour force participation rate (female/male pop. %)[e]	36.5 / 83.4	44.5 / 84.8	50.9 / 85.6
CPI: Consumer Price Index (2010=100)[e]	72	100	138[c]
Agricultural production index (2004-2006=100)	103	111	124[d]
Index of industrial production (2005=100)[f]	100	113	130[g]
International trade: exports (million current US$)	1 294	3 104	4 970[c]
International trade: imports (million current US$)	4 419	6 895	8 612[c]
International trade: balance (million current US$)	- 3 125	- 3 791	- 3 642[c]
Balance of payments, current account (million US$)	- 304	- 682	- 380[c]

Major trading partners

							2017
Export partners (% of exports)	United States	40.2	Germany	7.9	Belgium	7.0
Import partners (% of imports)	United States	34.7	China	15.0	Guatemala	8.6

Social indicators

	2005	2010	2018
Population growth rate (average annual %)[h]	2.4	2.1	1.8[b]
Urban population (% of total population)	48.6	51.9	57.1
Urban population growth rate (average annual %)[h]	3.8	3.4	3.0[b]
Fertility rate, total (live births per woman)[h]	3.8	3.2	2.6[b]
Life expectancy at birth (females/males, years)[h]	73.4 / 68.6	74.5 / 69.6	75.4 / 70.4[b]
Population age distribution (0-14/60+ years old, %)	39.9 / 5.5	36.6 / 5.8	31.0 / 7.1[a]
International migrant stock (000/% of total pop.)[i]	27.9 / 0.4	27.3 / 0.3	38.7 / 0.4[c]
Refugees and others of concern to the UNHCR (000)	0.1[j]	~0.0[j]	175.6[c]
Infant mortality rate (per 1 000 live births)[h]	31.2	29.4	27.8[b]
Health: Current expenditure (% of GDP)	7.2	8.2	7.6[b]
Health: Physicians (per 1 000 pop.)	0.4	...	...
Education: Government expenditure (% of GDP)	...	...	5.9[k]
Education: Primary gross enrol. ratio (f/m per 100 pop.)	105.4 / 105.5	104.9 / 105.2	95.8 / 96.6[d]
Education: Secondary gross enrol. ratio (f/m per 100 pop.)	... / ...	75.3 / 61.3	69.6 / 59.8[d]
Education: Tertiary gross enrol. ratio (f/m per 100 pop.)	19.0 / 13.2[a,l]	20.8 / 18.0	23.7 / 17.4[b]
Intentional homicide rate (per 100 000 pop.)	43.6	76.1	56.5[d]
Seats held by women in the National Parliament (%)	5.5	18.0	21.1

Environment and infrastructure indicators

	2005	2010	2018
Individuals using the Internet (per 100 inhabitants)	6.5[a,m]	11.1	30.0[a,d]
Research & Development expenditure (% of GDP)	~0.0[l]	...	...
Threatened species (number)	206[l]	240	301[c]
Forested area (% of land area)[e]	51.8	46.4	41.0[b]
CO2 emission estimates (million tons/tons per capita)	7.6 / 1.1	8.0 / 1.1	9.5 / 1.2[g]
Energy production, primary (Petajoules)	77	93	113[b]
Energy supply per capita (Gigajoules)	25	25	29[b]
Tourist/visitor arrivals at national borders (000)	673	863	880[b]
Important sites for terrestrial biodiversity protected (%)	57.5	57.6	65.0
Pop. using improved drinking water (urban/rural, %)	95.4 / 74.2	96.4 / 79.0	97.4 / 83.8[b]
Pop. using improved sanitation facilities (urban/rural, %)	80.4 / 61.1	83.9 / 70.3	86.7 / 77.7[b]
Net Official Development Assist. received (% of GNI)	7.51	4.20	2.05[d]

a Projected estimate (medium fertility variant). **b** 2015. **c** 2017. **d** 2016. **e** Estimate. **f** Data classified according to ISIC Rev. 3. **g** 2014. **h** Data refers to a 5-year period preceding the reference year. **i** Including refugees. **j** Data as at the end of December. **k** 2013. **l** 2004. **m** Population aged 5 years and over.

Hungary

Region	Eastern Europe	UN membership date	14 December 1955
Population (000, 2018)	9 689[a]	Surface area (km2)	93 024[b]
Pop. density (per km2, 2018)	107.0[a]	Sex ratio (m per 100 f)	90.8[a]
Capital city	Budapest	National currency	Forint (HUF)
Capital city pop. (000, 2018)	1 759.5	Exchange rate (per US$)	258.8[c]

Economic indicators

	2005	2010	2018
GDP: Gross domestic product (million current US$)	113 035	130 923	125 817[d]
GDP growth rate (annual %, const. 2010 prices)	4.4	0.7	2.2[d]
GDP per capita (current US$)	11 207.0	13 187.0	12 900.0[d]
Economy: Agriculture (% of Gross Value Added)[e]	4.3	3.5	4.4[d]
Economy: Industry (% of Gross Value Added)[e]	31.3	29.9	30.5[d]
Economy: Services and other activity (% of GVA)[e]	64.5	66.6	65.1[d]
Employment in agriculture (% of employed)	4.9	4.5[f]	4.8[f]
Employment in industry (% of employed)[f]	32.5	30.7	29.9
Employment in services & other sectors (% employed)[f]	62.7	64.8	65.4
Unemployment rate (% of labour force)	7.2	11.2	4.0[f]
Labour force participation rate (female/male pop. %)[f]	42.9 / 58.4	43.8 / 58.2	47.9 / 63.9
CPI: Consumer Price Index (2010=100)	77	100	114[c]
Agricultural production index (2004-2006=100)	97	80	88[d]
Index of industrial production (2005=100)	100	108[g]	122[g,h]
International trade: exports (million current US$)	62 272	94 749	113 382[c]
International trade: imports (million current US$)	65 920	87 432	104 284[c]
International trade: balance (million current US$)	- 3 648	7 317	9 098[c]
Balance of payments, current account (million US$)	- 7 883	346	3 743[c]

Major trading partners

						2017
Export partners (% of exports)	Germany	27.4	Romania	5.2	Italy	5.1
Import partners (% of imports)	Germany	26.5	Austria	6.2	Poland	5.6

Social indicators

	2005	2010	2018
Population growth rate (average annual %)[i]	- 0.3	- 0.3	- 0.3[b]
Urban population (% of total population)	66.4	68.9	71.4
Urban population growth rate (average annual %)[i]	0.3	0.4	0.2[b]
Fertility rate, total (live births per woman)[i]	1.3	1.3	1.3[b]
Life expectancy at birth (females/males, years)[i]	76.7 / 68.3	77.8 / 69.6	78.8 / 71.7[b]
Population age distribution (0-14/60+ years old, %)	15.5 / 21.4	14.9 / 22.1	14.3 / 26.3[a]
International migrant stock (000/% of total pop.)[j]	366.8 / 3.6	436.6 / 4.4	503.8 / 5.2[c]
Refugees and others of concern to the UNHCR (000)	8.9[k]	5.8[k]	6.0[c]
Infant mortality rate (per 1 000 live births)[i]	7.4	5.7	4.9[b]
Health: Current expenditure (% of GDP)	8.0	7.6	7.2[b]
Health: Physicians (per 1 000 pop.)	3.2	2.9	3.1[b]
Education: Government expenditure (% of GDP)	5.3	4.8	4.6[h]
Education: Primary gross enrol. ratio (f/m per 100 pop.)	97.1 / 99.1	100.5 / 101.2	101.7 / 102.0[d]
Education: Secondary gross enrol. ratio (f/m per 100 pop.)	95.8 / 96.7	96.4 / 97.7	102.3 / 102.3[d]
Education: Tertiary gross enrol. ratio (f/m per 100 pop.)	77.5 / 53.0	73.8 / 54.1	53.5 / 42.8[d]
Intentional homicide rate (per 100 000 pop.)	1.6	1.4	2.1[d]
Seats held by women in the National Parliament (%)	9.1	11.1	10.1

Environment and infrastructure indicators

	2005	2010	2018
Individuals using the Internet (per 100 inhabitants)	39.0[l]	65.0[l]	79.3[d]
Research & Development expenditure (% of GDP)	0.9	1.1	1.4[b]
Threatened species (number)	51[m]	47	66[c]
Forested area (% of land area)	22.1	22.6	22.9[f,b]
CO2 emission estimates (million tons/tons per capita)	58.0 / 5.8	50.2 / 5.0	42.1 / 4.3[h]
Energy production, primary (Petajoules)	434	496	471[b]
Energy supply per capita (Gigajoules)	115	111	107[b]
Tourist/visitor arrivals at national borders (000)	9 979	9 510	15 255[d]
Important sites for terrestrial biodiversity protected (%)	81.0	82.9	82.9
Pop. using improved drinking water (urban/rural, %)	99.7 / 98.4	100.0 / 100.0	100.0 / 100.0[b]
Pop. using improved sanitation facilities (urban/rural, %)	97.8 / 98.6	97.8 / 98.6	97.8 / 98.6[b]
Net Official Development Assist. disbursed (% of GNI)[n]	0.11	0.09	0.11[o,c]

a Projected estimate (medium fertility variant). **b** 2015. **c** 2017. **d** 2016. **e** Data classified according to ISIC Rev. 4. **f** Estimate. **g** Excluding water and waste management. **h** 2014. **i** Data refers to a 5-year period preceding the reference year. **j** Including refugees. **k** Data as at the end of December. **l** Population aged 16 to 74 years. **m** 2004. **n** Development Assistance Committee member (OECD). **o** Provisional data.

Iceland

Region	Northern Europe	UN membership date	19 November 1946
Population (000, 2018)	338[a]	Surface area (km2)	103 000[b]
Pop. density (per km2, 2018)	3.4[a]	Sex ratio (m per 100 f)	100.8[a]
Capital city	Reykjavik	National currency	Iceland Krona (ISK)
Capital city pop. (000, 2018)	216.4	Exchange rate (per US$)	104.4[c]

Economic indicators	2005	2010	2018
GDP: Gross domestic product (million current US$)	16 691	13 311	20 270[d]
GDP growth rate (annual %, const. 2010 prices)	6.7	- 3.6	7.2[d]
GDP per capita (current US$)	56 585.0	41 553.0	60 966.0[d]
Economy: Agriculture (% of Gross Value Added)[e]	5.7	7.4	5.7[d]
Economy: Industry (% of Gross Value Added)[e]	24.7	24.7	22.4[d]
Economy: Services and other activity (% of GVA)[e]	69.6	68.0	72.0[d]
Employment in agriculture (% of employed)	6.5	5.6[f]	3.1[f]
Employment in industry (% of employed)[f]	21.7	18.4	15.5
Employment in services & other sectors (% employed)[f]	71.8	76.0	81.4
Unemployment rate (% of labour force)	2.6	7.6	2.8[f]
Labour force participation rate (female/male pop. %)[f]	70.9 / 80.7	70.6 / 79.1	72.5 / 81.2
CPI: Consumer Price Index (2010=100)	67	100	122[c]
Agricultural production index (2004-2006=100)	99	110	126[c]
International trade: exports (million current US$)	3 091	4 603	4 850[c]
International trade: imports (million current US$)	4 979	3 914	6 945[c]
International trade: balance (million current US$)	- 1 888	689	- 2 094[c]
Balance of payments, current account (million US$)	- 2 653	- 881	879[c]

Major trading partners						2017
Export partners (% of exports)	Netherlands	25.5	Spain	13.5	United Kingdom	9.4
Import partners (% of imports)	Germany	10.6	Norway	9.1	China	6.9

Social indicators	2005	2010	2018
Population growth rate (average annual %)[g]	1.0	1.6	0.6[b]
Urban population (% of total population)	93.0	93.6	93.8
Urban population growth rate (average annual %)[g]	1.1	1.8	0.6[b]
Fertility rate, total (live births per woman)[g]	2.0	2.1	2.0[b]
Life expectancy at birth (females/males, years)[g]	82.6 / 78.8	83.2 / 79.6	83.8 / 80.6[b]
Population age distribution (0-14/60+ years old, %)	22.2 / 15.8	20.8 / 16.9	20.0 / 20.6[a]
International migrant stock (000/% of total pop.)	25.5 / 8.6	35.1 / 11.0	41.9 / 12.5[c]
Refugees and others of concern to the UNHCR (000)	0.4[h]	0.2[h]	0.8[c]
Infant mortality rate (per 1 000 live births)[g]	2.5	2.0	1.6[b]
Health: Current expenditure (% of GDP)	9.2	8.8	8.6[b]
Health: Physicians (per 1 000 pop.)	3.6	3.6	3.8[b]
Education: Government expenditure (% of GDP)	7.4	7.2	7.8[i]
Education: Primary gross enrol. ratio (f/m per 100 pop.)	95.7 / 98.0	99.6 / 99.0	98.6 / 98.7[b]
Education: Secondary gross enrol. ratio (f/m per 100 pop.)	112.1 / 110.5	108.2 / 106.5	119.6 / 118.6[b]
Education: Tertiary gross enrol. ratio (f/m per 100 pop.)	92.5 / 48.1	101.5 / 56.8	98.0 / 54.7[b]
Intentional homicide rate (per 100 000 pop.)	1.0	0.6	0.3[d]
Seats held by women in the National Parliament (%)	30.2	42.9	38.1

Environment and infrastructure indicators	2005	2010	2018
Individuals using the Internet (per 100 inhabitants)	87.0[j]	93.4[j,k]	98.2[f,d]
Research & Development expenditure (% of GDP)	2.7	2.7[l]	2.2[b]
Threatened species (number)	15[m]	17	27[c]
Forested area (% of land area)	0.4	0.4	0.5[f,b]
CO2 emission estimates (million tons/tons per capita)	2.2 / 7.5	2.0 / 6.2	2.0 / 6.1[n]
Energy production, primary (Petajoules)	127	252	285[b]
Energy supply per capita (Gigajoules)	534	875	950[b]
Tourist/visitor arrivals at national borders (000)	374	489	1 792[d]
Important sites for terrestrial biodiversity protected (%)	15.0	15.7	18.0
Pop. using improved drinking water (urban/rural, %)	100.0 / 100.0	100.0 / 100.0	100.0 / 100.0[b]
Pop. using improved sanitation facilities (urban/rural, %)	98.7 / 100.0	98.7 / 100.0	98.7 / 100.0[b]
Net Official Development Assist. disbursed (% of GNI)[o]	0.18	0.26	0.29[p,c]

a Projected estimate (medium fertility variant). **b** 2015. **c** 2017. **d** 2016. **e** Data classified according to ISIC Rev. 4. **f** Estimate. **g** Data refers to a 5-year period preceding the reference year. **h** Data as at the end of December. **i** 2013. **j** Population aged 16 to 74 years. **k** Users in the last 3 months. **l** 2009. **m** 2004. **n** 2014. **o** Development Assistance Committee member (OECD). **p** Provisional data.

India

Region	Southern Asia	UN membership date	30 October 1945
Population (000, 2018)	1 354 052 [a]	Surface area (km2)	3 287 263 [b]
Pop. density (per km2, 2018)	455.4 [a]	Sex ratio (m per 100 f)	107.5 [a]
Capital city	New Delhi	National currency	Indian Rupee (INR)
Capital city pop. (000, 2018)	28 513.7 [c]	Exchange rate (per US$)	63.9 [d]

Economic indicators	2005	2010	2018
GDP: Gross domestic product (million current US$)	812 059	1 650 635	2 259 642 [a]
GDP growth rate (annual %, const. 2010 prices)	9.3	10.3	7.1 [e]
GDP per capita (current US$)	710.0	1 341.0	1 706.0 [e]
Economy: Agriculture (% of Gross Value Added) [f]	19.5	18.9	17.4 [e]
Economy: Industry (% of Gross Value Added) [f]	33.6	32.5	28.8 [e]
Economy: Services and other activity (% of GVA) [f]	46.9	48.7	53.8 [e]
Employment in agriculture (% of employed) [g]	56.0	51.5	41.6
Employment in industry (% of employed) [g]	18.8	21.8	23.9
Employment in services & other sectors (% employed) [g]	25.2	26.7	34.5
Unemployment rate (% of labour force)	4.4	3.5	3.5 [g]
Labour force participation rate (female/male pop. %) [g]	36.8 / 83.1	28.6 / 80.5	27.0 / 78.8
CPI: Consumer Price Index (2010=100) [h]	66	100	160 [d]
Agricultural production index (2004-2006=100)	100	124	145 [e]
Index of industrial production (2005=100) [i,j]	100	152	163 [k]
International trade: exports (million current US$) [l]	100 353	220 408	216 913 [d]
International trade: imports (million current US$) [l]	140 862	350 029	337 414 [d]
International trade: balance (million current US$) [l]	- 40 509	- 129 621	- 120 501 [d]
Balance of payments, current account (million US$)	- 10 284	- 54 516	- 39 073 [d]

Major trading partners						2017
Export partners (% of exports)	United States	16.0	United Arab Emirates	9.6	China, Hong Kong SAR	5.0
Import partners (% of imports)	China	16.6	United States	5.7	United Arab Emirates	4.9

Social indicators	2005	2010	2018
Population growth rate (average annual %) [m]	1.7	1.5	1.2 [b]
Urban population (% of total population)	29.2	30.9	34.0
Urban population growth rate (average annual %) [m]	2.8	2.6	2.4 [b]
Fertility rate, total (live births per woman) [m]	3.1	2.8	2.4 [b]
Life expectancy at birth (females/males, years) [m]	64.4 / 62.7	66.5 / 64.7	69.1 / 66.2 [b]
Population age distribution (0-14/60+ years old, %)	32.8 / 7.3	30.9 / 7.8	27.4 / 9.6 [a]
International migrant stock (000/% of total pop.) [n]	5 923.6 / 0.5	5 436.0 / 0.4	5 188.6 / 0.4 [d]
Refugees and others of concern to the UNHCR (000)	142.4 [o]	193.7 [o]	206.5 [d]
Infant mortality rate (per 1 000 live births) [m]	59.9	49.8	41.3 [b]
Health: Current expenditure (% of GDP) [p,q]	3.8	3.3	3.9 [b]
Health: Physicians (per 1 000 pop.)	0.6	0.7	0.8 [e]
Education: Government expenditure (% of GDP)	3.2	3.4	3.8 [r]
Education: Primary gross enrol. ratio (f/m per 100 pop.)	101.5 / 104.3 [s]	110.4 / 108.1 [g]	123.9 / 108.1 [e]
Education: Secondary gross enrol. ratio (f/m per 100 pop.)	48.7 / 59.2 [g]	60.9 / 65.5	75.8 / 74.6 [e]
Education: Tertiary gross enrol. ratio (f/m per 100 pop.)	8.8 / 12.5	15.0 / 20.6	27.0 / 26.9 [e]
Intentional homicide rate (per 100 000 pop.)	3.9	3.8	3.2 [e]
Seats held by women in the National Parliament (%)	8.3	10.8	11.8

Environment and infrastructure indicators	2005	2010	2018
Individuals using the Internet (per 100 inhabitants) [g]	2.4	7.5	29.5 [e]
Research & Development expenditure (% of GDP)	0.8	0.8 [g]	0.6 [b]
Threatened species (number)	552 [t]	758	1 052 [d]
Forested area (% of land area)	22.8	23.5 [g]	23.8 [g,b]
CO2 emission estimates (million tons/tons per capita)	1 222.6 / 1.1	1 719.7 / 1.4	2 238.4 / 1.7 [k]
Energy production, primary (Petajoules)	18 315	22 598	23 538 [b]
Energy supply per capita (Gigajoules)	20	23	28 [b]
Tourist/visitor arrivals at national borders (000)	3 919 [u]	5 776 [u]	14 569 [v,e]
Important sites for terrestrial biodiversity protected (%)	22.6	22.6	26.1
Pop. using improved drinking water (urban/rural, %)	94.0 / 82.0	95.7 / 87.9	97.1 / 92.6 [b]
Pop. using improved sanitation facilities (urban/rural, %)	57.4 / 19.5	60.3 / 24.5	62.6 / 28.5 [b]
Net Official Development Assist. received (% of GNI)	0.23	0.17	0.12 [b]

a Projected estimate (medium fertility variant). b 2015. c Refers to the Delhi metropolitan area that is not restricted to state boundaries (National Capital Territory), includes contiguous suburban cities and towns, such as Faridabad, Gurgaon, and Ghaziabad. d 2017. e 2016. f Data classified according to ISIC Rev. 4. g Estimate. h Industrial workers. i Data classified according to ISIC Rev. 3. j Twelve months beginning 1 April of the year stated. k 2014. l Excluding military goods, fissionable materials, bunkers, ships and aircraft. m Data refers to a 5-year period preceding the reference year. n Including refugees. o Data as at the end of December. p Data revision. q Data refer to fiscal years beginning 1 April. r 2013. s 2003. t 2004. u Excluding nationals residing abroad. v Including nationals residing abroad.

Indonesia

Region	South-eastern Asia	UN membership date	28 September 1950
Population (000, 2018)	266 795[a]	Surface area (km2)	1 910 931[b]
Pop. density (per km2, 2018)	147.3[a]	Sex ratio (m per 100 f)	101.3[a]
Capital city	Jakarta	National currency	Rupiah (IDR)
Capital city pop. (000, 2018)	10 516.9[c]	Exchange rate (per US$)	13 548.0[d]

Economic indicators

	2005	2010	2018
GDP: Gross domestic product (million current US$)	304 372	755 094	932 259[e]
GDP growth rate (annual %, const. 2010 prices)	5.7	6.2	5.0[e]
GDP per capita (current US$)	1 343.0	3 113.0	3 570.0[e]
Economy: Agriculture (% of Gross Value Added)[f]	12.1	14.3	14.0[e]
Economy: Industry (% of Gross Value Added)[f]	43.1	43.9	40.8[e]
Economy: Services and other activity (% of GVA)[f]	44.8	41.8	45.3[e]
Employment in agriculture (% of employed)[g]	44.0	39.2	30.2
Employment in industry (% of employed)[g]	18.8	18.7	21.6
Employment in services & other sectors (% employed)[g]	37.2	42.2	48.2
Unemployment rate (% of labour force)	7.7	5.6	4.4[g]
Labour force participation rate (female/male pop. %)[g]	49.9 / 85.2	51.9 / 83.9	50.7 / 81.6
CPI: Consumer Price Index (2010=100)	69	100	142[d]
Agricultural production index (2004-2006=100)	98	123	143[e]
International trade: exports (million current US$)	85 660	157 779	168 810[d]
International trade: imports (million current US$)	57 701	135 663	157 388[d]
International trade: balance (million current US$)	27 959	22 116	11 422[d]
Balance of payments, current account (million US$)	278	5 144[h]	- 17 293[d]

Major trading partners

						2017
Export partners (% of exports)	China	13.6	United States	10.5	Japan	10.5
Import partners (% of imports)	China	21.9	Singapore	10.8	Japan	9.0

Social indicators

	2005	2010	2018
Population growth rate (average annual %)[i]	1.4	1.3	1.2[b]
Urban population (% of total population)	45.9	49.9	55.3
Urban population growth rate (average annual %)[i]	3.2	3.0	2.6[b]
Fertility rate, total (live births per woman)[i]	2.5	2.5	2.4[b]
Life expectancy at birth (females/males, years)[i]	68.5 / 64.9	69.8 / 65.6	70.7 / 66.6[b]
Population age distribution (0-14/60+ years old, %)	30.0 / 7.4	29.0 / 7.4	27.0 / 8.9[a]
International migrant stock (000/% of total pop.)[j]	289.6 / 0.1	305.4 / 0.1	345.9 / 0.1[d]
Refugees and others of concern to the UNHCR (000)	0.4[k]	2.9[k]	14.1[d]
Infant mortality rate (per 1 000 live births)[i]	36.5	29.7	25.0[b]
Health: Current expenditure (% of GDP)	2.8	3.5	3.3[b]
Health: Physicians (per 1 000 pop.)	0.1[l]	0.1	0.2[m]
Education: Government expenditure (% of GDP)	2.7[g]	2.8	3.6[b]
Education: Primary gross enrol. ratio (f/m per 100 pop.)	106.1 / 109.5[g]	112.2 / 108.0	101.4 / 105.4[e]
Education: Secondary gross enrol. ratio (f/m per 100 pop.)	59.8 / 60.4[g]	75.0 / 74.1	87.7 / 84.5[e]
Education: Tertiary gross enrol. ratio (f/m per 100 pop.)	14.7 / 18.5[n]	21.8 / 24.2	29.5 / 26.5[e]
Intentional homicide rate (per 100 000 pop.)	0.6[n]	0.4	0.5[e]
Seats held by women in the National Parliament (%)	11.3	18.0	19.8

Environment and infrastructure indicators

	2005	2010	2018
Individuals using the Internet (per 100 inhabitants)	3.6	10.9	25.4[a]
Research & Development expenditure (% of GDP)	-0.0[o,p]	0.1[h,o,q]	0.1[g,r]
Threatened species (number)	833[n]	1 142	1 281[d]
Forested area (% of land area)	54.0	52.1[g]	50.2[g,b]
CO2 emission estimates (million tons/tons per capita)	342.0 / 1.5	428.8 / 1.8	464.2 / 1.8[a]
Energy production, primary (Petajoules)	11 351	16 854	17 926[b]
Energy supply per capita (Gigajoules)	31	34	37[b]
Tourist/visitor arrivals at national borders (000)	5 002	7 003	11 519[e]
Important sites for terrestrial biodiversity protected (%)	21.3	22.8	23.5
Pop. using improved drinking water (urban/rural, %)	92.3 / 72.0	93.2 / 75.7	94.2 / 79.5[b]
Pop. using improved sanitation facilities (urban/rural, %)	68.1 / 38.6	70.4 / 43.5	72.3 / 47.5[b]
Net Official Development Assist. received (% of GNI)	0.93	0.19	- 0.01[e]

a Projected estimate (medium fertility variant). b 2015. c Refers to the functional urban area. d 2017. e 2016. f Data classified according to ISIC Rev. 4. g Estimate. h Break in the time series. i Data refers to a 5-year period preceding the reference year. j Including refugees. k Data as at the end of December. l 2003. m 2012. n 2004. o Partial data. p 2001. q 2009. r 2013. s 2014.

Iran (Islamic Republic of)

Region	Southern Asia	
Population (000, 2018)	82 012[a]	
Pop. density (per km2, 2018)	50.4[a]	
Capital city	Tehran	
Capital city pop. (000, 2018)	8 895.9	
UN membership date	24 October 1945	
Surface area (km2)	1 628 750[b,c]	
Sex ratio (m per 100 f)	101.1[a]	
National currency	Iranian Rial (IRR)	
Exchange rate (per US$)	36 074.0[d]	

Economic indicators	2005	2010	2018
GDP: Gross domestic product (million current US$)	226 452	491 099	425 403[e]
GDP growth rate (annual %, const. 2010 prices)	3.2	5.8	13.4[e]
GDP per capita (current US$)	3 216.0	6 586.0	5 299.0[e]
Economy: Agriculture (% of Gross Value Added)	6.2	6.4	9.8[e]
Economy: Industry (% of Gross Value Added)	47.7	43.4	34.3[e]
Economy: Services and other activity (% of GVA)	46.1	50.2	55.9[e]
Employment in agriculture (% of employed)[f]	24.8	19.2	16.6
Employment in industry (% of employed)[f]	30.4	32.2	32.4
Employment in services & other sectors (% employed)[f]	44.9	48.6	51.0
Unemployment rate (% of labour force)	12.1	13.5	11.9[f]
Labour force participation rate (female/male pop. %)[f]	19.4 / 74.3	15.9 / 70.0	16.6 / 71.1
CPI: Consumer Price Index (2010=100)	...	...	106[g,d]
Agricultural production index (2004-2006=100)	103	102	110[e]
International trade: exports (million current US$)[h,i]	60 012	83 785	33 103[f,d]
International trade: imports (million current US$)[h,i]	38 869[f]	54 697	29 519[f,d]
International trade: balance (million current US$)[h,i]	21 143	29 088	3 585[f,d]

Major trading partners						2017
Export partners (% of exports)	China	27.7[f]	Republic of Korea	12.9	India	12.3[f]
Import partners (% of imports)[f]	China	31.8	United Arab Emirates	11.8	Republic of Korea	7.3

Social indicators	2005	2010	2018
Population growth rate (average annual %)[j]	1.3	1.1	1.2[c]
Urban population (% of total population)	67.6	70.6	74.9
Urban population growth rate (average annual %)[j]	2.3	2.0	2.0[c]
Fertility rate, total (live births per woman)[j]	2.0	1.8	1.7[c]
Life expectancy at birth (females/males, years)[j]	72.3 / 70.0	74.6 / 71.0	76.2 / 74.0[c]
Population age distribution (0-14/60+ years old, %)	26.1 / 6.8	23.5 / 7.1	23.7 / 9.1[a]
International migrant stock (000/% of total pop.)[k]	2 588.9 / 3.6	2 761.6 / 3.7	2 699.2 / 3.3[d]
Refugees and others of concern to the UNHCR (000)	1 319.4[l]	1 085.3[l]	978.8[d]
Infant mortality rate (per 1 000 live births)[j]	25.0	18.9	14.8[c]
Health: Current expenditure (% of GDP)[m]	6.0	7.8	7.6[c]
Health: Physicians (per 1 000 pop.)	0.9	...	1.5[n]
Education: Government expenditure (% of GDP)	4.1	3.7	3.4[e]
Education: Primary gross enrol. ratio (f/m per 100 pop.)	98.2 / 100.7	104.8 / 105.7	111.6 / 105.8[c]
Education: Secondary gross enrol. ratio (f/m per 100 pop.)	74.1 / 76.9	80.6 / 82.2	89.1 / 88.8[c]
Education: Tertiary gross enrol. ratio (f/m per 100 pop.)	23.5 / 22.2	42.2 / 42.7	65.5 / 72.0[e]
Intentional homicide rate (per 100 000 pop.)	2.9[o]	3.0[p]	2.5[n]
Seats held by women in the National Parliament (%)	4.1	2.8	5.9

Environment and infrastructure indicators	2005	2010	2018
Individuals using the Internet (per 100 inhabitants)	8.1[f]	15.9[q]	53.2[e]
Research & Development expenditure (% of GDP)	0.6	0.3[r,s]	0.3[t]
Threatened species (number)	69[o]	102	134[d]
Forested area (% of land area)	6.6	6.6	6.6[f,c]
CO2 emission estimates (million tons/tons per capita)	468.8 / 6.7	573.0 / 7.7	649.5 / 8.3[n]
Energy production, primary (Petajoules)	13 006	14 283	13 637[c]
Energy supply per capita (Gigajoules)	104	116	126[c]
Tourist/visitor arrivals at national borders (000)	...	2 938	4 942[e]
Important sites for terrestrial biodiversity protected (%)	47.9	48.6	48.6
Pop. using improved drinking water (urban/rural, %)	98.0 / 88.8	97.8 / 90.9	97.7 / 92.1[c]
Pop. using improved sanitation facilities (urban/rural, %)	88.2 / 74.5	92.3 / 79.6	92.8 / 82.3[c]
Net Official Development Assist. received (% of GNI)	0.05	0.02	0.02[n]

a Projected estimate (medium fertility variant). b Land area only. c 2015. d 2017. e Estimate. f Estimate. g Index base: fiscal (solar) year 2016 (21 March 2016 - 20 March 2017)=100. h Year ending 20 March of the year stated. i Data include oil and gas. The value of oil exports and total exports are rough estimates based on information published in various petroleum industry journals. j Data refers to a 5-year period preceding the reference year. k Including refugees. l Data as at the end of December. m Provisional data. n 2014. o 2004. p 2009. q Population aged 6 years and over. r Excluding government. s Excluding private non-profit. t 2012.

Iraq

Region	Western Asia
Population (000, 2018)	39 340[a]
Pop. density (per km2, 2018)	90.6[a]
Capital city	Baghdad
Capital city pop. (000, 2018)	6 812.0

UN membership date	21 December 1945
Surface area (km2)	435 052[b]
Sex ratio (m per 100 f)	102.6[a]
National currency	Iraqi Dinar (IQD)
Exchange rate (per US$)	1 184.0[c]

Economic indicators	2005	2010	2018
GDP: Gross domestic product (million current US$)	36 268	117 138	160 021[d]
GDP growth rate (annual %, const. 2010 prices)	4.4	5.5	11.0[d]
GDP per capita (current US$)	1 343.0	3 808.0	4 301.0[d]
Economy: Agriculture (% of Gross Value Added)	6.9	5.1	4.1[d]
Economy: Industry (% of Gross Value Added)	63.3	55.4	39.8[d]
Economy: Services and other activity (% of GVA)	29.9	39.4	56.1[d]
Employment in agriculture (% of employed)[e]	23.0	23.1	19.2
Employment in industry (% of employed)[e]	18.3	18.7	19.5
Employment in services & other sectors (% employed)[e]	58.7	58.3	61.3
Unemployment rate (% of labour force)	18.0	11.2[e]	8.5[e]
Labour force participation rate (female/male pop. %)[e]	14.5 / 70.9	18.0 / 75.8	19.0 / 74.3
CPI: Consumer Price Index (2010=100)	59	100	119[c]
Agricultural production index (2004-2006=100)	102	103	75[d]
International trade: exports (million current US$)	19 773	52 483	24 266[e,c]
International trade: imports (million current US$)	12 861[e]	31 764	40 362[e,c]
International trade: balance (million current US$)	6 912[e]	20 718	- 16 096[e,c]
Balance of payments, current account (million US$)	- 3 335	6 488	3 843[d]

Major trading partners						2017
Export partners (% of exports)	Areas nes[f]	99.8[e]	Singapore	0.2	United Arab Emirates	~0.0[e]
Import partners (% of imports)[e]	Areas nes[f]	68.2	Turkey	8.3	China	7.4

Social indicators	2005	2010	2018
Population growth rate (average annual %)[g]	2.7	2.6	3.2[b]
Urban population (% of total population)	68.8	69.1	70.5
Urban population growth rate (average annual %)[g]	2.8	2.7	3.4[b]
Fertility rate, total (live births per woman)[g]	4.7	4.6	4.6[b]
Life expectancy at birth (females/males, years)[g]	71.0 / 66.9	71.2 / 65.1	71.4 / 67.0[b]
Population age distribution (0-14/60+ years old, %)	42.0 / 5.1	41.7 / 4.8	40.2 / 5.0[a]
International migrant stock (000/% of total pop.)[h,i]	132.9 / 0.5	117.4 / 0.4	366.6 / 1.0[c]
Refugees and others of concern to the UNHCR (000)	1 578.2[j]	1 796.3[j]	4 927.1[c]
Infant mortality rate (per 1 000 live births)[g]	34.7	33.3	32.1[b]
Health: Current expenditure (% of GDP)	2.9	3.3	3.4[b]
Health: Physicians (per 1 000 pop.)	...	0.6	0.9[k]
Education: Primary gross enrol. ratio (f/m per 100 pop.)	95.2 / 113.1[l]	98.7 / 117.0[m]	... / ...
Education: Secondary gross enrol. ratio (f/m per 100 pop.)	38.2 / 56.7[l]	45.6 / 61.0[m]	... / ...
Education: Tertiary gross enrol. ratio (f/m per 100 pop.)	11.9 / 20.0[e]	... / ...	... / ...
Intentional homicide rate (per 100 000 pop.)[n]	...	8.7	9.9[o]
Seats held by women in the National Parliament (%)	6.4[p]	25.5	25.3

Environment and infrastructure indicators	2005	2010	2018
Individuals using the Internet (per 100 inhabitants)	0.9[e]	2.5	21.2[e,d]
Research & Development expenditure (% of GDP)	...	~0.0[q]	~0.0[b]
Threatened species (number)	35[l]	60	72[c]
Forested area (% of land area)[e]	1.9	1.9	1.9[b]
CO2 emission estimates (million tons/tons per capita)	113.5 / 4.1	112.2 / 3.6	166.4 / 4.8[k]
Energy production, primary (Petajoules)	4 147	5 274	7 565[b]
Energy supply per capita (Gigajoules)	54	47	55[b]
Tourist/visitor arrivals at national borders (000)	127[r]	1 518	892[o]
Important sites for terrestrial biodiversity protected (%)	0.0	5.1	5.1
Pop. using improved drinking water (urban/rural, %)	94.4 / 57.1	94.0 / 65.2	93.8 / 70.1[b]
Pop. using improved sanitation facilities (urban/rural, %)	84.6 / 67.6	85.7 / 77.8	86.4 / 83.8[b]
Net Official Development Assist. received (% of GNI)	43.51	1.55	1.34[d]

a Projected estimate (medium fertility variant). b 2015. c 2017. d 2016. e Estimate. f Areas not elsewhere specified. g Data refers to a 5-year period preceding the reference year. h Including refugees. i Refers to foreign citizens. j Data as at the end of December. k 2014. l 2004. m 2007. n Excluding victims of terrorist attacks. o 2013. p 2000. q R&D budget instead of R&D expenditure or based on R&D budget. r 2001.

Ireland

Region	Northern Europe	UN membership date	14 December 1955
Population (000, 2018)	4 804 [a]	Surface area (km2)	69 797 [b]
Pop. density (per km2, 2018)	69.7 [a]	Sex ratio (m per 100 f)	98.5 [a]
Capital city	Dublin	National currency	Euro (EUR)
Capital city pop. (000, 2018)	1 201.4	Exchange rate (per US$)	0.8 [c]

Economic indicators

	2005	2010	2018
GDP: Gross domestic product (million current US$)	211 645	221 951	304 819 [d]
GDP growth rate (annual %, const. 2010 prices)	6.0	1.8	5.1 [d]
GDP per capita (current US$)	50 237.0	47 969.0	64 497.0 [d]
Economy: Agriculture (% of Gross Value Added) [e]	1.2	1.1	1.0 [d]
Economy: Industry (% of Gross Value Added) [e]	34.4	26.1	39.3 [d]
Economy: Services and other activity (% of GVA) [e]	64.5	72.9	59.7 [d]
Employment in agriculture (% of employed) [f]	6.0	4.6	5.3
Employment in industry (% of employed) [f]	27.7	19.6	19.0
Employment in services & other sectors (% employed) [f]	66.3	75.9	75.8
Unemployment rate (% of labour force)	4.3	13.8	6.0 [f]
Labour force participation rate (female/male pop. %) [i]	52.4 / 72.8	53.3 / 69.2	52.7 / 66.7
CPI: Consumer Price Index (2010=100) [g]	93	100	105 [c]
Agricultural production index (2004-2006=100)	98	101	110 [d]
Index of industrial production (2005=100)	100	109 [h]	128 [h,i]
International trade: exports (million current US$)	110 003	120 645	138 072 [c]
International trade: imports (million current US$)	70 284	64 601	88 828 [c]
International trade: balance (million current US$)	39 719	56 045	49 244 [c]
Balance of payments, current account (million US$)	- 7 150	2 319	42 719 [c]

Major trading partners

						2017
Export partners (% of exports)	United States	27.1	United Kingdom	11.8 [f]	Belgium	10.9
Import partners (% of imports)	United Kingdom	22.1	United States	20.6	France	13.3

Social indicators

	2005	2010	2018
Population growth rate (average annual %) [j]	1.8	1.9	0.3 [b]
Urban population (% of total population)	60.5	61.5	63.2
Urban population growth rate (average annual %) [j]	2.3	2.2	0.6 [b]
Fertility rate, total (live births per woman) [j]	2.0	2.0	2.0 [b]
Life expectancy at birth (females/males, years) [j]	80.4 / 75.3	82.0 / 77.4	83.0 / 78.7 [b]
Population age distribution (0-14/60+ years old, %)	20.2 / 14.8	20.7 / 16.1	21.5 / 19.4 [a]
International migrant stock (000/% of total pop.)	589.0 / 14.0	730.5 / 15.8	806.5 / 16.9 [c]
Refugees and others of concern to the UNHCR (000)	9.5 [k]	14.2 [k]	11.0 [c]
Infant mortality rate (per 1 000 live births) [j]	5.2	3.7	3.4 [b]
Health: Current expenditure (% of GDP)	7.6	10.5	7.8 [b]
Health: Physicians (per 1 000 pop.)	...	...	3.0 [d]
Education: Government expenditure (% of GDP)	4.5	6.0	4.9 [i]
Education: Primary gross enrol. ratio (f/m per 100 pop.)	106.2 / 106.8	106.9 / 106.4	100.8 / 100.8 [d]
Education: Secondary gross enrol. ratio (f/m per 100 pop.)	114.5 / 104.5	126.1 / 120.6	127.7 / 124.7 [d]
Education: Tertiary gross enrol. ratio (f/m per 100 pop.)	60.6 / 47.9	66.5 / 59.5	86.3 / 80.8 [b]
Intentional homicide rate (per 100 000 pop.)	1.2	1.1	0.8 [d]
Seats held by women in the National Parliament (%)	13.3	13.9	22.2

Environment and infrastructure indicators

	2005	2010	2018
Individuals using the Internet (per 100 inhabitants) [l]	41.6	69.8	82.2 [m,d]
Research & Development expenditure (% of GDP)	1.2	1.6 [f]	1.5 [f,i]
Threatened species (number)	22 [n]	27	50 [c]
Forested area (% of land area)	10.1	10.5	10.9 [f,b]
CO2 emission estimates (million tons/tons per capita)	43.5 / 10.5	40.1 / 8.7	34.1 / 7.3 [i]
Energy production, primary (Petajoules)	69	77	80 [b]
Energy supply per capita (Gigajoules)	147	132	118 [b]
Tourist/visitor arrivals at national borders (000) [o]	7 333	7 134 [p]	10 100 [d]
Important sites for terrestrial biodiversity protected (%)	86.7	89.3	89.9
Pop. using improved drinking water (urban/rural, %)	96.6 / 97.2	97.3 / 97.6	97.9 / 97.8 [b]
Pop. using improved sanitation facilities (urban/rural, %)	88.2 / 92.0	88.7 / 92.5	89.1 / 92.9 [b]
Net Official Development Assist. disbursed (% of GNI) [q]	0.42	0.52	0.30 [r,c]

a Projected estimate (medium fertility variant). b 2015. c 2017. d 2016. e Data classified according to ISIC Rev. 4. f Estimate. g Calculated by the Statistics Division of the United Nations from national indices. h Excluding water and waste management. i 2014. j Data refers to a 5-year period preceding the reference year. k Data as at the end of December. l Population aged 16 to 74 years. m Users in the last 3 months. n 2004. o Including tourists from Northern Ireland. p Break in the time series. q Development Assistance Committee member (OECD). r Provisional data.

Isle of Man

Region	Northern Europe	Population (000, 2018)	85[a]
Surface area (km2)	572[b]	Pop. density (per km2, 2018)	148.8[a]
Sex ratio (m per 100 f)	98.2[c,d]	Capital city	Douglas
National currency	Pound Sterling (GBP)	Capital city pop. (000, 2018)	27.2
Exchange rate (per US$)	0.7[e]		

Economic indicators	2005	2010	2018
Employment in agriculture (% of employed)[f]	1.4[g]	1.9[h]	...
Employment in industry (% of employed)[f]	16.1[g]	14.8[h]	...
Employment in services & other sectors (% of employed)[f]	82.5[g]	83.3[h]	...
Unemployment rate (% of labour force)	1.6[g]	2.4[h]	2.6[i,j,k]
Labour force participation rate (female/male pop. %)	55.7 / 71.4[g]	56.3 / 69.9[h]	57.5 / 69.3[j,l,m]
CPI: Consumer Price Index (2010=100)	...	...	161[n,o]

Social indicators	2005	2010	2018
Population growth rate (average annual %)[p]	1.0	1.0	0.8[b]
Urban population (% of total population)	51.9	52.0	52.6
Urban population growth rate (average annual %)[p]	1.0	1.0	0.9[b]
Population age distribution (0-14/60+ years old, %)[c]	17.3 / 22.1	16.4 / 24.1[q]	16.0 / 26.9[d]
International migrant stock (000/% of total pop.)	41.5 / 54.5	43.4 / 54.3	45.9 / 54.4[a]
Intentional homicide rate (per 100 000 pop.)	...	...	0.0[d]

Environment and infrastructure indicators	2005	2010	2018
Threatened species (number)	...	2	3[e]
Forested area (% of land area)[r]	6.1	6.1	6.1[b]
Energy production, primary (Petajoules)[r]	0	0	0[b]
Energy supply per capita (Gigajoules)	6[r]	2	3[r,b]

a Projected estimate (medium fertility variant). b 2015. c De jure population. d 2016. e 2017. f Data classified according to ISIC Rev. 3. g 2001. h 2006. i Population aged 15 to 64 years. j Break in the time series. k 2013. l Population aged 16 years and over. m 2011. n Index base: 2000=100. o 2014. p Data refers to a 5-year period preceding the reference year. q 2009. r Estimate.

Israel

Region	Western Asia	UN membership date	11 May 1949	
Population (000, 2018)	8 453[a]	Surface area (km2)	22 072[b]	
Pop. density (per km2, 2018)	390.6[a]	Sex ratio (m per 100 f)	98.8[a]	
Capital city	Jerusalem[c]	National currency	New Israeli Sheqel (ILS)	
Capital city pop. (000, 2018)	907.1[d]	Exchange rate (per US$)	3.5[e]	

Economic indicators

	2005	2010	2018
GDP: Gross domestic product (million current US$)	142 463	233 611	317 748[f]
GDP growth rate (annual %, const. 2010 prices)	4.1	5.5	4.0[f]
GDP per capita (current US$)	21 576.0	31 459.0	38 788.0[f]
Economy: Agriculture (% of Gross Value Added)[g]	1.8	1.7	1.3[f]
Economy: Industry (% of Gross Value Added)[g]	23.0	22.9	20.8[f]
Economy: Services and other activity (% of GVA)[g]	75.2	75.4	77.9[f]
Employment in agriculture (% of employed)[h]	2.0	1.6	1.1
Employment in industry (% of employed)[h]	21.6	20.2	17.2
Employment in services & other sectors (% employed)[h]	76.4	78.2	81.8
Unemployment rate (% of labour force)	11.3	8.5	4.3[h]
Labour force participation rate (female/male pop. %)[h]	55.0 / 68.8	57.0 / 69.4	59.3 / 69.0
CPI: Consumer Price Index (2010=100)	88	100	106[e]
Agricultural production index (2004-2006=100)	100	104	109[f]
Index of industrial production (2005=100)[i]	...	126	136[j]
International trade: exports (million current US$)[k]	42 771	58 413	53 791[e]
International trade: imports (million current US$)[k]	45 032	59 194	69 693[e]
International trade: balance (million current US$)[k]	- 2 262	- 781	- 15 901[e]
Balance of payments, current account (million US$)	4 540	8 372	10 392[e]

Major trading partners

							2017
Export partners (% of exports)	United States	27.0	United Kingdom	8.4[h]	Areas nes[l]	7.5	
Import partners (% of imports)	China	13.1	United States	11.8	Areas nes[l]	9.7	

Social indicators

	2005	2010	2018
Population growth rate (average annual %)[m]	1.9	2.3	1.6[b]
Urban population (% of total population)	91.5	91.8	92.4
Urban population growth rate (average annual %)[m]	1.9	2.4	1.7[b]
Fertility rate, total (live births per woman)[m]	2.9	2.9	3.0[b]
Life expectancy at birth (females/males, years)[m]	81.6 / 77.4	82.8 / 79.0	83.7 / 80.0[b]
Population age distribution (0-14/60+ years old, %)	27.9 / 13.2	27.3 / 14.9	27.8 / 16.3[a]
International migrant stock (000/% of total pop.)[n]	1 889.5 / 28.6	1 950.6 / 26.3	1 962.1 / 23.6[e]
Refugees and others of concern to the UNHCR (000)	1.5[o]	31.1[o]	63.7[e]
Infant mortality rate (per 1 000 live births)[m]	5.0	4.0	3.4[b]
Health: Current expenditure (% of GDP)	7.1	7.1	7.4[b]
Health: Physicians (per 1 000 pop.)	...	3.4	3.6[b]
Education: Government expenditure (% of GDP)	5.8	5.5	5.7[j]
Education: Primary gross enrol. ratio (f/m per 100 pop.)	103.8 / 103.3	104.5 / 104.0	104.1 / 103.2[f]
Education: Secondary gross enrol. ratio (f/m per 100 pop.)	104.4 / 105.0	103.3 / 100.9	105.0 / 103.2[f]
Education: Tertiary gross enrol. ratio (f/m per 100 pop.)	66.4 / 50.1	70.7 / 54.5[p]	75.2 / 53.7[f]
Intentional homicide rate (per 100 000 pop.)	2.5	2.0	1.4[b]
Seats held by women in the National Parliament (%)	15.0	19.2	27.5

Environment and infrastructure indicators

	2005	2010	2018
Individuals using the Internet (per 100 inhabitants)	25.2	67.5[q]	79.8[h,j]
Research & Development expenditure (% of GDP)[r]	4.0	3.9	4.3[b]
Threatened species (number)	57[s]	131	174[e]
Forested area (% of land area)	7.2	7.1	7.6[b]
CO2 emission estimates (million tons/tons per capita)	57.0 / 8.6	68.9 / 9.3	64.6 / 8.1[j]
Energy production, primary (Petajoules)	87	162	308[b]
Energy supply per capita (Gigajoules)	116	130	118[b]
Tourist/visitor arrivals at national borders (000)[t]	1 903	2 803	2 900[f]
Important sites for terrestrial biodiversity protected (%)	13.8	15.6	15.7
Pop. using improved drinking water (urban/rural, %)	100.0 / 100.0	100.0 / 100.0	100.0 / 100.0[b]
Pop. using improved sanitation facilities (urban/rural, %)	100.0 / 100.0	100.0 / 100.0	100.0 / 100.0[b]
Net Official Development Assist. disbursed (% of GNI)	0.07	0.07	0.10[u,e]

a Projected estimate (medium fertility variant). b 2015. c Designation and data provided by Israel. The position of the United Nations on Jerusalem is stated in A/RES/181 (II) and subsequent General Assembly and Security Council resolutions. d Including East Jerusalem. e 2017. f 2016. g Data classified according to ISIC Rev. 4. h Estimate. i Data refers to mining and manufacturing. j 2014. k Imports and exports net of returned goods. The figures also exclude Judea and Samaria and the Gaza area. l Areas not elsewhere specified. m Data refers to a 5-year period preceding the reference year. n Including refugees. o Data as at the end of December. p 2009. q Population aged 20 years and over. r Excluding Defence (all or mostly). s 2004. t Excluding nationals residing abroad. u Provisional data.

Italy

Region	Southern Europe	UN membership date	14 December 1955
Population (000, 2018)	59 291 [a]	Surface area (km2)	302 073 [b]
Pop. density (per km2, 2018)	201.6 [a]	Sex ratio (m per 100 f)	95.2 [a]
Capital city	Rome	National currency	Euro (EUR)
Capital city pop. (000, 2018)	4 209.7 [c]	Exchange rate (per US$)	0.8 [d]

Economic indicators

	2005	2010	2018
GDP: Gross domestic product (million current US$)	1 852 616	2 125 058	1 858 913 [a]
GDP growth rate (annual %, const. 2010 prices)	0.9	1.7	0.9 [e]
GDP per capita (current US$)	31 503.0	35 578.0	31 279.0 [e]
Economy: Agriculture (% of Gross Value Added) [f]	2.2	2.0	2.1 [e]
Economy: Industry (% of Gross Value Added) [f]	25.8	24.4	23.9 [e]
Economy: Services and other activity (% of GVA) [f]	71.9	73.7	74.0 [e]
Employment in agriculture (% of employed)	4.2	3.8 [g]	3.9 [g]
Employment in industry (% of employed) [g]	30.7	28.6	26.1
Employment in services & other sectors (% employed) [g]	65.1	67.6	70.0
Unemployment rate (% of labour force)	7.7	8.4	11.0 [g]
Labour force participation rate (female/male pop. %) [g]	37.9 / 61.0	37.8 / 58.9	39.4 / 58.0
CPI: Consumer Price Index (2010=100)	91 [h]	100	109 [h,d]
Agricultural production index (2004-2006=100)	100	97	92 [e]
Index of industrial production (2005=100)	100	89 [i]	80 [i,j]
International trade: exports (million current US$)	372 957	446 840	503 054 [d]
International trade: imports (million current US$)	384 836	486 984	451 416 [d]
International trade: balance (million current US$)	- 11 878	- 40 145	51 638 [d]
Balance of payments, current account (million US$)	- 17 023	- 73 018	54 333 [d]

Major trading partners

						2017
Export partners (% of exports)	Germany	12.5	France	10.3	United States	9.1
Import partners (% of imports)	Germany	16.3	France	8.8	China	7.1

Social indicators

	2005	2010	2018
Population growth rate (average annual %) [k]	0.5	0.3	- 0.1 [b]
Urban population (% of total population)	67.7	68.3	70.4
Urban population growth rate (average annual %) [k]	0.7	0.5	0.3 [b]
Fertility rate, total (live births per woman) [k]	1.3	1.4	1.4 [b]
Life expectancy at birth (females/males, years) [k]	83.1 / 77.3	84.1 / 78.8	84.7 / 79.9 [b]
Population age distribution (0-14/60+ years old, %)	14.1 / 25.1	14.0 / 26.9	13.4 / 29.8 [a]
International migrant stock (000/% of total pop.)	3 954.8 / 6.7	5 787.9 / 9.7	5 907.5 / 10.0 [d]
Refugees and others of concern to the UNHCR (000)	21.6 [l]	61.3 [l]	292.9 [d]
Infant mortality rate (per 1 000 live births) [k]	4.1	3.4	3.0 [b]
Health: Current expenditure (% of GDP)	8.4	9.0	9.0 [b]
Health: Physicians (per 1 000 pop.)	...	...	4.0 [e]
Education: Government expenditure (% of GDP)	4.2	4.4	4.1 [j]
Education: Primary gross enrol. ratio (f/m per 100 pop.)	100.7 / 101.8	101.4 / 102.4	100.8 / 101.6 [b]
Education: Secondary gross enrol. ratio (f/m per 100 pop.)	97.8 / 98.5	101.3 / 102.7	102.0 / 104.3 [b]
Education: Tertiary gross enrol. ratio (f/m per 100 pop.)	74.2 / 54.2	78.0 / 54.7	72.7 / 53.6 [b]
Intentional homicide rate (per 100 000 pop.)	1.0	0.9	0.7 [e]
Seats held by women in the National Parliament (%)	11.5	21.3	31.0

Environment and infrastructure indicators

	2005	2010	2018
Individuals using the Internet (per 100 inhabitants)	35.0 [m]	53.7 [m]	61.3 [n,e]
Research & Development expenditure (% of GDP)	1.0	1.2	1.3 [o,b]
Threatened species (number)	114 [p]	174	359 [d]
Forested area (% of land area)	29.8	30.7 [g]	31.6 [g,b]
CO2 emission estimates (million tons/tons per capita) [q]	473.4 / 8.1	405.4 / 6.8	320.4 / 5.4 []
Energy production, primary (Petajoules) [r]	1 269	1 384	1 509 [b]
Energy supply per capita (Gigajoules) [r]	134	123	107 [b]
Tourist/visitor arrivals at national borders (000) [s]	36 513	43 626	52 372 [e]
Important sites for terrestrial biodiversity protected (%)	75.1	78.0	78.0
Pop. using improved drinking water (urban/rural, %)	100.0 / 100.0	100.0 / 100.0	100.0 / 100.0 [b]
Pop. using improved sanitation facilities (urban/rural, %)	99.5 / 99.6	99.5 / 99.6	99.5 / 99.6 [b]
Net Official Development Assist. disbursed (% of GNI) [t]	0.29	0.15	0.29 [o,d]

a Projected estimate (medium fertility variant). b 2015. c Refers to the official Metropolitan City. d 2017. e 2016. f Data classified according to ISIC Rev. 4. g Estimate. h Calculated by the Statistics Division of the United Nations from national indices. i Excluding water and waste management. j 2014. k Data refers to a 5-year period preceding the reference year. l Data as at the end of December. m Population aged 16 to 74 years. n Population aged 6 years and over. o Provisional data. p 2004. q Including San Marino. r Data include San Marino and the Holy See. s Excluding seasonal and border workers. t Development Assistance Committee member (OECD).

Jamaica

Region	Caribbean	UN membership date	18 September 1962
Population (000, 2018)	2 899[a]	Surface area (km2)	10 990[b]
Pop. density (per km2, 2018)	267.7[a]	Sex ratio (m per 100 f)	99.0[a]
Capital city	Kingston	National currency	Jamaican Dollar (JMD)
Capital city pop. (000, 2018)	589.1	Exchange rate (per US$)	124.3[c]

Economic indicators

	2005	2010	2018
GDP: Gross domestic product (million current US$)	11 244	13 219	14 057[d]
GDP growth rate (annual %, const. 2010 prices)	0.9	- 1.5	1.4[d]
GDP per capita (current US$)	4 097.0	4 692.0	4 879.0[d]
Economy: Agriculture (% of Gross Value Added)	5.7	5.9	7.6[d]
Economy: Industry (% of Gross Value Added)	23.9	20.0	21.9[d]
Economy: Services and other activity (% of GVA)	70.4	74.1	70.5[d]
Employment in agriculture (% of employed)[e]	18.1	20.2	18.4
Employment in industry (% of employed)[e]	17.8	15.9	15.4
Employment in services & other sectors (% employed)[e]	64.1	63.8	66.2
Unemployment rate (% of labour force)	10.9	12.4	12.3[e]
Labour force participation rate (female/male pop. %)[e]	55.6 / 76.8	56.1 / 77.1	57.6 / 77.6
CPI: Consumer Price Index (2010=100)[f]	56	100	151[c]
Agricultural production index (2004-2006=100)	97	98	105[d]
International trade: exports (million current US$)	1 514	1 328	1 310[c]
International trade: imports (million current US$)	4 885	5 225	5 818[c]
International trade: balance (million current US$)	- 3 370	- 3 898	- 4 508[c]
Balance of payments, current account (million US$)	- 1 071	- 934	- 103[d]

Major trading partners

						2017
Export partners (% of exports)	United States	45.0	Netherlands	12.0	Canada	9.6
Import partners (% of imports)	United States	43.7	Japan	6.3	China	6.3

Social indicators

	2005	2010	2018
Population growth rate (average annual %)[g]	0.6	0.5	0.4[b]
Urban population (% of total population)	52.8	53.7	55.7
Urban population growth rate (average annual %)[g]	1.0	0.9	0.8[b]
Fertility rate, total (live births per woman)[g]	2.4	2.3	2.1[b]
Life expectancy at birth (females/males, years)[g]	75.6 / 70.0	76.8 / 71.6	77.9 / 73.1[b]
Population age distribution (0-14/60+ years old, %)	30.1 / 10.8	27.0 / 11.6	22.6 / 13.9[a]
International migrant stock (000/% of total pop.)	24.3 / 0.9	23.7 / 0.8	23.3 / 0.8[c]
Refugees and others of concern to the UNHCR (000)	...	~0.0[h]	~0.0[c]
Infant mortality rate (per 1 000 live births)[g]	20.0	17.9	15.0[b]
Health: Current expenditure (% of GDP)	4.1	5.4	5.9[b]
Health: Physicians (per 1 000 pop.)	0.8[i]	0.4[j]	0.5[d]
Education: Government expenditure (% of GDP)	4.6	6.4	5.4[c]
Education: Primary gross enrol. ratio (f/m per 100 pop.)	96.4 / 96.1[k]	... / ...	... / ...
Education: Secondary gross enrol. ratio (f/m per 100 pop.)	92.4 / 87.1	95.5 / 88.2	86.3 / 82.0[d]
Education: Tertiary gross enrol. ratio (f/m per 100 pop.)	25.5 / 11.7[l]	37.8 / 16.4	34.2 / 19.8[b]
Intentional homicide rate (per 100 000 pop.)	61.0	51.4	47.0[d]
Seats held by women in the National Parliament (%)	11.7	13.3	17.5

Environment and infrastructure indicators

	2005	2010	2018
Individuals using the Internet (per 100 inhabitants)	12.8[e]	27.7[m]	45.0[e,d]
Research & Development expenditure (% of GDP)	0.1[l]	...	...
Threatened species (number)	267[k]	282	311[c]
Forested area (% of land area)[e]	31.3	31.1	31.0[b]
CO2 emission estimates (million tons/tons per capita)	10.5 / 3.9	7.3 / 2.7	7.4 / 2.7[n]
Energy production, primary (Petajoules)	15	6	8[e,b]
Energy supply per capita (Gigajoules)	56	38	39[b]
Tourist/visitor arrivals at national borders (000)[o]	1 479	1 922	2 182[d]
Important sites for terrestrial biodiversity protected (%)	22.0	22.0	22.0
Pop. using improved drinking water (urban/rural, %)	97.6 / 89.1	97.5 / 89.3	97.5 / 89.4[b]
Pop. using improved sanitation facilities (urban/rural, %)	79.5 / 82.9	79.7 / 83.7	79.9 / 84.1[b]
Net Official Development Assist. received (% of GNI)	0.38	1.10	0.20[d]

a Projected estimate (medium fertility variant). **b** 2015. **c** 2017. **d** 2016. **e** Estimate. **f** Calculated by the Statistics Division of the United Nations from national indices. **g** Data refers to a 5-year period preceding the reference year. **h** Data as at the end of December. **i** 2003. **j** 2008. **k** 2004. **l** 2002. **m** Population aged 14 years and over. **n** 2014. **o** Including nationals residing abroad.

Japan

Region	Eastern Asia	UN membership date	18 December 1956
Population (000, 2018)	127 185[a]	Surface area (km2)	377 930[b,c]
Pop. density (per km2, 2018)	348.9[a]	Sex ratio (m per 100 f)	95.4[a]
Capital city	Tokyo	National currency	Yen (JPY)
Capital city pop. (000, 2018)	37 468.3[d]	Exchange rate (per US$)	112.9[e]

Economic indicators

	2005	2010	2018
GDP: Gross domestic product (million current US$)	4 755 410	5 700 098	4 936 212[f]
GDP growth rate (annual %, const. 2010 prices)	1.7	4.2	1.0[f]
GDP per capita (current US$)	37 054.0	44 341.0	38 640.0[f]
Economy: Agriculture (% of Gross Value Added)[g,h]	1.1	1.1	1.1[f]
Economy: Industry (% of Gross Value Added)[g,h]	30.1	28.5	28.0[f]
Economy: Services and other activity (% of GVA)[g,h]	68.8	70.4	71.0[f]
Employment in agriculture (% of employed)[i]	4.5	4.1	3.4
Employment in industry (% of employed)[i]	27.8	25.7	25.3
Employment in services & other sectors (% employed)[i]	67.7	70.2	71.3
Unemployment rate (% of labour force)	4.4	5.1	2.6[i]
Labour force participation rate (female/male pop. %)[i]	48.4 / 73.5	48.7 / 72.1	50.4 / 70.2
CPI: Consumer Price Index (2010=100)[j]	100	100	104[e]
Agricultural production index (2004-2006=100)	101	97	92[f]
International trade: exports (million current US$)	594 941	769 774	698 097[e]
International trade: imports (million current US$)	515 866	694 059	671 474[e]
International trade: balance (million current US$)	79 074	75 715	26 623[e]
Balance of payments, current account (million US$)	170 123	220 888	195 801[e]

Major trading partners

					2017
Export partners (% of exports)	United States	19.3	China	19.1	Republic of Korea	7.6
Import partners (% of imports)	China	24.5	United States	11.0	Australia	5.8

Social indicators

	2005	2010	2018
Population growth rate (average annual %)[k]	0.1	~0.0	- 0.1[l]
Urban population (% of total population)	86.0	90.8	91.6
Urban population growth rate (average annual %)[k]	1.9	1.1	~0.0[l]
Fertility rate, total (live births per woman)[k]	1.3	1.3	1.4[l]
Life expectancy at birth (females/males, years)[k]	85.2 / 78.3	86.0 / 79.2	86.4 / 80.0[l]
Population age distribution (0-14/60+ years old, %)	13.8 / 26.3	13.4 / 30.3	12.8 / 33.6[e]
International migrant stock (000/% of total pop.)[m]	2 012.9 / 1.6	2 134.2 / 1.7	2 321.5 / 1.8[e]
Refugees and others of concern to the UNHCR (000)	4.2[n]	7.0[n]	27.8[i,e]
Infant mortality rate (per 1 000 live births)[k]	3.0	2.6	2.2[l]
Health: Current expenditure (% of GDP)	7.8	9.2	10.9[l]
Health: Physicians (per 1 000 pop.)	2.1[o]	2.2	2.4[p]
Education: Government expenditure (% of GDP)	3.4	3.6	3.6[p]
Education: Primary gross enrol. ratio (f/m per 100 pop.)	100.6 / 100.1	101.8 / 101.4	99.0 / 98.6[l]
Education: Secondary gross enrol. ratio (f/m per 100 pop.)	98.5 / 97.9	100.8 / 100.1	102.5 / 101.8[l]
Education: Tertiary gross enrol. ratio (f/m per 100 pop.)	51.1 / 57.3	54.8 / 61.2	61.3 / 65.1[l]
Intentional homicide rate (per 100 000 pop.)	0.5	0.4	0.3[f]
Seats held by women in the National Parliament (%)	7.1	11.3	10.1

Environment and infrastructure indicators

	2005	2010	2018
Individuals using the Internet (per 100 inhabitants)	66.9[q]	78.2[q]	92.0[i,l]
Research & Development expenditure (% of GDP)	3.2	3.1	3.3[l]
Threatened species (number)	205[o]	330	404[e]
Forested area (% of land area)[l]	68.4	68.5	68.5[l]
CO2 emission estimates (million tons/tons per capita)	1 239.3 / 9.8	1 171.6 / 9.2	1 214.0 / 9.6[p]
Energy production, primary (Petajoules)	4 175	4 118	1 269[l]
Energy supply per capita (Gigajoules)	172	164	142[l]
Tourist/visitor arrivals at national borders (000)[r]	6 728	8 611	24 040[f]
Important sites for terrestrial biodiversity protected (%)	64.5	64.7	68.5
Pop. using improved drinking water (urban/rural, %)	100.0 / 100.0	100.0 / 100.0	100.0 / 100.0[l]
Pop. using improved sanitation facilities (urban/rural, %)	100.0 / 100.0	100.0 / 100.0	100.0 / 100.0[l]
Net Official Development Assist. disbursed (% of GNI)[s]	0.28	0.20	0.23[t,e]

a Projected estimate (medium fertility variant). **b** Data refer to 1 October. **c** 2007. **d** Major metropolitan areas. **e** 2017. **f** 2016. **g** Data classified according to ISIC Rev. 4. **h** At producers' prices. **i** Estimate. **j** Calculated by the Statistics Division of the United Nations from national indices. **k** Data refers to a 5-year period preceding the reference year. **l** 2015. **m** Refers to foreign citizens. **n** Data as at the end of December. **o** 2004. **p** 2014. **q** Population aged 6 years and over. **r** Excluding nationals residing abroad. **s** Development Assistance Committee member (OECD). **t** Provisional data.

Jordan

Region	Western Asia	UN membership date	14 December 1955	
Population (000, 2018)	9 904[a]	Surface area (km2)	89 318[b]	
Pop. density (per km2, 2018)	111.6[a]	Sex ratio (m per 100 f)	102.6[a]	
Capital city	Amman	National currency	Jordanian Dinar (JOD)	
Capital city pop. (000, 2018)	2 064.6	Exchange rate (per US$)	0.7[c]	

Economic indicators

	2005	2010	2018
GDP: Gross domestic product (million current US$)	12 589	26 425	38 655[d]
GDP growth rate (annual %, const. 2010 prices)	8.1	2.3	2.0[d]
GDP per capita (current US$)	2 203.0	3 679.0	4 088.0[d]
Economy: Agriculture (% of Gross Value Added)	3.0	3.2	4.1[d]
Economy: Industry (% of Gross Value Added)	26.9	28.7	27.4[d]
Economy: Services and other activity (% of GVA)	70.1	68.1	68.6[d]
Employment in agriculture (% of employed)[e]	3.9	3.7	3.7
Employment in industry (% of employed)[e]	26.6	26.4	26.8
Employment in services & other sectors (% employed)[e]	69.5	69.9	69.5
Unemployment rate (% of labour force)	14.8	12.5	14.7[e]
Labour force participation rate (female/male pop. %)[e]	12.2 / 67.6	15.3 / 67.3	14.0 / 63.5
CPI: Consumer Price Index (2010=100)	75	100	119[c]
Agricultural production index (2004-2006=100)	101	127	145[d]
Index of industrial production (2005=100)[f]	100	105	109[g]
International trade: exports (million current US$)	4 284	7 023	7 469[c]
International trade: imports (million current US$)	10 455	15 262	20 407[c]
International trade: balance (million current US$)	- 6 170	- 8 239	- 12 938[c]
Balance of payments, current account (million US$)	- 2 271	- 1 882[h]	- 4 251[c]

Major trading partners

						2017
Export partners (% of exports)	United States	21.5	Free zones	12.5	Saudi Arabia	11.3
Import partners (% of imports)	China	13.5	Saudi Arabia	13.5	United States	9.8

Social indicators

	2005	2010	2018
Population growth rate (average annual %)[i]	2.3	4.6	4.9[b]
Urban population (% of total population)	79.5	86.1	91.0
Urban population growth rate (average annual %)[i]	2.6	6.2	5.8[b]
Fertility rate, total (live births per woman)[i]	3.9	3.7	3.6[b]
Life expectancy at birth (females/males, years)[i]	73.8 / 70.8	74.6 / 71.5	75.5 / 72.2[b]
Population age distribution (0-14/60+ years old, %)	37.8 / 5.3	37.0 / 5.4	35.2 / 5.8[a]
International migrant stock (000/% of total pop.)[j,k]	2 325.4 / 40.7	2 723.0 / 37.9	3 233.6 / 33.3[c]
Refugees and others of concern to the UNHCR (000)	17.9[l]	453.2[l]	733.1[m,c]
Infant mortality rate (per 1 000 live births)[i]	22.4	19.7	17.1[b]
Health: Current expenditure (% of GDP)	8.9	8.1	6.3[b]
Health: Physicians (per 1 000 pop.)	2.4	2.5	3.4[b]
Education: Government expenditure (% of GDP)	...	...	3.9[d]
Education: Primary gross enrol. ratio (f/m per 100 pop.)	100.0 / 99.0[n]	... / ...	... / ...
Education: Secondary gross enrol. ratio (f/m per 100 pop.)	86.3 / 83.8	82.5 / 79.4	71.3 / 68.9[g]
Education: Tertiary gross enrol. ratio (f/m per 100 pop.)	39.0 / 35.9	39.7 / 34.9	37.5 / 35.0[d]
Intentional homicide rate (per 100 000 pop.)	1.2	1.6	1.5[d]
Seats held by women in the National Parliament (%)	5.5	6.4	15.4

Environment and infrastructure indicators

	2005	2010	2018
Individuals using the Internet (per 100 inhabitants)	12.9	27.2[o]	62.3[e,d]
Research & Development expenditure (% of GDP)	0.3[p]	0.4[q]	...
Threatened species (number)	30[n]	90	113[c]
Forested area (% of land area)[e]	1.1	1.1	1.1[b]
CO2 emission estimates (million tons/tons per capita)	21.1 / 4.0	21.2 / 3.3	26.5 / 3.6[g]
Energy production, primary (Petajoules)	10	9	8[b]
Energy supply per capita (Gigajoules)	54	46	48[b]
Tourist/visitor arrivals at national borders (000)[r]	2 987	4 207[h]	3 858[h,d]
Pop. using improved drinking water (urban/rural, %)	98.1 / 91.5	98.0 / 91.9	97.8 / 92.3[b]
Pop. using improved sanitation facilities (urban/rural, %)	98.4 / 97.2	98.5 / 98.2	98.6 / 98.9[b]
Net Official Development Assist. received (% of GNI)	5.53	3.64	7.14[d]

a Projected estimate (medium fertility variant). b 2015. c 2017. d 2016. e Estimate. f Data classified according to ISIC Rev. 3. g 2014. h Break in the time series. i Data refers to a 5-year period preceding the reference year. j Refers to foreign citizens. k Including refugees. l Data as at the end of December. m Includes Iraqi refugees registered with UNHCR. n 2004. o Population aged 5 years and over. p 2002. q 2008. r Including nationals residing abroad.

Kazakhstan

Region	Central Asia	UN membership date	02 March 1992
Population (000, 2018)	18 404 [a]	Surface area (km2)	2 724 902 [b]
Pop. density (per km2, 2018)	6.8 [a]	Sex ratio (m per 100 f)	93.9 [a]
Capital city	Astana	National currency	Tenge (KZT)
Capital city pop. (000, 2018)	1 068.1	Exchange rate (per US$)	332.3 [c]

Economic indicators

	2005	2010	2018
GDP: Gross domestic product (million current US$)	57 124	148 047	135 005 [d]
GDP growth rate (annual %, const. 2010 prices)	9.7	7.3	1.0 [d]
GDP per capita (current US$)	3 676.0	9 028.0	7 505.0 [d]
Economy: Agriculture (% of Gross Value Added) [e]	6.6	4.7	4.9 [d]
Economy: Industry (% of Gross Value Added) [e]	39.2	41.9	33.6 [d]
Economy: Services and other activity (% of GVA) [e]	54.2	53.4	61.4 [d]
Employment in agriculture (% of employed) [f]	32.4	28.3	17.7
Employment in industry (% of employed) [f]	18.0	18.7	20.8
Employment in services & other sectors (% employed) [f]	49.6	53.0	61.5
Unemployment rate (% of labour force)	8.1	5.8	5.1 [f]
Labour force participation rate (female/male pop. %) [f]	64.4 / 75.2	65.4 / 75.8	65.2 / 77.2
CPI: Consumer Price Index (2010=100)	61	100	169 [c]
Agricultural production index (2004-2006=100)	100	106	139 [d]
Index of industrial production (2005=100) [g]	100	115 [h]	...
International trade: exports (million current US$)	27 846	57 244	48 342 [c]
International trade: imports (million current US$)	17 333	24 024	29 346 [c]
International trade: balance (million current US$)	10 513	33 220	18 996 [c]
Balance of payments, current account (million US$)	- 1 036	1 386	- 5 353 [c]

Major trading partners

							2017
Export partners (% of exports)	Italy	17.9	China	12.0	Netherlands	9.8
Import partners (% of imports)	Russian Federation	39.1	China	16.0	Germany	5.1

Social indicators

	2005	2010	2018
Population growth rate (average annual %) [i]	0.6	1.1	1.6 [b]
Urban population (% of total population)	56.5	56.8	57.4
Urban population growth rate (average annual %) [i]	0.8	1.2	1.7 [b]
Fertility rate, total (live births per woman) [i]	2.0	2.5	2.7 [b]
Life expectancy at birth (females/males, years) [i]	70.4 / 59.1	71.9 / 60.8	73.9 / 64.3 [b]
Population age distribution (0-14/60+ years old, %)	24.5 / 10.1	24.0 / 9.9	28.3 / 11.3 [a]
International migrant stock (000/% of total pop.)	3 103.0 / 20.0	3 334.6 / 20.3	3 635.2 / 20.0 [c]
Refugees and others of concern to the UNHCR (000)	57.9 [j]	12.7 [j]	8.0 [c]
Infant mortality rate (per 1 000 live births) [i]	32.0	23.9	14.1 [b]
Health: Current expenditure (% of GDP)	4.0	4.2	3.9 [b]
Health: Physicians (per 1 000 pop.)	...	3.5	3.3 [k]
Education: Government expenditure (% of GDP)	2.3	3.1 [l]	3.0 [d]
Education: Primary gross enrol. ratio (f/m per 100 pop.)	101.4 / 101.5	108.3 / 107.7	108.8 / 107.1 [c]
Education: Secondary gross enrol. ratio (f/m per 100 pop.)	95.2 / 90.3 [m]	97.7 / 97.2	113.6 / 112.6 [c]
Education: Tertiary gross enrol. ratio (f/m per 100 pop.)	34.4 / 28.9 [m]	51.1 / 40.3	55.5 / 43.9 [c]
Intentional homicide rate (per 100 000 pop.) [n]	13.6 [c]	8.5	4.8 [b]
Seats held by women in the National Parliament (%)	10.4	17.8	27.1

Environment and infrastructure indicators

	2005	2010	2018
Individuals using the Internet (per 100 inhabitants)	3.0	31.6 [p]	76.8 [d]
Research & Development expenditure (% of GDP)	0.3	0.2	0.2 [b]
Threatened species (number)	53 [o]	73	82 [c]
Forested area (% of land area) [f]	1.2	1.2	1.2 [b]
CO2 emission estimates (million tons/tons per capita)	177.3 / 11.7	248.5 / 15.3	248.3 / 14.3 [k]
Energy production, primary (Petajoules)	5 131	6 770	7 338 [b]
Energy supply per capita (Gigajoules)	155	206	185 [b]
Tourist/visitor arrivals at national borders (000)	3 143	2 991	4 560 [k]
Important sites for terrestrial biodiversity protected (%)	9.6	14.8	16.3
Pop. using improved drinking water (urban/rural, %)	98.5 / 87.4	99.0 / 86.4	99.4 / 85.6 [b]
Pop. using improved sanitation facilities (urban/rural, %)	96.7 / 97.5	96.9 / 97.9	97.0 / 98.1 [b]
Net Official Development Assist. disbursed (% of GNI)	...	...	0.02 [d]
Net Official Development Assist. received (% of GNI)	0.43	0.17	0.05 [d]

a Projected estimate (medium fertility variant). **b** 2015. **c** 2017. **d** 2016. **e** Data classified according to ISIC Rev. 4. **f** Estimate. **g** Data classified according to ISIC Rev. 3. **h** 2008. **i** Data refers to a 5-year period preceding the reference year. **j** Data as at the end of December. **k** 2014. **l** 2009. **m** 2000. **n** Break in the time series. **o** 2004. **p** Population aged 16 to 74 years.

Kenya

Region	Eastern Africa	UN membership date	16 December 1963
Population (000, 2018)	50 951 [a]	Surface area (km2)	591 958 [b]
Pop. density (per km2, 2018)	89.5 [a]	Sex ratio (m per 100 f)	98.8 [a]
Capital city	Nairobi	National currency	Kenyan Shilling (KES)
Capital city pop. (000, 2018)	4 385.9	Exchange rate (per US$)	103.2 [c]

Economic indicators

	2005	2010	2018
GDP: Gross domestic product (million current US$)	21 506	40 000	70 526 [d]
GDP growth rate (annual %, const. 2010 prices)	5.9	8.4	5.8 [d]
GDP per capita (current US$)	597.0	987.0	1 455.0 [d]
Economy: Agriculture (% of Gross Value Added) [e]	23.2	27.1	34.5 [d]
Economy: Industry (% of Gross Value Added) [e]	22.3	20.3	18.5 [d]
Economy: Services and other activity (% of GVA) [e]	54.5	52.6	47.0 [d]
Employment in agriculture (% of employed) [f]	41.4	39.1	37.2
Employment in industry (% of employed) [f]	14.6	15.3	14.3
Employment in services & other sectors (% employed) [f]	44.0	45.6	48.5
Unemployment rate (% of labour force) [f]	10.5	12.1	11.4
Labour force participation rate (female/male pop. %) [f]	60.1 / 69.7	61.5 / 70.5	62.4 / 68.5
CPI: Consumer Price Index (2010=100)	56	100	172 [c]
Agricultural production index (2004-2006=100)	103	123	126 [d]
International trade: exports (million current US$)	3 420	5 169	5 805 [f,c]
International trade: imports (million current US$)	5 846	12 093	16 652 [f,c]
International trade: balance (million current US$)	- 2 426	- 6 924	- 10 847 [f,c]
Balance of payments, current account (million US$)	- 252	- 2 369	- 4 755 [c]

Major trading partners

							2017
Export partners (% of exports)	United States	10.5 [f]	Netherlands	9.3	Pakistan	8.3 [f]
Import partners (% of imports) [f]	China	35.7	India	8.0	Japan	4.6

Social indicators

	2005	2010	2018
Population growth rate (average annual %) [g]	2.7	2.7	2.7 [b]
Urban population (% of total population)	21.7	23.6	27.0
Urban population growth rate (average annual %) [g]	4.4	4.4	4.4 [b]
Fertility rate, total (live births per woman) [g]	5.0	4.6	4.1 [b]
Life expectancy at birth (females/males, years) [g]	54.5 / 51.0	61.3 / 58.1	67.8 / 63.0 [b]
Population age distribution (0-14/60+ years old, %)	43.8 / 3.7	43.2 / 3.8	40.1 / 4.3 [a]
International migrant stock (000/% of total pop.) [h]	756.9 / 2.1	927.0 / 2.2	1 078.6 / 2.2 [c]
Refugees and others of concern to the UNHCR (000)	268.2 [i]	751.0 [i]	504.5 [c]
Infant mortality rate (per 1 000 live births) [g]	62.2	49.4	39.4 [b]
Health: Current expenditure (% of GDP)	5.1	6.4	5.2 [b]
Health: Physicians (per 1 000 pop.)	0.1 [i]	0.2	0.2 [k]
Education: Government expenditure (% of GDP)	7.3	5.5	5.3 [b]
Education: Primary gross enrol. ratio (f/m per 100 pop.)	99.4 / 103.5	105.2 / 107.4 [l]	105.5 / 105.1 [d]
Education: Secondary gross enrol. ratio (f/m per 100 pop.)	46.6 / 48.8 [f]	54.9 / 60.7 [l]	... / ...
Education: Tertiary gross enrol. ratio (f/m per 100 pop.)	2.2 / 3.7 [l]	3.3 / 4.7 [l]	... / ...
Intentional homicide rate (per 100 000 pop.)	3.0	4.7	4.9 [d]
Seats held by women in the National Parliament (%)	7.1	9.8	21.8

Environment and infrastructure indicators

	2005	2010	2018
Individuals using the Internet (per 100 inhabitants)	3.1	7.2	26.0 [f,d]
Research & Development expenditure (% of GDP)	...	0.8 [m]	...
Threatened species (number)	229 [n]	338	480 [c]
Forested area (% of land area) [f]	7.1	7.4	7.8 [b]
CO2 emission estimates (million tons/tons per capita)	8.6 / 0.3	12.2 / 0.3	14.3 / 0.3 [k]
Energy production, primary (Petajoules)	338	650 [f]	761 [b]
Energy supply per capita (Gigajoules)	12	20 [f]	21 [b]
Tourist/visitor arrivals at national borders (000) [o]	1 399	1 470	1 268 [d]
Important sites for terrestrial biodiversity protected (%)	35.5	36.8	37.5
Pop. using improved drinking water (urban/rural, %)	85.4 / 47.9	83.3 / 52.9	81.6 / 56.8 [b]
Pop. using improved sanitation facilities (urban/rural, %)	29.5 / 27.6	30.5 / 28.8	31.2 / 29.7 [b]
Net Official Development Assist. received (% of GNI)	4.04	4.09	3.13 [d]

a Projected estimate (medium fertility variant). b 2015. c 2017. d 2016. e Data classified according to ISIC Rev. 4. f Estimate. g Data refers to a 5-year period preceding the reference year. h Including refugees. i Data as at the end of December. j 2002. k 2014. l 2009. m Break in the time series. n 2004. o Excluding nationals residing abroad.

Kiribati

Region	Micronesia	UN membership date	14 September 1999
Population (000, 2018)	118[a]	Surface area (km2)	726[b,c]
Pop. density (per km2, 2018)	146.2[a]	Sex ratio (m per 100 f)	97.3[a]
Capital city	Bairiki	National currency	Australian Dollar (AUD)
Capital city pop. (000)	3.2[c]	Exchange rate (per US$)	1.3[d]

Economic indicators

	2005	2010	2018
GDP: Gross domestic product (million current US$)	112	153	174[e]
GDP growth rate (annual %, const. 2010 prices)	5.0	- 1.6	4.2[e]
GDP per capita (current US$)	1 215.0	1 493.0	1 518.0[e]
Economy: Agriculture (% of Gross Value Added)[f]	21.8	24.6	23.5[e]
Economy: Industry (% of Gross Value Added)[f]	9.3	10.3	14.2[e]
Economy: Services and other activity (% of GVA)[f]	68.9	65.1	62.4[e]
Employment in agriculture (% of employed)	7.1[g]	22.1	...
Employment in industry (% of employed)	8.4[g]	16.1	...
Employment in services & other sectors (% employed)	81.1[g]	61.8	...
Unemployment rate (% of labour force)[h]	14.7	30.6	...
Labour force participation rate (female/male pop. %)	20.4 / 32.8[i,j]	52.3 / 66.8[i]	... / ...
CPI: Consumer Price Index (2010=100)[k]	...	100	100[c]
Agricultural production index (2004-2006=100)	95	60	61[e]
International trade: exports (million current US$)	4	4	11[k,d]
International trade: imports (million current US$)	74	73	183[k,d]
International trade: balance (million current US$)	- 70	- 69	- 172[k,d]
Balance of payments, current account (million US$)	...	–0	36[e]

Major trading partners

							2017
Export partners (% of exports)	Malaysia	33.2[k]	United States	21.2	Fiji	14.9[k]
Import partners (% of imports)[k]	Australia	21.8	Fiji	21.8	China	9.6

Social indicators

	2005	2010	2018
Population growth rate (average annual %)[l]	1.8	2.1	1.8[c]
Urban population (% of total population)	43.6	47.4	54.1
Urban population growth rate (average annual %)[l]	2.1	3.8	3.5[c]
Fertility rate, total (live births per woman)[l]	4.0	3.9	3.8[c]
Life expectancy at birth (females/males, years)[l]	67.5 / 61.6	68.1 / 62.0	68.9 / 62.4[c]
Population age distribution (0-14/60+ years old, %)	36.9 / 5.4	36.1 / 5.4	35.3 / 6.5[a]
International migrant stock (000/% of total pop.)	2.5 / 2.7	2.9 / 2.8	3.0 / 2.6[d]
Infant mortality rate (per 1 000 live births)[l]	51.6	49.3	46.9[c]
Health: Current expenditure (% of GDP)[m,n]	11.5	9.4	7.6[c]
Health: Physicians (per 1 000 pop.)	...	0.3[o]	0.2[p]
Education: Government expenditure (% of GDP)	12.0[q]	...	...
Education: Primary gross enrol. ratio (f/m per 100 pop.)	112.8 / 111.2	113.7 / 108.0[r]	106.4 / 103.7[e]
Education: Secondary gross enrol. ratio (f/m per 100 pop.)	95.3 / 83.1	91.5 / 82.9[o]	... / ...
Intentional homicide rate (per 100 000 pop.)	4.7[q]	3.9	7.5[s]
Seats held by women in the National Parliament (%)	4.8	4.3	6.5

Environment and infrastructure indicators

	2005	2010	2018
Individuals using the Internet (per 100 inhabitants)	4.0[k]	9.1	13.7[k,o]
Threatened species (number)	11[t]	90	104[d]
Forested area (% of land area)[k]	15.0	15.0	15.0[c]
CO2 emission estimates (million tons/tons per capita)	0.1 / 0.7	0.1 / 0.6	0.1 / 0.6[u]
Energy production, primary (Petajoules)	0	0	0[c]
Energy supply per capita (Gigajoules)	9[k]	8	8[k,c]
Tourist/visitor arrivals at national borders (000)[v]	4	5	6[e]
Important sites for terrestrial biodiversity protected (%)	12.5	52.5	52.5
Pop. using improved drinking water (urban/rural, %)	83.3 / 46.0	86.2 / 49.3	87.3 / 50.6[c]
Pop. using improved sanitation facilities (urban/rural, %)	48.7 / 27.2	50.5 / 29.6	51.2 / 30.6[c]
Net Official Development Assist. received (% of GNI)	17.46	10.50	23.22[a]

a Projected estimate (medium fertility variant). b Land area only. Excluding 84 square km of uninhabited islands. c 2015. d 2017. e 2016. f At factor cost. g Data classified according to ISIC Rev. 2. h De facto population. i Persons present (de facto). j Break in the time series. k Estimate. l Data refers to a 5-year period preceding the reference year. m General government expenditure (GGE) can be larger than the Gross domestic product (GDP) because government accounts for a very large part of domestic consumption and because a large part of domestic consumption in the country is accounted for by imports. n Data refer to fiscal years beginning 1 July. o 2008. p 2013. q 2001. r 2009. s 2012. t 2004. u 2014. v Air arrivals. Tarawa and Christmas Island.

Kuwait

Region	Western Asia	UN membership date	14 May 1963
Population (000, 2018)	4 197[a]	Surface area (km2)	17 818[b]
Pop. density (per km2, 2018)	235.5[a]	Sex ratio (m per 100 f)	134.8[a]
Capital city	Kuwait City	National currency	Kuwaiti Dinar (KWD)
Capital city pop. (000, 2018)	2 989.3[c]	Exchange rate (per US$)	0.3[d]

Economic indicators

	2005	2010	2018
GDP: Gross domestic product (million current US$)	80 798	115 416	110 346[e]
GDP growth rate (annual %, const. 2010 prices)	10.6	- 2.4	2.5[e]
GDP per capita (current US$)	35 490.0	38 497.0	27 229.0[e]
Economy: Agriculture (% of Gross Value Added)	0.3	0.4	0.4[e]
Economy: Industry (% of Gross Value Added)	60.2	58.2	58.8[e]
Economy: Services and other activity (% of GVA)	39.5	41.4	40.8[e]
Employment in agriculture (% of employed)[f]	2.7	3.1	3.6
Employment in industry (% of employed)[f]	20.7	25.7	26.6
Employment in services & other sectors (% employed)[f]	76.6	71.2	69.8
Unemployment rate (% of labour force)	2.0	1.8	2.1[f]
Labour force participation rate (female/male pop. %)[f]	46.3 / 82.3	48.2 / 84.6	46.9 / 83.7
CPI: Consumer Price Index (2010=100)	76	100	125[d]
Agricultural production index (2004-2006=100)	97	131	191[h]
Index of industrial production (2005=100)[g]	100	89	114[h]
International trade: exports (million current US$)	44 869[f]	62 698	54 807[d]
International trade: imports (million current US$)	15 801[f]	22 691	33 590[d]
International trade: balance (million current US$)	29 068[f]	40 007	21 217[d]
Balance of payments, current account (million US$)	30 071	36 989	- 7 591[d]

Major trading partners

						2017
Export partners (% of exports)	Areas nes[i]	90.5	India	1.4[f]	Saudi Arabia	1.2
Import partners (% of imports)	China	16.4	United States	10.3	United Arab Emirates	8.7

Social indicators

	2005	2010	2018
Population growth rate (average annual %)[j]	2.1	5.5	5.4[b]
Urban population (% of total population)	100.0	100.0	100.0
Urban population growth rate (average annual %)[j]	2.3	5.5	5.4[b]
Fertility rate, total (live births per woman)[j]	2.6	2.4	2.0[b]
Life expectancy at birth (females/males, years)[j]	74.4 / 72.6	74.8 / 73.0	75.5 / 73.5[b]
Population age distribution (0-14/60+ years old, %)	26.0 / 3.6	23.2 / 3.4	21.2 / 5.3[a]
International migrant stock (000/% of total pop.)[k,l]	1 333.3 / 58.6	1 871.5 / 62.4	3 123.4 / 75.5[d]
Refugees and others of concern to the UNHCR (000)	102.7[m]	96.5[m]	94.7[d]
Infant mortality rate (per 1 000 live births)[j]	10.2	9.6	8.4[b]
Health: Current expenditure (% of GDP)	2.4	2.8	4.0[b]
Health: Physicians (per 1 000 pop.)	...	2.4	2.6[b]
Education: Government expenditure (% of GDP)	4.7	3.8[f,n]	...
Education: Primary gross enrol. ratio (f/m per 100 pop.)	106.4 / 102.7	101.5 / 103.0	102.7 / 96.8[e]
Education: Secondary gross enrol. ratio (f/m per 100 pop.)	114.2 / 104.4[f]	99.0 / 96.8	101.4 / 94.0[b]
Education: Tertiary gross enrol. ratio (f/m per 100 pop.)	28.1 / 12.2[f,o]	... / ...	42.7 / 23.0[h]
Intentional homicide rate (per 100 000 pop.)	1.8	2.0	1.8[p]
Seats held by women in the National Parliament (%)	0.0	7.7	3.1

Environment and infrastructure indicators

	2005	2010	2018
Individuals using the Internet (per 100 inhabitants)	25.9	61.4[f]	78.4[f,a]
Research & Development expenditure (% of GDP)	0.1[q,r]	0.1[q,r]	0.3[s,t,u,h]
Threatened species (number)	20[o]	41	49[d]
Forested area (% of land area)[f]	0.3	0.4	0.4[b]
CO2 emission estimates (million tons/tons per capita)	71.5 / 31.6	89.6 / 29.3	95.4 / 25.4[v]
Energy production, primary (Petajoules)[w]	6 080	5 557	7 003[b]
Energy supply per capita (Gigajoules)[w]	500	441	375[b]
Tourist/visitor arrivals at national borders (000)	3 474	5 208	7 055[e]
Important sites for terrestrial biodiversity protected (%)	46.3	46.3	59.0
Pop. using improved drinking water (urban/rural, %)	99.0 / 99.0	99.0 / 99.0	99.0 / 99.0[b]
Pop. using improved sanitation facilities (urban/rural, %)	100.0 / 100.0	100.0 / 100.0	100.0 / 100.0[b]

a Projected estimate (medium fertility variant). b 2015. c Data refers to the Governorates of Capital, Hawalli, Al-Farwaniya and Mubarak Al-Kabeer. d 2017. e 2016. f Estimate. g Data classified according to ISIC Rev. 3. h 2013. i Areas not elsewhere specified. j Data refers to a 5-year period preceding the reference year. k Refers to foreign citizens. l Including refugees. m Data as at the end of December. n 2009. o 2004. p 2012. q Partial data. r Government only. s Break in the time series. t Excluding private non-profit. u Excluding business enterprise. v 2014. w The data for crude oil production include 50 per cent of the output of the Neutral Zone.

Kyrgyzstan

Region	Central Asia	UN membership date	02 March 1992	
Population (000, 2018)	6 133[a]	Surface area (km2)	199 949[b]	
Pop. density (per km2, 2018)	32.0[a]	Sex ratio (m per 100 f)	98.3[a]	
Capital city	Bishkek	National currency	Som (KGS)	
Capital city pop. (000, 2018)	996.3	Exchange rate (per US$)	68.8[c]	

Economic indicators

	2005	2010	2018
GDP: Gross domestic product (million current US$)	2 460	4 794	6 551[d]
GDP growth rate (annual %, const. 2010 prices)	- 0.2	- 0.5	3.8[d]
GDP per capita (current US$)	485.0	884.0	1 100.0[d]
Economy: Agriculture (% of Gross Value Added)[e]	31.3	18.8	14.4[d]
Economy: Industry (% of Gross Value Added)[e]	22.1	28.2	28.3[d]
Economy: Services and other activity (% of GVA)[e]	46.6	53.0	57.3[d]
Employment in agriculture (% of employed)[f]	38.5	29.9	26.1
Employment in industry (% of employed)[f]	17.6	22.8	22.4
Employment in services & other sectors (% employed)[f]	43.9	47.3	51.5
Unemployment rate (% of labour force)	8.1	8.6	7.4[f]
Labour force participation rate (female/male pop. %)[f]	54.1 / 76.1	52.2 / 76.6	48.0 / 75.9
CPI: Consumer Price Index (2010=100)	60	100	152[c]
Agricultural production index (2004-2006=100)	98	105	117[d]
Index of industrial production (2005=100)[g]	100	69	78[h]
International trade: exports (million current US$)	672	1 488	1 784[c]
International trade: imports (million current US$)	1 108	3 223	4 474[c]
International trade: balance (million current US$)	- 436	- 1 734	- 2 690[c]
Balance of payments, current account (million US$)	- 37	- 475[i]	- 347[c]

Major trading partners

						2017
Export partners (% of exports)	Switzerland	27.4	Kazakhstan	16.5	Russian Federation	14.7
Import partners (% of imports)	China	33.4	Russian Federation	26.4	Kazakhstan	13.1

Social indicators

	2005	2010	2018
Population growth rate (average annual %)[j]	0.6	1.3	1.6[b]
Urban population (% of total population)	35.3	35.3	36.4
Urban population growth rate (average annual %)[j]	0.6	1.3	1.8[b]
Fertility rate, total (live births per woman)[j]	2.5	2.8	3.1[b]
Life expectancy at birth (females/males, years)[j]	71.0 / 63.0	71.7 / 63.5	74.3 / 66.4[b]
Population age distribution (0-14/60+ years old, %)	31.0 / 7.1	29.9 / 6.4	32.1 / 7.8[a]
International migrant stock (000/% of total pop.)	312.9 / 6.2	231.5 / 4.3	200.3 / 3.3[c]
Refugees and others of concern to the UNHCR (000)	103.1[k]	304.2[k]	2.7[c]
Infant mortality rate (per 1 000 live births)[j]	37.8	30.3	19.6[b]
Health: Current expenditure (% of GDP)	7.5	7.1	8.2[b]
Health: Physicians (per 1 000 pop.)	..	1.9	1.9[i]
Education: Government expenditure (% of GDP)	4.9	5.8	6.0[b]
Education: Primary gross enrol. ratio (f/m per 100 pop.)	98.1 / 99.6	99.0 / 99.8	105.8 / 106.9[d]
Education: Secondary gross enrol. ratio (f/m per 100 pop.)	86.8 / 86.4	87.3 / 87.7	97.6 / 97.5[d]
Education: Tertiary gross enrol. ratio (f/m per 100 pop.)	47.5 / 37.8	47.7 / 36.6	51.6 / 40.4[d]
Intentional homicide rate (per 100 000 pop.)	8.3	19.8	4.5[d]
Seats held by women in the National Parliament (%)	10.0	25.6	19.2

Environment and infrastructure indicators

	2005	2010	2018
Individuals using the Internet (per 100 inhabitants)	10.5	16.3[f]	34.5[f,d]
Research & Development expenditure (% of GDP)	0.2	0.2	0.1[m,b]
Threatened species (number)	16[n]	40	44[c]
Forested area (% of land area)[f]	4.5	3.5	3.3[b]
CO2 emission estimates (million tons/tons per capita)	5.6 / 1.1	6.4 / 1.2	9.6 / 1.7[i]
Energy production, primary (Petajoules)	61	53	75[b]
Energy supply per capita (Gigajoules)	23	21	28[b]
Tourist/visitor arrivals at national borders (000)	183[o]	855	2 930[d]
Important sites for terrestrial biodiversity protected (%)	22.4	22.4	22.6
Pop. using improved drinking water (urban/rural, %)	96.3 / 74.6	96.5 / 80.4	96.7 / 86.2[b]
Pop. using improved sanitation facilities (urban/rural, %)	90.9 / 93.1	90.0 / 94.3	89.1 / 95.6[b]
Net Official Development Assist. received (% of GNI)	11.28	8.55	8.19[d]

a Projected estimate (medium fertility variant). b 2015. c 2017. d 2016. e Data classified according to ISIC Rev. 4. f Estimate. g Data classified according to ISIC Rev. 3. h 2011. i Break in the time series. j Data refers to a 5-year period preceding the reference year. k Data as at the end of December. l 2014. m Excluding private non-profit. n 2004. o 2002.

Lao People's Democratic Republic

Region	South-eastern Asia	UN membership date	14 December 1955
Population (000, 2018)	6 961 [a]	Surface area (km2)	236 800 [b]
Pop. density (per km2, 2018)	30.2 [a]	Sex ratio (m per 100 f)	99.6 [a]
Capital city	Vientiane	National currency	Lao Kip (LAK)
Capital city pop. (000, 2018)	664.8	Exchange rate (per US$)	8 307.3 [c]

Economic indicators	2005	2010	2018
GDP: Gross domestic product (million current US$)	2 946	7 313	15 806 [d]
GDP growth rate (annual %, const. 2010 prices)	6.8	8.1	7.0 [d]
GDP per capita (current US$)	512.0	1 171.0	2 339.0 [d]
Economy: Agriculture (% of Gross Value Added) [e]	29.1	23.6	19.5 [d]
Economy: Industry (% of Gross Value Added) [e]	26.2	30.9	32.5 [d]
Economy: Services and other activity (% of GVA) [e]	44.7	45.5	48.0 [d]
Employment in agriculture (% of employed) [f]	78.5 [f]	71.5	59.9 [f]
Employment in industry (% of employed) [f]	5.3	8.3	9.8
Employment in services & other sectors (% employed) [f]	16.2	20.2	30.4
Unemployment rate (% of labour force)	1.4	0.7	0.7 [f]
Labour force participation rate (female/male pop. %) [i]	77.9 / 79.8	76.8 / 79.3	77.0 / 79.8
CPI: Consumer Price Index (2010=100)	79 [g]	100 [g]	129 [c]
Agricultural production index (2004-2006=100)	100	132	219 [b]
International trade: exports (million current US$)	552 [f]	1 909	2 759 [f,c]
International trade: imports (million current US$)	874 [f]	1 837	4 804 [f,c]
International trade: balance (million current US$)	- 322 [f]	72	- 2 045 [f,c]
Balance of payments, current account (million US$)	- 174	29	- 1 234 [d]

Major trading partners						2017
Export partners (% of exports)	China	36.1 [f]	Thailand	31.3	Viet Nam	17.2 [f]
Import partners (% of imports) [f]	Thailand	61.9	China	18.2	Viet Nam	10.1

Social indicators	2005	2010	2018
Population growth rate (average annual %) [h]	1.5	1.6	1.3 [b]
Urban population (% of total population)	27.2	30.1	35.0
Urban population growth rate (average annual %) [h]	5.8	3.7	3.2 [b]
Fertility rate, total (live births per woman) [h]	3.9	3.4	2.9 [b]
Life expectancy at birth (females/males, years) [h]	61.7 / 59.0	64.5 / 61.8	66.8 / 63.9 [b]
Population age distribution (0-14/60+ years old, %)	40.3 / 5.5	36.3 / 5.6	32.5 / 6.4 [a]
International migrant stock (000/% of total pop.) [i,j]	20.4 / 0.4	32.5 / 0.5	45.5 / 0.7 [c]
Infant mortality rate (per 1 000 live births) [h]	69.2	56.7	47.3 [b]
Health: Current expenditure (% of GDP) [k]	4.8	3.2	2.8 [b]
Health: Physicians (per 1 000 pop.)	0.3	0.2 [l]	0.5 [m]
Education: Government expenditure (% of GDP)	2.4	1.7	2.9 [m]
Education: Primary gross enrol. ratio (f/m per 100 pop.)	104.6 / 119.6	118.7 / 128.6	108.3 / 112.6 [d]
Education: Secondary gross enrol. ratio (f/m per 100 pop.)	37.4 / 49.5	42.4 / 51.1	64.0 / 68.9 [d]
Education: Tertiary gross enrol. ratio (f/m per 100 pop.)	6.4 / 9.1	14.4 / 18.8	17.2 / 17.2 [d]
Intentional homicide rate (per 100 000 pop.)	9.6	8.0	7.0 [b]
Seats held by women in the National Parliament (%)	22.9	25.2	27.5

Environment and infrastructure indicators	2005	2010	2018
Individuals using the Internet (per 100 inhabitants)	0.9	7.0	21.9 [f,d]
Research & Development expenditure (% of GDP)	~0.0 [n,o]	...	...
Threatened species (number)	91 [p]	132	209 [c]
Forested area (% of land area)	73.1	77.2 [f]	81.3 [f,b]
CO2 emission estimates (million tons/tons per capita)	1.4 / 0.3	1.6 / 0.3	2.0 / 0.3 [m]
Energy production, primary (Petajoules)	73	117	185 [b]
Energy supply per capita (Gigajoules)	13	19	28 [b]
Tourist/visitor arrivals at national borders (000)	672	1 670	3 315 [d]
Important sites for terrestrial biodiversity protected (%)	44.0	45.5	45.5
Pop. using improved drinking water (urban/rural, %)	77.0 / 49.2	81.8 / 60.4	85.6 / 69.4 [b]
Pop. using improved sanitation facilities (urban/rural, %)	76.3 / 31.1	86.4 / 44.9	94.5 / 56.0 [b]
Net Official Development Assist. received (% of GNI)	11.14	6.19	2.63 [d]

a Projected estimate (medium fertility variant). b 2015. c 2017. d 2016. e Data classified according to ISIC Rev. 4. f Estimate. g Break in the time series. h Data refers to a 5-year period preceding the reference year. i Refers to foreign citizens. j Including refugees. k Data refer to fiscal years ending 30 September. l 2009. m 2014. n Partial data. o 2002. p 2004.

Latvia

Region	Northern Europe	UN membership date	17 September 1991
Population (000, 2018)	1 930[a]	Surface area (km2)	64 573[b]
Pop. density (per km2, 2018)	31.0[a]	Sex ratio (m per 100 f)	85.0[a]
Capital city	Riga	National currency	Euro (EUR)
Capital city pop. (000, 2018)	637.1	Exchange rate (per US$)	0.8[c]

Economic indicators

	2005	2010	2018
GDP: Gross domestic product (million current US$)	16 922	23 765	27 573[d]
GDP growth rate (annual %, const. 2010 prices)	10.7	- 3.9	2.1[d]
GDP per capita (current US$)	7 514.0	11 216.0	13 993.0[d]
Economy: Agriculture (% of Gross Value Added)[e]	4.3	4.4	4.0[d]
Economy: Industry (% of Gross Value Added)[e]	22.9	23.4	21.5[d]
Economy: Services and other activity (% of GVA)[e]	72.8	72.2	74.5[d]
Employment in agriculture (% of employed)	12.0	8.6[f]	7.3[f]
Employment in industry (% of employed)[f]	26.5	23.1	23.8
Employment in services & other sectors (% employed)[f]	61.5	68.3	68.8
Unemployment rate (% of labour force)	10.0	19.5	9.4[f]
Labour force participation rate (female/male pop. %)[f]	50.4 / 65.6	53.8 / 65.3	55.0 / 67.0
CPI: Consumer Price Index (2010=100)	72	100	111[c]
Agricultural production index (2004-2006=100)	105	108	139[d]
Index of industrial production (2005=100)	100	98[g]	111[g,h]
International trade: exports (million current US$)	5 303	8 851	12 895[c]
International trade: imports (million current US$)	8 770	11 143	15 886[c]
International trade: balance (million current US$)	- 3 468	- 2 292	- 2 991[c]
Balance of payments, current account (million US$)	- 1 988	494	- 246[c]

Major trading partners

							2017
Export partners (% of exports)	Lithuania	16.8	Estonia	11.6	Russian Federation	9.1
Import partners (% of imports)	Lithuania	18.6	Germany	11.3	Poland	9.1

Social indicators

	2005	2010	2018
Population growth rate (average annual %)[i]	- 1.1	- 1.2	- 1.2[b]
Urban population (% of total population)	68.0	67.8	68.1
Urban population growth rate (average annual %)[i]	- 1.2	- 1.3	- 1.2[b]
Fertility rate, total (live births per woman)[i]	1.3	1.5	1.5[b]
Life expectancy at birth (females/males, years)[i]	76.2 / 65.2	77.0 / 66.0	78.7 / 68.8[b]
Population age distribution (0-14/60+ years old, %)	14.7 / 22.5	14.1 / 23.6	15.6 / 26.6[a]
International migrant stock (000/% of total pop.)	376.7 / 16.7	313.8 / 14.8	256.9 / 13.2[c]
Refugees and others of concern to the UNHCR (000)	418.7[j]	327.0[j]	243.4[k,c]
Infant mortality rate (per 1 000 live births)[i]	9.9	7.8	6.5[b]
Health: Current expenditure (% of GDP)	8.9	8.6	5.8[b]
Health: Physicians (per 1 000 pop.)	3.7	3.1	3.2[b]
Education: Government expenditure (% of GDP)	4.9[l]	5.1	5.3[h]
Education: Primary gross enrol. ratio (f/m per 100 pop.)	91.8 / 96.0	108.7 / 108.7	98.0 / 98.8[b]
Education: Secondary gross enrol. ratio (f/m per 100 pop.)	99.5 / 99.5	94.6 / 97.0	111.7 / 112.8[b]
Education: Tertiary gross enrol. ratio (f/m per 100 pop.)	97.8 / 54.9	85.9 / 48.8	83.2 / 53.9[b]
Intentional homicide rate (per 100 000 pop.)	5.6	3.3	3.4[b]
Seats held by women in the National Parliament (%)	21.0	22.0	16.0

Environment and infrastructure indicators

	2005	2010	2018
Individuals using the Internet (per 100 inhabitants)	46.0[m]	68.4[m]	79.9[d]
Research & Development expenditure (% of GDP)	0.5	0.6	0.6[n,b]
Threatened species (number)	23[l]	18	30[c]
Forested area (% of land area)	53.0	53.9	54.0[f,b]
CO2 emission estimates (million tons/tons per capita)	7.5 / 3.3	8.1 / 3.9	7.0 / 3.5[h]
Energy production, primary (Petajoules)	78	95	98[b]
Energy supply per capita (Gigajoules)	82	97	91[b]
Tourist/visitor arrivals at national borders (000)[o]	1 116	1 373	1 793[d]
Important sites for terrestrial biodiversity protected (%)	97.2	97.3	97.3
Pop. using improved drinking water (urban/rural, %)	99.7 / 96.2	99.7 / 97.3	99.8 / 98.3[b]
Pop. using improved sanitation facilities (urban/rural, %)	88.0 / 73.9	89.4 / 77.7	90.8 / 81.5[b]
Net Official Development Assist. disbursed (% of GNI)	0.07	0.06	0.11[n,c]

a Projected estimate (medium fertility variant). **b** 2015. **c** 2017. **d** 2016. **e** Data classified according to ISIC Rev. 4. **f** Estimate. **g** Excluding water and waste management. **h** 2014. **i** Data refers to a 5-year period preceding the reference year. **j** Data as at the end of December. **k** Non-citizens of Latvia is the only category of residents who are not Latvian citizens, but who enjoy the right to reside in Latvia ex lege (all others require a resident permit) and an immediate right to acquire citizenship through registration and/or naturalisation (depending on age). **l** 2004. **m** Population aged 16 to 74 years. **n** Provisional data. **o** Non-resident departures. Survey of persons crossing the state border.

Lebanon

Region	Western Asia	UN membership date	24 October 1945
Population (000, 2018)	6 094 [a]	Surface area (km2)	10 452 [b]
Pop. density (per km2, 2018)	595.7 [a]	Sex ratio (m per 100 f)	100.7 [a]
Capital city	Beirut	National currency	Lebanese Pound (LBP)
Capital city pop. (000, 2018)	2 385.3 [c,d]	Exchange rate (per US$)	1 507.5 [e]

Economic indicators	2005	2010	2018
GDP: Gross domestic product (million current US$)	21 490	38 420	50 458 [f]
GDP growth rate (annual %, const. 2010 prices)	2.7	8.0	1.0 [f]
GDP per capita (current US$)	5 390.0	8 858.0	8 400.0 [f]
Economy: Agriculture (% of Gross Value Added) [g]	4.0	4.3	2.9 [f]
Economy: Industry (% of Gross Value Added) [g]	16.7	15.7	11.2 [f]
Economy: Services and other activity (% of GVA) [g]	79.3	80.1	85.9 [f]
Employment in agriculture (% of employed) [h]	3.4	2.5	3.2
Employment in industry (% of employed) [h]	18.8	19.2	20.2
Employment in services & other sectors (% employed) [h]	77.8	78.3	76.6
Unemployment rate (% of labour force) [h]	8.1	6.3	6.3
Labour force participation rate (female/male pop. %) [h]	20.4 / 70.7	22.3 / 67.8	23.3 / 71.1
CPI: Consumer Price Index (2010=100) [h]	...	100	119 [e]
Agricultural production index (2004-2006=100)	97	93	89 [f]
International trade: exports (million current US$)	1 879	4 254	2 843 [h,e]
International trade: imports (million current US$)	9 327	17 970	19 579 [h,a]
International trade: balance (million current US$)	- 7 448	- 13 716	- 16 736 [h,e]
Balance of payments, current account (million US$)	- 2 748	- 7 552	- 10 555 [f]

Major trading partners						2017
Export partners (% of exports) [h]	South Africa	21.1	Saudi Arabia	9.0	United Arab Emirates	8.0
Import partners (% of imports) [h]	China	11.2	Italy	7.5	United States	6.3

Social indicators	2005	2010	2018
Population growth rate (average annual %) [i]	4.2	1.7	6.0 [b]
Urban population (% of total population)	86.6	87.3	88.6
Urban population growth rate (average annual %) [i]	4.3	1.8	6.2 [b]
Fertility rate, total (live births per woman) [i]	2.0	1.6	1.7 [b]
Life expectancy at birth (females/males, years) [i]	77.4 / 73.9	79.7 / 76.0	80.9 / 77.3 [b]
Population age distribution (0-14/60+ years old, %)	27.9 / 10.7	23.7 / 11.9	22.6 / 12.3 [a]
International migrant stock (000/% of total pop.) [j]	756.8 / 19.0	820.7 / 18.9	1 939.2 / 31.9 [e]
Refugees and others of concern to the UNHCR (000)	3.0 [k]	9.5 [k]	1 021.0 [e]
Infant mortality rate (per 1 000 live births) [i]	13.8	10.6	9.2 [b]
Health: Current expenditure (% of GDP)	7.6	7.5	7.4 [b]
Health: Physicians (per 1 000 pop.)	3.4 [l]	2.7	2.4 [m]
Education: Government expenditure (% of GDP)	2.7	1.6	2.5 [n]
Education: Primary gross enrol. ratio (f/m per 100 pop.)	99.0 / 107.8 [h]	100.0 / 109.5	85.1 / 93.2 [f]
Education: Secondary gross enrol. ratio (f/m per 100 pop.)	80.8 / 80.2 [h]	76.0 / 74.5	60.1 / 59.9 [f]
Education: Tertiary gross enrol. ratio (f/m per 100 pop.)	45.2 / 43.0	49.3 / 47.4	45.8 / 39.6 [m]
Intentional homicide rate (per 100 000 pop.)	...	3.8	4.0 [f]
Seats held by women in the National Parliament (%)	2.3	3.1	3.1

Environment and infrastructure indicators	2005	2010	2018
Individuals using the Internet (per 100 inhabitants)	10.1 [o]	43.7 [h,p]	76.1 [h,f]
Threatened species (number)	26 [q]	50	87 [e]
Forested area (% of land area) [h]	13.3	13.4	13.4 [b]
CO2 emission estimates (million tons/tons per capita)	16.2 / 4.0	20.0 / 4.6	24.1 / 4.3 [m]
Energy production, primary (Petajoules)	10	9	8 [b]
Energy supply per capita (Gigajoules)	51	60	53 [b]
Tourist/visitor arrivals at national borders (000) [r]	1 140	2 168	1 688 [f]
Important sites for terrestrial biodiversity protected (%)	11.6	11.6	13.1
Pop. using improved drinking water (urban/rural, %)	91.7 / 91.7	97.7 / 97.7	99.0 / 99.0 [b]
Pop. using improved sanitation facilities (urban/rural, %)	82.0 / 82.0	80.9 / 80.9	80.7 / 80.7 [b]
Net Official Development Assist. received (% of GNI)	1.09	1.19	2.42 [f]

a Projected estimate (medium fertility variant). b 2015. c Estimates should be viewed with caution as these are derived from scarce data. d Excluding Syrian refugees. e 2017. f 2016. g Data classified according to ISIC Rev. 4. h Estimate. i Data refers to a 5-year period preceding the reference year. j Including refugees. k Data as at the end of December. l 2001. m 2014. n 2013. o Population aged 6 years and over. p Population aged 15 years and over. q 2004. r Excluding the Lebanon, Syria and Palestine nationalities.

Lesotho

Region	Southern Africa	UN membership date	17 October 1966
Population (000, 2018)	2 263[a]	Surface area (km2)	30 355[b]
Pop. density (per km2, 2018)	74.5[a]	Sex ratio (m per 100 f)	94.5[a]
Capital city	Maseru	National currency	Loti (LSL)
Capital city pop. (000, 2018)	201.9	Exchange rate (per US$)	12.3[c]

Economic indicators

	2005	2010	2018
GDP: Gross domestic product (million current US$)	1 559	2 394	2 241[d]
GDP growth rate (annual %, const. 2010 prices)	2.7	6.5	2.9[d]
GDP per capita (current US$)	800.0	1 173.0	1 017.0[d]
Economy: Agriculture (% of Gross Value Added)[e]	6.2	5.6	5.8[d]
Economy: Industry (% of Gross Value Added)[e]	37.7	32.8	32.3[d]
Economy: Services and other activity (% of GVA)[e]	56.1	61.7	61.8[d]
Employment in agriculture (% of employed)[f]	25.8	12.9	10.2
Employment in industry (% of employed)[f]	27.3	39.3	40.4
Employment in services & other sectors (% employed)[f]	46.9	47.8	49.4
Unemployment rate (% of labour force)[f]	37.2	25.9	28.5
Labour force participation rate (female/male pop. %)[f]	64.1 / 77.4	60.7 / 75.4	59.3 / 74.6
CPI: Consumer Price Index (2010=100)	71	100	143[c]
Agricultural production index (2004-2006=100)	105	107	96[d]
International trade: exports (million current US$)	650[f]	503	571[f,c]
International trade: imports (million current US$)	1 410[f]	1 277	1 608[f,c]
International trade: balance (million current US$)	- 760[f]	- 773	- 1 036[f,c]
Balance of payments, current account (million US$)	166[g]	- 158	- 166[c]

Major trading partners

						2017
Export partners (% of exports)[f]	United States	29.9[f]	South Africa	29.3	Belgium	28.1[f]
Import partners (% of imports)[f]	South Africa	86.7	Asia nes[h]	3.9	China	3.8

Social indicators

	2005	2010	2018
Population growth rate (average annual %)[i]	0.8	0.9	1.3[b]
Urban population (% of total population)	22.2	24.8	28.2
Urban population growth rate (average annual %)[i]	3.4	3.1	2.9[b]
Fertility rate, total (live births per woman)[i]	3.8	3.4	3.3[b]
Life expectancy at birth (females/males, years)[i]	46.4 / 44.6	50.2 / 47.6	54.7 / 50.1[b]
Population age distribution (0-14/60+ years old, %)	39.4 / 6.3	37.3 / 6.6	35.3 / 6.7[a]
International migrant stock (000/% of total pop.)[j,k]	6.3 / 0.3	6.4 / 0.4	6.7 / 0.3[c]
Refugees and others of concern to the UNHCR (000)	...	...	0.1[c]
Infant mortality rate (per 1 000 live births)[i]	86.8	74.1	59.8[b]
Health: Current expenditure (% of GDP)	5.3	6.2	8.4[b]
Health: Physicians (per 1 000 pop.)	~0.0[l]	...	...
Education: Government expenditure (% of GDP)	12.1	11.4[m]	...
Education: Primary gross enrol. ratio (f/m per 100 pop.)	117.0 / 117.2	109.0 / 111.8	102.1 / 105.7[d]
Education: Secondary gross enrol. ratio (f/m per 100 pop.)	44.4 / 34.5	59.7 / 42.3	60.2 / 44.5[d]
Education: Tertiary gross enrol. ratio (f/m per 100 pop.)	4.2 / 3.1	4.3 / 3.4[n]	10.9 / 7.3[b]
Intentional homicide rate (per 100 000 pop.)	...	37.4	41.2[b]
Seats held by women in the National Parliament (%)	11.7	24.2	22.1

Environment and infrastructure indicators

	2005	2010	2018
Individuals using the Internet (per 100 inhabitants)	2.6[f]	3.9[f]	27.4[d]
Research & Development expenditure (% of GDP)	0.1[o,p]	~0.0[o,q]	0.1[r,s,b]
Threatened species (number)	13[p]	16	18[c]
Forested area (% of land area)	1.4	1.4	1.6[b]
CO2 emission estimates (million tons/tons per capita)	2.0 / 1.0	2.3 / 1.1	2.5 / 1.2[t]
Energy production, primary (Petajoules)	25	27	31[b]
Energy supply per capita (Gigajoules)	23	26	27[b]
Tourist/visitor arrivals at national borders (000)	304	426	1 196[d]
Important sites for terrestrial biodiversity protected (%)	15.3	15.3	15.3
Pop. using improved drinking water (urban/rural, %)	93.6 / 76.0	94.1 / 76.5	94.6 / 77.0[b]
Pop. using improved sanitation facilities (urban/rural, %)	35.9 / 23.4	36.7 / 25.8	37.3 / 27.6[b]
Net Official Development Assist. received (% of GNI)	3.14	8.45	4.58[d]

a Projected estimate (medium fertility variant). b 2015. c 2017. d 2016. e Data classified according to ISIC Rev. 4. f Estimate. g Break in the time series. h Asia not elsewhere specified. i Data refers to a 5-year period preceding the reference year. j Refers to foreign citizens. k Including refugees. l 2003. m 2008. n 2006. o Partial data. p 2004. q 2009. r Excluding private non-profit. s Excluding business enterprise. t 2014.

Liberia

Region	Western Africa	UN membership date	02 November 1945	
Population (000, 2018)	4 854[a]	Surface area (km2)	111 369[b]	
Pop. density (per km2, 2018)	50.4[a]	Sex ratio (m per 100 f)	101.9[a]	
Capital city	Monrovia	National currency	Liberian Dollar (LRD)	
Capital city pop. (000, 2018)	1 418.3	Exchange rate (per US$)	125.4[c]	

Economic indicators

	2005	2010	2018
GDP: Gross domestic product (million current US$)	706	1 292	2 757[d]
GDP growth rate (annual %, const. 2010 prices)	5.3	7.3	- 0.5[d]
GDP per capita (current US$)	217.0	327.0	598.0[d]
Economy: Agriculture (% of Gross Value Added)	68.8	70.7	72.9[e,d]
Economy: Industry (% of Gross Value Added)	9.8	11.4	8.7[e,d]
Economy: Services and other activity (% of GVA)	21.5	18.0	18.4[e,d]
Employment in agriculture (% of employed)	53.0[f]	47.3	42.3[f]
Employment in industry (% of employed)[f]	9.3	10.8	12.0
Employment in services & other sectors (% employed)[f]	37.7	41.9	45.7
Unemployment rate (% of labour force)	5.6[f]	2.3	2.4[f]
Labour force participation rate (female/male pop. %)[f]	53.0 / 59.2	53.6 / 59.3	53.9 / 57.3
CPI: Consumer Price Index (2010=100)	62	100	181[c]
Agricultural production index (2004-2006=100)	102	104	113[d]
International trade: exports (million current US$)[f]	130	222	697[c]
International trade: imports (million current US$)[f]	309	710	464[c]
International trade: balance (million current US$)[f]	- 179	- 488	233[c]
Balance of payments, current account (million US$)	- 184	- 415	- 860[b]

Major trading partners

								2017
Export partners (% of exports)[f]	Areas nes[g]	20.9	Switzerland	17.3	United Arab Emirates	9.6		
Import partners (% of imports)[f]	Areas nes[g]	60.1	China	14.7	India	3.9		

Social indicators

	2005	2010	2018
Population growth rate (average annual %)[h]	2.5	3.8	2.6[b]
Urban population (% of total population)	46.1	47.8	51.2
Urban population growth rate (average annual %)[h]	3.2	4.6	3.4[b]
Fertility rate, total (live births per woman)[h]	5.7	5.2	4.8[b]
Life expectancy at birth (females/males, years)[h]	53.2 / 51.6	59.0 / 57.2	61.6 / 59.8[b]
Population age distribution (0-14/60+ years old, %)	43.3 / 4.9	43.3 / 4.8	41.5 / 4.9[a]
International migrant stock (000/% of total pop.)	87.2 / 2.7	99.1 / 2.5	98.6 / 2.1[c]
Refugees and others of concern to the UNHCR (000)	508.8[i]	26.6[i]	13.8[c]
Infant mortality rate (per 1 000 live births)[h]	96.9	71.8	59.0[b]
Health: Current expenditure (% of GDP)	8.5	10.0	15.2[b]
Health: Physicians (per 1 000 pop.)	~0.0[i]	~0.0	...
Education: Government expenditure (% of GDP)	...	3.2[k]	2.8[l]
Education: Primary gross enrol. ratio (f/m per 100 pop.)	95.7 / 129.9[m]	94.4 / 105.3[n]	89.3 / 98.7[b]
Education: Secondary gross enrol. ratio (f/m per 100 pop.)	29.7 / 40.8[m]	... / ...	32.6 / 42.0[b]
Education: Tertiary gross enrol. ratio (f/m per 100 pop.)	13.8 / 25.0[m]	6.5 / 12.1	9.0 / 14.3[l]
Intentional homicide rate (per 100 000 pop.)	...	3.3	3.2[l]
Seats held by women in the National Parliament (%)	5.3	12.5	9.9

Environment and infrastructure indicators

	2005	2010	2018
Individuals using the Internet (per 100 inhabitants)	~0.0[m]	2.3	7.3[f,d]
Threatened species (number)	94[j]	147	172[c]
Forested area (% of land area)	46.5	44.9	43.4[b]
CO2 emission estimates (million tons/tons per capita)	0.7 / 0.2	0.8 / 0.2	0.9 / 0.2[o]
Energy production, primary (Petajoules)	53	64	76[b]
Energy supply per capita (Gigajoules)	19	19	20[b]
Important sites for terrestrial biodiversity protected (%)	16.4	16.4	16.4
Pop. using improved drinking water (urban/rural, %)	80.4 / 55.2	84.5 / 58.9	88.6 / 62.6[b]
Pop. using improved sanitation facilities (urban/rural, %)	25.8 / 4.5	26.9 / 5.2	28.0 / 5.9[b]
Net Official Development Assist. received (% of GNI)	56.37	127.23	44.78[d]

a Projected estimate (medium fertility variant). b 2015. c 2017. d 2016. e Including taxes less subsidies on production and imports. f Estimate. g Areas not elsewhere specified. h Data refers to a 5-year period preceding the reference year. i Data as at the end of December. j 2004. k 2008. l 2012. m 2000. n 2009. o 2014.

Libya

Region	Northern Africa	UN membership date	14 December 1955
Population (000, 2018)	6 471 [a]	Surface area (km2)	1 676 198 [b]
Pop. density (per km2, 2018)	3.7 [a]	Sex ratio (m per 100 f)	101.6 [a]
Capital city	Tripoli	National currency	Libyan Dinar (LYD)
Capital city pop. (000, 2018)	1 157.7	Exchange rate (per US$)	1.4 [c]

Economic indicators	2005	2010	2018
GDP: Gross domestic product (million current US$)	45 451	80 942	42 960 [d]
GDP growth rate (annual %, const. 2010 prices)	10.3	4.3	2.0 [d]
GDP per capita (current US$)	7 846.0	13 121.0	6 826.0 [d]
Economy: Agriculture (% of Gross Value Added)	2.2	2.5	0.9 [d]
Economy: Industry (% of Gross Value Added)	75.7	74.0	67.1 [d]
Economy: Services and other activity (% of GVA)	22.2	23.5	32.0 [d]
Employment in agriculture (% of employed) [e]	8.7	7.3	11.2
Employment in industry (% of employed) [e]	28.3	31.6	25.4
Employment in services & other sectors (% employed) [e]	63.1	61.0	63.4
Unemployment rate (% of labour force) [e]	20.0	18.6	15.7
Labour force participation rate (female/male pop. %) [e]	27.4 / 75.5	29.3 / 77.3	25.8 / 79.1
CPI: Consumer Price Index (2010=100)	80	100	126 [f]
Agricultural production index (2004-2006=100)	101	112	117 [d]
International trade: exports (million current US$)	31 272 [e]	36 440	2 273 [e,c]
International trade: imports (million current US$)	6 058 [e]	17 674	5 743 [e,c]
International trade: balance (million current US$)	25 215 [e]	18 766	- 3 470 [e,c]
Balance of payments, current account (million US$)	14 945	16 801	- 4 705 [d]

Major trading partners						2017
Export partners (% of exports)	Italy	17.6 [e]	Germany	15.7	Spain	13.8 [e]
Import partners (% of imports) [e]	China	13.4	Italy	13.0	Turkey	9.3

Social indicators	2005	2010	2018
Population growth rate (average annual %) [g]	1.6	1.3	0.2 [b]
Urban population (% of total population)	77.1	78.1	80.1
Urban population growth rate (average annual %) [g]	1.7	1.5	0.5 [b]
Fertility rate, total (live births per woman) [g]	2.6	2.4	2.4 [b]
Life expectancy at birth (females/males, years) [g]	72.8 / 69.1	74.4 / 69.5	74.4 / 68.8 [b]
Population age distribution (0-14/60+ years old, %)	30.1 / 5.9	28.4 / 6.0	27.9 / 6.8 [a]
International migrant stock (000/% of total pop.) [h]	625.2 / 10.8	684.0 / 11.1	788.4 / 12.4 [c]
Refugees and others of concern to the UNHCR (000)	12.4 [i]	11.2 [i]	341.9 [c]
Infant mortality rate (per 1 000 live births) [g]	27.2	24.3	24.3 [b]
Health: Current expenditure (% of GDP) [e]	2.6	3.4	5.0 [j]
Health: Physicians (per 1 000 pop.)	1.2 [k]	1.9 [l]	2.1 [m]
Education: Primary gross enrol. ratio (f/m per 100 pop.)	101.7 / 102.8	107.0 / 111.5 [n]	... / ...
Education: Secondary gross enrol. ratio (f/m per 100 pop.)	100.8 / 84.5 [e]	106.0 / 90.2 [n]	... / ...
Education: Tertiary gross enrol. ratio (f/m per 100 pop.)	63.6 / 57.5 [e,o]	... / ...	... / ...
Intentional homicide rate (per 100 000 pop.)	3.7	3.1	2.5 [b]
Seats held by women in the National Parliament (%)	...	7.7	16.0

Environment and infrastructure indicators	2005	2010	2018
Individuals using the Internet (per 100 inhabitants) [o]	3.9	14.0	20.3 [d]
Threatened species (number)	25 [k]	44	63 [c]
Forested area (% of land area) [e]	0.1	0.1	0.1 [b]
CO2 emission estimates (million tons/tons per capita)	52.1 / 9.0	62.0 / 9.9	57.0 / 9.1 [m]
Energy production, primary (Petajoules)	4 062	4 294	1 496 [b]
Energy supply per capita (Gigajoules)	126	137	163 [b]
Tourist/visitor arrivals at national borders (000)	81	34 [p]	...
Important sites for terrestrial biodiversity protected (%)	4.6	4.6	4.6
Pop. using improved drinking water (urban/rural, %)	72.1 / 68.4 [q]	... / ...	... / ...
Pop. using improved sanitation facilities (urban/rural, %)	96.8 / 95.7	96.8 / 95.7	96.8 / 95.7 [b]
Net Official Development Assist. received (% of GNI)	0.05	0.01	1.85 [j]

a Projected estimate (medium fertility variant). b 2015. c 2017. d 2016. e Estimate. f 2013. g Data refers to a 5-year period preceding the reference year. h Refers to foreign citizens. i Data as at the end of December. j 2011. k 2004. l 2009. m 2014. n 2006. o 2003. p 2008. q 2000.

Liechtenstein

Region	Western Europe	UN membership date	18 September 1990
Population (000, 2018)	38[a]	Surface area (km2)	160[b]
Pop. density (per km2, 2018)	238.5[a]	Sex ratio (m per 100 f)	98.4[c,d]
Capital city	Vaduz	National currency	Swiss Franc (CHF)
Capital city pop. (000, 2018)	5.5	Exchange rate (per US$)	1.0[e]

Economic indicators	2005	2010	2018
GDP: Gross domestic product (million current US$)	4 046	5 621	6 194[d]
GDP growth rate (annual %, const. 2010 prices)	4.8	7.4	1.2[d]
GDP per capita (current US$)	116 095.0	156 127.0	164 437.0[d]
Economy: Agriculture (% of Gross Value Added)[f]	5.2	5.2	4.8[d]
Economy: Industry (% of Gross Value Added)[f]	38.6	39.0	40.2[d]
Economy: Services and other activity (% of GVA)[f]	56.1	55.9	55.0[d]
Unemployment rate (% of labour force)[g]	...	2.6	2.6[h]
Labour force participation rate (female/male pop. %)	52.8 / 73.7	52.6 / 70.9	53.5 / 70.6[h]
Agricultural production index (2004-2006=100)	100	101	97[d]

Social indicators	2005	2010	2018
Population growth rate (average annual %)[i]	0.9	0.7	0.8[b]
Urban population (% of total population)	14.7	14.5	14.3
Urban population growth rate (average annual %)[i]	0.4	0.3	0.5[b]
Fertility rate, total (live births per woman)	1.5	1.4	1.5[j]
Population age distribution (0-14/60+ years old, %)	17.5 / 16.8[c]	16.0 / 20.1	14.9 / 22.7[c,d]
International migrant stock (000/% of total pop.)	18.9 / 54.2	22.3 / 62.1	24.7 / 65.1[e]
Refugees and others of concern to the UNHCR (000)	0.2[k]	0.1[k]	0.3[e]
Education: Government expenditure (% of GDP)	2.4[l]	2.0[m]	2.6[n]
Education: Primary gross enrol. ratio (f/m per 100 pop.)[o]	108.5 / 109.9[l]	102.3 / 108.6	103.4 / 107.5[d]
Education: Secondary gross enrol. ratio (f/m per 100 pop.)[o]	103.9 / 117.2[l]	100.0 / 117.6	101.9 / 130.3[d]
Education: Tertiary gross enrol. ratio (f/m per 100 pop.)[o]	13.3 / 35.7[l]	27.4 / 44.3	24.8 / 45.3[d]
Intentional homicide rate (per 100 000 pop.)	0.0	2.8	0.0[d]
Seats held by women in the National Parliament (%)	12.0	24.0	12.0

Environment and infrastructure indicators	2005	2010	2018
Individuals using the Internet (per 100 inhabitants)	63.4	80.0[o]	98.1[o,d]
Threatened species (number)	8[l]	2	6[e]
Forested area (% of land area)[o]	43.1	43.1	43.1[b]
CO2 emission estimates (million tons/tons per capita)	... / ...	0.1 / 1.5	~0.0 / 1.1[p]
Energy production, primary (Petajoules)	...	1	1[b]
Energy supply per capita (Gigajoules)	...	81	76[b]
Tourist/visitor arrivals at national borders (000)	...	64	69[q,d]
Important sites for terrestrial biodiversity protected (%)	75.8	75.8	75.8
Net Official Development Assist. disbursed (% of GNI)	...	0.62	0.50[p]

a Projected estimate (medium fertility variant). b 2015. c De jure population. d 2016. e 2017. f Data classified according to ISIC Rev. 4. g Population aged 15 to 64 years. h 2013. i Data refers to a 5-year period preceding the reference year. j 2012. k Data as at the end of December. l 2004. m 2008. n 2011. o Estimate. p 2014. q Excluding long term tourists on campgrounds and in holiday flats.

Lithuania

Region	Northern Europe	UN membership date	17 September 1991
Population (000, 2018)	2 876[a]	Surface area (km2)	65 286[b]
Pop. density (per km2, 2018)	45.9[a]	Sex ratio (m per 100 f)	85.5[a]
Capital city	Vilnius	National currency	Euro (EUR)
Capital city pop. (000, 2018)	536.1	Exchange rate (per US$)	0.8[c]

Economic indicators

	2005	2010	2018
GDP: Gross domestic product (million current US$)	26 141	37 130	42 773[d]
GDP growth rate (annual %, const. 2010 prices)	7.7	1.6	2.3[d]
GDP per capita (current US$)	7 817.0	11 886.0	14 707.0[d]
Economy: Agriculture (% of Gross Value Added)[e]	4.8	3.3	3.3[d]
Economy: Industry (% of Gross Value Added)[e]	32.7	29.1	28.7[d]
Economy: Services and other activity (% of GVA)[e]	62.5	67.6	68.0[d]
Employment in agriculture (% of employed)[f]	14.3	8.8[f]	7.6[f]
Employment in industry (% of employed)[f]	29.1	24.6	24.7
Employment in services & other sectors (% employed)[f]	56.7	66.6	67.7
Unemployment rate (% of labour force)	8.3	17.8	7.4[f]
Labour force participation rate (female/male pop. %)[f]	50.6 / 62.9	52.5 / 62.3	55.9 / 66.1
CPI: Consumer Price Index (2010=100)[g]	78	100	113[c]
Agricultural production index (2004-2006=100)	106	100	131[d]
Index of industrial production (2005=100)	100	103	117[h]
International trade: exports (million current US$)	12 070	20 814	29 910[c]
International trade: imports (million current US$)	15 704	23 378	32 530[c]
International trade: balance (million current US$)	- 3 634	- 2 564	- 2 620[c]
Balance of payments, current account (million US$)	- 1 888	- 488	418[c]

Major trading partners

						2017
Export partners (% of exports)	Russian Federation	14.9	Latvia	9.9	Poland	8.1
Import partners (% of imports)	Russian Federation	13.0	Germany	12.3	Poland	10.6

Social indicators

	2005	2010	2018
Population growth rate (average annual %)[i]	- 0.9	- 1.4	- 1.3[b]
Urban population (% of total population)	66.6	66.8	67.7
Urban population growth rate (average annual %)[i]	- 1.0	- 1.3	- 1.1[b]
Fertility rate, total (live births per woman)[i]	1.3	1.4	1.6[b]
Life expectancy at birth (females/males, years)[i]	77.5 / 65.7	77.8 / 66.0	79.3 / 68.5[b]
Population age distribution (0-14/60+ years old, %)	16.8 / 21.1	14.8 / 22.4	15.0 / 25.7[a]
International migrant stock (000/% of total pop.)	201.2 / 6.0	160.8 / 5.1	124.7 / 4.3[c]
Refugees and others of concern to the UNHCR (000)	9.3[j]	4.6[j]	4.7[c]
Infant mortality rate (per 1 000 live births)[i]	7.7	6.0	4.4[b]
Health: Current expenditure (% of GDP)	5.6	6.8	6.5[b]
Health: Physicians (per 1 000 pop.)	...	3.9	4.4[b]
Education: Government expenditure (% of GDP)	4.9	5.3	4.5[h]
Education: Primary gross enrol. ratio (f/m per 100 pop.)	94.2 / 94.6	99.7 / 100.9	101.3 / 101.4[d]
Education: Secondary gross enrol. ratio (f/m per 100 pop.)	102.7 / 103.7	100.3 / 102.2	100.7 / 105.6[d]
Education: Tertiary gross enrol. ratio (f/m per 100 pop.)	98.0 / 62.9	103.2 / 68.7	77.5 / 55.2[d]
Intentional homicide rate (per 100 000 pop.)	11.1	7.0	5.2[d]
Seats held by women in the National Parliament (%)	22.0	19.1	21.3

Environment and infrastructure indicators

	2005	2010	2018
Individuals using the Internet (per 100 inhabitants)	36.2[k,l]	62.1[k,l]	74.4[d]
Research & Development expenditure (% of GDP)	0.7	0.8	1.0[m,b]
Threatened species (number)	17[n]	17	26[c]
Forested area (% of land area)	33.8	34.6	34.8[b]
CO2 emission estimates (million tons/tons per capita)	13.9 / 4.1	13.5 / 4.3	12.8 / 4.4[h]
Energy production, primary (Petajoules)	170	64	76[b]
Energy supply per capita (Gigajoules)	106	92	102[b]
Tourist/visitor arrivals at national borders (000)	2 000	1 507	2 296[d]
Important sites for terrestrial biodiversity protected (%)	89.6	91.6	91.6
Pop. using improved drinking water (urban/rural, %)	97.7 / 83.6	98.8 / 87.4	99.7 / 90.4[b]
Pop. using improved sanitation facilities (urban/rural, %)	94.7 / 76.1	95.9 / 79.4	97.2 / 82.8[b]
Net Official Development Assist. disbursed (% of GNI)	0.06	0.10	0.13[m,c]

a Projected estimate (medium fertility variant). **b** 2015. **c** 2017. **d** 2016. **e** Data classified according to ISIC Rev. 4. **f** Estimate. **g** Calculated by the Statistics Division of the United Nations from national indices. **h** 2014. **i** Data refers to a 5-year period preceding the reference year. **j** Data as at the end of December. **k** Users in the last 12 months. **l** Population aged 16 to 74 years. **m** Provisional data. **n** 2004.

Luxembourg

Region	Western Europe	UN membership date	24 October 1945
Population (000, 2018)	590[a]	Surface area (km2)	2 586[b]
Pop. density (per km2, 2018)	227.9[a]	Sex ratio (m per 100 f)	101.1[a]
Capital city	Luxembourg	National currency	Euro (EUR)
Capital city pop. (000, 2018)	119.8	Exchange rate (per US$)	0.8[c]

Economic indicators	2005	2010	2018
GDP: Gross domestic product (million current US$)	37 346	53 212	58 631[d]
GDP growth rate (annual %, const. 2010 prices)	3.2	4.9	3.1[d]
GDP per capita (current US$)	81 571.0	104 772.0	101 835.0[d]
Economy: Agriculture (% of Gross Value Added)[e]	0.4	0.3	0.3[d]
Economy: Industry (% of Gross Value Added)[e]	16.5	12.7	12.9[d]
Economy: Services and other activity (% of GVA)[e]	83.1	87.0	86.8[d]
Employment in agriculture (% of employed)[f]	1.7	1.1[f]	1.0[f]
Employment in industry (% of employed)[f]	17.3	13.4	11.7
Employment in services & other sectors (% employed)[f]	81.0	85.6	87.3
Unemployment rate (% of labour force)	4.5	4.4	5.6[f]
Labour force participation rate (female/male pop. %)[f]	45.4 / 64.7	48.8 / 65.4	52.3 / 63.3
CPI: Consumer Price Index (2010=100)	90	100	111[c]
Agricultural production index (2004-2006=100)	99	94	103[d]
Index of industrial production (2005=100)	100	89[h]	86[h,i]
International trade: exports (million current US$)	12 715	13 911	13 959[c]
International trade: imports (million current US$)	17 586	20 400	21 071[c]
International trade: balance (million current US$)	- 4 871	- 6 489	- 7 112[c]
Balance of payments, current account (million US$)	4 107	3 585	3 325[c]

Major trading partners							2017
Export partners (% of exports)	Germany	26.9	France	14.8	Belgium	11.6
Import partners (% of imports)	Belgium	24.3	Germany	24.1	France	11.8

Social indicators	2005	2010	2018
Population growth rate (average annual %)[j]	1.0	2.1	2.2[b]
Urban population (% of total population)	86.6	88.5	91.0
Urban population growth rate (average annual %)[j]	1.5	2.5	2.6[b]
Fertility rate, total (live births per woman)[j]	1.7	1.6	1.5[b]
Life expectancy at birth (females/males, years)[j]	81.4 / 75.1	82.2 / 76.7	83.4 / 78.8[b]
Population age distribution (0-14/60+ years old, %)	18.6 / 19.0	17.6 / 19.0	16.5 / 19.9[a]
International migrant stock (000/% of total pop.)	150.6 / 32.9	248.9 / 49.0	264.1 / 45.3[c]
Refugees and others of concern to the UNHCR (000)[k]	1.9	4.1	4.3[d]
Infant mortality rate (per 1 000 live births)[j]	5.0	2.3	3.4[b]
Health: Current expenditure (% of GDP)	7.2	7.0	6.0[b]
Health: Physicians (per 1 000 pop.)	...	2.8	2.9[d]
Education: Government expenditure (% of GDP)	3.6[l]	...	4.0[i]
Education: Primary gross enrol. ratio (f/m per 100 pop.)	100.9 / 100.7	98.1 / 97.1	98.6 / 98.6[b]
Education: Secondary gross enrol. ratio (f/m per 100 pop.)	97.9 / 92.9	102.9 / 99.9	103.9 / 100.1[b]
Education: Tertiary gross enrol. ratio (f/m per 100 pop.)	13.3 / 11.1[m]	19.2 / 17.3	20.8 / 18.7[b]
Intentional homicide rate (per 100 000 pop.)	0.9	2.0	0.7[i]
Seats held by women in the National Parliament (%)	23.3	20.0	28.3

Environment and infrastructure indicators	2005	2010	2018
Individuals using the Internet (per 100 inhabitants)	70.0[n]	90.6[n]	97.5[d]
Research & Development expenditure (% of GDP)	1.6	1.5	1.3[o,b]
Threatened species (number)	10[p]	5	11[c]
Forested area (% of land area)[f]	33.5	33.5	33.5[b]
CO2 emission estimates (million tons/tons per capita)	11.5 / 25.3	11.0 / 21.6	9.7 / 17.3[i]
Energy production, primary (Petajoules)	4	5	6[b]
Energy supply per capita (Gigajoules)	405	351	278[b]
Tourist/visitor arrivals at national borders (000)	913	805	1 054[d]
Important sites for terrestrial biodiversity protected (%)	62.8	62.8	78.7
Pop. using improved drinking water (urban/rural, %)	100.0 / 100.0	100.0 / 100.0	100.0 / 100.0[b]
Pop. using improved sanitation facilities (urban/rural, %)	97.5 / 98.7	97.5 / 98.6	97.5 / 98.5[b]
Net Official Development Assist. disbursed (% of GNI)[q]	0.79	1.05	1.00[o,c]

a Projected estimate (medium fertility variant). b 2015. c 2017. d 2016. e Data classified according to ISIC Rev. 4. f Estimate. g Calculated by the Statistics Division of the United Nations from national indices. h Excluding water and waste management. i 2014. j Data refers to a 5-year period preceding the reference year. k Data as at the end of December. l 2001. m 2003. n Population aged 16 to 74 years. o Provisional data. p 2004. q Development Assistance Committee member (OECD).

Madagascar

Region	Eastern Africa	UN membership date	20 September 1960
Population (000, 2018)	26 263 [a]	Surface area (km2)	587 295 [b]
Pop. density (per km2, 2018)	45.1 [a]	Sex ratio (m per 100 f)	99.5 [a]
Capital city	Antananarivo	National currency	Malagasy Ariary (MGA)
Capital city pop. (000, 2018)	3 058.4	Exchange rate (per US$)	3 230.2 [c]

Economic indicators

	2005	2010	2018
GDP: Gross domestic product (million current US$)	5 936	10 401	11 222 [d]
GDP growth rate (annual %, const. 2010 prices)	4.6	0.6	4.2 [d]
GDP per capita (current US$)	324.0	492.0	451.0 [d]
Economy: Agriculture (% of Gross Value Added)	32.4	28.4	34.6 [d]
Economy: Industry (% of Gross Value Added)	14.1	18.8	7.9 [d]
Economy: Services and other activity (% of GVA)	53.5	52.8	57.5 [d]
Employment in agriculture (% of employed) [e]	82.0	74.0	74.2
Employment in industry (% of employed) [e]	3.4	5.5	9.2
Employment in services & other sectors (% employed) [e]	14.6	20.5	16.5
Unemployment rate (% of labour force)	2.3	3.8	1.8 [e]
Labour force participation rate (female/male pop. %) [e]	84.2 / 89.1	87.1 / 91.0	83.8 / 89.5
CPI: Consumer Price Index (2010=100)	63	100	161 [c]
Agricultural production index (2004-2006=100)	103	123	118 [d]
Index of industrial production (2005=100) [f]	100	124 [g]	...
International trade: exports (million current US$)	836	1 082	2 312 [e,c]
International trade: imports (million current US$)	1 686	2 546	2 820 [e,c]
International trade: balance (million current US$)	- 850	- 1 464	- 508 [e,c]
Balance of payments, current account (million US$)	- 772 [h]	- 964	- 38 [d]

Major trading partners

						2017
Export partners (% of exports) [e]	France	23.8	United States	13.0	Germany	8.4
Import partners (% of imports) [e]	China	21.3	France	6.9	India	6.5

Social indicators

	2005	2010	2018
Population growth rate (average annual %) [i]	3.0	2.9	2.7 [b]
Urban population (% of total population)	28.8	31.9	37.2
Urban population growth rate (average annual %) [i]	4.2	4.9	4.7 [b]
Fertility rate, total (live births per woman) [i]	5.3	4.8	4.4 [b]
Life expectancy at birth (females/males, years) [i]	61.3 / 58.8	63.7 / 60.8	66.0 / 63.0 [b]
Population age distribution (0-14/60+ years old, %)	44.7 / 4.4	43.5 / 4.3	40.7 / 4.9 [a]
International migrant stock (000/% of total pop.) [j]	26.1 / 0.1	28.9 / 0.1	33.8 / 0.1 [c]
Refugees and others of concern to the UNHCR (000)	...	~0.0 [k]	0.1 [c]
Infant mortality rate (per 1 000 live births) [i]	58.0	45.5	36.8 [b]
Health: Current expenditure (% of GDP) [l]	5.5	5.4	5.2 [b]
Health: Physicians (per 1 000 pop.)	0.2	0.2	0.1 [m]
Education: Government expenditure (% of GDP)	3.8	3.2 [n]	2.1 [o]
Education: Primary gross enrol. ratio (f/m per 100 pop.)	135.8 / 142.0	142.4 / 145.0	144.0 / 143.7 [d]
Education: Secondary gross enrol. ratio (f/m per 100 pop.)	21.0 / 21.9 [e]	29.7 / 31.6 [n,a]	38.2 / 38.4 [d]
Education: Tertiary gross enrol. ratio (f/m per 100 pop.)	2.5 / 2.8	3.5 / 3.8	4.6 / 5.0 [b]
Intentional homicide rate (per 100 000 pop.)	10.0	9.2	7.7 [b]
Seats held by women in the National Parliament (%)	6.9	7.9	19.2

Environment and infrastructure indicators

	2005	2010	2018
Individuals using the Internet (per 100 inhabitants) [e]	0.6	1.7	4.7 [d]
Research & Development expenditure (% of GDP) [p]	0.2	0.1	~0.0 [h,q,r]
Threatened species (number)	530 [s]	663	1 324 [c]
Forested area (% of land area) [e]	22.1	21.6	21.4 [b]
CO2 emission estimates (million tons/tons per capita)	1.7 / 0.1	2.0 / 0.1	3.1 / 0.1 [f]
Energy production, primary (Petajoules)	104	124	132 [b]
Energy supply per capita (Gigajoules)	7	7	7 [b]
Tourist/visitor arrivals at national borders (000) [t]	277	196	293 [d]
Important sites for terrestrial biodiversity protected (%)	19.7	21.7	24.3
Pop. using improved drinking water (urban/rural, %)	77.5 / 27.8	79.6 / 31.5	81.6 / 35.3 [b]
Pop. using improved sanitation facilities (urban/rural, %)	16.9 / 8.3	17.5 / 8.5	18.0 / 8.7 [b]
Net Official Development Assist. received (% of GNI)	18.47	5.53	6.49 [d]

a Projected estimate (medium fertility variant). b 2015. c 2017. d 2016. e Estimate. f Data classified according to ISIC Rev. 3. g 2008. h Break in the time series. i Data refers to a 5-year period preceding the reference year. j Refers to foreign citizens. k Data as at the end of December. l Data revision. m 2012. n 2009. o 2013. p Partial data. q Government only. r 2014. s 2004. t Arrivals of non-resident tourists by air.

Malawi

Region	Eastern Africa	UN membership date	01 December 1964
Population (000, 2018)	19 165[a]	Surface area (km2)	118 484[b]
Pop. density (per km2, 2018)	203.3[a]	Sex ratio (m per 100 f)	98.2[a]
Capital city	Lilongwe	National currency	Malawi Kwacha (MWK)
Capital city pop. (000, 2018)	1 029.6	Exchange rate (per US$)	732.0[c]

Economic indicators	2005	2010	2018
GDP: Gross domestic product (million current US$)	3 656	6 960	5 318[d]
GDP growth rate (annual %, const. 2010 prices)	3.3	6.9	3.0[d]
GDP per capita (current US$)	280.0	459.0	294.0[d]
Economy: Agriculture (% of Gross Value Added)[e]	37.1	31.9	25.1[d]
Economy: Industry (% of Gross Value Added)[e]	16.8	16.4	16.4[d]
Economy: Services and other activity (% of GVA)[e]	46.1	51.7	58.5[d]
Employment in agriculture (% of employed)[f]	85.0	84.8	84.6
Employment in industry (% of employed)[f]	9.1	8.8	8.4
Employment in services & other sectors (% employed)[f]	5.9	6.5	6.9
Unemployment rate (% of labour force)	7.8	6.7[f]	6.1[f]
Labour force participation rate (female/male pop. %)[f]	74.2 / 80.1	73.1 / 81.8	72.4 / 82.1
CPI: Consumer Price Index (2010=100)[f]	64	100	342[c]
Agricultural production index (2004-2006=100)	86	156	146[d]
Index of industrial production (2005=100)	100[g]	...	...
International trade: exports (million current US$)	495	1 066	941[f,c]
International trade: imports (million current US$)	1 165	2 173	999[f,c]
International trade: balance (million current US$)	- 670	- 1 107	- 57[f,c]
Balance of payments, current account (million US$)	- 507	- 969	- 1 021[c]

Major trading partners						2017
Export partners (% of exports)	Belgium	10.6[f]	Zimbabwe	9.3	Mozambique	9.2[f]
Import partners (% of imports)[f]	South Africa	18.1	China	13.1	United Arab Emirates	11.0

Social indicators	2005	2010	2018
Population growth rate (average annual %)[h]	2.7	3.0	2.9[b]
Urban population (% of total population)	15.1	15.5	16.9
Urban population growth rate (average annual %)[h]	3.3	3.7	3.9[b]
Fertility rate, total (live births per woman)[h]	6.0	5.7	4.9[b]
Life expectancy at birth (females/males, years)[h]	48.9 / 45.7	55.2 / 51.5	63.1 / 58.2[b]
Population age distribution (0-14/60+ years old, %)	46.7 / 4.4	46.2 / 4.5	43.7 / 4.2[a]
International migrant stock (000/% of total pop.)[i]	221.7 / 1.7	217.7 / 1.4	237.1 / 1.3[c]
Refugees and others of concern to the UNHCR (000)	9.6[j]	15.2[j]	32.4[c]
Infant mortality rate (per 1 000 live births)[h]	99.1	79.7	66.5[b]
Health: Current expenditure (% of GDP)	6.1	7.2	9.3[b]
Health: Physicians (per 1 000 pop.)	~0.0[k]	~0.0[l]	...
Education: Government expenditure (% of GDP)	3.2[m]	3.5	4.7[d]
Education: Primary gross enrol. ratio (f/m per 100 pop.)	125.1 / 123.5	134.6 / 131.5	141.3 / 137.2[d]
Education: Secondary gross enrol. ratio (f/m per 100 pop.)	23.8 / 29.6	30.3 / 33.8	35.3 / 39.5[d]
Education: Tertiary gross enrol. ratio (f/m per 100 pop.)	0.3 / 0.6[f]	0.5 / 0.8	0.6 / 0.9[n]
Intentional homicide rate (per 100 000 pop.)	1.5	3.4	1.7[o]
Seats held by women in the National Parliament (%)	14.0	20.8	16.7

Environment and infrastructure indicators	2005	2010	2018
Individuals using the Internet (per 100 inhabitants)	0.4	2.3	9.6[f,d]
Threatened species (number)	50[k]	158	176[c]
Forested area (% of land area)	36.1	34.3	33.4[f,b]
CO2 emission estimates (million tons/tons per capita)	0.9 / 0.1	1.1 / 0.1	1.3 / 0.1[p]
Energy production, primary (Petajoules)	60	64	68[b]
Energy supply per capita (Gigajoules)	5	5	5[b]
Tourist/visitor arrivals at national borders (000)[q]	438	746	849[d]
Important sites for terrestrial biodiversity protected (%)	81.6	81.6	81.6
Pop. using improved drinking water (urban/rural, %)	93.8 / 67.9	94.8 / 76.5	95.7 / 89.1[b]
Pop. using improved sanitation facilities (urban/rural, %)	46.6 / 34.8	47.0 / 37.3	47.3 / 39.8[b]
Net Official Development Assist. received (% of GNI)	15.86	14.84	23.36[d]

a Projected estimate (medium fertility variant). b 2015. c 2017. d 2016. e Data classified according to ISIC Rev. 4. f Estimate. g Data classified according to ISIC Rev. 3. h Data refers to a 5-year period preceding the reference year. i Including refugees. j Data as at the end of December. k 2004. l 2009. m 2003. n 2011. o 2012. p 2014. q Departures.

Malaysia

Region	South-eastern Asia
Population (000, 2018)	32 042[a,b]
Pop. density (per km2, 2018)	97.5[a,b]
Capital city	Kuala Lumpur[d]
Capital city pop. (000, 2018)	7 563.9[e]

UN membership date	17 September 1957
Surface area (km2)	330 323[c]
Sex ratio (m per 100 f)	106.5[a,b]
National currency	Malaysian Ringgit (MYR)
Exchange rate (per US$)	4.1[f]

Economic indicators

	2005	2010	2018
GDP: Gross domestic product (million current US$)	143 534	255 018	296 531[g]
GDP growth rate (annual %, const. 2010 prices)	5.3	7.4	4.3[g]
GDP per capita (current US$)	5 594.0	9 071.0	9 508.0[g]
Economy: Agriculture (% of Gross Value Added)[h,i]	8.4	10.2	8.9[g]
Economy: Industry (% of Gross Value Added)[h,i]	46.9	40.9	40.2[g]
Economy: Services and other activity (% of GVA)[h,i]	44.7	48.9	50.9[g]
Employment in agriculture (% of employed)[j]	14.6	14.2	10.7
Employment in industry (% of employed)[j]	29.7	27.7	27.2
Employment in services & other sectors (% employed)[j]	55.6	58.0	62.1
Unemployment rate (% of labour force)	3.5	3.2	3.4[j]
Labour force participation rate (female/male pop. %)[j]	44.0 / 77.5	43.5 / 76.1	51.0 / 77.5
CPI: Consumer Price Index (2010=100)	88	100	120[f]
Agricultural production index (2004-2006=100)	100	111	123[g]
Index of industrial production (2005=100)[k]	100	107	116[l]
International trade: exports (million current US$)	141 624	198 791	216 428[f]
International trade: imports (million current US$)	114 290	164 586	193 856[f]
International trade: balance (million current US$)	27 334	34 204	22 572[f]
Balance of payments, current account (million US$)	19 980	25 644[m]	9 450[f]

Major trading partners

						2017
Export partners (% of exports)	Singapore	14.3	China	13.5	United States	9.5
Import partners (% of imports)	China	19.6	Singapore	11.1	United States	8.3

Social indicators

	2005	2010	2018
Population growth rate (average annual %)[b,n]	2.0	1.9	1.8[c]
Urban population (% of total population)[b]	66.6	70.9	76.0
Urban population growth rate (average annual %)[b,n]	3.5	3.1	2.7[c]
Fertility rate, total (live births per woman)[b,n]	2.5	2.2	2.1[c]
Life expectancy at birth (females/males, years)[b,n]	75.4 / 71.2	76.1 / 71.6	77.1 / 72.6[c]
Population age distribution (0-14/60+ years old, %)[b]	30.5 / 7.1	27.9 / 7.9	24.0 / 10.0[a]
International migrant stock (000/% of total pop.)[b,o,p]	1 722.3 / 6.7	2 406.0 / 8.6	2 703.6 / 8.5[f]
Refugees and others of concern to the UNHCR (000)	106.1[q]	212.9[q]	238.2[f]
Infant mortality rate (per 1 000 live births)[b,n]	6.8	6.8	6.5[c]
Health: Current expenditure (% of GDP)	2.9	3.3	4.0[c]
Health: Physicians (per 1 000 pop.)	0.7[r]	1.2	1.5[c]
Education: Government expenditure (% of GDP)	5.9[s]	5.0	4.8[g]
Education: Primary gross enrol. ratio (f/m per 100 pop.)	100.0 / 100.0	100.7 / 99.8	103.8 / 103.1[g]
Education: Secondary gross enrol. ratio (f/m per 100 pop.)	... / ...	... / ...	87.9 / 82.6[g]
Education: Tertiary gross enrol. ratio (f/m per 100 pop.)	... / ...	... / ...	48.3 / 40.3[g]
Intentional homicide rate (per 100 000 pop.)	2.4	1.9	2.1[l]
Seats held by women in the National Parliament (%)	9.1	9.9	10.4

Environment and infrastructure indicators

	2005	2010	2018
Individuals using the Internet (per 100 inhabitants)	48.6	56.3	78.8[g]
Research & Development expenditure (% of GDP)	0.6[s]	1.0	1.3[c]
Threatened species (number)	892[s]	1 180	1 272[f]
Forested area (% of land area)[j]	63.6	67.3	67.6[c]
CO2 emission estimates (million tons/tons per capita)	174.5 / 6.7	218.5 / 7.8	242.8 / 8.1[t]
Energy production, primary (Petajoules)	3 770	3 450	3 748[c]
Energy supply per capita (Gigajoules)	104	105	113[c]
Tourist/visitor arrivals at national borders (000)[u]	16 431	24 577	26 757[g]
Important sites for terrestrial biodiversity protected (%)	39.1	39.5	39.5
Pop. using improved drinking water (urban/rural, %)	98.5 / 90.2	99.6 / 91.7	100.0 / 93.0[c]
Pop. using improved sanitation facilities (urban/rural, %)	94.4 / 91.3	95.9 / 94.2	96.1 / 95.9[c]
Net Official Development Assist. received (% of GNI)	0.02	0.02	- 0.02[g]

a Projected estimate (medium fertility variant). b Including Sabah and Sarawak. c 2015. d Kuala Lumpur is the capital and Putrajaya is the administrative capital. e Refers to the Greater Kuala Lumpur. f 2017. g 2016. h At producers' prices. i Data classified according to ISIC Rev. 4. j Estimate. k Data classified according to ISIC Rev. 3. l 2013. m Break in the time series. n Data refers to a 5-year period preceding the reference year. o Including refugees. p Refers to foreign citizens. q Data as at the end of December. r 2002. s 2004. t 2014. u Including Singapore residents crossing the frontier by road through Johore Causeway.

Maldives

Region	Southern Asia	
Population (000, 2018)	444 [a]	
Pop. density (per km2, 2018)	1 480.9 [a]	
Capital city	Male	
Capital city pop. (000, 2018)	176.9	

UN membership date	21 September 1965	
Surface area (km2)	300 [b]	
Sex ratio (m per 100 f)	132.2 [a]	
National currency	Rufiyaa (MVR)	
Exchange rate (per US$)	15.4 [c]	

Economic indicators	2005	2010	2018
GDP: Gross domestic product (million current US$)	1 163	2 588	4 224 [d]
GDP growth rate (annual %, const. 2010 prices)	- 13.1	7.3	6.2 [d]
GDP per capita (current US$)	3 649.0	7 100.0	9 875.0 [d]
Economy: Agriculture (% of Gross Value Added) [e]	8.7	6.1	6.8 [d]
Economy: Industry (% of Gross Value Added) [e]	13.2	10.2	11.2 [d]
Economy: Services and other activity (% of GVA) [e]	78.1	83.8	82.0 [d]
Employment in agriculture (% of employed) [f]	14.4	15.0	7.2
Employment in industry (% of employed) [f]	26.1	16.1	24.7
Employment in services & other sectors (% employed) [f]	59.5	68.8	68.1
Unemployment rate (% of labour force) [f]	3.8	4.6	5.0
Labour force participation rate (female/male pop. %) [f]	50.4 / 75.6	50.1 / 78.6	43.3 / 82.5
CPI: Consumer Price Index (2010=100) [f]	73 [g]	100	136 [c]
Agricultural production index (2004-2006=100)	89	76	67 [d]
International trade: exports (million current US$)	154	74	175 [f,c]
International trade: imports (million current US$)	745	1 095	2 338 [f,c]
International trade: balance (million current US$)	- 591	- 1 021	- 2 163 [f,c]
Balance of payments, current account (million US$)	- 273	- 196	- 876 [c]

Major trading partners						2017
Export partners (% of exports)	Thailand	34.4 [f]	Sri Lanka	10.2	United States	8.9 [f]
Import partners (% of imports) [f]	United Arab Emirates	15.7	Singapore	14.3	China	13.4

Social indicators	2005	2010	2018
Population growth rate (average annual %) [h]	2.6	2.7	2.8 [b]
Urban population (% of total population)	33.8	36.4	39.8
Urban population growth rate (average annual %) [h]	6.5	4.2	3.9 [b]
Fertility rate, total (live births per woman) [h]	2.6	2.3	2.2 [b]
Life expectancy at birth (females/males, years) [h]	73.9 / 71.1	76.8 / 74.6	77.4 / 75.4 [b]
Population age distribution (0-14/60+ years old, %)	31.6 / 6.3	25.5 / 6.0	23.4 / 6.6 [a]
International migrant stock (000/% of total pop.) [i]	45.0 / 14.1	54.7 / 15.0	67.0 / 15.4 [c]
Infant mortality rate (per 1 000 live births) [h]	26.7	14.8	9.0 [b]
Health: Current expenditure (% of GDP)	8.8	9.3 [g,i]	11.5 [b]
Health: Physicians (per 1 000 pop.)	1.0 [k]	1.6	3.6 [b]
Education: Government expenditure (% of GDP)	5.0	4.1	4.3 [d]
Education: Primary gross enrol. ratio (f/m per 100 pop.)	117.0 / 121.1	105.4 / 109.3 [l]	101.7 / 101.4 [d]
Education: Secondary gross enrol. ratio (f/m per 100 pop.)	74.6 / 64.0 [f,k]	... / ...	... / ...
Education: Tertiary gross enrol. ratio (f/m per 100 pop.)	0.3 / 0.1 [m]	13.4 / 9.5 [n]	20.5 / 9.9 [o]
Intentional homicide rate (per 100 000 pop.)	1.3 [m]	1.6	0.8 [p]
Seats held by women in the National Parliament (%)	12.0	6.5	5.9

Environment and infrastructure indicators	2005	2010	2018
Individuals using the Internet (per 100 inhabitants)	6.9 [f,q]	26.5 [r]	59.1 [f,d]
Threatened species (number)	12 [k]	59	75 [c]
Forested area (% of land area) [f]	3.3	3.3	3.3 [b]
CO2 emission estimates (million tons/tons per capita)	0.6 / 2.1	0.9 / 2.8	1.3 / 3.7 [o]
Energy production, primary (Petajoules)	0	0	0 [b]
Energy supply per capita (Gigajoules)	30	40	52 [b]
Tourist/visitor arrivals at national borders (000) [s]	395	792	1 286 [d]
Important sites for terrestrial biodiversity protected (%)	0.0	0.0	0.0
Pop. using improved drinking water (urban/rural, %)	99.7 / 95.4	99.6 / 97.5	99.5 / 97.9 [b]
Pop. using improved sanitation facilities (urban/rural, %)	97.6 / 84.8	97.5 / 97.2	97.5 / 98.3 [b]
Net Official Development Assist. received (% of GNI)	7.03	5.55	0.63 [d]

a Projected estimate (medium fertility variant). b 2015. c 2017. d 2016. e Data classified according to ISIC Rev. 4. f Estimate. g Break in the time series. h Data refers to a 5-year period preceding the reference year. i Refers to foreign citizens. j Data revision. k 2004. l 2009. m 2003. n 2008. o 2014. p 2013. q Excluding mobile internet users. r Population aged 15 years and over. s Arrivals by air.

Mali

Region	Western Africa	UN membership date	28 September 1960
Population (000, 2018)	19 108 [a]	Surface area (km2)	1 240 192 [b]
Pop. density (per km2, 2018)	15.7 [a]	Sex ratio (m per 100 f)	100.3 [a]
Capital city	Bamako	National currency	CFA Franc, BCEAO (XOF) [c]
Capital city pop. (000, 2018)	2 446.7	Exchange rate (per US$)	546.9 [d]

Economic indicators

	2005	2010	2018
GDP: Gross domestic product (million current US$)	6 245	10 679	14 002 [e]
GDP growth rate (annual %, const. 2010 prices)	10.4	10.9	7.9 [e]
GDP per capita (current US$)	488.0	708.0	778.0 [e]
Economy: Agriculture (% of Gross Value Added)	34.4	34.9	39.8 [e]
Economy: Industry (% of Gross Value Added)	25.9	25.3	19.2 [e]
Economy: Services and other activity (% of GVA)	39.6	39.7	41.0 [e]
Employment in agriculture (% of employed) [f]	44.8	57.4	56.8
Employment in industry (% of employed) [f]	15.1	11.1	8.5
Employment in services & other sectors (% employed) [f]	40.1	31.5	34.7
Unemployment rate (% of labour force)	9.5 [f]	8.1	8.0 [f]
Labour force participation rate (female/male pop. %) [f]	38.2 / 69.9	49.9 / 80.5	61.1 / 82.8
CPI: Consumer Price Index (2010=100) [g]	86	100	110 [d]
Agricultural production index (2004-2006=100)	102	126	171 [e]
Index of industrial production (2005=100) [h,i]	100	74	91 [j]
International trade: exports (million current US$)	1 075	1 996	1 902 [f,d]
International trade: imports (million current US$)	1 544	4 704	5 000 [f,d]
International trade: balance (million current US$)	- 468	- 2 707	- 3 098 [f,d]
Balance of payments, current account (million US$)	- 438 [k]	- 1 190	...

Major trading partners

					2017
Export partners (% of exports)	South Africa	47.0 [f]	Switzerland	15.0	United Arab Emirates 7.6 [f]
Import partners (% of imports) [f]	Senegal	19.4	China	15.6	Côte d'Ivoire 9.8

Social indicators

	2005	2010	2018
Population growth rate (average annual %) [l]	3.1	3.3	2.9 [b]
Urban population (% of total population)	32.1	36.0	42.4
Urban population growth rate (average annual %) [l]	5.5	5.8	5.0 [b]
Fertility rate, total (live births per woman) [l]	6.8	6.7	6.4 [b]
Life expectancy at birth (females/males, years) [l]	50.6 / 49.3	54.6 / 53.4	56.9 / 55.6 [b]
Population age distribution (0-14/60+ years old, %)	46.9 / 4.6	47.5 / 4.2	47.5 / 3.9 [a]
International migrant stock (000/% of total pop.) [m]	256.8 / 2.0	336.6 / 2.2	383.7 / 2.1 [d]
Refugees and others of concern to the UNHCR (000)	13.1 [n]	15.3 [n]	83.9 [d]
Infant mortality rate (per 1 000 live births) [l]	106.6	89.1	78.5 [b]
Health: Current expenditure (% of GDP)	5.0	4.4	5.8 [b]
Health: Physicians (per 1 000 pop.)	0.1 [o]	0.1	...
Education: Government expenditure (% of GDP)	3.5	3.3	3.8 [b]
Education: Primary gross enrol. ratio (f/m per 100 pop.)	64.8 / 82.5	76.8 / 89.6	72.2 / 81.8 [e]
Education: Secondary gross enrol. ratio (f/m per 100 pop.)	19.6 / 31.8 [f]	31.9 / 46.4	36.6 / 49.1 [e]
Education: Tertiary gross enrol. ratio (f/m per 100 pop.)	1.4 / 2.8 [p]	3.6 / 8.6	3.2 / 7.7 [b]
Intentional homicide rate (per 100 000 pop.)	12.7	12.2	10.9 [b]
Seats held by women in the National Parliament (%)	10.2	10.2	8.8

Environment and infrastructure indicators

	2005	2010	2018
Individuals using the Internet (per 100 inhabitants)	0.5	2.0 [f]	11.1 [e]
Research & Development expenditure (% of GDP)	...	0.6 [q]	...
Threatened species (number)	25 [o]	29	42 [d]
Forested area (% of land area)	4.5	4.2 [f]	3.9 [f,b]
CO2 emission estimates (million tons/tons per capita)	0.9 / 0.1	1.0 / 0.1	1.4 / 0.1 [j]
Energy production, primary (Petajoules)	49	52	55 [b]
Energy supply per capita (Gigajoules)	5	5	5 [b]
Tourist/visitor arrivals at national borders (000)	...	169	173 [e]
Important sites for terrestrial biodiversity protected (%)	33.8	33.8	33.8
Pop. using improved drinking water (urban/rural, %)	79.1 / 46.1	87.8 / 55.1	96.5 / 64.1 [b]
Pop. using improved sanitation facilities (urban/rural, %)	34.8 / 13.3	36.2 / 14.7	37.5 / 16.1 [b]
Net Official Development Assist. received (% of GNI)	12.00	10.64	8.92 [e]

a Projected estimate (medium fertility variant). **b** 2015. **c** African Financial Community (CFA) Franc, Central Bank of West African States (BCEAO). **d** 2017. **e** 2016. **f** Estimate. **g** Bamako **h** Data classified according to ISIC Rev. 3. **i** Country data supplemented with data from the Observatoire Economique et Statistique d'Afrique Subsaharienne (Afristat). **j** 2014. **k** Break in the time series. **l** Data refers to a 5-year period preceding the reference year. **m** Including refugees. **n** Data as at the end of December. **o** 2004. **p** 2002. **q** Excluding business enterprise.

Malta

Region	Southern Europe	UN membership date	01 December 1964
Population (000, 2018)	432[a]	Surface area (km2)	315[b]
Pop. density (per km2, 2018)	1 350.3[a]	Sex ratio (m per 100 f)	100.9[a]
Capital city	Valletta	National currency	Euro (EUR)
Capital city pop. (000, 2018)	212.8[c]	Exchange rate (per US$)	0.8[d]

Economic indicators	2005	2010	2018
GDP: Gross domestic product (million current US$)	6 393	8 741	10 999[e]
GDP growth rate (annual %, const. 2010 prices)	3.8	3.5	5.5[e]
GDP per capita (current US$)	15 716.0	21 005.0	25 616.0[a]
Economy: Agriculture (% of Gross Value Added)[f]	2.2	1.7	1.4[e]
Economy: Industry (% of Gross Value Added)[f]	23.0	19.0	13.8[e]
Economy: Services and other activity (% of GVA)[f]	74.7	79.4	84.9[e]
Employment in agriculture (% of employed)[g]	2.1	1.3[g]	1.2[g]
Employment in industry (% of employed)[g]	29.8	25.5	19.1
Employment in services & other sectors (% employed)[g]	68.1	73.2	79.6
Unemployment rate (% of labour force)	6.9	6.8	4.2[g]
Labour force participation rate (female/male pop. %)[g]	29.6 / 67.5	34.1 / 66.4	42.3 / 66.4
CPI: Consumer Price Index (2010=100)	89	100	110[d]
Agricultural production index (2004-2006=100)	97	98	90[a]
Index of industrial production (2005=100)	100	102	97[h]
International trade: exports (million current US$)	2 431	3 717	3 193[g,d]
International trade: imports (million current US$)	3 865	5 732	6 827[g,d]
International trade: balance (million current US$)	- 1 435	- 2 015	- 3 634[g,d]
Balance of payments, current account (million US$)	- 418	- 420	1 721[d]

Major trading partners						2017
Export partners (% of exports)	United States	20.3[g]	Bunkers	10.7	Germany	10.7[g]
Import partners (% of imports)[g]	Italy	19.2	Cayman Islands	10.2	Canada	9.0

Social indicators	2005	2010	2018
Population growth rate (average annual %)[i]	0.5	0.5	0.5[b]
Urban population (% of total population)	93.6	94.1	94.6
Urban population growth rate (average annual %)[i]	0.8	0.5	0.6[b]
Fertility rate, total (live births per woman)[i]	1.5	1.4	1.4[b]
Life expectancy at birth (females/males, years)[i]	80.2 / 76.8	81.1 / 77.7	82.0 / 78.6[b]
Population age distribution (0-14/60+ years old, %)	17.7 / 18.8	15.2 / 22.9	14.5 / 26.6[a]
International migrant stock (000/% of total pop.)	24.6 / 6.0	33.0 / 7.9	45.5 / 10.6[d]
Refugees and others of concern to the UNHCR (000)	2.1[j]	7.4[j]	9.6[d]
Infant mortality rate (per 1 000 live births)[i]	6.9	5.8	4.8[b]
Health: Current expenditure (% of GDP)	8.7	8.2	9.6[b]
Health: Physicians (per 1 000 pop.)		3.1	3.9[b]
Education: Government expenditure (% of GDP)	4.5[k]	6.5	7.2[h]
Education: Primary gross enrol. ratio (f/m per 100 pop.)	95.7 / 98.0	99.3 / 98.7	106.6 / 102.6[e]
Education: Secondary gross enrol. ratio (f/m per 100 pop.)	100.3 / 104.5	98.0 / 109.7	97.8 / 93.8[e]
Education: Tertiary gross enrol. ratio (f/m per 100 pop.)	37.3 / 27.5	42.7 / 31.6	56.8 / 41.5[e]
Intentional homicide rate (per 100 000 pop.)	1.0	1.0	0.9[b]
Seats held by women in the National Parliament (%)	9.2	8.7	11.9

Environment and infrastructure indicators	2005	2010	2018
Individuals using the Internet (per 100 inhabitants)	41.2[i]	63.0[i]	77.3[e]
Research & Development expenditure (% of GDP)	0.5	0.6	0.8[m,b]
Threatened species (number)	25[k]	26	39[d]
Forested area (% of land area)[g]	1.1	1.1	1.1[b]
CO2 emission estimates (million tons/tons per capita)	2.7 / 6.6	2.6 / 6.2	2.3 / 5.6[h]
Energy production, primary (Petajoules)	0	0	1[b]
Energy supply per capita (Gigajoules)	91	86	65[b]
Tourist/visitor arrivals at national borders (000)[n]	1 171	1 339	1 966[e]
Important sites for terrestrial biodiversity protected (%)	99.4	99.4	99.4
Pop. using improved drinking water (urban/rural, %)	100.0 / 100.0	100.0 / 100.0	100.0 / 100.0[b]
Pop. using improved sanitation facilities (urban/rural, %)	100.0 / 100.0	100.0 / 100.0	100.0 / 100.0[b]
Net Official Development Assist. disbursed (% of GNI)	...	0.18	0.22[m,d]

a Projected estimate (medium fertility variant). b 2015. c Refers to the localities of the Northern Harbour and Southern Harbour. d 2017. e 2016. f Data classified according to ISIC Rev. 4. g Estimate. h 2014. i Data refers to a 5-year period preceding the reference year. j Data as at the end of December. k 2004. l Population aged 16 to 74 years. m Provisional data. n Departures by air and by sea.

Marshall Islands

Region	Micronesia	UN membership date	17 September 1991
Population (000, 2018)	53[a]	Surface area (km2)	181[b]
Pop. density (per km2, 2018)	295.4[a]	Sex ratio (m per 100 f)	104.5[c,d]
Capital city	Majuro	National currency	US Dollar (USD)
Capital city pop. (000, 2018)	30.7		

Economic indicators

	2005	2010	2018
GDP: Gross domestic product (million current US$)	138	165	183[d]
GDP growth rate (annual %, const. 2010 prices)	2.9	6.4	2.9[d]
GDP per capita (current US$)	2 651.0	3 143.0	3 449.0[d]
Economy: Agriculture (% of Gross Value Added)	9.2	15.6	17.0[d]
Economy: Industry (% of Gross Value Added)	9.2	11.6	10.7[d]
Economy: Services and other activity (% of GVA)	81.6	72.9	72.3[d]
Employment in agriculture (% of employed)	...	11.0[c,e]	...
Employment in industry (% of employed)	...	9.4[c,e]	...
Employment in services & other sectors (% employed)	...	79.6[c,e]	...
Unemployment rate (% of labour force)	...	...	4.7[c,f]
Labour force participation rate (female/male pop. %)	... / ...	... / ...	29.0 / 53.3[f]
Agricultural production index (2004-2006=100)	97	112	104[d]
International trade: exports (million current US$)[g]	11	17	26[h]
International trade: imports (million current US$)[g]	68	76	60[h]
International trade: balance (million current US$)[g]	- 57	- 60	- 35[h]
Balance of payments, current account (million US$)	- 3[c]	- 14	- 16[d]

Major trading partners

							2017
Export partners (% of exports)[g]	Spain	16.5	United States	15.2	Thailand	13.9	
Import partners (% of imports)	Areas nes[i]	87.4	United States	5.8	China	3.8	

Social indicators

	2005	2010	2018
Population growth rate (average annual %)[j]	-0.0	0.1	0.2[b]
Urban population (% of total population)	71.1	73.6	77.0
Urban population growth rate (average annual %)[j]	0.7	0.8	0.8[b]
Fertility rate, total (live births per woman)	...	...	4.1[f]
Life expectancy at birth (females/males, years)	70.6 / 67.0[k]	... / ...	72.5 / 71.3[c,f]
Population age distribution (0-14/60+ years old, %)	40.6 / 3.6[l,m,k]	40.9 / 4.5[l,m]	39.0 / 5.5[c,d]
International migrant stock (000/% of total pop.)	2.4 / 4.6	3.1 / 5.9	3.3 / 8.2[h]
Infant mortality rate (per 1 000 live births)	...	...	25.4[n,f]
Health: Current expenditure (% of GDP)[o,p]	26.3	19.3	22.1[b]
Health: Physicians (per 1 000 pop.)	...	0.6[q]	0.5[r]
Education: Government expenditure (% of GDP)	12.2[s]	...	...
Education: Primary gross enrol. ratio (f/m per 100 pop.)	129.9 / 103.0	107.9 / 107.4[t]	90.0 / 88.6[d]
Education: Secondary gross enrol. ratio (f/m per 100 pop.)	75.7 / 75.6	104.4 / 101.4[t]	76.5 / 69.8[d]
Education: Tertiary gross enrol. ratio (f/m per 100 pop.)	18.3 / 14.2[u]	... / ...	41.2 / 44.6[r]
Seats held by women in the National Parliament (%)	3.0	3.0	9.1

Environment and infrastructure indicators

	2005	2010	2018
Individuals using the Internet (per 100 inhabitants)	3.9	7.0[g]	29.8[a,d]
Threatened species (number)	13[k]	84	101[h]
Forested area (% of land area)[o]	70.2	70.2	70.2[b]
CO2 emission estimates (million tons/tons per capita)	0.1 / 1.7	0.1 / 2.0	0.1 / 1.9[v]
Energy production, primary (Petajoules)[g]	0	0	0[b]
Energy supply per capita (Gigajoules)[g]	35	41	42[b]
Tourist/visitor arrivals at national borders (000)	9[w]	5[x]	10[d]
Important sites for terrestrial biodiversity protected (%)	16.8	23.4	25.4
Pop. using improved drinking water (urban/rural, %)	92.5 / 96.5	93.1 / 97.2	93.5 / 97.6[b]
Pop. using improved sanitation facilities (urban/rural, %)	82.0 / 50.9	83.5 / 54.2	84.5 / 56.2[b]
Net Official Development Assist. received (% of GNI)	31.71	16.40	5.30[d]

a Projected estimate (medium fertility variant). b 2015. c Break in the time series. d 2016. e Data classified according to ISIC Rev. 3. f 2011. g Estimate. h 2017. i Areas not elsewhere specified. j Data refers to a 5-year period preceding the reference year. k 2004. l Projections are prepared by the Secretariat of the Pacific Community based on 1999 census of population and housing. m Estimates should be viewed with caution as these are derived from scarce data. n Data refers to a 3-year period up to and including the reference year. o Data refer to fiscal years ending 30 September. p Health expenditure indicators are high as they spend a lot on health using direct funding from the United States and also from their domestic funds. Current health expenditure is mostly government. q 2007. r 2012. s 2003. t 2009. u 2002. v 2014. w Air and sea arrivals. x Arrivals by air.

Martinique

Region	Caribbean	Population (000, 2018)	385[a]	
Surface area (km2)	1 128[b]	Pop. density (per km2, 2018)	363.3[a]	
Sex ratio (m per 100 f)	83.3[a]	Capital city	Fort-de-France	
National currency	Euro (EUR)	Capital city pop. (000, 2018)	79.4	
Exchange rate (per US$)	0.8[c]			

Economic indicators	2005	2010	2018
Employment in agriculture (% of employed)[d,e]	...	4.1	3.9[f]
Employment in industry (% of employed)[d,e]	...	11.9	11.8[f]
Employment in services & other sectors (% employed)[d,e]	...	85.3	69.0[f]
Unemployment rate (% of labour force)[e]	18.7	21.0	22.8[g,h]
Labour force participation rate (female/male pop. %)[e]	39.6 / 48.5	43.3 / 49.1	52.6 / 53.8[a,h]
CPI: Consumer Price Index (2010=100)[i]	...	100	106[j]
Agricultural production index (2004-2006=100)	99	82	79[j]

Social indicators	2005	2010	2018
Population growth rate (average annual %)[k]	0.5	- 0.1	- 0.5[b]
Urban population (% of total population)	89.3	89.0	89.0
Urban population growth rate (average annual %)[k]	0.4	- 0.2	- 0.5[b]
Fertility rate, total (live births per woman)[k]	1.9	2.1	2.0[b]
Life expectancy at birth (females/males, years)[k]	82.2 / 75.5	83.2 / 76.7	84.4 / 77.8[b]
Population age distribution (0-14/60+ years old, %)	21.1 / 18.0	19.6 / 20.6	17.6 / 26.4[a]
International migrant stock (000/% of total pop.)	57.0 / 14.4	59.6 / 15.1	61.8 / 16.0[c]
Infant mortality rate (per 1 000 live births)[k]	8.5	7.6	6.4[b]
Intentional homicide rate (per 100 000 pop.)	4.8	2.8[i]	...

Environment and infrastructure indicators	2005	2010	2018
Threatened species (number)	29[m]	31	48[c]
Forested area (% of land area)[n]	45.8	45.8	45.8[b]
CO2 emission estimates (million tons/tons per capita)	2.2 / 5.5	2.0 / 5.1	2.3 / 5.8[o]
Energy production, primary (Petajoules)[n]	0	1	1[b]
Energy supply per capita (Gigajoules)	73	69	79[n,b]
Tourist/visitor arrivals at national borders (000)	484	478	519[j]
Important sites for terrestrial biodiversity protected (%)	75.1	99.1	99.1
Pop. using improved drinking water (urban/rural, %)	95.5 / 99.8	100.0 / 99.8	100.0 / 99.8[b]
Pop. using improved sanitation facilities (urban/rural, %)	93.9 / 72.7	94.0 / 72.7	94.0 / 72.7[o]

a Projected estimate (medium fertility variant). b 2015. c 2017. d Population aged 15 to 64 years. e Excluding the institutional population. f 2012. g Break in the time series. h 2013. i Calculated by the Statistics Division of the United Nations from national indices. j 2016. k Data refers to a 5-year period preceding the reference year. l 2009. m 2004. n Estimate. o 2014.

Mauritania

Region	Western Africa	UN membership date	27 October 1961
Population (000, 2018)	4 540 [a]	Surface area (km2)	1 030 700 [b]
Pop. density (per km2, 2018)	4.4 [a]	Sex ratio (m per 100 f)	101.7 [a]
Capital city	Nouakchott	National currency	Ouguiya (MRU)
Capital city pop. (000, 2018)	1 205.4	Exchange rate (per US$)	35.3 [c]

Economic indicators	2005	2010	2018
GDP: Gross domestic product (million current US$)	2 184	4 338	4 667 [d]
GDP growth rate (annual %, const. 2010 prices)	9.0	4.8	1.7 [d]
GDP per capita (current US$)	698.0	1 202.0	1 085.0 [d]
Economy: Agriculture (% of Gross Value Added)	29.8	21.3	23.4 [d]
Economy: Industry (% of Gross Value Added)	32.4	40.9	36.1 [d]
Economy: Services and other activity (% of GVA)	37.9	37.8	40.4 [d]
Employment in agriculture (% of employed) [e]	77.9	77.3	75.5
Employment in industry (% of employed) [e]	8.9	7.6	7.2
Employment in services & other sectors (% employed) [e]	13.2	15.1	17.3
Unemployment rate (% of labour force) [e]	10.4	10.2	10.2
Labour force participation rate (female/male pop. %) [e]	30.2 / 71.4	30.4 / 69.2	31.1 / 67.7
CPI: Consumer Price Index (2010=100)	75	100	128 [c]
Agricultural production index (2004-2006=100)	100	109	120 [d]
International trade: exports (million current US$)	556	1 819	1 989 [c]
International trade: imports (million current US$)	1 342	1 708	3 522 [c]
International trade: balance (million current US$)	- 786	111	- 1 533 [c]
Balance of payments, current account (million US$)	...	...	- 709 [f,c]

Major trading partners						2017
Export partners (% of exports)	China	35.1	Switzerland	15.4	Spain	11.6
Import partners (% of imports)	Republic of Korea	18.1	United Arab Emirates	8.9	Norway	7.8

Social indicators	2005	2010	2018
Population growth rate (average annual %) [g]	2.9	2.8	2.9 [b]
Urban population (% of total population)	42.1	46.6	53.7
Urban population growth rate (average annual %) [g]	4.9	4.9	4.8 [b]
Fertility rate, total (live births per woman) [g]	5.3	5.1	4.9 [b]
Life expectancy at birth (females/males, years) [g]	61.9 / 58.6	62.8 / 59.8	64.1 / 61.2 [b]
Population age distribution (0-14/60+ years old, %)	42.1 / 4.8	41.2 / 4.8	39.7 / 5.1 [a]
International migrant stock (000/% of total pop.) [h,i]	58.1 / 1.9	84.7 / 2.3	168.4 / 3.8 [c]
Refugees and others of concern to the UNHCR (000)	30.2 [j]	27.0 [j]	79.7 [c]
Infant mortality rate (per 1 000 live births) [g]	75.6	72.4	68.0 [b]
Health: Current expenditure (% of GDP)	4.5	3.3	4.6 [b]
Health: Physicians (per 1 000 pop.)	0.1 [k]	0.1 [l]	...
Education: Government expenditure (% of GDP)	2.5 [e,k]	3.6	2.6 [e,d]
Education: Primary gross enrol. ratio (f/m per 100 pop.)	91.9 / 89.4	98.3 / 94.2	96.8 / 91.0 [d]
Education: Secondary gross enrol. ratio (f/m per 100 pop.)	20.7 / 23.6	18.6 / 21.8 [e]	31.1 / 32.0 [d]
Education: Tertiary gross enrol. ratio (f/m per 100 pop.)	1.5 / 4.3	2.5 / 6.2	3.5 / 6.9 [d]
Intentional homicide rate (per 100 000 pop.)	12.4	10.9	9.9 [b]
Seats held by women in the National Parliament (%)	3.7	22.1	25.2

Environment and infrastructure indicators	2005	2010	2018
Individuals using the Internet (per 100 inhabitants)	0.7	4.0 [e]	18.0 [e,d]
Threatened species (number)	26 [k]	58	86 [c]
Forested area (% of land area)	0.3	0.2	0.2 [b]
CO2 emission estimates (million tons/tons per capita)	1.6 / 0.5	2.2 / 0.6	2.7 / 0.7 [m]
Energy production, primary (Petajoules)	15	34	30 [b]
Energy supply per capita (Gigajoules)	12	12	13 [e,b]
Tourist/visitor arrivals at national borders (000)	30 [n]	...	...
Important sites for terrestrial biodiversity protected (%)	14.6	14.6	14.6
Pop. using improved drinking water (urban/rural, %)	50.4 / 45.9	55.4 / 52.9	58.4 / 57.1 [b]
Pop. using improved sanitation facilities (urban/rural, %)	46.0 / 10.9	53.2 / 12.7	57.5 / 13.8 [b]
Net Official Development Assist. received (% of GNI)	8.39	8.74	6.44 [d]

a Projected estimate (medium fertility variant). b 2015. c 2017. d 2016. e Estimate. f Break in the time series. g Data refers to a 5-year period preceding the reference year. h Refers to foreign citizens. i Including refugees. j Data as at the end of December. k 2004. l 2009. m 2014. n 2000.

Mauritius

Region	Eastern Africa
Population (000, 2018)	1 268[a,b]
Pop. density (per km2, 2018)	624.8[a,b]
Capital city	Port Louis
Capital city pop. (000, 2018)	149.4

UN membership date	24 April 1968
Surface area (km2)	1 969[c,d]
Sex ratio (m per 100 f)	97.7[a,b]
National currency	Mauritius Rupee (MUR)
Exchange rate (per US$)	33.5[e]

Economic indicators	2005	2010	2018
GDP: Gross domestic product (million current US$)	6 775	10 004	12 216[f]
GDP growth rate (annual %, const. 2010 prices)	1.8	4.4	3.7[f]
GDP per capita (current US$)	5 544.0	8 016.0	9 679.0[f]
Economy: Agriculture (% of Gross Value Added)	5.7	4.1[g]	3.5[g,f]
Economy: Industry (% of Gross Value Added)	26.6	25.3[g]	20.9[g,f]
Economy: Services and other activity (% of GVA)	67.8	70.7[g]	75.6[g,f]
Employment in agriculture (% of employed)[h]	10.0	8.5	7.1
Employment in industry (% of employed)[h]	32.4	28.8	25.7
Employment in services & other sectors (% employed)[h]	57.6	62.7	67.3
Unemployment rate (% of labour force)	9.6	7.7	7.0[h]
Labour force participation rate (female/male pop. %)[h]	41.1 / 76.8	42.8 / 74.1	45.1 / 72.2
CPI: Consumer Price Index (2010=100)[i]	73	100	125[e]
Agricultural production index (2004-2006=100)	98	99	92[f]
Index of industrial production (2005=100)[j]	100	112	117[k]
International trade: exports (million current US$)	2 144	1 850	2 103[e]
International trade: imports (million current US$)	3 160	4 402	5 269[e]
International trade: balance (million current US$)	- 1 016	- 2 553	- 3 167[e]
Balance of payments, current account (million US$)	- 324	- 1 006	- 878[e]

Major trading partners						2017
Export partners (% of exports)	France	15.8	United Kingdom	11.9	United States	11.2
Import partners (% of imports)	China	16.4	India	16.4	South Africa	8.5

Social indicators	2005	2010	2018
Population growth rate (average annual %)[b,l]	0.6	0.4	0.2[d]
Urban population (% of total population)[b]	42.1	41.6	40.8
Urban population growth rate (average annual %)[b,l]	0.3	0.2	- 0.1[d]
Fertility rate, total (live births per woman)[b,l]	1.9	1.7	1.5[d]
Life expectancy at birth (females/males, years)[b,l]	75.4 / 68.8	76.2 / 69.4	77.7 / 70.7[d]
Population age distribution (0-14/60+ years old, %)[b]	24.7 / 9.6	21.9 / 12.1	17.9 / 17.2[a]
International migrant stock (000/% of total pop.)[b,m]	19.6 / 1.6	24.8 / 2.0	28.7 / 2.3[e]
Refugees and others of concern to the UNHCR (000)	...	...	~0.0[e]
Infant mortality rate (per 1 000 live births)[b,l]	13.4	13.2	12.0[d]
Health: Current expenditure (% of GDP)	3.7	4.7	5.5[d]
Health: Physicians (per 1 000 pop.)	1.1[n]	1.2	2.0[d]
Education: Government expenditure (% of GDP)	4.2	3.6	5.1[e]
Education: Primary gross enrol. ratio (f/m per 100 pop.)	103.1 / 103.3	103.1 / 102.5	103.4 / 101.6[f]
Education: Secondary gross enrol. ratio (f/m per 100 pop.)	87.6 / 89.7[h]	91.3 / 87.2[h]	96.0 / 90.8[f]
Education: Tertiary gross enrol. ratio (f/m per 100 pop.)	21.7 / 21.0[h]	36.9 / 30.5	43.8 / 34.0[e]
Intentional homicide rate (per 100 000 pop.)	3.0	2.6	1.8[f]
Seats held by women in the National Parliament (%)	5.7	17.1	11.6

Environment and infrastructure indicators	2005	2010	2018
Individuals using the Internet (per 100 inhabitants)	15.2[b]	28.3[o]	53.2[h,i]
Research & Development expenditure (% of GDP)	0.4[p,q]	...	0.2[r,s,t]
Threatened species (number)	147[n]	222	257[e]
Forested area (% of land area)	18.8	18.9	19.0[h,d]
CO2 emission estimates (million tons/tons per capita)	3.3 / 2.6	3.9 / 3.2	4.2 / 3.3[u]
Energy production, primary (Petajoules)	12	11	12[d]
Energy supply per capita (Gigajoules)	45	50	52[d]
Tourist/visitor arrivals at national borders (000)	761	935	1 275[f]
Important sites for terrestrial biodiversity protected (%)	9.5	9.6	10.4
Pop. using improved drinking water (urban/rural, %)	99.8 / 99.2	99.9 / 99.6	99.9 / 99.8[d]
Pop. using improved sanitation facilities (urban/rural, %)	93.6 / 90.9	93.8 / 92.0	93.9 / 92.6[d]
Net Official Development Assist. received (% of GNI)	0.55	1.23	0.35[f]

a Projected estimate (medium fertility variant). b Including Agalega, Rodrigues and Saint Brandon. c Excluding the islands of Saint Brandon and Agalega. d 2015. e 2017. f 2016. g Data classified according to ISIC Rev. 4. h Estimate. i Calculated by the Statistics Division of the United Nations from national indices. j Data classified according to ISIC Rev. 3. k 2011. l Data refers to a 5-year period preceding the reference year. m Refers to foreign citizens. n 2004. o Population aged 5 years and over. p R&D budget instead of R&D expenditure or based on R&D budget. q Overestimated or based on overestimated data. r Excluding business enterprise. s Break in the time series. t 2012. u 2014.

Mayotte

Region	Eastern Africa	Population (000, 2018)	260[a]
Pop. density (per km2, 2018)	692.5[a]	Sex ratio (m per 100 f)	96.8[a]
Capital city	Mamoudzou	National currency	Euro (EUR)
Capital city pop. (000, 2018)	6.2	Exchange rate (per US$)	0.8[b]

Economic indicators	2005	2010	2018
International trade: exports (million current US$)	6	...	...
International trade: imports (million current US$)	309	...	...
International trade: balance (million current US$)	- 303	...	...

Social indicators	2005	2010	2018
Population growth rate (average annual %)[c]	3.4	3.2	2.8[d]
Urban population (% of total population)	50.2	49.0	46.1
Urban population growth rate (average annual %)[c]	4.4	2.7	2.0[d]
Fertility rate, total (live births per woman)[c]	4.8	4.6	4.1[d]
Life expectancy at birth (females/males, years)[c]	80.6 / 73.0	81.9 / 74.5	82.9 / 76.0[d]
Population age distribution (0-14/60+ years old, %)	42.4 / 4.8	42.9 / 5.1	40.2 / 5.9[a]
International migrant stock (000/% of total pop.)	63.2 / 35.5	72.8 / 34.9	74.4 / 29.4[b]
Infant mortality rate (per 1 000 live births)[c]	7.6	5.6	4.2[d]
Intentional homicide rate (per 100 000 pop.)	...	5.9[a]	...

Environment and infrastructure indicators	2005	2010	2018
Individuals using the Internet (per 100 inhabitants)	1.2[f]	...	...
Threatened species (number)	7[g]	69	88[b]
Forested area (% of land area)[h]	20.7	18.2	15.6[d]
Energy production, primary (Petajoules)	0	0	0[d]
Energy supply per capita (Gigajoules)	17[h]	20	21[d]
Important sites for terrestrial biodiversity protected (%)	15.6	54.1	54.1

a Projected estimate (medium fertility variant). b 2017. c Data refers to a 5-year period preceding the reference year.
d 2015. e 2009. f 2000. g 2004. h Estimate.

Mexico

Region	Central America	UN membership date	07 November 1945	
Population (000, 2018)	130 759[a]	Surface area (km2)	1 964 375[b]	
Pop. density (per km2, 2018)	67.3[a]	Sex ratio (m per 100 f)	99.2[a]	
Capital city	Mexico City	National currency	Mexican Peso (MXN)	
Capital city pop. (000, 2018)	21 580.8[c]	Exchange rate (per US$)	19.8[d]	

Economic indicators

	2005	2010	2018
GDP: Gross domestic product (million current US$)	877 477	1 057 801	1 076 914[e]
GDP growth rate (annual %, const. 2010 prices)	2.3	5.1	2.9[e]
GDP per capita (current US$)	8 089.0	9 016.0	8 444.0[e]
Economy: Agriculture (% of Gross Value Added)[f]	3.2	3.4	3.6[e]
Economy: Industry (% of Gross Value Added)[f]	34.2	33.7	31.3[e]
Economy: Services and other activity (% of GVA)[f]	62.6	62.9	65.1[e]
Employment in agriculture (% of employed)[g]	14.8	13.9	13.0
Employment in industry (% of employed)[g]	25.7	24.1	25.9
Employment in services & other sectors (% employed)[g]	59.5	62.0	61.2
Unemployment rate (% of labour force)	3.6	5.3	3.6[g]
Labour force participation rate (female/male pop. %)[g]	41.3 / 81.5	43.2 / 80.1	44.3 / 78.9
CPI: Consumer Price Index (2010=100)[h]	81	100	130[d]
Agricultural production index (2004-2006=100)	98	108	126[e]
Index of industrial production (2005=100)	100[i]	101	110[j]
International trade: exports (million current US$)[k,l]	214 207	298 305	409 451[d]
International trade: imports (million current US$)[k,l]	221 819	301 482	420 369[d]
International trade: balance (million current US$)[k,l]	- 7 612	- 3 177	- 10 918[d]
Balance of payments, current account (million US$)	- 9 053	- 5 241	- 19 354[d]

Major trading partners

						2017
Export partners (% of exports)	United States	80.0	Canada	2.8	Germany	1.7
Import partners (% of imports)	United States	46.4	China	17.6	Japan	4.3

Social indicators

	2005	2010	2018
Population growth rate (average annual %)[m]	1.3	1.6	1.4[b]
Urban population (% of total population)	76.3	77.8	80.2
Urban population growth rate (average annual %)[m]	1.7	2.0	1.8[b]
Fertility rate, total (live births per woman)[m]	2.6	2.4	2.3[b]
Life expectancy at birth (females/males, years)[m]	77.4 / 72.4	78.1 / 73.3	78.9 / 74.0[b]
Population age distribution (0-14/60+ years old, %)	32.3 / 7.7	29.8 / 8.4	26.3 / 10.4[a]
International migrant stock (000/% of total pop.)[n]	712.5 / 0.7	969.5 / 0.8	1 224.2 / 0.9[d]
Refugees and others of concern to the UNHCR (000)	3.4[o]	1.6[o]	13.9[d]
Infant mortality rate (per 1 000 live births)[m]	20.5	19.9	18.8[b]
Health: Current expenditure (% of GDP)	5.9	6.0	5.9[b]
Health: Physicians (per 1 000 pop.)	1.9[p]	1.9	2.2[b]
Education: Government expenditure (% of GDP)	4.9	5.2	5.3[j]
Education: Primary gross enrol. ratio (f/m per 100 pop.)	103.7 / 105.6	104.6 / 105.6	104.2 / 103.7[e]
Education: Secondary gross enrol. ratio (f/m per 100 pop.)	83.3 / 76.5	87.9 / 80.9	101.4 / 93.3[e]
Education: Tertiary gross enrol. ratio (f/m per 100 pop.)	23.8 / 23.0	26.8 / 25.8	37.3 / 36.5[e]
Intentional homicide rate (per 100 000 pop.)	9.1	22.0	19.3[e]
Seats held by women in the National Parliament (%)	22.6	27.6	42.6

Environment and infrastructure indicators

	2005	2010	2018
Individuals using the Internet (per 100 inhabitants)	17.2[q]	31.0[q,q]	59.5[e]
Research & Development expenditure (% of GDP)	0.4	0.5	0.6[g,b]
Threatened species (number)	748[r]	943	1 182[d]
Forested area (% of land area)	34.5	34.2	34.0[g,b]
CO2 emission estimates (million tons/tons per capita)	466.4 / 4.4	464.3 / 3.9	480.3 / 3.8[i]
Energy production, primary (Petajoules)	10 716	9 040	8 006[b]
Energy supply per capita (Gigajoules)	70	62	62[b]
Tourist/visitor arrivals at national borders (000)[s]	21 915	23 290	35 079[e]
Important sites for terrestrial biodiversity protected (%)	24.1	29.0	33.4
Pop. using improved drinking water (urban/rural, %)	95.0 / 79.8	96.2 / 86.7	97.2 / 92.1[b]
Pop. using improved sanitation facilities (urban/rural, %)	84.6 / 59.5	86.4 / 67.8	88.0 / 74.5[b]
Net Official Development Assist. received (% of GNI)	0.02	0.04	0.08[e]

a Projected estimate (medium fertility variant). b 2015. c Refers to the total population in 76 municipalities of the Metropolitan Area of Mexico City. d 2017. e 2016. f Data classified according to ISIC Rev. 4. g Estimate. h Calculated by the Statistics Division of the United Nations from national indices. i Including construction. j 2014. k Trade data include maquiladoras and exclude goods from customs-bonded warehouses. Total exports include revaluation and exports of silver. l Imports FOB. m Data refers to a 5-year period preceding the reference year. n Including refugees. o Data as at the end of December. p 2000. q December. r 2004. s Including nationals residing abroad.

Micronesia (Federated States of)

Region	Micronesia	
Population (000, 2018)	106[a]	
Pop. density (per km2, 2018)	151.8[a]	
Capital city	Palikir	
Capital city pop. (000, 2018)	7.0	

UN membership date	17 September 1991
Surface area (km2)	702[b]
Sex ratio (m per 100 f)	105.2[a]
National currency	US Dollar (USD)

Economic indicators

	2005	2010	2018
GDP: Gross domestic product (million current US$)	251	297	330[d]
GDP growth rate (annual %, const. 2010 prices)	2.1	2.0	-0.1[d]
GDP per capita (current US$)	2 360.0	2 862.0	3 144.0[d]
Economy: Agriculture (% of Gross Value Added)	24.2	26.7	27.3[d]
Economy: Industry (% of Gross Value Added)	5.7	7.8	6.9[d]
Economy: Services and other activity (% of GVA)	70.2	65.5	65.8[d]
CPI: Consumer Price Index (2010=100)	78	100	113[b]
Agricultural production index (2004-2006=100)	100	96	101[d]
International trade: exports (million current US$)[e]	13	23	3[f,c]
International trade: imports (million current US$)[e]	128	168	23[f,c]
International trade: balance (million current US$)[e]	-115	-145	-20[f,c]
Balance of payments, current account (million US$)	...	-25	...

Major trading partners
2017

Export partners (% of exports)[f]	Thailand	59.5	China	11.7	Philippines	11.5
Import partners (% of imports)	Republic of Korea	26.2[f]	United States	23.0[f]	Asia nes[g]	14.1

Social indicators

	2005	2010	2018
Population growth rate (average annual %)[h]	-0.2	-0.5	0.2[b]
Urban population (% of total population)	22.3	22.3	22.7
Urban population growth rate (average annual %)[h]	-0.2	-0.5	0.3[b]
Fertility rate, total (live births per woman)[h]	4.0	3.6	3.3[b]
Life expectancy at birth (females/males, years)[h]	68.2 / 66.9	69.1 / 67.6	69.8 / 67.7[b]
Population age distribution (0-14/60+ years old, %)	38.8 / 5.5	36.9 / 6.2	32.7 / 8.2[a]
International migrant stock (000/% of total pop.)	2.9 / 2.7	2.8 / 2.7	2.8 / 2.6[c]
Refugees and others of concern to the UNHCR (000)	...	...	~0.0[c]
Infant mortality rate (per 1 000 live births)[h]	37.9	34.9	33.2[b]
Health: Current expenditure (% of GDP)[i]	11.5	12.9	13.1[b]
Health: Physicians (per 1 000 pop.)	0.6	0.2[i]	...
Education: Government expenditure (% of GDP)	6.7[f,k]	...	12.5[b]
Education: Primary gross enrol. ratio (f/m per 100 pop.)	109.8 / 112.7	112.4 / 111.0[l]	95.7 / 95.4[b]
Education: Secondary gross enrol. ratio (f/m per 100 pop.)	86.7 / 80.1	... / ...	... / ...
Intentional homicide rate (per 100 000 pop.)	4.6	4.5	4.7[b]
Seats held by women in the National Parliament (%)	0.0	0.0	0.0

Environment and infrastructure indicators

	2005	2010	2018
Individuals using the Internet (per 100 inhabitants)	11.9	20.0[f]	33.4[d]
Threatened species (number)	30[m]	148	167[c]
Forested area (% of land area)[f]	91.4	91.6	91.8[b]
CO2 emission estimates (million tons/tons per capita)	0.1 / 1.1	0.1 / 1.1	0.2 / 1.4[n]
Energy production, primary (Petajoules)	0	0	0[b]
Energy supply per capita (Gigajoules)	16	17	22[f,b]
Tourist/visitor arrivals at national borders (000)[o]	19	45	30[d]
Important sites for terrestrial biodiversity protected (%)	1.3	1.3	1.3
Pop. using improved drinking water (urban/rural, %)	94.4 / 88.3	94.7 / 87.6	94.8 / 87.4[b]
Pop. using improved sanitation facilities (urban/rural, %)	72.6 / 35.0	81.6 / 45.0	85.1 / 49.0[b]
Net Official Development Assist. received (% of GNI)	41.10	20.79	13.05[d]

a Projected estimate (medium fertility variant). b 2015. c 2017. d 2016. e Imports FOB. f Estimate. g Asia not elsewhere specified. h Data refers to a 5-year period preceding the reference year. i Data refer to fiscal years ending 30 September. j 2009. k 2000. l 2007. m 2004. n 2014. o Arrivals in the States of Kosrae, Chuuk, Pohnpei and Yap; excluding FSM citizens.

Monaco

Region	Western Europe	UN membership date	28 May 1993
Population (000, 2018)	39 [a]	Surface area (km2)	2 [b]
Pop. density (per km2, 2018)	26 105.4 [a]	Sex ratio (m per 100 f)	94.7 [c,d]
Capital city	Monaco	National currency	Euro (EUR)
Capital city pop. (000, 2018)	38.9	Exchange rate (per US$)	0.8 [e]

Economic indicators	2005	2010	2018
GDP: Gross domestic product (million current US$)	4 203	5 362	6 468 [f]
GDP growth rate (annual %, const. 2010 prices)	1.6	2.2	3.2 [f]
GDP per capita (current US$)	124 374.0	144 561.0	168 004.0 [f]
Economy: Industry (% of Gross Value Added) [g,h]	12.2	12.9	18.3 [f]
Economy: Services and other activity (% of GVA) [g,h]	87.8	87.1	81.7 [f]
Unemployment rate (% of labour force)	3.6 [i,j]	...	...
Labour force participation rate (female/male pop. %)	35.1 / 57.3 [i,j]	... / ...	... / ...

Social indicators	2005	2010	2018
Population growth rate (average annual %) [k]	1.0	1.9	0.8 [b]
Urban population (% of total population)	100.0	100.0	100.0
Urban population growth rate (average annual %) [k]	1.0	1.9	0.6 [b]
Population age distribution (0-14/60+ years old, %)	13.2 / 28.9 [c,j]	12.7 / 31.2 [c,d]	... / ...
International migrant stock (000/% of total pop.)	21.3 / 63.1	21.1 / 57.0	21.3 / 54.9 [a]
Refugees and others of concern to the UNHCR (000) [l]	...	~0.0	~0.0 [f]
Health: Current expenditure (% of GDP) [m]	2.1	2.3	2.0 [b]
Health: Physicians (per 1 000 pop.)	...	...	6.6 [n]
Education: Government expenditure (% of GDP)	1.2 [o]	1.3	1.4 [f]
Intentional homicide rate (per 100 000 pop.)	3.0	0.0	0.0 [b]
Seats held by women in the National Parliament (%)	20.8	28.1	20.8

Environment and infrastructure indicators	2005	2010	2018
Individuals using the Internet (per 100 inhabitants)	55.5	75.0	95.2 [m,f]
Research & Development expenditure (% of GDP)	~0.0 [p]	...	...
Threatened species (number)	9 [o]	11	21 [e]
Tourist/visitor arrivals at national borders (000)	286	279	336 [f]
Pop. using improved drinking water (urban/rural, %)	100.0 / ...	100.0 / ...	100.0 / ... [b]
Pop. using improved sanitation facilities (urban/rural, %)	100.0 / ...	100.0 / ...	100.0 / ... [b]

a Projected estimate (medium fertility variant). b 2015. c De jure population. d 2008. e 2017. f 2016. g Data classified according to ISIC Rev. 4. h At producers' prices. i Population aged 17 years and over. j 2000. k Data refers to a 5-year period preceding the reference year. l Data as at the end of December. m Estimate. n 2014. o 2004. p Partial data.

Mongolia

Region	Eastern Asia
Population (000, 2018)	3 122[a]
Pop. density (per km2, 2018)	2.0[a]
Capital city	Ulaanbaatar
Capital city pop. (000, 2018)	1 520.4

UN membership date	27 October 1961
Surface area (km2)	1 564 116[b]
Sex ratio (m per 100 f)	97.8[a]
National currency	Tugrik (MNT)
Exchange rate (per US$)	2 427.1[c]

Economic indicators

	2005	2010	2018
GDP: Gross domestic product (million current US$)	2 926	7 189	11 160[d]
GDP growth rate (annual %, const. 2010 prices)	7.3	6.4	1.0[d]
GDP per capita (current US$)	1 158.0	2 650.0	3 686.0[d]
Economy: Agriculture (% of Gross Value Added)[e]	17.8	13.1	13.3[d]
Economy: Industry (% of Gross Value Added)[e]	37.4	37.0	35.3[d]
Economy: Services and other activity (% of GVA)[e]	44.8	50.0	51.4[d]
Employment in agriculture (% of employed)[f]	45.7	33.5	29.8
Employment in industry (% of employed)[f]	11.9	16.2	19.2
Employment in services & other sectors (% employed)[f]	42.5	50.2	51.0
Unemployment rate (% of labour force)	3.3	6.6	6.7[f]
Labour force participation rate (female/male pop. %)[f]	53.7 / 64.9	53.1 / 65.1	52.7 / 66.2
CPI: Consumer Price Index (2010=100)[g]	57	100	172[c]
Agricultural production index (2004-2006=100)	97	114	161[c]
Index of industrial production (2005=100)[h]	100	155	183[i]
International trade: exports (million current US$)	1 064	2 883[f]	6 112[f,c]
International trade: imports (million current US$)	1 183	3 172[f]	4 295[f,c]
International trade: balance (million current US$)	- 118	- 289[f]	1 817[f,c]
Balance of payments, current account (million US$)	88	- 885	- 1 155[c]

Major trading partners

						2017
Export partners (% of exports)[f]	China	79.0	United Kingdom	16.0	Russian Federation	1.1
Import partners (% of imports)[f]	China	31.1	Russian Federation	25.8	Japan	9.9

Social indicators

	2005	2010	2018
Population growth rate (average annual %)[j]	1.0	1.4	1.9[b]
Urban population (% of total population)	62.5	67.6	68.4
Urban population growth rate (average annual %)[j]	2.8	3.0	2.1[b]
Fertility rate, total (live births per woman)[j]	2.1	2.4	2.8[b]
Life expectancy at birth (females/males, years)[j]	67.7 / 60.8	70.3 / 62.4	72.7 / 64.5[b]
Population age distribution (0-14/60+ years old, %)	28.9 / 5.6	27.0 / 5.7	29.9 / 6.8[a]
International migrant stock (000/% of total pop.)[k]	11.5 / 0.5	16.1 / 0.6	18.2 / 0.6[c]
Refugees and others of concern to the UNHCR (000)	0.6[l]	0.3[l]	~0.0[c]
Infant mortality rate (per 1 000 live births)[j]	40.8	30.5	22.8[b]
Health: Current expenditure (% of GDP)	4.2	4.2	3.9[b]
Health: Physicians (per 1 000 pop.)	2.8[m]	2.8	3.3[b]
Education: Government expenditure (% of GDP)	4.3[n]	4.6	5.2[d]
Education: Primary gross enrol. ratio (f/m per 100 pop.)	98.0 / 98.0	124.2 / 127.1	103.0 / 105.4[d]
Education: Secondary gross enrol. ratio (f/m per 100 pop.)	95.0 / 85.6	94.8 / 88.4	100.6 / 100.0[d]
Education: Tertiary gross enrol. ratio (f/m per 100 pop.)	55.9 / 33.8	65.3 / 42.5	75.3 / 54.1[d]
Intentional homicide rate (per 100 000 pop.)	15.8	8.8	5.7[d]
Seats held by women in the National Parliament (%)	6.8	3.9	17.1

Environment and infrastructure indicators

	2005	2010	2018
Individuals using the Internet (per 100 inhabitants)	1.3[o]	10.2	22.3[d]
Research & Development expenditure (% of GDP)[p]	0.2	0.2	0.2[b]
Threatened species (number)	39[n]	36	41[c]
Forested area (% of land area)[f]	7.3	8.4	8.1[b]
CO2 emission estimates (million tons/tons per capita)	8.6 / 3.4	13.8 / 5.1	20.8 / 7.2[i]
Energy production, primary (Petajoules)	138	655	654[b]
Energy supply per capita (Gigajoules)	41	61	92[b]
Tourist/visitor arrivals at national borders (000)[q]	338	456	404[d]
Important sites for terrestrial biodiversity protected (%)	36.5	39.1	43.7
Pop. using improved drinking water (urban/rural, %)	71.6 / 41.3	69.0 / 50.3	66.4 / 59.2[b]
Pop. using improved sanitation facilities (urban/rural, %)	65.5 / 31.4	65.9 / 37.0	66.4 / 42.6[b]
Net Official Development Assist. received (% of GNI)	8.94	4.60	3.16[d]

a Projected estimate (medium fertility variant). b 2015. c 2017. d 2016. e Data classified according to ISIC Rev. 4. f Estimate. g Calculated by the Statistics Division of the United Nations from national indices. h Data classified according to ISIC Rev. 3. i 2014. j Data refers to a 5-year period preceding the reference year. k Refers to foreign citizens. l Data as at the end of December. m 2002. n 2004. o 2000. p Partial data. q Excluding diplomats and foreign residents in Mongolia.

Montenegro

Region	Southern Europe	UN membership date	28 June 2006
Population (000, 2018)	629[a]	Surface area (km2)	13 812[b]
Pop. density (per km2, 2018)	46.8[a]	Sex ratio (m per 100 f)	97.4[a]
Capital city	Podgorica	National currency	Euro (EUR)
Capital city pop. (000, 2018)	177.2[c]	Exchange rate (per US$)	0.8[d]

Economic indicators

	2005	2010	2018
GDP: Gross domestic product (million current US$)	2 279	4 138	4 374[e]
GDP growth rate (annual %, const. 2010 prices)	4.2	2.7	2.9[e]
GDP per capita (current US$)	3 697.0	6 628.0	6 958.0[e]
Economy: Agriculture (% of Gross Value Added)[f]	10.3	9.2	9.0[e]
Economy: Industry (% of Gross Value Added)[f]	22.1	20.5	19.1[e]
Economy: Services and other activity (% of GVA)[f]	67.6	70.3	71.8[e]
Employment in agriculture (% of employed)[g]	8.6	6.2	7.4
Employment in industry (% of employed)[g]	19.2	19.0	18.1
Employment in services & other sectors (% employed)[g]	72.1	74.8	74.6
Unemployment rate (% of labour force)	30.3	19.7	16.4[g]
Labour force participation rate (female/male pop. %)[g]	42.7 / 59.1	42.6 / 56.6	42.0 / 54.7
CPI: Consumer Price Index (2010=100)	82	100	113[h,d]
Agricultural production index (2004-2006=100)	...	63	66[e]
Index of industrial production (2005=100)	100	79[i]	64[i,j]
International trade: exports (million current US$)	...	437	421[d]
International trade: imports (million current US$)	...	2 182	2 611[d]
International trade: balance (million current US$)	...	- 1 745	- 2 190[d]
Balance of payments, current account (million US$)	...	- 952[k]	- 881[d]

Major trading partners

						2017
Export partners (% of exports)	Serbia	17.8	Bosnia-Herzegovina	12.7	Areas nes[l]	9.4
Import partners (% of imports)	Serbia	21.5	China	9.6	Germany	8.5

Social indicators

	2005	2010	2018
Population growth rate (average annual %)[m]	0.1	0.3	0.1[b]
Urban population (% of total population)	62.5	64.1	66.8
Urban population growth rate (average annual %)[m]	1.4	0.8	0.6[b]
Fertility rate, total (live births per woman)[m]	1.9	1.8	1.7[b]
Life expectancy at birth (females/males, years)[m]	76.2 / 70.6	76.5 / 71.9	78.8 / 74.0[b]
Population age distribution (0-14/60+ years old, %)	20.2 / 17.0	19.2 / 17.9	18.0 / 21.7[a]
International migrant stock (000/% of total pop.)	... / ...	78.5 / 12.6	71.0 / 11.3[d]
Refugees and others of concern to the UNHCR (000)	...	18.3[n]	13.0[d]
Infant mortality rate (per 1 000 live births)[m]	11.6	10.9	4.1[b]
Health: Current expenditure (% of GDP)	7.7	5.9	6.0[b]
Health: Physicians (per 1 000 pop.)	...	2.0	2.3[b]
Education: Primary gross enrol. ratio (f/m per 100 pop.)	112.6 / 112.8	109.6 / 111.2	94.6 / 97.4[e]
Education: Secondary gross enrol. ratio (f/m per 100 pop.)	95.8 / 93.3	101.0 / 99.7	90.5 / 90.6[e]
Education: Tertiary gross enrol. ratio (f/m per 100 pop.)	27.2 / 17.2	58.3 / 46.5	63.4 / 50.8[e]
Intentional homicide rate (per 100 000 pop.)	3.6	2.4	4.5[e]
Seats held by women in the National Parliament (%)	...	11.1	23.5

Environment and infrastructure indicators

	2005	2010	2018
Individuals using the Internet (per 100 inhabitants)	27.1[g]	37.5[g]	69.9[e]
Research & Development expenditure (% of GDP)	0.9	1.1[o]	0.4[d]
Threatened species (number)	...	72	98[d]
Forested area (% of land area)[g]	...	61.5	61.5[b]
CO2 emission estimates (million tons/tons per capita)	... / ...	2.6 / 4.1	2.2 / 3.5[i]
Energy production, primary (Petajoules)	25	35	30[b]
Energy supply per capita (Gigajoules)	67	77	66[b]
Tourist/visitor arrivals at national borders (000)	272	1 088	1 662[e]
Important sites for terrestrial biodiversity protected (%)	11.9	11.9	11.9
Pop. using improved drinking water (urban/rural, %)	99.3 / 95.6	99.8 / 97.4	100.0 / 99.2[b]
Pop. using improved sanitation facilities (urban/rural, %)	92.5 / 88.2	95.4 / 90.2	98.0 / 92.2[b]
Net Official Development Assist. received (% of GNI)	0.17	1.95	2.02[e]

a Projected estimate (medium fertility variant). b 2015. c Refers to the urban population of Podgorica municipality. d 2017. e 2016. f Data classified according to ISIC Rev. 4. g Estimate. h Calculated by the Statistics Division of the United Nations from national indices. i Excluding water and waste management. j 2014. k Break in the time series. l Areas not elsewhere specified. m Data refers to a 5-year period preceding the reference year. n Data as at the end of December. o 2007.

Montserrat

Region	Caribbean	Population (000, 2018)	5[a]
Surface area (km2)	103[b]	Pop. density (per km2, 2018)	52.0[a]
Sex ratio (m per 100 f)	106.0[c]	Capital city	Brades Estate
National currency	E. Caribbean Dollar (XCD)[d]	Capital city pop. (000, 2018)	0.5
Exchange rate (per US$)	2.7[e]		

Economic indicators	2005	2010	2018
GDP: Gross domestic product (million current US$)	49	56	62[c]
GDP growth rate (annual %, const. 2010 prices)	3.1	- 2.8	2.0[c]
GDP per capita (current US$)	10 229.0	11 228.0	12 044.0[c]
Economy: Agriculture (% of Gross Value Added)	0.9	1.1	1.7[c]
Economy: Industry (% of Gross Value Added)	16.7	13.3	12.9[c]
Economy: Services and other activity (% of GVA)	82.5	85.7	85.4[c]
Unemployment rate (% of labour force)	9.5[f,g]	...	5.6[h]
Labour force participation rate (female/male pop. %)	80.6 / 89.2[f,g]	... / ...	... / ...
CPI: Consumer Price Index (2010=100)[l]	87	100	109[e]
Agricultural production index (2004-2006=100)	100	98	104[c]
International trade: exports (million current US$)	1	1	5[i,e]
International trade: imports (million current US$)	30	29[i]	29[i,e]
International trade: balance (million current US$)	- 28	- 28	- 24[i,e]
Balance of payments, current account (million US$)	- 16	- 19	- 9[c]

Major trading partners						2017
Export partners (% of exports)	Mexico	73.4[i]	United States	7.4	France	6.1[i]
Import partners (% of imports)[i]	United States	47.6	Trinidad and Tobago	10.1	United Kingdom	9.8

Social indicators	2005	2010	2018
Population growth rate (average annual %)[j]	- 0.7	0.7	0.7[b]
Urban population (% of total population)	9.3	9.2	9.1
Urban population growth rate (average annual %)[j]	29.3	0.3	0.5[b]
Fertility rate, total (live births per woman)	1.7[k]	...	...
Population age distribution (0-14/60+ years old, %)	19.3 / 19.9[g]	19.6 / 19.0[l,m]	19.7 / 19.6[n,h]
International migrant stock (000/% of total pop.)	1.2 / 26.0	1.3 / 25.8	1.4 / 26.3[e]
Refugees and others of concern to the UNHCR (000)	...	~0.0[o]	...
Education: Government expenditure (% of GDP)	...	5.1[p]	...
Education: Primary gross enrol. ratio (f/m per 100 pop.)	118.7 / 114.6[i]	112.9 / 101.2[i,q]	... / ...
Education: Secondary gross enrol. ratio (f/m per 100 pop.)	122.5 / 111.0[i]	103.2 / 101.1[i,q]	... / ...
Intentional homicide rate (per 100 000 pop.)	20.9	20.4[r]	19.9[s]

Environment and infrastructure indicators	2005	2010	2018
Individuals using the Internet (per 100 inhabitants)	...	35.0	54.6[h]
Threatened species (number)	21[k]	35	55[e]
Forested area (% of land area)[i]	25.0	25.0	25.0[b]
CO2 emission estimates (million tons/tons per capita)	~0.0 / 6.6	0.1 / 13.0	~0.0 / 9.6[t]
Energy supply per capita (Gigajoules)	93[i]	175	149[b]
Tourist/visitor arrivals at national borders (000)	10	6	9[c]
Important sites for terrestrial biodiversity protected (%)	0.0	0.0	30.6
Pop. using improved drinking water (urban/rural, %)	98.9 / 99.0	98.9 / 99.0	99.0 / 99.0[b]
Pop. using improved sanitation facilities (urban/rural, %)	82.9 / 82.9	... / ...	... / ...

a Projected estimate (medium fertility variant). b 2015. c 2016. d East Caribbean Dollar. e 2017. f Break in the time series. g 2001. h 2011. i Estimate. j Data refers to a 5-year period preceding the reference year. k 2004. l Intercensus data. m 2006. n De jure population. o Data as at the end of December. p 2009. q 2007. r 2008. s 2012. t 2014.

Morocco

Region	Northern Africa	UN membership date	12 November 1956	
Population (000, 2018)	36 192[a]	Surface area (km2)	446 550[b]	
Pop. density (per km2, 2018)	81.1[a]	Sex ratio (m per 100 f)	98.2[a]	
Capital city	Rabat	National currency	Moroccan Dirham (MAD)	
Capital city pop. (000, 2018)	1 846.7[c]	Exchange rate (per US$)	9.3[d]	

Economic indicators	2005	2010	2018	
GDP: Gross domestic product (million current US$)[e]	62 545	93 217	103 607[f]	
GDP growth rate (annual %, const. 2010 prices)[e]	3.0	4.0	3.4[f]	
GDP per capita (current US$)[e]	2 049.0	2 876.0	2 937.0[f]	
Economy: Agriculture (% of Gross Value Added)[e]	13.1	14.4	13.6[f]	
Economy: Industry (% of Gross Value Added)[e]	28.9	28.6	29.5[f]	
Economy: Services and other activity (% of GVA)[e]	58.0	56.9	56.8[f]	
Employment in agriculture (% of employed)[g]	45.5	40.2	37.0	
Employment in industry (% of employed)[g]	19.5	22.0	19.5	
Employment in services & other sectors (% employed)[g]	35.0	37.8	43.5	
Unemployment rate (% of labour force)	11.0	9.1	9.3[g]	
Labour force participation rate (female/male pop. %)[g]	26.7 / 76.3	25.6 / 75.6	24.9 / 73.9	
CPI: Consumer Price Index (2010=100)[h]	90	100	109[f]	
Agricultural production index (2004-2006=100)	93	126	122[f]	
International trade: exports (million current US$)	11 185	17 765	21 249[g,d]	
International trade: imports (million current US$)	20 803	35 379	34 293[g,d]	
International trade: balance (million current US$)	- 9 618	- 17 614	- 13 044[g,d]	
Balance of payments, current account (million US$)	1 041	- 3 925	- 3 850[d]	

Major trading partners						2017
Export partners (% of exports)	Spain	23.3[g]	France	21.1	Italy	4.6[g]
Import partners (% of imports)[g]	Spain	15.7	France	13.2	China	9.1

Social indicators	2005	2010	2018
Population growth rate (average annual %)[i]	1.1	1.2	1.4[b]
Urban population (% of total population)	55.2	58.0	62.5
Urban population growth rate (average annual %)[i]	1.8	2.2	2.4[b]
Fertility rate, total (live births per woman)[i]	2.7	2.6	2.6[b]
Life expectancy at birth (females/males, years)[i]	71.4 / 68.5	74.4 / 71.3	76.0 / 73.7[b]
Population age distribution (0-14/60+ years old, %)	30.8 / 8.2	28.5 / 8.6	27.2 / 11.0[a]
International migrant stock (000/% of total pop.)[j]	54.4 / 0.2	70.9 / 0.2	95.8 / 0.3[d]
Refugees and others of concern to the UNHCR (000)	2.1[k]	1.1[k]	7.1[d]
Infant mortality rate (per 1 000 live births)[i]	36.6	33.2	28.1[b]
Health: Current expenditure (% of GDP)	4.8	5.9	5.5[b]
Health: Physicians (per 1 000 pop.)	0.5[l]	0.7[m]	0.6[n]
Education: Government expenditure (% of GDP)	...	5.3[m]	...
Education: Primary gross enrol. ratio (f/m per 100 pop.)	100.5 / 110.8	106.2 / 112.8	107.3 / 113.0[f]
Education: Secondary gross enrol. ratio (f/m per 100 pop.)	46.0 / 54.0	58.8 / 67.5	64.1 / 75.0[o]
Education: Tertiary gross enrol. ratio (f/m per 100 pop.)	10.5 / 13.0	13.7 / 15.2	30.7 / 33.2[f]
Intentional homicide rate (per 100 000 pop.)	1.5	1.4	1.2[b]
Seats held by women in the National Parliament (%)	10.8	10.5	20.5

Environment and infrastructure indicators	2005	2010	2018
Individuals using the Internet (per 100 inhabitants)	15.1[p,q]	52.0[g,r,s]	58.3[f]
Research & Development expenditure (% of GDP)	0.6[t]	0.7	...
Threatened species (number)	50[l]	157	207[d]
Forested area (% of land area)[g]	12.1	12.7	12.6[b]
CO2 emission estimates (million tons/tons per capita)	45.8 / 1.5	56.0 / 1.7	59.9 / 1.7[n]
Energy production, primary (Petajoules)	72	81	59[b]
Energy supply per capita (Gigajoules)	20	23	23[b]
Tourist/visitor arrivals at national borders (000)[u]	5 843	9 288	10 332[f]
Important sites for terrestrial biodiversity protected (%)	13.3	14.7	43.0
Pop. using improved drinking water (urban/rural, %)	96.9 / 61.0	98.1 / 63.7	98.7 / 65.3[b]
Pop. using improved sanitation facilities (urban/rural, %)	82.9 / 51.7	83.7 / 60.3	84.1 / 65.5[b]
Net Official Development Assist. received (% of GNI)	1.18	1.07	2.00[f]

a Projected estimate (medium fertility variant). b 2015. c Including Salé and Temara. d 2017. e Including Western Sahara. f 2016. g Estimate. h Calculated by the Statistics Division of the United Nations from national indices. i Data refers to a 5-year period preceding the reference year. j Refers to foreign citizens. k Data as at the end of December. l 2004. m 2009. n 2014. o 2012. p Population aged 12 to 65 years. q Users in the last month. r Living in electrified areas. s Population aged 6 to 74 years. t 2003. u Including nationals residing abroad.

Mozambique

Region	Eastern Africa	UN membership date	16 September 1975
Population (000, 2018)	30 529[a]	Surface area (km2)	799 380[b]
Pop. density (per km2, 2018)	38.8[a]	Sex ratio (m per 100 f)	95.6[a]
Capital city	Maputo	National currency	Mozambique Metical (MZN)
Capital city pop. (000, 2018)	1 101.8	Exchange rate (per US$)	59.0[c]

Economic indicators

	2005	2010	2018
GDP: Gross domestic product (million current US$)	7 724	10 154	10 930[d]
GDP growth rate (annual %, const. 2010 prices)	8.7	6.7	3.8[d]
GDP per capita (current US$)	369.0	419.0	379.0[d]
Economy: Agriculture (% of Gross Value Added)[e]	25.4	28.9	24.1[d]
Economy: Industry (% of Gross Value Added)[e]	20.7	18.6	21.1[d]
Economy: Services and other activity (% of GVA)[e]	53.8	52.5	54.8[d]
Employment in agriculture (% of employed)[f]	79.3	77.2	73.1
Employment in industry (% of employed)[f]	3.3	3.4	4.4
Employment in services & other sectors (% employed)[f]	17.4	19.3	22.5
Unemployment rate (% of labour force)[f]	21.7	22.2	24.9
Labour force participation rate (female/male pop. %)[f]	87.1 / 82.9	84.4 / 78.8	82.3 / 74.6
CPI: Consumer Price Index (2010=100)[g]	...	100	171[c]
Agricultural production index (2004-2006=100)	96	146	149[d]
International trade: exports (million current US$)	1 745	2 243	3 296[f,c]
International trade: imports (million current US$)	2 408	3 564	3 352[f,c]
International trade: balance (million current US$)	- 663	- 1 321	- 57[f,c]
Balance of payments, current account (million US$)	- 761	- 1 679	- 2 558[c]

Major trading partners

							2017
Export partners (% of exports)[f]	South Africa	21.0	Netherlands	20.9	India	20.2
Import partners (% of imports)[f]	South Africa	30.0	Singapore	8.1	China	7.9

Social indicators

	2005	2010	2018
Population growth rate (average annual %)[h]	2.9	2.9	2.9[b]
Urban population (% of total population)	30.0	31.8	36.0
Urban population growth rate (average annual %)[h]	3.5	4.1	4.5[b]
Fertility rate, total (live births per woman)[h]	5.8	5.6	5.4[b]
Life expectancy at birth (females/males, years)[h]	51.2 / 47.9	55.0 / 51.4	58.1 / 54.0[b]
Population age distribution (0-14/60+ years old, %)	45.6 / 4.8	45.7 / 4.8	44.5 / 4.8[a]
International migrant stock (000/% of total pop.)[i]	204.8 / 1.0	214.6 / 0.9	247.0 / 0.8[c]
Refugees and others of concern to the UNHCR (000)	6.0[j]	10.0[j]	42.7[c]
Infant mortality rate (per 1 000 live births)[h]	94.3	78.1	67.3[b]
Health: Current expenditure (% of GDP)[k]	6.4	5.1	5.4[b]
Health: Physicians (per 1 000 pop.)	~0.0[l]	~0.0	0.1[m]
Education: Government expenditure (% of GDP)	4.4	4.3[n]	6.5[m]
Education: Primary gross enrol. ratio (f/m per 100 pop.)	88.9 / 105.7	104.2 / 116.0	101.7 / 110.9[f,b]
Education: Secondary gross enrol. ratio (f/m per 100 pop.)	10.8 / 15.6	22.0 / 27.0	31.5 / 34.3[f,b]
Education: Tertiary gross enrol. ratio (f/m per 100 pop.)	0.9 / 1.9	3.6 / 5.6	6.2 / 7.9[d]
Intentional homicide rate (per 100 000 pop.)	5.2	3.6	3.4[o]
Seats held by women in the National Parliament (%)	34.8	39.2	39.6

Environment and infrastructure indicators

	2005	2010	2018
Individuals using the Internet (per 100 inhabitants)	0.9[f]	4.2	17.5[f,d]
Research & Development expenditure (% of GDP)	0.4[p,q,r]	0.4[s,t]	0.3[b]
Threatened species (number)	115[l]	209	309[c]
Forested area (% of land area)	51.0	49.6	48.2[b]
CO2 emission estimates (million tons/tons per capita)	1.8 / 0.1	2.7 / 0.1	8.4 / 0.3[u]
Energy production, primary (Petajoules)	429	517	810[b]
Energy supply per capita (Gigajoules)	18	17	19[b]
Tourist/visitor arrivals at national borders (000)	578[v]	1 718[w]	1 639[w,d]
Important sites for terrestrial biodiversity protected (%)	19.0	19.0	31.3
Pop. using improved drinking water (urban/rural, %)	77.0 / 31.0	79.2 / 34.8	80.6 / 37.0[b]
Pop. using improved sanitation facilities (urban/rural, %)	39.0 / 6.8	41.1 / 8.9	42.4 / 10.1[b]
Net Official Development Assist. received (% of GNI)	17.52	19.80	14.23[d]

a Projected estimate (medium fertility variant). b 2015. c 2017. d 2016. e Data classified according to ISIC Rev. 4. f Estimate. g Calculated by the Statistics Division of the United Nations from national indices. h Data refers to a 5-year period preceding the reference year. i Including refugees. j Data as at the end of December. k Data revision. l 2004. m 2013. n 2006. o 2011. p S&T budget instead of R&D expenditure. q Overestimated or based on overestimated data. r 2002. s Break in the time series. t Excluding business enterprise. u 2014. v The data correspond only to 12 border posts. w The data of all the border posts of the country are used.

Myanmar

Region	South-eastern Asia	UN membership date	19 April 1948
Population (000, 2018)	53 856[a]	Surface area (km2)	676 577[b]
Pop. density (per km2, 2018)	82.4[a]	Sex ratio (m per 100 f)	95.5[a]
Capital city	Nay Pyi Taw	National currency	Kyat (MMK)
Capital city pop. (000, 2018)	500.2	Exchange rate (per US$)	1 362.0[c]

Economic indicators	2005	2010	2018
GDP: Gross domestic product (million current US$)	11 931	41 445	65 698[d]
GDP growth rate (annual %, const. 2010 prices)	13.6	10.2	5.7[d]
GDP per capita (current US$)	246.0	826.0	1 242.0[d]
Economy: Agriculture (% of Gross Value Added)[e]	46.7	36.9	25.3[d]
Economy: Industry (% of Gross Value Added)[e]	17.5	26.5	34.9[d]
Economy: Services and other activity (% of GVA)[e]	35.8	36.7	39.8[d]
Employment in agriculture (% of employed)[f]	69.5	60.6	48.3
Employment in industry (% of employed)[f]	11.7	15.0	16.9
Employment in services & other sectors (% employed)[f]	18.8	24.4	34.8
Unemployment rate (% of labour force)[f]	0.9	0.8	0.8
Labour force participation rate (female/male pop. %)[f]	56.1 / 83.9	53.5 / 82.3	51.1 / 79.6
CPI: Consumer Price Index (2010=100)	45	100	145[c]
Agricultural production index (2004-2006=100)	99	135	137[d]
International trade: exports (million current US$)	3 776[f]	7 625	13 879[c]
International trade: imports (million current US$)	1 907[f]	4 164	19 253[c]
International trade: balance (million current US$)	1 869[f]	3 461	- 5 375[c]
Balance of payments, current account (million US$)	582	1 574	- 3 945[c]

Major trading partners						2017
Export partners (% of exports)	China	38.9	Thailand	19.4	Japan	6.5
Import partners (% of imports)	China	31.8	Singapore	15.2	Thailand	11.3

Social indicators	2005	2010	2018
Population growth rate (average annual %)[g]	1.0	0.7	0.9[b]
Urban population (% of total population)	27.9	28.9	30.6
Urban population growth rate (average annual %)[g]	1.7	1.3	1.5[b]
Fertility rate, total (live births per woman)[g]	2.9	2.6	2.3[b]
Life expectancy at birth (females/males, years)[g]	65.0 / 60.9	66.3 / 62.2	68.3 / 63.7[b]
Population age distribution (0-14/60+ years old, %)	30.9 / 7.0	30.0 / 7.5	26.3 / 9.7[a]
International migrant stock (000/% of total pop.)[h]	83.0 / 0.2	76.4 / 0.2	74.7 / 0.1[c]
Refugees and others of concern to the UNHCR (000)	236.5[i]	859.4[i]	1 277.8[c]
Infant mortality rate (per 1 000 live births)[g]	57.9	52.2	45.0[b]
Health: Current expenditure (% of GDP)[j,k,l]	1.8	1.9	4.9[b]
Health: Physicians (per 1 000 pop.)	0.4	0.5	0.6[m]
Education: Government expenditure (% of GDP)	...	...	2.2[c]
Education: Primary gross enrol. ratio (f/m per 100 pop.)	101.2 / 101.0	98.3 / 99.1	109.9 / 113.3[c]
Education: Secondary gross enrol. ratio (f/m per 100 pop.)	44.7 / 46.1	50.7 / 48.3	63.4 / 57.7[c]
Education: Tertiary gross enrol. ratio (f/m per 100 pop.)	... / ...	12.5 / 9.1[n]	19.0 / 13.0[c]
Intentional homicide rate (per 100 000 pop.)	1.4	1.6	2.3[d]
Seats held by women in the National Parliament (%)	...	...	10.2

Environment and infrastructure indicators	2005	2010	2018
Individuals using the Internet (per 100 inhabitants)	0.1	0.2	25.1[f,d]
Research & Development expenditure (% of GDP)	0.2[o,p]	...	...
Threatened species (number)	147[q]	249	321[c]
Forested area (% of land area)	51.0	48.6	44.5[f,b]
CO2 emission estimates (million tons/tons per capita)	11.6 / 0.3	12.5 / 0.3	21.6 / 0.4[f]
Energy production, primary (Petajoules)	927	969	1 141[b]
Energy supply per capita (Gigajoules)	13	13	16[b]
Tourist/visitor arrivals at national borders (000)	660	792	2 907[s,d]
Important sites for terrestrial biodiversity protected (%)	22.5	22.5	22.9
Pop. using improved drinking water (urban/rural, %)	88.0 / 66.0	91.4 / 72.0	92.7 / 74.4[b]
Pop. using improved sanitation facilities (urban/rural, %)	81.0 / 64.6	83.4 / 73.5	84.3 / 77.1[b]
Net Official Development Assist. received (% of GNI)	1.21	0.72	1.99[b]

a Projected estimate (medium fertility variant). b 2015. c 2017. d 2016. e At producers' prices. f Estimate. g Data refers to a 5-year period preceding the reference year. h Refers to foreign citizens. i Data as at the end of December. j Data refer to fiscal years beginning 1 April. k Data revision. l Country is still reporting data based on SHA1.0. m 2012. n 2007. o Partial data. p 2002. q 2004. r 2014. s Break in the time series.

Namibia

Region	Southern Africa	UN membership date	23 April 1990
Population (000, 2018)	2 588[a]	Surface area (km2)	824 116[b]
Pop. density (per km2, 2018)	3.1[a]	Sex ratio (m per 100 f)	94.8[a]
Capital city	Windhoek	National currency	Namibia Dollar (NAD)
Capital city pop. (000, 2018)	404.3	Exchange rate (per US$)	12.4[c]

Economic indicators

	2005	2010	2018
GDP: Gross domestic product (million current US$)	7 121	11 282	10 947[d]
GDP growth rate (annual %, const. 2010 prices)	2.5	6.0	1.1[d]
GDP per capita (current US$)	3 504.0	5 192.0	4 415.0[d]
Economy: Agriculture (% of Gross Value Added)	11.4	9.2	6.8[d]
Economy: Industry (% of Gross Value Added)	27.3	29.8	30.9[d]
Economy: Services and other activity (% of GVA)	61.3	61.1	62.3[d]
Employment in agriculture (% of employed)[e]	26.8	31.7	20.1
Employment in industry (% of employed)[e]	15.3	12.7	19.7
Employment in services & other sectors (% employed)[e]	57.9	55.6	60.2
Unemployment rate (% of labour force)	22.2[e]	22.1	23.3[e]
Labour force participation rate (female/male pop. %)[e]	52.0 / 64.4	54.6 / 63.8	59.0 / 65.6
CPI: Consumer Price Index (2010=100)[f]	71	100	146[c]
Agricultural production index (2004-2006=100)	104	90	93[d]
Index of industrial production (2005=100)[g]	100	116	127[h]
International trade: exports (million current US$)	2 726	5 848	5 573[e,c]
International trade: imports (million current US$)	2 525	5 980	8 101[e,c]
International trade: balance (million current US$)	201	- 131	- 2 529[e,c]
Balance of payments, current account (million US$)	333	- 534	- 296[c]

Major trading partners

						2017
Export partners (% of exports)	Switzerland	18.8[e]	South Africa	16.0	Botswana	14.1[e]
Import partners (% of imports)[e]	South Africa	57.2	Botswana	6.8	Zambia	4.1

Social indicators

	2005	2010	2018
Population growth rate (average annual %)[i]	1.4	1.3	2.2[b]
Urban population (% of total population)	36.6	41.6	50.0
Urban population growth rate (average annual %)[i]	3.8	3.9	4.6[b]
Fertility rate, total (live births per woman)[i]	3.8	3.6	3.6[b]
Life expectancy at birth (females/males, years)[i]	55.9 / 51.7	56.6 / 53.3	64.3 / 59.1[b]
Population age distribution (0-14/60+ years old, %)	39.8 / 5.0	38.4 / 5.2	36.5 / 5.6[a]
International migrant stock (000/% of total pop.)	106.3 / 5.2	102.4 / 4.7	95.1 / 3.8[c]
Refugees and others of concern to the UNHCR (000)	9.1[j]	8.8[j]	3.9[c]
Infant mortality rate (per 1 000 live births)[i]	59.4	46.6	36.4[b]
Health: Current expenditure (% of GDP)	12.4	9.5	8.9[b]
Health: Physicians (per 1 000 pop.)	0.3[k]	0.4[l]	...
Education: Government expenditure (% of GDP)	6.1[m]	8.3	...
Education: Primary gross enrol. ratio (f/m per 100 pop.)	108.2 / 109.5	105.8 / 109.2	109.1 / 113.5[h]
Education: Secondary gross enrol. ratio (f/m per 100 pop.)	66.9 / 59.9	69.0 / 60.1[l]	... / ...
Education: Tertiary gross enrol. ratio (f/m per 100 pop.)	6.3 / 7.4	10.4 / 8.2[n]	... / ...
Intentional homicide rate (per 100 000 pop.)	17.5[k]	14.4	17.1[o]
Seats held by women in the National Parliament (%)	25.0	26.9[p]	46.2

Environment and infrastructure indicators

	2005	2010	2018
Individuals using the Internet (per 100 inhabitants)	4.0[e]	11.6	31.0[e,d]
Research & Development expenditure (% of GDP)[q]	...	0.1[r]	0.3[s]
Threatened species (number)	69[k]	92	115[c]
Forested area (% of land area)[e]	9.3	8.9	8.4[b]
CO2 emission estimates (million tons/tons per capita)	2.3 / 1.1	3.1 / 1.4	3.8 / 1.6[s]
Energy production, primary (Petajoules)	17	17	20[b]
Energy supply per capita (Gigajoules)	26	30	31[b]
Tourist/visitor arrivals at national borders (000)	778	984	1 469[d]
Important sites for terrestrial biodiversity protected (%)	44.6	82.4	85.4
Pop. using improved drinking water (urban/rural, %)	98.4 / 74.2	98.3 / 79.4	98.2 / 84.6[b]
Pop. using improved sanitation facilities (urban/rural, %)	57.1 / 14.0	55.8 / 15.4	54.5 / 16.8[b]
Net Official Development Assist. received (% of GNI)	1.59	2.41	1.66[d]

a Projected estimate (medium fertility variant). b 2015. c 2017. d 2016. e Estimate. f Calculated by the Statistics Division of the United Nations from national indices. g Data classified according to ISIC Rev. 3. h 2013. i Data refers to a 5-year period preceding the reference year. j Data as at the end of December. k 2004. l 2007. m 2003. n 2008. o 2012. p Figure excludes 11 members yet to be sworn in. q Partial data. r Excluding government. s 2014.

Nauru

Region	Micronesia	
Population (000, 2018)	11 [a]	
Pop. density (per km2, 2018)	565.6 [a]	
Capital city	Yaren	
Capital city pop. (000, 2018)	11.3 [e]	

UN membership date	14 September 1999	
Surface area (km2)	21 [b]	
Sex ratio (m per 100 f)	101.9 [c,d]	
National currency	Australian Dollar (AUD)	
Exchange rate (per US$)	1.3 [f]	

Economic indicators	2005	2010	2018
GDP: Gross domestic product (million current US$)	26	62	103 [d]
GDP growth rate (annual %, const. 2010 prices)	- 12.1	20.1	10.4 [d]
GDP per capita (current US$)	2 600.0	6 234.0	9 119.0 [d]
Economy: Agriculture (% of Gross Value Added) [g]	7.8	4.3	3.2 [d]
Economy: Industry (% of Gross Value Added) [g]	- 6.5	48.0	58.5 [d]
Economy: Services and other activity (% of GVA) [g]	98.7	47.7	38.3 [d]
Unemployment rate (% of labour force)	22.7 [h,i]		23.0 [c,j]
Labour force participation rate (female/male pop. %)	69.6 / 86.8 [h,i]	... / ...	49.3 / 78.9 [j]
Agricultural production index (2004-2006=100)	100	106	114 [d]

Social indicators	2005	2010	2018
Population growth rate (average annual %) [k]	0.1	- 0.2	2.3 [b]
Urban population (% of total population)	100.0	100.0	100.0
Urban population growth rate (average annual %) [k]	0.2	- 0.2	2.3 [b]
Fertility rate, total (live births per woman)	...	...	3.9 [l,m]
Life expectancy at birth (females/males, years)	64.0 / 57.0 [n]	58.2 / 52.5 [o,p]	64.8 / 57.8 [c,l,m]
Population age distribution (0-14/60+ years old, %)	38.1 / 2.5 [i]	... / ...	39.5 / 4.0 [c,d]
International migrant stock (000/% of total pop.) [q]	2.3 / 22.3	2.1 / 21.1	3.7 / 32.7 [f]
Refugees and others of concern to the UNHCR (000)	...	...	0.8 [f]
Infant mortality rate (per 1 000 live births)	...	...	18.0 [l,m]
Health: Current expenditure (% of GDP) [r,s,t]	12.6	10.7	4.8 [b]
Health: Physicians (per 1 000 pop.)	1.0 [u]	1.0	1.4 [l]
Education: Primary gross enrol. ratio (f/m per 100 pop.) [v]	128.5 / 122.3	96.0 / 90.1 [w]	108.5 / 105.7 [d]
Education: Secondary gross enrol. ratio (f/m per 100 pop.) [v]	50.3 / 44.4	68.9 / 57.6 [w]	79.0 / 76.5 [d]
Intentional homicide rate (per 100 000 pop.)	...	...	0.0 [x]
Seats held by women in the National Parliament (%)	0.0	0.0	10.5

Environment and infrastructure indicators	2005	2010	2018
Individuals using the Internet (per 100 inhabitants)	...	...	54.0 [l]
Threatened species (number)	5 [u]	74	82 [f]
Forested area (% of land area) [v]	0.0	0.0	0.0 [b]
CO2 emission estimates (million tons/tons per capita)	0.1 / 6.1	~0.0 / 4.3	~0.0 / 4.8 [y]
Energy production, primary (Petajoules) [v]	...	0	0 [b]
Energy supply per capita (Gigajoules)	84 [v]	58	65 [v,b]
Important sites for terrestrial biodiversity protected (%)	0.0	0.0	0.0
Pop. using improved drinking water (urban/rural, %)	94.4 / ...	95.7 / ...	96.5 / ... [b]
Pop. using improved sanitation facilities (urban/rural, %)	65.7 / ...	65.6 / ...	65.6 / ... [b]
Net Official Development Assist. received (% of GNI)	...	48.74	17.72 [d]

a Projected estimate (medium fertility variant). b 2015. c Break in the time series. d 2016. e Refers to Nauru. f 2017. g At producers' prices. h Population aged 16 years and over. i 2002. j 2011. k Data refers to a 5-year period preceding the reference year. l Data refers to a 3-year period up to and including the reference year. m 2013. n 2000. o Data refers to a 6-year period up to and including the reference year. p 2007. q Refers to foreign citizens. r Data refer to fiscal years beginning 1 July. s General government expenditure (GGE) can be larger than the Gross domestic product (GDP) because government accounts for a very large part of domestic consumption and because a large part of domestic consumption in the country is accounted for by imports. t Indicators are sensitive to external funds flowing in to the country. u 2004. v Estimate. w 2008. x 2012. y 2014.

Nepal

Region	Southern Asia	UN membership date	14 December 1955
Population (000, 2018)	29 624[a]	Surface area (km2)	147 181[b]
Pop. density (per km2, 2018)	206.7[a]	Sex ratio (m per 100 f)	94.5[a]
Capital city	Kathmandu	National currency	Nepalese Rupee (NPR)
Capital city pop. (000, 2018)	1 329.7[c]	Exchange rate (per US$)	103.0[d]

Economic indicators

	2005	2010	2018
GDP: Gross domestic product (million current US$)	8 259	16 281	20 914[e]
GDP growth rate (annual %, const. 2010 prices)	3.1	4.8	0.4[e]
GDP per capita (current US$)	322.0	602.0	722.0[e]
Economy: Agriculture (% of Gross Value Added)	35.2	35.4	31.6[e]
Economy: Industry (% of Gross Value Added)	17.1	15.1	14.2[e]
Economy: Services and other activity (% of GVA)	47.7	49.5	54.2[e]
Employment in agriculture (% of employed)[f]	76.0	74.8	71.3
Employment in industry (% of employed)[f]	4.7	7.5	8.2
Employment in services & other sectors (% employed)[f]	19.3	17.7	20.5
Unemployment rate (% of labour force)[f]	1.5	2.1	2.7
Labour force participation rate (female/male pop. %)[f]	79.9 / 88.7	79.6 / 87.1	82.7 / 85.8
CPI: Consumer Price Index (2010=100)	...	...	117[g,d]
Agricultural production index (2004-2006=100)	100	114	140[d]
International trade: exports (million current US$)	863[f]	874	741[d]
International trade: imports (million current US$)	2 282[f]	5 116	10 038[d]
International trade: balance (million current US$)	- 1 419[f]	- 4 242	- 9 297[d]
Balance of payments, current account (million US$)	153	- 128	- 815[d]

Major trading partners

							2017
Export partners (% of exports)	India	56.7	United States	11.2	Turkey	6.4
Import partners (% of imports)	India	65.0	China	12.6	Areas nes[h]	2.0

Social indicators

	2005	2010	2018
Population growth rate (average annual %)[i]	1.5	1.1	1.2[b]
Urban population (% of total population)	15.1	16.8	19.7
Urban population growth rate (average annual %)[i]	4.0	3.1	3.2[b]
Fertility rate, total (live births per woman)[i]	3.6	3.0	2.3[b]
Life expectancy at birth (females/males, years)[i]	65.2 / 62.9	68.1 / 65.5	70.4 / 67.4[b]
Population age distribution (0-14/60+ years old, %)	39.7 / 6.7	37.0 / 7.4	30.2 / 8.8[a]
International migrant stock (000/% of total pop.)[j]	679.5 / 2.6	578.7 / 2.1	502.7 / 1.7[d]
Refugees and others of concern to the UNHCR (000)	538.6[k]	891.3[k]	24.4[d]
Infant mortality rate (per 1 000 live births)[i]	52.9	41.3	32.8[b]
Health: Current expenditure (% of GDP)[l]	4.5	5.0	6.1[b]
Health: Physicians (per 1 000 pop.)	0.2[m]		0.6[n]
Education: Government expenditure (% of GDP)	3.4	3.6	3.7[b]
Education: Primary gross enrol. ratio (f/m per 100 pop.)	110.2 / 120.4	146.9 / 137.6	138.4 / 130.1[d]
Education: Secondary gross enrol. ratio (f/m per 100 pop.)[f]	43.5 / 53.5	57.4 / 60.3	75.0 / 67.6[d]
Education: Tertiary gross enrol. ratio (f/m per 100 pop.)	5.6 / 10.3	11.0 / 17.9	12.2 / 11.4[e]
Intentional homicide rate (per 100 000 pop.)	3.4	3.0	2.2[e]
Seats held by women in the National Parliament (%)	5.9[o]	33.2	3.6[p]

Environment and infrastructure indicators

	2005	2010	2018
Individuals using the Internet (per 100 inhabitants)	0.8	7.9[q]	19.7[f,e]
Research & Development expenditure (% of GDP)	...	0.3[r,s]	...
Threatened species (number)	77[m]	93	104[d]
Forested area (% of land area)	25.4	25.4	25.4[b]
CO2 emission estimates (million tons/tons per capita)	3.1 / 0.1	5.1 / 0.2	8.0 / 0.3[h]
Energy production, primary (Petajoules)	349	384	430[b]
Energy supply per capita (Gigajoules)	14	17	18[b]
Tourist/visitor arrivals at national borders (000)[t]	375	603	753[e]
Important sites for terrestrial biodiversity protected (%)	50.3	54.6	54.6
Pop. using improved drinking water (urban/rural, %)	93.1 / 80.2	92.0 / 86.0	90.9 / 91.8[b]
Pop. using improved sanitation facilities (urban/rural, %)	47.8 / 26.7	51.9 / 35.1	56.0 / 43.5[b]
Net Official Development Assist. received (% of GNI)	5.19	5.05	4.94[e]

a Projected estimate (medium fertility variant). **b** 2015. **c** Refers to the municipality. **d** 2017. **e** 2016. **f** Estimate. **g** Index base: 2014/2015=100. **h** Areas not elsewhere specified. **i** Data refers to a 5-year period preceding the reference year. **j** Including refugees. **k** Data as at the end of December. **l** Data refer to fiscal years ending 15 July. **m** 2004. **n** 2014. **o** 2000. **p** Provisional data, **q** December. **r** Partial data. **s** R&D budget instead of R&D expenditure or based on R&D budget. **t** Including arrivals from India.

Netherlands

Region	Western Europe	UN membership date	10 December 1945
Population (000, 2018)	17 084[a]	Surface area (km2)	41 542[b]
Pop. density (per km2, 2018)	506.7[a]	Sex ratio (m per 100 f)	99.1[a]
Capital city	Amsterdam[c]	National currency	Euro (EUR)
Capital city pop. (000, 2018)	1 131.7	Exchange rate (per US$)	0.8[d]

Economic indicators	2005	2010	2018
GDP: Gross domestic product (million current US$)	678 517	836 390	777 228[a]
GDP growth rate (annual %, const. 2010 prices)	2.2	1.4	2.2[e]
GDP per capita (current US$)	41 456.0	50 135.0	45 753.0[e]
Economy: Agriculture (% of Gross Value Added)[f]	2.0	1.9	1.8[e]
Economy: Industry (% of Gross Value Added)[f]	24.0	22.1	20.0[e]
Economy: Services and other activity (% of GVA)[f]	74.0	76.0	78.2[e]
Employment in agriculture (% of employed)[g]	3.3	3.1	2.2[g]
Employment in industry (% of employed)[g]	20.5	17.6	16.4
Employment in services & other sectors (% employed)[g]	76.1	79.3	81.5
Unemployment rate (% of labour force)	4.7	4.4	4.3[g]
Labour force participation rate (female/male pop. %)[g]	56.6 / 72.3	58.2 / 71.3	57.9 / 68.9
CPI: Consumer Price Index (2010=100)	93	100	111[d]
Agricultural production index (2004-2006=100)	100	112	118[e]
Index of industrial production (2005=100)	100	107	103[h]
International trade: exports (million current US$)	349 813	492 646	494 558[g,d]
International trade: imports (million current US$)	310 591	439 987	441 338[g,d]
International trade: balance (million current US$)	39 222	52 659	53 220[g,d]
Balance of payments, current account (million US$)	41 600	61 820	84 830[d]

Major trading partners						2017
Export partners (% of exports)[g]	Germany	22.2[g]	Belgium	10.3	United Kingdom	9.0[g]
Import partners (% of imports)[g]	Germany	18.2	Belgium	10.5	China	9.0

Social indicators	2005	2010	2018
Population growth rate (average annual %)[i]	0.5	0.4	0.3[b]
Urban population (% of total population)	82.6	87.1	91.5
Urban population growth rate (average annual %)[i]	2.0	1.4	1.0[b]
Fertility rate, total (live births per woman)[i]	1.7	1.7	1.7[b]
Life expectancy at birth (females/males, years)[i]	81.0 / 76.2	82.2 / 78.0	83.1 / 79.4[b]
Population age distribution (0-14/60+ years old, %)	18.3 / 19.3	17.5 / 22.0	16.2 / 25.5[a]
International migrant stock (000/% of total pop.)	1 736.1 / 10.6	1 832.5 / 11.0	2 056.5 / 12.1[d]
Refugees and others of concern to the UNHCR (000)[j]	139.7	90.1	114.1[e]
Infant mortality rate (per 1 000 live births)[i]	4.9	4.1	3.5[b]
Health: Current expenditure (% of GDP)	9.3	10.4	10.7[b]
Health: Physicians (per 1 000 pop.)	...	...	3.5[b]
Education: Government expenditure (% of GDP)	5.2	5.6	5.5[h]
Education: Primary gross enrol. ratio (f/m per 100 pop.)	105.5 / 107.9	108.1 / 108.5	103.3 / 103.3[e]
Education: Secondary gross enrol. ratio (f/m per 100 pop.)	117.2 / 119.5	121.2 / 122.9	133.8 / 131.6[e]
Education: Tertiary gross enrol. ratio (f/m per 100 pop.)	61.1 / 56.4	67.3 / 60.3	85.3 / 75.6[e]
Intentional homicide rate (per 100 000 pop.)	1.1	0.9	0.6[e]
Seats held by women in the National Parliament (%)	36.7	42.0	36.0

Environment and infrastructure indicators	2005	2010	2018
Individuals using the Internet (per 100 inhabitants)	81.0[k,l]	90.7[k,l]	90.4[m,e]
Research & Development expenditure (% of GDP)	1.8	1.7	2.0[n,b]
Threatened species (number)	34[o]	24	40[d]
Forested area (% of land area)	10.8	11.1	11.2[g,b]
CO2 emission estimates (million tons/tons per capita)	181.5 / 11.1	183.1 / 11.0	167.3 / 9.9[h]
Energy production, primary (Petajoules)	2 610	2 917	1 990[b]
Energy supply per capita (Gigajoules)	205	207	179[b]
Tourist/visitor arrivals at national borders (000)	10 012	10 883	15 828[e]
Important sites for terrestrial biodiversity protected (%)	91.3	91.4	91.4
Pop. using improved drinking water (urban/rural, %)	100.0 / 100.0	100.0 / 100.0	100.0 / 100.0[b]
Pop. using improved sanitation facilities (urban/rural, %)	97.5 / 99.9	97.5 / 99.9	97.5 / 99.9[b]
Net Official Development Assist. disbursed (% of GNI)[p]	0.82	0.81	0.60[n,d]

a Projected estimate (medium fertility variant). b 2015. c Amsterdam is the capital and The Hague is the seat of government. d 2017. e 2016. f Data classified according to ISIC Rev. 4. g Estimate. h 2014. i Data refers to a 5-year period preceding the reference year. j Data as at the end of December. k Users in the last 12 months. l Population aged 16 to 74 years. m Population aged 12 years and over. n Provisional data. o 2004. p Development Assistance Committee member (OECD).

New Caledonia

Region	Melanesia	Population (000, 2018)	280[a]
Surface area (km2)	18 575[b]	Pop. density (per km2, 2018)	15.3[a]
Sex ratio (m per 100 f)	101.4[a]	Capital city	Nouméa
National currency	CFP Franc (XPF)[c]	Capital city pop. (000, 2018)	197.8
Exchange rate (per US$)	99.5[d]		

Economic indicators	2005	2010	2018
GDP: Gross domestic product (million current US$)	6 236	9 355	9 446[e]
GDP growth rate (annual %, const. 2010 prices)	3.6	6.9	3.0[e]
GDP per capita (current US$)	26 801.0	37 266.0	34 641.0[e]
Economy: Agriculture (% of Gross Value Added)	1.7	1.4	1.4[e]
Economy: Industry (% of Gross Value Added)	26.6	25.5	26.2[e]
Economy: Services and other activity (% of GVA)	71.7	73.1	72.4[e]
Employment in agriculture (% of employed)[f]	4.6	4.0	3.4
Employment in industry (% of employed)[f]	31.8	33.1	31.7
Employment in services & other sectors (% employed)[f]	63.7	63.0	65.0
Unemployment rate (% of labour force)[f]	15.8	14.2	14.8
Labour force participation rate (female/male pop. %)[f]	60.5 / 70.6	58.1 / 68.2	57.3 / 67.9
CPI: Consumer Price Index (2010=100)[g]	...	100	107[e]
Agricultural production index (2004-2006=100)	100	98	105[e]
International trade: exports (million current US$)	1 114	1 268	1 460[f,d]
International trade: imports (million current US$)	1 774	3 303	2 515[f,d]
International trade: balance (million current US$)	- 660	- 2 036	- 1 055[f,d]
Balance of payments, current account (million US$)	- 112	- 1 360	- 654[e]

Major trading partners						2017
Export partners (% of exports)	China	35.7[f]	Japan	15.9	Republic of Korea	15.1[f]
Import partners (% of imports)[f]	France	25.7	China	10.2	Singapore	8.2

Social indicators	2005	2010	2018
Population growth rate (average annual %)[h]	1.8	1.5	1.4[b]
Urban population (% of total population)	64.0	67.1	70.7
Urban population growth rate (average annual %)[h]	2.4	2.5	2.1[b]
Fertility rate, total (live births per woman)[h]	2.3	2.3	2.2[b]
Life expectancy at birth (females/males, years)[h]	77.2 / 71.3	78.3 / 72.4	79.3 / 73.7[b]
Population age distribution (0-14/60+ years old, %)	27.5 / 10.3	24.1 / 13.1	22.3 / 14.5[a]
International migrant stock (000/% of total pop.)	55.4 / 23.8	61.2 / 24.4	66.0 / 23.9[d]
Infant mortality rate (per 1 000 live births)[h]	17.4	15.1	13.0[b]
Intentional homicide rate (per 100 000 pop.)	...	3.2[i]	...

Environment and infrastructure indicators	2005	2010	2018
Individuals using the Internet (per 100 inhabitants)	32.4	42.0[f]	74.0[f,b]
Threatened species (number)	262[j]	415	526[d]
Forested area (% of land area)[f]	45.9	45.9	45.9[b]
CO2 emission estimates (million tons/tons per capita)	2.8 / 12.2	3.5 / 14.4	4.3 / 16.5[k]
Energy production, primary (Petajoules)	1	1	2[b]
Energy supply per capita (Gigajoules)	161	192	240[b]
Tourist/visitor arrivals at national borders (000)[l]	101	99	116[e]
Important sites for terrestrial biodiversity protected (%)	15.5	66.1	66.4
Pop. using improved drinking water (urban/rural, %)	95.5 / 95.5	98.0 / 98.0	98.5 / 98.5[b]
Pop. using improved sanitation facilities (urban/rural, %)	100.0 / 100.0	100.0 / 100.0	100.0 / 100.0[b]

a Projected estimate (medium fertility variant). b 2015. c Communauté financière du Pacifique (CFP) Franc. d 2017. e 2016. f Estimate. g Calculated by the Statistics Division of the United Nations from national indices. h Data refers to a 5-year period preceding the reference year. i 2009. j 2004. k 2014. l Including nationals residing abroad.

New Zealand

Region	Oceania	UN membership date	24 October 1945
Population (000, 2018)	4 750 [a]	Surface area (km2)	268 107 [b]
Pop. density (per km2, 2018)	18.0 [a]	Sex ratio (m per 100 f)	96.7 [a]
Capital city	Wellington	National currency	New Zealand Dollar (NZD)
Capital city pop. (000, 2018)	411.3	Exchange rate (per US$)	1.4 [c]

Economic indicators	2005	2010	2018
GDP: Gross domestic product (million current US$)	114 722	146 584	187 517 [d]
GDP growth rate (annual %, const. 2010 prices)	3.3	1.0	3.0 [d]
GDP per capita (current US$)	27 742.0	33 543.0	40 233.0 [d]
Economy: Agriculture (% of Gross Value Added) [e]	4.9	7.1	6.0 [d]
Economy: Industry (% of Gross Value Added) [e]	25.8	23.0	23.0 [d]
Economy: Services and other activity (% of GVA) [e]	69.3	69.9	71.1 [d]
Employment in agriculture (% of employed) [f]	7.2	6.9	6.5
Employment in industry (% of employed) [f]	22.2	21.0	20.1
Employment in services & other sectors (% employed) [f]	70.6	72.2	73.4
Unemployment rate (% of labour force)	3.8	6.1	5.0 [f]
Labour force participation rate (female/male pop. %) [f]	60.1 / 74.7	61.0 / 73.8	63.8 / 74.7
CPI: Consumer Price Index (2010=100) [g]	87	100	111 [c]
Agricultural production index (2004-2006=100)	99	104	117 [d]
Index of industrial production (2005=100) [h]	100	96	97 [i]
International trade: exports (million current US$)	21 729	30 932	38 050 [c]
International trade: imports (million current US$)	26 232	30 158	40 128 [c]
International trade: balance (million current US$)	- 4 504	774	- 2 078 [c]
Balance of payments, current account (million US$)	- 8 025	- 3 429	- 5 540 [c]

Major trading partners						2017
Export partners (% of exports)	China	22.3	Australia	16.4	United States	9.9
Import partners (% of imports)	China	19.3	Australia	12.2	United States	10.7

Social indicators	2005	2010	2018
Population growth rate (average annual %) [j]	1.4	1.1	1.1 [b]
Urban population (% of total population)	86.3	86.2	86.5
Urban population growth rate (average annual %) [j]	1.5	1.1	1.1 [b]
Fertility rate, total (live births per woman) [j]	1.9	2.1	2.0 [b]
Life expectancy at birth (females/males, years) [j]	81.3 / 76.8	82.3 / 78.3	83.1 / 79.5 [b]
Population age distribution (0-14/60+ years old, %)	21.5 / 16.4	20.5 / 18.4	19.8 / 21.3 [a]
International migrant stock (000/% of total pop.)	840.0 / 20.3	947.4 / 21.7	1 067.4 / 22.7 [c]
Refugees and others of concern to the UNHCR (000)	5.7 [k]	2.5 [k]	1.8 [c]
Infant mortality rate (per 1 000 live births) [j]	5.4	5.0	4.4 [b]
Health: Current expenditure (% of GDP)	8.3	9.7	9.3 [b]
Health: Physicians (per 1 000 pop.)	2.1 [l]	2.6	3.1 [b]
Education: Government expenditure (% of GDP)	6.3	7.0	6.3 [b]
Education: Primary gross enrol. ratio (f/m per 100 pop.)	99.3 / 100.1	101.3 / 101.0	99.2 / 98.5 [d]
Education: Secondary gross enrol. ratio (f/m per 100 pop.)	123.6 / 117.1	121.8 / 116.4	117.8 / 111.0 [d]
Education: Tertiary gross enrol. ratio (f/m per 100 pop.)	... / ...	98.7 / 67.4	96.4 / 68.2 [d]
Intentional homicide rate (per 100 000 pop.)	1.5 [m]	1.0	1.0 [i]
Seats held by women in the National Parliament (%)	28.3	33.6	38.3

Environment and infrastructure indicators	2005	2010	2018
Individuals using the Internet (per 100 inhabitants) [f]	62.7	80.5	88.5 [d]
Research & Development expenditure (% of GDP)	1.1	1.3 [n]	1.2 [o]
Threatened species (number)	149 [p]	153	199 [c]
Forested area (% of land area)	38.7	38.6	38.6 [f,b]
CO2 emission estimates (million tons/tons per capita)	34.1 / 8.3	31.8 / 7.3	34.7 / 7.7 [i]
Energy production, primary (Petajoules)	572	770	775 [b]
Energy supply per capita (Gigajoules)	181	191	209 [b]
Tourist/visitor arrivals at national borders (000)	2 353	2 435	3 370 [d]
Important sites for terrestrial biodiversity protected (%)	42.5	44.0	44.3
Pop. using improved drinking water (urban/rural, %)	100.0 / 100.0	100.0 / 100.0	100.0 / 100.0 [b]
Net Official Development Assist. disbursed (% of GNI) [q]	0.27	0.26	0.23 [r,c]

a Projected estimate (medium fertility variant). **b** 2015. **c** 2017. **d** 2016. **e** Data classified according to ISIC Rev. 4. **f** Estimate. **g** Calculated by the Statistics Division of the United Nations from national indices. **h** Twelve months ending 31 March of the year stated. **i** 2002. **j** Data refers to a 5-year period preceding the reference year. **k** Data as at the end of December. **l** 2002. **m** Data refer to offences, not victims, of intentional homicide. **n** 2009. **o** 2013. **p** 2004. **q** Development Assistance Committee member (OECD). **r** Provisional data.

Nicaragua

Region	Central America	UN membership date	24 October 1945
Population (000, 2018)	6 285[a]	Surface area (km2)	130 373[b]
Pop. density (per km2, 2018)	52.2[a]	Sex ratio (m per 100 f)	97.3[a]
Capital city	Managua	National currency	Cordoba Oro (NIO)
Capital city pop. (000, 2018)	1 047.9	Exchange rate (per US$)	30.8[c]

Economic indicators

	2005	2010	2018
GDP: Gross domestic product (million current US$)	6 300	8 759	13 230[d]
GDP growth rate (annual %, const. 2010 prices)	4.3	4.4	4.7[d]
GDP per capita (current US$)	1 171.0	1 526.0	2 151.0[d]
Economy: Agriculture (% of Gross Value Added)	17.8	18.7	17.3[d]
Economy: Industry (% of Gross Value Added)	22.9	24.2	26.8[d]
Economy: Services and other activity (% of GVA)	59.3	57.0	55.9[d]
Employment in agriculture (% of employed)[e]	28.9	32.2	28.8
Employment in industry (% of employed)[e]	19.7	16.5	17.7
Employment in services & other sectors (% employed)[e]	51.4	51.3	53.5
Unemployment rate (% of labour force)	5.6	7.8	4.4[e]
Labour force participation rate (female/male pop. %)[e]	44.1 / 82.1	47.1 / 82.9	50.6 / 83.9
CPI: Consumer Price Index (2010=100)	63.	100	147[c]
Agricultural production index (2004-2006=100)	104	118	132[c]
International trade: exports (million current US$)	866	1 848	4 926[c]
International trade: imports (million current US$)	2 536	4 191	7 704[c]
International trade: balance (million current US$)	- 1 670	- 2 343	- 2 778[c]
Balance of payments, current account (million US$)	-784[f]	- 780	- 694[c]

Major trading partners

						2017
Export partners (% of exports)	United States	58.6	Mexico	6.6	El Salvador	5.6
Import partners (% of imports)	United States	23.5	China	15.2	Mexico	11.0

Social indicators

	2005	2010	2018
Population growth rate (average annual %)[g]	1.4	1.3	1.2[b]
Urban population (% of total population)	55.9	56.9	58.5
Urban population growth rate (average annual %)[g]	1.6	1.6	1.5[b]
Fertility rate, total (live births per woman)[g]	2.8	2.6	2.3[b]
Life expectancy at birth (females/males, years)[g]	73.8 / 68.0	75.8 / 69.8	77.5 / 71.4[b]
Population age distribution (0-14/60+ years old, %)	36.0 / 6.1	32.8 / 6.5	28.6 / 8.7[a]
International migrant stock (000/% of total pop.)[h]	34.9 / 0.6	37.3 / 0.7	41.2 / 0.7[c]
Refugees and others of concern to the UNHCR (000)	0.2[i]	0.1[i]	0.7[c]
Infant mortality rate (per 1 000 live births)[g]	26.4	24.0	20.0[b]
Health: Current expenditure (% of GDP)	5.5	6.5	7.8[b]
Health: Physicians (per 1 000 pop.)	0.5	0.7	0.9[i]
Education: Government expenditure (% of GDP)	2.4[e,k]	4.5	...
Education: Primary gross enrol. ratio (f/m per 100 pop.)	120.2 / 121.9	122.7 / 123.8	... / ...
Education: Secondary gross enrol. ratio (f/m per 100 pop.)	74.1 / 63.7	78.8 / 69.8	... / ...
Education: Tertiary gross enrol. ratio (f/m per 100 pop.)	18.7 / 16.8[l]	... / ...	... / ...
Intentional homicide rate (per 100 000 pop.)	13.6	13.7	7.4[d]
Seats held by women in the National Parliament (%)	20.7	20.7	45.7

Environment and infrastructure indicators

	2005	2010	2018
Individuals using the Internet (per 100 inhabitants)	2.6	10.0[e]	24.6[a,d]
Research & Development expenditure (% of GDP)	~0.0[l]	...	0.1[m,b]
Threatened species (number)	90[n]	121	144[c]
Forested area (% of land area)	28.8	25.9	25.9[b]
CO2 emission estimates (million tons/tons per capita)	4.3 / 0.8	4.5 / 0.8	4.9 / 0.8[i]
Energy production, primary (Petajoules)	62	66	92[b]
Energy supply per capita (Gigajoules)	22	22	27[b]
Tourist/visitor arrivals at national borders (000)[o]	712	1 011	1 504[d]
Important sites for terrestrial biodiversity protected (%)	73.7	73.7	73.7
Pop. using improved drinking water (urban/rural, %)	96.3 / 63.7	98.2 / 67.3	99.3 / 69.4[b]
Pop. using improved sanitation facilities (urban/rural, %)	70.8 / 45.4	74.3 / 51.8	76.5 / 55.7[b]
Net Official Development Assist. received (% of GNI)	12.39	7.76	3.34[d]

a Projected estimate (medium fertility variant). **b** 2015. **c** 2017. **d** 2016. **e** Estimate. **f** Break in the time series. **g** Data refers to a 5-year period preceding the reference year. **h** Including refugees. **i** Data as at the end of December. **j** 2014. **k** 2003. **l** 2002. **m** Higher Education only. **n** 2004. **o** Including nationals residing abroad.

Niger

Region	Western Africa	UN membership date	20 September 1960
Population (000, 2018)	22 311[a]	Surface area (km2)	1 267 000[b]
Pop. density (per km2, 2018)	17.6[a]	Sex ratio (m per 100 f)	100.7[a]
Capital city	Niamey	National currency	CFA Franc, BCEAO (XOF)[c]
Capital city pop. (000, 2018)	1 213.8	Exchange rate (per US$)	546.9[d]

Economic indicators	2005	2010	2018
GDP: Gross domestic product (million current US$)	3 369	5 719	7 528[e]
GDP growth rate (annual %, const. 2010 prices)	7.4	8.4	5.0[e]
GDP per capita (current US$)	247.0	348.0	364.0[e]
Economy: Agriculture (% of Gross Value Added)	45.5	43.8	41.1[e]
Economy: Industry (% of Gross Value Added)	11.8	16.7	18.0[e]
Economy: Services and other activity (% of GVA)	42.7	39.4	40.8[e]
Employment in agriculture (% of employed)[f]	77.6	77.8	75.3
Employment in industry (% of employed)[f]	6.9	7.2	7.6
Employment in services & other sectors (% employed)[f]	15.5	15.1	17.1
Unemployment rate (% of labour force)	3.1	0.9[f]	0.4[f]
Labour force participation rate (female/male pop. %)[i]	67.8 / 90.9	67.7 / 91.1	67.5 / 90.6
CPI: Consumer Price Index (2010=100)[a,h]	89	100	109[d]
Agricultural production index (2004-2006=100)	102	146	173[d]
International trade: exports (million current US$)	486	479	639[f,d]
International trade: imports (million current US$)	736	2 273	1 617[f,d]
International trade: balance (million current US$)	- 250	- 1 794	- 978[f,d]
Balance of payments, current account (million US$)	- 312	- 1 136	- 1 181[e]

Major trading partners						2017
Export partners (% of exports)	France	31.3[f]	Thailand	11.8	Malaysia	11.1[f]
Import partners (% of imports)[f]	France	28.3	China	16.2	United States	7.8

Social indicators	2005	2010	2018
Population growth rate (average annual %)[i]	3.6	3.7	3.8[b]
Urban population (% of total population)	16.2	16.2	16.4
Urban population growth rate (average annual %)[i]	3.7	3.7	3.9[b]
Fertility rate, total (live births per woman)[i]	7.6	7.6	7.4[b]
Life expectancy at birth (females/males, years)[i]	52.0 / 50.8	55.6 / 54.2	59.5 / 57.6[b]
Population age distribution (0-14/60+ years old, %)	49.2 / 4.1	50.0 / 4.1	50.1 / 4.2[a]
International migrant stock (000/% of total pop.)[j]	124.5 / 0.9	126.5 / 0.8	295.6 / 1.4[d]
Refugees and others of concern to the UNHCR (000)	0.4[k]	0.3[k]	309.9[d]
Infant mortality rate (per 1 000 live births)[i]	88.1	74.8	65.8[b]
Health: Current expenditure (% of GDP)	7.2	6.2	7.2[b]
Health: Physicians (per 1 000 pop.)	~0.0[l]	~0.0[m]	...
Education: Government expenditure (% of GDP)	2.4[n]	3.7	6.0[b]
Education: Primary gross enrol. ratio (f/m per 100 pop.)	40.2 / 56.2	56.0 / 69.1	68.1 / 79.1[a]
Education: Secondary gross enrol. ratio (f/m per 100 pop.)	7.4 / 12.0	10.7 / 16.1	19.9 / 27.3[e]
Education: Tertiary gross enrol. ratio (f/m per 100 pop.)	0.6 / 1.7	0.8 / 2.2	0.9 / 2.6[o]
Intentional homicide rate (per 100 000 pop.)	...	...	4.4[o]
Seats held by women in the National Parliament (%)	12.4	9.7	17.0

Environment and infrastructure indicators	2005	2010	2018
Individuals using the Internet (per 100 inhabitants)[f]	0.2	0.8	4.3[b]
Threatened species (number)	15[l]	26	34[d]
Forested area (% of land area)[f]	1.0	1.0	0.9[b]
CO2 emission estimates (million tons/tons per capita)	0.7 / 0.1	1.2 / 0.1	2.1 / 0.1[p]
Energy production, primary (Petajoules)	70[f]	56	99[b]
Energy supply per capita (Gigajoules)	6[f]	4	5[b]
Tourist/visitor arrivals at national borders (000)	58	74	152[e]
Important sites for terrestrial biodiversity protected (%)	40.7	40.7	42.7
Pop. using improved drinking water (urban/rural, %)	86.4 / 41.2	94.8 / 45.3	100.0 / 48.6[b]
Pop. using improved sanitation facilities (urban/rural, %)	30.8 / 3.4	34.8 / 4.1	37.9 / 4.6[b]
Net Official Development Assist. received (% of GNI)	15.40	13.07	12.80[e]

a Projected estimate (medium fertility variant). b 2015. c African Financial Community (CFA) Franc, Central Bank of West African States (BCEAO). d 2017. e 2016. f Estimate. g Niamey h African population. i Data refers to a 5-year period preceding the reference year. j Including refugees. k Data as at the end of December. l 2004. m 2008. n 2003. o 2012. p 2014.

Nigeria

Region	Western Africa	UN membership date	07 October 1960
Population (000, 2018)	195 875[a]	Surface area (km2)	923 768[b]
Pop. density (per km2, 2018)	215.1[a]	Sex ratio (m per 100 f)	102.8[a]
Capital city	Abuja	National currency	Naira (NGN)
Capital city pop. (000, 2018)	2 918.5[c]	Exchange rate (per US$)	306.0[d]

Economic indicators	2005	2010	2018
GDP: Gross domestic product (million current US$)	180 502	369 062	404 649[e]
GDP growth rate (annual %, const. 2010 prices)	6.5	7.8	- 1.6[e]
GDP per capita (current US$)	1 299.0	2 327.0	2 176.0[e]
Economy: Agriculture (% of Gross Value Added)[f]	25.6	23.9	21.2[e]
Economy: Industry (% of Gross Value Added)[f]	23.7	25.3	18.4[e]
Economy: Services and other activity (% of GVA)[f]	50.7	50.8	60.4[e]
Employment in agriculture (% of employed)[g]	51.2	30.6	36.4
Employment in industry (% of employed)[g]	8.5	14.2	11.7
Employment in services & other sectors (% employed)[g]	40.4	55.3	51.9
Unemployment rate (% of labour force)[g]	4.3	3.9	7.0
Labour force participation rate (female/male pop. %)[g]	47.8 / 61.7	49.2 / 60.7	50.5 / 59.7
CPI: Consumer Price Index (2010=100)[h]	62	100	214[d]
Agricultural production index (2004-2006=100)	100	105	119[e]
International trade: exports (million current US$)	55 144[g]	86 568	44 466[d]
International trade: imports (million current US$)	21 314[g]	44 235	31 270[d]
International trade: balance (million current US$)	33 831[g]	42 333	13 196[d]
Balance of payments, current account (million US$)	36 529	13 111	10 381[d]

Major trading partners						2017
Export partners (% of exports)	India	17.9	United States	12.8	Spain	9.9
Import partners (% of imports)	China	18.7	Belgium	12.9	Netherlands	9.2

Social indicators	2005	2010	2018
Population growth rate (average annual %)[i]	2.6	2.6	2.7[b]
Urban population (% of total population)	39.1	43.5	50.3
Urban population growth rate (average annual %)[i]	4.8	4.8	4.6[b]
Fertility rate, total (live births per woman)[i]	6.1	5.9	5.7[b]
Life expectancy at birth (females/males, years)[i]	47.8 / 46.1	50.5 / 49.0	52.6 / 51.2[b]
Population age distribution (0-14/60+ years old, %)	43.7 / 4.6	44.0 / 4.5	43.8 / 4.5[a]
International migrant stock (000/% of total pop.)[i,k]	969.3 / 0.7	988.7 / 0.6	1 235.1 / 0.6[d]
Refugees and others of concern to the UNHCR (000)	12.7[l]	10.6[l]	2 478.3[d]
Infant mortality rate (per 1 000 live births)[i]	104.0	89.9	76.3[b]
Health: Current expenditure (% of GDP)	3.8	3.3	3.6[b]
Health: Physicians (per 1 000 pop.)	0.3	0.4[m]	...
Education: Primary gross enrol. ratio (f/m per 100 pop.)	92.6 / 109.8	80.9 / 89.1[g]	92.8 / 95.2[n]
Education: Secondary gross enrol. ratio (f/m per 100 pop.)	31.7 / 38.1	41.2 / 47.1	53.5 / 58.8[n]
Education: Tertiary gross enrol. ratio (f/m per 100 pop.)	8.7 / 12.3	8.1 / 11.0	8.3 / 12.0[o]
Intentional homicide rate (per 100 000 pop.)	11.8	10.7	9.8[b]
Seats held by women in the National Parliament (%)	4.7	7.0	5.6

Environment and infrastructure indicators	2005	2010	2018
Individuals using the Internet (per 100 inhabitants)[g]	3.5	11.5	25.7[e]
Research & Development expenditure (% of GDP)	...	0.2[p,q]	...
Threatened species (number)	232[r]	297	361[d]
Forested area (% of land area)[g]	12.2	9.9	7.7[b]
CO2 emission estimates (million tons/tons per capita)	106.1 / 0.8	91.5 / 0.6	96.3 / 0.6[s]
Energy production, primary (Petajoules)	9 734	10 595	10 603[b]
Energy supply per capita (Gigajoules)	32	31	32[b]
Tourist/visitor arrivals at national borders (000)	1 010	1 555	1 889[e]
Important sites for terrestrial biodiversity protected (%)	69.2	79.6	79.6
Pop. using improved drinking water (urban/rural, %)	79.0 / 44.2	79.9 / 50.7	80.8 / 57.3[b]
Pop. using improved sanitation facilities (urban/rural, %)	34.8 / 30.6	33.8 / 28.0	32.8 / 25.4[b]
Net Official Development Assist. received (% of GNI)	6.47	0.59	0.63[e]

a Projected estimate (medium fertility variant). b 2015. c Data refers to the urban agglomeration. d 2017. e 2016. f Data classified according to ISIC Rev. 4. g Estimate. h Rural and urban areas. i Data refers to a 5-year period preceding the reference year. j Refers to foreign citizens. k Including refugees. l Data as at the end of December. m 2009. n 2013. o 2011. p Excluding business enterprise. q 2007. r 2004. s 2014.

Niue

Region	Polynesia	Population (000, 2018)	2 [a]
Surface area (km2)	260 [b]	Pop. density (per km2, 2018)	6.2 [a]
Sex ratio (m per 100 f)	100.0 [c,d]	Capital city	Alofi
National currency	New Zealand Dollar (NZD)	Capital city pop. (000, 2018)	0.7
Exchange rate (per US$)	1.4 [e]		

Economic indicators	2005	2010	2018
Employment in agriculture (% of employed)	4.8 [c,f,g]	...	...
Employment in industry (% of employed)	9.3 [c,f,g]	...	...
Employment in services & other sectors (% employed)	85.9 [c,f,g]	...	...
Unemployment rate (% of labour force)	9.7 [c,g]	...	...
Labour force participation rate (female/male pop. %)	74.8 / 76.7 [h]	... / ...	... / ...
Agricultural production index (2004-2006=100)	100	97	101 [d]

Social indicators	2005	2010	2018
Population growth rate (average annual %) [i]	- 2.4	- 0.7	- 0.1 [b]
Urban population (% of total population)	35.2	38.7	44.8
Urban population growth rate (average annual %) [i]	- 1.1	1.2	1.9 [b]
Fertility rate, total (live births per woman)	...	...	2.6 [j,k]
Life expectancy at birth (females/males, years)	... / ...	76.0 / 67.0 [l]	76.3 / 70.1 [c,m,k]
Population age distribution (0-14/60+ years old, %)	26.1 / 15.1 [n]	25.7 / 16.8 [n]	22.8 / 20.1 [c,d]
International migrant stock (000/% of total pop.)	0.5 / 31.0	0.5 / 33.4	0.6 / 34.2 [e]
Infant mortality rate (per 1 000 live births)	...	...	8.1 [m,k]
Health: Current expenditure (% of GDP) [o,p,q]	10.1	9.8	6.3 [b]
Health: Physicians (per 1 000 pop.)	2.3 [r]	1.8 [s]	...
Education: Primary gross enrol. ratio (f/m per 100 pop.)	105.9 / 118.9 [t]	... / ...	125.3 / 132.5 [t,d]
Education: Secondary gross enrol. ratio (f/m per 100 pop.)	116.5 / 71.3 [t]	... / ...	114.1 / 104.1 [t,b]
Intentional homicide rate (per 100 000 pop.)	...	...	0.0 [u]

Environment and infrastructure indicators	2005	2010	2018
Individuals using the Internet (per 100 inhabitants)	51.7	77.0 [t]	79.6 [t,k]
Threatened species (number)	12 [r]	43	52 [e]
Forested area (% of land area) [t]	73.5	71.5	69.6 [b]
CO2 emission estimates (million tons/tons per capita)	~0.0 / 1.8	~0.0 / 1.9	~0.0 / 5.7 [v]
Energy production, primary (Petajoules)	0	0	0 [b]
Energy supply per capita (Gigajoules)	42	53	64 [b]
Tourist/visitor arrivals at national borders (000) [w]	3	6	8 [t,b]
Important sites for terrestrial biodiversity protected (%)	95.3	95.3	95.3
Pop. using improved drinking water (urban/rural, %)	98.8 / 98.8	98.5 / 98.6	98.4 / 98.6 [b]
Pop. using improved sanitation facilities (urban/rural, %)	89.9 / 89.9	100.0 / 100.0	100.0 / 100.0 [b]

a Projected estimate (medium fertility variant). b 2015. c Break in the time series. d 2016. e 2017. f Data classified according to ISIC Rev. 3. g 2002. h 2001. i Data refers to a 5-year period preceding the reference year. j Data refers to a 3-year period up to and including the reference year. k 2011. l 2006. m Data refers to a 5-year period up to and including the reference year. n De jure population. o Indicators are sensitive to external funds flowing in to the country. p Data refer to fiscal years beginning 1 July. q General government expenditure (GGE) can be larger than the Gross domestic product (GDP) because government accounts for a very large part of domestic consumption and because a large part of domestic consumption in the country is accounted for by imports. r 2004. s 2008. t Estimate. u 2012. v 2014. w Including Niueans residing usually in New Zealand.

Northern Mariana Islands

Region	Micronesia	Population (000, 2018)	55[a]
Surface area (km2)	457[b]	Pop. density (per km2, 2018)	120.0[a]
Sex ratio (m per 100 f)	107.1[c,d]	Capital city	Garapan
National currency	US Dollar (USD)	Capital city pop. (000)	4.0[e]

Economic indicators	2005	2010	2018
Employment in agriculture (% of employed)	1.5[c,f,g,h]	...	...
Employment in industry (% of employed)	47.2[c,f,g,h]	...	...
Employment in services & other sectors (% employed)	45.8[c,f,g,h]	...	...
Unemployment rate (% of labour force)[f]	6.5	11.2[c]	...
Labour force participation rate (female/male pop. %)	81.3 / 82.5[f,i]	66.6 / 77.6[c,f]	... / ...
International trade: exports (million current US$)[j]	1 254	1 453	1 787[k]
International trade: imports (million current US$)[j]	1 952	2 867	4 916[k]
International trade: balance (million current US$)[j]	- 699	- 1 414	- 3 129[k]

Major trading partners						2017
Export partners (% of exports)[j]	Areas nes[l]	91.1	Republic of Korea	3.6	Singapore	2.6
Import partners (% of imports)	Areas nes[l]	66.1[j]	China, Hong Kong SAR	13.5[j]	Republic of Korea	3.9

Social indicators	2005	2010	2018
Population growth rate (average annual %)[m]	- 1.6	- 3.2	0.1[b]
Urban population (% of total population)	90.6	90.9	91.6
Urban population growth rate (average annual %)[m]	- 1.5	- 3.1	0.2[b]
Fertility rate, total (live births per woman)	1.5	2.2	1.6[n]
Life expectancy at birth (females/males, years)	77.8 / 72.5[h]	79.9 / 74.4[o]	77.9 / 74.9[c,p]
Population age distribution (0-14/60+ years old, %)	22.9 / 3.7[q,r]	26.7 / 5.8	23.5 / 10.0[e,d]
International migrant stock (000/% of total pop.)	37.5 / 58.9	24.2 / 44.4	21.8 / 39.5[k]
Infant mortality rate (per 1 000 live births)	...	...	6.4[p]

Environment and infrastructure indicators	2005	2010	2018
Threatened species (number)	28[s]	85	102[k]
Forested area (% of land area)[j]	67.7	65.9	64.1[b]
Tourist/visitor arrivals at national borders (000)	507	379	531[d]
Important sites for terrestrial biodiversity protected (%)	3.8	40.6	40.6
Pop. using improved drinking water (urban/rural, %)	96.4 / 96.4	97.2 / 97.2	97.5 / 97.5[b]
Pop. using improved sanitation facilities (urban/rural, %)	76.2 / 76.2	78.7 / 78.7	79.7 / 79.7[b]

a Projected estimate (medium fertility variant). b 2015. c Break in the time series. d 2016. e 2010. f Population aged 16 years and over. g Data classified according to ISIC Rev. 2. h 2000. i 2003. j Estimate. k 2017. l Areas not elsewhere specified. m Data refers to a 5-year period preceding the reference year. n 2013. o 2009. p 2012. q Refers to the island of Saipan. r Estimates should be viewed with caution as these are derived from scarce data. s 2004.

Norway

Region	Northern Europe	UN membership date	27 November 1945
Population (000, 2018)	5 353 [a,b]	Surface area (km2)	386 194 [a,c]
Pop. density (per km2, 2018)	14.7 [a,b]	Sex ratio (m per 100 f)	102.0 [a,b]
Capital city	Oslo	National currency	Norwegian Krone (NOK)
Capital city pop. (000, 2018)	1 012.2	Exchange rate (per US$)	8.2 [d]

Economic indicators	2005	2010	2018
GDP: Gross domestic product (million current US$)	308 722	429 131	371 069 [e]
GDP growth rate (annual %, const. 2010 prices)	2.6	0.7	1.1 [e]
GDP per capita (current US$)	66 645.0	87 831.0	70 617.0 [e]
Economy: Agriculture (% of Gross Value Added) [f]	1.6	1.8	2.6 [e]
Economy: Industry (% of Gross Value Added) [f]	42.5	39.1	34.6 [e]
Economy: Services and other activity (% of GVA) [f]	55.9	59.2	62.8 [e]
Employment in agriculture (% of employed)	3.3	2.6 [g]	2.0 [g]
Employment in industry (% of employed) [g]	20.8	19.7	19.5
Employment in services & other sectors (% employed) [g]	75.8	77.8	78.5
Unemployment rate (% of labour force)	4.4	3.5	4.0 [g]
Labour force participation rate (female/male pop. %) [g]	60.7 / 70.3	61.8 / 69.7	60.8 / 67.4
CPI: Consumer Price Index (2010=100)	89	100	115 [d]
Agricultural production index (2004-2006=100)	99	102	107 [e]
Index of industrial production (2005=100)	100	88 [h]	85 [h,i]
International trade: exports (million current US$)	103 759	130 657	101 976 [d]
International trade: imports (million current US$)	55 488	77 330	85 526 [d]
International trade: balance (million current US$)	48 271	53 327	16 450 [d]
Balance of payments, current account (million US$)	49 967	50 258	20 169 [d]

Major trading partners						2017
Export partners (% of exports)	United Kingdom	21.1	Germany	15.5	Netherlands	9.9
Import partners (% of imports)	Sweden	11.5	Germany	11.1	China	9.8

Social indicators	2005	2010	2018
Population growth rate (average annual %) [a,j]	0.6	1.1	1.2 [c]
Urban population (% of total population) [a]	77.7	79.1	82.2
Urban population growth rate (average annual %) [a,j]	1.0	1.4	1.7 [c]
Fertility rate, total (live births per woman) [a,j]	1.8	1.9	1.8 [c]
Life expectancy at birth (females/males, years) [a,j]	81.8 / 76.8	82.8 / 78.3	83.6 / 79.5 [c]
Population age distribution (0-14/60+ years old, %) [a]	19.6 / 19.8	18.8 / 21.0	17.8 / 22.6 [b]
International migrant stock (000/% of total pop.) [a]	361.1 / 7.8	526.8 / 10.8	798.9 / 15.1 [d]
Refugees and others of concern to the UNHCR (000)	44.2 [k]	55.9 [k]	68.2 [d]
Infant mortality rate (per 1 000 live births) [a,j]	3.5	3.0	2.4 [c]
Health: Current expenditure (% of GDP)	8.3	8.9	10.0 [c]
Health: Physicians (per 1 000 pop.)		4.1	4.4 [c]
Education: Government expenditure (% of GDP)	6.9	6.7	7.7 [i]
Education: Primary gross enrol. ratio (f/m per 100 pop.)	98.7 / 98.4	99.2 / 98.9	100.1 / 100.3 [e]
Education: Secondary gross enrol. ratio (f/m per 100 pop.)	114.3 / 113.2	111.7 / 113.5	112.5 / 115.9 [e]
Education: Tertiary gross enrol. ratio (f/m per 100 pop.)	95.1 / 62.4	91.2 / 56.5	96.6 / 85.4 [e]
Intentional homicide rate (per 100 000 pop.)	0.7	0.6	0.5 [e]
Seats held by women in the National Parliament (%)	38.2	39.6	41.4

Environment and infrastructure indicators	2005	2010	2018
Individuals using the Internet (per 100 inhabitants)	82.0 [i]	93.4 [i]	97.3 [e]
Research & Development expenditure (% of GDP)	1.5	1.7	1.9 [m,c]
Threatened species (number)	33 [n]	36	64 [d]
Forested area (% of land area)	33.1	33.1	33.2 [g,c]
CO2 emission estimates (million tons/tons per capita)	42.4 / 9.2	60.1 / 12.3	47.6 / 9.2 [i]
Energy production, primary (Petajoules) [a]	9 372	8 759	8 615 [c]
Energy supply per capita (Gigajoules) [a]	242	291	234 [c]
Tourist/visitor arrivals at national borders (000)	3 824	4 767	5 960 [e]
Important sites for terrestrial biodiversity protected (%)	52.0	53.8	55.9
Pop. using improved drinking water (urban/rural, %)	100.0 / 100.0	100.0 / 100.0	100.0 / 100.0 [c]
Pop. using improved sanitation facilities (urban/rural, %)	98.0 / 98.3	98.0 / 98.3	98.0 / 98.3 [c]
Net Official Development Assist. disbursed (% of GNI) [o]	0.94	1.05	0.99 [m,d]

a Including Svalbard and Jan Mayen Islands. **b** Projected estimate (medium fertility variant). **c** 2015. **d** 2017. **e** 2016. **f** Data classified according to ISIC Rev. 4. **g** Estimate. **h** Excluding water and waste management. **i** 2014. **j** Data refers to a 5-year period preceding the reference year. **k** Data as at the end of December. **l** Population aged 16 to 74 years. **m** Provisional data. **n** 2004. **o** Development Assistance Committee member (OECD).

Oman

Region	Western Asia	UN membership date	07 October 1971
Population (000, 2018)	4 830[a]	Surface area (km2)	309 500[b]
Pop. density (per km2, 2018)	15.6[a]	Sex ratio (m per 100 f)	195.7[a]
Capital city	Muscat	National currency	Rial Omani (OMR)
Capital city pop. (000, 2018)	1 446.6[c]	Exchange rate (per US$)	0.4[d]

Economic indicators	2005	2010	2018
GDP: Gross domestic product (million current US$)	31 082	58 641	63 171[e]
GDP growth rate (annual %, const. 2010 prices)	2.5	4.8	3.1[e]
GDP per capita (current US$)	12 377.0	19 281.0	14 277.0[e]
Economy: Agriculture (% of Gross Value Added)	1.6	1.4	1.3[e]
Economy: Industry (% of Gross Value Added)	62.1	62.8	58.3[e]
Economy: Services and other activity (% of GVA)	36.3	35.9	40.4[e]
Employment in agriculture (% of employed)[f]	6.8	5.2	6.5
Employment in industry (% of employed)[f]	17.8	36.9	38.2
Employment in services & other sectors (% employed)[f]	75.4	58.0	55.3
Unemployment rate (% of labour force)[f]	19.1	18.2	16.2
Labour force participation rate (female/male pop. %)[f]	25.2 / 77.4	28.7 / 80.9	30.1 / 87.7
CPI: Consumer Price Index (2010=100)	76	100	112[d]
Agricultural production index (2004-2006=100)	112	119	144[e]
Index of industrial production (2005=100)[g]	100	165	181[h]
International trade: exports (million current US$)	18 692	36 600	17 652[f,d]
International trade: imports (million current US$)	8 970	19 775	18 893[f,d]
International trade: balance (million current US$)	9 722	16 825	- 1 241[f,d]
Balance of payments, current account (million US$)	5 178	4 634	- 12 319[e]

Major trading partners							2017
Export partners (% of exports)	China	43.6[f]	Areas nes[i]	10.3	United Arab Emirates	7.5[f]
Import partners (% of imports)[f]	United Arab Emirates	45.1	Areas nes[i]	11.2	China	4.8

Social indicators	2005	2010	2018
Population growth rate (average annual %)[j]	2.0	3.8	6.5[b]
Urban population (% of total population)	72.4	75.2	84.5
Urban population growth rate (average annual %)[j]	2.3	4.6	8.0[b]
Fertility rate, total (live births per woman)[j]	3.2	2.9	2.9[b]
Life expectancy at birth (females/males, years)[j]	75.5 / 71.4	77.6 / 73.2	78.7 / 74.5[b]
Population age distribution (0-14/60+ years old, %)	32.5 / 4.1	25.7 / 3.9	21.6 / 4.1[a]
International migrant stock (000/% of total pop.)[k]	666.2 / 26.5	816.2 / 26.8	2 073.3 / 44.7[d]
Refugees and others of concern to the UNHCR (000)	~0.0[l]	0.1[l]	0.7[d]
Infant mortality rate (per 1 000 live births)[j]	14.6	9.8	9.6[b]
Health: Current expenditure (% of GDP)	2.6	2.7	3.8[b]
Health: Physicians (per 1 000 pop.)	1.7	2.0	1.9[e]
Education: Government expenditure (% of GDP)	3.5	4.2[m]	6.2[e]
Education: Primary gross enrol. ratio (f/m per 100 pop.)	92.1 / 93.2	100.7 / 104.9[m]	110.1 / 107.2[e]
Education: Secondary gross enrol. ratio (f/m per 100 pop.)	86.0 / 89.3	97.1 / 101.8[m]	103.9 / 110.4[e]
Education: Tertiary gross enrol. ratio (f/m per 100 pop.)	19.1 / 17.9	28.5 / 19.7	59.7 / 32.8[a]
Intentional homicide rate (per 100 000 pop.)	2.1	1.6	0.7[h]
Seats held by women in the National Parliament (%)	2.4	0.0	1.2

Environment and infrastructure indicators	2005	2010	2018
Individuals using the Internet (per 100 inhabitants)	6.7	35.8[n]	69.8[e]
Research & Development expenditure (% of GDP)	...	...	0.2[b]
Threatened species (number)	55[o]	79	99[d]
Forested area (% of land area)	~0.0	~0.0	~0.0[f,b]
CO2 emission estimates (million tons/tons per capita)	29.9 / 12.3	47.4 / 16.1	61.2 / 14.4[h]
Energy production, primary (Petajoules)	2 356	2 793	3 481[b]
Energy supply per capita (Gigajoules)	183	264	285[b]
Tourist/visitor arrivals at national borders (000)	891	1 441	2 292[e]
Important sites for terrestrial biodiversity protected (%)	7.8	7.8	11.5
Pop. using improved drinking water (urban/rural, %)	90.8 / 79.9	94.1 / 84.3	95.5 / 86.1[b]
Pop. using improved sanitation facilities (urban/rural, %)	96.8 / 84.2	97.3 / 94.7	97.3 / 94.7[b]
Net Official Development Assist. received (% of GNI)	0.06	- 0.04	...

a Projected estimate (medium fertility variant). **b** 2015. **c** Refers to Muscat governorate. **d** 2017. **e** 2016. **f** Estimate. **g** Data classified according to ISIC Rev. 3. **h** 2014. **i** Areas not elsewhere specified. **j** Data refers to a 5-year period preceding the reference year. **k** Refers to foreign citizens. **l** Data as at the end of December. **m** 2009. **n** Population aged 5 years and over. **o** 2004.

Pakistan

Region	Southern Asia	UN membership date	30 September 1947
Population (000, 2018)	200 814[a]	Surface area (km2)	796 095[b]
Pop. density (per km2, 2018)	260.5[a]	Sex ratio (m per 100 f)	105.6[a]
Capital city	Islamabad	National currency	Pakistan Rupee (PKR)
Capital city pop. (000, 2018)	1 061.4	Exchange rate (per US$)	110.4[c]

Economic indicators	2005	2010	2018
GDP: Gross domestic product (million current US$)	117 708	174 508	282 506[d]
GDP growth rate (annual %, const. 2010 prices)	7.7	1.6	5.7[d]
GDP per capita (current US$)	765.0	1 023.0	1 462.0[d]
Economy: Agriculture (% of Gross Value Added)[e]	24.5	24.3	25.2[d]
Economy: Industry (% of Gross Value Added)[e]	21.2	20.6	19.2[d]
Economy: Services and other activity (% of GVA)[e]	54.3	55.1	55.6[d]
Employment in agriculture (% of employed)	43.1[f]	43.4	41.3[f]
Employment in industry (% of employed)[f]	20.3	21.4	23.9
Employment in services & other sectors (% employed)[f]	36.6	35.2	34.8
Unemployment rate (% of labour force)	7.7	0.6	4.2[f]
Labour force participation rate (female/male pop. %)[i]	19.3 / 84.1	21.7 / 80.1	25.1 / 82.6
CPI: Consumer Price Index (2010=100)	55	100[g]	157[c]
Agricultural production index (2004-2006=100)	100	111	128[c]
International trade: exports (million current US$)	16 050	21 413	21 878[c]
International trade: imports (million current US$)	25 097	37 537	57 440[c]
International trade: balance (million current US$)	- 9 046	- 16 124	- 35 562[c]
Balance of payments, current account (million US$)	- 3 606[a]	- 1 354	- 15 818[c]

Major trading partners						2017
Export partners (% of exports)	United States	18.3	United Kingdom	7.5	China	6.9
Import partners (% of imports)	China	26.8	United Arab Emirates	13.1	United States	4.9

Social indicators	2005	2010	2018
Population growth rate (average annual %)[h]	2.1	2.1	2.1[b]
Urban population (% of total population)	34.0	35.0	36.7
Urban population growth rate (average annual %)[h]	2.7	2.6	2.7[b]
Fertility rate, total (live births per woman)[h]	4.2	4.0	3.7[b]
Life expectancy at birth (females/males, years)[h]	64.2 / 62.5	65.3 / 63.5	66.8 / 65.0[b]
Population age distribution (0-14/60+ years old, %)	38.2 / 6.5	36.2 / 6.6	34.7 / 6.8[a]
International migrant stock (000/% of total pop.)[i]	3 171.1 / 2.1	3 941.6 / 2.3	3 398.2 / 1.7[c]
Refugees and others of concern to the UNHCR (000)	1 549.2[j]	4 151.0[j]	1 862.2[c]
Infant mortality rate (per 1 000 live births)[h]	84.0	76.9	69.8[b]
Health: Current expenditure (% of GDP)	2.9	2.6	2.7[b]
Health: Physicians (per 1 000 pop.)	0.8	0.9	1.0[b]
Education: Government expenditure (% of GDP)	2.3	2.3	2.8[c]
Education: Primary gross enrol. ratio (f/m per 100 pop.)	76.1 / 98.9	87.5 / 102.7	89.7 / 105.2[d]
Education: Secondary gross enrol. ratio (f/m per 100 pop.)	... / ...	31.0 / 40.2	41.1 / 50.7[d]
Education: Tertiary gross enrol. ratio (f/m per 100 pop.)	4.6 / 5.3	6.3 / 7.5[f,k]	9.0 / 10.4[d]
Intentional homicide rate (per 100 000 pop.)	6.4	7.7	4.4[d]
Seats held by women in the National Parliament (%)	21.3	22.2	20.6

Environment and infrastructure indicators	2005	2010	2018
Individuals using the Internet (per 100 inhabitants)	6.3	8.0[f]	15.5[d]
Research & Development expenditure (% of GDP)[l,m]	0.4	0.4[k]	0.2[b]
Threatened species (number)	72[n]	109	140[c]
Forested area (% of land area)[f]	2.5	2.2	1.9[b]
CO2 emission estimates (million tons/tons per capita)	136.6 / 0.8	161.4 / 1.0	166.3 / 0.9[o]
Energy production, primary (Petajoules)	2 020	2 255	2 415[b]
Energy supply per capita (Gigajoules)	17	18	18[b]
Tourist/visitor arrivals at national borders (000)	798	907	966[p]
Important sites for terrestrial biodiversity protected (%)	36.6	36.6	36.6
Pop. using improved drinking water (urban/rural, %)	94.9 / 86.7	94.4 / 88.3	93.9 / 89.9[b]
Pop. using improved sanitation facilities (urban/rural, %)	75.4 / 30.1	79.3 / 40.6	83.1 / 51.1[b]
Net Official Development Assist. received (% of GNI)	1.45	1.64	0.98[d]

a Projected estimate (medium fertility variant). b 2015. c 2017. d 2016. e Data classified according to ISIC Rev. 4. f Estimate. g Break in the time series. h Data refers to a 5-year period preceding the reference year. i Including refugees. j Data as at the end of December. k 2009. l Excluding business enterprise. m Excluding private non-profit. n 2004. o 2014. p 2012.

Palau

Region	Micronesia	UN membership date	15 December 1994
Population (000, 2018)	22[a]	Surface area (km2)	459[b]
Pop. density (per km2, 2018)	47.7[a]	Sex ratio (m per 100 f)	113.3[c,d]
Capital city	Melekeok	National currency	US Dollar (USD)
Capital city pop. (000, 2018)	11.4[e]		

Economic indicators

	2005	2010	2018
GDP: Gross domestic product (million current US$)	191	183	310[d]
GDP growth rate (annual %, const. 2010 prices)	0.2	3.0	1.9[d]
GDP per capita (current US$)	9 611.0	8 956.0	14 428.0[d]
Economy: Agriculture (% of Gross Value Added)[g]	4.4	4.5	3.4[d]
Economy: Industry (% of Gross Value Added)[g]	16.6	10.7	8.4[d]
Economy: Services and other activity (% of GVA)[g]	79.1	84.8	88.3[d]
Employment in agriculture (% of employed)[h]	7.1[i,j]	2.4[k,l]	...
Employment in industry (% of employed)[h]	13.8[i,j]	11.8[k,l]	...
Employment in services & other sectors (% employed)[h]	79.1[i,j]	85.9[k,l]	...
Unemployment rate (% of labour force)	4.2[h]	...	...
Labour force participation rate (female/male pop. %)	58.1 / 75.4[h]	... / ...	... / ...
CPI: Consumer Price Index (2010=100)	81	100	118[f]
International trade: exports (million current US$)	14[m]	12[m]	6[f]
International trade: imports (million current US$)	156[m]	107	158[f]
International trade: balance (million current US$)	- 143[m]	- 96[m]	- 151[f]
Balance of payments, current account (million US$)	- 40[c]	- 19	- 46[d]

Major trading partners

						2017
Export partners (% of exports)	Areas nes[n]	38.9	Japan	23.4[m]	Guam	14.5
Import partners (% of imports)	United States	35.8	Singapore	15.3	Japan	12.5

Social indicators

	2005	2010	2018
Population growth rate (average annual %)[o]	0.8	0.6	0.8[b]
Urban population (% of total population)	71.2	74.8	79.9
Urban population growth rate (average annual %)[o]	1.0	1.6	1.7[b]
Fertility rate, total (live births per woman)	1.5[i]	...	2.2[c,p,b]
Life expectancy at birth (females/males, years)	72.1 / 66.3	... / ...	77.8 / 68.1[c,b]
Population age distribution (0-14/60+ years old, %)	24.1 / 8.2[q]	... / ...	20.3 / 13.1[c,d]
International migrant stock (000/% of total pop.)	6.0 / 30.4	5.5 / 26.8	5.0 / 23.0[f]
Refugees and others of concern to the UNHCR (000)	...	...	~0.0[f]
Infant mortality rate (per 1 000 live births)			13.3[b]
Health: Current expenditure (% of GDP)[r,s]	9.0	11.5	10.6[b]
Health: Physicians (per 1 000 pop.)		1.4	1.2[t]
Education: Government expenditure (% of GDP)	7.6[m,u]	...	...
Education: Primary gross enrol. ratio (f/m per 100 pop.)	101.1 / 104.6[m,v]	... / ...	112.5 / 117.0[m,t]
Education: Secondary gross enrol. ratio (f/m per 100 pop.)	99.9 / 97.7[m,v]	... / ...	118.3 / 112.3[m,t]
Education: Tertiary gross enrol. ratio (f/m per 100 pop.)	52.3 / 25.6[m,u]	... / ...	78.1 / 50.6[m,w]
Intentional homicide rate (per 100 000 pop.)	...	...	3.1[x]
Seats held by women in the National Parliament (%)	0.0	0.0	12.5

Environment and infrastructure indicators

	2005	2010	2018
Threatened species (number)	21[v]	128	182[f]
Forested area (% of land area)[m]	87.6	87.6	87.6[b]
CO2 emission estimates (million tons/tons per capita)	0.3 / 13.1	0.3 / 12.3	0.3 / 12.4[l]
Energy supply per capita (Gigajoules)	156[m]	141	147[m,b]
Tourist/visitor arrivals at national borders (000)[y]	81	85	138[d]
Important sites for terrestrial biodiversity protected (%)	17.9	17.9	36.6
Pop. using improved drinking water (urban/rural, %)	97.1 / 84.4	97.0 / 86.0	97.0 / 86.0[b,z]
Pop. using improved sanitation facilities (urban/rural, %)	100.0 / 91.2	100.0 / 100.0	100.0 / 100.0[b]
Net Official Development Assist. received (% of GNI)	12.86	16.25	6.32[d]

a Projected estimate (medium fertility variant). **b** 2015. **c** Break in the time series. **d** 2016. **e** Refers to Koror. **f** 2017. **g** Data classified according to ISIC Rev. 4. **h** Population aged 16 years and over. **i** Data classified according to ISIC Rev. 2. **j** 2000. **k** Data classified according to ISIC Rev. 3. **l** 2008. **m** Estimate. **n** Areas not elsewhere specified. **o** Data refers to a 5-year period preceding the reference year. **p** Preliminary census results. **q** De jure population, **r** Data refer to fiscal years ending 30 September. **s** Data revision. **t** 2014. **u** 2002. **v** 2004. **w** 2013. **x** 2012. **y** Air arrivals (Palau International Airport). **z** 2011.

Panama

Region	Central America	
Population (000, 2018)	4 163[a]	
Pop. density (per km2, 2018)	56.0[a]	
Capital city	Panama City	
Capital city pop. (000, 2018)	1 783.5[c]	

UN membership date	13 November 1945	
Surface area (km2)	75 320[b]	
Sex ratio (m per 100 f)	100.4[a]	
National currency	Balboa (PAB)	
Exchange rate (per US$)	1.0[d]	

Economic indicators	2005	2010	2018
GDP: Gross domestic product (million current US$)	15 465	28 917	55 188[e]
GDP growth rate (annual %, const. 2010 prices)	7.2	5.8	4.9[e]
GDP per capita (current US$)	4 643.0	7 937.0	13 680.0[e]
Economy: Agriculture (% of Gross Value Added)	6.8	3.9	2.6[e]
Economy: Industry (% of Gross Value Added)	16.3	20.3	27.9[e]
Economy: Services and other activity (% of GVA)	76.9	75.8	69.6[e]
Employment in agriculture (% of employed)[f]	15.7	17.4	14.5
Employment in industry (% of employed)[f]	17.2	18.7	18.0
Employment in services & other sectors (% employed)[f]	67.1	63.9	67.5
Unemployment rate (% of labour force)[f]	9.8	6.5	6.2[d]
Labour force participation rate (female/male pop. %)[f]	47.9 / 81.1	49.0 / 82.0	50.5 / 80.4[d]
CPI: Consumer Price Index (2010=100)[g]	81	100	122[d]
Agricultural production index (2004-2006=100)	99	106	112[d]
International trade: exports (million current US$)	963	10 987	11 624[f,d]
International trade: imports (million current US$)	4 152	16 737	9 992[f,d]
International trade: balance (million current US$)	- 3 189	- 5 751	1 632[f,d]
Balance of payments, current account (million US$)	- 1 064	- 3 113	- 3 036[d]

Major trading partners						2017
Export partners (% of exports)[f]	United States	20.6	Colombia	9.5	Areas nes[h]	8.9
Import partners (% of imports)[f]	China	31.3	Singapore	18.9	United States	9.5

Social indicators	2005	2010	2018
Population growth rate (average annual %)[i]	1.9	1.8	1.7[b]
Urban population (% of total population)	63.7	65.1	67.7
Urban population growth rate (average annual %)[i]	2.4	2.2	2.2[b]
Fertility rate, total (live births per woman)[i]	2.7	2.6	2.6[b]
Life expectancy at birth (females/males, years)[i]	78.2 / 73.0	79.4 / 73.5	80.5 / 74.3[b]
Population age distribution (0-14/60+ years old, %)	30.4 / 8.8	29.1 / 9.7	27.1 / 11.7[a]
International migrant stock (000/% of total pop.)	117.6 / 3.5	157.3 / 4.3	190.7 / 4.7[d]
Refugees and others of concern to the UNHCR (000)	12.4[j]	17.6[j]	23.0[d]
Infant mortality rate (per 1 000 live births)[i]	19.8	16.8	15.2[b]
Health: Current expenditure (% of GDP)	6.6	6.6	7.0[b]
Health: Physicians (per 1 000 pop.)	1.4	1.4	1.6[k]
Education: Government expenditure (% of GDP)	3.6[f,l]	3.6[m]	3.2[n]
Education: Primary gross enrol. ratio (f/m per 100 pop.)	105.3 / 109.1	103.0 / 107.0	94.7 / 97.3[b]
Education: Secondary gross enrol. ratio (f/m per 100 pop.)	70.3 / 65.7	73.5 / 69.2	77.8 / 73.9[b]
Education: Tertiary gross enrol. ratio (f/m per 100 pop.)	52.5 / 32.1	53.7 / 35.1	58.0 / 36.8[b]
Intentional homicide rate (per 100 000 pop.)	10.9	12.6	9.7[e]
Seats held by women in the National Parliament (%)	16.7	8.5	18.3

Environment and infrastructure indicators	2005	2010	2018
Individuals using the Internet (per 100 inhabitants)	11.5	40.1[f]	54.0[f,a]
Research & Development expenditure (% of GDP)	0.2	0.1	0.1[k]
Threatened species (number)	310[j]	347	383[d]
Forested area (% of land area)	64.3	63.2[f]	62.1[f,b]
CO2 emission estimates (million tons/tons per capita)	6.8 / 2.1	9.2 / 2.5	8.8 / 2.3[e]
Energy production, primary (Petajoules)	32	26	36[b]
Energy supply per capita (Gigajoules)	37	40	44[b]
Tourist/visitor arrivals at national borders (000)	702	1 324	2 007[e]
Important sites for terrestrial biodiversity protected (%)	37.8	38.8	38.8
Pop. using improved drinking water (urban/rural, %)	97.8 / 80.2	97.7 / 84.4	97.7 / 88.6[b]
Pop. using improved sanitation facilities (urban/rural, %)	80.5 / 50.5	82.0 / 54.2	83.5 / 58.0[b]
Net Official Development Assist. received (% of GNI)	0.13	0.48	0.05[e]

a Projected estimate (medium fertility variant). b 2015. c Refers to the metropolitan area of Panama City. d 2017. e 2016. f Estimate. g Urban areas. h Areas not elsewhere specified. i Data refers to a 5-year period preceding the reference year. j Data as at the end of December. k 2013. l 2004. m 2008. n 2011. o 2014.

Papua New Guinea

Region	Melanesia	UN membership date	10 October 1975
Population (000, 2018)	8 418[a]	Surface area (km2)	462 840[b]
Pop. density (per km2, 2018)	18.6[a]	Sex ratio (m per 100 f)	103.5[a]
Capital city	Port Moresby	National currency	Kina (PGK)
Capital city pop. (000, 2018)	366.9	Exchange rate (per US$)	3.2[c]

Economic indicators	2005	2010	2018
GDP: Gross domestic product (million current US$)	7 312	14 205	19 694[d]
GDP growth rate (annual %, const. 2010 prices)	3.9	11.2	2.5[d]
GDP per capita (current US$)	1 158.0	1 998.0	2 436.0[d]
Economy: Agriculture (% of Gross Value Added)	22.7	20.3	20.1[d]
Economy: Industry (% of Gross Value Added)	34.0	33.6	28.1[d]
Economy: Services and other activity (% of GVA)	43.3	46.0	51.8[d]
Employment in agriculture (% of employed)	52.6[e]	25.8	20.4[e]
Employment in industry (% of employed)[e]	5.8	7.5	7.6
Employment in services & other sectors (% employed)[e]	41.6	66.7	72.0
Unemployment rate (% of labour force)	2.5[e]	2.0	2.7[e]
Labour force participation rate (female/male pop. %)[e]	70.9 / 73.9	70.2 / 73.0	68.9 / 70.8
CPI: Consumer Price Index (2010=100)	77	100[f]	136[d]
Agricultural production index (2004-2006=100)	99	112	122[d]
International trade: exports (million current US$)[e]	3 276	5 742	8 240[c]
International trade: imports (million current US$)[e]	1 728	3 950	3 578[c]
International trade: balance (million current US$)[e]	1 548	1 792	4 661[c]
Balance of payments, current account (million US$)	539	- 633	5 181[d]

Major trading partners							2017
Export partners (% of exports)[e]	Australia	26.0	Japan	24.4	China	19.1
Import partners (% of imports)[e]	Australia	30.7	China	16.2	Singapore	10.8

Social indicators	2005	2010	2018
Population growth rate (average annual %)[g]	2.5	2.4	2.2[b]
Urban population (% of total population)	13.1	13.0	13.2
Urban population growth rate (average annual %)[g]	2.4	2.2	2.2[b]
Fertility rate, total (live births per woman)[g]	4.4	4.1	3.8[b]
Life expectancy at birth (females/males, years)[g]	65.1 / 60.3	66.7 / 61.8	67.4 / 62.6[b]
Population age distribution (0-14/60+ years old, %)	39.1 / 5.1	38.3 / 5.4	35.6 / 6.2[a]
International migrant stock (000/% of total pop.)[h,i]	30.0 / 0.5	25.4 / 0.4	32.4 / 0.4[c]
Refugees and others of concern to the UNHCR (000)	10.1[j]	9.7[j]	9.5[c]
Infant mortality rate (per 1 000 live births)[g]	55.5	51.9	49.0[b]
Health: Current expenditure (% of GDP)	3.7	3.1	3.8[b]
Health: Physicians (per 1 000 pop.)	0.1[k]	0.1[l]	...
Education: Primary gross enrol. ratio (f/m per 100 pop.)	52.4 / 61.9	55.9 / 63.2[l]	106.6 / 117.9[m]
Education: Secondary gross enrol. ratio (f/m per 100 pop.)	... / ...	... / ...	34.0 / 45.2[m]
Intentional homicide rate (per 100 000 pop.)	8.3[k]	7.8[n]	...
Seats held by women in the National Parliament (%)	0.9	0.9	0.0

Environment and infrastructure indicators	2005	2010	2018
Individuals using the Internet (per 100 inhabitants)	1.7	1.3[o]	9.6[e,d]
Threatened species (number)	295[p]	453	493[c]
Forested area (% of land area)[e]	74.2	74.1	74.1[b]
CO2 emission estimates (million tons/tons per capita)	4.4 / 0.7	4.8 / 0.7	6.3 / 0.8[q]
Energy production, primary (Petajoules)	174	95	168[e,b]
Energy supply per capita (Gigajoules)	21	21	21[e,b]
Tourist/visitor arrivals at national borders (000)	69	140	184[b]
Important sites for terrestrial biodiversity protected (%)	7.3	7.3	7.3
Pop. using improved drinking water (urban/rural, %)	87.7 / 29.5	87.9 / 31.8	88.0 / 32.8[b]
Pop. using improved sanitation facilities (urban/rural, %)	58.4 / 13.1	57.0 / 13.3	56.4 / 13.3[b]
Net Official Development Assist. received (% of GNI)	5.89	5.62	3.52[q]

a Projected estimate (medium fertility variant). b 2015. c 2017. d 2016. e Estimate. f Break in the time series. g Data refers to a 5-year period preceding the reference year. h Including refugees. i Refers to foreign citizens. j Data as at the end of December. k 2000. l 2008. m 2007. n 2007. o Population aged 10 years and over. p 2004. q 2014.

Paraguay

Region	South America	UN membership date	24 October 1945
Population (000, 2018)	6 897[a]	Surface area (km2)	406 752[b]
Pop. density (per km2, 2018)	17.4[a]	Sex ratio (m per 100 f)	102.9[a]
Capital city	Asunción	National currency	Guaraní (PYG)
Capital city pop. (000, 2018)	3 222.2[c]	Exchange rate (per US$)	5 590.5[d]

Economic indicators

	2005	2010	2018
GDP: Gross domestic product (million current US$)	8 735	20 048	27 165[e]
GDP growth rate (annual %, const. 2010 prices)	2.1	13.1	4.0[e]
GDP per capita (current US$)	1 507.0	3 228.0	4 039.0[e]
Economy: Agriculture (% of Gross Value Added)	19.6	22.5	19.0[e]
Economy: Industry (% of Gross Value Added)	34.8	30.1	31.6[e]
Economy: Services and other activity (% of GVA)	45.7	47.4	49.4[e]
Employment in agriculture (% of employed)[f]	32.4	25.6	20.9
Employment in industry (% of employed)[f]	15.7	19.2	19.5
Employment in services & other sectors (% employed)[f]	51.9	55.2	59.6
Unemployment rate (% of labour force)	5.8	4.6	5.2[f]
Labour force participation rate (female/male pop. %)[f]	55.0 / 85.3	53.9 / 83.7	56.9 / 83.8
CPI: Consumer Price Index (2010=100)[g,h]	71	100	135[d]
Agricultural production index (2004-2006=100)	98	138	164[e]
Index of industrial production (2005=100)[i]	100	110	124[j]
International trade: exports (million current US$)	3 153	6 517	8 680[d]
International trade: imports (million current US$)	3 274	10 033	11 873[d]
International trade: balance (million current US$)	- 121	- 3 517	- 3 194[d]
Balance of payments, current account (million US$)	- 68	49	- 369[d]

Major trading partners

						2017
Export partners (% of exports)	Brazil	32.0	Argentina	13.1	Chile	7.3
Import partners (% of imports)	China	30.9	Brazil	23.0	Argentina	10.3

Social indicators

	2005	2010	2018
Population growth rate (average annual %)[k]	1.8	1.4	1.3[b]
Urban population (% of total population)	57.6	59.3	61.6
Urban population growth rate (average annual %)[k]	2.6	1.9	1.8[b]
Fertility rate, total (live births per woman)[k]	3.2	2.9	2.6[b]
Life expectancy at birth (females/males, years)[k]	72.9 / 68.7	73.9 / 69.7	74.9 / 70.7[b]
Population age distribution (0-14/60+ years old, %)	35.3 / 7.1	32.7 / 7.9	29.1 / 9.6[a]
International migrant stock (000/% of total pop.)	168.2 / 2.9	160.3 / 2.6	160.5 / 2.4[d]
Refugees and others of concern to the UNHCR (000)	0.1[l]	0.1[l]	0.2[d]
Infant mortality rate (per 1 000 live births)[k]	35.5	32.0	28.8[b]
Health: Current expenditure (% of GDP)	5.0	6.2	7.8[b]
Health: Physicians (per 1 000 pop.)	1.2[m]	...	1.3[n]
Education: Government expenditure (% of GDP)	3.4[o]	3.8	5.0[n]
Education: Primary gross enrol. ratio (f/m per 100 pop.)	110.3 / 113.5	101.8 / 105.9	104.3 / 107.6[n]
Education: Secondary gross enrol. ratio (f/m per 100 pop.)	67.8 / 66.0	70.2 / 66.5	79.1 / 74.2[n]
Education: Tertiary gross enrol. ratio (f/m per 100 pop.)	27.5 / 24.3	41.2 / 29.1	... / ...
Intentional homicide rate (per 100 000 pop.)	15.3	11.9	9.3[b]
Seats held by women in the National Parliament (%)	10.0	12.5	13.8

Environment and infrastructure indicators

	2005	2010	2018
Individuals using the Internet (per 100 inhabitants)	7.9[p,q]	19.8[p,q]	51.3[f,a]
Research & Development expenditure (% of GDP)	0.1	0.1[r]	0.1[s,b]
Threatened species (number)	50[o]	48	59[d]
Forested area (% of land area)[f]	46.5	42.7	38.6[b]
CO2 emission estimates (million tons/tons per capita)	3.8 / 0.7	5.1 / 0.8	5.7 / 0.9[i]
Energy production, primary (Petajoules)	288	327	329[b]
Energy supply per capita (Gigajoules)	31	38	39[b]
Tourist/visitor arrivals at national borders (000)[t]	341	465	1 308[e]
Important sites for terrestrial biodiversity protected (%)	23.3	23.3	23.3
Pop. using improved drinking water (urban/rural, %)	94.1 / 66.0	97.2 / 80.5	100.0 / 94.9[b]
Pop. using improved sanitation facilities (urban/rural, %)	87.6 / 59.9	92.3 / 69.2	95.5 / 78.4[b]
Net Official Development Assist. received (% of GNI)	0.70	0.65	0.34[e]

a Projected estimate (medium fertility variant). b 2015. c Refers to the district of Asunción and the 19 districts of Central Department. d 2017. e 2016. f Estimate. g Asunción metropolitan area. h Calculated by the Statistics Division of the United Nations from national indices. i Data classified according to ISIC Rev. 3. j 2014. k Data refers to a 5-year period preceding the reference year. l Data as at the end of December. m 2002. n 2012. o 2004. p Population aged 10 years and over. q Users in the last 3 months. r 2008. s Excluding business enterprise. t Excluding nationals residing abroad and crew members.

Peru

Region	South America	UN membership date	31 October 1945	
Population (000, 2018)	32 552[a]	Surface area (km2)	1 285 216[b]	
Pop. density (per km2, 2018)	25.4[a]	Sex ratio (m per 100 f)	99.8[a]	
Capital city	Lima	National currency	Sol (PEN)	
Capital city pop. (000, 2018)	10 390.6[c]	Exchange rate (per US$)	3.2[d]	

Economic indicators

	2005	2010	2018
GDP: Gross domestic product (million current US$)	76 080	147 528	192 210[e]
GDP growth rate (annual %, const. 2010 prices)	6.3	8.3	3.9[e]
GDP per capita (current US$)	2 755.0	5 022.0	6 049.0[e]
Economy: Agriculture (% of Gross Value Added)[f]	7.5	7.5	7.6[e]
Economy: Industry (% of Gross Value Added)[f]	37.7	39.1	32.5[e]
Economy: Services and other activity (% of GVA)[f]	54.7	53.5	59.9[e]
Employment in agriculture (% of employed)[g]	34.8	27.7	28.0
Employment in industry (% of employed)[g]	14.1	16.9	15.9
Employment in services & other sectors (% employed)[g]	51.1	55.4	56.0
Unemployment rate (% of labour force)	4.9	3.5	3.8[g]
Labour force participation rate (female/male pop. %)[g]	66.7 / 84.6	72.0 / 86.3	69.4 / 84.7
CPI: Consumer Price Index (2010=100)[h]	87	100	125[d]
Agricultural production index (2004-2006=100)	99	129	150[e]
Index of industrial production (2005=100)[i]	100	130	142[j]
International trade: exports (million current US$)[k]	17 114	35 807	44 238[d]
International trade: imports (million current US$)[k]	12 502	29 966	39 764[d]
International trade: balance (million current US$)[k]	4 612	5 842	4 474[d]
Balance of payments, current account (million US$)	1 148	- 3 782	- 2 720[d]

Major trading partners

						2017
Export partners (% of exports)	China	26.3	United States	15.7	Switzerland	5.3
Import partners (% of imports)	China	22.3	United States	20.3	Brazil	6.2

Social indicators

	2005	2010	2018
Population growth rate (average annual %)[l]	1.3	1.2	1.3[b]
Urban population (% of total population)	75.0	76.4	77.9
Urban population growth rate (average annual %)[l]	1.8	1.6	1.6[b]
Fertility rate, total (live births per woman)[l]	2.8	2.6	2.5[b]
Life expectancy at birth (females/males, years)[l]	74.3 / 69.0	75.9 / 70.5	76.8 / 71.5[b]
Population age distribution (0-14/60+ years old, %)	31.7 / 8.1	29.4 / 8.9	27.1 / 10.7[a]
International migrant stock (000/% of total pop.)	77.5 / 0.3	84.1 / 0.3	93.8 / 0.3[d]
Refugees and others of concern to the UNHCR (000)	1.2[m]	1.4[m]	12.2[d]
Infant mortality rate (per 1 000 live births)[l]	27.4	21.0	18.6[b]
Health: Current expenditure (% of GDP)	4.6	4.7	5.3[b]
Health: Physicians (per 1 000 pop.)	...	0.9[n]	1.1[o]
Education: Government expenditure (% of GDP)	2.8	2.9	3.8[e]
Education: Primary gross enrol. ratio (f/m per 100 pop.)	118.0 / 117.0	111.0 / 109.8	103.3 / 103.0[e]
Education: Secondary gross enrol. ratio (f/m per 100 pop.)	84.6 / 86.3	94.9 / 94.5	97.9 / 98.2[e]
Education: Tertiary gross enrol. ratio (f/m per 100 pop.)	33.6 / 32.8	35.4 / 33.3[p]	... / ...
Intentional homicide rate (per 100 000 pop.)	...	...	7.7[e]
Seats held by women in the National Parliament (%)	18.3	27.5	27.7

Environment and infrastructure indicators

	2005	2010	2018
Individuals using the Internet (per 100 inhabitants)	17.1[g]	34.8[q]	45.5[e]
Research & Development expenditure (% of GDP)	0.2[r]	...	0.1[b]
Threatened species (number)	508[r]	551	685[d]
Forested area (% of land area)[g]	59.0	58.4	57.8[b]
CO2 emission estimates (million tons/tons per capita)	37.1 / 1.4	57.6 / 1.9	61.7 / 2.0[s]
Energy production, primary (Petajoules)	455	786	961[b]
Energy supply per capita (Gigajoules)	20	27	30[b]
Tourist/visitor arrivals at national borders (000)[t,u]	1 571	2 299	3 744[v,e]
Pop. using improved drinking water (urban/rural, %)	90.0 / 59.1	90.7 / 64.2	91.4 / 69.2[b]
Pop. using improved sanitation facilities (urban/rural, %)	77.7 / 37.4	80.1 / 45.3	82.5 / 53.2[b]
Net Official Development Assist. received (% of GNI)	0.64	- 0.22	0.17[e]

a Projected estimate (medium fertility variant). **b** 2015. **c** Refers to the Province of Lima and the Constitutional Province of Callao. **d** 2017. **e** 2016. **f** Data classified according to ISIC Rev. 4. **g** Estimate. **h** Metropolitan Lima. **i** Data classified according to ISIC Rev. 3. **j** 2013. **k** Imports FOB. **l** Data refers to a 5-year period preceding the reference year. **m** Data as at the end of December. **n** 2009. **o** 2012. **p** 2006. **q** Population aged 6 years and over. **r** 2004. **s** 2014. **t** Including nationals residing abroad. **u** Including tourists with identity document other than a passport. **v** Provisional data.

Philippines

Region	South-eastern Asia	UN membership date	24 October 1945
Population (000, 2018)	106 512[a]	Surface area (km2)	300 000[b]
Pop. density (per km2, 2018)	357.2[a]	Sex ratio (m per 100 f)	101.2[a]
Capital city	Manila	National currency	Philippine Piso (PHP)
Capital city pop. (000, 2018)	13 482.5[c]	Exchange rate (per US$)	49.9[d]

Economic indicators	2005	2010	2018
GDP: Gross domestic product (million current US$)	103 072	199 591	304 906[e]
GDP growth rate (annual %, const. 2010 prices)	4.8	7.6	6.9[e]
GDP per capita (current US$)	1 195.0	2 130.0	2 951.0[e]
Economy: Agriculture (% of Gross Value Added)[f,g]	12.7	12.3	9.7[e]
Economy: Industry (% of Gross Value Added)[f,g]	33.9	32.6	30.9[e]
Economy: Services and other activity (% of GVA)[f,g]	53.5	55.1	59.5[e]
Employment in agriculture (% of employed)[h]	36.0	33.2	25.3
Employment in industry (% of employed)[h]	15.6	15.0	17.8
Employment in services & other sectors (% employed)[h]	48.5	51.8	56.8
Unemployment rate (% of labour force)	7.8	3.6	5.9[h]
Labour force participation rate (female/male pop. %)[h]	47.7 / 76.6	48.6 / 76.1	49.8 / 75.1
CPI: Consumer Price Index (2010=100)	...	...	112[i,d]
Agricultural production index (2004-2006=100)	99	112	113[e]
International trade: exports (million current US$)	41 255	51 498	68 713[d]
International trade: imports (million current US$)	49 487	58 468	101 889[d]
International trade: balance (million current US$)	- 8 233	- 6 970	- 33 177[d]
Balance of payments, current account (million US$)	1 990[j]	7 179	-2 518[d]

Major trading partners						2017
Export partners (% of exports)	Japan	15.8	United States	14.1	China, Hong Kong SAR	13.1
Import partners (% of imports)	China	18.1	Japan	11.6	Republic of Korea	8.7

Social indicators	2005	2010	2018
Population growth rate (average annual %)[k]	2.0	1.7	1.6[b]
Urban population (% of total population)	45.7	45.3	46.9
Urban population growth rate (average annual %)[k]	1.8	1.5	2.1[b]
Fertility rate, total (live births per woman)[k]	3.7	3.3	3.0[b]
Life expectancy at birth (females/males, years)[k]	70.8 / 64.4	71.5 / 64.8	72.1 / 65.4[b]
Population age distribution (0-14/60+ years old, %)	37.1 / 5.4	33.9 / 6.5	31.5 / 7.8[a]
International migrant stock (000/% of total pop.)[l,m]	257.5 / 0.3	208.6 / 0.2	218.5 / 0.2[d]
Refugees and others of concern to the UNHCR (000)	0.9[n]	139.9[n]	511.2[d]
Infant mortality rate (per 1 000 live births)[k]	28.1	25.0	22.2[b]
Health: Current expenditure (% of GDP)[o]	3.9	4.3	4.4[b]
Health: Physicians (per 1 000 pop.)	1.1[p]	...	...
Education: Government expenditure (% of GDP)	2.4	2.7[q]	...
Education: Primary gross enrol. ratio (f/m per 100 pop.)	105.4 / 106.5	107.5 / 108.6[q]	111.3 / 114.6[b]
Education: Secondary gross enrol. ratio (f/m per 100 pop.)	87.6 / 78.3	87.5 / 80.9[q]	92.1 / 84.8[b]
Education: Tertiary gross enrol. ratio (f/m per 100 pop.)	30.4 / 24.7	33.0 / 26.4	40.3 / 30.5[d]
Intentional homicide rate (per 100 000 pop.)[j]	7.5	9.5	11.0[e]
Seats held by women in the National Parliament (%)	15.3	21.0	29.5

Environment and infrastructure indicators	2005	2010	2018
Individuals using the Internet (per 100 inhabitants)	5.4[h]	25.0	55.5[h,e]
Research & Development expenditure (% of GDP)	0.1	0.1[q]	0.1[r]
Threatened species (number)	456[p]	697	783[d]
Forested area (% of land area)	23.7	22.9	27.0[b]
CO2 emission estimates (million tons/tons per capita)	74.8 / 0.9	84.9 / 0.9	105.7 / 1.1[s]
Energy production, primary (Petajoules)	762	924	999[b]
Energy supply per capita (Gigajoules)	17	18	20[b]
Tourist/visitor arrivals at national borders (000)[t]	2 623	3 520	5 967[e]
Important sites for terrestrial biodiversity protected (%)	38.7	41.4	41.7
Pop. using improved drinking water (urban/rural, %)	92.6 / 85.1	93.1 / 87.7	93.7 / 90.3[b]
Pop. using improved sanitation facilities (urban/rural, %)	74.3 / 60.8	76.1 / 65.8	77.9 / 70.8[b]
Net Official Development Assist. received (% of GNI)	0.44	0.20	0.08[e]

a Projected estimate (medium fertility variant). b 2015. c Refers to the National Capital Region. d 2017. e 2016. f Including taxes less subsidies on production and imports. g Data classified according to ISIC Rev. 4. h Estimate. i Index base: 2012=100. j Break in the time series. k Data refers to a 5-year period preceding the reference year. l Refers to foreign citizens. m Including refugees. n Data as at the end of December. o Data revision. p 2004. q 2009. r 2013. s 2014. t Including nationals residing abroad.

Poland

Region	Eastern Europe	UN membership date	24 October 1945
Population (000, 2018)	38 105[a]	Surface area (km2)	312 679[b]
Pop. density (per km2, 2018)	124.4[a]	Sex ratio (m per 100 f)	93.4[a]
Capital city	Warsaw	National currency	Zloty (PLN)
Capital city pop. (000, 2018)	1 767.8	Exchange rate (per US$)	3.5[c]

Economic indicators

	2005	2010	2018
GDP: Gross domestic product (million current US$)	306 127	479 321	471 402[d]
GDP growth rate (annual %, const. 2010 prices)	3.5	3.6	2.9[d]
GDP per capita (current US$)	7 980.0	12 507.0	12 332.0[d]
Economy: Agriculture (% of Gross Value Added)[e]	3.3	2.9	2.7[d]
Economy: Industry (% of Gross Value Added)[e]	32.8	33.2	33.7[d]
Economy: Services and other activity (% of GVA)[e]	63.9	63.9	63.6[d]
Employment in agriculture (% of employed)[f]	17.4	13.0[f]	10.3[f]
Employment in industry (% of employed)[f]	29.2	30.3	31.1
Employment in services & other sectors (% employed)[f]	53.4	56.6	58.6
Unemployment rate (% of labour force)	17.8	9.6	4.2[f]
Labour force participation rate (female/male pop. %)[f]	47.8 / 63.0	48.3 / 64.3	48.5 / 64.8
CPI: Consumer Price Index (2010=100)[g]	...	100	110[c]
Agricultural production index (2004-2006=100)	98	101	113[d]
Index of industrial production (2005=100)	100	134	154[h]
International trade: exports (million current US$)	89 378	157 065	221 308[c]
International trade: imports (million current US$)	101 539	174 128	217 979[c]
International trade: balance (million current US$)	- 12 161	- 17 063	3 329[c]
Balance of payments, current account (million US$)	- 7 981	- 25 875	1 584[c]

Major trading partners

							2017
Export partners (% of exports)	Germany	27.2	United Kingdom	6.4	Czechia	6.4
Import partners (% of imports)	Germany	22.7	China	12.1	Russian Federation	6.8

Social indicators

	2005	2010	2018
Population growth rate (average annual %)[i]	- 0.1	-0.0	-0.0[b]
Urban population (% of total population)	61.5	60.9	60.1
Urban population growth rate (average annual %)[i]	- 0.2	- 0.2	- 0.2[b]
Fertility rate, total (live births per woman)[i]	1.3	1.4	1.3[b]
Life expectancy at birth (females/males, years)[i]	78.8 / 70.4	79.8 / 71.3	81.0 / 72.9[b]
Population age distribution (0-14/60+ years old, %)	16.6 / 17.0	15.2 / 19.4	14.9 / 24.6[a]
International migrant stock (000/% of total pop.)	722.5 / 1.9	642.4 / 1.7	640.9 / 1.7[c]
Refugees and others of concern to the UNHCR (000)	6.3[j]	18.4[j]	25.7[c]
Infant mortality rate (per 1 000 live births)[i]	7.1	5.7	4.5[b]
Health: Current expenditure (% of GDP)	5.8	6.4	6.3[b]
Health: Physicians (per 1 000 pop.)	...	2.2	2.3[b]
Education: Government expenditure (% of GDP)	5.4	5.1	4.9[h]
Education: Primary gross enrol. ratio (f/m per 100 pop.)	94.3 / 94.8	96.2 / 97.0	110.6 / 109.6[d]
Education: Secondary gross enrol. ratio (f/m per 100 pop.)	99.3 / 99.9	95.8 / 96.2	105.5 / 108.5[d]
Education: Tertiary gross enrol. ratio (f/m per 100 pop.)	74.7 / 52.9	90.8 / 59.6	80.6 / 53.2[d]
Intentional homicide rate (per 100 000 pop.)	1.4[k]	1.1[k]	0.7[d]
Seats held by women in the National Parliament (%)	20.2	20.0	28.0

Environment and infrastructure indicators

	2005	2010	2018
Individuals using the Internet (per 100 inhabitants)[i]	38.8	62.3	73.3[m,d]
Research & Development expenditure (% of GDP)	0.6	0.7	1.0[b]
Threatened species (number)	46[n]	37	58[c]
Forested area (% of land area)	30.0	30.5	30.8[b]
CO2 emission estimates (million tons/tons per capita)	302.5 / 7.9	316.3 / 8.2	285.7 / 7.4[h]
Energy production, primary (Petajoules)	3 281	2 808	2 834[b]
Energy supply per capita (Gigajoules)	102	110	108[b]
Tourist/visitor arrivals at national borders (000)	15 200[o]	12 470[o]	17 471[d]
Important sites for terrestrial biodiversity protected (%)	73.4	87.9	88.1
Pop. using improved drinking water (urban/rural, %)	99.1 / 93.1	99.2 / 95.2	99.3 / 96.9[b]
Pop. using improved sanitation facilities (urban/rural, %)	95.2 / 83.3	96.5 / 90.8	97.5 / 96.7[b]
Net Official Development Assist. disbursed (% of GNI)[p]	0.07	0.08	0.13[q,c]

a Projected estimate (medium fertility variant). **b** 2015. **c** 2017. **d** 2016. **e** Data classified according to ISIC Rev. 4. **f** Estimate. **g** Calculated by the Statistics Division of the United Nations from national indices. **h** 2014. **i** Data refers to a 5-year period preceding the reference year. **j** Data as at the end of December. **k** Data refer to offences, not victims, of intentional homicide. **l** Population aged 16 to 74 years. **m** Users in the last 3 months. **n** 2004. **o** Border statistics are not collected any more, surveys used instead. **p** Development Assistance Committee member (OECD). **q** Provisional data.

Portugal

Region	Southern Europe	UN membership date	14 December 1955
Population (000, 2018)	10 291 [a]	Surface area (km2)	92 226 [b]
Pop. density (per km2, 2018)	112.4 [a]	Sex ratio (m per 100 f)	89.9 [a]
Capital city	Lisbon	National currency	Euro (EUR)
Capital city pop. (000, 2018)	2 927.3 [c]	Exchange rate (per US$)	0.8 [d]

Economic indicators

	2005	2010	2018
GDP: Gross domestic product (million current US$)	197 300	238 303	204 837 [e]
GDP growth rate (annual %, const. 2010 prices)	0.8	1.9	1.5 [e]
GDP per capita (current US$)	18 674.0	22 371.0	19 750.0 [e]
Economy: Agriculture (% of Gross Value Added) [f]	2.6	2.2	2.2 [e]
Economy: Industry (% of Gross Value Added) [f]	24.6	22.6	22.2 [e]
Economy: Services and other activity (% of GVA) [f]	72.7	75.2	75.6 [e]
Employment in agriculture (% of employed) [g]	12.0	11.2 [g]	6.7 [g]
Employment in industry (% of employed) [g]	30.4	27.3	24.6
Employment in services & other sectors (% employed) [g]	57.6	61.6	68.8
Unemployment rate (% of labour force)	7.6	10.8	7.8 [g]
Labour force participation rate (female/male pop. %) [g]	55.3 / 69.3	55.8 / 66.9	53.0 / 63.3
CPI: Consumer Price Index (2010=100) [h,i]	92	100	109 [d]
Agricultural production index (2004-2006=100)	97	105	108 [d]
Index of industrial production (2005=100)	100	92	88 [j]
International trade: exports (million current US$)	38 672	49 414	62 170 [d]
International trade: imports (million current US$)	63 904	77 682	77 834 [d]
International trade: balance (million current US$)	- 25 232	- 28 268	- 15 664 [d]
Balance of payments, current account (million US$)	- 19 538	- 24 202	1 167 [d]

Major trading partners

						2017
Export partners (% of exports)	Spain	25.2	France	12.5	Germany	11.3
Import partners (% of imports)	Spain	32.0	Germany	13.7	France	7.4

Social indicators

	2005	2010	2018
Population growth rate (average annual %) [k]	0.4	0.2	- 0.4 [b]
Urban population (% of total population)	57.5	60.6	65.2
Urban population growth rate (average annual %) [k]	1.5	1.2	0.5 [b]
Fertility rate, total (live births per woman) [k]	1.5	1.4	1.3 [b]
Life expectancy at birth (females/males, years) [k]	81.0 / 74.1	82.5 / 76.0	83.5 / 77.3 [b]
Population age distribution (0-14/60+ years old, %)	15.4 / 22.5	15.0 / 24.7	13.4 / 28.3 [a]
International migrant stock (000/% of total pop.)	771.2 / 7.3	762.8 / 7.2	880.2 / 8.5 [d]
Refugees and others of concern to the UNHCR (000) [l]	0.4	0.5	2.1 [e]
Infant mortality rate (per 1 000 live births) [k]	4.5	3.3	2.9 [b]
Health: Current expenditure (% of GDP)	9.4	9.8	9.0 [b]
Health: Physicians (per 1 000 pop.)	3.4	3.8	4.4 [i]
Education: Government expenditure (% of GDP)	5.1	5.4	5.1 [j]
Education: Primary gross enrol. ratio (f/m per 100 pop.)	114.6 / 120.3	109.4 / 112.7	103.3 / 107.1 [e]
Education: Secondary gross enrol. ratio (f/m per 100 pop.)	102.1 / 92.8	107.7 / 104.8	115.9 / 119.1 [e]
Education: Tertiary gross enrol. ratio (f/m per 100 pop.)	62.6 / 47.9	70.7 / 59.9	66.4 / 59.5 [e]
Intentional homicide rate (per 100 000 pop.)	1.3	1.2	0.6 [e]
Seats held by women in the National Parliament (%)	19.1	27.4	34.8

Environment and infrastructure indicators

	2005	2010	2018
Individuals using the Internet (per 100 inhabitants)	35.0 [m]	53.3 [m]	70.4 [e]
Research & Development expenditure (% of GDP)	0.8	1.5	1.3 [n,b]
Threatened species (number)	148 [o]	171	281 [d]
Forested area (% of land area) [g]	36.0	35.4	34.7 [b]
CO2 emission estimates (million tons/tons per capita)	65.3 / 6.2	48.1 / 4.5	45.1 / 4.3 [j]
Energy production, primary (Petajoules) [p]	151	242	222 [b]
Energy supply per capita (Gigajoules)	105	92	88 [b]
Tourist/visitor arrivals at national borders (000) [n,q]	5 769	6 756	11 223 [e]
Important sites for terrestrial biodiversity protected (%)	60.5	71.0	73.9
Pop. using improved drinking water (urban/rural, %)	99.2 / 98.3	99.7 / 99.5	100.0 / 100.0 [b]
Pop. using improved sanitation facilities (urban/rural, %)	98.7 / 95.2	99.2 / 98.7	99.6 / 99.8 [b]
Net Official Development Assist. disbursed (% of GNI) [r]	0.21	0.29	0.18 [n,d]

a Projected estimate (medium fertility variant). b 2015. c Refers to Grande Lisboa, the Peninsula of Setúbal, and the municipality Azambuja. d 2017. e 2016. f Data classified according to ISIC Rev. 4. g Estimate. h Excluding rent. i Calculated by the Statistics Division of the United Nations from national indices. j 2014. k Data refers to a 5-year period preceding the reference year. l Data as at the end of December. m Population aged 16 to 74 years. n Provisional data. o 2004. p Data includes the Azores and Madeira. q Includes establishments with 10 or more bed places: hotels, apartment hotels, "pousadas", tourist apartments and tourist villages, as well as other accommodation establishments: boarding houses, motels and inns. Includes camping sites and recreation centres. Does not include tourism in rural areas neither local accommodation. r Development Assistance Committee member (OECD).

Puerto Rico

Region	Caribbean	Population (000, 2018)	3 659[a]
Surface area (km2)	8 868[b]	Pop. density (per km2, 2018)	412.5[a]
Sex ratio (m per 100 f)	92.6[a]	Capital city	San Juan
National currency	US Dollar (USD)	Capital city pop. (000, 2018)	2 454.3[c]

Economic indicators	2005	2010	2018
GDP: Gross domestic product (million current US$)	83 915	98 381	105 035[d]
GDP growth rate (annual %, const. 2010 prices)	- 2.0	- 0.4	- 2.6[d]
GDP per capita (current US$)	22 286.0	26 470.0	28 636.0[d]
Economy: Agriculture (% of Gross Value Added)[e]	0.6	0.8	0.8[d]
Economy: Industry (% of Gross Value Added)[e]	47.3	50.7	50.4[d]
Economy: Services and other activity (% of GVA)[e]	52.1	48.4	48.8[d]
Employment in agriculture (% of employed)[f]	2.1	1.6	3.2
Employment in industry (% of employed)[f]	19.0	13.8	16.8
Employment in services & other sectors (% employed)[f]	78.9	84.7	80.1
Unemployment rate (% of labour force)	11.4	16.4	11.5[f]
Labour force participation rate (female/male pop. %)[f]	36.9 / 59.1	35.6 / 55.0	33.1 / 50.9
CPI: Consumer Price Index (2010=100)[g]	...	100	107[h]
Agricultural production index (2004-2006=100)	96	104	102[d]

Social indicators	2005	2010	2018
Population growth rate (average annual %)[i]	- 0.2	- 0.3	- 0.2[b]
Urban population (% of total population)	94.1	93.8	93.6
Urban population growth rate (average annual %)[i]	- 0.2	- 0.3	- 0.3[b]
Fertility rate, total (live births per woman)[i]	1.8	1.7	1.5[b]
Life expectancy at birth (females/males, years)[i]	80.9 / 72.7	81.8 / 73.8	83.2 / 75.2[b]
Population age distribution (0-14/60+ years old, %)	22.3 / 16.7	20.6 / 18.1	17.6 / 20.8[a]
International migrant stock (000/% of total pop.)	352.1 / 9.4	305.0 / 8.2	273.5 / 7.5[h]
Infant mortality rate (per 1 000 live births)[i]	8.0	7.0	6.3[b]
Education: Government expenditure (% of GDP)	...	...	6.0[i]
Education: Primary gross enrol. ratio (f/m per 100 pop.)	... / ...	95.8 / 92.5	87.5 / 86.0[b]
Education: Secondary gross enrol. ratio (f/m per 100 pop.)	... / ...	85.4 / 80.8	89.3 / 83.9[b]
Education: Tertiary gross enrol. ratio (f/m per 100 pop.)	... / ...	103.2 / 69.9	99.4 / 70.7[b]
Intentional homicide rate (per 100 000 pop.)	20.5	27.4	18.5[d]

Environment and infrastructure indicators	2005	2010	2018
Individuals using the Internet (per 100 inhabitants)	23.4[f]	45.3[k]	80.3[f,d]
Research & Development expenditure (% of GDP)	...	0.5[l]	0.4[b]
Threatened species (number)	97[m]	103	126[h]
Forested area (% of land area)	52.2	54.0[f]	55.9[f,b]
Energy production, primary (Petajoules)	0	0	1[b]
Energy supply per capita (Gigajoules)	6	7	16[b]
Tourist/visitor arrivals at national borders (000)[n]	3 686	3 186	3 736[d]
Important sites for terrestrial biodiversity protected (%)	34.0	34.0	34.0
Pop. using improved drinking water (urban/rural, %)	93.6 / 93.6[o]	... / ...	... / ...
Pop. using improved sanitation facilities (urban/rural, %)	99.3 / 99.3	99.3 / 99.3	99.3 / 99.3[b]

a Projected estimate (medium fertility variant). b 2015. c Refers to the Metropolitan Statistical Area. d 2016. e At producers' prices. f Estimate. g Calculated by the Statistics Division of the United Nations from national indices. h 2017. i Data refers to a 5 year period preceding the reference year. j 2014. k Population aged 12 years and over. l 2009. m 2004. n Arrivals of non-resident tourists by air. o 2000.

Qatar

Region	Western Asia	UN membership date	21 September 1971
Population (000, 2018)	2 695 [a]	Surface area (km2)	11 607 [b]
Pop. density (per km2, 2018)	232.1 [e]	Sex ratio (m per 100 f)	298.6 [a]
Capital city	Doha	National currency	Qatari Rial (QAR)
Capital city pop. (000, 2018)	633.4 [c]	Exchange rate (per US$)	3.6 [d]

Economic indicators

	2005	2010	2018
GDP: Gross domestic product (million current US$)	43 998	123 627	152 452 [e]
GDP growth rate (annual %, const. 2010 prices)	7.5	16.7	2.2 [e]
GDP per capita (current US$)	50 873.0	69 466.0	59 324.0 [e]
Economy: Agriculture (% of Gross Value Added) [f]	0.1	0.1	0.2 [e]
Economy: Industry (% of Gross Value Added) [f]	74.6	67.5	49.7 [e]
Economy: Services and other activity (% of GVA) [f]	25.3	32.4	50.1 [e]
Employment in agriculture (% of employed) [g]	3.1	1.5	1.2
Employment in industry (% of employed) [g]	40.4	57.2	54.6
Employment in services & other sectors (% employed) [g]	56.5	41.3	44.2
Unemployment rate (% of labour force)	1.6 [g]	0.4	0.2 [g]
Labour force participation rate (female/male pop. %) [g]	45.1 / 94.0	51.1 / 95.8	57.8 / 94.7
CPI: Consumer Price Index (2010=100)	...	...	108 [h,d]
Agricultural production index (2004-2006=100)	96	132	166 [e]
Index of industrial production (2005=100) [i]	100	190	226 [j]
International trade: exports (million current US$)	25 762	74 964	67 444 [g,d]
International trade: imports (million current US$)	10 061	23 240	29 451 [g,d]
International trade: balance (million current US$)	15 702	51 725	37 993 [g,d]
Balance of payments, current account (million US$)	...	...	6 426 [d]

Major trading partners

					2017
Export partners (% of exports)	Japan	19.1 [g]	Republic of Korea	15.6	India	12.9 [g]
Import partners (% of imports) [g]	United States	14.4	China	10.4	Germany	9.3

Social indicators

	2005	2010	2018
Population growth rate (average annual %) [k]	7.6	14.4	6.6 [b]
Urban population (% of total population)	97.4	98.5	99.1
Urban population growth rate (average annual %) [k]	7.8	14.7	6.7 [b]
Fertility rate, total (live births per woman) [k]	3.0	2.2	2.0 [b]
Life expectancy at birth (females/males, years) [k]	78.1 / 75.6	78.6 / 75.9	79.4 / 76.8 [b]
Population age distribution (0-14/60+ years old, %)	21.7 / 2.5	13.1 / 1.8	13.9 / 3.1 [a]
International migrant stock (000/% of total pop.) [l]	646.0 / 74.7	1 456.4 / 81.8	1 721.4 / 65.2 [d]
Refugees and others of concern to the UNHCR (000)	0.1 [m]	1.3 [m]	1.5 [d]
Infant mortality rate (per 1 000 live births) [k]	9.4	7.8	7.2 [b]
Health: Current expenditure (% of GDP)	2.6	1.8	3.1 [b]
Health: Physicians (per 1 000 pop.)	2.6	3.9	2.0 [j]
Education: Government expenditure (% of GDP)	4.0	4.5	3.6 [j]
Education: Primary gross enrol. ratio (f/m per 100 pop.)	103.7 / 107.1	105.9 / 104.7	103.4 / 104.0 [e]
Education: Secondary gross enrol. ratio (f/m per 100 pop.)	96.0 / 102.3	103.3 / 99.2	100.7 / 85.8 [e]
Education: Tertiary gross enrol. ratio (f/m per 100 pop.)	31.1 / 8.8 [g]	25.6 / 4.8	47.1 / 6.4 [e]
Intentional homicide rate (per 100 000 pop.)	0.7	0.2	0.4 [j]
Seats held by women in the National Parliament (%)		0.0	9.8

Environment and infrastructure indicators

	2005	2010	2018
Individuals using the Internet (per 100 inhabitants)	24.7	69.0	94.3 [g,e]
Research & Development expenditure (% of GDP)	...	...	0.5 [n]
Threatened species (number)	12 [o]	32	39 [d]
Forested area (% of land area) [g]	0.0	0.0	0.0 [b]
CO2 emission estimates (million tons/tons per capita)	51.0 / 62.1	72.5 / 41.1	107.9 / 49.7 [j]
Energy production, primary (Petajoules)	3 718	7 428	9 225 [b]
Energy supply per capita (Gigajoules)	886	660	848 [b]
Tourist/visitor arrivals at national borders (000)	...	1 700	2 938 [e]
Important sites for terrestrial biodiversity protected (%)	50.0	50.0	50.0
Pop. using improved drinking water (urban/rural, %)	99.7 / 99.7	100.0 / 100.0	100.0 / 100.0 [b]
Pop. using improved sanitation facilities (urban/rural, %)	98.8 / 98.8	98.3 / 98.2	98.0 / 98.0 [b]

a Projected estimate (medium fertility variant). b 2015. c Does not include the populations from the industrial area and zone 58. d 2017. e 2016. f Data classified according to ISIC Rev. 4. g Estimate. h Index base: 2013=100. i Data classified according to ISIC Rev. 3. j 2014. k Data refers to a 5-year period preceding the reference year. l Refers to foreign citizens. m Data as at the end of December. n 2012. o 2004.

Republic of Korea

Region	Eastern Asia
Population (000, 2018)	51 164 [a]
Pop. density (per km2, 2018)	526.2 [a]
Capital city	Seoul
Capital city pop. (000, 2018)	9 963.5 [c]

UN membership date	17 September 1991
Surface area (km2)	100 284 [b]
Sex ratio (m per 100 f)	100.1 [a]
National currency	South Korean Won (KRW)
Exchange rate (per US$)	1 070.5 [d]

Economic indicators	2005	2010	2018
GDP: Gross domestic product (million current US$)	898 137	1 094 499	1 411 246 [e]
GDP growth rate (annual %, const. 2010 prices)	3.9	6.5	2.8 [e]
GDP per capita (current US$)	18 439.0	22 088.0	27 785.0 [e]
Economy: Agriculture (% of Gross Value Added) [f]	3.1	2.5	2.2 [e]
Economy: Industry (% of Gross Value Added) [f]	37.5	38.3	38.6 [e]
Economy: Services and other activity (% of GVA) [f]	59.4	59.3	59.2 [e]
Employment in agriculture (% of employed) [g]	7.9	6.6	4.8
Employment in industry (% of employed) [g]	26.8	25.0	24.6
Employment in services & other sectors (% employed) [g]	65.2	68.5	70.6
Unemployment rate (% of labour force)	3.7	3.7	3.7 [g]
Labour force participation rate (female/male pop. %) [g]	50.4 / 74.0	49.5 / 72.2	52.2 / 73.2
CPI: Consumer Price Index (2010=100) [h]	86	100	113 [d]
Agricultural production index (2004-2006=100)	100	101	103 [e]
Index of industrial production (2005=100)	100	139 [i]	151 [i,j]
International trade: exports (million current US$)	284 418	466 381	573 627 [d]
International trade: imports (million current US$)	261 236	425 208	478 469 [d]
International trade: balance (million current US$)	23 183	41 173	95 158 [d]
Balance of payments, current account (million US$)	12 655	28 850	78 460 [d]

Major trading partners						2017
Export partners (% of exports)	China	24.7	United States	12.0	Viet Nam	8.3
Import partners (% of imports)	China	20.5	Japan	11.5	United States	10.6

Social indicators	2005	2010	2018
Population growth rate (average annual %) [k]	0.6	0.3	0.4 [b]
Urban population (% of total population)	81.3	81.9	81.5
Urban population growth rate (average annual %) [k]	1.0	0.5	0.3 [b]
Fertility rate, total (live births per woman) [k]	1.2	1.2	1.2 [b]
Life expectancy at birth (females/males, years) [k]	80.6 / 73.6	82.7 / 76.0	84.4 / 77.9 [b]
Population age distribution (0-14/60+ years old, %)	18.8 / 12.8	16.1 / 15.3	13.4 / 21.1 [a]
International migrant stock (000/% of total pop.) [l]	485.5 / 1.0	919.3 / 1.9	1 151.9 / 2.3 [d]
Refugees and others of concern to the UNHCR (000)	0.6 [m]	1.2 [m]	9.4 [d]
Infant mortality rate (per 1 000 live births) [k]	5.0	3.5	3.0 [b]
Health: Current expenditure (% of GDP)	5.1	6.5	7.4 [b]
Health: Physicians (per 1 000 pop.)	1.8	2.0	2.3 [e]
Education: Government expenditure (% of GDP)	3.9	4.7 [n]	5.1 [b]
Education: Primary gross enrol. ratio (f/m per 100 pop.)	100.7 / 101.4	101.7 / 101.7	97.8 / 97.4 [b]
Education: Secondary gross enrol. ratio (f/m per 100 pop.)	98.2 / 96.0	96.1 / 96.6	100.3 / 100.1 [b]
Education: Tertiary gross enrol. ratio (f/m per 100 pop.)	70.9 / 110.8	86.8 / 116.7	80.6 / 104.6 [b]
Intentional homicide rate (per 100 000 pop.)	...	...	0.7 [e]
Seats held by women in the National Parliament (%)	13.0	14.7	17.0

Environment and infrastructure indicators	2005	2010	2018
Individuals using the Internet (per 100 inhabitants)	73.5 [o]	83.7 [o]	92.7 [e]
Research & Development expenditure (% of GDP)	2.6 [p]	3.5	4.2 [b]
Threatened species (number)	55 [q]	64	111 [d]
Forested area (% of land area)	64.6	64.0 [g]	63.4 [g,b]
CO2 emission estimates (million tons/tons per capita)	462.9 / 9.8	566.7 / 11.6	587.2 / 11.7 [e]
Energy production, primary (Petajoules)	1 776	1 855	2 116 [b]
Energy supply per capita (Gigajoules)	186	213	226 [b]
Tourist/visitor arrivals at national borders (000)	6 023	8 798	17 242 [e]
Important sites for terrestrial biodiversity protected (%)	27.3	36.4	36.6
Pop. using improved drinking water (urban/rural, %)	99.1 / 83.2	99.7 / 87.9	99.7 / 87.9 [b,r]
Pop. using improved sanitation facilities (urban/rural, %)	100.0 / 100.0	100.0 / 100.0	100.0 / 100.0 [b]
Net Official Development Assist. disbursed (% of GNI) [s]	0.10	0.12	0.14 [t,d]

a Projected estimate (medium fertility variant). b 2015. c Refers to Seoul Special City. d 2017. e 2016. f Data classified according to ISIC Rev. 4. g Estimate. h Calculated by the Statistics Division of the United Nations from national indices. i Excluding water and waste management. j 2014. k Data refers to a 5-year period preceding the reference year. l Refers to foreign citizens. m Data as at the end of December. n 2009. o Population aged 3 years and over. p Excluding social sciences and humanities. q 2004. r 2012. s Development Assistance Committee member (OECD). t Provisional data.

Republic of Moldova

Region	Eastern Europe	UN membership date	02 March 1992	
Population (000, 2018)	4 041 [a,b]	Surface area (km2)	33 846 [c]	
Pop. density (per km2, 2018)	123.0 [a,b]	Sex ratio (m per 100 f)	92.1 [a,b]	
Capital city	Chisinau	National currency	Moldovan Leu (MDL)	
Capital city pop. (000, 2018)	509.7	Exchange rate (per US$)	17.1 [d]	

Economic indicators	2005	2010	2018
GDP: Gross domestic product (million current US$)	2 988	5 812	6 773 [e]
GDP growth rate (annual %, const. 2010 prices)	7.5	7.1	4.3 [e]
GDP per capita (current US$)	719.0	1 423.0	1 668.0 [e]
Economy: Agriculture (% of Gross Value Added)	19.1	14.1	14.0 [e]
Economy: Industry (% of Gross Value Added)	22.3	20.0	20.3 [e]
Economy: Services and other activity (% of GVA)	58.6	65.9	65.7 [e]
Employment in agriculture (% of employed)	40.6 [f]	27.5	32.6 [f]
Employment in industry (% of employed) [f]	16.0	18.6	17.2
Employment in services & other sectors (% employed) [f]	43.3	53.8	50.2
Unemployment rate (% of labour force)	7.3	7.4	4.4 [f]
Labour force participation rate (female/male pop. %) [f]	46.4 / 50.9	38.9 / 45.4	38.9 / 45.6
CPI: Consumer Price Index (2010=100) [g,h]	...	100	154 [d]
Agricultural production index (2004-2006=100)	100	93	111 [e]
Index of industrial production (2005=100) [i]	100	82	94 [j]
International trade: exports (million current US$)	1 091	1 541	2 425 [d]
International trade: imports (million current US$)	2 292	3 855	4 831 [d]
International trade: balance (million current US$)	- 1 201	- 2 314	- 2 406 [d]
Balance of payments, current account (million US$)	- 226	- 481	- 617 [d]

Major trading partners						2017
Export partners (% of exports)	Romania	24.8	Russian Federation	10.5	Italy	9.7
Import partners (% of imports)	Romania	14.4	Russian Federation	11.8	Ukraine	10.6

Social indicators	2005	2010	2018
Population growth rate (average annual %) [b,k]	- 0.2	- 0.4	- 0.1 [c]
Urban population (% of total population) [b]	42.8	42.6	42.6
Urban population growth rate (average annual %) [b,k]	- 1.0	- 0.4	- 0.2 [c]
Fertility rate, total (live births per woman) [b,k]	1.2	1.3	1.3 [c]
Life expectancy at birth (females/males, years) [b,k]	71.6 / 63.6	72.1 / 64.4	75.2 / 66.7 [c]
Population age distribution (0-14/60+ years old, %) [b]	18.5 / 13.6	16.5 / 14.1	15.8 / 18.0 [a]
International migrant stock (000/% of total pop.) [b]	174.0 / 4.2	157.7 / 3.9	140.0 / 3.5 [d]
Refugees and others of concern to the UNHCR (000)	1.8 [l]	2.3 [l]	5.2 [d]
Infant mortality rate (per 1 000 live births) [b,k]	18.9	15.5	14.3 [c]
Health: Current expenditure (% of GDP) [m]	9.6	12.2	10.2 [c]
Health: Physicians (per 1 000 pop.)	...	2.4	3.2 [c]
Education: Government expenditure (% of GDP)	7.2	9.1	6.7 [e]
Education: Primary gross enrol. ratio (f/m per 100 pop.) [f]	97.2 / 98.6	93.3 / 93.7	91.9 / 92.9 [c]
Education: Secondary gross enrol. ratio (f/m per 100 pop.) [f]	90.0 / 86.2	89.0 / 87.0	86.5 / 85.8 [c]
Education: Tertiary gross enrol. ratio (f/m per 100 pop.) [f]	42.9 / 29.5	43.7 / 32.7	47.4 / 35.3 [c]
Intentional homicide rate (per 100 000 pop.)	7.1	6.5	3.2 [n]
Seats held by women in the National Parliament (%)	15.8	23.8	22.8

Environment and infrastructure indicators	2005	2010	2018
Individuals using the Internet (per 100 inhabitants)	14.6	32.3 [j]	71.0 [e]
Research & Development expenditure (% of GDP)	0.4	0.4	0.4 [c]
Threatened species (number)	27 [o]	27	35 [d]
Forested area (% of land area) [f]	11.0	11.8	12.4 [c]
CO2 emission estimates (million tons/tons per capita)	4.9 / 1.3	4.9 / 1.2	4.9 / 1.2 [n]
Energy production, primary (Petajoules)	4	8	15 [c]
Energy supply per capita (Gigajoules)	24	22	21 [c]
Tourist/visitor arrivals at national borders (000) [h]	67	64	121 [e]
Important sites for terrestrial biodiversity protected (%)	23.6	23.6	23.6
Pop. using improved drinking water (urban/rural, %)	96.8 / 77.4	96.9 / 79.6	96.9 / 81.4 [c]
Pop. using improved sanitation facilities (urban/rural, %)	87.1 / 63.1	87.5 / 65.3	87.8 / 67.1 [c]
Net Official Development Assist. received (% of GNI)	5.07	7.51	4.58 [e]

a Projected estimate (medium fertility variant). b Including the Transnistria region. c 2015. d 2017. e 2016. f Estimate. g Data refer to 8 cities only. h Excluding the left side of the river Nistru and the municipality of Bender. i Data classified according to ISIC Rev. 3. j 2013. k Data refers to a 5-year period preceding the reference year. l Data as at the end of December. m Excluding the Transnistria region. n 2014. o 2004.

Réunion

Region	Eastern Africa	Population (000, 2018)	883[a]
Surface area (km2)	2 513[b]	Pop. density (per km2, 2018)	353.3[a]
Sex ratio (m per 100 f)	93.9[a]	Capital city	Saint-Denis
National currency	Euro (EUR)	Capital city pop. (000, 2018)	147.2
Exchange rate (per US$)	0.8[c]		

Economic indicators	2005	2010	2018
Employment in agriculture (% of employed)[e]	...	4.2[d]	4.3[f,g]
Employment in industry (% of employed)[e]	...	14.1[d]	12.7[f,g]
Employment in services & other sectors (% employed)[e]	...	67.1[d]	81.7[f,g]
Unemployment rate (% of labour force)[e]	30.1	28.9	28.9[f,h]
Labour force participation rate (female/male pop. %)[e]	41.1 / 60.3	45.3 / 59.9	49.1 / 61.3[f,h]
CPI: Consumer Price Index (2010=100)	...	...	127[i,j]
Agricultural production index (2004-2006=100)	99	105	102[k]

Social indicators	2005	2010	2018
Population growth rate (average annual %)[l]	1.4	1.0	0.8[b]
Urban population (% of total population)	96.3	98.5	99.6
Urban population growth rate (average annual %)[l]	2.5	1.4	0.9[b]
Fertility rate, total (live births per woman)[l]	2.4	2.4	2.4[b]
Life expectancy at birth (females/males, years)[l]	80.6 / 73.0	81.9 / 74.5	82.9 / 76.0[b]
Population age distribution (0-14/60+ years old, %)	26.9 / 10.3	25.4 / 12.2	23.2 / 17.0[a]
International migrant stock (000/% of total pop.)	115.1 / 14.5	123.0 / 14.8	129.2 / 14.7[c]
Infant mortality rate (per 1 000 live births)[l]	7.6	5.6	4.2[b]
Intentional homicide rate (per 100 000 pop.)	3.2	1.8[m]	...

Environment and infrastructure indicators	2005	2010	2018
Individuals using the Internet (per 100 inhabitants)	28.1	...	...
Threatened species (number)	48[n]	104	130[c]
Forested area (% of land area)[o]	34.0	35.2	35.1[b]
CO2 emission estimates (million tons/tons per capita)	3.4 / 4.3	4.2 / 5.0	4.2 / 4.9[j]
Energy production, primary (Petajoules)	7	8	9[b]
Energy supply per capita (Gigajoules)	61	70	69[b]
Tourist/visitor arrivals at national borders (000)[p]	409	420	458[k]
Important sites for terrestrial biodiversity protected (%)	0.6	45.8	45.8
Pop. using improved drinking water (urban/rural, %)	99.2 / 97.8	99.2 / 97.8	99.2 / 97.8[b]
Pop. using improved sanitation facilities (urban/rural, %)	98.4 / 95.2	98.4 / 95.2	98.4 / 95.3[b]

a Projected estimate (medium fertility variant). b 2015. c 2017. d Population aged 15 to 64 years. e Excluding the institutional population. f Break in the time series. g 2012. h 2013. i Index base: 2000=100. j 2014. k 2016. l Data refers to a 5-year period preceding the reference year. m 2009. n 2004. o Estimate. p Arrivals by air.

Romania

Region	Eastern Europe	UN membership date	14 December 1955
Population (000, 2018)	19 581 a	Surface area (km2)	238 391 b
Pop. density (per km2, 2018)	85.1 a	Sex ratio (m per 100 f)	94.0 a
Capital city	Bucharest	National currency	Romanian Leu (RON)
Capital city pop. (000, 2018)	1 821.4	Exchange rate (per US$)	3.9 c

Economic indicators	2005	2010	2018
GDP: Gross domestic product (million current US$)	99 699	167 998	186 691 d
GDP growth rate (annual %, const. 2010 prices)	4.2	- 0.8	4.8 d
GDP per capita (current US$)	4 652.0	8 219.0	9 439.0 d
Economy: Agriculture (% of Gross Value Added) e	9.5	6.3	4.3 d
Economy: Industry (% of Gross Value Added) e	36.0	41.3	32.4 d
Economy: Services and other activity (% of GVA) e	54.5	52.4	63.3 d
Employment in agriculture (% of employed) f	32.3	31.0	22.3 f
Employment in industry (% of employed) f	30.5	28.3	28.5
Employment in services & other sectors (% employed) f	37.3	40.7	49.2
Unemployment rate (% of labour force)	7.2	7.0	5.1 f
Labour force participation rate (female/male pop. %) f	46.3 / 61.2	46.3 / 64.3	43.7 / 62.8
CPI: Consumer Price Index (2010=100)	74	100 g	114 c
Agricultural production index (2004-2006=100)	95	90	95 d
Index of industrial production (2005=100)	100	123 h	155 h,i
International trade: exports (million current US$)	27 730	49 413	70 627 c
International trade: imports (million current US$)	40 463	62 007	85 318 c
International trade: balance (million current US$)	- 12 733	- 12 593	- 14 691 c
Balance of payments, current account (million US$)	- 8 541 g	- 8 478	- 7 111 c

Major trading partners						2017
Export partners (% of exports)	Germany	23.0	Italy	11.2	France	6.8
Import partners (% of imports)	Germany	20.1	Italy	10.0	Hungary	7.5

Social indicators	2005	2010	2018
Population growth rate (average annual %) j	- 0.6	- 0.9	- 0.6 b
Urban population (% of total population)	53.2	53.8	54.0
Urban population growth rate (average annual %) j	- 0.6	- 0.7	- 0.6 b
Fertility rate, total (live births per woman) j	1.3	1.4	1.5 b
Life expectancy at birth (females/males, years) j	75.2 / 67.9	76.7 / 69.5	78.4 / 71.4 b
Population age distribution (0-14/60+ years old, %)	15.9 / 19.6	15.8 / 21.4	15.2 / 25.3 a
International migrant stock (000/% of total pop.)	145.2 / 0.7	166.1 / 0.8	370.8 / 1.9 c
Refugees and others of concern to the UNHCR (000)	2.7 k	1.7 k	3.8 c
Infant mortality rate (per 1 000 live births) j	16.9	12.0	8.7 b
Health: Current expenditure (% of GDP)	5.5	5.7	5.0 b
Health: Physicians (per 1 000 pop.)	2.0 l	2.5	2.7 m
Education: Government expenditure (% of GDP)	3.5	3.5	3.1 i
Education: Primary gross enrol. ratio (f/m per 100 pop.)	107.7 / 109.2	96.8 / 98.3	88.9 / 90.0 d
Education: Secondary gross enrol. ratio (f/m per 100 pop.)	84.5 / 82.9	96.8 / 97.6	88.6 / 89.3 d
Education: Tertiary gross enrol. ratio (f/m per 100 pop.)	50.8 / 40.2	75.9 / 55.3	53.3 / 43.0 d
Intentional homicide rate (per 100 000 pop.) n	2.1	2.0	1.2 d
Seats held by women in the National Parliament (%)	11.4	11.4	20.7

Environment and infrastructure indicators	2005	2010	2018
Individuals using the Internet (per 100 inhabitants)	21.5 f,o	39.9 o	59.5 d
Research & Development expenditure (% of GDP)	0.4	0.5	0.5 b
Threatened species (number)	63 p	64	104 c
Forested area (% of land area)	27.8	28.3	29.8 f,b
CO2 emission estimates (million tons/tons per capita)	96.5 / 4.4	78.4 / 3.9	70.0 / 3.6 i
Energy production, primary (Petajoules)	1 173	1 155	1 116 b
Energy supply per capita (Gigajoules)	75	73	69 b
Tourist/visitor arrivals at national borders (000)	5 839	7 498	10 223 d
Important sites for terrestrial biodiversity protected (%)	14.8	65.0	77.3
Pop. using improved drinking water (urban/rural, %)	98.1 / 83.2	99.7 / 93.7	100.0 / 100.0 b
Pop. using improved sanitation facilities (urban/rural, %)	90.7 / 58.4	91.5 / 61.1	92.2 / 63.3 b
Net Official Development Assist. disbursed (% of GNI)	...	0.07	0.15 d

a Projected estimate (medium fertility variant). b 2015. c 2017. d 2016. e Data classified according to ISIC Rev. 4. f Estimate. g Break in the time series. h Excluding water and waste management. i 2014. j Data refers to a 5-year period preceding the reference year. k Data as at the end of December. l 2002. m 2013. n Data refer to offences, not victims, of intentional homicide. o Population aged 16 to 74 years. p 2004.

Russian Federation

Region	Eastern Europe	UN membership date	24 October 1945
Population (000, 2018)	143 965[a]	Surface area (km2)	17 098 246[b]
Pop. density (per km2, 2018)	8.8[a]	Sex ratio (m per 100 f)	86.8[a]
Capital city	Moscow	National currency	Russian Ruble (RUB)
Capital city pop. (000, 2018)	12 409.7	Exchange rate (per US$)	57.6[c]

Economic indicators

	2005	2010	2018
GDP: Gross domestic product (million current US$)	764 016	1 524 917	1 246 015[d]
GDP growth rate (annual %, const. 2010 prices)	6.4	4.5	- 0.2[d]
GDP per capita (current US$)	5 320.0	10 652.0	8 655.0[d]
Economy: Agriculture (% of Gross Value Added)	5.0	3.9	4.7[d]
Economy: Industry (% of Gross Value Added)	38.1	34.7	32.4[d]
Economy: Services and other activity (% of GVA)	57.0	61.4	62.8[d]
Employment in agriculture (% of employed)	10.2[e]	7.8	6.6[e]
Employment in industry (% of employed)[e]	29.8	27.7	26.8
Employment in services & other sectors (% employed)[e]	60.0	64.5	66.6
Unemployment rate (% of labour force)	7.2	7.4	5.0[e]
Labour force participation rate (female/male pop. %)[e]	55.9 / 68.3	56.5 / 70.8	56.3 / 71.4
CPI: Consumer Price Index (2010=100)	61	100	168[c]
Agricultural production index (2004-2006=100)	99	99	139[d]
Index of industrial production (2005=100)[f]	100	109	121[g]
International trade: exports (million current US$)	241 452	397 068	403 406[e,c]
International trade: imports (million current US$)	98 707	228 912	228 213[c]
International trade: balance (million current US$)	142 744	168 156	175 194[e,c]
Balance of payments, current account (million US$)	84 389	67 452	35 173[c]

Major trading partners

						2017
Export partners (% of exports)	Areas nes[h]	11.0[e]	China	9.7[e]	Netherlands	8.8
Import partners (% of imports)	China	21.2	Germany	10.0	United States	5.6

Social indicators

	2005	2010	2018
Population growth rate (average annual %)[i]	- 0.4	- 0.1	0.1[b]
Urban population (% of total population)	73.5	73.7	74.4
Urban population growth rate (average annual %)[i]	- 0.4	-0.0	0.2[b]
Fertility rate, total (live births per woman)[i]	1.3	1.4	1.7[b]
Life expectancy at birth (females/males, years)[i]	72.0 / 58.6	73.7 / 61.0	75.9 / 84.7[b]
Population age distribution (0-14/60+ years old, %)	15.2 / 17.2	14.9 / 18.0	17.8 / 21.5[a]
International migrant stock (000/% of total pop.)	11 667.6 / 8.1	11 194.7 / 7.8	11 651.5 / 8.1[c]
Refugees and others of concern to the UNHCR (000)	483.1[j]	132.6[j]	282.6[c]
Infant mortality rate (per 1 000 live births)[i]	16.2	10.7	8.3[b]
Health: Current expenditure (% of GDP)	5.1	5.3	5.6[k,b]
Health: Physicians (per 1 000 pop.)	...	5.0	4.0[b]
Education: Government expenditure (% of GDP)	3.8	4.1[l]	3.8[m]
Education: Primary gross enrol. ratio (f/m per 100 pop.)	95.4 / 95.2	99.5 / 99.0[n]	102.3 / 101.8[d]
Education: Secondary gross enrol. ratio (f/m per 100 pop.)	82.5 / 83.4	84.3 / 85.7[n]	104.0 / 105.6[d]
Education: Tertiary gross enrol. ratio (f/m per 100 pop.)	84.3 / 61.3	86.9 / 64.3[n]	89.3 / 74.7[d]
Intentional homicide rate (per 100 000 pop.)	24.8	14.9[o,n]	10.8[p,d]
Seats held by women in the National Parliament (%)	9.8	14.0	15.8

Environment and infrastructure indicators

	2005	2010	2018
Individuals using the Internet (per 100 inhabitants)	15.2	43.0[q]	76.4[r,s,d]
Research & Development expenditure (% of GDP)	1.1	1.1	1.1[b]
Threatened species (number)	151[t]	126	235[c]
Forested area (% of land area)	49.4	49.8[e]	49.8[e,b]
CO2 emission estimates (million tons/tons per capita)	1 615.1 / 11.2	1 670.5 / 11.7	1 705.3 / 11.9[e]
Energy production, primary (Petajoules)	50 506	53 679	56 024[b]
Energy supply per capita (Gigajoules)	190	202	208[b]
Tourist/visitor arrivals at national borders (000)	22 201	22 281	24 571[d]
Important sites for terrestrial biodiversity protected (%)	26.8	26.8	26.9
Pop. using improved drinking water (urban/rural, %)	98.5 / 87.6	98.7 / 89.6	98.9 / 91.2[b]
Pop. using improved sanitation facilities (urban/rural, %)	77.3 / 58.6	77.1 / 58.7	77.0 / 58.7[b]
Net Official Development Assist. disbursed (% of GNI)	...	0.03	0.08[u,v,c]

a Projected estimate (medium fertility variant). **b** 2015. **c** 2017. **d** 2016. **e** Estimate. **f** Data classified according to ISIC Rev. 3. **g** 2014. **h** Areas not elsewhere specified. **i** Data refers to a 5-year period preceding the reference year. **j** Data as at the end of December. **k** From 2015 the data is adjusted by WHO in accordance with United Nations General Assembly Resolution A/RES/68/262. **l** 2008. **m** 2012. **n** 2009. **o** Break in the time series. **p** Include victims of attempted homicide. **q** Population aged 16 to 74 years. **r** Population aged 15 to 72 years. **s** Users in the last 12 months. **t** 2004. **u** Some of the debt relief reported may correspond to the credits. Statistics currently published on ODA by Russia and the estimates from the previous Chairman's reports should not be used at the same time. **v** Provisional data.

Rwanda

Region	Eastern Africa	UN membership date	18 September 1962
Population (000, 2018)	12 501 [a]	Surface area (km2)	26 338 [b]
Pop. density (per km2, 2018)	506.7 [a]	Sex ratio (m per 100 f)	96.2 [a]
Capital city	Kigali	National currency	Rwanda Franc (RWF)
Capital city pop. (000, 2018)	1 057.8	Exchange rate (per US$)	843.3 [c]

Economic indicators

	2005	2010	2018
GDP: Gross domestic product (million current US$)	2 581	5 774	8 474 [d]
GDP growth rate (annual %, const. 2010 prices)	9.4	7.3	5.9 [d]
GDP per capita (current US$)	287.0	563.0	711.0 [d]
Economy: Agriculture (% of Gross Value Added) [e]	39.3	30.2	31.5 [d]
Economy: Industry (% of Gross Value Added) [e]	13.8	15.8	17.6 [d]
Economy: Services and other activity (% of GVA) [e]	46.9	53.9	50.8 [d]
Employment in agriculture (% of employed) [f]	85.6	79.6	65.7
Employment in industry (% of employed) [f]	3.4	5.5	8.3
Employment in services & other sectors (% employed) [f]	11.0	14.8	26.0
Unemployment rate (% of labour force) [f]	1.7	3.0	1.4
Labour force participation rate (female/male pop. %) [f]	85.2 / 86.8	86.1 / 87.6	86.0 / 86.2
CPI: Consumer Price Index (2010=100) [g,h]	...	100	135 [c]
Agricultural production index (2004-2006=100)	101	139	140 [d]
International trade: exports (million current US$)	150	242	984 [f,c]
International trade: imports (million current US$)	374	1 405	1 794 [f,c]
International trade: balance (million current US$)	- 224	- 1 163	- 810 [f,c]
Balance of payments, current account (million US$)	...	- 427 [i]	- 628 [c]

Major trading partners

							2017
Export partners (% of exports)	Dem. Rep. of Congo	31.8 [f]	Kenya	16.0	United Arab Emirates	14.0 [f]
Import partners (% of imports) [f]	China	21.2	Uganda	11.2	Kenya	7.8

Social indicators

	2005	2010	2018
Population growth rate (average annual %) [j]	2.3	2.6	2.5 [b]
Urban population (% of total population)	16.9	16.9	17.2
Urban population growth rate (average annual %) [j]	4.8	2.6	2.6 [b]
Fertility rate, total (live births per woman) [j]	5.4	4.8	4.2 [b]
Life expectancy at birth (females/males, years) [j]	51.5 / 49.6	61.5 / 58.6	67.1 / 63.1 [b]
Population age distribution (0-14/60+ years old, %)	41.7 / 4.1	41.8 / 4.1	39.8 / 5.0 [a]
International migrant stock (000/% of total pop.) [k]	432.8 / 4.8	436.8 / 4.3	443.1 / 3.6 [c]
Refugees and others of concern to the UNHCR (000)	64.4 [l]	55.7 [l]	173.8 [c]
Infant mortality rate (per 1 000 live births) [j]	90.7	59.8	44.0 [b]
Health: Current expenditure (% of GDP) [m]	7.5	9.3	7.9 [b]
Health: Physicians (per 1 000 pop.)	-0.0 [n]	0.1	0.1 [b]
Education: Government expenditure (% of GDP)	5.7 [o]	4.9	3.5 [f,d]
Education: Primary gross enrol. ratio (f/m per 100 pop.)	138.1 / 137.2	146.9 / 143.3	136.8 / 137.3 [d]
Education: Secondary gross enrol. ratio (f/m per 100 pop.)	15.4 / 17.3	32.8 / 33.1	38.4 / 34.9 [d]
Education: Tertiary gross enrol. ratio (f/m per 100 pop.)	2.0 / 3.5 [n]	5.0 / 6.4	6.9 / 9.1 [d]
Intentional homicide rate (per 100 000 pop.)	...	2.8	2.5 [b]
Seats held by women in the National Parliament (%)	48.8	56.3	61.3

Environment and infrastructure indicators

	2005	2010	2018
Individuals using the Internet (per 100 inhabitants) [f]	0.6	8.0	20.0 [d]
Threatened species (number)	37 [n]	55	62 [c]
Forested area (% of land area) [f]	15.6	18.1	19.5 [b]
CO2 emission estimates (million tons/tons per capita)	0.5 / 0.1	0.6 / 0.1	0.8 / 0.1 [p]
Energy production, primary (Petajoules)	63	76	85 [f,b]
Energy supply per capita (Gigajoules)	8	8	8 [f,b]
Tourist/visitor arrivals at national borders (000)	113 [q,o]	504	932 [d]
Important sites for terrestrial biodiversity protected (%)	45.7	45.7	45.7
Pop. using improved drinking water (urban/rural, %)	85.9 / 65.9	86.2 / 68.9	66.6 / 71.9 [b]
Pop. using improved sanitation facilities (urban/rural, %)	59.6 / 50.4	59.1 / 56.7	58.5 / 62.9 [b]
Net Official Development Assist. received (% of GNI)	22.41	18.03	14.06 [d]

a Projected estimate (medium fertility variant). **b** 2015. **c** 2017. **d** 2016. **e** Data classified according to ISIC Rev. 4. **f** Estimate. **g** Calculated by the Statistics Division of the United Nations from national indices. **h** Urban areas. **i** Break in the time series. **j** Data refers to a 5-year period preceding the reference year. **k** Including refugees. **l** Data as at the end of December. **m** Data revision. **n** 2004. **o** 2001. **p** 2014. **q** January-November.

Saint Helena

Region	Western Africa	Population (000, 2018)	4 [a,b]
Surface area (km2)	308 [a,c]	Pop. density (per km2, 2018)	10.4 [a,b]
Capital city	Jamestown	National currency	Saint Helena Pound (SHP)
Capital city pop. (000, 2018)	0.6	Exchange rate (per US$)	0.7 [d]

Economic indicators

	2005	2010	2018
Employment in agriculture (% of employed)	...	7.3 [e,f,g]	...
Employment in industry (% of employed)	...	20.0 [e,f,g]	...
Employment in services & other sectors (% employed)	...	72.7 [e,f,g]	...
Unemployment rate (% of labour force)	5.2	2.0	...
International trade: exports (million current US$) [h,i]	1	~0	~0 [d]
International trade: imports (million current US$) [h,i]	12	20	55 [d]
International trade: balance (million current US$) [h,i]	- 12	- 20	- 55 [d]

Major trading partners

						2017
Export partners (% of exports) [h]	United States	45.6	Japan	13.8	Czechia	10.3
Import partners (% of imports) [h]	South Africa	42.5	United Kingdom	42.2	Greece	6.3

Social indicators

	2005	2010	2018
Population growth rate (average annual %) [a,j]	- 3.6	- 0.5	- 0.7 [c]
Urban population (% of total population) [a]	39.9	39.5	39.8
Urban population growth rate (average annual %) [a,j]	- 3.8	- 0.7	- 0.7 [c]
International migrant stock (000/% of total pop.) [a]	0.5 / 11.4	0.6 / 13.6	0.6 / 15.0 [d]
Intentional homicide rate (per 100 000 pop.)	0.0	0.0 [k]	...

Environment and infrastructure indicators

	2005	2010	2018
Individuals using the Internet (per 100 inhabitants)	15.9	24.9	37.6 [h,i]
Threatened species (number) [a]	60 [m]	60	100 [d]
Forested area (% of land area) [h]	5.1	5.1	5.1 [c]
CO2 emission estimates (million tons/tons per capita)	~0.0 / 2.0	~0.0 / 2.9	~0.0 / 3.1 [n]
Energy production, primary (Petajoules)	0	0	0 [c]
Energy supply per capita (Gigajoules)	33	38	37 [h,c]
Important sites for terrestrial biodiversity protected (%) [a]	0.6	16.7	54.8

a Including Ascension and Tristan da Cunha. b Projected estimate (medium fertility variant). c 2015. d 2017. e Population aged 15 to 69 years. f Data classified according to ISIC Rev. 3. g 2008. h Estimate. i Year ending 31 March of the following year. j Data refers to a 5-year period preceding the reference year. k 2009. l 2012. m 2004. n 2014.

Saint Kitts and Nevis

Region	Caribbean	UN membership date	23 September 1983
Population (000, 2018)	56 [a]	Surface area (km2)	261 [b]
Pop. density (per km2, 2018)	214.8 [a]	Sex ratio (m per 100 f)	97.0 [c,d]
Capital city	Basseterre	National currency	E. Caribbean Dollar (XCD) [e]
Capital city pop. (000, 2018)	14.4	Exchange rate (per US$)	2.7 [f]

Economic indicators	2005	2010	2018
GDP: Gross domestic product (million current US$)	543	705	910 [g]
GDP growth rate (annual %, const. 2010 prices)	8.8	- 2.2	2.2 [g]
GDP per capita (current US$)	11 178.0	13 708.0	16 597.0 [g]
Economy: Agriculture (% of Gross Value Added)	1.9	1.6	1.1 [g]
Economy: Industry (% of Gross Value Added)	25.4	28.1	28.0 [g]
Economy: Services and other activity (% of GVA)	72.6	70.3	70.9 [g]
Employment in agriculture (% of employed)	0.2 [h,i,j]	...	...
Employment in industry (% of employed)	48.8 [h,i,j]	...	...
Employment in services & other sectors (% employed)	42.1 [h,i,j]	...	...
Unemployment rate (% of labour force)	5.1 [j]	...	...
Labour force participation rate (female/male pop. %)	74.9 / 62.8 [h,j]	... / ...	... / ...
CPI: Consumer Price Index (2010=100) [k]	82	100	106 [f]
Agricultural production index (2004-2006=100)	91	35	39 [g]
International trade: exports (million current US$)	34	32	33 [f]
International trade: imports (million current US$)	210	270	309 [f]
International trade: balance (million current US$)	- 176	- 238	- 276 [f]
Balance of payments, current account (million US$)	- 65	- 139	- 102 [g]

Major trading partners						2017
Export partners (% of exports)	United States	88.7	Saint Lucia	6.0 [k]	Trinidad and Tobago	6.5
Import partners (% of imports)	United States	67.0	Trinidad and Tobago	4.4	Canada	2.7

Social indicators	2005	2010	2018
Population growth rate (average annual %) [l]	1.4	1.1	1.1 [b]
Urban population (% of total population)	32.0	31.3	30.8
Urban population growth rate (average annual %) [l]	0.9	0.7	0.8 [b]
Population age distribution (0-14/60+ years old, %)	28.0 / 9.9 [m]	... / ...	... / ...
International migrant stock (000/% of total pop.)	6.7 / 13.7	7.2 / 14.1	7.6 / 13.7 [f]
Refugees and others of concern to the UNHCR (000)	...	...	-0.0 [b]
Health: Current expenditure (% of GDP)	5.1	5.7	5.6 [b]
Health: Physicians (per 1 000 pop.)	1.1 [j]	...	...
Education: Government expenditure (% of GDP)	3.9	4.3 [n]	2.8 [b]
Intentional homicide rate (per 100 000 pop.)	16.5	40.8	34.2 [o]
Seats held by women in the National Parliament (%)	0.0	6.7	13.3

Environment and infrastructure indicators	2005	2010	2018
Individuals using the Internet (per 100 inhabitants)	34.0 [k]	63.0	76.8 [k,g]
Threatened species (number)	19 [p]	36	52 [f]
Forested area (% of land area)	42.3	42.3	42.3 [k,b]
CO2 emission estimates (million tons/tons per capita)	0.2 / 4.0	0.2 / 4.2	0.2 / 4.2 [q]
Energy production, primary (Petajoules)	1	0	0 [k,b]
Energy supply per capita (Gigajoules)	67 [k]	61	60 [k,b]
Tourist/visitor arrivals at national borders (000) [r]	141	98	122 [g]
Important sites for terrestrial biodiversity protected (%)	29.2	29.2	29.2
Pop. using improved drinking water (urban/rural, %)	98.3 / 98.3	98.3 / 98.3	98.3 / 98.3 [b]
Pop. using improved sanitation facilities (urban/rural, %)	87.3 / 87.3	... / ...	... / ...
Net Official Development Assist. received (% of GNI)	0.51	1.70	3.92 [s]

a Projected estimate (medium fertility variant). **b** 2015. **c** Provisional data. **d** 2011. **e** East Caribbean Dollar. **f** 2017. **g** 2016. **h** Break in the time series. **i** Data classified according to ISIC Rev. 2. **j** 2001. **k** Estimate, **l** Data refers to a 5-year period preceding the reference year. **m** 2000. **n** 2007. **o** 2012. **p** 2004. **q** 2014. **r** Arrivals of non-resident tourists by air. **s** 2013.

Saint Lucia

Region	Caribbean	UN membership date	18 September 1979
Population (000, 2018)	180[a]	Surface area (km2)	539[b,c]
Pop. density (per km2, 2018)	294.5[a]	Sex ratio (m per 100 f)	95.8[a]
Capital city	Castries	National currency	E. Caribbean Dollar (XCD)[d]
Capital city pop. (000, 2018)	22.3	Exchange rate (per US$)	2.7[e]

Economic indicators

	2005	2010	2018
GDP: Gross domestic product (million current US$)	935	1 244	1 397[f]
GDP growth rate (annual %, const. 2010 prices)	- 1.7	- 1.0	0.7[f]
GDP per capita (current US$)	5 714.0	7 210.0	7 848.0[f]
Economy: Agriculture (% of Gross Value Added)	3.5	2.9	3.0[f]
Economy: Industry (% of Gross Value Added)	18.7	15.5	13.5[f]
Economy: Services and other activity (% of GVA)	77.8	81.6	83.5[f]
Employment in agriculture (% of employed)[g]	13.8	14.6	15.3
Employment in industry (% of employed)[g]	20.3	18.4	17.4
Employment in services & other sectors (% employed)[g]	65.9	67.0	67.2
Unemployment rate (% of labour force)	18.7	20.6	20.4[g]
Labour force participation rate (female/male pop. %)[g]	57.3 / 75.6	58.9 / 75.3	61.4 / 75.9
CPI: Consumer Price Index (2010=100)[g]	87	100	108[e]
Agricultural production index (2004-2006=100)	91	87	65[f]
International trade: exports (million current US$)	64	215	104[g,e]
International trade: imports (million current US$)	486	647	731[g,e]
International trade: balance (million current US$)	- 422	- 432	- 627[g,e]
Balance of payments, current account (million US$)	- 129	- 203	- 31[f]

Major trading partners

						2017
Export partners (% of exports)[g]	United States	43.2[g]	Areas nes[h]	12.4	Trinidad and Tobago	8.4[g]
Import partners (% of imports)[g]	United States	46.9	Trinidad and Tobago	12.7	Areas nes[h]	5.0

Social indicators

	2005	2010	2018
Population growth rate (average annual %)[i]	0.8	1.1	0.5[c]
Urban population (% of total population)	23.1	18.4	18.7
Urban population growth rate (average annual %)[i]	- 2.9	- 3.4	0.6[c]
Fertility rate, total (live births per woman)[i]	1.8	1.6	1.5[c]
Life expectancy at birth (females/males, years)[i]	74.0 / 70.1	76.6 / 71.4	77.6 / 72.2[c]
Population age distribution (0-14/60+ years old, %)	27.7 / 9.8	23.2 / 12.1	18.5 / 14.1[a]
International migrant stock (000/% of total pop.)	11.5 / 7.0	12.1 / 7.0	12.9 / 7.2[e]
Refugees and others of concern to the UNHCR (000)	...	~0.0[j]	~0.0[e]
Infant mortality rate (per 1 000 live births)[i]	14.2	11.8	10.9[c]
Health: Current expenditure (% of GDP)	5.6	6.6	6.0[c]
Health: Physicians (per 1 000 pop.)	0.5	0.1[k]	
Education: Government expenditure (% of GDP)	5.1	3.9[g]	5.7[f]
Education: Primary gross enrol. ratio (f/m per 100 pop.)	100.5 / 105.1	98.1 / 103.3[l]	... / ...
Education: Secondary gross enrol. ratio (f/m per 100 pop.)	84.0 / 71.5	94.1 / 95.2	88.3 / 87.4[f]
Education: Tertiary gross enrol. ratio (f/m per 100 pop.)	19.0 / 7.0	18.0 / 7.0	25.4 / 13.0[f]
Intentional homicide rate (per 100 000 pop.)	25.0	25.5	19.3[m]
Seats held by women in the National Parliament (%)	11.1	11.1	16.7

Environment and infrastructure indicators

	2005	2010	2018
Individuals using the Internet (per 100 inhabitants)	21.6	43.3	46.7[g,f]
Threatened species (number)	29[n]	46	62[e]
Forested area (% of land area)[g]	34.3	33.8	33.3[e]
CO2 emission estimates (million tons/tons per capita)	0.4 / 2.2	0.4 / 2.3	0.4 / 2.2[m]
Energy production, primary (Petajoules)	0	0	0[c]
Energy supply per capita (Gigajoules)	33[g]	33	33[c]
Tourist/visitor arrivals at national borders (000)[o]	318	306	348[f]
Important sites for terrestrial biodiversity protected (%)	40.3	46.0	46.0
Pop. using improved drinking water (urban/rural, %)	98.0 / 94.0	98.8 / 94.9	99.5 / 95.6[c]
Pop. using improved sanitation facilities (urban/rural, %)	82.8 / 86.6	83.9 / 89.5	84.7 / 91.9[c]
Net Official Development Assist. received (% of GNI)	1.21	3.42	1.12[f]

a Projected estimate (medium fertility variant). **b** Refers to habitable area. Excludes Saint Lucia's Forest Reserve. **c** 2015. **d** East Caribbean Dollar. **e** 2017. **f** 2016. **g** Estimate. **h** Areas not elsewhere specified. **i** Data refers to a 5-year period preceding the reference year. **j** Data as at the end of December. **k** 2009. **l** 2007. **m** 2014. **o** Excluding nationals residing abroad.

Saint Pierre and Miquelon

Region	Northern America	Population (000, 2018)	6[a]
Surface area (km2)	242[b]	Pop. density (per km2, 2018)	27.6[a]
Sex ratio (m per 100 f)	98.2[c]	Capital city	Saint-Pierre
National currency	Euro (EUR)	Capital city pop. (000, 2018)	5.7
Exchange rate (per US$)	0.8[d]		

Economic indicators	2005	2010	2018
Agricultural production index (2004-2006=100)	94	110	115[e]
International trade: exports (million current US$)[f]	31	137	780[d]
International trade: imports (million current US$)[f]	216	747	2 991[d]
International trade: balance (million current US$)[f]	- 185	- 610	- 2 211[d]

Major trading partners						2017
Export partners (% of exports)[f]	Canada	39.6	France	15.3	Portugal	14.8
Import partners (% of imports)[f]	France	58.7	Canada	34.2	Netherlands	3.0

Social indicators	2005	2010	2018
Population growth rate (average annual %)[g]	~0.0	-0.0	-0.0[b]
Urban population (% of total population)	89.9	89.9	89.9
Urban population growth rate (average annual %)[g]	0.1	-0.0	0.1[b]
Population age distribution (0-14/60+ years old, %)	... / ...	19.1 / 17.8[c]	... / ...
International migrant stock (000/% of total pop.)	1.1 / 18.3	1.0 / 16.2	1.0 / 15.7[d]
Intentional homicide rate (per 100 000 pop.)	...	15.9[h]	...

Environment and infrastructure indicators	2005	2010	2018
Threatened species (number)	2[i]	4	12[d]
Forested area (% of land area)[f]	13.0	12.6	12.2[b]
CO2 emission estimates (million tons/tons per capita)	0.1 / 10.5	0.1 / 11.3	0.1 / 12.2[j]
Energy production, primary (Petajoules)	0	0	0[b]
Energy supply per capita (Gigajoules)[f]	149	160	175[b]

a Projected estimate (medium fertility variant). b 2015. c 2006. d 2017. e 2016. f Estimate. g Data refers to a 5-year period preceding the reference year. h 2009. i 2004. j 2014.

Saint Vincent and the Grenadines

Region	Caribbean	UN membership date	16 September 1980
Population (000, 2018)	110[a]	Surface area (km2)	389[b]
Pop. density (per km2, 2018)	282.6[a]	Sex ratio (m per 100 f)	101.7[a]
Capital city	Kingstown	National currency	E. Caribbean Dollar (XCD)[c]
Capital city pop. (000, 2018)	26.6	Exchange rate (per US$)	2.7[d]

Economic indicators

	2005	2010	2018
GDP: Gross domestic product (million current US$)	551	681	765[e]
GDP growth rate (annual %, const. 2010 prices)	2.5	- 3.3	1.3[e]
GDP per capita (current US$)	5 065.0	6 232.0	6 980.0[e]
Economy: Agriculture (% of Gross Value Added)	6.2	7.1	8.2[e]
Economy: Industry (% of Gross Value Added)	18.6	19.2	17.4[e]
Economy: Services and other activity (% of GVA)	75.1	73.7	74.4[e]
Employment in agriculture (% of employed)[f]	7.2	6.8	6.0
Employment in industry (% of employed)[f]	12.6	13.1	12.7
Employment in services & other sectors (% employed)[f]	80.3	80.0	81.3
Unemployment rate (% of labour force)[f]	18.9	18.8	18.3
Labour force participation rate (female/male pop. %)[f]	54.7 / 80.8	57.3 / 81.0	58.7 / 80.1
CPI: Consumer Price Index (2010=100)[f]	81	100[g]	107[d]
Agricultural production index (2004-2006=100)	104	119	110[b]
International trade: exports (million current US$)	40	42	39[f,d]
International trade: imports (million current US$)	240	379	315[f,d]
International trade: balance (million current US$)	- 201	- 338	- 276[f,d]
Balance of payments, current account (million US$)	- 102	- 208	- 122[e]

Major trading partners

						2017
Export partners (% of exports)	Barbados	17.8[f]	Saint Lucia	17.2	Antigua and Barbuda	14.5[f]
Import partners (% of imports)[f]	United States	38.2	Trinidad and Tobago	17.6	United Kingdom	7.2

Social indicators

	2005	2010	2018
Population growth rate (average annual %)[h]	0.2	0.1	~0.0[b]
Urban population (% of total population)	47.0	49.0	52.2
Urban population growth rate (average annual %)[h]	1.0	0.9	0.8[b]
Fertility rate, total (live births per woman)[h]	2.2	2.1	2.0[b]
Life expectancy at birth (females/males, years)[h]	73.3 / 68.3	74.0 / 69.8	74.9 / 70.7[b]
Population age distribution (0-14/60+ years old, %)	28.5 / 9.4	26.5 / 9.5	23.5 / 12.2[a]
International migrant stock (000/% of total pop.)	4.4 / 4.0	4.5 / 4.1	4.6 / 4.2[d]
Infant mortality rate (per 1 000 live births)[h]	21.2	18.5	16.5[b]
Health: Current expenditure (% of GDP)	3.7	4.4	4.2[b]
Health: Physicians (per 1 000 pop.)	0.6[i]	...	...
Education: Government expenditure (% of GDP)	6.4	5.1	5.8[e]
Education: Primary gross enrol. ratio (f/m per 100 pop.)	112.3 / 123.9	101.2 / 108.8	102.1 / 104.6[e]
Education: Secondary gross enrol. ratio (f/m per 100 pop.)	99.5 / 79.5	108.8 / 106.3	106.2 / 107.6[e]
Intentional homicide rate (per 100 000 pop.)	23.9	22.9	36.5[e]
Seats held by women in the National Parliament (%)	22.7	21.7	13.0

Environment and infrastructure indicators

	2005	2010	2018
Individuals using the Internet (per 100 inhabitants)[f]	9.2	33.7	55.6[e]
Research & Development expenditure (% of GDP)	0.1[i]	...	...
Threatened species (number)	24[k]	38	58[d]
Forested area (% of land area)[f]	66.7	69.2	69.2[b]
CO2 emission estimates (million tons/tons per capita)	0.2 / 2.0	0.2 / 2.0	0.2 / 1.9[l]
Energy production, primary (Petajoules)	0	0	0[b]
Energy supply per capita (Gigajoules)	31[f]	31	31[f,b]
Tourist/visitor arrivals at national borders (000)[m]	96	72	79[e]
Important sites for terrestrial biodiversity protected (%)	42.7	42.7	42.7
Pop. using improved drinking water (urban/rural, %)	95.1 / 95.1	95.1 / 95.1	95.1 / 95.1[b]
Pop. using improved sanitation facilities (urban/rural, %)	76.1 / 76.1	... / ...	... / ...
Net Official Development Assist. received (% of GNI)	1.51	2.52	1.19[e]

a Projected estimate (medium fertility variant). **b** 2015. **c** East Caribbean Dollar. **d** 2017. **e** 2016. **f** Estimate. **g** Break in the time series. **h** Data refers to a 5-year period preceding the reference year. **i** 2001. **j** 2002. **k** 2004. **l** 2014. **m** Arrivals of non-resident tourists by air.

Samoa

Region	Polynesia
Population (000, 2018)	198[a]
Pop. density (per km2, 2018)	69.9[a]
Capital city	Apia
Capital city pop. (000, 2018)	36.1

UN membership date	15 December 1976
Surface area (km2)	2 842[b]
Sex ratio (m per 100 f)	106.6[a]
National currency	Tala (WST)
Exchange rate (per US$)	2.5[c]

Economic indicators

	2005	2010	2018
GDP: Gross domestic product (million current US$)	434	679	822[d]
GDP growth rate (annual %, const. 2010 prices)	5.1	4.3	5.8[d]
GDP per capita (current US$)	2 414.0	3 648.0	4 214.0[d]
Economy: Agriculture (% of Gross Value Added)[e]	12.3	9.1	10.4[d]
Economy: Industry (% of Gross Value Added)[e]	30.6	25.8	22.7[d]
Economy: Services and other activity (% of GVA)[e]	57.2	65.1	66.9[d]
Employment in agriculture (% of employed)[f]	7.1	5.9	5.8
Employment in industry (% of employed)[f]	14.8	15.3	15.0
Employment in services & other sectors (% employed)[f]	78.1	78.8	79.2
Unemployment rate (% of labour force)[f]	2.1	4.8	8.1
Labour force participation rate (female/male pop. %)[i]	24.6 / 40.8	24.3 / 40.4	23.7 / 38.7
CPI: Consumer Price Index (2010=100)[f,g]	76	100	112[c]
Agricultural production index (2004-2006=100)	101	107	118[d]
International trade: exports (million current US$)	87	70	44[c]
International trade: imports (million current US$)	239	310	356[c]
International trade: balance (million current US$)	- 151	- 240	- 312[c]
Balance of payments, current account (million US$)	- 48[h]	- 44	- 32[d]

Major trading partners

						2017
Export partners (% of exports)	American Samoa	26.6	Australia	21.4	New Zealand	19.7
Import partners (% of imports)	New Zealand	26.4	Singapore	16.6	United States	11.1

Social indicators

	2005	2010	2018
Population growth rate (average annual %)[i]	0.6	0.7	0.8[b]
Urban population (% of total population)	21.2	20.1	18.2
Urban population growth rate (average annual %)[i]	- 0.1	- 0.4	- 0.4[b]
Fertility rate, total (live births per woman)[i]	4.4	4.5	4.2[b]
Life expectancy at birth (females/males, years)[i]	73.6 / 67.2	75.4 / 69.1	77.4 / 71.1[b]
Population age distribution (0-14/60+ years old, %)	39.6 / 6.9	38.3 / 7.2	36.4 / 8.7[a]
International migrant stock (000/% of total pop.)	5.7 / 3.2	5.1 / 2.8	4.9 / 2.5[c]
Refugees and others of concern to the UNHCR (000)	...	...	~0.0[c]
Infant mortality rate (per 1 000 live births)[i]	25.7	21.3	18.0[b]
Health: Current expenditure (% of GDP)[j]	5.2	5.3	5.6[b]
Health: Physicians (per 1 000 pop.)	0.3	0.3	...
Education: Government expenditure (% of GDP)	3.8[f,k]	5.1[l]	4.1[d]
Education: Primary gross enrol. ratio (f/m per 100 pop.)	109.8 / 109.0	109.9 / 111.5	106.3 / 107.0[d]
Education: Secondary gross enrol. ratio (f/m per 100 pop.)	88.2 / 78.2	93.6 / 82.3	88.6 / 80.3[d]
Education: Tertiary gross enrol. ratio (f/m per 100 pop.)	7.2 / 7.8[m]	... / ...	... / ...
Intentional homicide rate (per 100 000 pop.)	...	8.6	3.1[n]
Seats held by women in the National Parliament (%)	6.1	8.2	10.0

Environment and infrastructure indicators

	2005	2010	2018
Individuals using the Internet (per 100 inhabitants)	3.4	7.0[f]	29.4[f,d]
Threatened species (number)	18[o]	78	93[c]
Forested area (% of land area)[f]	60.4	60.4	60.4[b]
CO2 emission estimates (million tons/tons per capita)	0.2 / 0.9	0.2 / 1.0	0.2 / 1.0[p]
Energy production, primary (Petajoules)	2	2[f]	1[f,b]
Energy supply per capita (Gigajoules)	21[f]	24[f]	29[b]
Tourist/visitor arrivals at national borders (000)	102	122	134[d]
Important sites for terrestrial biodiversity protected (%)	31.2	31.2	36.5
Pop. using improved drinking water (urban/rural, %)	97.2 / 95.0	97.4 / 97.7	97.5 / 99.3[b]
Pop. using improved sanitation facilities (urban/rural, %)	93.6 / 91.5	93.4 / 91.2	93.3 / 91.1[b]
Net Official Development Assist. received (% of GNI)	9.95	23.71	11.56[d]

a Projected estimate (medium fertility variant). b 2015. c 2017. d 2016. e At producers' prices. f Estimate. g Excluding rent. h Break in the time series. i Data refers to a 5-year period preceding the reference year. j Data refer to fiscal years beginning 1 July. k 2002. l 2008. m 2000. n 2013. o 2004. p 2014.

San Marino

Region	Southern Europe	UN membership date	02 March 1992
Population (000, 2018)	34[a]	Surface area (km2)	61[b]
Pop. density (per km2, 2018)	559.3[a]	Sex ratio (m per 100 f)	94.9[c,b]
Capital city	San Marino	National currency	Euro (EUR)
Capital city pop. (000, 2018)	4.5	Exchange rate (per US$)	0.8[d]

Economic indicators	2005	2010	2018
GDP: Gross domestic product (million current US$)	2 027	2 139	1 591[e]
GDP growth rate (annual %, const. 2010 prices)	2.3	- 4.6	1.0[e]
GDP per capita (current US$)	69 338.0	68 767.0	47 910.0[e]
Economy: Agriculture (% of Gross Value Added)[f]	~0.0	~0.0	~0.0[e]
Economy: Industry (% of Gross Value Added)[f]	38.2	35.4	34.8[e]
Economy: Services and other activity (% of GVA)[f]	61.8	64.6	65.1[e]
Employment in agriculture (% of employed)	0.5[g]	0.3[h]	...
Employment in industry (% of employed)	39.3[g]	34.3[h]	...
Employment in services & other sectors (% employed)	60.2[g]	65.4[h]	...
Unemployment rate (% of labour force)	...	4.4	6.6[h,i,j]
Labour force participation rate (female/male pop. %)	53.8 / 79.2[k]	... / ...	... / ...
CPI: Consumer Price Index (2010=100)	...	...	109[l,d]

Social indicators	2005	2010	2018
Population growth rate (average annual %)[m]	1.3	1.2	1.2[b]
Urban population (% of total population)	94.5	95.7	97.2
Urban population growth rate (average annual %)[m]	1.5	1.5	1.4[b]
Fertility rate, total (live births per woman)	1.3[n]	...	...
Life expectancy at birth (females/males, years)	84.0 / 77.4[o]	... / ...	86.4 / 81.7[p]
Population age distribution (0-14/60+ years old, %)	15.2 / 21.5[c,n]	20.9 / 21.6[q,r,s]	15.0 / 24.1[c,b]
International migrant stock (000/% of total pop.)[t]	4.2 / 14.4	4.4 / 14.1	5.2 / 15.7[d]
Health: Current expenditure (% of GDP)	4.1	5.8	6.8[b]
Health: Physicians (per 1 000 pop.)	...	...	6.4[j]
Education: Government expenditure (% of GDP)	...	2.3	2.4[u]
Education: Primary gross enrol. ratio (f/m per 100 pop.)[v]	... / ...	100.6 / 88.8	92.6 / 93.9[w]
Education: Secondary gross enrol. ratio (f/m per 100 pop.)[v]	... / ...	98.2 / 96.3	95.9 / 93.5[w]
Education: Tertiary gross enrol. ratio (f/m per 100 pop.)[v]	... / ...	77.3 / 53.0	69.9 / 50.5[w]
Intentional homicide rate (per 100 000 pop.)	0.0	0.0	0.0[u]
Seats held by women in the National Parliament (%)	16.7	16.7	26.7

Environment and infrastructure indicators	2005	2010	2018
Individuals using the Internet (per 100 inhabitants)	50.3	54.2[x]	49.6[g]
Threatened species (number)	...	0	1[d]
Forested area (% of land area)[y]	0.0	0.0	0.0[b]
Tourist/visitor arrivals at national borders (000)[y]	50	120	60[e]

a Projected estimate (medium fertility variant). b 2015. c Population statistics are compiled from registers. d 2017. e 2016. f Data classified according to ISIC Rev. 4. g Data classified according to ISIC Rev. 3. h Break in the time series. i Population aged 14 years and over. j 2014. k 2003. l Index base: December 2010=100. m Data refers to a 5-year period preceding the reference year. n 2004. o 2000. p 2013. q Provisional data. r Population aged 0 to 20 years. s Population aged 61 years and over. t Refers to foreign citizens. u 2011. v Estimate. w 2012. x 2009. y Including Italian tourists.

Sao Tome and Principe

Region	Middle Africa	UN membership date	16 September 1975
Population (000, 2018)	209 [a]	Surface area (km2)	964 [b]
Pop. density (per km2, 2018)	217.5 [a]	Sex ratio (m per 100 f)	99.2 [a]
Capital city	Sao Tome	National currency	Dobra (STN)
Capital city pop. (000, 2018)	80.1	Exchange rate (per US$)	20.5 [c]

Economic indicators	2005	2010	2018
GDP: Gross domestic product (million current US$)	126	197	343 [d]
GDP growth rate (annual %, const. 2010 prices)	7.1	6.7	0.1 [d]
GDP per capita (current US$)	811.0	1 130.0	1 715.0 [d]
Economy: Agriculture (% of Gross Value Added)	18.3	11.8	11.5 [d]
Economy: Industry (% of Gross Value Added)	14.9	18.2	16.7 [d]
Economy: Services and other activity (% of GVA)	66.8	70.1	71.9 [d]
Employment in agriculture (% of employed) [e]	27.9	23.9	16.0
Employment in industry (% of employed) [e]	17.2	16.1	13.9
Employment in services & other sectors (% employed) [e]	54.9	60.0	70.2
Unemployment rate (% of labour force)	16.5	14.6 [e]	13.4 [e]
Labour force participation rate (female/male pop. %) [e]	38.8 / 73.5	40.1 / 75.5	41.2 / 75.3
CPI: Consumer Price Index (2010=100)	39	100	172 [c]
Agricultural production index (2004-2006=100)	101	104	109 [d]
International trade: exports (million current US$)	3	6	11 [c]
International trade: imports (million current US$)	50	112	147 [c]
International trade: balance (million current US$)	- 46	- 106	- 136 [c]
Balance of payments, current account (million US$)	- 36	- 88	- 73 [c]

Major trading partners						2017
Export partners (% of exports)	Netherlands	29.8	Spain	16.6	France	16.1
Import partners (% of imports)	Portugal	54.5	Angola	19.8	China	5.0

Social indicators	2005	2010	2018
Population growth rate (average annual %) [f]	2.3	2.3	2.2 [b]
Urban population (% of total population)	59.2	65.0	72.8
Urban population growth rate (average annual %) [f]	4.4	4.2	3.8 [b]
Fertility rate, total (live births per woman) [f]	5.1	4.9	4.7 [b]
Life expectancy at birth (females/males, years) [f]	65.6 / 62.0	67.4 / 63.6	68.2 / 64.0 [b]
Population age distribution (0-14/60+ years old, %)	44.1 / 5.6	44.1 / 4.7	42.4 / 4.4 [a]
International migrant stock (000/% of total pop.) [g]	3.4 / 2.2	2.7 / 1.5	2.3 / 1.1 [c]
Infant mortality rate (per 1 000 live births) [f]	51.8	46.0	43.8 [b]
Health: Current expenditure (% of GDP)	12.1	5.3	9.8 [b]
Health: Physicians (per 1 000 pop.)	0.5 [h]	...	...
Education: Government expenditure (% of GDP)	5.3	9.7	3.7 [i]
Education: Primary gross enrol. ratio (f/m per 100 pop.)	124.0 / 129.0	117.1 / 118.3	108.1 / 112.4 [c]
Education: Secondary gross enrol. ratio (f/m per 100 pop.)	43.8 / 41.3	52.0 / 51.1	96.0 / 83.5 [c]
Education: Tertiary gross enrol. ratio (f/m per 100 pop.)	... / ...	4.2 / 4.3	13.3 / 12.8 [b]
Intentional homicide rate (per 100 000 pop.)	...	3.4	3.4 [i]
Seats held by women in the National Parliament (%)	9.1	7.3	18.2

Environment and infrastructure indicators	2005	2010	2018
Individuals using the Internet (per 100 inhabitants)	13.8 [e]	18.8	28.0 [e,d]
Threatened species (number)	61 [h]	70	94 [c]
Forested area (% of land area) [e]	58.3	55.8	55.8 [b]
CO2 emission estimates (million tons/tons per capita)	0.1 / 0.5	0.1 / 0.6	0.1 / 0.6 [i]
Energy production, primary (Petajoules)	1	1	1 [b]
Energy supply per capita (Gigajoules)	13 [e]	14	14 [e,b]
Tourist/visitor arrivals at national borders (000)	16	8	29 [d]
Important sites for terrestrial biodiversity protected (%)	0.0	58.0	58.0
Pop. using improved drinking water (urban/rural, %)	91.6 / 80.6	97.7 / 91.5	98.9 / 93.6 [b]
Pop. using improved sanitation facilities (urban/rural, %)	33.1 / 18.4	39.5 / 22.5	40.8 / 23.3 [b]
Net Official Development Assist. received (% of GNI)	26.58	25.35	13.36 [d]

a Projected estimate (medium fertility variant). **b** 2015. **c** 2017. **d** 2016. **e** Estimate. **f** Data refers to a 5-year period preceding the reference year. **g** Refers to foreign citizens. **h** 2004. **i** 2014. **j** 2011.

Saudi Arabia

Region	Western Asia	UN membership date	24 October 1945
Population (000, 2018)	33 554 [a]	Surface area (km2)	2 206 714 [b]
Pop. density (per km2, 2018)	15.6 [a]	Sex ratio (m per 100 f)	134.0 [a]
Capital city	Riyadh	National currency	Saudi Riyal (SAR)
Capital city pop. (000, 2018)	6 906.6	Exchange rate (per US$)	3.8 [c]

Economic indicators

	2005	2010	2018
GDP: Gross domestic product (million current US$)	328 461	528 207	639 617 [d]
GDP growth rate (annual %, const. 2010 prices)	5.6	5.0	1.4 [d]
GDP per capita (current US$)	13 740.0	19 260.0	19 817.0 [d]
Economy: Agriculture (% of Gross Value Added) [e]	3.2	2.6	2.7 [d]
Economy: Industry (% of Gross Value Added) [e]	61.8	58.2	43.1 [d]
Economy: Services and other activity (% of GVA) [e]	35.0	39.1	54.2 [d]
Employment in agriculture (% of employed) [f]	4.0	4.3	6.4
Employment in industry (% of employed) [f]	20.0	21.4	22.6
Employment in services & other sectors (% employed) [f]	75.9	74.4	71.1
Unemployment rate (% of labour force)	6.0	5.6	5.6 [f]
Labour force participation rate (female/male pop. %) [f]	17.7 / 74.0	18.2 / 74.4	22.3 / 79.7
CPI: Consumer Price Index (2010=100) [g]	81	100	116 [c]
Agricultural production index (2004-2006=100)	100	103	106 [d]
Index of industrial production (2005=100) [h]	100	112	135 [i]
International trade: exports (million current US$)	180 278	250 577	251 648 [f,c]
International trade: imports (million current US$)	57 233	103 622	123 934 [f,c]
International trade: balance (million current US$)	123 045	146 955	127 714 [f,c]
Balance of payments, current account (million US$)	90 060 [j]	66 751	- 23 843 [d]

Major trading partners

					2017
Export partners (% of exports)	Areas nes [k]	79.0 [f]	United Arab Emirates 3.2	China	2.0 [f]
Import partners (% of imports) [f]	China	14.5	United States 13.4	Germany	6.3

Social indicators

	2005	2010	2018
Population growth rate (average annual %) [l]	2.8	2.7	2.8 [b]
Urban population (% of total population)	81.0	82.1	83.8
Urban population growth rate (average annual %) [l]	3.1	3.0	3.1 [b]
Fertility rate, total (live births per woman) [l]	3.6	3.2	2.7 [b]
Life expectancy at birth (females/males, years) [l]	74.6 / 71.5	74.8 / 71.9	75.6 / 72.7 [b]
Population age distribution (0-14/60+ years old, %)	33.8 / 4.4	29.8 / 4.5	24.9 / 5.8 [a]
International migrant stock (000/% of total pop.) [m,n]	6 501.8 / 27.2	8 430.0 / 30.7	12 185.3 / 37.0 [c]
Refugees and others of concern to the UNHCR (000)	311.0 [o]	70.7 [o]	70.2 [c]
Infant mortality rate (per 1 000 live births) [l]	17.5	14.7	13.0 [b]
Health: Current expenditure (% of GDP)	3.4	3.5	5.8 [b]
Health: Physicians (per 1 000 pop.)	0.7 [p]	2.4	2.6 [i]
Education: Government expenditure (% of GDP)	5.4	5.1 [q]	...
Education: Primary gross enrol. ratio (f/m per 100 pop.)	94.7 / 96.2 [f]	105.6 / 106.5	115.2 / 117.3 [d]
Education: Secondary gross enrol. ratio (f/m per 100 pop.) [f]	84.4 / 89.7	88.6 / 100.0 [r]	101.5 / 131.3 [i]
Education: Tertiary gross enrol. ratio (f/m per 100 pop.)	35.2 / 23.8	39.1 / 34.0	66.7 / 66.5 [d]
Intentional homicide rate (per 100 000 pop.)	1.2	1.0 [s]	1.5 [b]
Seats held by women in the National Parliament (%)	0.0	0.0	19.9

Environment and infrastructure indicators

	2005	2010	2018
Individuals using the Internet (per 100 inhabitants)	12.7	41.0	73.8 [d]
Research & Development expenditure (% of GDP) [u]	~0.0 [t]	0.9 [j,v]	0.8 [v,w]
Threatened species (number)	41 [x]	103	131 [c]
Forested area (% of land area) [f]	0.5	0.5	0.5 [b]
CO2 emission estimates (million tons/tons per capita)	397.6 / 16.5	518.5 / 18.4	601.0 / 19.5 [i]
Energy production, primary (Petajoules) [y]	24 162	22 115	28 571 [b]
Energy supply per capita (Gigajoules) [y]	252	274	354 [b]
Tourist/visitor arrivals at national borders (000)	8 037	10 850	18 049 [d]
Important sites for terrestrial biodiversity protected (%)	21.0	21.0	21.0
Pop. using improved drinking water (urban/rural, %)	96.7 / 96.7	97.0 / 97.0	97.0 / 97.0 [b]
Pop. using improved sanitation facilities (urban/rural, %)	99.7 / 99.7	100.0 / 100.0	100.0 / 100.0 [b]
Net Official Development Assist. received (% of GNI)	0.01	- 0.03 [s]	

a Projected estimate (medium fertility variant). **b** 2015. **c** 2017. **d** 2016. **e** Data classified according to ISIC Rev. 4. **f** Estimate. **g** Calculated by the Statistics Division of the United Nations from national indices. **h** Data classified according to ISIC Rev. 3. **i** 2014. **j** Break in the time series. **k** Areas not elsewhere specified. **l** Data refers to a 5-year period preceding the reference year. **m** Refers to foreign citizens. **n** Including refugees. **o** Data as at the end of December. **p** 2001. **q** 2008. **s** 2007. **t** Partial data. **u** R&D budget instead of R&D expenditure or based on R&D budget. **v** Overestimate or based on overestimated data. **w** 2013. **x** 2004. **y** The data for crude oil production include 50 per cent of the output of the Neutral Zone.

Senegal

Region	Western Africa	UN membership date	28 September 1960	
Population (000, 2018)	16 294 [a]	Surface area (km2)	196 712 [b,c]	
Pop. density (per km2, 2018)	84.6 [a]	Sex ratio (m per 100 f)	96.7 [a]	
Capital city	Dakar	National currency	CFA Franc, BCEAO (XOF) [d]	
Capital city pop. (000, 2018)	2 978.4 [e]	Exchange rate (per US$)	546.9 [f]	

Economic indicators

	2005	2010	2018
GDP: Gross domestic product (million current US$)	8 708	12 926	14 605 [g]
GDP growth rate (annual %, const. 2010 prices)	5.6	4.2	6.5 [g]
GDP per capita (current US$)	774.0	1 001.0	948.0 [g]
Economy: Agriculture (% of Gross Value Added)	16.8	17.5	17.1 [g]
Economy: Industry (% of Gross Value Added)	23.6	23.4	23.4 [g]
Economy: Services and other activity (% of GVA)	59.6	59.2	59.6 [g]
Employment in agriculture (% of employed)	40.6	53.3	52.8
Employment in industry (% of employed) [h]	17.4	19.6	20.2
Employment in services & other sectors (% employed) [h]	42.0	27.0	27.0
Unemployment rate (% of labour force) [h]	8.9	10.2	4.8
Labour force participation rate (female/male pop. %) [h]	34.2 / 69.8	42.4 / 69.6	45.9 / 69.9
CPI: Consumer Price Index (2010=100) [i,j]	...	100	109 [f]
Agricultural production index (2004-2006=100)	110	151	145 [g]
Index of industrial production (2005=100) [k]	100 [l]	104	102 [m]
International trade: exports (million current US$)	1 471	2 088	2 989 [f]
International trade: imports (million current US$)	3 498	4 782	6 729 [f]
International trade: balance (million current US$)	- 2 027	- 2 694	- 3 740 [f]
Balance of payments, current account (million US$)	- 676 [n]	- 589	...

Major trading partners

							2017
Export partners (% of exports)	Mali	19.8	Switzerland	10.1 [h]	Bunkers	5.1	
Import partners (% of imports)	France	14.7	China	9.7	Nigeria	7.9	

Social indicators

	2005	2010	2018
Population growth rate (average annual %) [o]	2.6	2.8	3.0 [c]
Urban population (% of total population)	41.7	43.8	47.2
Urban population growth rate (average annual %) [o]	3.3	3.7	3.9 [c]
Fertility rate, total (live births per woman) [o]	5.3	5.1	5.0 [c]
Life expectancy at birth (females/males, years) [o]	60.6 / 57.3	63.8 / 61.0	67.5 / 63.8 [c]
Population age distribution (0-14/60+ years old, %)	43.7 / 4.9	43.2 / 4.7	42.7 / 4.7 [a]
International migrant stock (000/% of total pop.) [p]	230.3 / 2.1	256.1 / 2.0	265.6 / 1.7 [f]
Refugees and others of concern to the UNHCR (000)	23.4 [q]	24.2 [q]	17.9 [f]
Infant mortality rate (per 1 000 live births) [o]	61.1	51.1	43.9 [c]
Health: Current expenditure (% of GDP)	4.6	4.0	4.0 [c]
Health: Physicians (per 1 000 pop.)	0.1 [f]	0.1 [s]	0.1 [g]
Education: Government expenditure (% of GDP)	5.1	6.5	7.1 [c]
Education: Primary gross enrol. ratio (f/m per 100 pop.)	77.5 / 80.6	85.4 / 80.9	87.9 / 78.4 [g]
Education: Secondary gross enrol. ratio (f/m per 100 pop.)	18.9 / 25.2	33.3 / 38.2	48.4 / 47.8 [h,g]
Education: Tertiary gross enrol. ratio (f/m per 100 pop.)	... / ...	5.5 / 9.3 [h]	7.9 / 13.2 [g]
Intentional homicide rate (per 100 000 pop.)	9.3	8.5	7.4 [c]
Seats held by women in the National Parliament (%)	19.2	22.7	41.8

Environment and infrastructure indicators

	2005	2010	2018
Individuals using the Internet (per 100 inhabitants)	4.8	8.0 [h]	25.7 [h,g]
Research & Development expenditure (% of GDP)	...	0.5	...
Threatened species (number)	47 [r]	82	123 [f]
Forested area (% of land area) [h]	45.0	44.0	43.0 [c]
CO2 emission estimates (million tons/tons per capita)	5.8 / 0.6	7.7 / 0.6	8.9 / 0.6 [m]
Energy production, primary (Petajoules)	52	86	80 [c]
Energy supply per capita (Gigajoules)	11	13	11 [c]
Tourist/visitor arrivals at national borders (000)	769	900 [h]	1 007 [h,c]
Important sites for terrestrial biodiversity protected (%)	41.1	41.1	41.2
Pop. using improved drinking water (urban/rural, %)	91.4 / 56.9	92.2 / 62.1	92.9 / 67.3 [c]
Pop. using improved sanitation facilities (urban/rural, %)	62.5 / 28.7	63.9 / 31.2	65.4 / 33.8 [c]
Net Official Development Assist. received (% of GNI)	8.20	7.32	5.17 [g]

a Projected estimate (medium fertility variant). b Surface area is based on the 2002 population and housing census. c 2015. d African Financial Community (CFA) Franc, Central Bank of West African States (BCEAO). e Refers to the sum of the Departments of Dakar, Pikine and Guédiawaye, in Dakar Region. f 2017. g 2016. h Estimate. i Calculated by the Statistics Division of the United Nations from national indices. j Data refer to the national index. k Data classified according to ISIC Rev. 3. l Country data supplemented with data from the Observatoire Economique et Statistique d'Afrique Subsaharienne (Afristat). m 2014. n Break in the time series. o Data refers to a 5-year period preceding the reference year. p Including refugees. q Data as at the end of December. r 2004. s 2008.

Serbia

Region	Southern Europe
Population (000, 2018)	8 762 [a,b]
Pop. density (per km2, 2018)	100.2 [a,b]
Capital city	Belgrade
Capital city pop. (000, 2018)	1 389.4 [e]

UN membership date	01 November 2000
Surface area (km2)	88 499 [c,d]
Sex ratio (m per 100 f)	95.6 [a,b]
National currency	Serbian Dinar (RSD)
Exchange rate (per US$)	99.1 [f]

Economic indicators

	2005	2010	2018
GDP: Gross domestic product (million current US$) [g]	26 252	39 460	38 300 [h]
GDP growth rate (annual %, const. 2010 prices) [g]	5.5	0.6	2.8 [h]
GDP per capita (current US$) [g]	3 528.0	5 412.0	5 426.0 [h]
Economy: Agriculture (% of Gross Value Added) [g,i]	12.0	10.2	7.9 [h]
Economy: Industry (% of Gross Value Added) [g,i]	29.3	28.4	31.3 [h]
Economy: Services and other activity (% of GVA) [g,i]	58.7	61.4	60.8 [h]
Employment in agriculture (% of employed) [j]	23.3 [j]	22.6	18.7 [j]
Employment in industry (% of employed) [j]	27.6	22.3	24.5
Employment in services & other sectors (% employed) [j]	49.1	55.0	56.8
Unemployment rate (% of labour force)	20.8	19.2	13.1 [j]
Labour force participation rate (female/male pop. %) [j]	45.4 / 64.5	42.9 / 59.4	45.6 / 61.2
CPI: Consumer Price Index (2010=100)	65	100	139 [f]
Agricultural production index (2004-2006=100)	...	103	105 [h]
Index of industrial production (2005=100)	100	97 [k]	96 [k,l]
International trade: exports (million current US$)	...	9 795	16 959 [f]
International trade: imports (million current US$)	...	16 735	22 146 [f]
International trade: balance (million current US$)	...	- 6 940	- 5 187 [f]
Balance of payments, current account (million US$)	...	- 2 692	- 2 355 [f]

Major trading partners

					2017
Export partners (% of exports)	Italy	13.2	Germany	12.6	Bosnia-Herzegovina 8.0
Import partners (% of imports)	Germany	12.7	Italy	10.0	China 8.2

Social indicators

	2005	2010	2018
Population growth rate (average annual %) [b,m]	- 0.6	- 0.4	- 0.4 [d]
Urban population (% of total population) [b]	53.9	55.0	56.1
Urban population growth rate (average annual %) [b,m]	- 0.2	-0.0	- 0.1 [d]
Fertility rate, total (live births per woman) [b,m]	1.7	1.6	1.6 [d]
Life expectancy at birth (females/males, years) [b,m]	75.4 / 69.4	76.1 / 70.6	77.5 / 71.8 [d]
Population age distribution (0-14/60+ years old, %) [b]	18.6 / 19.0	17.3 / 21.0	16.3 / 24.8 [a]
International migrant stock (000/% of total pop.) [b]	845.1 / 9.2	826.1 / 9.1	801.9 / 9.1 [f]
Refugees and others of concern to the UNHCR (000) [b]	486.9 [n]	312.6 [n]	254.3 [f]
Infant mortality rate (per 1 000 live births) [b,m]	14.1	12.4	9.8 [d]
Health: Current expenditure (% of GDP) [g]	8.7	10.1	9.4 [d]
Health: Physicians (per 1 000 pop.)	...	2.5	2.5 [i]
Education: Government expenditure (% of GDP)	...	4.6	4.0 [d]
Education: Primary gross enrol. ratio (f/m per 100 pop.) [j]	103.0 / 102.5	95.6 / 96.1	100.5 / 100.7 [h]
Education: Secondary gross enrol. ratio (f/m per 100 pop.) [j]	90.0 / 87.3	92.4 / 90.5	96.9 / 95.6 [h]
Education: Tertiary gross enrol. ratio (f/m per 100 pop.) [j]	50.1 / 38.6	55.6 / 42.8	70.9 / 53.9 [h]
Intentional homicide rate (per 100 000 pop.)	1.6	1.4	1.4 [h]
Seats held by women in the National Parliament (%)	...	21.0	34.4

Environment and infrastructure indicators

	2005	2010	2018
Individuals using the Internet (per 100 inhabitants)	26.3 [j,o]	40.9	67.1 [h]
Research & Development expenditure (% of GDP) [q]	0.4 [p]	0.7	0.9 [d]
Threatened species (number)	...	46	71 [f]
Forested area (% of land area) [j]	...	31.0	31.1 [d]
CO2 emission estimates (million tons/tons per capita)	... / ...	46.0 / 5.1	37.7 / 4.3 [l]
Energy production, primary (Petajoules) [r]	431	440	449 [d]
Energy supply per capita (Gigajoules) [r]	68	72	69 [d]
Tourist/visitor arrivals at national borders (000)	453	683	1 281 [h]
Important sites for terrestrial biodiversity protected (%)	24.1	26.3	30.2
Pop. using improved drinking water (urban/rural, %)	99.5 / 99.1	99.4 / 99.0	99.4 / 98.9 [d]
Pop. using improved sanitation facilities (urban/rural, %)	97.9 / 95.4	98.1 / 94.8	98.2 / 94.2 [d]
Net Official Development Assist. received (% of GNI)	4.12	1.71	1.78 [h]

a Projected estimate (medium fertility variant). b Including Kosovo. c Changes in total area per year are the result of new measuring and correcting of the administrative borders between former Yugoslavian countries. d 2015. e Refers to the urban population of Belgrade area. f 2017. g Excluding Kosovo and Metohija. h 2016. i Data classified according to ISIC Rev. 4. j Estimate. k Excluding water and waste management. l 2014. m Data refers to a 5-year period preceding the reference year. n Data as at the end of December. o Population aged 16 to 74 years. p Do not correspond exactly to Frascati Manual recommendations. q Excluding data from some regions, provinces or states. r Excluding Kosovo.

Seychelles

Region	Eastern Africa	UN membership date	21 September 1976
Population (000, 2018)	95[a]	Surface area (km2)	457[b]
Pop. density (per km2, 2018)	207.0[a]	Sex ratio (m per 100 f)	97.2[a]
Capital city	Victoria	National currency	Seychelles Rupee (SCR)
Capital city pop. (000, 2018)	28.1	Exchange rate (per US$)	13.8[c]

Economic indicators

	2005	2010	2018
GDP: Gross domestic product (million current US$)	919	970	1 434[d]
GDP growth rate (annual %, const. 2010 prices)	9.0	5.9	1.5[d]
GDP per capita (current US$)	10 357.0	10 612.0	15 217.0[d]
Economy: Agriculture (% of Gross Value Added)[e]	3.8	2.7	2.0[d]
Economy: Industry (% of Gross Value Added)[e]	19.4	16.5	12.6[d]
Economy: Services and other activity (% of GVA)[e]	76.8	80.8	85.4[d]
Employment in agriculture (% of employed)	...	...	3.6[f,g,h]
Employment in industry (% of employed)	...	...	17.9[f,g,h]
Employment in services & other sectors (% employed)	...	...	78.2[f,g,h]
Unemployment rate (% of labour force)	5.5	...	4.1[f,g,i,h]
Labour force participation rate (female/male pop. %)	... / ...	... / ...	61.9 / 68.3[f,g,i,h]
CPI: Consumer Price Index (2010=100)[j]	54	100	123[c]
Agricultural production index (2004-2006=100)	99	92	99[d]
International trade: exports (million current US$)	340	418	497[k,c]
International trade: imports (million current US$)	675	1 180	2 141[k,c]
International trade: balance (million current US$)	- 335	- 763	- 1 644[k,c]
Balance of payments, current account (million US$)	- 174	- 214	- 296[c]

Major trading partners

					2017
Export partners (% of exports)	United Arab Emirates 26.3[k]	France 22.8	United Kingdom 15.4[k]
Import partners (% of imports)[k]	Cayman Islands 30.8	United Arab Emirates 15.3	France 8.9

Social indicators

	2005	2010	2018
Population growth rate (average annual %)[l]	1.8	0.6	0.5[b]
Urban population (% of total population)	51.7	53.3	56.7
Urban population growth rate (average annual %)[l]	2.3	1.2	1.3[b]
Fertility rate, total (live births per woman)[l]	2.2	2.3	2.4[b]
Life expectancy at birth (females/males, years)[l]	76.8 / 67.9	77.3 / 68.0	77.9 / 68.7[b]
Population age distribution (0-14/60+ years old, %)	24.9 / 9.2	22.8 / 10.0	22.4 / 13.8[a]
International migrant stock (000/% of total pop.)	9.0 / 10.1	11.4 / 12.5	12.9 / 13.6[c]
Refugees and others of concern to the UNHCR (000)	...	...	~0.0[c]
Infant mortality rate (per 1 000 live births)[l]	10.6	10.2	10.2[b]
Health: Current expenditure (% of GDP)	3.9	3.6	3.4[b]
Health: Physicians (per 1 000 pop.)	1.2	1.1	1.0[m]
Education: Government expenditure (% of GDP)	5.4[n]	4.8[o]	3.6[h]
Education: Primary gross enrol. ratio (f/m per 100 pop.)	108.0 / 110.1	112.1 / 108.8	112.4 / 113.2[d]
Education: Secondary gross enrol. ratio (f/m per 100 pop.)	84.8 / 79.0	77.0 / 72.5[k]	96.1 / 89.9[d]
Education: Tertiary gross enrol. ratio (f/m per 100 pop.)	... / ...	... / ...	27.2 / 14.7[d]
Intentional homicide rate (per 100 000 pop.)	11.4[p]	9.8	12.7[d]
Seats held by women in the National Parliament (%)	29.4	23.5	21.2

Environment and infrastructure indicators

	2005	2010	2018
Individuals using the Internet (per 100 inhabitants)	25.4	41.0[k]	56.5[k,d]
Research & Development expenditure (% of GDP)	0.3	...	...
Threatened species (number)	84[p]	190	439[c]
Forested area (% of land area)	88.4	88.4[k]	88.4[k,b]
CO2 emission estimates (million tons/tons per capita)	0.7 / 8.3	0.4 / 4.8	0.5 / 5.2[q]
Energy production, primary (Petajoules)	0	0	0[b]
Energy supply per capita (Gigajoules)	115	66	65[b]
Tourist/visitor arrivals at national borders (000)	129	175	303[d]
Important sites for terrestrial biodiversity protected (%)	19.5	19.7	19.7
Pop. using improved drinking water (urban/rural, %)	95.7 / 95.7	95.7 / 95.7	95.7 / 95.7[b]
Pop. using improved sanitation facilities (urban/rural, %)	98.4 / 98.4	98.4 / 98.4	98.4 / 98.4[b]
Net Official Development Assist. received (% of GNI)	1.85	5.89	0.40[d]

a Projected estimate (medium fertility variant). b 2015. c 2017. d 2016. e Data classified according to ISIC Rev. 4. f Excluding some areas. g Excluding the institutional population. h 2011. i Break in the time series. j Calculated by the Statistics Division of the United Nations from national indices. k Estimate. l Data refers to a 5-year period preceding the reference year. m 2012. n 2003. o 2006. p 2004. q 2014.

Sierra Leone

Region	Western Africa	UN membership date	27 September 1961
Population (000, 2018)	7 720 [a]	Surface area (km2)	72 300 [b]
Pop. density (per km2, 2018)	107.0 [a]	Sex ratio (m per 100 f)	98.2 [a]
Capital city	Freetown	National currency	Leone (SLL)
Capital city pop. (000, 2018)	1 135.9	Exchange rate (per US$)	7 537.0 [c]

Economic indicators	2005	2010	2018
GDP: Gross domestic product (million current US$)	1 650	2 578	3 675 [d]
GDP growth rate (annual %, const. 2010 prices)	4.5	5.3	6.1 [d]
GDP per capita (current US$)	292.0	399.0	497.0 [d]
Economy: Agriculture (% of Gross Value Added)	51.0	55.2	59.9 [d]
Economy: Industry (% of Gross Value Added)	11.6	8.1	5.8 [d]
Economy: Services and other activity (% of GVA)	37.4	36.7	34.3 [d]
Employment in agriculture (% of employed) [e]	65.9	63.7	59.8
Employment in industry (% of employed) [e]	6.1	6.4	6.2
Employment in services & other sectors (% employed) [e]	28.0	29.8	34.0
Unemployment rate (% of labour force) [e]	3.6	4.3	4.4
Labour force participation rate (female/male pop. %) [e]	64.4 / 65.7	60.5 / 61.9	57.0 / 58.6
CPI: Consumer Price Index (2010=100) [f]	...	100	176 [c]
Agricultural production index (2004-2006=100)	94	147	195 [d]
International trade: exports (million current US$)	154	319 [e]	324 [e,c]
International trade: imports (million current US$)	341	776 [e]	893 [e,c]
International trade: balance (million current US$)	- 187	- 457 [e]	- 569 [e,c]
Balance of payments, current account (million US$)	- 105	- 585	- 162 [d]

Major trading partners						2017
Export partners (% of exports) [e]	Côte d'Ivoire	34.7	United States	31.0	Belgium	19.3
Import partners (% of imports) [e]	China	12.6	United States	9.8	India	7.8

Social indicators	2005	2010	2018
Population growth rate (average annual %) [g]	4.3	2.6	2.3 [b]
Urban population (% of total population)	36.9	38.9	42.1
Urban population growth rate (average annual %) [g]	5.0	3.7	3.3 [b]
Fertility rate, total (live births per woman) [g]	6.1	5.6	4.8 [b]
Life expectancy at birth (females/males, years) [g]	42.6 / 40.1	46.7 / 45.0	50.7 / 49.6 [b]
Population age distribution (0-14/60+ years old, %)	44.4 / 4.1	44.0 / 4.1	41.7 / 4.2 [a]
International migrant stock (000/% of total pop.) [h]	149.6 / 2.6	97.5 / 1.5	95.2 / 1.3 [c]
Refugees and others of concern to the UNHCR (000)	66.3 [i]	8.6 [i]	0.7 [c]
Infant mortality rate (per 1 000 live births) [g]	134.9	116.9	94.4 [b]
Health: Current expenditure (% of GDP)	9.8	9.2	18.3 [b]
Health: Physicians (per 1 000 pop.)	~0.0	~0.0	...
Education: Government expenditure (% of GDP)	2.8 [e]	2.6	2.9 [d]
Education: Primary gross enrol. ratio (f/m per 100 pop.)	60.9 / 87.1 [k]	... / ...	115.2 / 114.4 [d]
Education: Secondary gross enrol. ratio (f/m per 100 pop.)	20.0 / 28.3 [e,k]	... / ...	38.6 / 42.4 [d]
Education: Tertiary gross enrol. ratio (f/m per 100 pop.)	1.1 / 2.7 [e,l]	... / ...	... / ...
Intentional homicide rate (per 100 000 pop.)	1.7	2.5	1.7 [b]
Seats held by women in the National Parliament (%)	14.5	13.2	12.4

Environment and infrastructure indicators	2005	2010	2018
Individuals using the Internet (per 100 inhabitants)	0.2	0.6 [e]	11.8 [a,d]
Threatened species (number)	86 [j]	131	177 [c]
Forested area (% of land area) [e]	39.1	37.8	42.2 [b]
CO2 emission estimates (million tons/tons per capita)	0.5 / 0.1	0.7 / 0.1	1.3 / 0.2 [m]
Energy production, primary (Petajoules)	50	52	54 [b]
Energy supply per capita (Gigajoules)	11	10	10 [b]
Tourist/visitor arrivals at national borders (000) [n]	40	39	55 [d]
Important sites for terrestrial biodiversity protected (%)	55.4	69.0	80.3
Pop. using improved drinking water (urban/rural, %)	78.8 / 36.8	81.9 / 42.3	84.9 / 47.8 [b]
Pop. using improved sanitation facilities (urban/rural, %)	22.3 / 5.9	22.5 / 6.4	22.8 / 6.9 [b]
Net Official Development Assist. received (% of GNI)	21.38	17.33	21.11 [d]

a Projected estimate (medium fertility variant). **b** 2015. **c** 2017. **d** 2016. **e** Estimate. **f** Calculated by the Statistics Division of the United Nations from national indices. **g** Data refers to a 5-year period preceding the reference year. **h** Including refugees. **i** Data as at the end of December. **j** 2004. **k** 2001. **l** 2002. **m** 2014. **n** Arrivals by air.

Singapore

Region	South-eastern Asia	UN membership date	21 September 1965	
Population (000, 2018)	5 792 [a]	Surface area (km2)	719 [b,c]	
Pop. density (per km2, 2018)	8 274.1 [a]	Sex ratio (m per 100 f)	97.7 [a]	
Capital city	Singapore	National currency	Singapore Dollar (SGD)	
Capital city pop. (000, 2018)	5 791.9	Exchange rate (per US$)	1.3 [d]	

Economic indicators

	2005	2010	2018
GDP: Gross domestic product (million current US$)	127 418	236 420	296 946 [e]
GDP growth rate (annual %, const. 2010 prices)	7.5	15.2	2.0 [e]
GDP per capita (current US$)	28 372.0	46 592.0	52 814.0 [e]
Economy: Agriculture (% of Gross Value Added) [f,g]	0.1	~0.0	~0.0 [e]
Economy: Industry (% of Gross Value Added) [g,h]	32.4	27.6	26.1 [e]
Economy: Services and other activity (% of GVA) [g]	67.6	72.3	73.8 [e]
Employment in agriculture (% of employed) [i]	0.9	0.1	0.1
Employment in industry (% of employed) [i]	21.8	30.4	16.2
Employment in services & other sectors (% employed) [i]	77.2	69.5	83.7
Unemployment rate (% of labour force)	5.6	3.2	1.8 [i]
Labour force participation rate (female/male pop. %) [i]	52.4 / 76.3	57.1 / 77.2	60.3 / 76.5
CPI: Consumer Price Index (2010=100)	88	100	113 [d]
Agricultural production index (2004 2006=100)	90	92	115 [d]
International trade: exports (million current US$)	230 344	351 867	373 255 [d]
International trade: imports (million current US$)	200 724	310 791	327 710 [d]
International trade: balance (million current US$)	29 619	41 076	45 545 [d]
Balance of payments, current account (million US$)	28 105	55 421	60 989 [d]

Major trading partners

						2017
Export partners (% of exports)	China	14.5	China, Hong Kong SAR	12.3	Malaysia	10.6
Import partners (% of imports)	China	13.8	Malaysia	11.9	United States	10.6

Social indicators

	2005	2010	2018
Population growth rate (average annual %) [i]	2.8	2.4	1.7 [c]
Urban population (% of total population)	100.0	100.0	100.0
Urban population growth rate (average annual %) [i]	2.8	2.4	1.7 [c]
Fertility rate, total (live births per woman) [i]	1.3	1.3	1.2 [c]
Life expectancy at birth (females/males, years) [i]	81.8 / 76.7	83.7 / 78.7	84.5 / 80.1 [c]
Population age distribution (0-14/60+ years old, %)	19.1 / 12.6	17.3 / 14.1	14.7 / 20.4 [a]
International migrant stock (000/% of total pop.)	1 710.6 / 38.1	2 164.8 / 42.7	2 623.4 / 46.0 [d]
Refugees and others of concern to the UNHCR (000)	~0.0 [k]	~0.0 [k]	~0.0 [d]
Infant mortality rate (per 1 000 live births) [i]	2.5	2.2	2.1 [c]
Health: Current expenditure (% of GDP) [l,m]	3.0	3.2	4.3 [c]
Health: Physicians (per 1 000 pop.)	1.5	1.7	2.3 [c]
Education: Government expenditure (% of GDP)	3.2	3.1	2.9 [n]
Education: Primary gross enrol. ratio (f/m per 100 pop.)	... / ...	... / ...	100.7 / 100.9 [i,e]
Education: Secondary gross enrol. ratio (f/m per 100 pop.)	... / ...	... / ...	107.7 / 108.6 [i,e]
Intentional homicide rate (per 100 000 pop.)	0.5	0.4	0.3 [e]
Seats held by women in the National Parliament (%)	16.0	23.4	23.0

Environment and infrastructure indicators

	2005	2010	2018
Individuals using the Internet (per 100 inhabitants)	61.0 [o]	71.0 [i,p]	81.0 [i,e]
Research & Development expenditure (% of GDP)	2.2	2.0	2.2 [q]
Threatened species (number)	85 [r]	277	293 [d]
Forested area (% of land area) [i]	23.7	23.3	23.1 [c]
CO2 emission estimates (million tons/tons per capita)	30.4 / 7.1	55.6 / 11.0	56.4 / 10.2 [q]
Energy production, primary (Petajoules)	...	25	28 [c]
Energy supply per capita (Gigajoules)	189	218	220 [c]
Tourist/visitor arrivals at national borders (000)	7 079	9 161	12 914 [e]
Important sites for terrestrial biodiversity protected (%)	21.1	21.1	21.1
Pop. using improved drinking water (urban/rural, %)	100.0 / ...	100.0 / ...	100.0 / ... [c]
Pop. using improved sanitation facilities (urban/rural, %)	100.0 / ...	100.0 / ...	100.0 / ... [c]

a Projected estimate (medium fertility variant). **b** The land area of Singapore comprises the mainland and other islands. **c** 2015. **d** 2017. **e** 2016. **f** Including mining and quarrying. **g** Data classified according to ISIC Rev. 4. **h** Excluding mining and quarrying. **i** Estimate. **j** Data refers to a 5-year period preceding the reference year. **k** Data as at the end of December. **l** Data refer to fiscal years beginning 1 April. **m** Medisave is classified as Social insurance scheme, considering that it is a compulsory payment. **n** 2013. **o** Population aged 15 years and over. **p** Population aged 7 years and over. **q** 2014. **r** 2004.

Sint Maarten (Dutch part)

Region	Caribbean	Population (000, 2018)	41 [a]
Surface area (km2)	34 [b]	Pop. density (per km2, 2018)	1 192.7 [a]
Sex ratio (m per 100 f)	95.7 [c,d]	Capital city	Philipsburg
National currency	Neth. Ant. Guilder (ANG) [e]	Capital city pop. (000, 2018)	40.6 [f]
Exchange rate (per US$)	1.8 [g]		

Economic indicators	2005	2010	2018
GDP: Gross domestic product (million current US$)	708	896	1 072 [h]
GDP growth rate (annual %, const. 2010 prices)	...	1.1	0.4 [h]
GDP per capita (current US$)	21 762.0	27 065.0	27 116.0 [h]
Economy: Agriculture (% of Gross Value Added)	0.3	0.1	0.1 [h]
Economy: Industry (% of Gross Value Added)	16.4	13.4	9.2 [h]
Economy: Services and other activity (% of GVA)	83.3	86.5	90.7 [h]
Balance of payments, current account (million US$)	...	...	47 [g]

Social indicators	2005	2010	2018
Population growth rate (average annual %) [i]	0.4	0.4	3.1 [b]
Urban population (% of total population)	100.0	100.0	100.0
Urban population growth rate (average annual %) [i]	0.4	0.4	3.1 [b]
Life expectancy at birth (females/males, years)	... / ...	77.2 / 72.0 [j]	77.1 / 69.2 [k,l]
Population age distribution (0-14/60+ years old, %)	... / ...	... / ...	21.0 / 10.4 [c,j]
International migrant stock (000/% of total pop.)	13.1 / 40.3	26.2 / 79.1	28.3 / 70.4 [g]
Refugees and others of concern to the UNHCR (000)	...	~0.0 [m]	~0.0 [g]

Environment and infrastructure indicators	2005	2010	2018
Threatened species (number)			51 [g]
CO2 emission estimates (million tons/tons per capita)	... / ...	... / ...	0.7 / 19.5 [d]
Energy supply per capita (Gigajoules)	...	...	305 [n,b]
Tourist/visitor arrivals at national borders (000) [o]	468	443	528 [h]
Important sites for terrestrial biodiversity protected (%)	6.4	6.4	6.4

a Projected estimate (medium fertility variant). **b** 2015. **c** De jure population. **d** 2014. **e** Netherlands Antillean Guilder. **f** Refers to the total population of Sint Maarten. **g** 2017. **h** 2016. **i** Data refers to a 5-year period preceding the reference year. **j** Data refers to a 3-year period up to and including the reference year. **k** Data refers to a 2-year period up to and including the reference year. **l** 2013. **m** Data as at the end of December. **n** Estimate. **o** Arrivals by air. Including arrivals to Saint Martin (French part).

Slovakia

Region	Eastern Europe	UN membership date	19 January 1993
Population (000, 2018)	5 450[a]	Surface area (km2)	49 035[b,c]
Pop. density (per km2, 2018)	113.3[a]	Sex ratio (m per 100 f)	94.6[a]
Capital city	Bratislava	National currency	Euro (EUR)
Capital city pop. (000, 2018)	429.9	Exchange rate (per US$)	0.8[d]

Economic indicators	2005	2010	2018
GDP: Gross domestic product (million current US$)	48 965	89 501	89 769[e]
GDP growth rate (annual %, const. 2010 prices)	6.8	5.0	3.3[e]
GDP per capita (current US$)	9 069.0	16 561.0	16 489.0[e]
Economy: Agriculture (% of Gross Value Added)[f]	3.6	2.8	3.7[e]
Economy: Industry (% of Gross Value Added)[f]	36.1	35.2	34.8[e]
Economy: Services and other activity (% of GVA)[f]	60.3	62.0	61.5[e]
Employment in agriculture (% of employed)[g]	4.8	3.2[g]	2.8[g]
Employment in industry (% of employed)[g]	38.8	37.1	36.1
Employment in services & other sectors (% employed)[g]	56.4	59.6	61.1
Unemployment rate (% of labour force)	16.3	14.4	6.8[g]
Labour force participation rate (female/male pop. %)[g]	51.3 / 68.6	50.6 / 67.6	52.2 / 67.4
CPI: Consumer Price Index (2010=100)	87	100	110[d]
Agricultural production index (2004-2006=100)	102	82	98[e]
Index of industrial production (2005=100)	100	127[h]	158[h,i]
International trade: exports (million current US$)	32 210[g]	63 999	84 525[d]
International trade: imports (million current US$)	34 226	64 382	82 994[d]
International trade: balance (million current US$)	- 2 016[g]	- 383	1 532[d]
Balance of payments, current account (million US$)	- 5 125	- 4 211	- 2 044[d]

Major trading partners						2017
Export partners (% of exports)	Germany	20.6	Czechia	11.5	Poland	7.6
Import partners (% of imports)	Germany	16.7	Czechia	10.3	Europe nes[j]	8.6

Social indicators	2005	2010	2018
Population growth rate (average annual %)[k]	-0.0	-0.0	0.1[c]
Urban population (% of total population)	55.6	54.7	53.7
Urban population growth rate (average annual %)[k]	- 0.2	- 0.3	- 0.2[c]
Fertility rate, total (live births per woman)[k]	1.2	1.3	1.4[c]
Life expectancy at birth (females/males, years)[k]	77.8 / 69.8	78.6 / 70.8	79.8 / 72.6[c]
Population age distribution (0-14/60+ years old, %)	16.8 / 16.1	15.3 / 17.8	15.5 / 22.3[a]
International migrant stock (000/% of total pop.)	130.5 / 2.4	146.3 / 2.7	184.6 / 3.4[d]
Refugees and others of concern to the UNHCR (000)	3.1[l]	1.6[l]	2.5[d]
Infant mortality rate (per 1 000 live births)[k]	7.3	6.2	5.7[c]
Health: Current expenditure (% of GDP)	6.6	7.8	6.9[c]
Health: Physicians (per 1 000 pop.)	...	3.3[m]	3.4[c]
Education: Government expenditure (% of GDP)	3.8	4.1	4.6[c]
Education: Primary gross enrol. ratio (f/m per 100 pop.)	97.6 / 98.8	101.0 / 101.9	98.1 / 98.9[c]
Education: Secondary gross enrol. ratio (f/m per 100 pop.)	93.7 / 92.8	92.8 / 91.8	91.5 / 90.5[c]
Education: Tertiary gross enrol. ratio (f/m per 100 pop.)	45.6 / 35.4	69.6 / 45.0	64.3 / 41.6[i]
Intentional homicide rate (per 100 000 pop.)	1.7	1.5	1.0[e]
Seats held by women in the National Parliament (%)	16.7	18.0	20.0

Environment and infrastructure indicators	2005	2010	2018
Individuals using the Internet (per 100 inhabitants)[n]	55.2	75.7[o]	80.5[o,e]
Research & Development expenditure (% of GDP)	0.5	0.6	1.2[c]
Threatened species (number)	48[p]	34	54[d]
Forested area (% of land area)	40.2	40.3	40.3[c]
CO2 emission estimates (million tons/tons per capita)	39.4 / 7.3	36.2 / 6.7	30.7 / 5.6[i]
Energy production, primary (Petajoules)	265	250	265[c]
Energy supply per capita (Gigajoules)	144	136	125[c]
Tourist/visitor arrivals at national borders (000)[q]	1 515	1 327	2 027[e]
Important sites for terrestrial biodiversity protected (%)	73.1	76.3	83.6
Pop. using improved drinking water (urban/rural, %)	100.0 / 99.8	100.0 / 100.0	100.0 / 100.0[c]
Pop. using improved sanitation facilities (urban/rural, %)	99.4 / 98.2	99.4 / 98.2	99.4 / 98.2[c]
Net Official Development Assist. disbursed (% of GNI)[r]	...	0.09	0.12[s,d]

a Projected estimate (medium fertility variant). b Excluding inland water. c 2015. d 2017. e 2016. f Data classified according to ISIC Rev. 4. g Estimate. h Excluding water and waste management. i 2014. j Europe not elsewhere specified. k Data refers to a 5-year period preceding the reference year. l Data as at the end of December. m 2009. n Population aged 16 to 74 years. o Users in the last 3 months. p 2004. q Non-resident tourists staying in commercial accommodation only (representing approximately 25% of all tourists). r Development Assistance Committee member (OECD). s Provisional data.

Slovenia

Region	Southern Europe	UN membership date	22 May 1992
Population (000, 2018)	2 081 [a]	Surface area (km2)	20 273 [b]
Pop. density (per km2, 2018)	103.3 [a]	Sex ratio (m per 100 f)	98.7 [a]
Capital city	Ljubljana	National currency	Euro (EUR)
Capital city pop. (000, 2018)	286.5	Exchange rate (per US$)	0.8 [c]

Economic indicators

	2005	2010	2018
GDP: Gross domestic product (million current US$)	36 345	48 014	44 709 [d]
GDP growth rate (annual %, const. 2010 prices)	4.0	1.2	3.1 [d]
GDP per capita (current US$)	18 206.0	23 477.0	21 517.0 [d]
Economy: Agriculture (% of Gross Value Added) [e]	2.6	2.0	2.2 [d]
Economy: Industry (% of Gross Value Added) [e]	34.1	30.6	32.3 [d]
Economy: Services and other activity (% of GVA) [e]	63.3	67.4	65.5 [d]
Employment in agriculture (% of employed)	9.1	8.8 [f]	4.8 [f]
Employment in industry (% of employed) [f]	37.1	32.6	31.8
Employment in services & other sectors (% employed) [f]	53.8	58.6	63.4
Unemployment rate (% of labour force)	6.5	7.2	6.7 [f]
Labour force participation rate (female/male pop. %) [f]	52.8 / 66.0	53.2 / 65.5	51.4 / 60.4
CPI: Consumer Price Index (2010=100)	87	100	107 [c]
Agricultural production index (2004-2006=100)	99	91	88 [d]
Index of industrial production (2005=100)	100	103 [g]	104 [g,h]
International trade: exports (million current US$)	17 896	24 435	28 773 [c]
International trade: imports (million current US$)	19 626	26 592	28 192 [c]
International trade: balance (million current US$)	- 1 730	- 2 157	581 [c]
Balance of payments, current account (million US$)	- 680	- 55	3 132 [c]

Major trading partners

						2017
Export partners (% of exports)	Germany	20.3	Italy	11.5	Croatia	8.0
Import partners (% of imports)	Germany	17.1	Italy	14.4	Austria	8.1

Social indicators

	2005	2010	2018
Population growth rate (average annual %) [i]	0.1	0.5	0.3 [b]
Urban population (% of total population)	51.5	52.7	54.5
Urban population growth rate (average annual %) [i]	0.4	0.9	0.7 [b]
Fertility rate, total (live births per woman) [i]	1.2	1.4	1.6 [b]
Life expectancy at birth (females/males, years) [i]	80.4 / 72.8	82.0 / 75.0	83.2 / 77.2 [b]
Population age distribution (0-14/60+ years old, %)	14.0 / 20.8	14.1 / 22.2	15.1 / 26.8 [a]
International migrant stock (000/% of total pop.)	197.3 / 9.9	253.8 / 12.4	244.8 / 11.8 [c]
Refugees and others of concern to the UNHCR (000)	1.2 [j]	4.6 [j]	0.9 [c]
Infant mortality rate (per 1 000 live births) [i]	4.0	3.2	2.5 [b]
Health: Current expenditure (% of GDP)	8.0	8.6	8.5 [b]
Health: Physicians (per 1 000 pop.)	...	2.4	2.8 [b]
Education: Government expenditure (% of GDP)	5.6	5.6	5.3 [h]
Education: Primary gross enrol. ratio (f/m per 100 pop.)	99.3 / 101.0	98.5 / 99.4	99.6 / 99.2 [b]
Education: Secondary gross enrol. ratio (f/m per 100 pop.)	96.8 / 97.4	98.1 / 99.2	109.9 / 109.6 [b]
Education: Tertiary gross enrol. ratio (f/m per 100 pop.)	93.4 / 65.6	107.3 / 72.3	95.6 / 65.3 [b]
Intentional homicide rate (per 100 000 pop.)	1.0	0.7	0.5 [d]
Seats held by women in the National Parliament (%)	12.2	14.4	36.7

Environment and infrastructure indicators

	2005	2010	2018
Individuals using the Internet (per 100 inhabitants)	46.8 [k]	70.0 [l]	75.5 [d]
Research & Development expenditure (% of GDP)	1.4	2.1	2.2 [m,b]
Threatened species (number)	74 [n]	95	143 [c]
Forested area (% of land area)	61.7	61.9	62.0 [b]
CO2 emission estimates (million tons/tons per capita)	15.9 / 7.9	15.3 / 7.5	12.8 / 6.2 [h]
Energy production, primary (Petajoules)	146	157	142 [b]
Energy supply per capita (Gigajoules)	153	149	133 [b]
Tourist/visitor arrivals at national borders (000)	1 555	1 869	3 032 [d]
Important sites for terrestrial biodiversity protected (%)	86.1	86.1	88.7
Pop. using improved drinking water (urban/rural, %)	99.8 / 99.4	99.7 / 99.4	99.7 / 99.4 [b]
Pop. using improved sanitation facilities (urban/rural, %)	99.1 / 99.1	99.1 / 99.1	99.1 / 99.1 [b]
Net Official Development Assist. disbursed (% of GNI) [o]	0.11	0.13	0.16 [m,c]

a Projected estimate (medium fertility variant). **b** 2015. **c** 2017. **d** 2016. **e** Data classified according to ISIC Rev. 4. **f** Estimate. **g** Excluding water and waste management. **h** 2014. **i** Data refers to a 5-year period preceding the reference year. **j** Data as at the end of December. **k** Users in the last 3 months. **l** Population aged 16 to 74 years. **m** Provisional data. **n** 2004. **o** Development Assistance Committee member (OECD).

Solomon Islands

Region	Melanesia	UN membership date	19 September 1978
Population (000, 2018)	623[a]	Surface area (km2)	28 896[b]
Pop. density (per km2, 2018)	22.3[a]	Sex ratio (m per 100 f)	103.4[a]
Capital city	Honiara	National currency	Solomon Is. Dollar (SBD)[c]
Capital city pop. (000, 2018)	81.8	Exchange rate (per US$)	7.9[d]

Economic indicators

	2005	2010	2018
GDP: Gross domestic product (million current US$)	429	720	1 134[e]
GDP growth rate (annual %, const. 2010 prices)	12.8	10.6	3.2[e]
GDP per capita (current US$)	914.0	1 363.0	1 892.0[e]
Economy: Agriculture (% of Gross Value Added)	30.4	28.7	26.9[e]
Economy: Industry (% of Gross Value Added)	7.5	13.3	15.2[e]
Economy: Services and other activity (% of GVA)	62.1	57.9	57.9[e]
Employment in agriculture (% of employed)[f]	71.2	69.5	69.7
Employment in industry (% of employed)[f]	8.4	9.1	9.8
Employment in services & other sectors (% employed)[f]	20.5	21.4	20.6
Unemployment rate (% of labour force)[f]	2.2	2.1	2.1
Labour force participation rate (female/male pop. %)[f]	63.9 / 81.7	63.4 / 81.4	62.4 / 80.3
CPI: Consumer Price Index (2010=100)	66	100	127[d]
Agricultural production index (2004-2006=100)	103	111	113[e]
International trade: exports (million current US$)	70	215	500[d]
International trade: imports (million current US$)	139	328	572[d]
International trade: balance (million current US$)	- 68	- 112	- 72[d]
Balance of payments, current account (million US$)	- 90	- 144	- 46[d]

Major trading partners

						2017
Export partners (% of exports)	China	65.2	Italy	7.7	Switzerland	3.9
Import partners (% of imports)	Australia	19.9	Singapore	13.8	New Zealand	13.2

Social indicators

	2005	2010	2018
Population growth rate (average annual %)[g]	2.6	2.3	2.1[b]
Urban population (% of total population)	17.8	20.0	23.7
Urban population growth rate (average annual %)[g]	5.0	4.7	4.3[b]
Fertility rate, total (live births per woman)[g]	4.6	4.4	4.1[b]
Life expectancy at birth (females/males, years)[g]	66.0 / 63.5	68.8 / 66.1	71.1 / 68.3[b]
Population age distribution (0-14/60+ years old, %)	41.3 / 4.8	40.8 / 5.1	38.5 / 5.5[a]
International migrant stock (000/% of total pop.)	3.3 / 0.7	2.8 / 0.5	2.5 / 0.4[d]
Refugees and others of concern to the UNHCR (000)	...	...	~0.0[e]
Infant mortality rate (per 1 000 live births)[g]	49.9	38.7	30.0[b]
Health: Current expenditure (% of GDP)	10.1	7.4	8.0[b]
Health: Physicians (per 1 000 pop.)	0.2	0.2[h]	0.2[i]
Education: Government expenditure (% of GDP)	...	10.0	...
Education: Primary gross enrol. ratio (f/m per 100 pop.)	97.8 / 103.2	113.1 / 116.0	114.0 / 115.4[e]
Education: Secondary gross enrol. ratio (f/m per 100 pop.)	27.4 / 33.2	44.9 / 51.9	47.0 / 49.5[j]
Intentional homicide rate (per 100 000 pop.)	5.5	3.8[h]	...
Seats held by women in the National Parliament (%)	0.0	0.0	2.0

Environment and infrastructure indicators

	2005	2010	2018
Individuals using the Internet (per 100 inhabitants)	0.8	5.0[f]	11.0[f,a]
Threatened species (number)	74[k]	220	245[d]
Forested area (% of land area)[f]	80.1	79.1	78.1[b]
CO2 emission estimates (million tons/tons per capita)	0.2 / 0.3	0.2 / 0.4	0.2 / 0.4[l]
Energy production, primary (Petajoules)[f]	3	3	3[b]
Energy supply per capita (Gigajoules)[f]	12	11	10[b]
Tourist/visitor arrivals at national borders (000)	9[m]	20	23[e]
Important sites for terrestrial biodiversity protected (%)	7.1	9.5	9.5
Pop. using improved drinking water (urban/rural, %)	93.2 / 77.2	93.2 / 77.2	93.2 / 77.2[b]
Pop. using improved sanitation facilities (urban/rural, %)	81.4 / 15.0	81.4 / 15.0	81.4 / 15.0[b]
Net Official Development Assist. received (% of GNI)	47.69	68.51	15.22[b]

a Projected estimate (medium fertility variant). b 2015. c Solomon Islands Dollar. d 2017. e 2016. f Estimate. g Data refers to a 5-year period preceding the reference year. h 2008. i 2013. j 2012. k 2004. l 2014. m Without first quarter.

Somalia

Region	Eastern Africa	UN membership date	20 September 1960
Population (000, 2018)	15 182[a]	Surface area (km2)	637 657[b]
Pop. density (per km2, 2018)	24.2[a]	Sex ratio (m per 100 f)	99.3[a]
Capital city	Mogadishu	National currency	Somali Shilling (SOS)
Capital city pop. (000, 2018)	2 081.6[c]	Exchange rate (per US$)	24 300.0[d,e]

Economic indicators

	2005	2010	2018
GDP: Gross domestic product (million current US$)	2 316	1 071	1 318[f]
GDP growth rate (annual %, const. 2010 prices)	3.0	2.6	2.6[f]
GDP per capita (current US$)	222.0	89.0	92.0[f]
Economy: Agriculture (% of Gross Value Added)	60.1	60.2	60.2[f]
Economy: Industry (% of Gross Value Added)	7.4	7.4	7.4[f]
Economy: Services and other activity (% of GVA)	32.6	32.5	32.5[f]
Employment in agriculture (% of employed)[g]	86.7	86.4	86.2
Employment in industry (% of employed)[g]	7.2	7.4	7.6
Employment in services & other sectors (% employed)[g]	6.1	6.2	6.2
Unemployment rate (% of labour force)[g]	5.9	6.0	5.9
Labour force participation rate (female/male pop. %)[g]	17.5 / 76.0	17.5 / 75.0	18.7 / 74.3
Agricultural production index (2004-2006=100)	103	105	108[f]
International trade: exports (million current US$)[g]	379	568	1 003[e]
International trade: imports (million current US$)[g]	469	496	537[e]
International trade: balance (million current US$)[g]	- 90	72	466[e]

Major trading partners 2017

Export partners (% of exports)[g]	Saudi Arabia	48.6	Oman	20.5	United Arab Emirates	10.8
Import partners (% of imports)[g]	China	18.9	United Arab Emirates	17.8	India	15.9

Social indicators

	2005	2010	2018
Population growth rate (average annual %)[h]	2.9	2.9	2.9[b]
Urban population (% of total population)	36.3	39.3	45.0
Urban population growth rate (average annual %)[h]	4.6	4.5	4.8[b]
Fertility rate, total (live births per woman)[h]	7.5	7.1	6.6[b]
Life expectancy at birth (females/males, years)[h]	53.1 / 50.0	54.8 / 51.6	56.5 / 53.3[b]
Population age distribution (0-14/60+ years old, %)	47.9 / 4.3	47.7 / 4.3	46.3 / 4.4[a]
International migrant stock (000/% of total pop.)[g,i]	20.7 / 0.2	24.0 / 0.2	44.9 / 0.3[a]
Refugees and others of concern to the UNHCR (000)	400.6[j]	1 489.8[j]	1 620.6[e]
Infant mortality rate (per 1 000 live births)[h]	97.0	89.8	79.5[b]
Health: Physicians (per 1 000 pop.)	...	~0.0[k]	~0.0[l]
Education: Primary gross enrol. ratio (f/m per 100 pop.)	... / ...	16.8 / 30.3[m]	... / ...
Education: Secondary gross enrol. ratio (f/m per 100 pop.)	... / ...	3.8 / 8.2[m]	... / ...
Intentional homicide rate (per 100 000 pop.)	5.0	5.3	4.3[b]
Seats held by women in the National Parliament (%)	...	6.9	24.4

Environment and infrastructure indicators

	2005	2010	2018
Individuals using the Internet (per 100 inhabitants)[g]	1.1	1.2[n]	1.9[f]
Threatened species (number)	64[o]	128	175[e]
Forested area (% of land area)[g]	11.4	10.8	10.1[b]
CO2 emission estimates (million tons/tons per capita)	0.6 / 0.1	0.6 / 0.1	0.6 / 0.1[l]
Energy production, primary (Petajoules)	103	124	129[b]
Energy supply per capita (Gigajoules)	13	13	13[b]
Important sites for terrestrial biodiversity protected (%)	0.0	0.0	0.0
Pop. using improved drinking water (urban/rural, %)	60.5 / 11.0	69.6 / 8.8	69.6 / 8.8[p]
Pop. using improved sanitation facilities (urban/rural, %)	50.0 / 7.4	52.0 / 6.3	52.0 / 6.3[p]
Net Official Development Assist. received (% of GNI)	...	...	20.42[f]

a Projected estimate (medium fertility variant). b 2015. c Data refers to the urban agglomeration. d UN operational exchange rate. e 2017. f 2016. g Estimate. h Data refers to a 5-year period preceding the reference year. i Including refugees. j Data as at the end of December. k 2006. l 2014. m 2007. n 2009. o 2004. p 2011.

South Africa

Region	Southern Africa	UN membership date	07 November 1945
Population (000, 2018)	57 398 [a]	Surface area (km2)	1 221 037 [b]
Pop. density (per km2, 2018)	47.3 [a]	Sex ratio (m per 100 f)	96.3 [a]
Capital city	Pretoria [c]	National currency	Rand (ZAR)
Capital city pop. (000, 2018)	2 378.4	Exchange rate (per US$)	12.3 [d]

Economic indicators

	2005	2010	2018
GDP: Gross domestic product (million current US$)	257 772	375 348	295 440 [e]
GDP growth rate (annual %, const. 2010 prices)	5.3	3.0	0.3 [e]
GDP per capita (current US$)	5 280.0	7 276.0	5 274.0 [e]
Economy: Agriculture (% of Gross Value Added)	2.7	2.6	2.4 [e]
Economy: Industry (% of Gross Value Added)	30.3	30.2	28.9 [e]
Economy: Services and other activity (% of GVA)	67.1	67.2	68.6 [e]
Employment in agriculture (% of employed) [f]	7.5	4.9	5.5
Employment in industry (% of employed) [f]	25.7	24.4	23.4
Employment in services & other sectors (% employed) [f]	66.8	70.7	71.2
Unemployment rate (% of labour force)	23.8	24.7	28.5 [f]
Labour force participation rate (female/male pop. %) [f]	45.9 / 51.8	44.7 / 60.5	47.9 / 62.0
CPI: Consumer Price Index (2010=100) [g,h]	74	100	146 [d]
Agricultural production index (2004-2006=100)	103	117	117 [d]
International trade: exports (million current US$) [i,j]	46 991	82 626	88 268 [d]
International trade: imports (million current US$) [i,j]	55 033	82 949	83 031 [d]
International trade: balance (million current US$) [i,j]	- 8 042	- 323	5 237 [d]
Balance of payments, current account (million US$)	- 8 015	- 5 492	- 8 607 [d]

Major trading partners

						2017
Export partners (% of exports)	China	9.8	United States	7.5	Germany	6.6
Import partners (% of imports)	China	18.3	Germany	11.5	United States	6.6

Social indicators

	2005	2010	2018
Population growth rate (average annual %) [k]	1.3	1.1	1.4 [b]
Urban population (% of total population)	59.5	62.2	66.4
Urban population growth rate (average annual %) [k]	2.2	2.0	2.2 [b]
Fertility rate, total (live births per woman) [k]	2.8	2.6	2.6 [b]
Life expectancy at birth (females/males, years) [k]	56.7 / 51.2	55.6 / 50.6	63.0 / 56.1 [b]
Population age distribution (0-14/60+ years old, %)	31.7 / 6.7	30.4 / 7.2	28.8 / 8.5 [a]
International migrant stock (000/% of total pop.) [l]	1 210.9 / 2.5	2 096.9 / 4.1	4 036.7 / 7.1 [d]
Refugees and others of concern to the UNHCR (000)	169.9 [m]	229.7 [m]	308.2 [d]
Infant mortality rate (per 1 000 live births) [k]	60.5	52.7	36.5 [b]
Health: Current expenditure (% of GDP) [n]	6.7	7.4	8.2 [b]
Health: Physicians (per 1 000 pop.)	0.7 [o]	0.7	0.8 [e]
Education: Government expenditure (% of GDP)	5.1	5.7	5.9 [e]
Education: Primary gross enrol. ratio (f/m per 100 pop.)	100.7 / 104.5	95.8 / 99.9	99.0 / 106.6 [b]
Education: Secondary gross enrol. ratio (f/m per 100 pop.)	93.1 / 87.2	94.7 / 89.4	102.0 / 103.5 [b]
Education: Tertiary gross enrol. ratio (f/m per 100 pop.)	... / ...	... / ...	23.2 / 16.4 [e]
Intentional homicide rate (per 100 000 pop.)	38.0	30.8	34.0 [e]
Seats held by women in the National Parliament (%)	32.8	44.5	42.4

Environment and infrastructure indicators

	2005	2010	2018
Individuals using the Internet (per 100 inhabitants)	7.5	24.0 [f]	54.0 [f,a]
Research & Development expenditure (% of GDP)	0.9	0.7	0.7 [q]
Threatened species (number)	357 [o]	441	581 [d]
Forested area (% of land area)	7.6	7.6	7.6 [f,b]
CO2 emission estimates (million tons/tons per capita)	416.9 / 8.7	474.1 / 9.2	489.8 / 9.1 [p]
Energy production, primary (Petajoules)	6 648	6 906	7 049 [b]
Energy supply per capita (Gigajoules)	114	122	117 [b]
Tourist/visitor arrivals at national borders (000)	7 369 [r]	8 074 [s]	10 044 [t,a]
Important sites for terrestrial biodiversity protected (%)	33.5	35.1	37.7
Pop. using improved drinking water (urban/rural, %)	98.9 / 74.2	99.2 / 77.8	99.6 / 81.4 [b]
Pop. using improved sanitation facilities (urban/rural, %)	67.2 / 50.6	68.4 / 55.5	69.6 / 60.5 [b]
Net Official Development Assist. received (% of GNI)	0.27	0.28	0.41 [e]

a Projected estimate (medium fertility variant). b 2015. c Pretoria is the administrative capital, Cape Town is the legislative capital and Bloemfontein is the judiciary capital. d 2017. e 2016. f Estimate. g Calculated by the Statistics Division of the United Nations from national indices. h Urban areas. i Exports include gold. j Imports FOB. k Data refers to a 5-year period preceding the reference year. l Including refugees. m Data as at the end of December. n Data refer to fiscal years ending 31 March. o 2004. p 2014. q 2013. r Excluding arrivals for work and contract workers. s Break in the time series. t Excluding transit.

South Sudan

Region	Eastern Africa	UN membership date	14 July 2011
Population (000, 2018)	12 919 [a]	Surface area (km2)	658 841 [b]
Pop. density (per km2, 2018)	21.1 [a]	Sex ratio (m per 100 f)	100.5 [a]
Capital city	Juba	National currency	S. Sudanese Pound (SSP) [c]
Capital city pop. (000, 2018)	368.9	Exchange rate (per US$)	127.9 [d]

Economic indicators		2005	2010	2018
GDP: Gross domestic product (million current US$)		...	15 206	8 534 [e]
GDP growth rate (annual %, const. 2010 prices)		...	- 1.8	0.3 [e]
GDP per capita (current US$)		...	1 510.0	534.0 [e]
Economy: Agriculture (% of Gross Value Added)		...	5.1	4.1 [e]
Economy: Industry (% of Gross Value Added)		...	55.4	39.8 [e]
Economy: Services and other activity (% of GVA)		...	39.4	56.1 [e]
Employment in agriculture (% of employed) [f]		56.5	54.1	65.4
Employment in industry (% of employed) [f]		18.8	19.8	19.5
Employment in services & other sectors (% employed) [f]		24.6	26.1	15.2
Unemployment rate (% of labour force) [f]		12.2	12.1	11.5
Labour force participation rate (female/male pop. %) [f]		70.6 / 77.2	70.6 / 75.9	70.9 / 73.8
CPI: Consumer Price Index (2010=100)		...	100	4 584 [d]
International trade: exports (million current US$)		...	...	1 840 [f,d]
International trade: imports (million current US$)		...	...	886 [f,d]
International trade: balance (million current US$)		...	...	953 [f,d]
Balance of payments, current account (million US$)		...	...	- 965 [d]

Major trading partners						2017
Export partners (% of exports)	China	95.9 [f]	India	3.8	Uganda	0.1 [f]
Import partners (% of imports) [f]	Uganda	69.0	China	12.4	United States	3.2

Social indicators	2005	2010	2018
Population growth rate (average annual %) [g]	3.8	4.3	3.3 [b]
Urban population (% of total population)	17.2	17.9	19.6
Urban population growth rate (average annual %) [g]	4.6	5.1	4.4 [b]
Fertility rate, total (live births per woman) [g]	6.0	5.6	5.2 [b]
Life expectancy at birth (females/males, years) [g]	51.3 / 49.1	53.3 / 51.3	56.0 / 54.1 [b]
Population age distribution (0-14/60+ years old, %)	44.3 / 5.1	43.3 / 5.3	41.5 / 5.1 [a]
International migrant stock (000/% of total pop.) [h]	... / ...	257.9 / 2.6	845.2 / 6.7 [a]
Refugees and others of concern to the UNHCR (000)	...	...	2 222.1 [d]
Infant mortality rate (per 1 000 live births) [g]	101.4	89.1	77.7 [b]
Health: Current expenditure (% of GDP)	...	...	2.5 [f,b]
Education: Government expenditure (% of GDP)	...	...	1.8 [e]
Education: Primary gross enrol. ratio (f/m per 100 pop.)	... / ...	... / ...	55.1 / 77.8 [b]
Education: Secondary gross enrol. ratio (f/m per 100 pop.)	... / ...	... / ...	6.9 / 12.8 [b]
Intentional homicide (per 100 000 pop.)	...	...	13.9 [i]
Seats held by women in the National Parliament (%)	...	...	28.5

Environment and infrastructure indicators	2005	2010	2018
Individuals using the Internet (per 100 inhabitants) [f]	...	7.0	17.9 [b]
Threatened species (number)	...	...	49 [d]
CO2 emission estimates (million tons/tons per capita)	... / ...	... / ...	1.5 / 0.1 [i]
Energy production, primary (Petajoules)	...	...	321 [b]
Energy supply per capita (Gigajoules)	...	...	2 [b]
Important sites for terrestrial biodiversity protected (%)	30.3	33.6	33.6
Pop. using improved drinking water (urban/rural, %)	... / ...	... / ...	66.7 / 56.9 [b]
Pop. using improved sanitation facilities (urban/rural, %)	... / ...	... / ...	16.4 / 4.5 [b]
Net Official Development Assist. received (% of GNI)	...	...	21.07 [b]

a Projected estimate (medium fertility variant). b 2015. c South Sudanese Pound. d 2017. e 2016. f Estimate. g Data refers to a 5-year period preceding the reference year. h Including refugees. i 2012. j 2014.

Spain

Region	Southern Europe	UN membership date	14 December 1955
Population (000, 2018)	46 398[a,b]	Surface area (km2)	505 944[c]
Pop. density (per km2, 2018)	93.0[a,b]	Sex ratio (m per 100 f)	96.3[a,b]
Capital city	Madrid	National currency	Euro (EUR)
Capital city pop. (000, 2018)	6 497.1	Exchange rate (per US$)	0.8[d]

Economic indicators	2005	2010	2018
GDP: Gross domestic product (million current US$)	1 157 248	1 431 617	1 237 255[e]
GDP growth rate (annual %, const. 2010 prices)	3.7	−0.0	3.3[e]
GDP per capita (current US$)	26 276.0	30 598.0	26 695.0[e]
Economy: Agriculture (% of Gross Value Added)[f]	3.0	2.6	2.8[e]
Economy: Industry (% of Gross Value Added)[f]	30.4	26.0	23.5[e]
Economy: Services and other activity (% of GVA)[f]	66.5	71.4	73.8[e]
Employment in agriculture (% of employed)	5.3	4.2[g]	4.0[g]
Employment in industry (% of employed)[g]	29.6	23.0	19.3
Employment in services & other sectors (% employed)[g]	65.1	72.8	76.6
Unemployment rate (% of labour force)	9.2	19.9	15.4[g]
Labour force participation rate (female/male pop. %)[g]	46.1 / 68.0	51.5 / 67.3	52.0 / 63.3
CPI: Consumer Price Index (2010=100)[i]	89[h]	100	108[d]
Agricultural production index (2004-2006=100)	95	103	104[e]
Index of industrial production (2005=100)	100	83[j]	76[j,k]
International trade: exports (million current US$)	192 798	246 265	319 622[d]
International trade: imports (million current US$)	289 611	315 547	350 922[d]
International trade: balance (million current US$)	- 96 812	- 69 282	- 31 300[d]
Balance of payments, current account (million US$)	- 87 005	- 56 363	25 622[d]

Major trading partners						2017
Export partners (% of exports)	France	14.7	Germany	10.9	Italy	7.8
Import partners (% of imports)	Germany	12.5	France	10.7	China	8.3

Social indicators	2005	2010	2018
Population growth rate (average annual %)[e,l]	1.5	1.2	- 0.2[c]
Urban population (% of total population)[a]	77.3	78.4	80.3
Urban population growth rate (average annual %)[a,l]	1.7	1.5	0.1[c]
Fertility rate, total (live births per woman)[a,l]	1.3	1.4	1.3[c]
Life expectancy at birth (females/males, years)[a,l]	83.3 / 76.5	84.3 / 78.1	85.3 / 79.6[c]
Population age distribution (0-14/60+ years old, %)[a]	14.3 / 21.6	14.6 / 22.4	14.6 / 25.8[b]
International migrant stock (000/% of total pop.)[a]	4 107.2 / 9.3	6 280.1 / 13.4	5 947.1 / 12.8[d]
Refugees and others of concern to the UNHCR (000)	5.4[m]	6.6[m]	36.4[d]
Infant mortality rate (per 1 000 live births)[a,l]	4.0	3.4	2.9[c]
Health: Current expenditure (% of GDP)	7.7	9.0	9.2[c]
Health: Physicians (per 1 000 pop.)	4.5	3.8	3.9[c]
Education: Government expenditure (% of GDP)	4.1	4.8	4.3[k]
Education: Primary gross enrol. ratio (f/m per 100 pop.)	102.2 / 103.6	105.2 / 105.7	104.5 / 103.3[e]
Education: Secondary gross enrol. ratio (f/m per 100 pop.)	121.1 / 113.6	125.5 / 122.8	128.4 / 127.5[e]
Education: Tertiary gross enrol. ratio (f/m per 100 pop.)	74.2 / 60.4	87.1 / 70.3	99.2 / 83.5[e]
Intentional homicide rate (per 100 000 pop.)	1.2	0.9	0.6[e]
Seats held by women in the National Parliament (%)	36.0	36.6	39.1

Environment and infrastructure indicators	2005	2010	2018
Individuals using the Internet (per 100 inhabitants)	47.9[n,o]	65.8[p]	80.6[e]
Research & Development expenditure (% of GDP)	1.1	1.4	1.2[c]
Threatened species (number)	153[q]	240	617[d]
Forested area (% of land area)	34.6	36.5	36.8[c]
CO2 emission estimates (million tons/tons per capita)	353.5 / 8.1	270.9 / 5.8	234.0 / 5.1[k]
Energy production, primary (Petajoules)[r]	1 256	1 419	1 368[c]
Energy supply per capita (Gigajoules)[r]	136	115	106[c]
Tourist/visitor arrivals at national borders (000)	55 914	52 677	75 315[h,e]
Important sites for terrestrial biodiversity protected (%)	53.0	54.6	56.3
Pop. using improved drinking water (urban/rural, %)	100.0 / 100.0	100.0 / 100.0	100.0 / 100.0[c]
Pop. using improved sanitation facilities (urban/rural, %)	99.9 / 100.0	99.8 / 100.0	99.8 / 100.0[c]
Net Official Development Assist. disbursed (% of GNI)[s]	0.27	0.43	0.19[t,d]

a Including Canary Islands, Ceuta and Melilla. **b** Projected estimate (medium fertility variant). **c** 2015. **d** 2017. **e** 2016. **f** Data classified according to ISIC Rev. 4. **g** Estimate. **h** Break in the time series. **i** Calculated by the Statistics Division of the United Nations from national indices. **j** Excluding water and waste management. **k** 2014. **l** Data refers to a 5-year period preceding the reference year. **m** Data as at the end of December. **n** Users in the last 12 months. **o** Population aged 16 to 74 years. **p** Population aged 10 years and over. **q** 2004. **r** Data include the Canary Islands. **s** Development Assistance Committee member (OECD). **t** Provisional data.

Sri Lanka

Region	Southern Asia	UN membership date	14 December 1955
Population (000, 2018)	20 950 [a]	Surface area (km2)	65 610 [b]
Pop. density (per km2, 2018)	334.1 [a]	Sex ratio (m per 100 f)	92.4 [a]
Capital city	Colombo [c]	National currency	Sri Lanka Rupee (LKR)
Capital city pop. (000, 2018)	599.8	Exchange rate (per US$)	152.9 [d]

Economic indicators	2005	2010	2018
GDP: Gross domestic product (million current US$)	27 932	56 726	81 322 [e]
GDP growth rate (annual %, const. 2010 prices)	6.2	8.0	4.4 [e]
GDP per capita (current US$)	1 431.0	2 808.0	3 910.0 [e]
Economy: Agriculture (% of Gross Value Added) [f]	8.8	9.5	8.2 [e]
Economy: Industry (% of Gross Value Added) [f]	31.0	29.7	29.6 [e]
Economy: Services and other activity (% of GVA) [f]	60.1	60.9	62.2 [e]
Employment in agriculture (% of employed) [g]	33.8	33.6	26.0
Employment in industry (% of employed) [g]	27.3	24.9	25.7
Employment in services & other sectors (% employed) [g]	38.9	41.5	48.3
Unemployment rate (% of labour force)	7.7	4.9	4.1 [g]
Labour force participation rate (female/male pop. %) [g]	36.9 / 76.7	34.8 / 76.3	34.9 / 73.9
CPI: Consumer Price Index (2010=100)	58 [h,i,j]	100 [h,j]	123 [k,d]
Agricultural production index (2004-2006=100)	102	123	128 [e]
International trade: exports (million current US$)	6 160	8 304	11 741 [d]
International trade: imports (million current US$)	8 307	12 354	21 316 [d]
International trade: balance (million current US$)	- 2 147	- 4 050	- 9 575 [d]
Balance of payments, current account (million US$)	- 650	- 1 075	- 2 309 [d]

Major trading partners						2017
Export partners (% of exports)	United States	24.9	United Kingdom	8.9	India	6.7
Import partners (% of imports)	India	21.1	China	19.7	United Arab Emirates	7.3

Social indicators	2005	2010	2018
Population growth rate (average annual %) [l]	0.8	0.7	0.5 [b]
Urban population (% of total population)	18.3	18.2	18.5
Urban population growth rate (average annual %) [l]	0.7	0.6	0.5 [b]
Fertility rate, total (live births per woman) [l]	2.3	2.3	2.1 [b]
Life expectancy at birth (females/males, years) [l]	77.1 / 69.6	77.7 / 70.6	78.0 / 71.2 [b]
Population age distribution (0-14/60+ years old, %)	25.6 / 10.4	25.4 / 11.8	23.7 / 15.4 [a]
International migrant stock (000/% of total pop.) [m]	39.5 / 0.2	38.0 / 0.2	40.0 / 0.2 [d]
Refugees and others of concern to the UNHCR (000)	352.1 [n]	435.3 [n]	41.7 [d]
Infant mortality rate (per 1 000 live births) [l]	13.1	10.1	8.2 [b]
Health: Current expenditure (% of GDP) [i]	3.8	3.0	3.0 [b]
Health: Physicians (per 1 000 pop.)	0.5	0.7	0.9 [b]
Education: Government expenditure (% of GDP)	...	1.7	3.5 [e]
Education: Primary gross enrol. ratio (f/m per 100 pop.)	99.1 / 99.9	98.4 / 101.0	100.8 / 103.0 [e]
Education: Secondary gross enrol. ratio (f/m per 100 pop.)	... / ...	97.5 / 96.3	99.3 / 96.0 [e]
Education: Tertiary gross enrol. ratio (f/m per 100 pop.)	... / ...	20.9 / 11.7	22.9 / 14.8 [e]
Intentional homicide rate (per 100 000 pop.) [i]	6.2	3.8	2.5 [e]
Seats held by women in the National Parliament (%)	4.9	5.8	5.8

Environment and infrastructure indicators	2005	2010	2018
Individuals using the Internet (per 100 inhabitants)	1.8 [g]	12.0	32.1 [g,e]
Research & Development expenditure (% of GDP)	0.2 [i,o]	0.1	0.1 [p]
Threatened species (number)	394 [o]	552	587 [d]
Forested area (% of land area)	33.8	33.5	33.0 [b]
CO2 emission estimates (million tons/tons per capita)	12.1 / 0.6	13.3 / 0.7	18.4 / 0.9 [q]
Energy production, primary (Petajoules)	163	184	181 [b]
Energy supply per capita (Gigajoules)	16	18	21 [b]
Tourist/visitor arrivals at national borders (000) [r]	549	654	2 051 [e]
Important sites for terrestrial biodiversity protected (%)	41.7	47.5	49.8
Pop. using improved drinking water (urban/rural, %)	96.2 / 82.9	97.5 / 89.6	98.5 / 95.0 [b]
Pop. using improved sanitation facilities (urban/rural, %)	86.2 / 86.5	87.2 / 92.7	88.1 / 96.7 [b]
Net Official Development Assist. received (% of GNI)	4.83	1.03	0.46 [e]

a Projected estimate (medium fertility variant). b 2015. c Colombo is the capital and Sri Jayewardenepura Kotte is the legislative capital. d 2017. e 2016. f Data classified according to ISIC Rev. 4. g Estimate. h Colombo i Break in the time series. j Calculated by the Statistics Division of the United Nations from national indices. k Index base: 2013=100. l Data refers to a 5-year period preceding the reference year. m Including refugees. n Data as at the end of December. o 2004. p 2013. q 2014. r Excluding nationals residing abroad.

State of Palestine

Region	Western Asia	Population (000, 2018)	5 053 a,b
Surface area (km2)	6 020 c	Pop. density (per km2, 2018)	839.3 a,b
Sex ratio (m per 100 f)	102.9 a,b	Capital city	East Jerusalem d
Capital city pop. (000, 2018)	275.1 d		

Economic indicators	2005	2010	2018
GDP: Gross domestic product (million current US$)	4 832	8 913	13 397 e
GDP growth rate (annual %, const. 2010 prices)	10.8	8.1	4.1 e
GDP per capita (current US$)	1 351.0	2 192.0	2 796.0 e
Economy: Agriculture (% of Gross Value Added) f	5.8	6.4	4.4 e
Economy: Industry (% of Gross Value Added) f	25.8	23.3	22.5 e
Economy: Services and other activity (% of GVA) f	68.3	70.2	73.1 e
Employment in agriculture (% of employed) g	14.6	12.8	9.7
Employment in industry (% of employed) g	26.3	25.7	29.4
Employment in services & other sectors (% employed) g	59.2	61.5	61.0
Unemployment rate (% of labour force)	23.5	23.7	28.6 g
Labour force participation rate (female/male pop. %) g	14.1 / 67.0	14.8 / 66.4	19.8 / 72.1
CPI: Consumer Price Index (2010=100)	81	100	111 h
Agricultural production index (2004-2006=100)	96	75	87 e
Index of industrial production (2005=100)	100	115	130 i
International trade: exports (million current US$)	335	576	1 035 g,h
International trade: imports (million current US$)	2 668	3 959	5 624 g,h
International trade: balance (million current US$)	- 2 332	- 3 383	- 4 589 g,h
Balance of payments, current account (million US$)	- 1 365	- 1 307	- 1 564 h

Major trading partners						2017
Export partners (% of exports)	Israel	83.2 g	Jordan	5.6	United Arab Emirates	2.5 g
Import partners (% of imports) g	Israel	58.2	Turkey	8.9	China	7.1

Social indicators	2005	2010	2018
Population growth rate (average annual %) b,j	2.1	2.6	2.7 c
Urban population (% of total population) b	73.1	74.1	76.2
Urban population growth rate (average annual %) b,j	2.4	2.9	3.1 c
Fertility rate, total (live births per woman) b,j	5.0	4.6	4.2 c
Life expectancy at birth (females/males, years) b,j	72.9 / 69.5	73.9 / 70.2	74.8 / 71.1 c
Population age distribution (0-14/60+ years old, %) b	45.6 / 4.0	42.4 / 4.3	39.3 / 4.7 a
International migrant stock (000/% of total pop.) b,k	266.6 / 7.5	258.0 / 6.3	253.7 / 5.2 h
Refugees and others of concern to the UNHCR (000)	...	...	~0.0 c
Infant mortality rate (per 1 000 live births) b,j	24.9	22.3	20.0 c
Education: Government expenditure (% of GDP)	...	6.7	5.7 e
Education: Primary gross enrol. ratio (f/m per 100 pop.)	87.9 / 88.5	90.1 / 91.9	94.0 / 93.9 e
Education: Secondary gross enrol. ratio (f/m per 100 pop.)	91.7 / 87.7	89.0 / 82.4	88.0 / 79.9 e
Education: Tertiary gross enrol. ratio (f/m per 100 pop.)	41.2 / 40.6	54.9 / 41.1	52.8 / 33.3 e
Intentional homicide rate (per 100 000 pop.)	2.4	0.8	0.7 e

Environment and infrastructure indicators	2005	2010	2018
Individuals using the Internet (per 100 inhabitants) g	16.0 l	37.4	61.2 e
Research & Development expenditure (% of GDP) m	...	0.4	0.5 n
Threatened species (number)	4 o	18	31 h
Forested area (% of land area) g	1.5	1.5	1.5 c
CO2 emission estimates (million tons/tons per capita)	2.7 / 0.8	2.0 / 0.5	2.8 / 0.6 i
Energy production, primary (Petajoules)	8	9	9 c
Energy supply per capita (Gigajoules)	16	13	16 c
Tourist/visitor arrivals at national borders (000)	88	522	400 e
Important sites for terrestrial biodiversity protected (%)	2.5	2.5	2.5
Pop. using improved drinking water (urban/rural, %)	78.9 / 84.1	64.8 / 82.8	50.7 / 81.5 c
Pop. using improved sanitation facilities (urban/rural, %)	91.6 / 86.2	92.5 / 89.1	93.0 / 90.2 c
Net Official Development Assist. received (% of GNI)	19.61	26.41	16.04 e

a Projected estimate (medium fertility variant). b Including East Jerusalem. c 2015. d Designation and data provided by the State of Palestine. The position of the United Nations on Jerusalem is stated in A/RES/181 (II) and subsequent General Assembly and Security Council resolutions. e 2016. f Data classified according to ISIC Rev. 4. g Estimate. h 2017. i 2014. j Data refers to a 5-year period preceding the reference year. k Refugees are not part of the foreign-born migrant stock in the State of Palestine. l Population aged 10 years and over. m Excluding business enterprise. n 2013. o 2004.

Sudan

Region	Northern Africa	UN membership date	12 November 1956
Population (000, 2018)	41 512ᵃ	Pop. density (per km2, 2018)	23.5ᵃ
Sex ratio (m per 100 f)	99.9ᵃ	Capital city	Khartoum
National currency	Sudanese Pound (SDG)	Capital city pop. (000, 2018)	5 534.1
Exchange rate (per US$)	6.7ᵇ		

Economic indicators

	2005	2010	2018
GDP: Gross domestic product (million current US$)	...	54 459	82 887ᶜ
GDP growth rate (annual %, const. 2010 prices)	...	8.8	3.0ᶜ
GDP per capita (current US$)	...	1 584.0	2 094.0ᶜ
Economy: Agriculture (% of Gross Value Added)	...	42.8	31.7ᶜ
Economy: Industry (% of Gross Value Added)	...	13.9	20.8ᶜ
Economy: Services and other activity (% of GVA)	...	43.4	47.6ᶜ
Employment in agriculture (% of employed)ᵈ	54.8	49.2	53.2
Employment in industry (% of employed)ᵈ	21.4	22.6	19.2
Employment in services & other sectors (% employed)ᵈ	23.8	28.2	27.6
Unemployment rate (% of labour force)ᵈ	13.0	12.9	12.8
Labour force participation rate (female/male pop. %)ᵈ	24.5 / 74.0	23.0 / 72.7	23.5 / 69.8
CPI: Consumer Price Index (2010=100)	60	100	350ᵈ
International trade: exports (million current US$)	...	...	4 061ᵈ·ᵇ
International trade: imports (million current US$)	...	...	9 163ᵈ·ᵇ
International trade: balance (million current US$)	...	...	-5 102ᵈ·ᵇ
Balance of payments, current account (million US$)	-2 473	-1 725ᶠ	-5 033ᵇ

Major trading partners

							2017
Export partners (% of exports)	China	56.4ᵈ	United Arab Emirates	14.4	Saudi Arabia	14.4ᵈ
Import partners (% of imports)ᵈ	China	22.8	Jordan	8.6	India	8.5

Social indicators

	2005	2010	2018
Population growth rate (average annual %)ᵍ	2.5	2.1	2.3ᵉ
Urban population (% of total population)	32.8	33.1	34.6
Urban population growth rate (average annual %)ᵍ	2.7	2.3	2.8ᵉ
Fertility rate, total (live births per woman)ᵍ	5.3	5.0	4.8ᵉ
Life expectancy at birth (females/males, years)ᵍ	61.3 / 57.5	63.2 / 59.8	65.1 / 62.1ᵉ
Population age distribution (0-14/60+ years old, %)	43.5 / 4.9	43.0 / 5.1	40.5 / 5.6ᵃ
International migrant stock (000/% of total pop.)ʰ	... / ...	578.4 / 1.7	735.8 / 1.8ᵇ
Refugees and others of concern to the UNHCR (000)	1 029.7ⁱ	1 951.5ⁱ	2 867.8ᵇ
Infant mortality rate (per 1 000 live births)ᵍ	61.8	53.7	48.7ᵉ
Health: Current expenditure (% of GDP)ᵈ	4.1ʲ	5.3ʲ	6.3ᵉ
Health: Physicians (per 1 000 pop.)	0.2ᵏ	0.3ⁱ	...
Education: Government expenditure (% of GDP)	1.6	2.2ᵐ	...
Education: Primary gross enrol. ratio (f/m per 100 pop.)	59.2 / 67.5	68.1 / 75.8	70.3 / 76.7ᵉ
Education: Secondary gross enrol. ratio (f/m per 100 pop.)	37.3 / 40.2	39.6 / 45.6	45.5 / 46.1ᵉ
Education: Tertiary gross enrol. ratio (f/m per 100 pop.)	13.0 / 11.5	17.3 / 14.7	17.5 / 16.5ʰ
Intentional homicide rate (per 100 000 pop.)	...	5.2ⁱ	...
Seats held by women in the National Parliament (%)	...	...	30.5

Environment and infrastructure indicators

	2005	2010	2018
Individuals using the Internet (per 100 inhabitants)	1.3	16.7ᵈ	28.0ᵈ·ᶜ
Research & Development expenditure (% of GDP)	0.3ᵒ	...	...
Threatened species (number)	55ᵏ	112	133ᵇ
CO2 emission estimates (million tons/tons per capita)	... / ...	... / ...	15.4 / 0.4ⁿ
Energy production, primary (Petajoules)	...	...	658ᵉ
Energy supply per capita (Gigajoules)	...	...	16ᵉ
Tourist/visitor arrivals at national borders (000)ᵖ	246	495	741ᵉ
Important sites for terrestrial biodiversity protected (%)	9.1	18.6	25.0
Net Official Development Assist. received (% of GNI)	7.43	3.35	0.94ᶜ

a Projected estimate (medium fertility variant). b 2017. c 2016. d Estimate. e 2015. f Break in the time series. g Data refers to a 5-year period preceding the reference year. h Including refugees. i Data as at the end of December. j Including South Sudan. k 2004. l 2008. m 2009. n 2014. o Overestimated or based on overestimated data. p Including nationals residing abroad.

Suriname

Region	South America	UN membership date	04 December 1975
Population (000, 2018)	568[a]	Surface area (km2)	163 820[b]
Pop. density (per km2, 2018)	3.6[a]	Sex ratio (m per 100 f)	100.7[a]
Capital city	Paramaribo	National currency	Surinam Dollar (SRD)
Capital city pop. (000, 2018)	239.5[c]	Exchange rate (per US$)	7.5[d]

Economic indicators	2005	2010	2018
GDP: Gross domestic product (million current US$)	2 193	4 368	3 278[e]
GDP growth rate (annual %, const. 2010 prices)	3.9	5.2	- 5.1[e]
GDP per capita (current US$)	4 395.0	8 303.0	5 871.0[e]
Economy: Agriculture (% of Gross Value Added)	11.3	10.2	9.7[e]
Economy: Industry (% of Gross Value Added)	37.4	37.9	31.8[e]
Economy: Services and other activity (% of GVA)	51.3	51.9	58.4[e]
Employment in agriculture (% of employed)[f]	7.0	4.2	2.6
Employment in industry (% of employed)[f]	24.2	23.0	24.4
Employment in services & other sectors (% employed)[f]	68.8	72.8	73.0
Unemployment rate (% of labour force)	9.8[f]	7.6	8.1[f]
Labour force participation rate (female/male pop. %)[f]	38.9 / 65.5	41.0 / 65.4	41.9 / 65.1
CPI: Consumer Price Index (2010=100)	69	100	264[d]
Agricultural production index (2004-2006=100)	99	137	146[e]
International trade: exports (million current US$)	997	2 026	1 441[d]
International trade: imports (million current US$)	1 050	1 397	1 209[d]
International trade: balance (million current US$)	- 53	628	232[d]
Balance of payments, current account (million US$)	- 144	651	- 2[d]

Major trading partners			2017
Export partners (% of exports)	Switzerland 32.0	China, Hong Kong SAR 22.5	Belgium 10.8
Import partners (% of imports)	United States 31.8	Netherlands 13.8	Trinidad and Tobago 9.7

Social indicators	2005	2010	2018
Population growth rate (average annual %)[g]	1.1	1.1	1.0[b]
Urban population (% of total population)	66.7	66.3	66.1
Urban population growth rate (average annual %)[g]	1.2	1.0	0.9[b]
Fertility rate, total (live births per woman)[g]	2.8	2.6	2.5[b]
Life expectancy at birth (females/males, years)[g]	71.7 / 64.8	73.1 / 66.4	74.2 / 67.8[b]
Population age distribution (0-14/60+ years old, %)	30.8 / 8.5	28.7 / 9.1	26.2 / 10.6[a]
International migrant stock (000/% of total pop.)[h]	33.7 / 6.7	39.7 / 7.5	47.7 / 8.5[d]
Refugees and others of concern to the UNHCR (000)	...	~0.0[i]	0.1[d]
Infant mortality rate (per 1 000 live births)[g]	24.2	22.2	17.4[b]
Health: Current expenditure (% of GDP)	7.7	5.4	6.5[b]
Health: Physicians (per 1 000 pop.)	0.8[j]		
Education: Primary gross enrol. ratio (f/m per 100 pop.)	104.6 / 106.7	115.9 / 116.7	121.0 / 120.9[e]
Education: Secondary gross enrol. ratio (f/m per 100 pop.)	79.3 / 59.6	81.1 / 63.2	89.7 / 68.1[b]
Education: Tertiary gross enrol. ratio (f/m per 100 pop.)	15.8 / 9.6[k]	... / ...	... / ...
Intentional homicide rate (per 100 000 pop.)	13.8	8.3[j]	...
Seats held by women in the National Parliament (%)	19.6	25.5	25.5

Environment and infrastructure indicators	2005	2010	2018
Individuals using the Internet (per 100 inhabitants)	6.4	31.6	45.4[f,e]
Threatened species (number)	59[j]	65	83[d]
Forested area (% of land area)[f]	98.5	98.4	98.3[b]
CO2 emission estimates (million tons/tons per capita)	1.6 / 3.2	2.4 / 4.6	2.0 / 3.7[m]
Energy production, primary (Petajoules)	32	43	40[b]
Energy supply per capita (Gigajoules)	53	77	54[b]
Tourist/visitor arrivals at national borders (000)	161	205	256[e]
Important sites for terrestrial biodiversity protected (%)	51.2	51.2	51.2
Pop. using improved drinking water (urban/rural, %)	97.9 / 79.2	98.0 / 85.8	98.1 / 88.4[b]
Pop. using improved sanitation facilities (urban/rural, %)	89.2 / 62.6	88.6 / 61.7	88.4 / 61.4[b]
Net Official Development Assist. received (% of GNI)	2.62	2.43	0.47[e]

a Projected estimate (medium fertility variant). b 2015. c Refers to the total population of the District of Paramaribo. d 2017. e 2016. f Estimate. g Data refers to a 5-year period preceding the reference year. h Refers to foreign citizens. i Data as at the end of December. j 2004. k 2002. l 2008. m 2014.

Sweden

Region	Northern Europe	UN membership date	19 November 1946
Population (000, 2018)	9 983[a]	Surface area (km2)	438 574[b]
Pop. density (per km2, 2018)	24.3[a]	Sex ratio (m per 100 f)	100.3[a]
Capital city	Stockholm	National currency	Swedish Krona (SEK)
Capital city pop. (000, 2018)	1 583.0[c]	Exchange rate (per US$)	8.2[d]

Economic indicators

	2005	2010	2018
GDP: Gross domestic product (million current US$)	389 043	488 378	514 476[e]
GDP growth rate (annual %, const. 2010 prices)	2.8	6.0	3.3[e]
GDP per capita (current US$)	43 042.0	52 009.0	52 297.0[e]
Economy: Agriculture (% of Gross Value Added)[f]	1.1	1.6	1.3[e]
Economy: Industry (% of Gross Value Added)[f]	29.7	28.9	24.5[e]
Economy: Services and other activity (% of GVA)[f]	69.2	69.4	74.2[e]
Employment in agriculture (% of employed)[g]	2.0	2.1	1.8
Employment in industry (% of employed)[g]	22.1	19.9	18.0
Employment in services & other sectors (% employed)[g]	75.9	78.0	80.2
Unemployment rate (% of labour force)	7.7	8.6	6.7[g]
Labour force participation rate (female/male pop. %)[g]	59.6 / 68.0	58.9 / 67.4	60.8 / 67.3
CPI: Consumer Price Index (2010=100)	93	100	106[d]
Agricultural production index (2004-2006=100)	100	95	100[e]
Index of industrial production (2005=100)	100	93[h]	88[h,i]
International trade: exports (million current US$)	130 264	158 411	153 106[d]
International trade: imports (million current US$)	111 351	148 788	153 856[d]
International trade: balance (million current US$)	18 912	9 622	- 751[d]
Balance of payments, current account (million US$)	23 583	29 196	17 097[d]

Major trading partners

						2017
Export partners (% of exports)	Germany	10.7	Norway	10.1	Finland	6.9
Import partners (% of imports)	Germany	18.7	Netherlands	8.9	Norway	8.1

Social indicators

	2005	2010	2018
Population growth rate (average annual %)[j]	0.4	0.8	0.8[b]
Urban population (% of total population)	84.3	85.1	87.4
Urban population growth rate (average annual %)[j]	0.4	0.9	1.1[b]
Fertility rate, total (live births per woman)[j]	1.7	1.9	1.9[b]
Life expectancy at birth (females/males, years)[j]	82.3 / 77.9	83.1 / 79.0	83.7 / 80.0[b]
Population age distribution (0-14/60+ years old, %)	17.4 / 23.5	16.5 / 24.9	17.7 / 25.6[a]
International migrant stock (000/% of total pop.)	1 125.8 / 12.5	1 337.2 / 14.2	1 747.7 / 17.6[d]
Refugees and others of concern to the UNHCR (000)	96.4[k]	110.8[k]	339.0[d]
Infant mortality rate (per 1 000 live births)[j]	3.2	2.6	2.4[b]
Health: Current expenditure (% of GDP)	8.3	8.5	11.0[b]
Health: Physicians (per 1 000 pop.)	...	3.9	4.2[i]
Education: Government expenditure (% of GDP)	6.6	6.6	7.7[i]
Education: Primary gross enrol. ratio (f/m per 100 pop.)	95.7 / 95.9	101.2 / 101.7	125.5 / 120.5[b]
Education: Secondary gross enrol. ratio (f/m per 100 pop.)	103.8 / 104.3	97.6 / 98.6	150.0 / 131.5[b]
Education: Tertiary gross enrol. ratio (f/m per 100 pop.)	99.9 / 64.8	89.6 / 58.5	75.6 / 49.6[b]
Intentional homicide rate (per 100 000 pop.)	0.9	1.0	1.1[e]
Seats held by women in the National Parliament (%)	45.3	46.4	43.6

Environment and infrastructure indicators

	2005	2010	2018
Individuals using the Internet (per 100 inhabitants)	84.8[l]	90.0[m]	91.5[a]
Research & Development expenditure (% of GDP)	3.4[n]	3.2[g]	3.3[o,b]
Threatened species (number)	36[p]	29	54[d]
Forested area (% of land area)	68.8	68.4	68.9[b]
CO2 emission estimates (million tons/tons per capita)	51.6 / 5.7	52.0 / 5.5	43.4 / 4.5[i]
Energy production, primary (Petajoules)	1 430	1 364	1 408[b]
Energy supply per capita (Gigajoules)	237	225	193[b]
Tourist/visitor arrivals at national borders (000)	7 627[q]	...	19 945[i]
Important sites for terrestrial biodiversity protected (%)	56.7	57.8	58.8
Pop. using improved drinking water (urban/rural, %)	100.0 / 100.0	100.0 / 100.0	100.0 / 100.0[b]
Pop. using improved sanitation facilities (urban/rural, %)	99.2 / 99.6	99.2 / 99.6	99.2 / 99.6[b]
Net Official Development Assist. disbursed (% of GNI)[r]	0.94	0.97	1.01[o,d]

a Projected estimate (medium fertility variant). b 2015. c Refers to "tätort" (according to the administrative divisions of 2005). d 2017. e 2016. f Data classified according to ISIC Rev. 4. g Estimate. h Excluding water and waste management. i 2014. j Data refers to a 5-year period preceding the reference year. k Data as at the end of December. l Population aged 16 to 74 years. m Population aged 16 to 75 years. n Break in the time series. o Provisional data. p 2004. q 2003. r Development Assistance Committee member (OECD).

Switzerland

Region	Western Europe	UN membership date	10 September 2002
Population (000, 2018)	8 544 [a]	Surface area (km2)	41 291 [b]
Pop. density (per km2, 2018)	216.2 [a]	Sex ratio (m per 100 f)	98.3 [a]
Capital city	Bern	National currency	Swiss Franc (CHF)
Capital city pop. (000, 2018)	422.2	Exchange rate (per US$)	1.0 [c]

Economic indicators	2005	2010	2018
GDP: Gross domestic product (million current US$)	408 697	583 783	668 851 [d]
GDP growth rate (annual %, const. 2010 prices)	3.1	3.0	1.4 [d]
GDP per capita (current US$)	55 153.0	74 538.0	79 609.0 [d]
Economy: Agriculture (% of Gross Value Added) [e]	0.9	0.7	0.7 [d]
Economy: Industry (% of Gross Value Added) [e]	27.0	26.6	25.8 [d]
Economy: Services and other activity (% of GVA) [e]	72.1	72.7	73.5 [d]
Employment in agriculture (% of employed) [f]	3.9	3.5	3.4 [f]
Employment in industry (% of employed) [f]	22.5	22.4	20.6
Employment in services & other sectors (% employed) [f]	73.6	74.1	76.0
Unemployment rate (% of labour force)	4.4	4.8	4.9 [f]
Labour force participation rate (female/male pop. %) [f]	59.5 / 75.0	59.9 / 74.3	62.8 / 73.9
CPI: Consumer Price Index (2010=100) [g]	96	100	98 [c]
Agricultural production index (2004-2006=100)	99	103	101 [d]
Index of industrial production (2005=100)	100	119 [h]	130 [h,i]
International trade: exports (million current US$)	130 930	195 609	299 309 [c]
International trade: imports (million current US$)	126 574	176 281	267 501 [c]
International trade: balance (million current US$)	4 356	19 329	31 807 [c]
Balance of payments, current account (million US$)	55 573	86 701	66 558 [c]

Major trading partners						2017
Export partners (% of exports)	Germany	15.2	United States	12.3	China	8.2
Import partners (% of imports)	Germany	20.7	United States	8.0	Italy	7.5

Social indicators	2005	2010	2018
Population growth rate (average annual %) [j]	0.7	1.1	1.2 [b]
Urban population (% of total population)	73.5	73.6	73.8
Urban population growth rate (average annual %) [j]	0.7	1.1	1.2 [b]
Fertility rate, total (live births per woman) [j]	1.4	1.5	1.5 [b]
Life expectancy at birth (females/males, years) [j]	83.1 / 77.7	84.1 / 79.3	84.8 / 80.5 [b]
Population age distribution (0-14/60+ years old, %)	16.3 / 21.3	15.1 / 22.8	14.9 / 24.5 [a]
International migrant stock (000/% of total pop.)	1 805.4 / 24.4	2 075.2 / 26.5	2 506.4 / 29.6 [c]
Refugees and others of concern to the UNHCR (000)	63.4 [k]	61.9 [k]	114.8 [o]
Infant mortality rate (per 1 000 live births) [j]	4.6	4.2	3.9 [b]
Health: Current expenditure (% of GDP)	10.3	10.7	12.1 [b]
Health: Physicians (per 1 000 pop.)	...	3.8	4.2 [d]
Education: Government expenditure (% of GDP)	5.2	4.9	5.1 [i]
Education: Primary gross enrol. ratio (f/m per 100 pop.)	101.8 / 102.1	102.3 / 102.8	104.0 / 104.8 [d]
Education: Secondary gross enrol. ratio (f/m per 100 pop.)	92.1 / 97.9	94.3 / 97.2	100.3 / 104.2 [d]
Education: Tertiary gross enrol. ratio (f/m per 100 pop.)	42.4 / 48.9	52.5 / 53.0	58.4 / 57.3 [d]
Intentional homicide rate (per 100 000 pop.)	1.0	0.7	0.5 [d]
Seats held by women in the National Parliament (%)	25.0	29.0	32.5

Environment and infrastructure indicators	2005	2010	2018
Individuals using the Internet (per 100 inhabitants)	70.1 [l,m]	83.9 [l,m]	89.4 [d]
Research & Development expenditure (% of GDP)	2.7 [n]	2.7 [o]	3.0 [p]
Threatened species (number)	49 [n]	45	74 [c]
Forested area (% of land area)	30.8	31.3	31.7 [f,b]
CO2 emission estimates (million tons/tons per capita)	41.3 / 5.5	39.0 / 5.0	35.3 / 4.3 [i]
Energy production, primary (Petajoules) [q]	458	526	509 [b]
Energy supply per capita (Gigajoules) [q]	145	139	123 [b]
Tourist/visitor arrivals at national borders (000)	7 229	8 628	9 205 [d]
Important sites for terrestrial biodiversity protected (%)	28.5	35.2	35.2
Pop. using improved drinking water (urban/rural, %)	100.0 / 100.0	100.0 / 100.0	100.0 / 100.0 [b]
Pop. using improved sanitation facilities (urban/rural, %)	99.9 / 99.9	99.9 / 99.8	99.9 / 99.8 [b]
Net Official Development Assist. disbursed (% of GNI) [r]	0.42	0.39	0.46 [s,c]

a Projected estimate (medium fertility variant). b 2015. c 2017. d 2016. e Data classified according to ISIC Rev. 4. f Estimate. g Calculated by the Statistics Division of the United Nations from national indices. h Excluding water and waste management. i 2014. j Data refers to a 5-year period preceding the reference year. k Data as at the end of December. l Users in the last 6 months. m Population aged 14 years and over. n 2004. o 2008. p 2012. q Including Liechtenstein. r Development Assistance Committee member (OECD). s Provisional data.

Syrian Arab Republic

Region	Western Asia	UN membership date	24 October 1945
Population (000, 2018)	18 284[a]	Surface area (km2)	185 180[b]
Pop. density (per km2, 2018)	99.6[a]	Sex ratio (m per 100 f)	101.9[a]
Capital city	Damascus	National currency	Syrian Pound (SYP)
Capital city pop. (000, 2018)	2 319.5[c]	Exchange rate (per US$)	436.5[d]

Economic indicators	2005	2010	2018
GDP: Gross domestic product (million current US$)	28 397	60 465	22 163[e]
GDP growth rate (annual %, const. 2010 prices)	6.2	3.4	- 3.4[e]
GDP per capita (current US$)	1 552.0	2 877.0	1 203.0[e]
Economy: Agriculture (% of Gross Value Added)[f]	20.3	19.7	20.5[e]
Economy: Industry (% of Gross Value Added)[f]	31.2	30.7	30.2[e]
Economy: Services and other activity (% of GVA)[f]	48.5	49.6	49.3[e]
Employment in agriculture (% of employed)[g]	21.2	15.2	23.0
Employment in industry (% of employed)[g]	26.5	34.3	33.0
Employment in services & other sectors (% employed)[g]	52.2	50.6	44.0
Unemployment rate (% of labour force)	9.9[g]	8.6	12.1[g]
Labour force participation rate (female/male pop. %)[g]	16.2 / 76.2	13.2 / 72.8	11.6 / 69.7
CPI: Consumer Price Index (2010=100)	...	100	663[e]
Agricultural production index (2004-2006=100)	100	89	79[e]
Index of industrial production (2005=100)[h]	100	98	...
International trade: exports (million current US$)	6 450	11 353	949[g,d]
International trade: imports (million current US$)	7 898	17 562	1 773[g,d]
International trade: balance (million current US$)	- 1 448	- 6 209	- 824[g,d]
Balance of payments, current account (million US$)	299	- 367	...

Major trading partners						2017
Export partners (% of exports)[g]	Lebanon	16.9	Egypt	13.7	Saudi Arabia	11.3
Import partners (% of imports)[g]	Turkey	28.0	China	20.1	Russian Federation	5.7

Social indicators	2005	2010	2018
Population growth rate (average annual %)[i]	2.2	2.8	- 2.3[b]
Urban population (% of total population)	53.8	55.6	54.2
Urban population growth rate (average annual %)[i]	2.9	3.4	- 3.6[b]
Fertility rate, total (live births per woman)[i]	3.8	3.4	3.1[b]
Life expectancy at birth (females/males, years)[i]	75.9 / 71.4	77.3 / 72.0	76.3 / 84.4[b]
Population age distribution (0-14/60+ years old, %)	39.1 / 4.9	36.4 / 5.1	35.7 / 7.1[a]
International migrant stock (000/% of total pop.)[j,k]	876.4 / 4.6	1 785.1 / 8.5	1 013.8 / 5.5[d]
Refugees and others of concern to the UNHCR (000)	328.0[l]	1 308.1[l]	6 544.6[d]
Infant mortality rate (per 1 000 live births)[i]	17.7	15.0	17.9[b]
Health: Current expenditure (% of GDP)	4.1	3.4	3.6[m]
Health: Physicians (per 1 000 pop.)	1.6	1.5	1.5[n]
Education: Government expenditure (% of GDP)	5.4[o]	5.1[p]	...
Education: Primary gross enrol. ratio (f/m per 100 pop.)	118.4 / 121.9	116.5 / 120.8	74.7 / 77.3[q]
Education: Secondary gross enrol. ratio (f/m per 100 pop.)	68.1 / 71.2	72.4 / 72.3	49.3 / 49.3[q]
Education: Tertiary gross enrol. ratio (f/m per 100 pop.)	17.1 / 19.1	24.0 / 27.8	42.7 / 36.0[q]
Intentional homicide rate (per 100 000 pop.)	2.4	2.2	...
Seats held by women in the National Parliament (%)	12.0	12.4	13.2

Environment and infrastructure indicators	2005	2010	2018
Individuals using the Internet (per 100 inhabitants)	5.6[g]	20.7	31.9[g,e]
Threatened species (number)	29[o]	78	132[d]
Forested area (% of land area)[g]	2.5	2.7	2.7[b]
CO2 emission estimates (million tons/tons per capita)	50.6 / 2.8	61.6 / 3.0	30.7 / 1.7[n]
Energy production, primary (Petajoules)	1 171	1 165	196[b]
Energy supply per capita (Gigajoules)	40	44	23[b]
Tourist/visitor arrivals at national borders (000)[r]	3 571	8 546[s]	5 070[s,t]
Important sites for terrestrial biodiversity protected (%)	1.1	1.1	1.1
Pop. using improved drinking water (urban/rural, %)	94.0 / 82.5	92.8 / 85.9	92.3 / 87.2[b]
Pop. using improved sanitation facilities (urban/rural, %)	95.6 / 87.2	96.0 / 92.8	96.2 / 95.1[b]
Net Official Development Assist. received (% of GNI)	0.25	0.21[u]	...

a Projected estimate (medium fertility variant). b 2015. c Estimates should be viewed with caution as these are derived from scarce data. d 2017. e 2016. f Including taxes less subsidies on production and imports. g Estimate. h Data classified according to ISIC Rev. 3. i Data refers to a 5-year period preceding the reference year. j Refers to foreign citizens. k Including refugees. l Data as at the end of December. m 2012. n 2014. o 2004. p 2009. q 2013. r Including nationals residing abroad. s Including Iraqi nationals. t 2011. u 2007.

Tajikistan

Region	Central Asia	UN membership date	02 March 1992
Population (000, 2018)	9 107[a]	Surface area (km2)	142 600[b]
Pop. density (per km2, 2018)	65.1[a]	Sex ratio (m per 100 f)	100.8[a]
Capital city	Dushanbe	National currency	Somoni (TJS)
Capital city pop. (000, 2018)	872.7	Exchange rate (per US$)	8.8[c]

Economic indicators	2005	2010	2018
GDP: Gross domestic product (million current US$)	2 312	5 642	6 952[d]
GDP growth rate (annual %, const. 2010 prices)	6.7	6.5	6.9[d]
GDP per capita (current US$)	337.0	738.0	796.0[d]
Economy: Agriculture (% of Gross Value Added)	23.8	21.8	23.3[d]
Economy: Industry (% of Gross Value Added)	30.7	27.9	29.6[d]
Economy: Services and other activity (% of GVA)	45.6	50.3	47.1[d]
Employment in agriculture (% of employed)[e]	56.7	53.1	51.2
Employment in industry (% of employed)[e]	16.2	15.5	16.5
Employment in services & other sectors (% employed)[e]	27.1	31.4	32.3
Unemployment rate (% of labour force)[e]	11.2	11.7	10.3
Labour force participation rate (female/male pop. %)[e]	47.3 / 69.5	46.9 / 71.4	45.4 / 73.5
CPI: Consumer Price Index (2010=100)[f]	...	100	160[c]
Agricultural production index (2004-2006=100)	99	124	159[d]
Index of industrial production (2005=100)[g]	100	114	145[h]
International trade: exports (million current US$)[e]	905	1 207	1 198[c]
International trade: imports (million current US$)[e]	1 329	2 659	2 775[c]
International trade: balance (million current US$)[e]	- 424	- 1 452	- 1 577[c]
Balance of payments, current account (million US$)	- 19	- 540[i]	- 35[c]

Major trading partners						2017
Export partners (% of exports)[e]	Kazakhstan	29.8	Turkey	18.6	Switzerland	14.9
Import partners (% of imports)[e]	China	51.1	Russian Federation	19.1	Kazakhstan	12.7

Social indicators	2005	2010	2018
Population growth rate (average annual %)[j]	2.0	2.2	2.2[b]
Urban population (% of total population)	26.5	26.5	27.1
Urban population growth rate (average annual %)[j]	2.0	2.2	2.4[b]
Fertility rate, total (live births per woman)[j]	3.6	3.5	3.5[b]
Life expectancy at birth (females/males, years)[j]	69.6 / 63.6	71.9 / 66.0	73.5 / 67.7[b]
Population age distribution (0-14/60+ years old, %)	38.1 / 5.1	35.7 / 4.9	35.3 / 6.0[a]
International migrant stock (000/% of total pop.)	280.4 / 4.1	278.2 / 3.6	273.3 / 3.1[c]
Refugees and others of concern to the UNHCR (000)	1.1[k]	7.1[k]	18.1[c]
Infant mortality rate (per 1 000 live births)[j]	62.9	48.9	38.9[b]
Health: Current expenditure (% of GDP)	5.2	5.8	6.9[b]
Health: Physicians (per 1 000 pop.)	2.0	1.7	1.7[h]
Education: Government expenditure (% of GDP)	3.5	4.0	5.2[b]
Education: Primary gross enrol. ratio (f/m per 100 pop.)	96.9 / 100.2	98.0 / 100.4	98.1 / 99.5[c]
Education: Secondary gross enrol. ratio (f/m per 100 pop.)	73.6 / 88.5	78.3 / 89.7	82.7 / 92.0[l]
Education: Tertiary gross enrol. ratio (f/m per 100 pop.)	13.4 / 28.0	15.8 / 29.9	26.4 / 35.2[c]
Intentional homicide rate (per 100 000 pop.)	2.3	2.4	1.6[m]
Seats held by women in the National Parliament (%)	12.7	17.5	19.0

Environment and infrastructure indicators	2005	2010	2018
Individuals using the Internet (per 100 inhabitants)	0.3	11.6[e]	20.5[e,d]
Research & Development expenditure (% of GDP)	0.1	0.1[n,o]	0.1[n,o,b]
Threatened species (number)	24[p]	40	45[c]
Forested area (% of land area)	2.9	2.9[e]	3.0[e,b]
CO2 emission estimates (million tons/tons per capita)	2.4 / 0.4	2.5 / 0.3	5.2 / 0.6[h]
Energy production, primary (Petajoules)	66	65	82[b]
Energy supply per capita (Gigajoules)	15	12	13[b]
Tourist/visitor arrivals at national borders (000)	5[q]	160	414[b]
Important sites for terrestrial biodiversity protected (%)	20.5	20.5	21.0
Pop. using improved drinking water (urban/rural, %)	92.6 / 54.5	92.8 / 61.3	93.1 / 66.7[b]
Pop. using improved sanitation facilities (urban/rural, %)	92.9 / 91.7	93.4 / 93.8	93.8 / 95.5[b]
Net Official Development Assist. received (% of GNI)	11.30	6.21	4.09[d]

a Projected estimate (medium fertility variant). b 2015. c 2017. d 2016. e Estimate. f Calculated by the Statistics Division of the United Nations from national indices. g Data classified according to ISIC Rev. 3. h 2014. i Break in the time series. j Data refers to a 5-year period preceding the reference year. k Data as at the end of December. l 2013. m 2011. n Excluding private non-profit. o Excluding business enterprise. p 2004. q 2001.

Thailand

Region	South-eastern Asia	UN membership date	16 December 1946
Population (000, 2018)	69 183[a]	Surface area (km2)	513 120[b]
Pop. density (per km2, 2018)	135.4[a]	Sex ratio (m per 100 f)	95.0[a]
Capital city	Bangkok	National currency	Baht (THB)
Capital city pop. (000, 2018)	10 156.3	Exchange rate (per US$)	32.7[c]

Economic indicators	2005	2010	2018
GDP: Gross domestic product (million current US$)	189 318	341 105	407 026[d]
GDP growth rate (annual %, const. 2010 prices)	4.2	7.5	4.3[d]
GDP per capita (current US$)	2 894.0	5 075.0	5 911.0[d]
Economy: Agriculture (% of Gross Value Added)[e]	9.2	10.5	8.3[d]
Economy: Industry (% of Gross Value Added)[e]	38.6	40.0	35.8[d]
Economy: Services and other activity (% of GVA)[e]	52.2	49.5	55.8[d]
Employment in agriculture (% of employed)[f]	42.6[f]	38.2	32.0[f]
Employment in industry (% of employed)[f]	20.3	20.6	22.5
Employment in services & other sectors (% employed)[f]	37.1	41.1	45.5
Unemployment rate (% of labour force)	1.4	0.6	1.3[f]
Labour force participation rate (female/male pop. %)[f]	65.7 / 81.5	64.5 / 80.8	60.3 / 77.0
CPI: Consumer Price Index (2010=100)[g]	87	100	111[c]
Agricultural production index (2004-2006=100)	98	114	118[d]
International trade: exports (million current US$)	110 110	195 312	233 695[f,c]
International trade: imports (million current US$)	118 164	182 393	225 681[f,c]
International trade: balance (million current US$)	- 8 054	12 918	8 013[f,c]
Balance of payments, current account (million US$)	- 7 642[h]	11 486	48 126[c]

Major trading partners					2017
Export partners (% of exports)	United States	11.4[f]	China	11.0	Japan	9.5[f]
Import partners (% of imports)[f]	China	21.6	Japan	15.8	United States	6.2

Social indicators	2005	2010	2018
Population growth rate (average annual %)[i]	0.8	0.5	0.4[b]
Urban population (% of total population)	37.4	43.9	49.9
Urban population growth rate (average annual %)[i]	4.3	3.7	2.1[b]
Fertility rate, total (live births per woman)[i]	1.6	1.6	1.5[b]
Life expectancy at birth (females/males, years)[i]	74.9 / 67.7	76.6 / 69.8	78.4 / 70.8[b]
Population age distribution (0-14/60+ years old, %)	21.3 / 11.1	19.2 / 12.9	17.0 / 17.6[a]
International migrant stock (000/% of total pop.)[i]	2 163.4 / 3.3	3 224.1 / 4.8	3 588.9 / 5.2[c]
Refugees and others of concern to the UNHCR (000)	149.4[k]	649.4[k]	593.5[c]
Infant mortality rate (per 1 000 live births)[i]	16.7	13.4	11.2[b]
Health: Current expenditure (% of GDP)[l,m]	3.4	3.6	3.8[b]
Health: Physicians (per 1 000 pop.)	0.3[n]	0.4	0.5[b]
Education: Government expenditure (% of GDP)	3.9	3.5	4.1[o]
Education: Primary gross enrol. ratio (f/m per 100 pop.)	100.4 / 103.3	96.2 / 97.4	97.5 / 103.5[b]
Education: Secondary gross enrol. ratio (f/m per 100 pop.)	75.4 / 71.9[f]	85.3 / 79.6	118.1 / 123.0[b]
Education: Tertiary gross enrol. ratio (f/m per 100 pop.)	47.2 / 42.0	56.5 / 44.3	54.2 / 37.8[b]
Intentional homicide rate (per 100 000 pop.)	7.3	5.4	3.2[d]
Seats held by women in the National Parliament (%)	8.8	13.3	4.8

Environment and infrastructure indicators	2005	2010	2018
Individuals using the Internet (per 100 inhabitants)	15.0	22.4	47.5[d]
Research & Development expenditure (% of GDP)	0.2	0.2[p]	0.6[b]
Threatened species (number)	221[n]	477	611[c]
Forested area (% of land area)[f]	31.5	31.8	32.1[b]
CO2 emission estimates (million tons/tons per capita)	247.5 / 3.7	281.9 / 4.2	316.2 / 4.7[q]
Energy production, primary (Petajoules)	2 144	2 952	2 929[b]
Energy supply per capita (Gigajoules)	61	74	80[b]
Tourist/visitor arrivals at national borders (000)	11 567[r]	15 936	32 530[d]
Important sites for terrestrial biodiversity protected (%)	68.0	71.0	71.7
Pop. using improved drinking water (urban/rural, %)	97.0 / 92.6	97.4 / 95.6	97.6 / 98.0[b]
Pop. using improved sanitation facilities (urban/rural, %)	89.6 / 95.3	89.9 / 96.1	89.9 / 96.1[b]
Net Official Development Assist. disbursed (% of GNI)	...	~0.00	0.05[d]
Net Official Development Assist. received (% of GNI)	- 0.09	- 0.01	0.06[d]

a Projected estimate (medium fertility variant). b 2015. c 2017. d 2016. e At producers' prices. f Estimate. g Calculated by the Statistics Division of the United Nations from national indices. h Break in the time series. i Data refers to a 5-year period preceding the reference year. j Including refugees. k Data as at the end of December. l Data refer to fiscal years ending 30 September. m Data revision. n 2004. o 2013. p 2009. q 2014. r Including nationals residing abroad.

The former Yugoslav Republic of Macedonia

Region	Southern Europe	UN membership date	08 April 1993
Population (000, 2018)	2 085[a]	Surface area (km2)	25 713[b]
Pop. density (per km2, 2018)	82.7[a]	Sex ratio (m per 100 f)	100.0[a]
Capital city	Skopje	National currency	Denar (MKD)
Capital city pop. (000, 2018)	584.2	Exchange rate (per US$)	51.3[c]

Economic indicators	2005	2010	2018
GDP: Gross domestic product (million current US$)	6 259	9 407	10 746[d]
GDP growth rate (annual %, const. 2010 prices)	4.7	3.4	2.9[d]
GDP per capita (current US$)	3 038.0	4 543.0	5 163.0[d]
Economy: Agriculture (% of Gross Value Added)[e]	11.3	11.7	10.5[d]
Economy: Industry (% of Gross Value Added)[e]	23.7	24.4	28.4[d]
Economy: Services and other activity (% of GVA)[e]	64.9	63.9	61.1[d]
Employment in agriculture (% of employed)[f]	19.5	19.3	16.0
Employment in industry (% of employed)[f]	32.4	29.6	29.7
Employment in services & other sectors (% employed)[f]	48.1	51.1	54.3
Unemployment rate (% of labour force)	37.2	32.0	22.8[f]
Labour force participation rate (female/male pop. %)[f]	42.0 / 63.8	42.8 / 68.6	42.5 / 67.4
CPI: Consumer Price Index (2010=100)	87	100	111[c]
Agricultural production index (2004-2006=100)	100	115	123[d]
Index of industrial production (2005=100)	100	100[g]	113[g,h]
International trade: exports (million current US$)	2 041	3 351	5 670[c]
International trade: imports (million current US$)	3 228	5 474	7 719[c]
International trade: balance (million current US$)	- 1 187	- 2 123	- 2 049[c]
Balance of payments, current account (million US$)	- 159	- 198	- 129[c]

Major trading partners					2017
Export partners (% of exports)	Germany	47.0	Serbia	8.4	Bulgaria	5.9
Import partners (% of imports)	Germany	11.8	United Kingdom	10.1	Greece	8.0

Social indicators	2005	2010	2018
Population growth rate (average annual %)[i]	0.2	0.1	0.1[b]
Urban population (% of total population)	57.5	57.1	58.0
Urban population growth rate (average annual %)[i]	- 0.1	- 0.1	0.2[b]
Fertility rate, total (live births per woman)[i]	1.6	1.5	1.5[b]
Life expectancy at birth (females/males, years)[i]	76.4 / 71.3	76.3 / 72.1	77.2 / 73.2[b]
Population age distribution (0-14/60+ years old, %)	20.2 / 15.3	17.9 / 16.4	16.6 / 19.9[a]
International migrant stock (000/% of total pop.)	127.7 / 6.2	129.7 / 6.3	131.0 / 6.3[c]
Refugees and others of concern to the UNHCR (000)	4.4[j]	3.3[j]	1.2[c]
Infant mortality rate (per 1 000 live births)[i]	12.9	10.8	9.0[b]
Health: Current expenditure (% of GDP)	8.4	7.0	6.1[b]
Health: Physicians (per 1 000 pop.)	...	2.7	2.9[b]
Education: Government expenditure (% of GDP)	3.3[k]	...	...
Education: Primary gross enrol. ratio (f/m per 100 pop.)	92.5 / 94.5	86.7 / 88.0	93.7 / 94.1[b]
Education: Secondary gross enrol. ratio (f/m per 100 pop.)	80.2 / 82.8[f]	81.0 / 83.4	81.2 / 82.6[b]
Education: Tertiary gross enrol. ratio (f/m per 100 pop.)	34.1 / 24.6	40.4 / 34.7	45.9 / 36.7[b]
Intentional homicide rate (per 100 000 pop.)	2.1	2.1	1.6[h]
Seats held by women in the National Parliament (%)	19.2	32.5	37.5

Environment and infrastructure indicators	2005	2010	2018
Individuals using the Internet (per 100 inhabitants)	26.4[f,l]	51.9[m]	72.2[d]
Research & Development expenditure (% of GDP)	0.2	0.2	0.4[b]
Threatened species (number)	29[n]	90	110[c]
Forested area (% of land area)[f]	38.3	39.6	39.6[b]
CO2 emission estimates (million tons/tons per capita)	11.3 / 5.5	8.6 / 4.2	7.5 / 3.6[h]
Energy production, primary (Petajoules)	108	68	58[b]
Energy supply per capita (Gigajoules)	80	59	57[b]
Tourist/visitor arrivals at national borders (000)	197	262	510[d]
Important sites for terrestrial biodiversity protected (%)	20.8	21.1	21.1
Pop. using improved drinking water (urban/rural, %)	99.8 / 98.6	99.8 / 98.8	99.8 / 98.9[b]
Pop. using improved sanitation facilities (urban/rural, %)	93.8 / 84.7	96.5 / 83.4	97.2 / 82.6[b]
Net Official Development Assist. received (% of GNI)	3.70	2.10	1.61[d]

a Projected estimate (medium fertility variant). b 2015. c 2017. d 2016. e Data classified according to ISIC Rev. 4. f Estimate. g Excluding water and waste management. h 2014. i Data refers to a 5-year period preceding the reference year. j Data as at the end of December. k 2002. l Population aged 16 to 74 years. m Population aged 15 to 74 years. n 2004.

Timor-Leste

Region	South-eastern Asia	UN membership date	27 September 2002
Population (000, 2018)	1 324[a]	Surface area (km2)	14 919[b]
Pop. density (per km2, 2018)	89.0[a]	Sex ratio (m per 100 f)	103.2[a]
Capital city	Dili	National currency	US Dollar (USD)
Capital city pop. (000, 2018)	281.1		

Economic indicators

	2005	2010	2018
GDP: Gross domestic product (million current US$)	1 850	3 999	2 703[d]
GDP growth rate (annual %, const. 2010 prices)	52.7	- 1.3	5.0[d]
GDP per capita (current US$)	1 802.0	3 604.0	2 131.0[d]
Economy: Agriculture (% of Gross Value Added)[e]	7.3	4.8	7.0[d]
Economy: Industry (% of Gross Value Added)[e]	76.7	79.9	69.2[d]
Economy: Services and other activity (% of GVA)[e]	16.0	15.3	23.8[d]
Employment in agriculture (% of employed)[f]	60.4	50.8	24.9
Employment in industry (% of employed)[f]	7.8	9.3	15.4
Employment in services & other sectors (% employed)[f]	31.8	39.9	59.7
Unemployment rate (% of labour force)	7.2[f]	3.3	3.5[f]
Labour force participation rate (female/male pop. %)[f]	31.6 / 66.4	26.5 / 56.2	24.7 / 52.1
CPI: Consumer Price Index (2010=100)[f]	74	100	142[c]
Agricultural production index (2004-2006=100)	101	124	111[d]
International trade: exports (million current US$)	43	42[f]	197[f,c]
International trade: imports (million current US$)	102	298[f]	724[f,c]
International trade: balance (million current US$)	- 58	- 256[f]	- 527[f,c]
Balance of payments, current account (million US$)	...	1 671	- 339[c]

Major trading partners

							2017
Export partners (% of exports)[f]	Singapore	52.2	Thailand	30.7	United States	4.0
Import partners (% of imports)[f]	Indonesia	36.9	China	28.4	Viet Nam	8.8

Social indicators

	2005	2010	2018
Population growth rate (average annual %)[g]	3.3	1.6	2.2[b]
Urban population (% of total population)	26.0	27.7	30.6
Urban population growth rate (average annual %)[g]	4.7	2.8	3.5[b]
Fertility rate, total (live births per woman)[g]	7.0	6.5	5.9[b]
Life expectancy at birth (females/males, years)[g]	63.0 / 60.0	67.6 / 65.2	69.5 / 66.1[b]
Population age distribution (0-14/60+ years old, %)	49.2 / 4.3	45.6 / 5.1	43.5 / 5.5[a]
International migrant stock (000/% of total pop.)	11.3 / 1.1	11.5 / 1.0	12.1 / 0.9[c]
Refugees and others of concern to the UNHCR (000)	~0.0[h]	~0.0[h]	~0.0[c]
Infant mortality rate (per 1 000 live births)[g]	64.0	50.2	43.9[b]
Health: Current expenditure (% of GDP)[i]	1.3	1.3	3.1[b]
Health: Physicians (per 1 000 pop.)	0.1[j]	0.1	0.1[k]
Education: Government expenditure (% of GDP)	...	11.0	7.5[l]
Education: Primary gross enrol. ratio (f/m per 100 pop.)	85.2 / 93.2	116.3 / 121.4	108.3 / 110.8[d]
Education: Secondary gross enrol. ratio (f/m per 100 pop.)	51.8 / 53.2	60.8 / 60.6	77.1 / 71.7[d]
Education: Tertiary gross enrol. ratio (f/m per 100 pop.)	9.3 / 8.1[f,m]	15.8 / 21.9	... / ...
Intentional homicide rate (per 100 000 pop.)	4.5	3.5	3.9[b]
Seats held by women in the National Parliament (%)	25.3	29.2	32.3

Environment and infrastructure indicators

	2005	2010	2018
Individuals using the Internet (per 100 inhabitants)	0.1	3.0[f]	25.2[f,d]
Threatened species (number)	11[i]	18	24[c]
Forested area (% of land area)[f]	53.7	49.9	46.1[b]
CO2 emission estimates (million tons/tons per capita)	0.2 / 0.2	0.2 / 0.2	0.5 / 0.4[l]
Energy production, primary (Petajoules)	201	186	147[f,b]
Energy supply per capita (Gigajoules)[f]	4	4	7[b]
Tourist/visitor arrivals at national borders (000)[n]	...	40	66[d]
Important sites for terrestrial biodiversity protected (%)	14.9	38.7	38.7
Pop. using improved drinking water (urban/rural, %)	79.9 / 54.2	90.8 / 58.7	95.2 / 60.5[b]
Pop. using improved sanitation facilities (urban/rural, %)	59.5 / 30.1	66.3 / 27.7	69.0 / 26.8[b]
Net Official Development Assist. received (% of GNI)	22.16	8.85	7.77[b]

a Projected estimate (medium fertility variant). b 2015. c 2017. d 2016. e Data classified according to ISIC Rev. 4. f Estimate. g Data refers to a 5-year period preceding the reference year. h Data as at the end of December. i Data revision. j 2004. k 2011. l 2014. m 2002. n Arrivals by air at Dili Airport.

Togo

Region	Western Africa	UN membership date	20 September 1960
Population (000, 2018)	7 991 [a]	Surface area (km2)	56 785 [b]
Pop. density (per km2, 2018)	146.9 [a]	Sex ratio (m per 100 f)	99.4 [a]
Capital city	Lomé	National currency	CFA Franc, BCEAO (XOF) [c]
Capital city pop. (000, 2018)	1 745.7	Exchange rate (per US$)	546.9 [d]

Economic indicators	2005	2010	2018
GDP: Gross domestic product (million current US$)	2 281	3 426	4 449 [a]
GDP growth rate (annual %, const. 2010 prices)	- 4.7	6.1	5.0 [e]
GDP per capita (current US$)	401.0	527.0	585.0 [e]
Economy: Agriculture (% of Gross Value Added)	32.9	33.8	28.7 [e]
Economy: Industry (% of Gross Value Added)	15.9	16.0	17.3 [e]
Economy: Services and other activity (% of GVA)	51.2	50.3	54.0 [e]
Employment in agriculture (% of employed) [f]	42.5	38.4	36.9
Employment in industry (% of employed) [f]	17.9	18.3	17.3
Employment in services & other sectors (% employed) [f]	39.6	43.4	45.8
Unemployment rate (% of labour force) [f]	1.9	1.9	1.8
Labour force participation rate (female/male pop. %) [f]	80.5 / 80.7	77.0 / 80.3	75.6 / 79.3
CPI: Consumer Price Index (2010=100) [g]	78	100	110 [d]
Agricultural production index (2004-2006=100)	97	123	142 [e]
Index of industrial production (2005=100)	100 [h]	124	156 [i]
International trade: exports (million current US$)	360	648	749 [d]
International trade: imports (million current US$)	593	1 205	1 615 [d]
International trade: balance (million current US$)	- 233	- 557	- 866 [d]
Balance of payments, current account (million US$)	- 204	- 200	- 461 [b]

Major trading partners						2017
Export partners (% of exports)	Burkina Faso	17.9	Benin	14.3 [f]	Ghana	7.6
Import partners (% of imports)	China	19.6	France	10.8	Japan	5.1

Social indicators	2005	2010	2018
Population growth rate (average annual %) [j]	2.7	2.7	2.6 [b]
Urban population (% of total population)	35.2	37.5	41.7
Urban population growth rate (average annual %) [j]	4.0	4.0	4.0 [b]
Fertility rate, total (live births per woman) [j]	5.3	5.0	4.7 [b]
Life expectancy at birth (females/males, years) [j]	54.7 / 53.0	56.4 / 55.1	59.8 / 58.3 [b]
Population age distribution (0-14/60+ years old, %)	42.6 / 4.5	42.5 / 4.4	41.3 / 4.6 [a]
International migrant stock (000/% of total pop.) [k,l]	203.4 / 3.6	255.3 / 3.9	264.0 / 3.6 [d]
Refugees and others of concern to the UNHCR (000)	18.7 [m]	14.2 [m]	13.3 [d]
Infant mortality rate (per 1 000 live births) [j]	77.3	63.2	55.7 [b]
Health: Current expenditure (% of GDP)	4.2	6.3	6.6 [b]
Health: Physicians (per 1 000 pop.)	~0.0 [n]	0.1 [o]	...
Education: Government expenditure (% of GDP)	3.4	4.4	5.1 [e]
Education: Primary gross enrol. ratio (f/m per 100 pop.)	104.1 / 122.5	120.6 / 133.7	120.8 / 127.0 [e]
Education: Secondary gross enrol. ratio (f/m per 100 pop.)	31.3 / 58.8	30.7 / 57.9 [f,p]	... / ...
Education: Tertiary gross enrol. ratio (f/m per 100 pop.)	... / ...	... / ...	7.4 / 17.1 [e]
Intentional homicide rate (per 100 000 pop.)	10.7	9.6	9.0 [b]
Seats held by women in the National Parliament (%)	6.2	11.1	17.6

Environment and infrastructure indicators	2005	2010	2018
Individuals using the Internet (per 100 inhabitants) [f]	1.8	3.0	11.3 [e]
Research & Development expenditure (% of GDP) [q]	...	0.3	0.3 [r,j]
Threatened species (number)	32 [n]	54	80 [d]
Forested area (% of land area) [f]	7.1	5.3	3.5 [b]
CO2 emission estimates (million tons/tons per capita)	1.3 / 0.3	2.6 / 0.4	2.6 / 0.4 [l]
Energy production, primary (Petajoules)	84	99	113 [b]
Energy supply per capita (Gigajoules)	18	20	20 [b]
Tourist/visitor arrivals at national borders (000)	81	202	338 [e]
Important sites for terrestrial biodiversity protected (%)	75.0	97.0	97.0
Pop. using improved drinking water (urban/rural, %)	86.6 / 40.5	89.0 / 42.3	91.4 / 44.2 [b]
Pop. using improved sanitation facilities (urban/rural, %)	24.1 / 4.5	24.4 / 3.7	24.7 / 2.9 [b]
Net Official Development Assist. received (% of GNI)	3.97	14.61	4.08 [e]

a Projected estimate (medium fertility variant). b 2015. c African Financial Community (CFA) Franc, Central Bank of West African States (BCEAO). d 2017. e 2016. f Estimate. g WAEMU harmonized consumer price index. h Country data supplemented with data from the Observatoire Economique et Statistique d'Afrique Subsaharienne (Afristat). i 2014. j Data refers to a 5-year period preceding the reference year. k Refers to foreign citizens. l Including refugees. m Data as at the end of December. n 2004. o 2008. p 2007. q Excluding business enterprise. r Excluding private non-profit.

Tokelau

Region	Polynesia	Population (000, 2018)	1 [a]
Surface area (km2)	12 [b]	Pop. density (per km2, 2018)	131.9 [a]
Sex ratio (m per 100 f)	100.0 [c,d]	Capital city	Tokelau [e]
National currency	New Zealand Dollar (NZD)	Exchange rate (per US$)	1.4 [f]

Economic indicators

	2005	2010	2018
Agricultural production index (2004-2006=100)	100	108	115 [d]
International trade: exports (million current US$) [g]	~0	~0	~0 [f]
International trade: imports (million current US$) [g]	1	1	1 [f]
International trade: balance (million current US$) [g]	- 1	- 1	- 1 [f]

Major trading partners

						2017
Export partners (% of exports) [g]	Indonesia	70.7	Bangladesh	6.8	France	5.0
Import partners (% of imports) [g]	Nigeria	69.5	Germany	9.1	Samoa	6.9

Social indicators

	2005	2010	2018
Population growth rate (average annual %) [h]	- 5.0	- 1.3	1.9 [b]
Urban population (% of total population)	0.0	0.0	0.0
Urban population growth rate (average annual %) [h]	0.0	0.0	0.0 [b]
Fertility rate, total (live births per woman)	...	...	2.1 [i]
Population age distribution (0-14/60+ years old, %)	40.7 / 9.5 [j]	36.6 / 11.3 [k]	28.3 / 12.2 [c,d]
International migrant stock (000/% of total pop.)	0.3 / 21.4	0.4 / 37.6	0.5 / 38.8 [f]
Education: Primary gross enrol. ratio (f/m per 100 pop.)	132.6 / 101.8 [g,l]	... / ...	95.2 / 107.7 [g,d]
Education: Secondary gross enrol. ratio (f/m per 100 pop.)	75.8 / 83.3 [g,l]	... / ...	70.7 / 69.6 [g,d]

Environment and infrastructure indicators

	2005	2010	2018
Threatened species (number)	6 [m]	41	49 [f]
Forested area (% of land area) [g]	0.0	0.0	0.0 [b]
Important sites for terrestrial biodiversity protected (%)	2.6	2.6	2.6
Pop. using improved drinking water (urban/rural, %)	... / 96.2	... / 99.1	... / 100.0 [b]
Pop. using improved sanitation facilities (urban/rural, %)	... / 71.4	... / 83.3	... / 90.5 [b]

a Projected estimate (medium fertility variant). **b** 2015. **c** Break in the time series. **d** 2016. **e** The "capital" rotates yearly between the three atolls of Atafu, Fakaofo and Nukunomu, each with fewer than 500 inhabitants in 2011. **f** 2017. **g** Estimate. **h** Data refers to a 5-year period preceding the reference year. **i** 2012. **j** 2001. **k** 2006. **l** 2003. **m** 2004.

Tonga

Region	Polynesia	UN membership date	14 September 1999
Population (000, 2018)	109[a]	Surface area (km2)	747[b]
Pop. density (per km2, 2018)	151.4[a]	Sex ratio (m per 100 f)	100.7[a]
Capital city	Nuku'alofa	National currency	Pa'anga (TOP)
Capital city pop. (000, 2018)	22.9	Exchange rate (per US$)	2.2[c]

Economic indicators	2005	2010	2018
GDP: Gross domestic product (million current US$)	262	374	401[d]
GDP growth rate (annual %, const. 2010 prices)	1.6	3.6	3.4[d]
GDP per capita (current US$)	2 589.0	3 590.0	3 748.0[d]
Economy: Agriculture (% of Gross Value Added)	20.2	18.2	19.3[d]
Economy: Industry (% of Gross Value Added)	19.1	19.9	19.4[d]
Economy: Services and other activity (% of GVA)	60.6	61.8	61.3[d]
Employment in agriculture (% of employed)[e]	31.9	31.6	31.6
Employment in industry (% of employed)[e]	30.3	30.6	31.7
Employment in services & other sectors (% employed)[e]	37.7	37.8	36.7
Unemployment rate (% of labour force)[e]	3.0	1.1	1.2
Labour force participation rate (female/male pop. %)[e]	45.5 / 75.2	45.4 / 75.0	45.1 / 74.1
CPI: Consumer Price Index (2010=100)[e]	77	100	113[d]
Agricultural production index (2004-2006=100)	98	135	137[d]
International trade: exports (million current US$)	10	8	10[e,c]
International trade: imports (million current US$)	120	159	212[e,c]
International trade: balance (million current US$)	- 110	- 151	- 201[e,c]
Balance of payments, current account (million US$)	- 21	- 80	- 56[b]

Major trading partners						2017
Export partners (% of exports)	United States	27.4[e]	Republic of Korea	20.6	New Zealand	17.6[e]
Import partners (% of imports)[e]	New Zealand	31.7	China	20.8	Netherlands	11.2

Social indicators	2005	2010	2018
Population growth rate (average annual %)[f]	0.6	0.6	0.4[b]
Urban population (% of total population)	23.2	23.4	23.1
Urban population growth rate (average annual %)[f]	0.7	0.8	0.3[b]
Fertility rate, total (live births per woman)[f]	4.2	4.0	3.8[h]
Life expectancy at birth (females/males, years)[f]	73.5 / 68.8	74.7 / 69.0	75.6 / 69.6[b]
Population age distribution (0-14/60+ years old, %)	38.2 / 8.3	37.4 / 8.0	35.4 / 8.7[a]
International migrant stock (000/% of total pop.)	4.3 / 4.3	4.6 / 4.4	5.0 / 4.6[c]
Refugees and others of concern to the UNHCR (000)	...	~0.0[g]	...
Infant mortality rate (per 1 000 live births)[f]	23.5	22.0	20.6[b]
Health: Current expenditure (% of GDP)[h]	4.6	4.9	5.9[b]
Health: Physicians (per 1 000 pop.)	0.3[i]	0.6	...
Education: Government expenditure (% of GDP)	3.9[j]	...	...
Education: Primary gross enrol. ratio (f/m per 100 pop.)	110.1 / 113.4	107.3 / 109.4	107.4 / 108.6[k]
Education: Secondary gross enrol. ratio (f/m per 100 pop.)	116.3 / 105.5[i]	107.2 / 100.4	94.2 / 86.4[k]
Education: Tertiary gross enrol. ratio (f/m per 100 pop.)	8.0 / 4.8[l]	... / ...	... / ...
Intentional homicide rate (per 100 000 pop.)	4.0	1.0	1.0[m]
Seats held by women in the National Parliament (%)	0.0	3.1	7.4

Environment and infrastructure indicators	2005	2010	2018
Individuals using the Internet (per 100 inhabitants)[e]	4.9	16.0	40.0[d]
Threatened species (number)	16[j]	58	79[c]
Forested area (% of land area)	12.5[e]	12.5	12.5[b]
CO2 emission estimates (million tons/tons per capita)	0.1 / 1.1	0.1 / 1.1	0.1 / 1.1[k]
Energy production, primary (Petajoules)	0	0	0[b]
Energy supply per capita (Gigajoules)	16[e]	16	16[b]
Tourist/visitor arrivals at national borders (000)[n]	42	47	59[c]
Important sites for terrestrial biodiversity protected (%)	9.3	9.3	9.3
Pop. using improved drinking water (urban/rural, %)	97.6 / 99.0	98.8 / 99.3	99.7 / 99.6[b]
Pop. using improved sanitation facilities (urban/rural, %)	97.4 / 90.7	97.5 / 89.7	97.6 / 89.0[b]
Net Official Development Assist. received (% of GNI)	12.12	18.48	20.91[d]

a Projected estimate (medium fertility variant). **b** 2015. **c** 2017. **d** 2016. **e** Estimate. **f** Data refers to a 5-year period preceding the reference year. **g** Data as at the end of December. **h** Data refer to fiscal years beginning 1 July. **i** 2002. **j** 2004. **k** 2014. **l** 2003. **m** 2012. **n** Arrivals by air.

Trinidad and Tobago

Region	Caribbean	UN membership date	18 September 1962
Population (000, 2018)	1 373 [a]	Surface area (km2)	5 127 [b]
Pop. density (per km2, 2018)	267.6 [a]	Sex ratio (m per 100 f)	96.9 [a]
Capital city	Port of Spain	National currency	TT Dollar (TTD) [c]
Capital city pop. (000, 2018)	544.4 [d]	Exchange rate (per US$)	6.8 [e]

Economic indicators

	2005	2010	2018
GDP: Gross domestic product (million current US$)	15 982	22 123	24 086 [f]
GDP growth rate (annual %, const. 2010 prices)	6.2	3.3	- 2.3 [f]
GDP per capita (current US$)	12 323.0	16 658.0	17 646.0 [f]
Economy: Agriculture (% of Gross Value Added)	0.5	0.4	0.4 [f]
Economy: Industry (% of Gross Value Added)	56.7	51.3	37.8 [f]
Economy: Services and other activity (% of GVA)	42.8	48.3	61.8 [f]
Employment in agriculture (% of employed) [g]	4.3	3.7	3.6
Employment in industry (% of employed) [g]	31.1	30.2	26.8
Employment in services & other sectors (% employed) [g]	64.5	66.1	69.6
Unemployment rate (% of labour force)	8.0	5.9	5.1 [g]
Labour force participation rate (female/male pop. %) [g]	53.5 / 76.2	52.5 / 75.4	51.0 / 73.2
CPI: Consumer Price Index (2010=100) [h]	65	100	140 [e]
Agricultural production index (2004-2006=100)	99	96	96 [f]
Index of industrial production (2005=100) [i]	100	159	142 [j]
International trade: exports (million current US$)	9 611	10 982	8 863 [g,e]
International trade: imports (million current US$)	5 694	6 480	6 425 [g,e]
International trade: balance (million current US$)	3 918	4 502	2 439 [g,e]
Balance of payments, current account (million US$)	3 881	4 172	2 325 [e]

Major trading partners

						2017
Export partners (% of exports)	United States	41.7 [g]	Argentina	6.8	Colombia	4.1 [g]
Import partners (% of imports) [g]	United States	32.0	Gabon	12.5	China	7.1

Social indicators

	2005	2010	2018
Population growth rate (average annual %) [k]	0.5	0.5	0.5 [b]
Urban population (% of total population)	55.0	54.0	53.2
Urban population growth rate (average annual %) [k]	0.1	0.1	0.2 [b]
Fertility rate, total (live births per woman) [k]	1.8	1.8	1.8 [b]
Life expectancy at birth (females/males, years) [k]	72.5 / 65.1	73.0 / 65.8	73.8 / 66.9 [b]
Population age distribution (0-14/60+ years old, %)	21.8 / 10.8	20.7 / 12.4	20.5 / 15.5 [a]
International migrant stock (000/% of total pop.)	44.8 / 3.5	48.2 / 3.6	50.2 / 3.7 [e]
Refugees and others of concern to the UNHCR (000)	...	0.1 [i]	0.7 [e]
Infant mortality rate (per 1 000 live births) [k]	28.9	26.6	24.8 [b]
Health: Current expenditure (% of GDP)	4.9	5.2	6.0 [b]
Health: Physicians (per 1 000 pop.)	0.8 [m]	1.8	1.8 [n]
Education: Government expenditure (% of GDP)	3.1 [m]	...	...
Education: Primary gross enrol. ratio (f/m per 100 pop.)	97.8 / 100.7 [g]	104.3 / 108.0	... / ...
Education: Secondary gross enrol. ratio (f/m per 100 pop.)	88.5 / 82.6 [g,o]	... / ...	... / ...
Education: Tertiary gross enrol. ratio (f/m per 100 pop.)	13.4 / 10.6 [o]	... / ...	... / ...
Intentional homicide rate (per 100 000 pop.)	29.8	35.6	30.9 [b]
Seats held by women in the National Parliament (%)	19.4	26.8	31.0

Environment and infrastructure indicators

	2005	2010	2018
Individuals using the Internet (per 100 inhabitants) [g]	29.0	48.5	73.3 [f]
Research & Development expenditure (% of GDP)	0.1	~0.0	0.1 [j]
Threatened species (number)	33 [o]	48	69 [e]
Forested area (% of land area)	44.8	44.1	45.7 [b]
CO2 emission estimates (million tons/tons per capita)	38.2 / 29.0	47.9 / 36.1	46.3 / 34.2 [j]
Energy production, primary (Petajoules)	1 464	1 786	1 577 [b]
Energy supply per capita (Gigajoules)	516	636	600 [b]
Tourist/visitor arrivals at national borders (000) [p]	463	388	410 [f]
Important sites for terrestrial biodiversity protected (%)	40.7	40.7	40.7
Pop. using improved drinking water (urban/rural, %)	94.1 / 94.1	95.0 / 95.0	95.1 / 95.1 [b]
Pop. using improved sanitation facilities (urban/rural, %)	91.1 / 91.1	91.4 / 91.4	91.5 / 91.5 [b]
Net Official Development Assist. received (% of GNI)	-0.01	0.02	...

a Projected estimate (medium fertility variant). **b** 2015. **c** Trinidad and Tobago Dollar. **d** Data refers to the urban agglomeration. **e** 2017. **f** 2016. **g** Estimate. **h** Data refer to the Retail Price Index. **i** Data classified according to ISIC Rev. 3. **j** 2014. **k** Data refers to a 5-year period preceding the reference year. **l** Data as at the end of December. **m** 2003. **n** 2011. **o** 2004. **p** Arrivals by air.

Tunisia

Region	Northern Africa	
Population (000, 2018)	11 659[a]	
Pop. density (per km2, 2018)	75.0[a]	
Capital city	Tunis	
Capital city pop. (000, 2018)	2 290.8[c]	
UN membership date	12 November 1956	
Surface area (km2)	163 610[b]	
Sex ratio (m per 100 f)	97.7[a]	
National currency	Tunisian Dinar (TND)	
Exchange rate (per US$)	2.3[d]	

Economic indicators

	2005	2010	2018
GDP: Gross domestic product (million current US$)	32 272	44 051	41 704[d]
GDP growth rate (annual %, const. 2010 prices)	4.0	3.0	1.0[d]
GDP per capita (current US$)	3 194.0	4 140.0	3 657.0[d]
Economy: Agriculture (% of Gross Value Added)[e]	10.0	8.1	9.8[d]
Economy: Industry (% of Gross Value Added)[e]	28.8	31.1	26.0[d]
Economy: Services and other activity (% of GVA)[e]	61.3	60.8	64.2[d]
Employment in agriculture (% of employed)[f]	20.8	17.7	13.5
Employment in industry (% of employed)[f]	42.2	44.9	42.7
Employment in services & other sectors (% employed)[f]	37.0	37.3	43.8
Unemployment rate (% of labour force)	12.9	13.0	15.1[f]
Labour force participation rate (female/male pop. %)[i]	23.9 / 68.6	24.5 / 69.7	24.1 / 70.3
CPI: Consumer Price Index (2010=100)[f]	82	100[g]	138[h]
Agricultural production index (2004-2006=100)	102	106	117[d]
Index of industrial production (2005=100)	100	115	112[i]
International trade: exports (million current US$)	10 494	16 427	14 532[f,h]
International trade: imports (million current US$)	13 174	22 215	20 715[f,h]
International trade: balance (million current US$)	- 2 681	- 5 789	- 6 183[f,h]
Balance of payments, current account (million US$)	- 299	- 2 104	- 3 694[d]

Major trading partners

						2017
Export partners (% of exports)	France	32.0[f]	Italy	17.4	Germany	10.5[f]
Import partners (% of imports)[f]	France	15.4	Italy	14.5	China	9.3

Social indicators

	2005	2010	2018
Population growth rate (average annual %)[j]	0.8	1.0	1.2[b]
Urban population (% of total population)	65.2	66.7	68.9
Urban population growth rate (average annual %)[j]	1.4	1.5	1.6[b]
Fertility rate, total (live births per woman)[j]	2.0	2.0	2.3[b]
Life expectancy at birth (females/males, years)[j]	76.3 / 71.4	77.0 / 72.3	77.1 / 73.0[b]
Population age distribution (0-14/60+ years old, %)	25.5 / 10.0	23.3 / 10.4	24.0 / 12.6[a]
International migrant stock (000/% of total pop.)	35.0 / 0.3[k]	43.2 / 0.4[k]	57.7 / 0.5[l,h]
Refugees and others of concern to the UNHCR (000)	0.1[m]	0.1[m]	0.6[h]
Infant mortality rate (per 1 000 live births)[j]	23.0	18.7	18.5[b]
Health: Current expenditure (% of GDP)	5.4	5.9	6.7[b]
Health: Physicians (per 1 000 pop.)	0.9	1.2	1.3[b]
Education: Government expenditure (% of GDP)	6.5	6.3	6.6[b]
Education: Primary gross enrol. ratio (f/m per 100 pop.)	109.3 / 114.0	105.3 / 109.0	113.2 / 116.2[d]
Education: Secondary gross enrol. ratio (f/m per 100 pop.)	88.3 / 81.4	93.4 / 87.5	97.9 / 88.1[d]
Education: Tertiary gross enrol. ratio (f/m per 100 pop.)	35.1 / 28.6	42.6 / 27.8	41.2 / 24.1[d]
Intentional homicide rate (per 100 000 pop.)	2.6	2.7	3.0[n]
Seats held by women in the National Parliament (%)	22.8	27.6	31.3

Environment and infrastructure indicators

	2005	2010	2018
Individuals using the Internet (per 100 inhabitants)	9.7	36.8	50.9[f,d]
Research & Development expenditure (% of GDP)	0.7	0.7	0.6[f,b]
Threatened species (number)	36[o]	75	96[h]
Forested area (% of land area)	5.9	6.4	6.7[f,b]
CO2 emission estimates (million tons/tons per capita)	22.7 / 2.3	27.7 / 2.6	28.8 / 2.6[i]
Energy production, primary (Petajoules)	274	341	260[b]
Energy supply per capita (Gigajoules)	35	40	40[b]
Tourist/visitor arrivals at national borders (000)	6 378[p]	7 828	5 724[d]
Important sites for terrestrial biodiversity protected (%)	16.0	27.2	40.8
Pop. using improved drinking water (urban/rural, %)	98.6 / 82.4	99.6 / 88.4	100.0 / 93.2[b]
Pop. using improved sanitation facilities (urban/rural, %)	96.2 / 66.0	96.9 / 73.7	97.4 / 79.8[b]
Net Official Development Assist. received (% of GNI)	1.20	1.31	1.55[d]

a Projected estimate (medium fertility variant). **b** 2015. **c** Refers to Grand Tunis. **d** 2016. **e** At factor cost. **f** Estimate. **g** Break in the time series. **h** 2017. **i** 2014. **j** Data refers to a 5-year period preceding the reference year. **k** Refers to foreign citizens. **l** Including refugees. **m** Data as at the end of December. **n** 2012. **o** 2004. **p** Excluding nationals residing abroad.

Turkey

Region	Western Asia	
Population (000, 2018)	81 917[a]	
Pop. density (per km2, 2018)	106.4[a]	
Capital city	Ankara	
Capital city pop. (000, 2018)	4 919.1[c]	

UN membership date	24 October 1945
Surface area (km2)	783 562[b]
Sex ratio (m per 100 f)	97.2[a]
National currency	Turkish Lira (TRY)
Exchange rate (per US$)	3.8[d]

Economic indicators

	2005	2010	2018
GDP: Gross domestic product (million current US$)	501 423	771 877	863 712[e]
GDP growth rate (annual %, const. 2010 prices)	9.0	8.5	3.2[e]
GDP per capita (current US$)	7 384.0	10 672.0	10 863.0[e]
Economy: Agriculture (% of Gross Value Added)[f]	10.6	10.3	7.0[e]
Economy: Industry (% of Gross Value Added)[f]	29.0	28.0	32.0[e]
Economy: Services and other activity (% of GVA)[f]	60.4	61.8	61.0[e]
Employment in agriculture (% of employed)[g]	25.7	23.7	18.8
Employment in industry (% of employed)[g]	26.3	26.2	26.9
Employment in services & other sectors (% employed)[g]	48.0	50.1	54.3
Unemployment rate (% of labour force)	10.6	10.7	11.1[g]
Labour force participation rate (female/male pop. %)[g]	23.3 / 70.1	27.0 / 69.6	32.2 / 71.7
CPI: Consumer Price Index (2010=100)[g,i]	66[h]	100	175[d]
Agricultural production index (2004-2006=100)	101	110	129[e]
Index of industrial production (2005=100)	100	116[j]	140[j,k]
International trade: exports (million current US$)	73 476	113 883	157 055[d]
International trade: imports (million current US$)	116 774	185 544	233 792[d]
International trade: balance (million current US$)	- 43 298	- 71 661	- 76 737[d]
Balance of payments, current account (million US$)	- 20 980[h]	- 44 616	- 47 378[d]

Major trading partners

								2017
Export partners (% of exports)	Germany	9.6	United Kingdom	6.1[g]	United Arab Emirates	5.8		
Import partners (% of imports)	China	10.0	Germany	9.1	Russian Federation	8.3		

Social indicators

	2005	2010	2018
Population growth rate (average annual %)[l]	1.4	1.3	1.6[b]
Urban population (% of total population)	67.8	70.8	75.1
Urban population growth rate (average annual %)[l]	2.4	2.1	2.4[b]
Fertility rate, total (live births per woman)[l]	2.4	2.2	2.1[b]
Life expectancy at birth (females/males, years)[l]	74.9 / 68.0	76.9 / 69.9	78.1 / 71.5[b]
Population age distribution (0-14/60+ years old, %)	28.6 / 9.6	26.9 / 10.4	24.6 / 12.3[a]
International migrant stock (000/% of total pop.)[m]	1 319.2 / 1.9	1 367.0 / 1.9	4 882.0 / 6.0[d]
Refugees and others of concern to the UNHCR (000)	8.7[n]	17.8[n]	3 470.1[d]
Infant mortality rate (per 1 000 live births)[l]	24.7	16.4	12.6[b]
Health: Current expenditure (% of GDP)	4.9	5.1	4.1[b]
Health: Physicians (per 1 000 pop.)	1.5	1.7	1.7[k]
Education: Government expenditure (% of GDP)	3.0[o]	2.8[p]	4.4[k]
Education: Primary gross enrol. ratio (f/m per 100 pop.)	100.5 / 105.8	100.6 / 102.0	102.9 / 103.6[b]
Education: Secondary gross enrol. ratio (f/m per 100 pop.)	76.1 / 91.6	80.5 / 87.9	101.7 / 104.4[b]
Education: Tertiary gross enrol. ratio (f/m per 100 pop.)	27.9 / 38.2	50.5 / 62.1	88.9 / 101.8[b]
Intentional homicide rate (per 100 000 pop.)	4.9	4.2	4.3[q]
Seats held by women in the National Parliament (%)	4.4	9.1	14.6

Environment and infrastructure indicators

	2005	2010	2018
Individuals using the Internet (per 100 inhabitants)	15.5[r,s]	39.8[r,s]	58.3[e]
Research & Development expenditure (% of GDP)	0.6	0.8	1.0[k]
Threatened species (number)	92[b]	150	388[d]
Forested area (% of land area)	13.9	14.6	15.2[b]
CO2 emission estimates (million tons/tons per capita)	237.4 / 3.5	298.0 / 4.1	346.0 / 4.5[k]
Energy production, primary (Petajoules)	1 004	1 352	1 314[b]
Energy supply per capita (Gigajoules)	52	61	66[b]
Tourist/visitor arrivals at national borders (000)	20 273	31 364[t]	30 289[t,e]
Important sites for terrestrial biodiversity protected (%)	2.1	2.2	2.3
Pop. using improved drinking water (urban/rural, %)	98.3 / 90.3	99.7 / 95.9	100.0 / 100.0[b]
Pop. using improved sanitation facilities (urban/rural, %)	97.3 / 76.5	97.8 / 81.0	98.3 / 85.5[b]
Net Official Development Assist. disbursed (% of GNI)	0.17	0.13	0.95[u,d]
Net Official Development Assist. received (% of GNI)	0.08	0.14	0.43[d]

a Projected estimate (medium fertility variant). **b** 2015. **c** Refers to Altindag, Cankaya, Etimesgut, Golbasi, Keçioren, Mamak, Sincan and Yenimahalle. **d** 2017. **e** 2016. **f** Data classified according to ISIC Rev. 4. **g** Estimate. **h** Break in the time series. **i** Calculated by the Statistics Division of the United Nations from national indices. **j** Excluding water and waste management. **k** 2014. **l** Data refers to a 5-year period preceding the reference year. **m** Including refugees. **n** Data as at the end of December. **o** 2004. **p** 2006. **q** 2012. **r** Users in the last 12 months. **s** Population aged 16 to 74 years. **t** Turkish citizens resident abroad are included. **u** Provisional data.

Turkmenistan

Region	Central Asia	UN membership date	02 March 1992
Population (000, 2018)	5 852[a]	Surface area (km2)	488 100[b]
Pop. density (per km2, 2018)	12.5[a]	Sex ratio (m per 100 f)	97.0[a]
Capital city	Ashgabat	National currency	Turkmen. Manat (TMT)[c]
Capital city pop. (000, 2018)	810.2	Exchange rate (per US$)	3.5[d,e]

Economic indicators	2005	2010	2018
GDP: Gross domestic product (million current US$)	14 182	22 583	36 180[f]
GDP growth rate (annual %, const. 2010 prices)	13.0	9.2	6.2[f]
GDP per capita (current US$)	2 983.0	4 439.0	6 389.0[f]
Economy: Agriculture (% of Gross Value Added)	18.8	14.5	13.4[f]
Economy: Industry (% of Gross Value Added)	37.6	48.4	51.0[f]
Economy: Services and other activity (% of GVA)	43.6	37.0	35.6[f]
Employment in agriculture (% of employed)[g]	19.1	12.6	7.9
Employment in industry (% of employed)[g]	36.6	45.1	44.8
Employment in services & other sectors (% employed)[g]	44.2	42.3	47.2
Unemployment rate (% of labour force)	3.8[g]	4.0	3.3[g]
Labour force participation rate (female/male pop. %)[g]	52.5 / 75.2	52.9 / 76.2	53.2 / 78.2
Agricultural production index (2004-2006=100)	104	98	102[f]
International trade: exports (million current US$)[g]	3 009	3 335	3 813[e]
International trade: imports (million current US$)[g]	2 217	2 400	2 679[e]
International trade: balance (million current US$)[g]	792	935	1 135[e]

Major trading partners						2017
Export partners (% of exports)[g]	China	78.6	Turkey	4.9	Afghanistan	4.9
Import partners (% of imports)[g]	Turkey	26.6	Germany	10.9	China	9.3

Social indicators	2005	2010	2018
Population growth rate (average annual %)[h]	1.0	1.4	1.8[b]
Urban population (% of total population)	47.1	48.5	51.6
Urban population growth rate (average annual %)[h]	1.5	2.0	2.5[b]
Fertility rate, total (live births per woman)[h]	2.8	2.6	3.0[b]
Life expectancy at birth (females/males, years)[h]	68.2 / 60.3	69.6 / 62.2	70.8 / 63.9[b]
Population age distribution (0-14/60+ years old, %)	32.6 / 6.1	29.5 / 6.1	30.8 / 7.6[a]
International migrant stock (000/% of total pop.)	213.1 / 4.5	198.0 / 3.9	195.1 / 3.4[e]
Refugees and others of concern to the UNHCR (000)	12.0[i]	20.1[i]	3.4[e]
Infant mortality rate (per 1 000 live births)	62.1	54.2	46.9[b]
Health: Current expenditure (% of GDP)	9.6	5.0	6.3[b]
Health: Physicians (per 1 000 pop.)	4.4[j]	2.3	2.3[k]
Education: Government expenditure (% of GDP)	...	...	3.0[l]
Education: Primary gross enrol. ratio (f/m per 100 pop.)	... / ...	... / ...	87.5 / 89.2[k]
Education: Secondary gross enrol. ratio (f/m per 100 pop.)	... / ...	... / ...	84.0 / 87.6[k]
Education: Tertiary gross enrol. ratio (f/m per 100 pop.)	... / ...	... / ...	6.2 / 9.7[k]
Intentional homicide rate (per 100 000 pop.)	4.3	4.2[m]	...
Seats held by women in the National Parliament (%)	26.0[n]	16.8	25.8

Environment and infrastructure indicators	2005	2010	2018
Individuals using the Internet (per 100 inhabitants)[g]	1.0	3.0	18.0[f]
Threatened species (number)	40[o]	45	54[e]
Forested area (% of land area)[g]	8.8	8.8	8.8[b]
CO2 emission estimates (million tons/tons per capita)	48.3 / 10.2	57.3 / 11.4	68.4 / 12.9[k]
Energy production, primary (Petajoules)	2 584	1 982	3 407[e]
Energy supply per capita (Gigajoules)	170	189	216[b]
Tourist/visitor arrivals at national borders (000)	12	8[p]	...
Important sites for terrestrial biodiversity protected (%)	14.4	14.6	14.6
Pop. using improved drinking water (urban/rural, %)	89.1 / 34.6	... / ...	... / ...
Pop. using improved sanitation facilities (urban/rural, %)	77.0 / 49.9	... / ...	... / ...
Net Official Development Assist. received (% of GNI)	0.39	0.21	0.10[f]

a Projected estimate (medium fertility variant). b 2015. c Turkmenistan New Manat. d UN operational exchange rate. e 2017. f 2016. g Estimate. h Data refers to a 5-year period preceding the reference year. i Data as at the end of December. j 2002. k 2014. l 2012. m 2006. n 2000. o 2004. p 2007.

Turks and Caicos Islands

Region	Caribbean	Population (000, 2018)	36[a]
Surface area (km2)	948[b,c]	Pop. density (per km2, 2018)	37.9[a]
Sex ratio (m per 100 f)	104.1[d,e,f]	Capital city	Cockburn Town
National currency	US Dollar (USD)	Capital city pop. (000)	0.1[g]

Economic indicators	2005	2010	2018
GDP: Gross domestic product (million current US$)	579	687	918[h]
GDP growth rate (annual %, const. 2010 prices)	14.4	1.0	4.4[h]
GDP per capita (current US$)	21 879.0	22 159.0	26 291.0[h]
Economy: Agriculture (% of Gross Value Added)	1.2	0.6	0.6[h]
Economy: Industry (% of Gross Value Added)	19.7	12.4	10.5[h]
Economy: Services and other activity (% of GVA)	79.1	86.9	88.9[h]
Employment in agriculture (% of employed)[i]	1.4	1.2[j,k]	...
Employment in industry (% of employed)[i]	16.8	23.1[j,k]	...
Employment in services & other sectors (% employed)[i]	70.9	74.0[j,k]	...
Unemployment rate (% of labour force)	8.0	8.3[j,k]	...
International trade: exports (million current US$)	15	16[l]	4[l,f]
International trade: imports (million current US$)	304	302[l]	370[l,f]
International trade: balance (million current US$)	- 289	- 286[l]	- 366[l,f]
Balance of payments, current account (million US$)	...	...	253[h]

Major trading partners						2017
Export partners (% of exports)	Bahamas	30.2[l]	Zimbabwe	25.1	United States	21.9[l]
Import partners (% of imports)[l]	United States	89.9	Dominican Republic	1.4	Japan	1.1

Social indicators	2005	2010	2018
Population growth rate (average annual %)[m]	6.7	3.2	2.0[c]
Urban population (% of total population)	87.7	90.2	93.1
Urban population growth rate (average annual %)[m]	7.5	3.7	2.5[c]
Life expectancy at birth (females/males, years)	77.3 / 75.1[n]	... / ...	77.8 / 75.8[o]
Population age distribution (0-14/60+ years old, %)	26.6 / 5.2[g]	... / ...	19.2 / 7.6[a,d,f]
International migrant stock (000/% of total pop.)	13.1 / 49.6	17.2 / 55.5	24.5 / 69.2[f]
Refugees and others of concern to the UNHCR (000)	...	...	~0.0[f]
Education: Government expenditure (% of GDP)	...	...	3.3[c]
Intentional homicide rate (per 100 000 pop.)	0.0	6.6[p]	5.9[q]

Environment and infrastructure indicators	2005	2010	2018
Threatened species (number)	20[r]	34	60[f]
Forested area (% of land area)[l]	36.2	36.2	36.2[c]
CO2 emission estimates (million tons/tons per capita)	0.1 / 4.0	0.2 / 6.1	0.2 / 6.1[q]
Energy production, primary (Petajoules)	0	0	0[c]
Energy supply per capita (Gigajoules)[l]	57	84	84[c]
Tourist/visitor arrivals at national borders (000)	176	281	454[h]
Important sites for terrestrial biodiversity protected (%)	28.0	28.0	28.0
Pop. using improved drinking water (urban/rural, %)	87.0 / 87.0	... / ...	... / ...
Pop. using improved sanitation facilities (urban/rural, %)	81.4 / 81.4	... / ...	... / ...

a Projected estimate (medium fertility variant). b Including low water level for all islands (area to shoreline). c 2015. d Estimates should be viewed with caution as these are derived from scarce data. e De jure population. f 2017. g 2001. h 2016. i Data classified according to ISIC Rev. 3. j Break in the time series. k 2008. l Estimate. m Data refers to a 5-year period preceding the reference year. n 2002. o 2012. p 2009. q 2014. r 2004.

Tuvalu

Region	Polynesia	UN membership date	05 September 2000
Population (000, 2018)	11 [a]	Surface area (km2)	26 [b]
Pop. density (per km2, 2018)	376.2 [a]	Sex ratio (m per 100 f)	102.0 [c]
Capital city	Funafuti	National currency	Australian Dollar (AUD)
Capital city pop. (000, 2018)	7.0	Exchange rate (per US$)	1.3 [d]

Economic indicators	2005	2010	2018
GDP: Gross domestic product (million current US$)	22	32	37 [c]
GDP growth rate (annual %, const. 2010 prices)	- 4.1	- 3.1	3.0 [c]
GDP per capita (current US$)	2 162.0	3 005.0	3 307.0 [c]
Economy: Agriculture (% of Gross Value Added)	22.2	27.6	24.3 [c]
Economy: Industry (% of Gross Value Added)	8.3	4.7	8.2 [c]
Economy: Services and other activity (% of GVA)	69.4	67.7	67.5 [c]
Unemployment rate (% of labour force)	6.5	...	...
Labour force participation rate (female/male pop. %)	47.9 / 69.6	... / ...	... / ...
Agricultural production index (2004-2006=100)	100	104	111 [b]
International trade: exports (million current US$)	~0	~0 [e]	~0 [e,d]
International trade: imports (million current US$)	13	12 [e]	12 [e,d]
International trade: balance (million current US$)	- 13	- 12 [e]	- 12 [e,d]
Balance of payments, current account (million US$)	- 4	- 14	...

Major trading partners						2017
Export partners (% of exports) [e]	Thailand	93.3	Japan	4.2	Bosnia-Herzegovina	0.4
Import partners (% of imports) [e]	Singapore	27.7	Japan	23.3	Fiji	14.3

Social indicators	2005	2010	2018
Population growth rate (average annual %) [f]	1.2	1.0	0.9 [b]
Urban population (% of total population)	49.7	54.8	62.4
Urban population growth rate (average annual %) [f]	2.8	2.9	2.6 [b]
Fertility rate, total (live births per woman)	3.7 [g]	...	3.6 [h,i]
Life expectancy at birth (females/males, years)	... / ...	71.9 / 67.4	... / ...
Population age distribution (0-14/60+ years old, %)	36.2 / 8.6 [g]	... / ...	31.1 / 9.9 [c]
International migrant stock (000/% of total pop.) [j]	0.2 / 1.8	0.2 / 1.5	0.1 / 1.3 [d]
Infant mortality rate (per 1 000 live births)	...	10.3	...
Health: Current expenditure (% of GDP) [k]	11.1	14.4	15.0 [b]
Health: Physicians (per 1 000 pop.)	1.0 [l]	1.2 [m]	...
Education: Primary gross enrol. ratio (f/m per 100 pop.)	97.6 / 101.4	97.6 / 102.4 [n]	118.8 / 119.6 [b]
Education: Secondary gross enrol. ratio (f/m per 100 pop.)	74.1 / 67.4 [e,o]	... / ...	108.2 / 85.0 [e,b]
Intentional homicide rate (per 100 000 pop.)	0.0	9.5	18.0 [l]
Seats held by women in the National Parliament (%)	0.0	0.0	6.7

Environment and infrastructure indicators	2005	2010	2018
Individuals using the Internet (per 100 inhabitants)	5.2 [p]	25.0 [e]	46.0 [e,c]
Threatened species (number)	8 [q]	85	96 [d]
Forested area (% of land area) [g]	33.3	33.3	33.3 [b]
CO2 emission estimates (million tons/tons per capita)	~0.0 / ...	~0.0 / ...	~0.0 / ... [r]
Energy production, primary (Petajoules)	...	...	0 [b]
Energy supply per capita (Gigajoules)	13 [e]	13	14 [e,b]
Tourist/visitor arrivals at national borders (000)	1	2	2 [c]
Pop. using improved drinking water (urban/rural, %)	96.9 / 95.3	98.3 / 97.0	98.3 / 97.0 [b]
Pop. using improved sanitation facilities (urban/rural, %)	84.0 / 78.3	86.3 / 80.2	86.3 / 80.2 [b,s]
Net Official Development Assist. received (% of GNI)	24.65	27.46	44.44 [c]

a Projected estimate (medium fertility variant). b 2015. c 2016. d 2017. e Estimate. f Data refers to a 5-year period preceding the reference year. g 2002. h Break in the time series. i 2012. j Refers to foreign citizens. k Data revision. l 2003. m 2009. n 2006. o 2001. p 2000. q 2004. r 2014. s 2013.

Uganda

Region	Eastern Africa	UN membership date	25 October 1962
Population (000, 2018)	44 271 [a]	Surface area (km2)	241 550 [b]
Pop. density (per km2, 2018)	221.6 [a]	Sex ratio (m per 100 f)	99.0 [a]
Capital city	Kampala	National currency	Uganda Shilling (UGX)
Capital city pop. (000, 2018)	2 986.4 [c]	Exchange rate (per US$)	3 635.1 [d]

Economic indicators	2005	2010	2018
GDP: Gross domestic product (million current US$)	11 154	19 803	25 308 [e]
GDP growth rate (annual %, const. 2010 prices)	10.0	8.2	2.3 [e]
GDP per capita (current US$)	391.0	584.0	610.0 [e]
Economy: Agriculture (% of Gross Value Added) [f]	28.6	26.1	25.5 [e]
Economy: Industry (% of Gross Value Added) [f]	22.2	20.4	22.7 [e]
Economy: Services and other activity (% of GVA) [f]	49.1	53.5	51.8 [e]
Employment in agriculture (% of employed) [g]	75.3	71.1	68.4
Employment in industry (% of employed) [g]	5.7	7.1	7.0
Employment in services & other sectors (% employed) [g]	19.0	21.8	24.6
Unemployment rate (% of labour force)	1.9	4.0 [g]	2.2 [g]
Labour force participation rate (female/male pop. %) [g]	65.0 / 76.1	65.9 / 76.0	66.7 / 74.9
CPI: Consumer Price Index (2010=100)	...	...	168 [h,d]
Agricultural production index (2004-2006=100)	100	89	92 [e]
International trade: exports (million current US$)	813	1 619	2 852 [g,d]
International trade: imports (million current US$)	2 054	4 664	4 809 [g,d]
International trade: balance (million current US$)	- 1 241	- 3 046	- 1 957 [g,d]
Balance of payments, current account (million US$)	51	- 1 609	- 1 128 [d]

Major trading partners						2017
Export partners (% of exports) [g]	Kenya	16.3 [g]	United Arab Emirates	15.0	South Sudan	9.7 [g]
Import partners (% of imports) [g]	China	18.4	India	17.3	Kenya	9.5

Social indicators	2005	2010	2018
Population growth rate (average annual %) [i]	3.4	3.4	3.4 [b]
Urban population (% of total population)	17.0	19.4	23.8
Urban population growth rate (average annual %) [i]	6.2	6.1	6.0 [b]
Fertility rate, total (live births per woman) [i]	6.7	6.4	5.9 [b]
Life expectancy at birth (females/males, years) [i]	52.1 / 47.8	56.7 / 53.6	60.7 / 56.5 [b]
Population age distribution (0-14/60+ years old, %)	49.8 / 3.6	49.3 / 3.4	47.4 / 3.3 [a]
International migrant stock (000/% of total pop.) [i]	653.0 / 2.3	529.2 / 1.6	1 692.1 / 3.9 [d]
Refugees and others of concern to the UNHCR (000)	260.7 [k]	594.4 [k]	1 489.7 [d]
Infant mortality rate (per 1 000 live births) [i]	79.4	68.2	60.2 [b]
Health: Current expenditure (% of GDP) [l]	11.3	10.7	7.3 [b]
Health: Physicians (per 1 000 pop.)	0.1	...	0.1 [b]
Education: Government expenditure (% of GDP)	5.0 [m]	2.4	2.3 [n]
Education: Primary gross enrol. ratio (f/m per 100 pop.)	119.2 / 120.2	117.7 / 115.9	101.3 / 98.3 [e]
Education: Secondary gross enrol. ratio (f/m per 100 pop.)	17.0 / 21.1 [m]	21.6 / 26.3 [o]	... / ...
Education: Tertiary gross enrol. ratio (f/m per 100 pop.)	2.7 / 4.4 [m]	3.5 / 4.4	4.0 / 5.2 [n]
Intentional homicide rate (per 100 000 pop.)	8.7	9.3	11.5 [n]
Seats held by women in the National Parliament (%)	23.9	31.5	34.3

Environment and infrastructure indicators	2005	2010	2018
Individuals using the Internet (per 100 inhabitants)	1.7	12.5	21.9 [g,e]
Research & Development expenditure (% of GDP)	0.2	0.5	...
Threatened species (number)	134 [m]	166	196 [d]
Forested area (% of land area)	17.2	13.7	10.4 [b]
CO2 emission estimates (million tons/tons per capita)	2.2 / 0.1	3.9 / 0.1	5.2 / 0.1 [n]
Energy production, primary (Petajoules)	390	477	595 [b]
Energy supply per capita (Gigajoules)	15	16	17 [b]
Tourist/visitor arrivals at national borders (000)	468	946	1 323 [e]
Important sites for terrestrial biodiversity protected (%)	61.0	72.0	72.0
Pop. using improved drinking water (urban/rural, %)	89.0 / 60.8	92.6 / 69.1	95.5 / 75.8 [b]
Pop. using improved sanitation facilities (urban/rural, %)	28.4 / 15.1	28.5 / 16.3	28.5 / 17.3 [b]
Net Official Development Assist. received (% of GNI)	13.66	8.52	7.00 [e]

a Projected estimate (medium fertility variant). b 2015. c Data includes Kira, Makindye Ssabagabo and Nansana. d 2017. e 2016. f Data classified according to ISIC Rev. 4. g Estimate. h Index base: 1 July 2009 - 30 June 2010=100. i Data refers to a 5-year period preceding the reference year. j Including refugees. k Data as at the end of December. l Unlike other countries, in Uganda Fiscal Years starting on July 1 and ending in June 30 are converted to the previous year and that is a special request from the country. m 2004. n 2014. o 2007.

Ukraine

Region	Eastern Europe	UN membership date	24 October 1945	
Population (000, 2018)	44 009 [a,b]	Surface area (km2)	603 500 [c]	
Pop. density (per km2, 2018)	76.0 [a,b]	Sex ratio (m per 100 f)	86.0 [a,b]	
Capital city	Kyiv	National currency	Hryvnia (UAH)	
Capital city pop. (000, 2018)	2 956.7	Exchange rate (per US$)	28.1 [d]	

Economic indicators

	2005	2010	2018
GDP: Gross domestic product (million current US$)	89 239	136 012 [e]	93 270 [e,f]
GDP growth rate (annual %, const. 2010 prices)	3.1	0.3 [e]	2.3 [e,f]
GDP per capita (current US$)	1 903.0	2 970.0 [e]	2 099.0 [e,f]
Economy: Agriculture (% of Gross Value Added) [g]	10.0	8.4 [e]	13.7 [e,f]
Economy: Industry (% of Gross Value Added) [g]	34.1	29.3 [e]	27.1 [e,f]
Economy: Services and other activity (% of GVA) [g]	55.8	62.3 [e]	59.2 [e,f]
Employment in agriculture (% of employed) [h]	19.4	20.3	14.4
Employment in industry (% of employed) [h]	26.0	25.7	25.7
Employment in services & other sectors (% employed) [h]	54.6	54.0	59.9
Unemployment rate (% of labour force)	7.2	8.1	9.0 [h]
Labour force participation rate (female/male pop. %) [h]	48.5 / 62.9	48.4 / 63.0	46.6 / 62.7
CPI: Consumer Price Index (2010=100)	51	100	235 [d]
Agricultural production index (2004-2006=100)	100	107	153 [f]
Index of industrial production (2005=100) [i]	100	94	99 [j]
International trade: exports (million current US$)	34 228	51 430	43 428 [d]
International trade: imports (million current US$)	36 122	60 737	49 439 [d]
International trade: balance (million current US$)	- 1 894	- 9 307	- 6 011 [d]
Balance of payments, current account (million US$)	2 534	- 3 016	- 2 088 [d]

Major trading partners

						2017
Export partners (% of exports)	Russian Federation	9.1	Poland	6.3 [h]	Turkey	5.8
Import partners (% of imports)	Russian Federation	14.6	China	11.4	Germany	10.5

Social indicators

	2005	2010	2018
Population growth rate (average annual %) [a,k]	- 0.6	- 0.5	- 0.5 [c]
Urban population (% of total population) [a]	67.8	68.6	69.4
Urban population growth rate (average annual %) [a,k]	- 0.6	- 0.2	- 0.4 [c]
Fertility rate, total (live births per woman) [a,k]	1.1	1.4	1.5 [c]
Life expectancy at birth (females/males, years) [a,k]	73.4 / 61.8	73.8 / 62.2	76.0 / 66.1 [c]
Population age distribution (0-14/60+ years old, %) [a]	14.6 / 20.4	14.1 / 21.0	15.8 / 23.5 [b]
International migrant stock (000/% of total pop.) [a]	5 050.3 / 10.8	4 818.8 / 10.5	4 964.3 / 11.2 [d]
Refugees and others of concern to the UNHCR (000)	76.9 [l]	46.4 [l]	1 845.0 [d]
Infant mortality rate (per 1 000 live births) [a,k]	14.8	12.6	8.8 [c]
Health: Current expenditure (% of GDP) [e]	6.1	6.4	6.1 [c]
Health: Physicians (per 1 000 pop.)	...	3.5	3.0 [m]
Education: Government expenditure (% of GDP)	6.1	7.3 [n]	5.9 [m]
Education: Primary gross enrol. ratio (f/m per 100 pop.)	106.2 / 106.6	99.1 / 98.5	100.9 / 98.9 [m]
Education: Secondary gross enrol. ratio (f/m per 100 pop.)	91.8 / 99.2 [h]	94.3 / 96.7 [h]	95.7 / 97.8 [m]
Education: Tertiary gross enrol. ratio (f/m per 100 pop.)	78.0 / 63.1	89.5 / 71.2	89.5 / 77.6 [m]
Intentional homicide rate (per 100 000 pop.)	6.5	4.3	6.3 [m]
Seats held by women in the National Parliament (%)	5.3	8.0	12.3

Environment and infrastructure indicators

	2005	2010	2018
Individuals using the Internet (per 100 inhabitants)	3.7 [h,o,p]	23.3	52.5 [h,i]
Research & Development expenditure (% of GDP)	1.0	0.8	0.6 [q,c]
Threatened species (number)	55 [r]	61	102 [d]
Forested area (% of land area)	16.5	16.5	16.7 [h,c]
CO2 emission estimates (million tons/tons per capita)	333.9 / 7.1	304.6 / 6.7	227.3 / 5.1 [m]
Energy production, primary (Petajoules)	3 328	3 238	2 552 [c]
Energy supply per capita (Gigajoules)	125	120	84 [c]
Tourist/visitor arrivals at national borders (000)	17 631	21 203	13 333 [f]
Important sites for terrestrial biodiversity protected (%)	23.3	23.3	23.7
Pop. using improved drinking water (urban/rural, %)	98.4 / 94.6	97.0 / 96.2	95.5 / 97.8 [c]
Pop. using improved sanitation facilities (urban/rural, %)	97.2 / 90.7	97.3 / 91.8	97.4 / 92.6 [c]
Net Official Development Assist. received (% of GNI)	0.48	0.49	1.65 [f]

a Including Crimea. **b** Projected estimate (medium fertility variant). **c** 2015. **d** 2017. **e** Excludes the temporarily occupied territory of the Autonomous Republic of Crimea and Sevastopol. **f** 2016. **g** Data classified according to ISIC Rev. 4. **h** Estimate. **i** Data classified according to ISIC Rev. 3. **j** 2012. **k** Data refers to a 5-year period preceding the reference year. **l** Data as at the end of December. **m** 2014. **n** 2009. **o** Population aged 15 to 59 years. **p** Users in the last month. **q** Excluding data from some regions, provinces or states. **r** 2004.

United Arab Emirates

Region	Western Asia	UN membership date	09 December 1971
Population (000, 2018)	9 542[a]	Surface area (km2)	83 600[b]
Pop. density (per km2, 2018)	114.1[a]	Sex ratio (m per 100 f)	257.9[a]
Capital city	Abu Dhabi	National currency	UAE Dirham (AED)[c]
Capital city pop. (000, 2018)	1 419.7	Exchange rate (per US$)	3.7[d]

Economic indicators

	2005	2010	2018
GDP: Gross domestic product (million current US$)	182 978	289 787	348 744[e]
GDP growth rate (annual %, const. 2010 prices)	4.9	1.6	3.0[e]
GDP per capita (current US$)	39 955.0	35 038.0	37 622.0[e]
Economy: Agriculture (% of Gross Value Added)[f]	1.3	0.8	0.8[e]
Economy: Industry (% of Gross Value Added)[f]	54.0	52.5	40.2[e]
Economy: Services and other activity (% of GVA)[f]	44.7	46.7	59.0[e]
Employment in agriculture (% of employed)[g]	4.9	0.8	0.3
Employment in industry (% of employed)[g]	40.1	29.3	38.7
Employment in services & other sectors (% employed)[g]	55.0	69.9	61.0
Unemployment rate (% of labour force)	3.1	3.8[g]	1.8[g]
Labour force participation rate (female/male pop. %)[g]	37.2 / 92.5	42.9 / 93.3	40.6 / 91.7
CPI: Consumer Price Index (2010=100)	...	100[h]	113[d]
Agricultural production index (2004-2006=100)	106	108	101[e]
International trade: exports (million current US$)	115 453	198 362	220 453[g,d]
International trade: imports (million current US$)	80 814	187 001	237 797[g,d]
International trade: balance (million current US$)	34 639	11 361	- 17 345[g,d]

Major trading partners

						2017
Export partners (% of exports)[g]	Areas nes[i]	51.4	Asia nes[j]	13.9	India	3.8
Import partners (% of imports)[g]	Areas nes[i]	30.2	China	8.3	United States	7.6

Social indicators

	2005	2010	2018
Population growth rate (average annual %)[k]	7.5	11.8	2.0[b]
Urban population (% of total population)	82.3	84.1	86.5
Urban population growth rate (average annual %)[k]	8.0	12.3	2.4[b]
Fertility rate, total (live births per woman)[k]	2.4	2.0	1.8[b]
Life expectancy at birth (females/males, years)[k]	76.3 / 74.1	77.3 / 75.2	78.2 / 76.0[b]
Population age distribution (0-14/60+ years old, %)	18.4 / 1.7	13.4 / 1.5	13.9 / 2.6[a]
International migrant stock (000/% of total pop.)[i,m]	3 281.0 / 71.6	7 316.6 / 88.5	8 312.5 / 88.4[d]
Refugees and others of concern to the UNHCR (000)	0.2[n]	0.6[n]	1.7[d]
Infant mortality rate (per 1 000 live births)[k]	9.2	6.9	6.2[b]
Health: Current expenditure (% of GDP)	2.3	3.9	3.5[b]
Health: Physicians (per 1 000 pop.)	1.6	1.5	1.6[o]
Education: Primary gross enrol. ratio (f/m per 100 pop.)	... / ...	98.9 / 96.9	108.9 / 112.8[e]
Education: Secondary gross enrol. ratio (f/m per 100 pop.)	... / ...	... / ...	93.0 / 98.6[e]
Education: Tertiary gross enrol. ratio (f/m per 100 pop.)	... / ...	29.9 / 10.7	53.2 / 26.7[e]
Intentional homicide rate (per 100 000 pop.)	1.2	0.8	0.9[e]
Seats held by women in the National Parliament (%)	0.0	22.5	22.5

Environment and infrastructure indicators

	2005	2010	2018
Individuals using the Internet (per 100 inhabitants)	40.0[g]	68.0	90.6[p,q,e]
Research & Development expenditure (% of GDP)	...	...	0.9[b]
Threatened species (number)	23[r]	48	56[d]
Forested area (% of land area)[g]	3.7	3.8	3.9[b]
CO2 emission estimates (million tons/tons per capita)	116.1 / 28.5	160.8 / 19.3	211.4 / 23.2[o]
Energy production, primary (Petajoules)	7 293	7 496	9 682[b]
Energy supply per capita (Gigajoules)	453	316	392[b]
Tourist/visitor arrivals at national borders (000)	7 126[s]	...	...
Important sites for terrestrial biodiversity protected (%)	0.0	13.2	30.8
Pop. using improved drinking water (urban/rural, %)	99.6 / 100.0	99.6 / 100.0	99.6 / 100.0[b]
Pop. using improved sanitation facilities (urban/rural, %)	98.0 / 95.2	98.0 / 95.2	98.0 / 95.2[b]
Net Official Development Assist. disbursed (% of GNI)[t]	...	0.14	1.31[u,d]

a Projected estimate (medium fertility variant). **b** 2015. **c** United Arab Emirates Dirham. **d** 2017. **e** 2016. **f** At producers' prices. **g** Estimate. **h** Break in the time series. **i** Areas not elsewhere specified. **j** Asia not elsewhere specified. **k** Data refers to a 5-year period preceding the reference year. **l** Refers to foreign citizens. **m** Including refugees. **n** Data as at the end of December. **o** 2014. **p** Population aged 15 to 74 years. **q** Users in the last 3 months. **r** 2004. **s** Arrivals in hotels only. Including domestic tourism and nationals of the country residing abroad. **t** Data reported at activity level, represent flows from all government agencies. Commitments are set equal to disbursements for agencies other than the Abu Dhabi Fund for Development. **u** Provisional data.

United Kingdom

Region	Northern Europe	UN membership date	24 October 1945
Population (000, 2018)	66 574[a]	Surface area (km2)	242 495[b]
Pop. density (per km2, 2018)	275.2[a]	Sex ratio (m per 100 f)	97.5[a]
Capital city	London	National currency	Pound Sterling (GBP)
Capital city pop. (000, 2018)	9 046.5[c]	Exchange rate (per US$)	0.7[d]

Economic indicators

	2005	2010	2018
GDP: Gross domestic product (million current US$)	2 520 709	2 441 173	2 647 899[e]
GDP growth rate (annual %, const. 2010 prices)	3.1	1.7	1.8[e]
GDP per capita (current US$)	41 812.0	38 561.0	40 249.0[e]
Economy: Agriculture (% of Gross Value Added)[f]	0.6	0.7	0.6[e]
Economy: Industry (% of Gross Value Added)[f]	21.9	20.0	20.2[e]
Economy: Services and other activity (% of GVA)[f]	77.5	79.3	79.2[e]
Employment in agriculture (% of employed)[g]	1.4	1.2[g]	1.1[g]
Employment in industry (% of employed)[g]	22.2	19.2	18.2
Employment in services & other sectors (% employed)[g]	76.4	79.6	80.7
Unemployment rate (% of labour force)	4.8	7.8	4.2[g]
Labour force participation rate (female/male pop. %)[g]	54.7 / 69.2	55.5 / 68.6	56.9 / 68.1
CPI: Consumer Price Index (2010=100)[h]	87	100	116[e]
Agricultural production index (2004-2006=100)	100	102	103[e]
Index of industrial production (2005=100)	100	92	90[i]
International trade: exports (million current US$)	392 744	422 014	443 734[d]
International trade: imports (million current US$)	528 461	627 618	640 365[d]
International trade: balance (million current US$)	- 135 717	- 205 603	- 196 631[d]
Balance of payments, current account (million US$)	- 52 165	- 92 499	- 106 505[d]

Major trading partners

						2017
Export partners (% of exports)	United States	13.3	Germany	10.5	France	7.4
Import partners (% of imports)	Germany	13.9	China	9.3	United States	9.2

Social indicators

	2005	2010	2018
Population growth rate (average annual %)[j]	0.4	1.0	0.6[b]
Urban population (% of total population)	79.9	81.3	83.4
Urban population growth rate (average annual %)[j]	0.8	1.3	1.0[b]
Fertility rate, total (live births per woman)[j]	1.7	1.9	1.9[b]
Life expectancy at birth (females/males, years)[j]	80.6 / 76.1	81.8 / 77.5	82.8 / 79.0[b]
Population age distribution (0-14/60+ years old, %)	18.0 / 21.2	17.5 / 22.7	17.8 / 24.2[a]
International migrant stock (000/% of total pop.)	5 926.2 / 9.8	7 604.6 / 12.0	8 841.7 / 13.4[d]
Refugees and others of concern to the UNHCR (000)	316.6[k]	253.3[k]	152.7[d]
Infant mortality rate (per 1 000 live births)[j]	5.3	4.8	4.1[b]
Health: Current expenditure (% of GDP)	7.2	8.5	9.9[b]
Health: Physicians (per 1 000 pop.)	...	2.7	2.8[b]
Education: Government expenditure (% of GDP)	5.0	5.8	5.6[b]
Education: Primary gross enrol. ratio (f/m per 100 pop.)	106.2 / 106.3	104.5 / 105.0	101.8 / 102.0[b]
Education: Secondary gross enrol. ratio (f/m per 100 pop.)	107.0 / 103.9	103.2 / 102.9	127.5 / 123.6[b]
Education: Tertiary gross enrol. ratio (f/m per 100 pop.)	68.9 / 49.5	67.9 / 50.7	65.8 / 49.2[b]
Intentional homicide rate (per 100 000 pop.)	1.4	1.2	1.2[e]
Seats held by women in the National Parliament (%)	18.1	19.5	32.0

Environment and infrastructure indicators

	2005	2010	2018
Individuals using the Internet (per 100 inhabitants)	70.0[i]	85.0[i]	94.8[e]
Research & Development expenditure (% of GDP)	1.6	1.7[g]	1.7[g,b]
Threatened species (number)	55[m]	73	102[d]
Forested area (% of land area)	12.5	12.6	13.0[g,b]
CO2 emission estimates (million tons/tons per capita)	542.6 / 9.0	493.2 / 7.8	419.8 / 6.5[i]
Energy production, primary (Petajoules)[n]	8 483	6 217	4 926[b]
Energy supply per capita (Gigajoules)[n]	153	135	116[b]
Tourist/visitor arrivals at national borders (000)	28 039	28 295	35 814[e]
Important sites for terrestrial biodiversity protected (%)	81.7	83.8	84.4
Pop. using improved drinking water (urban/rural, %)	100.0 / 100.0	100.0 / 100.0	100.0 / 100.0[b]
Pop. using improved sanitation facilities (urban/rural, %)	99.1 / 99.6	99.1 / 99.6	99.1 / 99.6[b]
Net Official Development Assist. disbursed (% of GNI)[o]	0.47	0.57	0.70[p,d]

a Projected estimate (medium fertility variant). b 2015. c Data refer to "Urban area" (Greater London). d 2017. e 2016. f Data classified according to ISIC Rev. 4. g Estimate. h Calculated by the Statistics Division of the United Nations from national indices. i 2014. j Data refers to a 5-year period preceding the reference year. k Data as at the end of December. l Population aged 16 to 74 years. m 2004. n Shipments of coal and oil to Jersey, Guernsey and the Isle of Man from the United Kingdom are not classed as exports. Supplies of coal and oil to these islands are, therefore, included as part of UK supply. Exports of natural gas to the Isle of Man included with the exports to Ireland. o Development Assistance Committee member (OECD). p Provisional data.

United Republic of Tanzania

Region	Eastern Africa	UN membership date	14 December 1961
Population (000, 2018)	59 091 [a,b]	Surface area (km2)	947 303 [c]
Pop. density (per km2, 2018)	66.7 [a,b]	Sex ratio (m per 100 f)	97.9 [a,b]
Capital city	Dodoma	National currency	Tanzanian Shilling (TZS)
Capital city pop. (000, 2018)	261.6	Exchange rate (per US$)	2 230.1 [d]

Economic indicators

	2005	2010	2018
GDP: Gross domestic product (million current US$) [e]	18 072	31 105	47 653 [f]
GDP growth rate (annual %, const. 2010 prices) [e]	7.4	6.4	7.0 [f]
GDP per capita (current US$) [e]	471.0	694.0	881.0 [f]
Economy: Agriculture (% of Gross Value Added) [e,g]	30.1	31.7	31.2 [f]
Economy: Industry (% of Gross Value Added) [e,g]	20.8	21.5	27.0 [f]
Economy: Services and other activity (% of GVA) [e,g]	49.1	46.8	41.9 [f]
Employment in agriculture (% of employed) [h]	74.7	72.2	66.0
Employment in industry (% of employed) [h]	4.8	5.4	6.0
Employment in services & other sectors (% employed) [h]	20.5	22.4	28.0
Unemployment rate (% of labour force) [h]	4.4	3.0	2.3
Labour force participation rate (female/male pop. %) [h]	81.8 / 84.4	81.9 / 84.4	79.4 / 87.5
CPI: Consumer Price Index (2010=100) [e]	66	100	175 [f]
Agricultural production index (2004-2006=100)	98	128	165 [f]
International trade: exports (million current US$)	1 672	4 051	4 500 [h,d]
International trade: imports (million current US$)	3 247	8 013	7 706 [h,d]
International trade: balance (million current US$)	- 1 575	- 3 962	- 3 206 [h,d]
Balance of payments, current account (million US$)	- 1 093	- 2 211 [i]	- 2 009 [f]

Major trading partners

						2017
Export partners (% of exports)	Switzerland	16.2 [h]	India	14.8	South Africa	13.3 [h]
Import partners (% of imports) [h]	China	20.8	India	18.1	United Arab Emirates	7.5

Social indicators

	2005	2010	2018
Population growth rate (average annual %) [b,i]	2.8	3.1	3.1 [c]
Urban population (% of total population) [b]	24.8	28.1	33.8
Urban population growth rate (average annual %) [b,j]	5.0	5.6	5.5 [c]
Fertility rate, total (live births per woman) [b,j]	5.7	5.6	5.2 [c]
Life expectancy at birth (females/males, years) [b,j]	55.4 / 52.0	60.1 / 57.5	64.8 / 60.8 [c]
Population age distribution (0-14/60+ years old, %) [b]	45.3 / 4.6	45.3 / 4.7	44.7 / 4.7 [a]
International migrant stock (000/% of total pop.) [b,k]	770.8 / 2.0	308.6 / 0.7	492.6 / 0.9 [d]
Refugees and others of concern to the UNHCR (000)	630.6 [l]	273.8 [l]	511.9 [d]
Infant mortality rate (per 1 000 live births) [b,j]	67.1	52.4	44.0 [c]
Health: Current expenditure (% of GDP)	...	...	6.1 [e,m,c]
Health: Physicians (per 1 000 pop.)	~0.0 [n]	...	~0.0 [o]
Education: Government expenditure (% of GDP)	4.6	4.6	3.5 [o]
Education: Primary gross enrol. ratio (f/m per 100 pop.)	99.7 / 104.9	97.7 / 97.1	82.0 / 79.5 [c]
Education: Secondary gross enrol. ratio (f/m per 100 pop.)	... / ...	27.1 / 34.3	30.3 / 33.1 [p]
Education: Tertiary gross enrol. ratio (f/m per 100 pop.)	0.9 / 2.0 [h]	1.9 / 2.4	2.7 / 5.2 [c]
Intentional homicide rate (per 100 000 pop.)	7.6 [q]	8.4	7.0 [c]
Seats held by women in the National Parliament (%)	21.4	30.7	37.2

Environment and infrastructure indicators

	2005	2010	2018
Individuals using the Internet (per 100 inhabitants) [h]	1.1	2.9	13.0 [c]
Research & Development expenditure (% of GDP) [s]	...	0.4 [r]	0.5 [p]
Threatened species (number)	416 [q]	691	1 082 [d]
Forested area (% of land area)	56.4	54.1 [h]	52.0 [h,c]
CO2 emission estimates (million tons/tons per capita)	5.5 / 0.1	7.1 / 0.1	11.6 / 0.2 [o]
Energy production, primary (Petajoules)	665	782	958 [c]
Energy supply per capita (Gigajoules)	19	19	20 [c]
Tourist/visitor arrivals at national borders (000)	590	754	1 233 [f]
Important sites for terrestrial biodiversity protected (%)	52.5	57.0	57.0
Pop. using improved drinking water (urban/rural, %)	83.0 / 45.4	80.1 / 45.5	77.2 / 45.5 [c]
Pop. using improved sanitation facilities (urban/rural, %)	21.3 / 7.6	26.3 / 7.9	31.3 / 8.3 [c]
Net Official Development Assist. received (% of GNI)	9.00	9.53	4.96 [f]

a Projected estimate (medium fertility variant). **b** Including Zanzibar. **c** 2015. **d** 2017. **e** Tanzania mainland only, excluding Zanzibar. **f** 2016. **g** Data classified according to ISIC Rev. 4. **h** Estimate. **i** Break in the time series. **j** Data refers to a 5-year period preceding the reference year. **k** Including refugees. **l** Data as at the end of December. **m** Data revision. **n** 2002. **o** 2014. **p** 2013. **q** 2004. **r** Partial data. **s** Excluding business enterprise.

United States of America

Region	Northern America	UN membership date	24 October 1945
Population (000, 2018)	326 767 [a]	Surface area (km2)	9 833 517 [b]
Pop. density (per km2, 2018)	35.7 [a]	Sex ratio (m per 100 f)	98.0 [a]
Capital city	Washington, D.C.	National currency	US Dollar (USD)
Capital city pop. (000, 2018)	5 206.6		

Economic indicators	2005	2010	2018
GDP: Gross domestic product (million current US$)	13 093 726	14 964 372	18 624 475 [d]
GDP growth rate (annual %, const. 2010 prices)	3.3	2.5	1.5 [d]
GDP per capita (current US$)	44 366.0	48 485.0	57 808.0 [d]
Economy: Agriculture (% of Gross Value Added) [e,f]	1.0	1.1	1.0 [d]
Economy: Industry (% of Gross Value Added) [e,f]	21.5	20.2	19.2 [d]
Economy: Services and other activity (% of GVA) [e,f]	77.5	78.8	79.9 [d]
Employment in agriculture (% of employed) [g]	1.6	1.6	1.6
Employment in industry (% of employed) [g]	21.0	18.5	18.8
Employment in services & other sectors (% employed) [g]	77.4	79.9	79.6
Unemployment rate (% of labour force)	5.1	9.6	4.3 [g]
Labour force participation rate (female/male pop. %) [g]	58.2 / 72.2	57.5 / 69.9	55.5 / 68.0
CPI: Consumer Price Index (2010=100) [h]	90	100	112 [c]
Agricultural production index (2004-2006=100)	100	106	117 [d]
Index of industrial production (2005=100)	100	96 [i]	108 [i,j]
International trade: exports (million current US$) [k]	904 339	1 278 099	1 546 069 [c]
International trade: imports (million current US$) [k]	1 732 321	1 968 260	2 408 395 [c]
International trade: balance (million current US$) [k]	- 827 981	- 690 161	- 862 326 [c]
Balance of payments, current account (million US$)	- 745 246	- 430 702	- 466 248 [c]

Major trading partners						2017
Export partners (% of exports)	Canada	18.2	Mexico	15.7	China	8.4
Import partners (% of imports)	China	21.8	Mexico	13.2	Canada	12.7

Social indicators	2005	2010	2018
Population growth rate (average annual %) [l]	0.9	0.9	0.7 [b]
Urban population (% of total population)	79.9	80.8	82.3
Urban population growth rate (average annual %) [l]	1.1	1.1	0.9 [b]
Fertility rate, total (live births per woman) [l]	2.0	2.0	1.9 [b]
Life expectancy at birth (females/males, years) [l]	79.7 / 74.5	80.6 / 75.6	81.2 / 76.5 [b]
Population age distribution (0-14/60+ years old, %)	20.9 / 16.7	20.2 / 18.4	18.8 / 22.0 [a]
International migrant stock (000/% of total pop.)	39 258.3 / 13.3	44 183.6 / 14.3	49 777.0 / 15.3 [c]
Refugees and others of concern to the UNHCR (000)	549.2 [m]	270.9 [m]	971.5 [n,c]
Infant mortality rate (per 1 000 live births) [l]	7.0	6.8	6.0 [b]
Health: Current expenditure (% of GDP)	14.5	16.4	16.8 [b]
Health: Physicians (per 1 000 pop.)	2.7 [o]	2.4	2.6 [i]
Education: Government expenditure (% of GDP)	...	5.4	5.0 [i]
Education: Primary gross enrol. ratio (f/m per 100 pop.)	98.1 / 99.2	99.2 / 100.1	99.4 / 99.2 [b]
Education: Secondary gross enrol. ratio (f/m per 100 pop.)	95.5 / 93.6	93.6 / 92.5	97.7 / 96.7 [b]
Intentional homicide rate (per 100 000 pop.)	5.7	4.8	5.4 [d]
Seats held by women in the National Parliament (%)	14.9	16.8	19.5

Environment and infrastructure indicators	2005	2010	2018
Individuals using the Internet (per 100 inhabitants)	68.0 [g]	71.7 [p]	76.2 [g,d]
Research & Development expenditure (% of GDP) [q]	2.5	2.7	2.8 [r,b]
Threatened species (number)	1 143 [o]	1 152	1 513 [c]
Forested area (% of land area)	33.3	33.7	33.9 [g,b]
CO2 emission estimates (million tons/tons per capita) [s]	5 789.7 / 19.3	5 395.5 / 17.2	5 254.3 / 16.2 [i]
Energy production, primary (Petajoules) [t]	68 124	71 882	84 007 [b]
Energy supply per capita (Gigajoules) [t]	325	297	282 [b]
Tourist/visitor arrivals at national borders (000)	49 206	60 010	75 608 [u,d]
Pop. using improved drinking water (urban/rural, %)	99.5 / 96.7	99.4 / 97.6	99.4 / 98.2 [b]
Pop. using improved sanitation facilities (urban/rural, %)	99.9 / 99.6	100.0 / 99.9	100.0 / 100.0 [b]
Net Official Development Assist. disbursed (% of GNI) [v]	0.23	0.20	0.18 [r,c]

a Projected estimate (medium fertility variant). b 2015. c 2017. d 2016. e Including taxes less subsidies on production and imports. f Data classified according to ISIC Rev. 4. g Estimate. h Urban areas. i Excluding water and waste management. j 2014. k Including the trade of the U.S. Virgin Islands and Puerto Rico but excluding shipments of merchandise between the United States and its other possessions (Guam and American Samoa). Data include imports and exports of non-monetary gold. l Data refers to a 5-year period preceding the reference year. m Data as at the end of December. n Pending asylum applications for U.S. Citizenship and Immigration Services at start-2017 and mid-2017 are multiplied by inflation factor (1.518). o 2004. p Population aged 3 years and over. q Excluding most or all capital expenditures. r Provisional data. s Including overseas territories. t Oil and coal trade statistics include overseas territories. u Break in the time series. v Development Assistance Committee member (OECD).

United States Virgin Islands

Region	Caribbean	Population (000, 2018)	105[a]
Surface area (km2)	347[b]	Pop. density (per km2, 2018)	299.8[a]
Sex ratio (m per 100 f)	91.0[a]	Capital city	Charlotte Amalie
National currency	US Dollar (USD)	Capital city pop. (000, 2018)	52.3

Economic indicators	2005	2010	2018
Employment in agriculture (% of employed)[c]	2.3	2.2	2.7
Employment in industry (% of employed)[c]	11.0	11.1	11.7
Employment in services & other sectors (% employed)[c]	86.7	86.7	85.6
Unemployment rate (% of labour force)[c]	7.7	7.3	7.0
Labour force participation rate (female/male pop. %)[c]	60.1 / 70.0	59.4 / 68.4	57.0 / 64.2
Agricultural production index (2004-2006=100)	99	107	107[d]

Social indicators	2005	2010	2018
Population growth rate (average annual %)[e]	- 0.2	- 0.3	- 0.2[b]
Urban population (% of total population)	93.7	94.6	95.7
Urban population growth rate (average annual %)[e]	0.1	- 0.1	- 0.1[b]
Fertility rate, total (live births per woman)[e]	2.1	2.4	2.3[b]
Life expectancy at birth (females/males, years)[e]	79.5 / 74.9	80.3 / 75.5	81.5 / 76.7[b]
Population age distribution (0-14/60+ years old, %)	22.4 / 16.6	20.8 / 20.4	20.0 / 26.0[a]
International migrant stock (000/% of total pop.)	56.6 / 52.6	56.7 / 53.4	56.7 / 54.1[f]
Infant mortality rate (per 1 000 live births)[e]	11.6	10.7	9.3[b]
Intentional homicide rate (per 100 000 pop.)	34.3	52.8	49.3[g]

Environment and infrastructure indicators	2005	2010	2018
Individuals using the Internet (per 100 inhabitants)[c]	27.3	31.2	59.6[d]
Threatened species (number)	31[h]	33	58[f]
Forested area (% of land area)	53.5	51.9	50.3[b]
Energy production, primary (Petajoules)	...	...	0[c,b]
Energy supply per capita (Gigajoules)	...	...	1[c,b]
Tourist/visitor arrivals at national borders (000)	594	572	642[b]
Important sites for terrestrial biodiversity protected (%)	33.1	34.0	39.4
Pop. using improved drinking water (urban/rural, %)	100.0 / 100.0	100.0 / 100.0	100.0 / 100.0[b]
Pop. using improved sanitation facilities (urban/rural, %)	96.4 / 96.4	96.4 / 96.4	96.4 / 96.4[b]

a Projected estimate (medium fertility variant). b 2015. c Estimate. d 2016. e Data refers to a 5-year period preceding the reference year. f 2017. g 2012. h 2004.

Uruguay

Region	South America	UN membership date	18 December 1945
Population (000, 2018)	3 470 [a]	Surface area (km2)	173 626 [b]
Pop. density (per km2, 2018)	19.8 [a]	Sex ratio (m per 100 f)	93.5 [a]
Capital city	Montevideo	National currency	Peso Uruguayo (UYU)
Capital city pop. (000, 2018)	1 737.0 [c]	Exchange rate (per US$)	28.8 [d]

Economic indicators	2005	2010	2018	
GDP: Gross domestic product (million current US$)	17 363	40 285	52 420 [e]	
GDP growth rate (annual %, const. 2010 prices)	7.5	7.8	1.5 [e]	
GDP per capita (current US$)	5 221.0	11 938.0	15 221.0 [e]	
Economy: Agriculture (% of Gross Value Added)	9.8	8.0	6.6 [e]	
Economy: Industry (% of Gross Value Added)	26.6	27.3	27.8 [e]	
Economy: Services and other activity (% of GVA)	63.6	64.7	65.6 [e]	
Employment in agriculture (% of employed)	5.7 [f]	11.6	8.0 [f]	
Employment in industry (% of employed) [f]	22.9	21.4	19.8	
Employment in services & other sectors (% employed) [f]	71.4	67.0	72.2	
Unemployment rate (% of labour force)	12.2	7.2	8.3 [f]	
Labour force participation rate (female/male pop. %) [f]	52.5 / 74.4	55.3 / 76.7	56.3 / 74.6	
CPI: Consumer Price Index (2010=100) [g]	71	100	175 [d]	
Agricultural production index (2004-2006=100)	101	119	118 [d]	
International trade: exports (million current US$)	3 422	6 724	7 889 [d]	
International trade: imports (million current US$)	3 879	8 622	8 458 [d]	
International trade: balance (million current US$)	- 457	- 1 898	- 568 [d]	
Balance of payments, current account (million US$)	42	- 731	926 [d]	

Major trading partners						2017
Export partners (% of exports)	China	18.8	Brazil	16.5 [f]	Free zones	16.4
Import partners (% of imports)	China	20.0	Brazil	19.5	Argentina	12.6

Social indicators	2005	2010	2018
Population growth rate (average annual %) [h]	~0.0	0.3	0.3 [b]
Urban population (% of total population)	93.3	94.4	95.3
Urban population growth rate (average annual %) [h]	0.3	0.5	0.5 [b]
Fertility rate, total (live births per woman) [h]	2.2	2.1	2.0 [b]
Life expectancy at birth (females/males, years) [h]	78.9 / 71.6	79.7 / 72.5	80.4 / 73.2 [b]
Population age distribution (0-14/60+ years old, %)	23.8 / 17.9	22.5 / 18.4	20.9 / 19.7 [a]
International migrant stock (000/% of total pop.)	82.3 / 2.5	76.3 / 2.3	79.6 / 2.3 [a]
Refugees and others of concern to the UNHCR (000)	0.1 [i]	0.2 [i]	1.1 [d]
Infant mortality rate (per 1 000 live births) [h]	14.4	13.4	12.7 [b]
Health: Current expenditure (% of GDP)	8.6	8.4	9.2 [b]
Health: Physicians (per 1 000 pop.)	3.7 [j]	3.9 [k]	...
Education: Government expenditure (% of GDP)	2.7	2.9 [j]	4.4 [m]
Education: Primary gross enrol. ratio (f/m per 100 pop.)	112.4 / 115.3	110.2 / 113.9	106.2 / 108.6 [b]
Education: Secondary gross enrol. ratio (f/m per 100 pop.)	108.5 / 94.2	96.2 / 84.6	... / ...
Education: Tertiary gross enrol. ratio (f/m per 100 pop.)	57.9 / 33.2	58.0 / 34.5 [l]	... / ...
Intentional homicide rate (per 100 000 pop.)	5.7	6.1	7.7 [e]
Seats held by women in the National Parliament (%)	12.1	14.1	20.2

Environment and infrastructure indicators	2005	2010	2018
Individuals using the Internet (per 100 inhabitants)	20.1	46.4 [n]	66.4 [e]
Research & Development expenditure (% of GDP)	0.2 [j]	0.3	0.3 [o]
Threatened species (number)	50 [p]	80	106 [b]
Forested area (% of land area)	8.7	9.9	10.5 [b]
CO2 emission estimates (million tons/tons per capita)	5.8 / 1.7	6.4 / 1.9	6.7 / 2.0 [o]
Energy production, primary (Petajoules)	45	89	126 [f,b]
Energy supply per capita (Gigajoules)	38	51	62 [b]
Tourist/visitor arrivals at national borders (000)	1 808	2 353	3 037 [e]
Important sites for terrestrial biodiversity protected (%)	10.4	20.7	20.8
Pop. using improved drinking water (urban/rural, %)	99.0 / 82.6	99.6 / 88.3	100.0 / 93.9 [b]
Pop. using improved sanitation facilities (urban/rural, %)	95.0 / 87.1	95.8 / 89.8	96.6 / 92.6 [b]
Net Official Development Assist. received (% of GNI)	0.10	0.12	0.04 [b]

a Projected estimate (medium fertility variant). b 2015. c Data refer to the department of Montevideo and localities of the departments of Canelones and San José (Cerámicas del Sur and Ciudad del Plata). d 2017. e 2016. f Estimate. g Calculated by the Statistics Division of the United Nations from national indices. h Data refers to a 5-year period preceding the reference year. i Data as at the end of December. j 2002. k 2008. l 2006. m 2011. n Population aged 6 years and over. o 2014. p 2004.

Uzbekistan

Region	Central Asia	UN membership date	02 March 1992
Population (000, 2018)	32 365[a]	Surface area (km2)	448 969[b]
Pop. density (per km2, 2018)	76.1[a]	Sex ratio (m per 100 f)	99.4[a]
Capital city	Tashkent	National currency	Uzbekistan Sum (UZS)
Capital city pop. (000, 2018)	2 464.0	Exchange rate (per US$)	8 125.0[c,d]

Economic indicators	2005	2010	2018
GDP: Gross domestic product (million current US$)	14 396	39 526	67 779[e]
GDP growth rate (annual %, const. 2010 prices)	7.0	8.5	6.0[e]
GDP per capita (current US$)	543.0	1 382.0	2 155.0[e]
Economy: Agriculture (% of Gross Value Added)	29.5	19.8	17.6[e]
Economy: Industry (% of Gross Value Added)	29.1	33.3	32.9[e]
Economy: Services and other activity (% of GVA)	41.4	46.9	49.5[e]
Employment in agriculture (% of employed)[f]	34.7	27.2	21.4
Employment in industry (% of employed)[f]	32.2	37.1	37.7
Employment in services & other sectors (% employed)[f]	33.1	35.7	40.9
Unemployment rate (% of labour force)[f]	8.3	8.2	6.9
Labour force participation rate (female/male pop. %)[f]	52.3 / 74.6	53.0 / 75.7	53.8 / 78.0
Agricultural production index (2004-2006=100)	100	127	167[e]
Index of industrial production (2005=100)[g]	100	165	175[h]
International trade: exports (million current US$)[f]	4 458	11 587	13 894[d]
International trade: imports (million current US$)[f]	3 657	8 381	12 998[d]
International trade: balance (million current US$)[f]	801	3 206	896[d]

Major trading partners						2017
Export partners (% of exports)[f]	Switzerland	37.9	China	19.2	Russian Federation	10.6
Import partners (% of imports)[f]	Russian Federation	23.7	China	19.4	Kazakhstan	11.3

Social indicators	2005	2010	2018
Population growth rate (average annual %)[i]	1.3	1.5	1.6[b]
Urban population (% of total population)	48.5	51.0	50.5
Urban population growth rate (average annual %)[i]	2.3	2.5	1.5[b]
Fertility rate, total (live births per woman)[i]	2.5	2.5	2.4[b]
Life expectancy at birth (females/males, years)[i]	71.0 / 64.5	72.2 / 66.1	73.5 / 68.1[b]
Population age distribution (0-14/60+ years old, %)	32.6 / 6.6	29.1 / 6.2	28.0 / 7.9[a]
International migrant stock (000/% of total pop.)	1 329.3 / 5.0	1 220.1 / 4.3	1 159.2 / 3.6[d]
Refugees and others of concern to the UNHCR (000)	44.5[i]	0.3[j]	86.4[d]
Infant mortality rate (per 1 000 live births)[i]	49.5	40.7	31.3[b]
Health: Current expenditure (% of GDP)	5.3	5.5	6.2[b]
Health: Physicians (per 1 000 pop.)	...	2.6	2.5[k]
Education: Primary gross enrol. ratio (f/m per 100 pop.)	96.7 / 96.8	92.8 / 94.5	102.3 / 103.9[d]
Education: Secondary gross enrol. ratio (f/m per 100 pop.)	87.3 / 89.9	89.6 / 89.6	92.4 / 93.6[d]
Education: Tertiary gross enrol. ratio (f/m per 100 pop.)	8.2 / 11.9	7.6 / 11.1	6.9 / 11.3[d]
Intentional homicide rate (per 100 000 pop.)	3.4	3.0[i]	...
Seats held by women in the National Parliament (%)	17.5	22.0	16.0

Environment and infrastructure indicators	2005	2010	2018
Individuals using the Internet (per 100 inhabitants)	3.3	15.9[f]	46.8[f,a]
Research & Development expenditure (% of GDP)	0.2	0.2	0.2[b]
Threatened species (number)	31[m]	50	59[d]
Forested area (% of land area)	7.7	7.7[f]	7.6[f,b]
CO2 emission estimates (million tons/tons per capita)	117.2 / 4.5	104.2 / 3.7	105.2 / 3.6[k]
Energy production, primary (Petajoules)	2 446	2 309	2 344[b]
Energy supply per capita (Gigajoules)	79	65	60[b]
Tourist/visitor arrivals at national borders (000)	242	975	1 969[n]
Important sites for terrestrial biodiversity protected (%)	11.7	15.9	15.9
Pop. using improved drinking water (urban/rural, %)	98.1 / 81.8	98.5 / 80.9	98.5 / 80.9[b,o]
Pop. using improved sanitation facilities (urban/rural, %)	99.2 / 96.2	100.0 / 100.0	100.0 / 100.0[b]
Net Official Development Assist. received (% of GNI)	1.18	0.58	0.67[e]

a Projected estimate (medium fertility variant). **b** 2015. **c** UN operational exchange rate. **d** 2017. **e** 2016. **f** Estimate. **g** Data classified according to ISIC Rev. 3. **h** 2011. **i** Data refers to a 5-year period preceding the reference year. **j** Data as at the end of December. **k** 2014. **l** 2008. **m** 2004. **n** 2013. **o** 2012.

Vanuatu

Region	Melanesia	UN membership date	15 September 1981
Population (000, 2018)	282[a]	Surface area (km2)	12 189[b]
Pop. density (per km2, 2018)	23.1[a]	Sex ratio (m per 100 f)	102.3[a]
Capital city	Port Vila	National currency	Vatu (VUV)
Capital city pop. (000, 2018)	52.7	Exchange rate (per US$)	107.5[c]

Economic indicators	2005	2010	2018
GDP: Gross domestic product (million current US$)	395	701	838[d]
GDP growth rate (annual %, const. 2010 prices)	5.3	1.6	4.0[d]
GDP per capita (current US$)	1 886.0	2 966.0	3 097.0[d]
Economy: Agriculture (% of Gross Value Added)[e]	24.1	21.9	27.0[d]
Economy: Industry (% of Gross Value Added)[e]	8.5	13.0	9.6[d]
Economy: Services and other activity (% of GVA)[e]	67.4	65.0	63.5[d]
Employment in agriculture (% of employed)[f]	64.2	61.4	64.7
Employment in industry (% of employed)[f]	5.5	6.9	6.0
Employment in services & other sectors (% employed)[f]	30.3	31.7	29.4
Unemployment rate (% of labour force)[f]	5.6	5.4	5.2
Labour force participation rate (female/male pop. %)[f]	61.5 / 79.1	61.2 / 79.5	61.5 / 79.7
CPI: Consumer Price Index (2010=100)	84	100	108[d]
Agricultural production index (2004-2006=100)	100	128	124[d]
International trade: exports (million current US$)	38[f]	46	38[f,c]
International trade: imports (million current US$)	149[f]	276	313[f,c]
International trade: balance (million current US$)	- 111[f]	- 230	- 275[f,c]
Balance of payments, current account (million US$)	- 34	- 42[g]	- 82[b]

Major trading partners						2017
Export partners (% of exports)	Mauritania	28.4[f]	Japan	27.9	Philippines	8.1[f]
Import partners (% of imports)[f]	China	18.0	Australia	14.9	New Zealand	8.7

Social indicators	2005	2010	2018
Population growth rate (average annual %)[h]	2.5	2.4	2.3[b]
Urban population (% of total population)	23.1	24.5	25.3
Urban population growth rate (average annual %)[h]	3.7	3.6	2.7[b]
Fertility rate, total (live births per woman)[h]	4.1	3.6	3.4[b]
Life expectancy at birth (females/males, years)[h]	70.3 / 66.7	72.1 / 68.2	73.6 / 69.4[b]
Population age distribution (0-14/60+ years old, %)	39.7 / 5.2	38.2 / 5.7	35.8 / 6.8[a]
International migrant stock (000/% of total pop.)	2.8 / 1.3	3.0 / 1.3	3.2 / 1.2[b]
Refugees and others of concern to the UNHCR (000)	...	~0.0[i]	~0.0[b]
Infant mortality rate (per 1 000 live births)[h]	34.6	28.6	24.3[b]
Health: Current expenditure (% of GDP)[j]	1.9	2.8	3.5[b]
Health: Physicians (per 1 000 pop.)	0.1[k]	0.1[l]	0.2[m]
Education: Government expenditure (% of GDP)	8.4[n]	5.0[o]	5.5[b]
Education: Primary gross enrol. ratio (f/m per 100 pop.)	116.1 / 119.2	121.9 / 123.0	118.7 / 120.7[b]
Education: Secondary gross enrol. ratio (f/m per 100 pop.)	39.5 / 45.8[k]	59.5 / 59.6	56.4 / 53.4[b]
Education: Tertiary gross enrol. ratio (f/m per 100 pop.)	3.5 / 5.9[f,k]	... / ...	... / ...
Intentional homicide rate (per 100 000 pop.)	2.5	2.3	2.1[b]
Seats held by women in the National Parliament (%)	3.8	3.8	0.0

Environment and infrastructure indicators	2005	2010	2018
Individuals using the Internet (per 100 inhabitants)	5.1	8.0	24.0[f,d]
Threatened species (number)	29[k]	121	137[c]
Forested area (% of land area)[f]	36.1	36.1	36.1[b]
CO2 emission estimates (million tons/tons per capita)	0.1 / 0.3	0.1 / 0.5	0.2 / 0.6[p]
Energy production, primary (Petajoules)	1	1	1[b]
Energy supply per capita (Gigajoules)	8	11	11[b]
Tourist/visitor arrivals at national borders (000)	62	97	95[d]
Important sites for terrestrial biodiversity protected (%)	6.4	6.4	6.4
Pop. using improved drinking water (urban/rural, %)	96.8 / 77.8	97.8 / 85.4	98.9 / 92.9[b]
Pop. using improved sanitation facilities (urban/rural, %)	59.3 / 46.0	64.1 / 53.8	65.1 / 55.4[b]
Net Official Development Assist. received (% of GNI)	10.81	15.96	12.32[p]

a Projected estimate (medium fertility variant). b 2015. c 2017. d 2016. e Data classified according to ISIC Rev. 4. f Estimate. g Break in the time series. h Data refers to a 5-year period preceding the reference year. i Data as at the end of December. j Government expenditures show fluctuations due to variations in capital investment. k 2004. l 2008. m 2012. n 2003. o 2009. p 2014.

Venezuela (Bolivarian Republic of)

Region	South America	UN membership date	15 November 1945
Population (000, 2018)	32 381 [a]	Surface area (km2)	912 050 [b]
Pop. density (per km2, 2018)	36.7 [a]	Sex ratio (m per 100 f)	98.9 [a]
Capital city	Caracas	National currency	Bolívar (VEF)
Capital city pop. (000, 2018)	2 934.6 [c]	Exchange rate (per US$)	10.0 [d]

Economic indicators

	2005	2010	2018
GDP: Gross domestic product (million current US$)	145 514	393 806	291 376 [e]
GDP growth rate (annual %, const. 2010 prices)	10.3	- 1.5	- 16.5 [e]
GDP per capita (current US$)	5 433.0	13 566.0	9 230.0 [e]
Economy: Agriculture (% of Gross Value Added)	4.0	5.7	5.6 [e]
Economy: Industry (% of Gross Value Added)	56.9	51.0	39.2 [e]
Economy: Services and other activity (% of GVA)	39.2	43.4	55.3 [e]
Employment in agriculture (% of employed) [f]	9.8	9.1	10.0
Employment in industry (% of employed) [f]	21.0	23.9	23.6
Employment in services & other sectors (% employed) [f]	69.3	67.0	66.4
Unemployment rate (% of labour force)	11.4	8.4	7.7 [f]
Labour force participation rate (female/male pop. %) [f]	49.7 / 80.6	50.6 / 79.3	50.4 / 77.3
CPI: Consumer Price Index (2010=100) [g]	...	100	772 [b]
Agricultural production index (2004-2006=100)	101	111	109 [e]
International trade: exports (million current US$)	55 413	66 963	11 563 [f,d]
International trade: imports (million current US$)	21 848	32 343	6 771 [f,d]
International trade: balance (million current US$)	33 565	34 620	4 792 [f,d]
Balance of payments, current account (million US$)	25 447 [h]	5 585	- 3 870 [e]

Major trading partners

						2017
Export partners (% of exports) [f]	United States	44.5	China	22.5	India	15.0
Import partners (% of imports) [f]	United States	33.3	China	21.4	Mexico	8.6

Social indicators

	2005	2010	2018
Population growth rate (average annual %) [i]	1.8	1.6	1.4 [b]
Urban population (% of total population)	88.0	88.1	88.2
Urban population growth rate (average annual %) [i]	1.9	1.6	1.4 [b]
Fertility rate, total (live births per woman) [i]	2.7	2.5	2.4 [b]
Life expectancy at birth (females/males, years) [i]	77.2 / 68.8	77.7 / 69.4	78.2 / 69.9 [b]
Population age distribution (0-14/60+ years old, %)	31.7 / 7.4	29.8 / 8.3	27.3 / 10.2 [a]
International migrant stock (000/% of total pop.)	1 070.6 / 4.0	1 331.5 / 4.6	1 426.3 / 4.5 [d]
Refugees and others of concern to the UNHCR (000)	206.3 [j]	217.4 [j]	172.8 [d]
Infant mortality rate (per 1 000 live births)	18.1	15.9	13.8 [b]
Health: Current expenditure (% of GDP)	4.0	4.5	3.2 [b]
Health: Physicians (per 1 000 pop.)	1.9 [k]	...	...
Education: Government expenditure (% of GDP)	...	6.9 [l]	...
Education: Primary gross enrol. ratio (f/m per 100 pop.)	101.6 / 103.7	99.9 / 102.9	95.2 / 97.8 [e]
Education: Secondary gross enrol. ratio (f/m per 100 pop.)	77.5 / 68.6	84.7 / 77.2	88.9 / 82.5 [e]
Education: Tertiary gross enrol. ratio (f/m per 100 pop.)	41.2 / 38.4 [f,m]	97.7 / 57.8 [f,n]	... / ...
Intentional homicide rate (per 100 000 pop.)	37.2	45.1	56.3 [e]
Seats held by women in the National Parliament (%)	9.7	17.5	22.2

Environment and infrastructure indicators

	2005	2010	2018
Individuals using the Internet (per 100 inhabitants)	12.6	37.4 [f]	60.0 [f,e]
Threatened species (number)	219 [o]	270	328 [d]
Forested area (% of land area) [f]	54.1	53.9	52.9 [b]
CO2 emission estimates (million tons/tons per capita)	165.1 / 6.2	189.1 / 6.5	185.2 / 6.1 [p]
Energy production, primary (Petajoules)	8 283	8 139	7 337 [b]
Energy supply per capita (Gigajoules)	103	111	79 [b]
Tourist/visitor arrivals at national borders (000)	706	526	601 [e]
Important sites for terrestrial biodiversity protected (%)	67.4	67.4	67.4
Pop. using improved drinking water (urban/rural, %)	94.2 / 74.6	94.7 / 76.6	95.0 / 77.9 [b]
Pop. using improved sanitation facilities (urban/rural, %)	94.5 / 61.3	96.4 / 66.7	97.5 / 69.9 [b]
Net Official Development Assist. received (% of GNI)	0.03	0.01	0.01 [q]

a Projected estimate (medium fertility variant). **b** 2015. **c** Refers to multiple municipalities and parishes (see source). **d** 2017. **e** 2016. **f** Estimate. **g** Calculated by the Statistics Division of the United Nations from national indices. **h** Break in the time series. **i** Data refers to a 5-year period preceding the reference year. **j** Data as at the end of December. **k** 2001. **l** 2009. **m** 2003. **n** 2008. **o** 2004. **p** 2014. **q** 2013.

Viet Nam

Region	South-eastern Asia	UN membership date	20 September 1977
Population (000, 2018)	96 491 [a]	Surface area (km2)	330 967 [b]
Pop. density (per km2, 2018)	311.2 [a]	Sex ratio (m per 100 f)	98.0 [a]
Capital city	Hanoi	National currency	Dong (VND)
Capital city pop. (000, 2018)	4 282.7 [c]	Exchange rate (per US$)	22 425.0 [d]

Economic indicators	2005	2010	2018
GDP: Gross domestic product (million current US$)	57 633	115 932	205 276 [e]
GDP growth rate (annual %, const. 2010 prices)	7.5	6.4	6.2 [e]
GDP per capita (current US$)	684.0	1 310.0	2 171.0 [e]
Economy: Agriculture (% of Gross Value Added) [f]	19.3 [g]	21.0	18.1 [e]
Economy: Industry (% of Gross Value Added) [f]	38.1 [g]	36.7	36.4 [e]
Economy: Services and other activity (% of GVA) [f]	42.6 [g]	42.2	45.5 [e]
Employment in agriculture (% of employed) [h]	54.6	48.8	39.6
Employment in industry (% of employed) [h]	18.9	21.4	25.3
Employment in services & other sectors (% employed) [h]	26.5	29.7	35.1
Unemployment rate (% of labour force)	2.3 [h]	2.6	2.1 [h]
Labour force participation rate (female/male pop. %) [h]	72.5 / 81.4	72.5 / 81.6	73.2 / 83.4
CPI: Consumer Price Index (2010=100)	60	100	156 [d]
Agricultural production index (2004-2006=100)	100	120	138 [e]
Index of industrial production (2005=100)	100	156	199 [i]
International trade: exports (million current US$)	32 447	72 237	203 526 [h,d]
International trade: imports (million current US$)	36 761	84 839	218 338 [h,d]
International trade: balance (million current US$)	- 4 314	- 12 602	- 14 813 [h,d]
Balance of payments, current account (million US$)	- 560	- 4 276	6 124 [d]

Major trading partners						2017
Export partners (% of exports)	United States	21.7 [h]	China	12.4	Japan	8.3 [h]
Import partners (% of imports) [h]	China	28.6	Republic of Korea	18.4	Japan	8.6

Social indicators	2005	2010	2018
Population growth rate (average annual %) [j]	1.0	1.0	1.1 [b]
Urban population (% of total population)	27.3	30.4	35.9
Urban population growth rate (average annual %) [j]	3.2	3.1	3.2 [b]
Fertility rate, total (live births per woman) [j]	1.9	1.9	2.0 [b]
Life expectancy at birth (females/males, years) [j]	78.7 / 68.9	79.6 / 69.7	80.3 / 70.7 [b]
Population age distribution (0-14/60+ years old, %)	27.2 / 8.6	23.7 / 8.9	23.0 / 11.6 [a]
International migrant stock (000/% of total pop.) [k,l]	51.8 / 0.1	61.8 / 0.1	76.1 / 0.1 [d]
Refugees and others of concern to the UNHCR (000)	17.4 [m]	12.1 [m]	11.0 [d]
Infant mortality rate (per 1 000 live births) [j]	25.3	22.2	19.3 [b]
Health: Current expenditure (% of GDP) [n]	5.0	5.9	5.7 [b]
Health: Physicians (per 1 000 pop.)	0.6	0.7	0.8 [e]
Education: Government expenditure (% of GDP)	...	5.1	5.7 [o]
Education: Primary gross enrol. ratio (f/m per 100 pop.)	94.5 / 99.5	102.2 / 107.6	110.1 / 109.8 [e]
Education: Tertiary gross enrol. ratio (f/m per 100 pop.)	13.3 / 18.7	22.7 / 22.6	31.3 / 25.3 [e]
Intentional homicide rate (per 100 000 pop.)	1.2	1.5	1.5 [p]
Seats held by women in the National Parliament (%)	27.3	25.8	26.7

Environment and infrastructure indicators	2005	2010	2018
Individuals using the Internet (per 100 inhabitants)	12.7	30.6	46.5 [h,e]
Research & Development expenditure (% of GDP)	0.2 [q]	...	0.4 [o]
Threatened species (number)	289 [r]	424	616 [d]
Forested area (% of land area) [h]	42.2	45.6	47.6 [b]
CO2 emission estimates (million tons/tons per capita)	98.1 / 1.2	142.7 / 1.6	166.9 / 1.8 [i]
Energy production, primary (Petajoules)	2 612	2 747	3 043 [b]
Energy supply per capita (Gigajoules)	21	26	32 [b]
Tourist/visitor arrivals at national borders (000)	3 477	5 050	10 013 [e]
Important sites for terrestrial biodiversity protected (%)	27.2	30.0	40.9
Pop. using improved drinking water (urban/rural, %)	95.5 / 80.4	97.3 / 88.6	99.1 / 96.9 [b]
Pop. using improved sanitation facilities (urban/rural, %)	82.6 / 53.4	88.5 / 61.6	94.4 / 69.7 [b]
Net Official Development Assist. received (% of GNI)	3.38	3.38	1.52 [e]

a Projected estimate (medium fertility variant). b 2015. c Refers to urban population in the city districts. d 2017. e 2016. f Data classified according to ISIC Rev. 4. g At producers' prices. h Estimate. i 2014. j Data refers to a 5-year period preceding the reference year. k Including refugees. l Refers to foreign citizens. m Data as at the end of December. n Data revision. o 2013. p 2011. q 2002. r 2004.

Wallis and Futuna Islands

Region	Polynesia	Population (000, 2018)	12[a]
Surface area (km2)	142[b]	Pop. density (per km2, 2018)	83.4[a]
Sex ratio (m per 100 f)	93.4[c,d]	Capital city	Matu-Utu
National currency	CFP Franc (XPF)[e]	Capital city pop. (000, 2018)	1.0
Exchange rate (per US$)	99.5[f]		

Economic indicators

	2005	2010	2018
Agricultural production index (2004-2006=100)	102	105	112[d]
International trade: exports (million current US$)[g]	1	1	1[f]
International trade: imports (million current US$)[g]	51	35[g]	57[g,f]
International trade: balance (million current US$)[g]	- 50	- 34	- 55[f]

Major trading partners

					2017
Export partners (% of exports)[g]	Singapore	29.7	United Kingdom	22.5	France	8.8
Import partners (% of imports)[g]	France	26.4	New Caledonia	20.7	Fiji	18.4

Social indicators

	2005	2010	2018
Population growth rate (average annual %)[h]	0.1	- 1.6	- 2.1[b]
Urban population (% of total population)	0.0	0.0	0.0
Urban population growth rate (average annual %)[h]	0.0	0.0	0.0[b]
Fertility rate, total (live births per woman)	...	...	2.1[i]
Life expectancy at birth (females/males, years)	75.5 / 73.1[j]	... / ...	78.7 / 72.8[c,j]
Population age distribution (0-14/60+ years old, %)	... / ...	... / ...	25.5 / 15.4[d]
International migrant stock (000/% of total pop.)	2.4 / 16.2	2.8 / 20.7	2.8 / 23.6[f]
Infant mortality rate (per 1 000 live births)	...	5.2[k,l]	...

Environment and infrastructure indicators

	2005	2010	2018
Individuals using the Internet (per 100 inhabitants)	6.7	8.2	9.0[g,m]
Threatened species (number)	13[n]	74	89[f]
Forested area (% of land area)	41.5	41.6	41.6[b]
CO2 emission estimates (million tons/tons per capita)	~0.0 / 1.9	~0.0 / 2.1	~0.0 / 1.6[o]
Energy supply per capita (Gigajoules)	26	27	26[b]
Important sites for terrestrial biodiversity protected (%)	0.0	0.0	0.0

a Projected estimate (medium fertility variant). b 2015. c Break in the time series. d 2016. e Communauté financière du Pacifique (CFP) Franc. f 2017. g Estimate. h Data refers to a 5-year period preceding the reference year. i 2013. j 2003. k Data refers to a 4-year period up to and including the reference year. l 2008. m 2012. n 2004. o 2014.

Western Sahara

Region	Northern Africa	Population (000, 2018)	567[a]
Surface area (km2)	266 000[b,c]	Pop. density (per km2, 2018)	2.1[a]
Sex ratio (m per 100 f)	109.9[a]	Capital city	El Aaiún
National currency	Moroccan Dirham (MAD)	Capital city pop. (000, 2018)	232.4
Exchange rate (per US$)	9.3[d]		

Economic indicators	2005	2010	2018
Employment in agriculture (% of employed)[e]	38.0	34.6	30.6
Employment in industry (% of employed)[e]	29.2	30.2	30.9
Employment in services & other sectors (% employed)[e]	32.8	35.2	38.4
Unemployment rate (% of labour force)[e]	8.1	7.9	7.3
Labour force participation rate (female/male pop. %)[e]	26.9 / 79.0	28.1 / 79.5	28.9 / 79.6
Agricultural production index (2004-2006=100)	100	102	107[f]

Social indicators	2005	2010	2018
Population growth rate (average annual %)[e]	6.6	1.9	1.8[c]
Urban population (% of total population)	86.0	86.3	86.7
Urban population growth rate (average annual %)[e]	6.7	1.9	1.9[c]
Fertility rate, total (live births per woman)[g]	2.8	2.6	2.6[c]
Life expectancy at birth (females/males, years)[g]	65.8 / 62.3	68.1 / 64.7	70.3 / 66.9[c]
Population age distribution (0-14/60+ years old, %)	31.5 / 3.6	29.4 / 3.8	27.7 / 5.7[a]
International migrant stock (000/% of total pop.)[e]	3.9 / 0.9	4.5 / 0.9	5.4 / 1.0[d]
Infant mortality rate (per 1 000 live births)[g]	52.9	43.1	34.1[c]

Environment and infrastructure indicators	2005	2010	2018
Threatened species (number)	19[h]	39	49[d]
Forested area (% of land area)[e]	2.7	2.7	2.7[c]

a Projected estimate (medium fertility variant). b Comprising the Northern Region (former Saguia el Hamra) and Southern Region (former Rio de Oro). c 2015. d 2017. e Estimate. f 2016. g Data refers to a 5-year period preceding the reference year. h 2004.

Yemen

Region	Western Asia
Population (000, 2018)	28 915[a]
Pop. density (per km2, 2018)	54.8[a]
Capital city	Sana'a
Capital city pop. (000, 2018)	2 779.3[c]

UN membership date	30 September 1947
Surface area (km2)	527 968[b]
Sex ratio (m per 100 f)	102.1[a]
National currency	Yemeni Rial (YER)
Exchange rate (per US$)	214.9[d]

Economic indicators

	2005	2010	2018
GDP: Gross domestic product (million current US$)	19 041	29 031	25 374[e]
GDP growth rate (annual %, const. 2010 prices)	5.1	7.8	- 9.8[e]
GDP per capita (current US$)	925.0	1 230.0	920.0[e]
Economy: Agriculture (% of Gross Value Added)	9.6	12.1	15.4[e]
Economy: Industry (% of Gross Value Added)	43.8	34.4	31.0[e]
Economy: Services and other activity (% of GVA)	46.5	53.4	53.6[e]
Employment in agriculture (% of employed)[f]	30.1	24.1	47.7
Employment in industry (% of employed)[f]	15.7	19.0	12.2
Employment in services & other sectors (% employed)[f]	54.2	56.9	40.1
Unemployment rate (% of labour force)[f]	16.1	17.8	16.1[d]
Labour force participation rate (female/male pop. %)[f]	23.6 / 71.3	24.8 / 71.4	26.2 / 73.7[d]
CPI: Consumer Price Index (2010=100)[f]	60[g]	100	158[h]
Agricultural production index (2004-2006=100)	98	136	141[e]
International trade: exports (million current US$)	5 608	6 437	637[f,d]
International trade: imports (million current US$)	5 400	9 255	7 162[f,d]
International trade: balance (million current US$)	208	- 2 818	- 6 525[f,d]
Balance of payments, current account (million US$)	624	- 1 054	- 3 026[b]

Major trading partners

						2017
Export partners (% of exports)[f]	Saudi Arabia	32.2	Oman	17.0	Areas nes[i]	10.6
Import partners (% of imports)[f]	United Arab Emirates	11.5	China	10.8	Saudi Arabia	8.6

Social indicators

	2005	2010	2018
Population growth rate (average annual %)[j]	2.8	2.7	2.6[b]
Urban population (% of total population)	28.9	31.8	36.6
Urban population growth rate (average annual %)[j]	4.8	4.6	4.4[b]
Fertility rate, total (live births per woman)[j]	5.9	5.0	4.4[b]
Life expectancy at birth (females/males, years)[j]	62.4 / 59.7	64.1 / 61.4	65.6 / 62.8[b]
Population age distribution (0-14/60+ years old, %)	45.7 / 4.2	42.5 / 4.4	39.6 / 4.6[a]
International migrant stock (000/% of total pop.)[k,l]	171.1 / 0.8	285.8 / 1.2	384.3 / 1.4[d]
Refugees and others of concern to the UNHCR (000)	82.8[m]	508.6[m]	3 206.8[d]
Infant mortality rate (per 1 000 live births)[j]	67.9	53.0	47.2[b]
Health: Current expenditure (% of GDP)[f]	4.6	5.2	6.0[b]
Health: Physicians (per 1 000 pop.)	0.3[n]	0.3[o]	0.3[h]
Education: Government expenditure (% of GDP)	9.2[f,p]	5.2[q]	...
Education: Primary gross enrol. ratio (f/m per 100 pop.)	74.4 / 100.6	81.2 / 99.5	86.1 / 98.6[e]
Education: Secondary gross enrol. ratio (f/m per 100 pop.)	29.7 / 60.7	33.2 / 53.4	42.8 / 58.9[e]
Education: Tertiary gross enrol. ratio (f/m per 100 pop.)	5.1 / 13.9	6.4 / 14.6	6.1 / 13.7[r]
Intentional homicide rate (per 100 000 pop.)	4.6	4.7	6.7[s]
Seats held by women in the National Parliament (%)	0.3	0.3	0.0

Environment and infrastructure indicators

	2005	2010	2018
Individuals using the Internet (per 100 inhabitants)	1.0[f]	12.4	24.6[f,e]
Threatened species (number)	195[n]	269	298[d]
Forested area (% of land area)[f]	1.0	1.0	1.0[b]
CO2 emission estimates (million tons/tons per capita)	20.0 / 1.0	23.4 / 1.0	22.7 / 0.9[h]
Energy production, primary (Petajoules)	844	804	172[b]
Energy supply per capita (Gigajoules)	13	14	5[b]
Tourist/visitor arrivals at national borders (000)	336	1 025[t]	367[t,b]
Important sites for terrestrial biodiversity protected (%)	20.0	31.1	31.1
Pop. using improved drinking water (urban/rural, %)	75.9 / 48.5	72.0 / 46.5	72.0 / 46.5[u]
Pop. using improved sanitation facilities (urban/rural, %)	88.7 / 30.4	92.5 / 34.1	92.5 / 34.1[u]
Net Official Development Assist. received (% of GNI)	1.96	2.29	7.09[e]

a Projected estimate (medium fertility variant). b 2015. c Data refers to the urban agglomeration. d 2017. e 2016. f Estimate. g Break in the time series. h 2014. i Areas not elsewhere specified. j Data refers to a 5-year period preceding the reference year. k Refers to foreign citizens. l Including refugees. m Data as at the end of December. n 2004. o 2009. p 2001. q 2008. r 2011. s 2013. t Including nationals residing abroad. u 2012.

Zambia

Region	Eastern Africa	UN membership date	01 December 1964
Population (000, 2018)	17 609ᵃ	Surface area (km2)	752 612ᵇ
Pop. density (per km2, 2018)	23.7ᵃ	Sex ratio (m per 100 f)	98.5ᵃ
Capital city	Lusaka	National currency	Zambian Kwacha (ZMW)
Capital city pop. (000, 2018)	2 523.8	Exchange rate (per US$)	9.9ᶜ

Economic indicators	2005	2010	2018
GDP: Gross domestic product (million current US$)	8 332	20 265	21 063ᵈ
GDP growth rate (annual %, const. 2010 prices)	7.2	10.3	3.6ᵈ
GDP per capita (current US$)	691.0	1 463.0	1 270.0ᵈ
Economy: Agriculture (% of Gross Value Added)	15.5	10.0ᵉ	5.1ᵉ,ᵈ
Economy: Industry (% of Gross Value Added)	28.6	34.1ᵉ	35.8ᵉ,ᵈ
Economy: Services and other activity (% of GVA)	55.9	55.9ᵉ	59.2ᵉ,ᵈ
Employment in agriculture (% of employed)ᶠ	72.8	63.4	53.0
Employment in industry (% of employed)ᶠ	6.8	8.8	12.0
Employment in services & other sectors (% employed)ᶠ	20.4	27.8	35.0
Unemployment rate (% of labour force)	10.4ᶠ	13.2	7.8ᶠ
Labour force participation rate (female/male pop. %)ᶠ	73.7 / 85.7	71.1 / 82.2	70.1 / 79.6
CPI: Consumer Price Index (2010=100)	60	100ᵍ	181ᶜ
Agricultural production index (2004-2006=100)	100	164	183ᵈ
Index of industrial production (2005=100)ʰ	100	141	157ⁱ
International trade: exports (million current US$)	1 810	7 200	8 363ᶠ,ᶜ
International trade: imports (million current US$)	2 558	5 321	9 145ᶠ,ᶜ
International trade: balance (million current US$)	- 748	1 879	-782ᶠ,ᶜ
Balance of payments, current account (million US$)	- 232ᵍ	1 525	- 1 006ᶜ

Major trading partners					2017
Export partners (% of exports)	Switzerland	44.3ᶠ	China	14.5	Singapore	7.8ᶠ
Import partners (% of imports)ᶠ	South Africa	30.9	Dem. Rep. of Congo	11.2	China	8.2

Social indicators	2005	2010	2018
Population growth rate (average annual %)ʲ	2.7	2.8	3.0ᵇ
Urban population (% of total population)	36.9	39.4	43.5
Urban population growth rate (average annual %)ʲ	3.9	4.1	4.3ᵇ
Fertility rate, total (live births per woman)ʲ	6.0	5.6	5.2ᵇ
Life expectancy at birth (females/males, years)ʲ	48.4 / 45.3	54.7 / 51.2	61.9 / 57.5ᵇ
Population age distribution (0-14/60+ years old, %)	47.0 / 3.9	46.8 / 3.8	44.5 / 3.7ᵃ
International migrant stock (000/% of total pop.)ᵏ	252.7 / 2.1	149.6 / 1.1	157.0 / 0.9ᶜ
Refugees and others of concern to the UNHCR (000)	185.7ˡ	57.9ˡ	58.5ᶜ
Infant mortality rate (per 1 000 live births)ʲ	82.2	65.2	53.8ᵇ
Health: Current expenditure (% of GDP)	7.4	4.6	5.4ᵇ
Health: Physicians (per 1 000 pop.)	0.1	0.1	0.1ᵈ
Education: Government expenditure (% of GDP)	1.7	1.1ᵐ	...
Education: Primary gross enrol. ratio (f/m per 100 pop.)	107.4 / 112.5	105.9 / 104.5	102.7 / 102.0ⁱ
Education: Tertiary gross enrol. ratio (f/m per 100 pop.)	... / ...	... / ...	3.5 / 4.6ⁿ
Intentional homicide rate (per 100 000 pop.)	7.6ᵒ	5.9	5.3ᵇ
Seats held by women in the National Parliament (%)	12.0	14.0	18.0

Environment and infrastructure indicators	2005	2010	2018
Individuals using the Internet (per 100 inhabitants)	2.9ᶠ	10.0	25.5ᶠ,ᵈ
Research & Development expenditure (% of GDP)	~0.0ᵖ	0.3ᵍ,ᵐ	...
Threatened species (number)	39ᵍ	67	88ᶜ
Forested area (% of land area)ᶠ	67.7	66.5	65.4ᵇ
CO2 emission estimates (million tons/tons per capita)	2.3 / 0.2	2.7 / 0.2	4.5 / 0.3ᶠ
Energy production, primary (Petajoules)	280	319	385ᵇ
Energy supply per capita (Gigajoules)	27	25	27ᵇ
Tourist/visitor arrivals at national borders (000)	669	815	956ᵈ
Important sites for terrestrial biodiversity protected (%)	46.3	48.3	48.3
Pop. using improved drinking water (urban/rural, %)	86.7 / 40.3	86.2 / 45.8	85.6 / 51.3ᵇ
Pop. using improved sanitation facilities (urban/rural, %)	56.9 / 32.9	56.3 / 34.3	55.6 / 35.7ᵇ
Net Official Development Assist. received (% of GNI)	15.18	4.86	5.10ᵈ

a Projected estimate (medium fertility variant). b 2015. c 2017. d 2016. e Data classified according to ISIC Rev. 4. f Estimate. g Break in the time series. h Data classified according to ISIC Rev. 3. i 2013. j Data refers to a 5-year period preceding the reference year. k Including refugees. l Data as at the end of December. m 2008. n 2012. o 2000. p Partial data. q 2004. r 2014.

Zimbabwe

Region	Eastern Africa	UN membership date	25 August 1980
Population (000, 2018)	16 913[a]	Surface area (km2)	390 757[b]
Pop. density (per km2, 2018)	43.7[a]	Sex ratio (m per 100 f)	95.1[a]
Capital city	Harare	National currency	Zimbabwe Dollar (ZWL)
Capital city pop. (000, 2018)	1 515.0		

Economic indicators	2005	2010	2018
GDP: Gross domestic product (million current US$)	6 223	10 052	16 124[d]
GDP growth rate (annual %, const. 2010 prices)	- 4.1	15.4	0.7[d]
GDP per capita (current US$)	481.0	714.0	998.0[d]
Economy: Agriculture (% of Gross Value Added)	12.3	13.4	11.2[d]
Economy: Industry (% of Gross Value Added)	41.9	28.4	24.3[d]
Economy: Services and other activity (% of GVA)	45.9	58.1	64.5[d]
Employment in agriculture (% of employed)[e]	72.6	69.0	68.6
Employment in industry (% of employed)[e]	10.4	9.4	7.4
Employment in services & other sectors (% employed)[e]	17.0	21.6	24.0
Unemployment rate (% of labour force)[e]	4.5	5.3	5.1
Labour force participation rate (female/male pop. %)[e]	77.1 / 88.2	77.4 / 88.4	78.9 / 89.3
CPI: Consumer Price Index (2010=100)	...	100	106[f]
Agricultural production index (2004-2006=100)	92	98	100[d]
International trade: exports (million current US$)	1 394	3 199	3 465[e,f]
International trade: imports (million current US$)	2 072	5 852	5 449[e,f]
International trade: balance (million current US$)	- 679	- 2 653	- 1 985[e,f]
Balance of payments, current account (million US$)	...	- 1 444	- 591[d]

Major trading partners						2017
Export partners (% of exports)	South Africa	79.4[e]	Mozambique	9.5	United Arab Emirates	4.1[e]
Import partners (% of imports)[e]	South Africa	41.3	Singapore	21.5	China	7.0

Social indicators	2005	2010	2018
Population growth rate (average annual %)[g]	1.1	1.7	2.3[b]
Urban population (% of total population)	34.1	33.2	32.2
Urban population growth rate (average annual %)[g]	1.3	1.2	1.8[b]
Fertility rate, total (live births per woman)[g]	4.0	4.0	4.0[b]
Life expectancy at birth (females/males, years)[g]	45.5 / 42.7	49.4 / 47.2	59.0 / 56.1[b]
Population age distribution (0-14/60+ years old, %)	41.8 / 4.5	41.5 / 4.3	41.0 / 4.2[a]
International migrant stock (000/% of total pop.)[h]	392.7 / 3.0	397.9 / 2.8	403.9 / 2.4[f]
Refugees and others of concern to the UNHCR (000)	14.0[i]	4.9[i]	11.0[f]
Infant mortality rate (per 1 000 live births)[g]	67.2	58.3	46.5[b]
Health: Current expenditure (% of GDP)	...	11.6	10.3[b]
Health: Physicians (per 1 000 pop.)	0.2[j]	0.1	0.1[k]
Education: Government expenditure (% of GDP)	...	1.8	7.5[k]
Education: Primary gross enrol. ratio (f/m per 100 pop.)	97.2 / 98.5[l]	... / ...	97.9 / 99.5[m]
Education: Secondary gross enrol. ratio (f/m per 100 pop.)	36.8 / 40.8[l]	... / ...	46.7 / 47.6[m]
Education: Tertiary gross enrol. ratio (f/m per 100 pop.)	... / ...	5.4 / 6.8	8.0 / 8.9[b]
Intentional homicide rate (per 100 000 pop.)	10.4	5.0	6.7[n]
Seats held by women in the National Parliament (%)	10.0	15.0	33.2

Environment and infrastructure indicators	2005	2010	2018
Individuals using the Internet (per 100 inhabitants)[e]	2.4	8.4	23.1[d]
Threatened species (number)	43[j]	55	89[f]
Forested area (% of land area)[e]	44.6	40.4	36.4[b]
CO2 emission estimates (million tons/tons per capita)	10.8 / 0.8	7.8 / 0.6	12.0 / 0.8[k]
Energy production, primary (Petajoules)	379	368	449[b]
Energy supply per capita (Gigajoules)	33	28	30[b]
Tourist/visitor arrivals at national borders (000)	1 559	2 239	2 168[d]
Important sites for terrestrial biodiversity protected (%)	80.7	80.7	85.9
Pop. using improved drinking water (urban/rural, %)	98.0 / 68.9	97.5 / 68.1	97.0 / 67.3[b]
Pop. using improved sanitation facilities (urban/rural, %)	50.3 / 32.5	49.8 / 31.7	49.3 / 30.8[b]
Net Official Development Assist. received (% of GNI)	6.80	7.54	4.19[d]

a Projected estimate (medium fertility variant). b 2015. c 2005. d 2016. e Estimate. f 2017. g Data refers to a 5-year period preceding the reference year. h Including refugees. i Data as at the end of December. j 2004. k 2014. l 2003. m 2013. n 2012.

Technical notes

Below are brief descriptions of the indicators presented in the world, regional and country profiles. The terms are arranged in alphabetical order.

Agricultural production index is calculated by the Laspeyres formula based on the sum of price-weighted quantities of different agricultural commodities produced. The commodities covered in the computation of indices of agricultural production are all crops and livestock products originating in each country. Practically all products are covered, with the main exception of fodder crops. Production quantities of each commodity are weighted by the average international commodity prices in the base period and summed for each year. To obtain the index, the aggregate for a given year is divided by the average aggregate for the base period 2004-2006. Indices are calculated without any deductions for feed and seed and are referred to as "gross" by the Food and Agriculture Organization of the United Nations (FAO).
Source of the data: Food and Agriculture Organization of the United Nations (FAO), Rome, FAOSTAT database, last accessed May 2018.

Balance of payments is a statement summarizing the economic transactions between the residents of a country and non-residents during a specific period, usually a year. It includes transactions in goods, services, income, transfers and financial assets and liabilities. Generally, the balance of payments is divided into two major components: the current account and the capital and financial account. The data on balance of payments correspond to the current account category. The current account is a record of all transactions in the balance of payments covering the exports and imports of goods and services, payments of income, and current transfers between residents of a country and non-residents.
Source of the data: International Monetary Fund (IMF), Washington, D.C., Balance of Payment (BOP) Statistics database, last accessed April 2018.

Capital city and capital city population is the designation of any specific city as a capital city as reported by the country or area. The city can be the seat of the government as determined by the country. Some countries designate more than one city to be a capital city with a specific title function (e.g., administrative and/or legislative capital). The data refer to the year 2018, unless otherwise stated in a footnote.
Source of the data: United Nations Population Division (UNPD), New York, "World Urbanization Prospects (WUP): The 2018 Revision", last accessed May 2018.

CO_2 emission estimates represent the volume of carbon dioxide (CO_2) produced during the combustion of solid, liquid, and gaseous fuels, from gas flaring and the manufacture of cement. Original data were converted to CO_2 emissions by using the conversion formula: 1 gram Carbon = 3.667 grams CO_2.
Source of the data: Carbon Dioxide Information Analysis Center (CDIAC) of the Oak Ridge National Laboratory, Tennessee, database on national CO2 emission estimates, last accessed March 2017.

Technical notes (*continued*)

CPI: Consumer price index measures the period-to-period proportional change in the prices of a fixed set of consumer goods and services of constant quantity and characteristics, acquired, used or paid for by the reference population. The index is constructed as a weighted average of a large number of elementary aggregate indices. Each of the elementary aggregate indices is estimated using a sample of prices for a defined set of goods and services obtained in, or by residents of, a specific region from a given set of outlets or other sources of consumption. The indices here generally refer to "all items" and to the country as a whole, unless otherwise stated in a footnote.
Source of the data: *United Nations Statistics Division (UNSD), New York, Monthly Bulletin of Statistics (MBS), last accessed May 2018.*

Economy: agriculture, industry and services and other activity presents the shares of the components of Gross Value Added (GVA) at current prices by kind of economic activity; agriculture (agriculture, hunting, forestry and fishing), industry (mining and quarrying, manufacturing, electricity, gas and water supply; and construction) and in services and other sectors based on the sections of the International Standard Industrial Classification of All Economic Activities (ISIC), Revision 3, unless a different revision is stated in a footnote.
Source of the data: *United Nations Statistics Division (UNSD), New York, National Accounts Statistics: Analysis of Main Aggregates (AMA) database, last accessed December 2017.*

Education: Government expenditure shows the trends in general government expenditures for educational affairs and services at pre-primary, primary, secondary and tertiary levels and subsidiary services to education, expressed as a percentage of the gross domestic product.
Source of the data: *United Nations Educational, Scientific and Cultural Organization (UNESCO), Montreal, the UNESCO Institute for Statistics (UIS) statistics database, last accessed May 2018.*

Education: Primary, secondary and tertiary gross enrolment ratio is the total enrolment in the primary, secondary and tertiary levels of education, regardless of age, expressed as a percentage of the <u>eligible</u> official school-age population corresponding to the same level of education in a given school year. Education at the primary level provides the basic elements of education (e.g. at elementary school or primary school). Education at the secondary level is provided at middle school, secondary school, high school, teacher-training school at this level and schools of a vocational or technical nature. Education at the tertiary level is that which is provided at university, teachers' college, higher professional school, and which requires, as a minimum condition of admission, the successful completion of education at the second level, or evidence of the attainment of an equivalent level of knowledge. Enrolment is measured at the beginning of the school or academic year. The gross enrolment ratio at each level will include all pupils whatever their ages, whereas the population is limited to the range of official school ages. Therefore, for countries with almost universal education among the school-age population, the gross enrolment ratio can exceed 100 if the actual age distribution of pupils extends beyond the official school ages.

Source of the data: United Nations Educational, Scientific and Cultural Organization
(UNESCO), Montreal, the UNESCO Institute for Statistics (UIS) statistics database, last
accessed May 2018.

Employment in agricultural, industrial and services and other sectors: The "employed"
comprise all persons above a specified age who, during a specified brief period, either one
week or one day, were in "paid employment" or in "self-employment", see ILO's Current
International Recommendations on Labour Statistics. The data refer to those 15 years and
over, unless otherwise stated in a footnote, who perform any work at all in the reference
period, for pay or profit in agriculture (agriculture, forestry and fishing), industry (mining and
quarrying; manufacturing; electricity, gas, steam and air conditioning supply; water supply,
sewerage, waste management and remediation activities; and construction) and in services
and other sectors based on the sections of the International Standard Industrial Classification
of All Economic Activities (ISIC), Revision 4, unless an earlier revision is stated in a footnote.
Source of the data: International Labour Organization (ILO), Geneva, Key Indicators of the
Labour Market (KILM 9th edition) and the ILOSTAT database, last accessed March 2018.

Energy production, primary, is the capture or extraction of fuels or energy from natural
energy flows, the biosphere and natural reserves of fossil fuels within the national territory in
a form suitable for use. Inert matter removed from the extracted fuels and quantities
reinjected, flared or vented are not included. The resulting products are referred to as
"primary" products. It excludes secondary production, that is, the manufacture of energy
products through the process of transforming primary and/or other secondary fuels or energy.
Data are provided in a common energy unit (Petajoule) and refer to the following primary
energy sources: hard coal, brown coal, peat, oil shale, conventional crude oil, natural gas
liquids (NGL), other hydrocarbons, additives and oxygenates, natural gas, fuelwood, wood
residues and by-products, bagasse, animal waste, black liquor, other vegetal material and
residues, biogasoline, biodiesels, bio jet kerosene, other liquid biofuels, biogases, industrial
waste, municipal waste, nuclear, solar photovoltaic, solar thermal, hydro, wind, geothermal,
and tide, wave and other marine sources. Peat, biomass and wastes are included only when
the production is for energy purposes. See International Recommendations for Energy
Statistics (2011) and 2015 Energy Balances for a complete description of the methodology.
Source of the data: United Nations Statistics Division (UNSD), New York, Energy Statistics
Yearbook 2015, last accessed December 2017.

Energy supply per capita is defined as primary energy production plus imports minus exports
minus international marine bunkers minus international aviation bunkers minus stock changes.
For imports, exports, international bunkers and stock changes, it includes secondary energy
products, in addition to primary products.
Source of the data: United Nations Statistics Division (UNSD), New York, Energy Statistics
Yearbook 2015, last accessed December 2017.

Exchange rate in units of national currency per US dollar refers to end-of-period quotations.
The exchange rates are classified into broad categories, reflecting both the role of the

Technical notes (*continued*)

authorities in the determination of the exchange and/or the multiplicity of exchange rates in a country. The market rate is used to describe exchange rates determined largely by market forces; the official rate is an exchange rate determined by the authorities, sometimes in a flexible manner. For countries maintaining multiple exchange arrangements, the rates are labelled principal rate, secondary rate, and tertiary rate.

Source of the data: International Monetary Fund (IMF), Washington, D.C., the International Financial Statistics (IFS) database supplemented by United Nations Department of Management (DM), UN Treasury operational rates of exchange, last accessed May 2018.

Fertility rate is the total fertility rate, a widely used summary indicator of fertility. It refers to the number of children that would be born per woman, assuming no female mortality at child bearing ages and the age-specific fertility rates of a specified country and reference period. The data are an average over five-year ranges; 2000-2005 data are labelled "2005", 2005-2010 data are labelled "2010" and 2010-2015 data are labelled "2018", unless otherwise stated in a footnote.

Source of the data: United Nations Population Division (UNPD), New York, "World Population Prospects (WPP): The 2017 Revision"; supplemented by data from the United Nations Statistics Division (UNSD), New York, Demographic Yearbook 2015 and the Pacific Community (SPC) Statistics and Demography Programme for small countries or areas, last accessed June 2017.

Forested area refers to the percentage of land area occupied by forest. Forest is defined in the Food and Agriculture Organization's Global Forest Resources Assessment as land spanning more than 0.5 hectares with trees higher than 5 metres and a canopy cover of more than 10 percent, or trees able to reach these thresholds in situ. It does not include land that is predominantly under agricultural or urban land use. Data are calculated from the forest estimates divided by the land area.

Source of the data: Food and Agriculture Organization of the United Nations (FAO), Rome, FAOSTAT database, last accessed January 2018.

GDP: Gross domestic product is an aggregate measure of production equal to the sum of gross value added of all resident producer units plus that part (possibly the total) of taxes on products, less subsidies on products, that is not included in the valuation of output. It is also equal to the sum of the final uses of goods and services (all uses except intermediate consumption) measured at purchasers' prices, less the value of imports of goods and services, and equal to the sum of primary incomes distributed by resident producer units (see System of National Accounts 2008). The data are in current United States (US) dollars and are estimates of the total production of goods and services of the countries represented in economic terms, not as a measure of the standard of living of their inhabitants. To have comparable coverage for as many countries as possible, these US dollar estimates are based on official GDP data in national currency, supplemented by national currency estimates prepared by the Statistics Division using additional data from national and international sources. The estimates given here are in most cases those accepted by the United Nations General Assembly's Committee on Contributions for determining United Nations members' contributions to the United Nations regular budget. The exchange rates for

the conversion of GDP national currency data into US dollars are the average market rates published by the International Monetary Fund, in International Financial Statistics (IFS). Official exchange rates are used only when free market rates are not available. For non-members of the Fund, the conversion rates used are the average of UN Treasury rates of exchange. It should be noted that the conversion from local currency into US dollars introduces deficiencies in comparability over time and among countries which should be considered when using the data. For example, comparability over time is distorted when exchange rate fluctuations differ substantially from domestic inflation rates.
Source of the data: United Nations Statistics Division (UNSD), New York, National Accounts Statistics: Analysis of Main Aggregates (AMA) database, last accessed December 2017.

GDP growth rate is derived on the basis of constant 2010 price series in national currency. The figures are computed as the geometric mean of annual rates of growth expressed in percentages.
Source of the data: United Nations Statistics Division (UNSD), New York, National Accounts Statistics: Analysis of Main Aggregates (AMA) database, last accessed December 2017.

GDP per capita estimates are the value of all goods and services produced in the economy divided by the population.
Source of the data: United Nations Statistics Division (UNSD), New York, National Accounts Statistics: Analysis of Main Aggregates (AMA) database, last accessed December 2017.

Health: Physicians includes generalist medical practitioners and specialist medical practitioners, expressed as the number of physicians per 1 000 population. The classification of health workers used is based on criteria for vocational education and training, regulation of health professions, and activities and tasks of jobs, i.e. a framework for categorizing key workforce variables according to shared characteristics.
Source of the data: World Health Organisation (WHO), Geneva, WHO Global Health Workforce statistics database, last accessed April 2018.

Health: Current expenditure refers to all health care goods and services used or consumed during a year excluding capital spending, or rather "gross capital formation", which is the purchase of new assets used repeatedly over several years. These estimates are in line with the 2011 System of Health Accounts (SHA). Current expenditure is expressed as a proportion of Gross Domestic Product (GDP).
Source of the data: World Health Organization (WHO), Geneva, WHO Global Health Expenditure database, last accessed March 2018.

Important sites for terrestrial biodiversity protected shows land which contributes significantly to the global persistence of biodiversity measured as a proportion of which is wholly covered by a designated protected area. Data are based on spatial overlap between polygons for Key Biodiversity Areas from the World Database of key Biodiversity Areas and polygons for protected areas from the World Database on Protected Areas. Figures for each region are calculated as the proportion of each Key Biodiversity Area covered by protected areas, averaged (i.e. calculated as the mean) across all Key Biodiversity Areas within the region.

Source of the data: United Nations Environment Programme (UNEP) World Conservation Monitoring Centre (WCWC), Cambridge, Sustainable Development Goals (SDGs) statistics database, last accessed May 2018.

Index of Industrial production generally cover industry (mining and quarrying; manufacturing; electricity, gas, steam and air conditioning supply; water supply, sewerage, waste management and remediation activities; and construction) based on the sections (i.e. B, C, D and E) of the International Standard Industrial Classification of All Economic Activities (ISIC), Revision 4, unless a different revision/set of sections is stated in a footnote.

Source of the data: United Nations Statistics Division (UNSD), New York, Statistical Yearbook 2013 (58th issue), last accessed November 2015.

Individuals using the Internet refer to the percentage of people who used the Internet from any location and for any purpose, irrespective of the device and network used. It can be via a computer (i.e. desktop or laptop computer, tablet or similar handheld computer), mobile phone, games machine, digital TV, etc. Access can be via a fixed or mobile network. There are certain data limits to this indicator, insofar as estimates have to be calculated for many developing countries which do not yet collect information and communications technology household statistics.

Source of the data: International Telecommunication Union (ITU), Geneva, the ITU database, last accessed April 2018.

Infant mortality rate is the ratio of infant deaths (the deaths of children under one year of age) in a given year to the total number of live births in the same year, expressed as a rate per 1 000 live births. The data are an average over five-year ranges; 2000-2005 data are labelled "2005", 2005-2010 data are labelled "2010" and 2010-2015 data are labelled "2018", unless otherwise stated in a footnote.

Source of the data: United Nations Population Division (UNPD), New York, "World Population Prospects (WPP): The 2017 Revision"; supplemented by data from the United Nations Statistics Division (UNSD), New York, Demographic Yearbook 2015 and the Pacific Community (SPC) Statistics and Demography Programme for small countries or areas, last accessed June 2017.

Intentional homicide rate: The rates are the annual number of unlawful deaths purposefully inflicted on a person by another person, reported for the year per 100 000. For most countries, country information on causes of death is not available for most causes. Estimates are therefore based on cause of death modelling and death registration data from other countries in the region. Further country-level information and data on specific causes was also used.

Source of the data: United Nations Office on Drugs and Crime (UNODC), Vienna, UNODC Statistics database, last accessed May 2018.

International migrant stock generally represents the number of persons born in a country other than that in which they live. When information on country of birth was not recorded, data on the number of persons having foreign citizenship was used instead. In the absence of any empirical data, estimates were imputed. Data refer to mid-year. Figures for international migrant stock as a percentage of the population are the outcome of dividing the estimated international migrant stock by the estimated total population and multiplying the result by 100.

Source of the data: United Nations Population Division (UNPD), New York, "International migrant stock: The 2017 Revision", last accessed January 2018.

International trade: Exports, imports and balance show the movement of goods out of and into a country. Goods simply being transported through a country (goods in transit) or temporarily admitted (except for goods for inward processing) do not add to the stock of material resources of a country and are not included in the international merchandise trade statistics. In the "general trade system", the definition of the statistical territory of a country coincides with its economic territory. In the "special trade system", the definition of the statistical territory comprises only a particular part of the economic territory, mainly that part which coincides with the free circulation area for goods. "The free circulation area" is a part of the economic territory of a country within which goods "may be disposed of without Customs restrictions". In the case of exports, the transaction value is the value at which the goods were sold by the exporter, including the cost of transportation and insurance, to bring the goods onto the transporting vehicle at the frontier of the exporting country (an FOB-type valuation). In the case of imports, the transaction value is the value at which the goods were purchased by the importer plus the cost of transportation and insurance to the frontier of the importing country (a CIF-type valuation). Both imports and exports are shown in United States dollars. Conversion from national currencies is made by means of currency conversion factors based on official exchange rates (par values or weighted averages). All regional aggregations are calculated as the sum of their components.

Source of the data: United Nations Statistics Division (UNSD), New York, Commodity Trade Statistics Database (UN COMTRADE), last accessed May 2018.

Labour force participation rate is calculated by expressing the number of persons in the labour force as a percentage of the working-age population. The labour force is the sum of the number of persons employed and the number of unemployed (see ILO's current International Recommendations on Labour Statistics). The working-age population is the population above a certain age, prescribed for the measurement of economic characteristics. The data refer to the age group of 15 years and over and are based on ILO's modelled estimates, unless otherwise stated in a footnote.

Source of the data: International Labour Organization (ILO), Geneva, Key Indicators of the Labour Market (KILM 9th edition) and the ILOSTAT database, last accessed March 2018.

Life expectancy at birth is the average number of years of life at birth (age 0) for males and females according to the expected mortality rates by age estimated for the reference year and population. The data are an average over five-year ranges; 2000-2005 data are labelled

"2005", 2005-2010 data are labelled "2010" and 2010-2015 data are labelled "2018", unless otherwise stated in a footnote.

Source of the data: United Nations Population Division (UNPD), New York, "World Population Prospects (WPP): The 2017 Revision"; supplemented by data from the United Nations Statistics Division (UNSD), New York, Demographic Yearbook 2015 and the Pacific Community (SPC) Statistics and Demography Programme for small countries or areas, last accessed June 2017.

Major trading partners show the three largest trade partners (countries of last known destination and origin or consignment) in international merchandise trade transactions. In some cases a special partner is shown (i.e. Areas nes, bunkers, etc.) instead of a country and refers to one of the following special categories. Areas not elsewhere specified (i.e. Areas nes) is used (a) for low value trade, (b) if the partner designation was unknown to the country or if an error was made in the partner assignment and (c) for reasons of confidentiality. If a specific geographical location can be identified within Areas nes, then they are recorded accordingly (i.e. Asia nes). Bunkers are ship stores and aircraft supplies, which consists mostly of fuels and food. Free zones belong to the geographical and economic territory of a country but not to its customs territory. For the purposes of trade statistics, the transactions between the customs territory and the free zones are recorded, if the reporting country uses the Special Trade System. Free zones can be commercial free zones (duty free shops) or industrial free zones. Data are expressed as percentages of total exports and of total imports of the country, area or special partner.

Source of the data: United Nations Statistics Division (UNSD), New York, Commodity Trade Statistics Database (UN COMTRADE), last accessed May 2018.

National currency refers to those notes and coins in circulation that are commonly used to make payments. The official currency names and the ISO currency codes are those officially in use, and may be subject to change.

Source of the data: International Organisation for Standardization (ISO), Geneva, Currency Code Services – ISO 4217 Maintenance Agency, last accessed May 2018.

Net Official Development Assistance received or disbursed is defined as those flows to developing countries and multilateral institutions provided by official agencies, including state and local governments, or by their executive agencies, each transaction of which meets the following tests: i) it is administered with the promotion of the economic development and welfare of developing countries as its main objective; and ii) it is concessional in character and conveys a grant element of at least 25 per cent. It is expressed as a percentage of Gross National Income of either the donor or recipient. The multilateral institutions include the World Bank Group, regional banks, financial institutions of the European Union and a number of United Nations institutions, programmes and trust funds.

Source of the data: Organisation for Economic Co-operation and Development (OECD), Paris, the OECD Development Assistance Committee (DAC) statistics database, last accessed May 2018.

Population refers to the medium fertility projected de facto population as of 1 July 2018, unless otherwise stated in a footnote. The total population of a country may comprise either all usual residents of the country (de jure population) or all persons present in the country (de facto population) at the time of the census; for purposes of international comparisons, the de facto definition is used, unless otherwise stated in a footnote.
Source of the data: United Nations Population Division (UNPD), New York, "World Population Prospects (WPP): The 2017 Revision", last accessed June 2017.

Population age distribution refers to the percentage of the population aged 0-14 years and aged 60 years and older at the mid-year unless otherwise stated in a footnote.
Source of the data: United Nations Population Division (UNPD), New York, "World Population Prospects (WPP): The 2017 Revision"; supplemented by data from the United Nations Statistics Division (UNSD), New York, Demographic Yearbook 2015 and the Pacific Community (SPC) Statistics and Demography Programme for small countries or areas, last accessed June 2017.

Population density refers to the medium fertility projected population as of 1 July 2018 per square kilometre of surface area, unless otherwise stated in a footnote.
Source of the data: United Nations Population Division (UNPD), New York, "World Population Prospects (WPP): The 2017 Revision", last accessed June 2017.

Population growth rate is the average annual percentage change in total population size. The data are an average over five-year ranges; 2000-2005 data are labelled "2005", 2005-2010 data are labelled "2010" and 2010-2015 data are labelled "2018", unless otherwise stated in a footnote.
Source of the data: United Nations Population Division (UNPD), New York, "World Population Prospects (WPP): The 2017 Revision", last accessed June 2017.

Population using improved drinking water sources is the percentage of the population in urban and rural areas, according to national definitions, who use any of the following types of water supply for drinking: piped water, public tap, borehole or pump, protected well, protected spring or rainwater. Improved water sources do not include vendor-provided water, bottled water, tanker trucks or unprotected wells and springs. Use of an improved drinking water source is a proxy for the use of safe drinking water.
Source of the data: World Health Organization (WHO) and the United Nations Children's Fund (UNICEF), Geneva and New York, the WHO/UNICEF Joint Monitoring Programme (JMP) for Water and Sanitation database, last accessed October 2015.

Population using improved sanitation facilities refers to the percentage of the population in urban and rural areas, according to national definitions, with access to facilities that hygienically separate human excreta from human, animal and insect contact. Facilities such as sewers or septic tanks, poor flush latrines and simple pit or ventilated improved pit latrines are assumed to be adequate, provided that they are not public. To be effective, facilities must be correctly constructed and properly maintained. Sanitation facilities are not considered

improved when shared with other households, or open to public use. Use of an improved sanitation facility is a proxy for access to basic sanitation.
Source of the data: World Health Organization (WHO) and the United Nations Children's Fund (UNICEF), Geneva and New York, the WHO/UNICEF Joint Monitoring Programme (JMP) for Water and Sanitation database, last accessed October 2015.

Refugees and others of concern to the UNHCR: The 1951 United Nations Convention relating to the Status of Refugees states that a refugee is someone who, owing to a well-founded fear of being persecuted for reasons of race, religion, nationality, political opinion or membership in a particular social group, is outside the country of his or her nationality and is unable to, or owing to such fear, is unwilling to avail himself or herself of the protection of that country; or who, not having a nationality and being outside the country of his or her former habitual residence, is unable or, owing to such fear, unwilling to return to it. In this series, refugees refer to persons granted a humanitarian status and/or those granted temporary protection. Included are persons who have been granted temporary protection on a group basis. The series also includes returned refugees, asylum-seekers, stateless persons and persons displaced internally within their own country and others of concern to UNHCR.
Source of the data: United Nations High Commissioner for Refugees (UNHCR), Geneva, UNHCR population statistics database, last accessed February 2018.

Region is based on macro geographical regions arranged according to continents and component geographical regions used for statistical purposes as at 31 July 2017.
Source of the data: United Nations Statistics Division (UNSD), New York, Statistical Yearbook 2017 edition (60th issue) Annex I - Country and area nomenclature, regional and other groupings (based on Series M49: Standard Country or Area codes and Geographical Regions for Statistical Use), last accessed October 2017.

Research & Development expenditure refers to expenditure on creative work undertaken on a systematic basis in order to increase the stock of knowledge, including knowledge of humanity, culture and society, and the use of this stock of knowledge to devise new applications, expressed as a percentage of Gross Domestic Product (GDP). It is the total intramural expenditure on R&D performed on the national territory during a given period. It includes R&D performed within a country and funded from abroad but excludes payments made abroad for R&D.
Source of the data: United Nations Educational, Scientific and Cultural Organization (UNESCO), Montreal, the UNESCO Institute for Statistics (UIS) statistics database, last accessed November 2017.

Seats held by women in the National Parliament refer to the number of women in the lower chamber of the National Parliament expressed as a percentage of total occupied seats in the lower or single House, situation as of 1 February 2018.
Source of the data: Inter-Parliamentary Union (IPU), Geneva, Women in National Parliament dataset and the Sustainable Development Goals (SDGs) statistics database, last accessed March 2018.

Sex ratio is calculated as the ratio of the medium fertility projected population of men to that of 100 women as of 1 July 2018, unless otherwise stated in a footnote.
Source of the data: United Nations Population Division (UNPD), New York, "World Population Prospects (WPP): The 2017 Revision"; supplemented by data from the United Nations Statistics Division (UNSD), New York, Demographic Yearbook 2015 and the Pacific Community (SPC) Statistics and Demography Programme for small countries or areas, last accessed June 2017.

Surface area refers to land area plus inland water, unless otherwise stated in a footnote.
Source of the data: United Nations Statistics Division (UNSD), New York, Demographic Yearbook 2015 and the demographic statistics database, last accessed June 2017.

Threatened species represents the number of plants and animals that are most in need of conservation attention and are compiled by the World Conservation Union IUCN/ Species Survival Commission (SSC).
Source of the data: International Union for Conservation of Nature (IUCN), Gland and Cambridge, IUCN Red List of Threatened Species publication, last accessed May 2017.

Tourist/visitor arrivals at national borders is any person who travels to a country other than that in which he or she has his or her usual residence but outside his/her usual environment for a period not exceeding 12 months and whose main purpose of visit is other than the exercise of an activity remunerated from with the country visited, and who stays at least one night in a collective or private accommodation in the country visited (see Recommendations on Tourism Statistics of the United Nations and the World Tourism Organization). The data refer to arrivals of non-resident tourists at national borders, unless otherwise stated in a footnote.
Source of the data: World Tourism Organization (UNWTO), Madrid, the UNWTO statistics database, last accessed January 2018.

UN membership date: The United Nations (UN) is an intergovernmental organization whose members are the countries of the world. Currently there are 193 Member States of the United Nations, some of which joined the UN by signing and ratifying the Charter of the United Nations in 1945; the other countries joined the UN later, through the adoption of a resolution admitting them to membership. The process usually follows these steps: first, the country applies for membership and makes a declaration accepting the obligations of the Charter; second, the Security Council adopts a resolution recommending that the General Assembly admit the country to membership and finally the General Assembly adopts a resolution admitting the country.
Source of the data: United Nations (UN), Department of Public Information (DPI), News and Media Division, New York, Member states and date of admission, last accessed May 2018.

Unemployment refers to persons above a specified age who during a specified reference period were: "without work", i.e. were not in paid employment or self-employment as defined under employment; "currently available for work", i.e. were available for paid employment or

Technical notes (*continued*)

self-employment during the reference period; and "seeking work", i.e. had taken specific steps in a specified recent period to seek paid employment or self-employment (see ILO's current International Recommendations on Labour Statistics). The data refer to the 15 years and over age group and are based on ILO's modelled estimates, unless otherwise stated in a footnote.

Source of the data: International Labour Organization (ILO), Geneva, Key Indicators of the Labour Market (KILM 9th edition) and the ILOSTAT database, last accessed March 2018.

Urban population is based on the number of persons at the mid-year defined as urban according to national definitions of this concept. In most cases these definitions are those used in the most recent population census.

Source of the data: United Nations Population Division (UNPD), New York, "World Urbanization Prospects (WUP): The 2018 Revision", last accessed May 2018.

Urban population growth rate is based on the number of persons defined as urban according to national definitions of this concept. In most cases these definitions are those used in the most recent population census. The data are an average over five-year ranges; 2000-2005 data are labelled "2005", 2005-2010 data are labelled "2010" and 2010-2015 data are labelled "2018", unless otherwise stated in a footnote.

Source of the data: United Nations Population Division (UNPD), New York, "World Urbanization Prospects (WUP): The 2018 Revision", last accessed May 2018.

Statistical sources and references

Statistical sources

Carbon Dioxide Information Analysis Center (CDIAC) of the Oak Ridge National Laboratory, Tennessee, database on national CO_2 emission estimates, available at http://cdiac.ess-dive.lbl.gov/trends/emis/meth_reg.html.

Food and Agriculture Organization of the United Nations (FAO), Rome, FAOSTAT database, available at http://www.fao.org/faostat/en/#home.

International Labour Organization (ILO), Geneva, the ILOSTAT database, available at http://www.ilo.org/ilostat.
_____, Key Indicators of the Labour Market (KILM 9th edition), available at http://www.ilo.org/global/statistics-and-databases/research-and-databases/kilm/lang--en/index.htm.

International Monetary Fund (IMF), Washington, D.C., Balance of Payment (BOP) Statistics database, available at http://data.imf.org/bop.
_____, the International Financial Statistics (IFS) database, available at http://data.imf.org/ifs.

International Organisation for Standardization (ISO), Geneva, Currency Code Services – ISO 4217 Maintenance Agency, available at https://www.iso.org/iso-4217-currency-codes.html.

International Telecommunication Union (ITU), Geneva, the ITU Database, available at http://www.itu.int/en/ITU-D/statistics/Pages/default.aspx.

International Union for Conservation of Nature (IUCN), Gland and Cambridge, IUCN Red List of Threatened Species publication, available at http://www.iucnredlist.org/about/summary-statistics.

Inter-Parliamentary Union (IPU), Geneva, Women in National Parliament dataset, available at http://www.ipu.org/wmn-e/classif.htm.

Organisation for Economic Co-operation and Development (OECD), Paris, the OECD Development Assistance Committee (DAC) statistics database, available at http://stats.oecd.org/.

Pacific Community (SPC) Statistics and Demography Programme, Nouméa, Population and demographic indicators, available at http://sdd.spc.int/en/.

United Nations (UN), Department of Economic and Social Affairs (DESA), Population Division (UNPD), New York, "International migrant stock: The 2017 Revision", available at http://www.un.org/en/development/desa/population/migration/data/index.shtml.
_____, "World Population Prospects (WPP): The 2017 Revision", available at https://esa.un.org/unpd/wpp/.
_____, "World Urbanization Prospects (WUP): The 2018 Revision", available at https://esa.un.org/unpd/wup/.

Statistical sources and references (*continued*)

United Nations (UN), Department of Economic and Social Affairs (DESA), Statistics Division (UNSD), New York, Commodity Trade statistics database (UN COMTRADE), available at https://comtrade.un.org/.

_____, Demographic Yearbook (Series R, United Nations publication), available at https://unstats.un.org/unsd/demographic-social/products/dyb/.

_____, Energy Statistics Yearbook (Series J, United Nations publication), available at http://unstats.un.org/unsd/energy/yearbook/default.htm.

_____, Monthly Bulletin of Statistics (Series Q, United Nations publication), available at http://unstats.un.org/unsd/mbs/.

_____, National Accounts Statistics: Analysis of Main Aggregates (AMA) database (Series X, United Nations publication), available at http://unstats.un.org/unsd/snaama/introduction.asp.

_____, Statistical Yearbook (Series S, United Nations publication), available at https://unstats.un.org/unsd/publications/statistical-yearbook/.

_____, Sustainable Development Goals (SDGs) statistics database, available at https://unstats.un.org/sdgs/indicators/database.

United Nations (UN), Department of Management (DM), Office of Programme Planning, Budget and Accounts (OPPBA), New York, UN Treasury operational rates of exchange, available at https://treasury.un.org/operationalrates.

United Nations (UN), Department of Public Information (DPI), News and Media Division, New York, Member states and date of admission, available at http://www.un.org/en/member-states/index.html.

United Nations Educational, Scientific and Cultural Organization (UNESCO), Montreal, the UNESCO Institute for Statistics (UIS) statistics database, available at http://data.uis.unesco.org/.

United Nations High Commissioner for Refugees (UNHCR), Geneva, UNHCR population statistics database, available at http://popstats.unhcr.org

United Nations Office on Drugs and Crime (UNODC), Vienna, UNODC Statistics database, available at https://data.unodc.org/.

World Health Organization (WHO) and the United Nations Children's Fund (UNICEF), Geneva and New York, the WHO/UNICEF Joint Monitoring Programme (JMP) for Water and Sanitation database, available at www.wssinfo.org.

World Health Organization (WHO), Geneva, WHO Global Health Expenditure database, available at http://apps.who.int/nha/database.

_____, WHO Global Health Workforce statistics database, available at http://www.who.int/hrh/statistics/hwfstats/en/.

World Tourism Organization (UNWTO), Madrid, the UNWTO statistics database, available at http://www.e-unwto.org/loi/unwtotfb.

References

Food and Agriculture Organization of the United Nations (2015). Global Forest Resources Assessment 2015, available at http://www.fao.org/forest-resources-assessment/en/.

International Labour Organization (2000). Current International Recommendations on Labour Statistics, 2000 Edition, available at http://www.ilo.org/global/publications/ilo-bookstore/order-online/books/WCMS_PUBL_9221108465_EN/lang--en/index.htm.

International Monetary Fund (2009). Balance of Payments and International Investment Position Manual, Sixth Edition, available at https://www.imf.org/external/pubs/ft/bop/2007/bopman6.htm.

United Nations (1951 and 1967). Convention relating to the Status of Refugees of 1951 (United Nations, Treaty Series, vol. 189 (1954), No. 2545, p. 137), art. 1) and Protocol relating to the Status of Refugees of 1967 (United Nations, Treaty Series, vol. 606 (1967), No. 8791, p. 267), available at https://treaties.un.org/doc/Publication/UNTS/Volume%20189/volume-189-I-2545-English.pdf and https://treaties.un.org/doc/Publication/UNTS/Volume%20606/volume-606-I-8791-English.pdf.

United Nations (1982). Concepts and Methods in Energy Statistics, with Special Reference to Energy Accounts and Balances: A Technical Report. Statistical Office, Series F, No. 29 and Corr. 1 (United Nations publication, Sales No. E.82.XVII.13 and corrigendum), available at http://unstats.un.org/unsd/publication/SeriesF/SeriesF_29E.pdf.

United Nations (2008). International Standard Industrial Classification of All Economic Activities (ISIC), Rev. 4. Statistics Division, Series M, No. 4, Rev.4 (United Nations publication, Sales No. E.08.XVII.25), available at http://unstats.un.org/unsd/publication/SeriesM/seriesm_4rev4e.pdf.

United Nations (2008). Principles and Recommendations for Population and Housing Censuses Rev. 2. Statistics Division, Series M, No. 67, Rev. 2 (United Nations publication, Sales No. E.07.XVII.8), available at http://unstats.un.org/unsd/publication/SeriesM/Seriesm_67rev2e.pdf.

United Nations (2010). International Merchandise Trade Statistics: Concepts and Definitions, Statistics Division, Series M, No.52, Rev.3, (United Nations publication, Sales No. E.10.XVII.13), available at http://unstats.un.org/unsd/publication/SeriesM/SeriesM_52rev3E.pdf.

United Nations (2011). International Recommendations for Energy Statistics (IRES), Statistics Division, available at http://unstats.un.org/unsd/statcom/doc11/BG-IRES.pdf.

United Nations (2013). International Merchandise Trade Statistics: Compilers Manual Revision 1 (IMTS 2010-CM), Statistics Division , Series F, No. 87, Rev.1 (United Nations publication, Sales No. E.13.XVII.8), available at https://unstats.un.org/unsd/trade/publications/seriesf_87Rev1_e_cover.pdf.

United Nations (2018). Standard Country or Area Codes for Statistical Use, Statistics Division, Series M, No. 49, available at http://unstats.un.org/unsd/methods/m49/m49.htm

Statistical sources and references (*continued*)

United Nations, European Commission, International Monetary Fund, Organisation for Economic Cooperation and Development and World Bank (2009). System of National Accounts 2008, Statistics Division, Series M, No. 2, Rev.5 (United Nations publication, Sales No. E.08.XVII.29), available at http://unstats.un.org/unsd/nationalaccount/sna2008.asp.

World Health Organization (2007). International Statistical Classification of Diseases and Related Health Problems, Tenth Revision (ICD-10), (Geneva) available at http://www.who.int/classifications/icd/en/.

United Nations and World Tourism Organization (2008). International Recommendations for Tourism Statistics 2008, Statistics Division, Series M, No. 83/Rev.1 (United Nations publication, Sales No. E.08.XVII.28), available at http://unstats.un.org/unsd/publication/SeriesM/SeriesM_83rev1e.pdf.

Related statistical products

The World Statistics Pocketbook can also be viewed online in PDF format as well as an app for Android and Apple devices at http://unstats.un.org/unsd/pocketbook/ and in UNdata at http://data.un.org/en/index.html.

Other statistical publications offering a broad cross-section of information which may be of interest to users of the World Statistics Pocketbook include:
1. The Monthly Bulletin of Statistics (MBS) in print and the Monthly Bulletin of Statistics Online, available at http://unstats.un.org/unsd/mbs/.
2. The Statistical Yearbook (SYB) in print and online in PDF format, available at http://unstats.un.org/unsd/publications/statistical-yearbook/.

Both publications are available for sale in print format (see below for instructions on how to order). For more information about other publications and online databases prepared by the United Nations Statistics Division, please visit: https://unstats.un.org/unsd/publications/. For additional information about the work of the United Nations Statistics Division, please visit http://unstats.un.org/unsd. To order United Nations publications, please visit https://shop.un.org or contact:

United Nations Publications
300 East 42nd Street
New York, NY 10017
Tel: 1-888-254-4286 / Fax: 1-800-338-4550 / E-mail: publications@un.org

Please provide the Statistical Dissemination Section – which is responsible for producing the World Statistics Pocketbook, the Monthly Bulletin of Statistics and the Statistical Yearbook – your feedback and suggestions regarding these statistical products, as well as the utility of the data, by contacting statistics@un.org.